"Value-pa
comprehensive..."

—Los Angeles Times

"Unbeatable..."

—The Washington Post

Let's Go
AUSTRIA

is the best book for anyone traveling on a budget. Here's why:

■ No other guidebook has as many budget listings.

Take Salzburg, for example. We list 14 accommodations for under $13 a night. We tell you how to get there the cheapest way, whether by bus, plane, or bike, and where to get an inexpensive and satisfying meal once you've arrived. We give hundreds of money-saving tips that anyone can use, plus invaluable advice on discounts and deals for students, children, families, and senior travelers.

■ Let's Go researchers have to make it on their own.

Our Harvard-Radcliffe researcher-writers travel on budgets as tight as your own—no expense accounts, no free hotel rooms.

■ Let's Go is completely revised each year.

We don't just update the prices, we go back to the place. If a charming café has become an overpriced tourist trap, we'll replace the listing with a new and better one.

■ No other guidebook includes all this:

Honest, engaging coverage of both the cities and the countryside; up-to-the-minute prices, directions, addresses, phone numbers, and opening hours; in-depth essays on local culture, history, and politics; comprehensive listings on transportation between and within regions and cities; straight advice on work and study, budget accommodations, sights, nightlife, and food; detailed city and regional maps; and much more.

■ Let's Go is for anyone who wants to see Austria on a budget.

Books by Let's Go, Inc.

EUROPE

Let's Go: Europe

Let's Go: Austria

Let's Go: Britain & Ireland

Let's Go: France

Let's Go: Germany & Switzerland

Let's Go: Greece & Turkey

Let's Go: Ireland

Let's Go: Italy

Let's Go: London

Let's Go: Paris

Let's Go: Rome

Let's Go: Spain & Portugal

NORTH & CENTRAL AMERICA

Let's Go: USA & Canada

Let's Go: Alaska & The Pacific Northwest

Let's Go: California & Hawaii

Let's Go: New York City

Let's Go: Washington, D.C.

Let's Go: Mexico

MIDDLE EAST & ASIA

Let's Go: Israel & Egypt

Let's Go: Thailand

Let's Go

The Budget Guide to

AUSTRIA 1994

Justin M. Levitt
Editor

Marc David Zelanko
Assistant Editor

Written by
Let's Go, Inc.
A subsidiary of
Harvard Student Agencies, Inc.

St. Martin's Press ■ New York

HELPING LET'S GO

If you have suggestions or corrections, or just want to share your discoveries, drop us a line. We read every piece of correspondence, whether a 10-page letter, a velveteen Elvis postcard, or, as in one case, a collage. All suggestions are passed along to our researcher-writers. Please note that mail received after May 5, 1994 will probably be too late for the 1995 book, but will be retained for the following edition. Address mail to:

Let's Go: Austria
Let's Go, Inc.
1 Story Street
Cambridge, MA 02138
USA

In addition to the invaluable travel advice our readers share with us, many are kind enough to offer their services as researchers or editors. Unfortunately, the charter of Let's Go, Inc. and Harvard Student Agencies, Inc. enables us to employ only currently enrolled Harvard students.

Distributed outside the U.S. and Canada by Pan Macmillan Ltd.

ISBN: 0-312-10002-7

First edition
10 9 8 7 6 5 4 3 2 1

Let's Go: **Austria** is written by the Publishing Division of Let's Go, Inc., 1 Story Street, Cambridge, MA 02138.

Let's Go® is a registered trademark of Let's Go, Inc.
Printed in the U.S.A. on recycled paper with biodegradable soy ink.

Editor	Justin M. Levitt
Assistant Editor	Marc David Zelanko
Managing Editor	Pete Keith
Publishing Director	Mark N. Templeton
Production Manager	Edward Owen
Office Coordinator	Susan P. Krause
Assistant General Manager	Anne E. Chisholm
Researcher-Writers	
Northeast Austria (Lower Austria, Burgenland, Vienna)	Edward J. Collins, Jr.
Prague and Budapest	Julio DePietro
Northwest Austria (Upper Austria, Salzburg)	Adam Freudenheim
West Austria (Tyrol, Vorarlberg)	Sucharita Mulpuru
South Austria (Styria, Carinthia, East Tyrol)	James Charles Rhee
Bratislava (Near Vienna)	Geneviève Roach
Sales Group Manager	Swati Y. Rao
Sales Group Assistant Manager	Paul Kyong Hwan Kim
Sales Group Representatives	Jonathan N. Adolph Wendy A. Gribb Ashley Hubka Carolyn B. Rendell Tara E. Walpert
President	Martín E. Escobari
General Manager	Richard M. Olken
Contributor	Henry K. Hall

Acknowledgments

Our five stalwart researchers constructed *Let's Go: APB* nearly from scratch. The greatest testimonial to their effort is this guide—their guide—which sprawls on for 440-odd pages. That they completed their task at all is astounding—that they performed with such style, with art, and, above all, with dedication, is superhuman. We have no resources left to thank them sufficiently, but their work displays a worth we would belittle with mere description.

We owe Vienna and Lower Austria to **Ted Collins.** Ted was fastidious and consummately devoted to The Cause™. He checked each detail, down to the stability of tourist office furnishings, and then portrayed every nuance in supple prose. Ted provided us with enough anecdotes for a miniseries and enough pamphlets to fill a swimming pool. This budding teenage heartthrob wowed the crowds while finding time to overhaul his beloved capital city.

Julio DePietro delivered some of the most brilliant text these eyes have seen. We took our orders from his marginalia (copy?) most willingly. We would gladly have kept this sleuth all to ourselves. He managed, somehow, to keep track of the forest while describing every birch, oak, pine, maple, dogwood... This summer, Julio spring-cleaned Prague and Budapest.

Adam Freudenheim enthusiastically attacked the Salzburg sector, giving every town 110% percent. Adam has a great personality, too spunky for words. The smile on this trooper's face 5000 miles away was evident even through his copy. Adam was bright-eyed and bushy-tailed to the end. We'll never forget his efforts.

Sucharita Mulpuru traveled to an unhealthy number of "quaint" Tyrolean ski hamlets. She outpaced her itinerary, producing outstanding copy that kept us chortling late—(late!)—into the night. Sucharita created substance from void; she somehow understood exactly what we were looking for. And we'll never get lost in West Austria again.

James Rhee faced apocalyptic weather and sucking chest wounds while traversing some of the most unnerving terrain in Southeast Austria. Undaunted, he wowed us with golden research and writing. A verbal alchemist, James was wittily thorough, and thoroughly witty. The mountains of exemplary copy testify to his fanatical dedication.

Henry Hall filled some gaping nooks and crannies in our Prague coverage. From the bagel end of the business, **Rob Brooker** translated lox and less kosher victuals into Hungarian. **Conor O'Dwyer** expanded Prague restaurants to superlative proportions. **Gabriele Wolf**, at the Austrian National Tourist Office, submerged us in pamphlets, and was still willing to talk to us after insipid phone call #11. Many, many others have earned our everlasting gratitude: special thanks to **Kelley Curry** of Planned Parenthood, the fine folks at **Boston Public Library** telephone reference, **Gene Krause,** and **"J."** over at Berkeley.

Pete K. was good cop and bad cop, but always concerned friend, inspiring us through the God-awful hours. **Mark T.,** Let's Go *über-meister*, deflated us gently as we inflated the book. **Ed** and **Sue** became midwives during this painful labor. The 1-2 bites of every meal we tithed to **Amy** earned us the opportunity to answer her phone. **Mimi** funked with a smile and impeccable style. **Justin** "Purveyor of Much Coffee and Man of Mighty Monikers" **B.** transcribed mightily for us many tall tales.

Deborah, who cooked up some creative cuisine, knows the extent of our devotion. **Jahan's** ebullience and newfound friendship floated the spirits of this landlocked ship. **Goo®! David G.,** the consummate mensch, brought a *gespichl* of the 'burbs to the office—oy. We dedicate our sanity to **Ben P., Dov,** and **David L.** And for all of the smiles and support—if only we could have filled our pages with acknos instead of Ecru, Aubergine, and Drab: **Dan, ¡Alex!, Mira, Beth, Adina, Natasha, Brian, Liz, JT, Maia, Jane, Selya, Jews.**

Justin would have floundered without SuperFind **Marc.** He was a compatriot in misery and an impeccable colleague. He served us all by excising my worthless humor; *his* talented touch elevates the guide. May he never release that emphysemic doppelgänger ap-parent-ly trapped inside his frame. You are a wonderful individual, my friend. To the magnificent folks at **110 Line** and **109 Beacon**—just head to the index. **Ashley, Mike,** and **Elena:** I can only afford 6 words. Most of all, **Mom, Dad,** and **Brendon,** thank you for the long-distance love.

Marc tips his summer's cap to **Justin**—first editor, then partner, now co-conspirator and dear friend. Dusty, your competence, brilliance, and grace will forever inspire me. We wrote a gem. To **Jon, Jon, Ali, Jamie, Janine, Josh, Michael, Naomi,** and **Mr. Blayne**—my devotion. Finally, yet first and foremost, I thank **Mom, Dad,** and **Amy.** Without you, I'm nothing. With you, I'm me. I love you all so much.

Contents

Maps

About Let's Go

Back in 1960, a few students at Harvard got together to produce a 20-page pamphlet offering a collection of tips on budget travel in Europe. For three years, Harvard Student Agencies, a student-run nonprofit corporation, had been doing a brisk business booking charter flights to Europe; this modest, mimeographed packet was offered to passengers as an extra. The following year, students traveling to Europe researched the first full-fledged edition of *Let's Go: Europe*, a pocket-sized book featuring advice on shoestring travel, irreverent write-ups of sights, and a decidedly youthful slant.

Throughout the 60s, the guides reflected the times: one section of the 1968 *Let's Go: Europe* talked about "Street Singing in Europe on No Dollars a Day." During the 70s, *Let's Go* gradually became a large-scale operation, adding regional European guides and expanding coverage into North Africa and Asia. The 80s saw the arrival of *Let's Go: USA & Canada* and *Let's Go: Mexico*, as well as regional North American guides; in the 90s we introduced five in-depth city guides to Paris, London, Rome, New York, and Washington, DC.

This year we're proud to announce three new guides: *Let's Go: Austria* (including Prague and Budapest), *Let's Go: Ireland*, and *Let's Go: Thailand* (including Honolulu, Tokyo, and Singapore), bringing our total number of titles up to twenty.

We've seen a lot in thirty-four years. *Let's Go: Europe* is now the world's #1 best selling international guide, translated into seven languages. And our guides are still researched, written, and produced entirely by students who know first-hand how to see the world on the cheap.

Every spring, we recruit nearly 100 researchers and an editorial team of 50 to write our books anew. Come summertime, after several months of training, researchers hit the road for seven weeks of exploration, from Bangkok to Budapest, Anchorage to Ankara. With pen and notebook in hand, a few changes of underwear stuffed in our backpacks, and a budget as tight as yours, we visit every *pensione*, *palapa*, pizzeria, café, club, campground, or castle we can find to make sure you'll get the most out of *your* trip.

We've put the best of our discoveries into the book you're now holding. A brand-new edition of each guide hits the shelves every year, only months after it was researched, so you know you're getting the most reliable, up-to-date, and comprehensive information available. And even as you read this, work on next year's editions is well underway.

At *Let's Go*, we think of budget travel not only as a means of cutting down on costs, but as a way of breaking down a few walls as well. Living cheap and simple on the road brings you closer to the real people and places you've been saving up to visit. This book will ease your anxieties and answer your questions about the basics—to help *you* get off the beaten track and explore. We encourage you to put *Let's Go* away now and then and strike out on your own. As any seasoned traveler will tell you, the best discoveries are often those you make yourself. If you find something worth sharing, drop us a line and let us know. We're at Let's Go, Inc., 1 Story Street, Cambridge, MA, 02138, USA.

Happy travels!

How To Use This Book

Let's Go: Austria is written for the adventurous budget traveler. In the summer of 1993, we sent our roving researchers out on a shoestring budget with your concerns in mind: how to get from place to place, savor the local cuisine, take in the sights, absorb the culture, enjoy the evenings, and get some sleep, all in the most economical way possible. We introduce you to Austria and its primary gateway cities, Prague and Budapest, so you can get to know them safely, intimately, and, best of all, cheaply.

Even without Vienna, Austria would be one of Europe's most charming destinations. Yet, Austria's capital is undeniably the main attraction—a world-class cultural center so top-heavy with genius that virtuosi Franz Lizst, Gustav Mahler, Joseph Haydn, and Oskar Kokoschka rank among the second-rate talents. Prague and Budapest are the *other* grand cities of Central Europe, long dormant but recently "rediscovered" by delighted Western throngs.

Before and during a visit to Austria, Prague, and Budapest, your copy of *Let's Go* will serve you well. In the **Planning Your Trip** section, we guide you through the immense preparation required before you depart. If a travel concern has crossed your mind, it's in the guide—**Useful Addresses, Money, Safety and Security, Packing,** and 70 pages brimming with frank insider tips. We exhaust the possibilities for traveling to and moving around Austria, Prague, and Budapest. You'll find over two dozen budget railpasses; then scan ahead for comprehensive coverage of bike, bus, plane, ferry, motorcycle, car, and foot power. For every destination, we'll share the most practical information about **Getting Around, Accommodations, Keeping in Touch,** and even those wacky Austrian **Idiosyncracies.**

After Idiosyncracies, turn the (recycled) page to enter **Österreich 101,** a breezy primer that condenses Austria's fascinating history and culture. In the back of the book dwell the **Appendix** and **Glossary**—flip-to references of the strange and useful, liberally swaddled in translations of German, Czech, and Hungarian.

For each entry, **Orientation and Practical Information** maps out the town and compiles the crucial information you'd otherwise get by condensing a phone book, a best friend, and a personal excursion engineer. For larger cities, *Let's Go* has this year introduced a revolutionary **new map design,** featuring helpful quadrant indicators—cross referenced in text, as in (*map**B3*)—and hotel and hostel icons that make it easier than ever to reach your pillow at night. Plus information about airports, public transportation, budget travel offices, American Express, currency exchange, hospitals, gay and lesbian resources, English-language bookstores, and even laundromats. With your purse in mind, the **Accommodations** and **Food** sections offer ranked evaluations of lodgings, restaurants, and grocers. Then follows a write-up of each town's **Sights** in readable prose that is—with any luck—sometimes witty. In addition to the area's well-known and oft-trampled attractions, *Let's Go* escorts you to offbeat and unusual sights that other guides ignore. In most locales, we deliver the outdoors as well, with extensive coverage of **skiing, hiking,** and **watersports.** In more populous cities, we conclude with **Entertainment** opportunities, from quaffing some wine to quaking from Wagner, and then bust through the city limits with **daytrips** to out-of-the-way nooks and crannies.

Read or at least skim as much of the **Essentials** as you can. Look it over before you leave—in the bathroom, on the bus to work, in bed; there's brilliant stuff there if you take the time to wade through it. Much of the information presented here applies everywhere in the book but, given space constraints, will not be repeated *ad nauseam.* These helpful hints can make a good trip spectacular.

Organization

Let's Go: Austria tackles Central Europe from west to east, the path followed by most travelers who enter Austria from the tourist-laden realms of France, Italy, Germany, and Switzerland (see these *Let's Go* companion volumes—they're almost as good as the guide you're reading). Each chapter in this book features a major city which anchors the region; the chapters are not necessarily constructed around provincial boundaries, as Austrians largely ignore these political divisions.

The book's Genesis is West Austria, the stereotypical fantasy picture-book land with the best skiing in the country, and Alpine Olympic host Innsbruck. Central Tyrol and the stunning Großglockner Road follow. Next comes the Salzburger Land, radiating from the acclaimed residence of everyone's favorite singing nun. The Salzburger lakes, too, are alive with the sound of music. The following chapter describes Northwest Austria and the Danube city of Linz; Southeast Austria, next in line, is blessed by both Klagenfurt and Graz. The next section presents Lower Austria, a gateway to Vienna, the final Austrian delight. From the capital, it's just a baby step over the border, north into the Czech Republic or east into Hungary. Prague and Budapest round out the coverage in the guide

How Not to Use This Book

Let's Go is as comprehensive as a book this size can be, but other important sources of information exist; consult the publications of some of the organizations listed in the Useful Travel Organizations section and elsewhere throughout the Essentials. Never surrender your independence of mind. If *Let's Go* really is your bible, don't be a naive scriptural literalist. Our researchers, despite Herculean efforts, have not uncovered *all* of Europe's treasures—the most memorable and worthwhile discoveries will be the ones you make yourself. Put down the book and explore. *Let's Go* is thoroughly updated every year, but you still may discover a number of facts or numbers that have changed since our researchers were in the field in the summer of 1993: prices rise, bus schedules change, cooks die. Prepare to roll with the punches.

A NOTE TO OUR READERS

The information for this book is gathered by *Let's Go*'s researchers during the late spring and summer months. Each listing is derived from the assigned researcher's opinion based upon his or her visit at a particular time. The opinions are expressed in a candid and forthright manner. Other travelers might disagree. Those traveling at a different time may have different experiences since prices, dates, hours, and conditions are always subject to change. You are urged to check beforehand to avoid inconvenience and surprises. Travel always involves a certain degree of risk, especially in low-cost areas. When traveling, especially on a budget, you should always take particular care to ensure your safety.

Topography and Political Divisions
Danube (Donau)
NIEDERÖSTERREICH
Inn
Danube
Vienna
OBERÖSTERREICH
Inn
VORARLBERG
Lake Constance
Enns
Zugspitze
Kaiser Range
Dachstein
Enns
Inn
Salzach
BURGENLAND
SALZBURG
The Arlberg
TIROL
Stubai Glacier
Grossglockner
Mur
STEIERMARK
OST-TIROL
KÄRNTEN
Ötztaler Alps
Drau
Mura
Drava
N
0
50 miles
0
50 kilometers
GERMANY
Munich
Braunau am Inn
Salzburg
Hallein
Bregenz
Reutte
Kufstein
Jenbach
St. Johann im Pongau
Ehrwald
Seefeld
Kitzbühel
Zell am See
Feldkirch
Imst
Innsbruck
Zell am Ziller
Lech
Krimml
Bludenz
Zürs
St. Anton am Arlberg
Fulpmes
Mayrhofen
Badgastein
Heiligenblut
Pfunds
Lienz
LIECHTENSTEIN
SWITZERLAND
ITALY
0
50 miles
0
50 kilometers
N

Austria (Österreich)

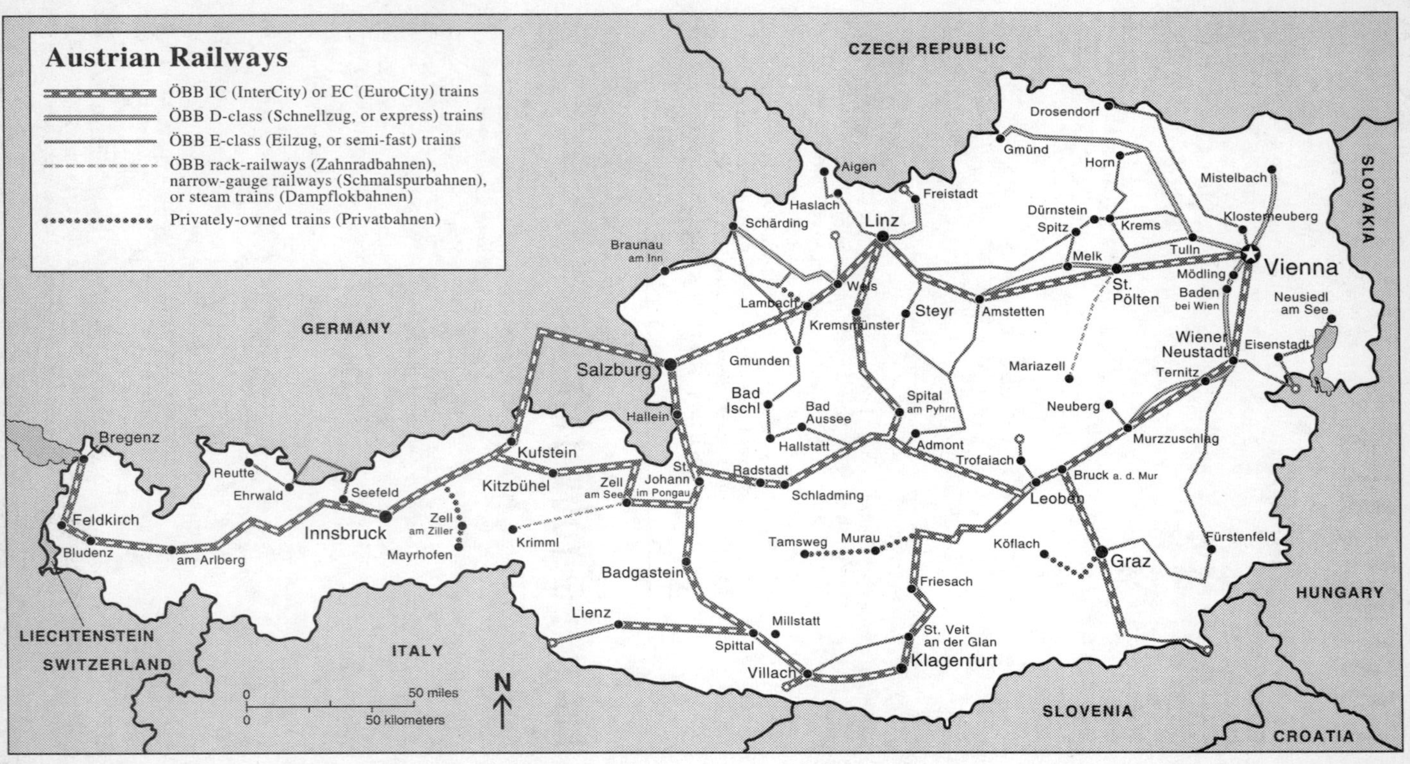
Austrian Railways
ÖBB IC (InterCity) or EC (EuroCity) trains
ÖBB D-class (Schnellzug, or express) trains
ÖBB E-class (Eilzug, or semi-fast) trains
ÖBB rack-railways (Zahnradbahnen), narrow-gauge railways (Schmalspurbahnen), or steam trains (Dampflokbahnen)
Privately-owned trains (Privatbahnen)
CZECH REPUBLIC
SLOVAKIA
GERMANY
HUNGARY
SLOVENIA
CROATIA
ITALY
LIECHTENSTEIN
SWITZERLAND
N
0
50 miles
0
50 kilometers
Drosendorf
Gmünd
Horn
Mistelbach
Aigen
Freistadt
Haslach
Linz
Dürnstein
Spitz
Krems
Klosterneuberg
Schärding
Tulln
Vienna
Braunau am Inn
Melk
St. Pölten
Mödling
Baden bei Wien
Neusiedl am See
Wels
Lambach
Kremsmünster
Steyr
Amstetten
Wiener Neustadt
Eisenstadt
Gmunden
Salzburg
Mariazell
Ternitz
Bad Ischl
Bad Aussee
Spital am Pyhrn
Neuberg
Hallein
Hallstatt
Admont
Trofaiach
Murzzuschlag
Bregenz
Kufstein
Reutte
Ehrwald
Seefeld
Kitzbühel
Zell am See
St. Johann im Pongau
Radstadt
Schladming
Bruck a. d. Mur
Leoben
Feldkirch
Zell am Ziller
Innsbruck
Krimml
Tamsweg
Murau
Köflach
Fürstenfeld
Graz
Bludenz
am Arlberg
Mayrhofen
Badgastein
Friesach
Lienz
Millstatt
Spittal
St. Veit an der Glan
Klagenfurt
Villach

ESSENTIALS

US$1	= 11.4 Schillings (AS)	10 AS =	US$0.88
CDN$1	= 8.59 AS	10 AS =	CDN$1.16
UK£1	= 17.4 AS	10 AS =	UK£0.57
IR£1	= 16.3 AS	10 AS =	IR£0.61
AUS$1	= 7.38 AS	10 AS =	AUS$1.36
NZ$1	= 6.20 AS	10 AS =	NZ$1.61
SAR1	= 3.38 AS	10 AS =	SAR2.96
DM1	= 7.03 AS	10 AS =	DM1.42
SK1	= 0.35 AS	10 AS =	SK28.5
KČS1	= 0.40 AS	10 AS =	KČS25.1
FT1	= 0.12 AS	10 AS =	FT81.2

Country Code: 43 **International Dialing Prefix: 900 from Vienna**
00 from elsewhere

Price Warning

Let's Go includes exchange rates and prices so you can match your plans to your resources. Remember that the numbers listed were compiled in the summer of 1993, when Let's Go Researcher-Writers for this edition were in the field. Although inflation in Austria is minimal by global standards (around 3%), prices in service industries (such as hotels) tend to increase at a faster rate, and exchange rate fluctuations can always skew your estimates. Check the financial pages of a newspaper before setting off on your trip; do not assume the hotel proprietor is trying to cheat you if he or she asks for a higher price than the one listed in this guide.

PLANNING YOUR TRIP

A successful trip requires, along with some cash and a taste for adventure, a generous helping of forethought. Fortunately, billion-dollar industries are devoted entirely to helping the intimidated traveler tackle the offerings of Austria, Prague, and Budapest. The many organizations listed below, especially national tourist offices, will send you a mound (or three) of literature. Dive in and plan a trip tailored to your specific interests. Strongly resist the urge to see everything. A madcap schedule will only detract from your trip. If you try to see Vienna, Salzburg, Innsbruck, and Prague all in a week, you'll probably come away from your vacation with nothing but vague, discomfiting memories of train stations and unwashed schoolchildren rampaging though the halls of youth hostels.

Select your traveling companions as carefully as you would choose a spouse or an automobile air freshener. Ah, how quickly when traveling can organized become bossy, relaxed slothful, and zany annoying. Traveling with fifteen fraternity brothers or sorority sisters or frarority hermaphrodites—or even just one—may effectively insulate you from local culture. On the other hand, companions will share in food and lodging costs, provide extra safety in numbers, and serve as an invaluable source of energy and comfort. If you choose to travel with others, discuss your trip in detail before you leave to make sure your general interests and sight-seeing agendas are compatible. Keep in mind that, despite the obvious drawbacks, going solo can be the best way to travel; freedom of movement tends to counterbalance potentially depressing loneliness. Anyway, you are sure to meet other travelers along the way who will seem like close friends after a day or two of concerted frolicking.

WHEN TO GO

In July and August, airfares, temperatures, and tempers rise right along with the population of tourists. And, as any good business responds to the flow of its customers, in the winter months some hostels close and some sights abbreviate their hours. May and June combine the best of both touristic worlds: the sights are open and uncrowded. Crowds in ski areas follow different fluctuations, kind of like weather or sink drainage spirals in the southern hemisphere. Winter sports gear up in November and continue even into May, depending on the location. High-season (*Hauptsaison*) for skiing is mid-December to mid-January and February to March; glacier skiing ignores any imposed schedule. Austrians flock to tourist spots *en masse* with the onset of school vacations; airports and train stations become jammed, and road traffic can be measured in meters per hour. Try your best to avoid trekking across Austria the day after school lets out. Schoolchildren are scary as individuals, and pack behavior defies all explanation. Austrian schools vacate in the summer and for three term-time holidays: Winter break (Christmas Eve until about Jan. 5), Spring break (one week between Feb. 1 and Feb. 20, depending on the region), and Easter break (March 30 to April 5).

A FEW GENTLE SUGGESTIONS

> *Travel, in the younger sort, is a part of education; in the elder, a part of experience. He that travelleth into a country before he hath some entrance into the language, goeth to school, and not to travel.*
>
> *Francis Bacon*

Many budget travelers find themselves succumbing to a budget obsession when traveling: to stay in the cheapest lodgings, no matter how miserable; to eat grim, insipid food; to yearn only to spend fewer *Schillings* than yesterday. These are a few of our least favorite things. Perhaps the worst sin of the entire *Let's Go* series is its perpetuation of this mindset among travelers, many of whom have spent years saving enough money to go abroad, just to end up traveling with the same attitude. When you hit the travel doldrums, use some of your money to cushion the shocks. A rich meal or a quiet evening in a soothing *Pension* might add 100 *Schillings* to your bill but may make you feel rich and pampered rather than destitute and ignored. Better to go home raving about three lovely weeks of down pillows and *Sacher Torte* than bitching about four weeks of night-train accommodations and grocery store cuisine. You're on a vacation, not a crusade.

You will probably learn the most about new and foreign cultures by dissolving discreetly into them. Even the most rudimentary effort at integration goes a long way. Talk to the people around you, in their own language if possible; even a few phrases of German, Czech, or Hungarian will be appreciated. (See the Appendix and the Glossary at the end of this guide for some helpful language hints.) A statue of Mozart, whatever its other virtues, is a poor conversationalist; an Austrian with *Lederhosen* and a nose ring is far more interesting. An afternoon of relaxation at a park in Salzburg or a café in Vienna (cafés, after all, are made for people-watching) will teach you more about a country and its people than hours spent in a museum.

There's no faster way to acquaint yourself with a people than to convince them (and yourself) that you're part of their culture. Of course, most tourists find themselves unable to shake the aura that identifies them as outsiders from four blocks away; any foreigner is bound at first to appear, well, foreign. But don't be discouraged; make an effort to assimilate. You will be rewarded for your efforts.

On that note, take the time to meet *people*. Unless you're desperately homesick, eat *Schnitzel* instead of Pizza Hut. A photo of Walter and Gisela Schmidt who put you up for the night in Graz will contain more memories than a postcard of the *Dom.* Many Europeans are sincerely interested in other lands and peoples but have a very strong sense of their own cultural history; if you insult or belittle it, you'll only seem ignorant. Keep in mind that you are a guest, not an overlord. Don't expect things to work the way they do at home; half the fun is untangling a new system.

Above all, don't automatically equate "our way" with "better." Remember that many Europeans speak no English; ask humbly (you're the one who should speak their language) "*Sprechen Sie Englisch?*" before launching into a question. Better yet, try to learn a little German, and don't be afraid to test it out. You can learn the pronunciation system, plus the words for yes, no, where is, how much, and the numbers up to ten, in about fifteen minutes. Really. **Berlitz** sells *Self-Teacher* books, available in most bookstores, for about US$12. Such paperbacks cost much less than cassette tapes and, if you're motivated, are probably just as effective. Travelers who are unable to yell "Fire!" or "Help!" in a foreign language subject themselves voluntarily and unnecessarily to a potentially calamitous handicap.

In any case, learn at least one phrase: thank you—in German, *danke* (DAHNK-uh); in Czech, *děkuji* (DYEH-kuh-yih); in Hungarian, *köszönöm* (KOE-soe-noem).

■■■ USEFUL ADDRESSES

■ National Tourist Offices

These outposts can provide copious help in planning your trip; have them mail you brochures well before you leave. They will provide information on most towns and regions as well as specific information for travelers with special concerns. Most information—but not all—is available in English.

Austrian National Tourist Offices

U.S.: In **New York,** 500 Fifth Ave. #2009, New York, NY 10110 (tel. (212) 944-6880; fax 730-4568); **Chicago,** 500 N. Michigan Ave. #1950, Chicago, IL 60611 (tel. (312) 644-8029); **Los Angeles,** 11601 Wilshire Blvd. #2480, Los Angeles, CA 90025 (tel. (310) 477-3332).

Canada: In **Montreal,** 1010 Sherbrooke St. W. #1410, Montreal, Quebec, H3A 2R7 (tel. (514) 849-3708 or (514) 849-3709); **Toronto,** 2 Bloor St. E. #3330, Toronto, Ontario, M4W 1A8 (tel. (416) 967-3381); **Vancouver,** Granville Sq. #1380, 200 Granville St., Vancouver, British Columbia V6C 1S4 (tel. (604) 683-8695).

United Kingdom: 30 St. George St., London, W1R OAL (tel. (71) 629 04 61; fax 499 60 38).

Ireland: Honorary Representation for Ireland, Merrion Hall, Strand Rd., Sandymount, P.O. Box 2506, Dublin 4 (tel. (01) 283 04 88; fax 283 05 31).

Australia: 36 Carrington St., First floor, Sydney NSW 2000 (tel. (2) 299 36 21; fax 299 38 08).

New Zealand: Honorary Representation for New Zealand, 76 Symonds St., Auckland (tel. (9) 373 40 78; fax 373 40 76).

South Africa: Cradock Heights, 2nd floor, 21 Cradock Ave., Rosebank, 2196 Johannesburg (tel. (11) 442 72 35; fax 442 83 04).

Czech Republic: Opletalova 39, CZ-1100 Prague 1 (tel. 22 17 48; fax 22 24 01).

Hungary: Vaci u. 40, Apt. 20, H-1056 Budapest (tel. 118 78 24; fax 117 15 46).

Czech Travel Bureau (Čedok)

Formerly a National Tourist Office, Čedok has since transformed itself into a travel wholesaler and tour operator. Contact Čedok for travel arrangements, but not for brochures and hand-holding. The Czech Embassy in your home country might assist you with such services (see Embassies and Consulates below). In the U.S., contact Čedok at 10 E. 40th St. #3604, New York, NY 10016 (tel. (212) 689-9720; fax 481-0597).

Hungarian National Tourist Offices

IBUSZ Travel, Inc. was established in 1992, replacing IBUSZ Hungarian Travel Co. Today's IBUSZ is a subsidiary of IBUSZ Hungarian Travel Co., owned by private investors and one of Hungary's largest banks, with headquarters in Budapest. IBUSZ enters its 92nd year of service in 1994 and remains the largest full-service travel company in Hungary.

U.S.: In **New Jersey,** One Parker Plaza #1104, Fort Lee, NJ 07024 (tel. (800) 367-7878 or (201) 592-8585). **Chicago,** 233 North Michigan Ave. #1308 (tel. (312) 819-3510; fax 819-3151).

United Kingdom: Danube Travel Ltd., 6 Conduit St., London, W1R 9TG (tel. (071) 491-3588).

■ Embassies and Consulates

A consulate looks after the interests of its country's nationals who visit or live in a foreign country. You should make sure your consulate is cognizant of your presence in Austria, Prague, or Budapest if you plan on staying there for more than a few weeks. To facilitate this, many consulates have registration cards you can fill out and remit.

If you are seriously ill or in trouble, your embassy can provide a list of local lawyers or doctors; it can also contact your relatives. If you are arrested, consular officials can visit you in custody. In extreme cases, they can offer emergency financial assistance, including transferring money from your home country. In Austria, embassies are largely located in Vienna, consulates in Innsbruck and Salzburg.

Refer to the Embassies and Consulates Section in the Practical Information section of each city for the addresses of your home country's offices there.

Austrian Consulates

U.S.: 950 Third Ave., 20th Floor, New York, NY 10022 (tel. (212) 737-6400).

Canada: 1131 Kensington Rd., NW, Calgary, Alberta T2N 3P4 (tel. (403) 283-6526; fax 283-4909).

United Kingdom: 18 Belgrave Mews West, London, SW1X 8HU (tel. (071) 235 37 31, fax 232 80 25).

Ireland: 15 Ailesbury Court Apartments, 93 Ailesbury Rd., Dublin 4 (tel. (00353/1) 269 45 77; fax 283 08 60).

Australia: 12 Talbot St., Forrest ACT 2603, Canberra (tel. (06) 295 13 76; fax 239 67 51).

New Zealand: 28A Tizard Rd., Birkenhead, Auckland 10 (tel. (06649) 480 84 95).

South Africa: 33 Bellevue Rd., Berea, Durban 4001 (tel. (031) 21 54 08; fax 309 13 40).

Czech Consulates (Velvyslanectvi Ceske Republicky)

U.S.: Consular Section, 3900 Spring of Freedom St., NW, Washington, DC 20008, (tel. (202) 363-6315); visa office, tel. (202) 363-6308; fax (202) 966-8540.

Canada: 50 Rideau Terrace, Ottowa, Ontario, K1N 2AI (tel. (613) 749 15 66; fax 749 03 16).

United Kingdom: 26 Kensington Palace Gardens, London W84 QY (tel. (071) 727 49 18; fax 727 96 54).

Ireland: Trade Mission of the Czech Republic, Confederation House of Irish Industry, Kildare St., Dublin 2 (tel. (31) 71 49 81; fax 679 86 38).

Australia: 38 Culgoe Circuit, O'Malley, Canberra ACT 2606 (tel. (6) 290 13 86; fax 290 00 06).

South Africa: 936 Pretorius St., Arcadia, P.O. Box 3326, 0001 Pretoria (tel. (12) 342 34 77; fax 43 20 33).

Hungarian Consulates

U.S.: 223 E. 52nd St., New York, NY 10022 (tel. (212) 879-4127).

Canada: In **Toronto:** 102 Bloor St. W., Suite 45, Toronto, Ontario, M5S 1M8 (tel. (416) 923-8981; fax 923-2732). In **Montreal:** 1200 McGill College St., Suite 2030, Montreal, Quebec H3B 4G7 (tel. (514) 393-1555; fax 393-3528).

United Kingdom: 35 Easton Place, London SW1 X8BY (tel. (071) 235 71 91; fax 823 13 48).

Ireland: 2 Fitzwilliam Place, Dublin 2 (tel. (031) 61 29 03; fax 61 28 80).

Australia: Suite 405, Edgecliff Centre 203-233, New South Head Road, Edgecliff, NSW 2027 SY (tel. (612) 328 78 59; fax 327 18 29).

South Africa: P.O. Box 27077 Sunnyside 0132, 959 Arcadia Street, Arcadia (tel. (012) 43 30 30; fax 43 30 29).

■ Travel Organizations

Council on International Educational Exchange (CIEE/Council Travel), 205 E. 42nd St., NY 10017 (tel. (212) 661-1450; (800) 223-7402 for charter flight tickets only). Provides low cost travel arrangements (flights worldwide, charter tickets, Eurail passes, and individual country rail passes), books (including *Let's Go* guides and *Where to Stay U.S.A.),* insurance, and travel gear. Information on academics, work, voluntary service, homestays, and professional opportunities abroad. Work-exchange programs that help you find jobs overseas. HI memberships. ISIC, FIYTO, and ITIC cards. Write away for *Student Travels* (free), CIEE's new biannual travel magazine for college students. **Council Travel** and **Council Charter** are CIEE's two budget subsidiaries. CIEE operates 43 offices throughout the U.S., including those listed below and branches in Providence, RI; Amherst and Cambridge, MA; and Berkeley, La Jolla, and Long Beach, CA.

Boston, 729 Boylston St. #201, Boston, MA 02116 (tel. (617) 266-1926).

Chicago, 1153 N. Dearborn St., Chicago, IL 60610 (tel. (312) 951-0585).

Dallas, 6923 Snider Plaza B, Dallas, TX 75205 (tel. (214) 363-9941).

Los Angeles, 1093 Broxton Ave. #220, Los Angeles, CA 90024 (tel. (310) 208-3551).

Portland, 715 SW Morrison #600, Portland, OR 97205 (tel. (503) 228-1900).

San Diego, 953 Garnet Ave., San Diego, CA 94108 (tel. (619) 270-6401).

San Francisco, 919 Irving St. #102, San Francisco, CA 94122 (tel. (415) 566-6222).

Seattle, 1314 NE 43rd St. #210, Seattle, WA 98105 (tel. (206) 632-2448).

CIEE International Affiliates. If you can't locate an affiliated office in your country, contact CIEE's main office in New York or the **International Student Travel Confederation (ISTC),** Store Kongensgade 40H, 1264 Copenhagen K, Denmark (tel. +45 33 93 93 03).:

Canada: Travel CUTS (Canadian University Travel Services Ltd.), 187 College St., Toronto, Ontario M5T 1P7 (tel. (416) 979-2406).

United Kingdom: London Student Travel, 52 Grosvenor Gardens, London WC1 (tel. (071) 730 34 02).

Australia: SSA/STA Swap Program, P.O. Box 399 (First floor), 220 Faraday St., Carlton South, Melbourne, Victoria 3053 (tel. (03) 347 69 11).

STA Travel, 17 E. 45th St., New York, NY 10017 (tel. (212) 986-9643 or (800) 777-0112). A worldwide youth travel organization. Over 100 offices. Offers bargain flights, railpasses, accommodations, tours, insurance, and ISICs. Ten offices in the U.S., including:

Boston: 273 Newbury St., Boston, MA 02116 (tel. (617) 266-6014).

Los Angeles: 7202 Melrose Ave., Los Angeles, CA 90046 (tel. (213) 934-8722).

Philadelphia: University City Travel, 3730 Walnut St., Philadelphia, PA 19104 (tel. (215) 382-2928).

San Francisco: 51 Grant Ave., San Francisco, CA 94108 (tel. (415) 391-8407).

United Kingdom: Main offices are at 86 Old Brompton Rd., London SW7 3LQ, and 117 Euston Rd., London NW1 2SX (tel. (071) 937 99 21 for European Travel; 937 99 71 for North American; 937 99 62 for Long Haul Travel; 937 17 33 for Round the World Travel).

New Zealand: 10 High St., Auckland (tel. (09) 309 9995).

Federation of International Youth Travel Organisations (FIYTO), Bredgage 25H, DK-1260, Copenhagen K, Denmark (tel +45 33 33 96 00; fax +45 33 93 96 76). Sells the GO 25 Card and lists organizations that provide special services and discounts to card-carrying members of Hostelling International (see Youth and Student Identification).

Hostelling International (HI), 9 Guessens Rd., Welwyn Garden City, Herts., AL8 6QW, England (tel. (707) 33 24 87). Formerly known as the **International Youth Hostel Federation (IYHF).** This office handles international administration and policy matters; address general inquiries to the relevant national hostel associations (see Hostel Membership for addresses).

Austrian Airlines, tel. (800) 843-0002 or (212) 307-6226 in the U.S., (800) 387-1477 in Canada.

CSA, 545 Fifth Ave., New York, NY 10017 (tel. (212) 682-5833; fax 682-5836). The national airline of the Czech Republic, with non-stop flights from New York, Chicago, Vienna, Tel Aviv, and 13 other cities.

Chicago, 35 E. Wacker Dr., Chicago, IL 60601 (tel. (800) 628-6107 and (312) 201-1781; fax (312) 201-1783).

Montreal, 2020 rue Universite, Montreal, Quebec H3A 2A5 (tel. (514) 844-4200; fax 844-5742).

Toronto, 401 Bay St., Simpson Tower #1510, Toronto, Ontario M5H 2Y4 (tel. (416) 363-3174; fax 363-0239).

ÖKISTA (Österreichisches Komittee für Internationalen Studienaustausch), Garnisongasse 7, A-1090 Wien (tel. (0222) 401 48 0; fax 401 48 290). Pretty much the equivalent of Council Travel, Austrian-style. Low prices on airline tickets. Four other offices in Vienna, and offices in Graz, Innsbruck, Linz, Salzburg, and Klagenfurt. See Budget Travel under Practical Information for each city.

Campus Travel, 52 Grosvenor Gardens, London SW1W 0AG (tel. (071) 730 88 32; fax 730 57 39). Offers student discount flights, ISICs, and other services.

Educational Travel Centre (ETC), 438 N. Frances St., Madison, WI 53703 (tel. (608) 256-5551). Flight information, HI cards, coachpasses, and railpasses. Ask for the free pamphlet *Taking Off.*

International Student Exchange Flights (ISE), 5010 East Shea Blvd., #A104, Scottsdale, AZ 85254 (tel. (602) 951-1177). Budget student flights, railpasses, traveler's checks, and travel guides, including the *Let's Go* series. Free catalog.

German Rail, Inc., 20 Park Plaza, Boston, MA 02116 (tel. (617) 542-0577). Offices in Atlanta, Dallas, San Francisco, Los Angeles, Rosemont (Rosemont?), and Toronto. Sells rail tickets for trains throughout Europe.

■ Publications

European Association of Music Festivals, 122, rue de Lausanne, 1202, Geneva, Switzerland (tel. +41 (22) 732 28 03; fax +41 (22) 738 40 12). Publishes the booklet, *Festivals,* which lists the dates and programs of major European music and theater festivals. Don't let high prices discourage you from "high culture"; student rates and standing room discounts are often available.

Forsyth Travel Library, P.O. Box 2975, Shawnee Mission, KS 66201 (tel. (800) 367-7984). Call or write for their catalog of maps, guidebooks, railpasses, and timetables.

Superintendent of Documents, U.S. Government Printing Office, Washington, DC 20402 (tel. (202) 783-3238). Publishes *Tips for Travelers* (US$1), *Your Trip Abroad* (US$1.25), *Safe Trip Abroad* (US$1), and *Health Information for International Travel* (US$5). Prices include postage.

Wide World Books and Maps, 1911 N. 45th St., Seattle, WA 98103 (tel. (206) 634-3453). Sells hard-to-find maps. Open Mon.-Fri. 10am-7pm, Sat. 10am-6pm, Sun. noon-5pm.

Zephyr Press, 13 Robinson St., Somerville, MA 02145. Publishes the invaluable *People to People* books, which introduce readers to individuals who live in the Czech Republic, Slovakia, and Hungary. Using the addresses and personal descriptions provided, you can write ahead to the participants and frolic with them once you arrive.

■■■ DOCUMENTS 'N FORMALITIES

Be sure to file all applications several weeks or months in advance of your planned departure date. Remember, you rely on government agencies to complete these transactions, and a backlog in processing could spoil even the best-laid plans; many a mouse's trip has been shelved by a bureaucratic snarl. An agency might deem your applications inadequate, so you should leave enough leeway to have them rejected and resubmitted—maybe several times. Most offices suggest that you apply in the winter off-season (between August and December) for speedier service.

When you travel, always carry on your person two or more forms of identification, including at least one photo ID. A passport combined with a driver's license or birth certificate usually serves as adequate proof of your identity and citizenship. Many establishments, especially banks, require several IDs before cashing traveler's checks. Never carry your passport, travel ticket, identification documents, money, traveler's checks, insurance, and credit cards all together, or you risk being left entirely without ID or funds in case of theft or loss. It is wise to carry a half dozen extra passport-size photos that you can attach to the sundry IDs you'll eventually acquire or trade with your new friends overseas; photo shops and many department stores can snap inexpensive head-shots, and photo booths exist at many rail stations.

If you plan an extended stay in Austria, Prague, or Budapest, you might want to register your passport with the nearest embassy or consulate.

For general information about documents, formalities, and prudent travel abroad, procure the booklet *Your Trip Abroad* from the U.S. Department of State, Bureau of Consular Affairs, Public Affairs, Room 5807, Washington, DC 20520-4818.

■ Entrance Requirements

Citizens of the U.S., Canada, the U.K., Ireland, Australia, New Zealand, and South Africa all need valid passports to enter Austria, the Czech Republic, or Hungary, and to re-enter their own country. Be advised that these countries may deny you entrance if your passport expires in fewer than six months. Also, returning to your home country with an expired passport may result in a hefty fine. If your travel plans extend beyond Austria, the Czech Republic, and Hungary, remember that some countries on the European continent and elsewhere require a separate visa.

When you enter Austria, the Czech Republic, or Hungary, dress neatly and carry proof of your financial independence, such as a visa to the next country on your itinerary, an air ticket to depart, or enough money to cover the cost of your living expenses. The standard period of admission is from one to six months in Austria and the Czech Republic and one month in Hungary. To stay longer, you must present evidence that you will be able to support yourself for an extended period of time, and authorities often require a medical examination. Admission as a visitor does not include the right to work, which is authorized only by a work permit (see Alternatives to Tourism below). Entering these countries to study does not require a special visa, but immigration officers will want to see proof of acceptance from an Austrian, Czech, or Hungarian school, proof that the course of study will take up most of your time in the country, and, as always, proof that you can support yourself. A verbal promise of "intended" employment may not suffice for border officials; have a copy of a contract or a letter from the foreign office just in case.

■ Passports

As a precaution in case your passport is lost or stolen, be sure before you leave to *photocopy the pages of your passport that contain your photograph and identifying information.* Especially important is your passport number. Carry this photocopy in a safe place apart from your passport, perhaps with a traveling companion, and leave another copy at home. Better yet, carry a photocopy of all the pages of the passport, including all visa stamps, apart from your actual passport, and leave a duplicate copy with a relative or friend. These measures will help prove your citizenship and facilitate the issuing of a new passport. Consulates also recommend that you carry an expired passport or an official copy of your birth certificate (not necessarily the one issued at birth, of course) in a part of your baggage separate from other documents. You can request a duplicate birth certificate from the Bureau of Vital Records and Statistics in your state or province of birth.

Losing your passport can generate a monumental hassle. It may take weeks to process a replacement, and your new passport may be valid only for a limited time. In addition, any visas stamped in your old passport will be irretrievably lost. If you do lose your passport, *immediately* notify the local police and the nearest embassy or consulate of your home government. To expedite its replacement, you will need to know all the information that you had previously recorded and photocopied and show identification and proof of citizenship. Some consulates can issue new passports within two days if you provide adequate proof of citizenship. In an emergency, ask for **immediate temporary traveling papers** that permit you to return to your home country. Remember that your passport is a public, not private, document; it legally belongs to your nation's government.

Applying for a passport is complicated, so make sure your questions are answered in advance; you don't want to wait two hours in a flickering-fluorescent-lit passport office just to be told you'll have to return tomorrow because your application is insufficient.

United States Passports

U.S. citizens may apply for a passport, valid for 10 years (5 yr. if under 18) at any one of several thousand federal or state courthouses or post offices authorized to accept passport applications, or at a **U.S. Passport Agency,** located in Boston, Chicago, Honolulu, Houston, Los Angeles, Miami, New Orleans, New York, Philadelphia, San Francisco, Seattle, Stamford, and Washington, DC. Refer to the "U.S. Government, State Department" section of the telephone directory or call your local post office for addresses. Parents must apply, in person, for children under age 13. You must apply in person if this is your first passport or if you are under 18.

For a U.S. passport, you must submit the following along with a completed application form: (1) proof of U.S. citizenship (either a certified birth certificate, naturalization papers, or a previous passport); (2) valid identification bearing your signature and either your photo or a personal description (e.g. an unexpired driver's license or passport, student ID card, or government ID card); and (3) two identical t passport-size (2 in. by 2 in.) photographs with a white or off-white background taken within the past six months. Bring these items and $65 (under 18 $40) in check (traveler's, certified, or personal) or money order. Write your date of birth on the check, and photocopy the data page for your personal records. You can renew your passport by mail (or in person) for $55. Your old passport can serve as both (1) and (2) and must be enclosed with the application and photos.

Processing usually takes three to four weeks, perhaps fewer from a Passport Agency. Passports are processed according to the departure date indicated on the application form. During peak travel season (March through August), processing may take even longer. File your application as early as possible. If you fail to indicate a departure date, the agency will assume you are not planning any immediate travel (read: It may take *months*). In any event, your passport will be mailed to you. You may pay for express mail return of your passport. Passport agencies offer **rush service:** if you have proof that you are departing within five working days (e.g. an airplane ticket), a Passport Agency will issue a passport while you wait (and wait, and wait). Arrive at dawn, well before the office opens, and expect to remain there at least until the end of the day. Of course, rush service is risky.

Abroad, a U.S. embassy or consulate can usually issue new passports, given proof of citizenship. For more information, contact the U.S. Passport Information's helpful

24-hour recorded message (tel. (202) 647-0518), which offers general information, agency locations, business hours, etc., or call the recorded message of the passport agency nearest you.

If your passport is lost or stolen in the U.S., report it in writing to Passport Services, 1425 K St., NW, Department of State, Washington, DC 20522-1705, or to the nearest passport agency.

Canadian Passports

Canadian passport application forms in English and French are available at all passport offices, post offices, and most travel agencies. Along with the application form, a citizen must provide: (1) citizenship documentation (an old passport does not suffice as proof); (2) two identical passport-size photographs less than one year old that indicate the photographer, the studio address, and the date the photos were taken; and (3) a CDN$35 fee (paid in cash, money order, certified check, or bank draft). Both photographs must be signed by the applicant, and the application form and one of the photographs must be certified by a guarantor (someone who has known the applicant for two years and whose profession falls into one of the categories listed in the application form). Citizens may apply in person at any one of 29 regional Passport Offices across Canada. Travel agents can direct the applicant to the nearest location. Citizens who reside in the U.S. can contact a Canadian diplomatic mission; those outside Canada and the U.S. should contact the nearest embassy or consulate. You can apply by mail by sending a completed application form with appropriate documentation and the CDN$35 fee to Passport Office, External Affairs, Ottawa, Ontario, K1A 0G3.

The processing time is approximately five business days for in-person applications and three weeks for mailed ones. Service is usually faster in winter, the off-peak travel season. Applicants over age 16 should file form A; those younger than 16 should use Form B. Children may be included on a parent's passport. A passport is valid for five years and is not renewable—citizens must apply for a new passport when the old one expires.

For additional **information**, call the **24-hour recorded message** (tel. (800) 567-6868, Metro Toronto 973-3251, Montreal 283-2152). Refer to the booklet, *Bon Voyage, But...,* for further help and a list of Canadian embassies and consulates abroad. It is available free of charge from any passport office or from: Info-Export (BPTE), External Affairs, Ottawa, Ontario, K1A 0G2, Canada (tel. (613) 996-8885).

United Kingdom Passports

British citizens can obtain either a full passport or a more restricted Visitor's Passport. For a **full passport** valid for 10 years (5 yr. if under 16), apply in person or by mail to the London Passport Office or by mail to a passport office located in Liverpool, Newport, Peterborough, Glasgow, or Belfast. Along with a completed application, you must submit: (1) a birth certificate and marriage certificate (if applicable); (2) two identical, recent photos signed by a guarantor (a professional who is not a relative who has known you for two years); and (3) the £18 fee. Children under 16 may be included on a parent's passport. Processing usually takes four to six weeks. The London office offers same-day walk-in rush service; arrive early. For a **Visitor's Passport,** valid for one year in Western Europe only, apply in person at major post offices. You must bring identification, two identical photos, and the fee (around £9).

Irish Passports

Irish citizens can apply for a passport by mail to one of the following two passport offices: Department of Foreign Affairs, Passport Office, Setanta Centre, Molesworth St., Dublin 2 (tel. (01) 6711633), or Passport Office, 1A South Mall, Cork (tel. (021) 272 525). You can obtain an application form at a local *Garda* station or request one from a passport office. First-time applicants should send their long-form birth certificate and two identical photographs. To renew, citizens should send the old passport (save a photocopy before you send it off) and two photos. Passports cost £45 and are valid for 10 years. Citizens younger than 18 or older than 65 can request a three-year passport that costs £10.

Australian Passports

Australian citizens must apply for a passport in person at a local post office, a passport office, or an Australian diplomatic mission overseas. An appointment may be necessary at any of the three. Passport offices are located in Adelaide, Brisbane, Canberra, Darwin, Hobart, Melbourne, Newcastle, Perth, and Sydney. A parent may file an application for a child who is under 18 and unmarried. Along with your application, you must submit: (1) proof of citizenship (such as an expired passport, a birth certificate, or a citizens certificate from the Immigration service); (2) proof of your present name; (3) two identical, signed photographs (45mm by 35mm) less than six months old; (4) other forms of ID (such as a driver's license, credit card, rate notice, etc.). Application fees are adjusted every three months; call the toll-free **information** service for current details (tel. 13 12 32).

New Zealand Passports

Applicants for New Zealand passports must contact their local Link Centre, travel agent, or New Zealand Representative for an application form, which they must complete and mail to the New Zealand Passport Office, Documents of National Identity Division, Department of Internal Affairs, Box 10-526, Wellington (tel. (04) 474 81 00). You must submit along with a completed application: (1) proof of citizenship; (2) proof of identity; and (3) two certified photos. The standard processing time is 10 working days from receipt of a correct application; applications marked as "urgent" receive priority. The application fee is NZ$56.25 for an application submitted in New Zealand and NZ$110 for one submitted overseas (if under age 16, NZ$25.30 and NZ$49.50, respectively).

Citizens applying from overseas should send the passport application to the nearest embassy, high commission, or consulate that is authorized to issue passports. Unless you need the passport urgently, the application will be processed in New Zealand.

South African Passports

South African citizens can apply for a passport at any Home Affairs Office. Two photos, either a birth certificate or an identity book, and the R30 fee must accompany a completed application. For further information, contact the Home Affairs Office nearest you.

■ Visas

A visa is an endorsement that a foreign government stamps into a passport; it allows the bearer to stay in that country for a specified purpose and period of time. Most visas cost US$10-30 and allow you to spend about a month in a country, within six months to a year from the date of issue. Regulations are adjusted frequently, so check the country's visa requirements and restrictions as close to your departure date as possible.

If you want to **extend your stay** beyond the visa limit, apply for a visa at the country's embassy or consulate in your home country well before your departure (see Useful Addresses: Embassies and Consulates above). Unless you are a student, extending your visit once you are abroad is more difficult. In that case, you must contact the country's immigration officials or local police well before your time is up, and you must show sound proof of financial resources (see Entrance Requirements above).

The U.S. Department of State publishes a helpful pamphlet for American citizens called *Foreign Visa Requirements.* Send a check for 50¢ per pamphlet to the Consumer Information Center, Dept. 454V, Pueblo, CO 81009 (tel. (719) 948 3334); the office, we might add, also offers the ever-popular pamphlets *Hair: A Personal Statement, Metric Measures Up,* and *The Duck Stamp Story.* For more **information,** write to the Bureau of Consular Affairs, Passport Services, 1425 K St., NW, Department of State, Washington, DC 20522-1705.

To get a **visa by mail,** apply to the embassies or consulates of your destination countries; you usually have to submit your passport and fill out a form they supply, and the process will take several weeks. Begin *early*. You can often pay a company in your country's capital to procure a visa for you, an especially useful service if you need the documents quickly and want to circumvent a bloated governmental bureaucracy. Check the phone book; in the USA, contact **Visa Center, Inc.,** 507 Fifth Ave. #904, New York, NY 10017 (tel. (212) 986-0924). This organization is one of many that can secure visas for travel to and from all possible countries. The service charge varies, but the average cost for a U.S. citizen is US$15-20 per visa.

Austria

U.S., Canadian, British, Irish, Australian, and New Zealand tourists need not obtain a visa to visit Austria. These citizens must carry only a valid passport to remain in the country for three months, except Brits, who may stay for 6 months with a valid passport. Citizens of these countries who wish to stay longer than the allotted time or who enter Austria for a purpose other than tourism (study, employment, establishing a residence), and citizens of South Africa, must carry a visa as well as a passport. Visas will be issued by the Austrian embassy or consulate in your home country.

The Czech Republic

Visa requirements for visitors to the Czech Republic have been eroding steadily since the 1989 revolution. Citizens of the U.S., Ireland, and the U.K. need not obtain a visa to visit the Czech Republic and may stay for 30, 90, and 180 days, respectively, though some unofficial organizations in Central Europe might tell you otherwise to secure an unnecessary visa fee. For the latest information, contact the Czech Embassy in your home country or your own embassy in the Czech Republic.

Other foreigners need visas, available from any Czech Embassy or Consulate upon presentation of a visa application, or at the appropriate Czech border crossing points for cars: Rozvadov, Dolni, Dvoriste, or Hate. Processing a visa application through the mail is amazingly efficient; the entire undertaking usually takes only two days, plus postage time. Applications presented to the Embassy in person are generally granted on the spot. The visa application consists of: (1) a travel document (such as a passport); (2) a photograph; (3) a stamped, self-addressed envelope; and (4) the fee (CDN$44 or the equivalent), paid by cashier's check or money order. Visas are free for children under 15.

Special double entry visas allow visitors to enter the Czech Republic twice. To obtain this visa, you must present two applications, two photographs, and a visa fee equivalent to US$31.

A visa may be used at any time within six months from the date of issue. Bearers of a Czech tourist visa must register their stay with the Czech passport authorities within 48 hours after arrival to the Czech Republic. These visas may then be extended at the local passport or visa authorities for up to six months while the visitor is in the Czech Republic.

The visa section of the Czech consulate in the U.S. is open Monday to Friday from 8:30 to 11:30am. Call (202) 363-6308 for 24-hour recorded **information.**

Hungary

Citizens of the U.S., Canada, the U.K., Ireland, and South Africa only need a valid passport to travel through Hungary for transit or tourism. Citizens of Australia and New Zealand must obtain visas from the Hungarian Consulate before they arrive. Along with two completed applications, you must submit a valid passport and two passport-size photos. The fee is AUS$25, payable in money order, bank check, or cash. This fee is waived for children under 14 who are included on a parent's passport, but they must complete a separate application, including photographs. Visas are issued within two working days; while-you-wait rush service is available for an extra AUS$15 fee. The Australian Consulate also processes applications from New Zealanders, though it may take longer. Contact the Consulate General of the Republic of Hungary #405, Edgecliff Centre, 203-233 New South Head Rd., Edgecliff, NSW 2027, Sydney, Australia (tel. (02) 328 78 59, fax (02) 327 18 29). Visa application forms and all their accoutrements may be submitted in person Mon., Wed., and Fri. 10am-1pm, or by mail (if you include a self-addressed, stamped envelope).

After 30 days in the country, *all* visitors must register with the police; after 90 days, you must inform **KEOKH,** at the Foreign National Office, Andrassy út 12, Budapest (tel. (1) 118 08 00), where a residence permit will be issued for 800 Ft.

■ Customs

Unless you plan to import a BMW or a barnyard beast, you will probably pass right over the customs barrier with minimal ado. The many rules and regulations of customs and duties hardly pose a threat to the budget traveler. Austria, the Czech Republic, and Hungary prohibit or restrict the importation of firearms, explosives, ammunition, fireworks, controlled drugs, most plants and animals, lottery tickets, and obscene literature and films. Guidelines for the Czech Republic have been eroding steadily since the 1989 revolution. For the latest information, contact the Czech Embassy. To preclude an international hullabaloo when you transport prescription drugs, ensure that bottles are clearly marked, and carry a copy of the prescription to show the customs officer. Place the medicines in your carry-on baggage to further avoid suspicion. In addition, officials may seize articles manufactured from protected species, such as certain reptiles and big cats that roar.

Upon returning home, you must declare all articles that you have acquired abroad and must pay a duty on the value of those articles that exceed the allowance established by your country's customs service. Holding onto receipts for purchases made abroad will help you ascertain values when you return. It is wise to *make a list,* including serial numbers, of any valuables you carry with you from home (and maybe rethink why you are traveling with valuables in the first place). If you register this list with customs before your departure and have a customs official stamp it, you will avoid import duty charges and ensure an easy passage upon your return. Be especially careful to document items manufactured abroad.

Keep in mind that goods and gifts purchased at duty-free shops abroad are *not* exempt from duty or sales tax at your point of return; you must declare these items along with other purchases. "Duty-free" only exempts you from paying a tax in the country of purchase.

Entering Austria, the Czech Republic, and Hungary

Visitors entering these countries must declare all baggage and belongings at the point of entry. You need not register or pay a duty on items, such as clothing, that you import for personal use during your journey, provided that you will, in turn, export them as well.

Austria

Travelers over 17 may import the following items duty-free after declaring them: (1) 400 cigarettes or 100 cigars or 500g tobacco; (2) 2.25L wine; and (3) 1L alcohol if you arrive from a non-European country. If you arrive from a European country, the limits are: (1) 200 cigarettes or 50 cigars or 250g tobacco; (2) 2.25L wine; (3) and 1L alcohol. A duty is placed on amounts that exceed these. If, on the way to Austria, a stopover of more than 24 hours has been made in any European country, customs exemptions can only be granted for the latter, more limited quantities. In addition, each traveler may import one bottle of cologne, one bottle of perfume, and souvenir items with a total retail value not to exceed 400 AS. To import the maximum two cats or dogs per person, a visitor must present a valid certificate of vaccination against rabies with an authorized German translation of the certificate.

The Czech Republic

Travelers over 18 may import (1) 2L wine; (2) 1L spirits; (3) 250 cigarettes or a corresponding amount of tobacco products. According to the Embassy of the Czech Republic (see Embassies and Consulates above), "All dogs and other small animals (cats, rabbits, guinea-pigs, hamsters, *small carnivorous animals,* fowls, pigeons, *birds,* parrots, *apes*) shall be accompanied by a Certificate of Origin and Veterinary Health Certificate issued within three days prior to shipment and signed by a State Veterinary Officer or a veterinary surgeon authorized by the Government of the country of origin."

Hungary

According to the Hungarian Embassy in New York City, travelers over 18 may import (1) 200 cigarettes; (2) 2L wine; and (3) 1L spirits. Small animals must be accompanied by a certificate from a veterinarian that attests to the pet's health and vaccination (English is acceptable). Hunters may import a rifle and bullets.

Returning Home

Returning to the United States

U.S. citizens returning home may bring $400 worth of accompanying goods duty-free but must pay a 10% tax on the next $1000. You must declare all purchases, so remember to have sales slips ready. Goods are considered duty-free if they are for personal or household use (this includes gifts) but this cannot include more than 100 cigars, 200 cigarettes (1 carton), and 1L of wine or liquor. You must be over 21 to bring liquor into the U.S. To be eligible for the duty-free allowance, you must have remained abroad for at least 48 hours and cannot have used this exemption or any part of it within the preceding 30 days.

You can mail unsolicited gifts duty-free if they are worth less than $50, though you may not mail liquor, tobacco, or perfume. Officials occasionally spot check parcels, so mark the price and nature of the gift and the words "Unsolicited Gift" on the package. If you send back a non-gift parcel or a gift worth more than $50, the Postal Service will collect a duty for its value plus a handling charge to deliver it. If you mail home personal goods of U.S. origin, you can avoid duty charges by marking the package "American goods returned." For more information, consult the brochure, *Know Before You Go,* available from R. Woods, Consumer Information Center, Pueblo, CO 81009 (item 477Y). You can direct other questions to the U.S. Customs Service, P.O. Box 7407, Washington, DC 20044 (tel. (202) 927-6724). Foreign nationals living in the U.S. are subject to different regulations; refer to the leaflet *Customs Hints for Visitors (Nonresidents).*

Returning to Canada

Canadian citizens who remain abroad for at least one week may bring back up to CDN$300 worth of goods duty-free once every calendar year; goods that exceed the allowance will be taxed at 20%. You are permitted to ship goods home under this exemption as long as you declare them when you arrive. Citizens over the legal age (which varies by province) may import in-person (not through the mail) up to 200 cigarettes, 50 cigars, 400g loose tobacco, 1.14L wine or alcohol, and 355ml beer; the value of these products is included in the CDN$300 allowance. For more information, contact External Affairs, Communications Branch, Mackenzie Ave., Ottawa, Ontario, K1A 0I5 (tel. (613) 957-0275).

Returning to the United Kingdom

British citizens are allowed an exemption of up to £36 of goods purchased outside the EC, including not more than 200 cigarettes, 100 cigarillos, 50 cigars, or 250kg of tobacco; and no more than 2L of still table wine plus 1L of alcohol over 22% by volume. You must be over 17 to import liquor or tobacco. For more information about U.K. customs, contact Her Majesty's Customs and Excise, Custom House, Heathrow Airport North, Hounslow, Middlesex, TW6 2LA (tel. (081) 750 16 03, fax 750 15 49). *HM Customs & Excise Notice #1* explains the allowances for people travelling to the U.K. both from within and without the European Community.

Returning to Ireland

Irish citizens may return home with the equivalent of IR£34 (under 17 IR£17) of goods purchased outside the EC, including: 1) 200 cigarettes, 100 cigarillos, 50 cigars, or 250g tobacco, or apportioned fractions thereof; 2) 1L liquor or 2L wine, or apportioned fractions thereof; 3) 2L still wine; 4) 50g perfume; and 5) 0.25L toilet water. Citizens under 17 are not entitled to any allowance for tobacco or alcoholic products. For more information, contact The Revenue Commissioners, Dublin Castle (tel. (01) 679 27 77, fax (01) 671 20 21).

Returning to Australia and New Zealand

Australian citizens may import AUS$400 (under 18 AUS$200) of goods duty-free, including 250 cigarettes, 250g tobacco, and 1L alcohol. You must be over 18 to import tobacco or alcohol products. For information, contact the nearest Australian consulate, or the Australian Customs Service, 5 Constitution Ave., Canberra, ACT, 2601.

Each New Zealand citizen may bring home up to NZ$700 worth of goods duty-free if they are intended for personal use or are unsolicited gifts. The concession is 200 cigarettes (1 carton), 250g of tobacco, or 50 cigars, or a combination of all three not to exceed 250g. You may also bring in 4.5L of beer or wine and 1.125L of liquor. Only travelers over 17 may bring tobacco or alcoholic beverages into the country. For more information, consult *New Zealand Customs Guide for Travelers,* available from customs offices, or contact New Zealand Customs, 50 Anzac Avenue, Box 29, Auckland (tel. (09) 377 35 20; fax 309 29 78).

Returning to South Africa

Each South African citizen may import items worth up to R500 duty-free, not including: 400 cigarettes, 50 cigars, 250g tobacco, 2L wine, 1L of spirits, 250mL toilet water, and 50mL perfume. Amounts exceeding this limit are fully dutiable. Golf clubs, watches, firearms, and furs do not fall within the duty-free allowances for travelers who have been absent from the Republic for less than six months, and goods acquired abroad and sent to the Republic as unaccompanied baggage do not qualify for any allowances. You may not export or import South African Bank notes in excess of R500.

Persons who require specific information or advice concerning customs and excise duties can address their inquiries to: The Commissioner for Customs and Excise, Private Bag X47, Pretoria, 0001. This agency distributes the pamphlet, *South African Customs Information,* for visitors and residents who travel abroad. South Africans in the U.S. should contact: South African Mission, 3201 New Mexico Ave. #390, NW, Washington, DC 20016 (tel. (202) 232-4400; fax 364-6008).

■ Hostel Membership

Hostelling International (HI) is the new and universal trademark name adopted by the International Youth Hostel Federation (IYHF). The 6,000 official youth hostels worldwide will normally display the new HI logo (a blue triangle enclosing a white pine tree and hut) alongside the symbol of one of the 70 national hostel associations.

A one-year Hostelling International (HI) membership permits you to stay at youth hostels all over Austria, Prague, and Budapest at unbeatable prices. And, despite the name, you need not be a youth; travelers over 25 pay only a slight surcharge for a bed. You can save yourself potential trouble by procuring a membership card before you leave home. Some hostels do not sell them on the spot, and it may even be cheaper (or more expensive) in your home country depending on currency exchange rates.

One-year hostel membership cards are available from some travel agencies, including Council Travel and STA Travel (see Useful Travel Organizations above), and from the following HI national affiliates:

International Youth Hostel Federation (IYHF) Headquarters, 9 Guessens Rd., Welwyn Garden City, Herts. AL8 6QW, England (tel. (0707) 33 24 87).

American Youth Hostels (AYH), 733 15th St. #840, NW, Washington, DC, 20005 (tel. (202) 783-6161; fax 783-6171); also dozens of regional offices across the U.S. (call above number for information). Fee $25, under 18 $10, over 54 $15. AYH is the U.S. member of IYHF. 200 hostels in U.S. Contact AYH for ISICs, student and charter flights, travel equipment, literature on budget travel, and information on summer positions as a group leader for domestic outings; to lead, you must be over 21 and complete a 7-day, US$350 course.

Hostelling International—Canada (HI-C), National Office, 1600 James Naismith Dr. #608, Gloucester, Ontario K1B 5N4 (tel. (613) 748-5638). 1-yr. membership fee CDN$26.75, under 18 CDN$12.84; 2-yr. fee CDN$37.45.

Youth Hostels Association of England and Wales (YHA), Trevelyan House, 8 St. Stephen's Hill, St. Albans, Herts AL1 2DY (tel. (0727) 855 215). Fee £9, under 18 £3.

Youth Hostel Association of Northern Ireland (YHANI), 56 Bradbury Pl., Belfast BT7 1RU (tel. (0232) 324 733).

An Óige (Irish Youth Hostel Association), 61 Mountjoy Sq., Dublin 7, Ireland (tel. (01) 30 45 55; fax 30 58 08). Fee £9, under 18 £3.

Australian Youth Hostels Association (AYHA), Level 3, 10 Mallett St., Camperdown, New South Wales, 2050 (tel. (02) 565 16 99; fax 565 13 25). Fee AUS$40.

Youth Hostels Association of New Zealand, P.O. Box 436, corner of Manchester and Gloucester St., Christchurch 1 (tel. 64 3 379 99 70; fax 64 3 365 44 76). Fee NZ$24.

The guides, *Budget Accommodation Vol. 1: Europe and the Mediterranean* and *Vol. 2: Africa, America, Asia, Australia, and New Zealand* (each US$14, including postage and handling), list up-to-date information on HI hostels. They contain English, French, German, and Spanish translations and are available from any hostel association.

HI has recently instituted an **International Booking Network.** To reserve space in high season, obtain an International Booking Voucher from any national youth hostel association (in your home country or the one you will visit) and send it to a participating hostel four to eight weeks in advance of your stay, along with US$2 in local currency. You can contact some hostels, indicated in this guide, by fax. If your plans are firm enough to allow it, pre-booking is wise. Effective use of this pre-application is the way populous school groups always manage to reserve rooms before you do.

■ Youth and Student Identification

In the world of budget travel, youth has its privileges. Two main forms of student and youth identification are accepted worldwide; they are extremely useful, especially for the insurance packages that accompany them.

The **International Student Identity Card (ISIC)** is the most widely accepted form of student identification. Over one million students flash it every year. Using this card can garner you discounts for sights, theaters, museums, accommodations, train, ferry, and airplane travel, and other services throughout Austria, Prague, and Budapest. Present the card wherever you go, and ask about discounts, even when none are advertised. Cardholders are automatically eligible for accident insurance of up to US$3000 as well as $100 per day of in-hospital care for up to 60 days. In addition, students with an ISIC have access to a toll-free Traveler's Assistance hotline whose multilingual staff can provide assistance in medical, legal, and financial emergencies overseas.

Many student-travel offices issue ISICs (see Useful Addresses above). When you apply for the card, procure a copy of the International Student Identity Card Handbook, which lists by country some of the available discounts.

To apply, supply in person or by mail: (1) current, dated proof of your degree-seeking student status (a letter on school stationary signed and sealed by the registrar, a photocopied grade report, or a Bursar's receipt with school seal that indicates full payment for fall 1993, spring 1994, or summer 1994 sessions); (2) a 1½ x 2" photo (vending machine-size) with your name printed and signed on the back; (3) proof of your birthdate and nationality; and (4) the name, address, and phone number of a beneficiary; in the event of the insured's death, payment will be made to the beneficiary. Mail these items to CIEE or another participating bureau (see Useful Addresses above). Applicants must be at least 12 years old and must be a student at a secondary or post-secondary school. The 1994 card is valid from Sept. 1993 through Dec. 1994. The fee is $15.

Because of the proliferation of phony and improperly issued ISIC cards, many airlines and some other services now require double proof of student identity. It is wise to have a signed letter from the registrar attesting to your student status and stamped with the school seal, or carry your school ID card.

The new, US$16 **International Teacher Identity Card (ITIC)** offers identical discounts, in theory, but because of its recent introduction, many establishments are reluctant to honor the card. The application process is the same as the process to obtain an ISIC.

Federation of International Youth Travel Organizations (FIYTO) issues its own discount card to travelers who are not students but are under 26. Also known as the **International Youth Discount Travel Card** or the **GO 25 Card,** this one-year card offers many of the same benefits as the ISIC, and most organizations that sell the ISIC also sell Go 25. A brochure that lists discounts is free when you purchase the card. The card discounts, for example, the Juniorhotel Praha (tel. 29 29 84) in Prague, by 140 kčs, as well as most museums, often by 50%. It also discounts many Austrian hotels and hostels by 10%, as well as language schools, museums, and recreational facilities in Austrian cities. To apply for the card in person, bring: (1) proof of birthdate (a copy of your birth certificate, a passport, or a valid driver's license); and (2) a passport-sized photo (with your name printed on the back). The fee is US$10, CDN$12, and £4. For more information, contact FIYTO at Bredgage 25H, DK-1260, Copenhagen K, Denmark (tel. (+45) 33 33 96 00, fax (+45) 33 93 96 76).

■ International Driver's License

To drive in Austria, Prague, or Budapest, your driver's license must be accompanied by an International Driver's Permit (IDP) or by an official validation from the country's consulate or National Tourist Office. The IDP smooths out difficulties with foreign police officers, especially if you do not speak their language, and serves as an additional piece of identification; the Austrian National Tourist office "strongly recommends" that you carry it. Know that most car rental agencies do not require the permit, and that some drivers choose to risk driving without one. All vehicles must be covered by third-party liability insurance.

Your IDP must be issued in your own country *before* you depart. U.S. license holders can obtain an International Driving Permit (US$10), valid for one year, at any **American Automobile Association (AAA)** office or by writing to its main office, AAA Florida, Travel Agency Services Department, 1000 AAA Drive, Heathrow, FL 32746-5080 (tel. (800) 222-4357 or (407) 444-7883; fax (407) 444-7380). You may also procure an IDP from the **American Automobile Touring Alliance,** Bayside Plaza, 188 The Embarcadero, San Francisco, CA 94105.

International Student Identity Card
ISIC
SHAW
AMY
3/5/73
9/26/93
U.S.
NORTHWESTERN UNIV.
STUDENT
ISIC920545135

COUNCIL

Canadian license holders can obtain an IDP ($10CDN) through any **Canadian Automobile Association (CAA)** branch office in Canada, or by writing to CAA Toronto, 60 Commerce Valley Dr. East, Markham, Ontario, L3T 7P9 (tel. (416) 771-3170).

Applicants in the U.S. or Canada must be over 18 and must submit (1) a completed application; (2) two recent passport-size photos; (3) a valid U.S. or Canadian driver's license.

Most credit cards cover standard insurance. If you rent, lease, or borrow a car, you will need a green card, or International Insurance Certificate, to prove that you have liability insurance. Obtain it through the car rental agency; most of them include coverage in their prices. If you lease a car, you can obtain a green card from the dealer. Some travel agents offer the card, and it may be available at the border. Verify whether your auto insurance applies abroad; even if it does, you will still need a green card to certify this to foreign officials.

■■■ MONEY

If you stay in hostels and prepare your own food, expect to spend anywhere from US$15-50 per day, depending on local cost of living and your needs. Transportation will increase these figures. Don't sacrifice your health or safety for a cheaper tab.

No matter how low your budget, if you plan to travel for more than a couple of days, you'll need to keep handy a much larger amount of cash than you do at home. Carrying it around with you, however, even in a money belt, is risky, and personal checks from home may not be acceptable no matter how many forms of identity you have (even banks eschew them). Inevitably you will have to rely on some combination of the innovations of the modern financial world, but keep their shortcomings in mind.

■ Currency and Exchange

Currency exchange (*Wechsel* in German) commissions can quickly add up to a major expense. To minimize your losses, convert fairly large sums at one time, and carry the cash in a moneybelt or neck pouch. Post offices generally offer the best exchange rates and charge the smallest commissions. Tote bills or checks of your own currency in small denominations, especially for those moments when you are forced to exchange money at train stations or, worse yet, at luxury hotels or restaurants. It is a good idea to convert a small amount of money (about US$100) to local currency before you go. Why? Well, you might find yourself stuck with no money if you arrive after banking hours or on a holiday, and pre-conversion allows you to breeze through the airport while others languish at exchange counter lines. Since you lose money with every transaction, it is wise to convert in large sums (provided the exchange rate is either staying constant or deteriorating), but try not to exchange more than you will need.

Austrian Currency

There are no restrictions on importing Austrian or foreign money into Austria. Foreign currencies may also be brought out without limitation, but you may only export 15,000 AS, unless you obtain a special permit. The basic unit of currency in Austria is the **Schilling,** abbreviated variously as AS, öS, AUS, or, within Austria, simply as S. Each *Schilling* is subdivided into 100 **Groschen** (g). Coins come in 5, 10, 20, and 50g, and 1, 5, 10, and 20 AS denominations. Bills come in 20, 50, 100, 500, 1000, and 5000 AS amounts.

Banks throughout Austria are usually open Mon.-Wed. and Fri. 8am-12:30pm and 1:30-3pm, Thurs. 8am-12:30 and 1:30-5:30pm. In Vienna, most banks are open Mon.-Wed. and Fri. 8am-3pm, Thurs. 8am-5:30pm. The primary national banking chains are **Sparkasse, Creditanstalt, HypoBank,** and **Raiffaissen.** The best place to **exchange money** is the post office. Exchange rates are standardized among banks and exchange counters, while stores, hotels, and restaurants that accept payment in U.S. dollars apply a slightly lower rate o. exchange. Exchange offices at airports and rail terminals are usually open daily 8am-8pm—in Vienna, 8am-10pm.

Many banks offer cash advances with a **Visa card** (the **Zentralsparkasse** and **Kommerzialbank** do this at most branches). **American Express** has offices in Vienna, Salzburg, Innsbruck, Linz, Klagenfurt, and Graz. Banks are legally required to charge a commission for cashing foreign traveler's checks. American Express charges the legal minimum for its checks, and their exchange rates are generally comparable to banks.

Czech Republic Currency

Czech currency comes in banknotes of 10, 20, 50, 100, 200, 500, and 1000 crowns, or **koruny** (abbreviated kčs); the crown is subdivided into 100 **haléř** (h). Coins come in 5, 10, 20, or 50 h, and 1, 2, 5, and 10, 20, and 50 kčs denominations. Currency may not be imported or exported. You should save your receipts when you change dollars into *koruny* so you can change them back into dollars as you depart the Czech Republic. The Republic's **cash situation** is in flux; bills from erstwhile Czechoslovakia are still used, but all old bill of 100 kčs or more must be stamped to be valid. Unsuspecting tourists may be slipped unstamped bills, so beware; examine each 100, 500, or 1000 kčs note before accepting it. New Czech bills and coins are gradually being introduced, and new 200 and 1000 kčs bills are already circulating. New bills of 50, 100, and 500 kčs are set to occupy pocketbooks and wallets by 1994. In addition to the old, still-valid Czechoslovak coins, two new denominations, 20 and 50 kčs, have been minted. **American Express** has an office in Prague. Official exchange counters abound, and many downtown locations keep extended hours. The official floating rate is now virtually identical to the black market street rate, so it makes little sense to take the risks of unlicensed exchanges.

Hungarian Currency

The Hungarian currency, the **Forint,** circulates in coins of 1, 2, 5, 10, and 20 Ft and old-fashioned banknotes of 50, 100, 500, 1000, and 5000 Ft. If you hold these notes in front of a light, you'll notice a handy metal strip that signifies they are genuine. You may also encounter fractions of the Forint called fillérs, small coins hardly still in use. You can exchange money with ease in Budapest's District V (inner Pest) day or night, and at ATMs anywhere. Since the collapse of the black market, it is no longer worth exchanging money illegally. The street rate is only a tad better than the official one; worse yet, the risk of a charlatan swindling you is prohibitively high. **American Express** has an office in Budapest.

■ Traveler's Checks

Traveler's checks are the safest and most convenient way to carry large sums of money—would Karl Malden lie to you? They are refundable if lost or stolen, and many issuing agencies offer additional services such as refund hotlines, message relaying, travel insurance, and emergency assistance. The major brands are sold by agencies and banks everywhere, usually for a 1-2% commission or a set fee. The **American Automobile Association (AAA)** offers commission-free American Express travelers cheques to its members. Buying checks in small denominations ($20 checks rather than $50 or higher) is safer and more convenient—otherwise, after a small purchase, you'll still be carrying a large sum of cash. When possible, procure checks in the currency of the nation you will visit, or you will have to convert them after you arrive and pay twice the fee. When you purchase traveler's checks, you must sign each check at the top; a matching signature on the bottom is required to redeem the check. In Austria, traveler's checks are honored almost universally. Commissions vary widely among the nine *Länder* and even among branches of the same bank; while the Sparkasse in Nassereith charges 40 AS per check, Sparkasse in Salzburg charges 100 AS (US$10 per check). Rural areas tend to

offer the most generous commissions. In Prague and Budapest, traveler's checks are less recognized, but most banks will, perhaps reluctantly, exchange them. Post offices generally offer the best exchange rates.

Call any of the toll-free numbers below to find out the advantages of a particular type of check and the name of the issuing agency nearest you.

American Express: Call (800) 221-7282 in the U.S. and Canada, (0800) 52 13 13 in the U.K., and (02) 886 06 89 in Australia, New Zealand, and the South Pacific with questions or to report lost or stolen cheques. Elsewhere, call collect to the U.S. (tel. (801) 964-6665) for referral to offices in individual countries. AmEx travelers cheques are the most widely recognized and the easiest to replace if lost or stolen —just call the information number or the AmEx Travel office nearest you. AmEx offices cash their own cheques commission-free (except where prohibited by the national government). AmEx also sells cheques that can be signed by either of two people traveling together ("Cheque for Two"), although the fee makes this a less appealing option. AmEx offers additional conveniences, such as a plethora of offices abroad and its mail-holding service (see Keeping in Touch below). Cheques are available in 7 currencies. AAA members can obtain AmEx travelers cheques commission-free at AAA offices. Ask for the pint-size *Traveler's Companion* booklet, which lists addresses for the travel offices as well as stolen check hotlines for each country.

Barclays: Sells Visa traveler's checks. For lost or stolen checks, call Visa (tel. 800) 645-6556); for Barclays information, call (800) 221-2426 in the U.S. and Canada, (202) 67 12 12 in the U.K.; from elsewhere, call New York collect (212) 858-8500. Branches exist in almost every city and town in the U.K. Commission on check purchases varies from branch to branch (usually 1-3%). Barclays branches cash any Visa traveler's checks without a commission. Checks in four currencies.

Citicorp: Sells Visa traveler's checks (tel. (800) 645-6556 in the U.S. and Canada, (071) 982 40 40 in London, from elsewhere call collect to the U.S. (tel. (813) 623-1709). Commission is 1-2% on check purchases. Check holders are automatically enrolled in the **Travel Assist Hotline** (tel. (800) 523-1199) for 45 days after checks are bought. This service provides travelers with English-speaking doctor, lawyer, and interpreter referrals as well as traveler's check refund assistance. Citicorp also has a World Courier Service that guarantees hand-delivery of traveler's checks anywhere—yes, anywhere.

Thomas Cook: Thomas Cook and MasterCard International have formed a "global alliance" under which Thomas Cook distributes traveler's checks with both the MasterCard and Thomas Cook insignias printed on them. Thomas Cook handles the distribution of checks in U.S. dollars as well as checks in 10 other currencies. In the U.S., call (800) 223-7373 for refunds, (800) 223-4030 for orders. From elsewhere, call collect (212) 974-5696. Some Thomas Cook Currency Services offices (located in major cities around the globe) do not charge any fee for purchase of checks, while some charge a 1-2% commission. You can buy MasterCard traveler's checks from Thomas Cook at any bank displaying a MasterCard sign.

Visa: tel. (800) 227-6811 in the U.S. and Canada; from abroad, call collect to New York (212) 858-8500 or London (071) 937 80 91. Similar to the Thomas Cook/MasterCard alliance, Visa and Barclay's Bank have formed a coalition under which Visa checks can be cashed for free at any Barclay's bank. Checks available in many currencies.

Procuring a refund on lost or stolen checks can be time-consuming. To accelerate the process and avoid red tape, record check numbers as you cash them to help sniff out exactly which checks are missing. *Furthermore, keep check receipts and the record of which checks you've cashed separate from the checks themselves.* Leave a photocopy of check serial numbers with someone at home as a backup in case you lose your copy. Never countersign checks until you're prepared to cash them. Most importantly, always keep some cash stowed away for emergencies.

If you suspect your checks were filched...

Don't panic. Search around you and through your things. Once you are sure they're gone, look for the receipts. Take a deep breath, and head for a phone. If you use American Express checks, look for the local office or call their toll-free number (an English-speaking operator is on call 24 hrs.) If the office is open, the staff will ask which checks you have cashed and which were stolen; you will probably need to show various forms of identification. They can usually issue you new checks on the spot (or, if by phone, the next working day). If you think that your checks were stolen, and not sinking to the bottom of the Danube, you may speed the process if you file a police report at the nearest station.

■ Credit Cards

Budget travelers will have little day-to-day use for credit cards in Austria, Prague, and Budapest; few inexpensive establishments or transit authorities honor them, and those enticing, pricier places accept them all too willingly. Nonetheless, a little plastic can prove an invaluable ally. In an emergency, a credit card can get you a cash advance or pay for an unexpected ticket home. Some cards even cover car rental collision insurance, saving you a hefty fee. Try to pay for large purchases abroad by credit card; the credit card company gets a better exchange rate than you can. You can often reduce conversion fees by charging a purchase instead of changing traveler's checks. Credit cards are a wonderful safety valve as well; you can't stop payment on a fraudulent purchase if you paid with cash.

Visa and **MasterCard** are the most commonly welcomed credit cards in Europe, followed by **American Express.** Note that the ubiquitous European **Carte Bleue** and **EuroCard** and the British **Barclaycard** and **Access,** are the exact equivalents of Visa and MasterCard, respectively; look for the familiar logos rather than the names. You may need to remind businesses that accept EuroCard and Carte Bleue that your MasterCard or Visa is the American counterpart. The EuroCard/MasterCard is accepted at over 22,000 restaurants, hotels, and shops throughout Austria. If you need a cash advance, banks associated with the Big Three credit companies will give you an instant cash advance in the local currency, up to the amount of your remaining credit line. Unfortunately, in most cases you'll pay mortifying interest rates.

If you are a student and your income level is low, you may have difficulty acquiring a recognized credit card. American Express, as well as some of the larger national banks, have credit card offers geared especially towards students. Otherwise, you may have to find someone older and more entrenched in the financial establishment (try a parent) to co-sign your application. If a family member already has a credit card, their company can effortlessly issue an additional card in your name, with the bills sent directly to your loved ones. When using the credit card, just be sure to pay your bill as soon as you receive your statement; you'll incur hefty interest rates if you neglect to pay your balance each month.

American Express (tel. (800) 528-4800) demands the highest annual fee ($55) of the major credit corporations, but—sing along now—membership *does* have its privileges. AmEx cardholders can cash personal checks at AmEx offices abroad (up to US$1000, with the Gold card US$5000). Members can also access Global Assist, a 24-hour hotline that offers information and legal assistance in emergencies (tel. (800) 333-2639 in the U.S. and Canada; from abroad call Washington, DC collect (202) 554-2639). Cardholders can take advantage of the American Express Travel Service; benefits include assistance in changing airline, hotel, and car rental reservations, sending mailgrams and international cables, and holding your mail at more than 1500 AmEx offices around the world. In addition, there's a Purchase Protection Plan for cardholders that will refund or replace deficient products you buy with the card (certain restrictions apply). **MasterCard** (tel. (800) 999-0454) and **Visa** (tel. (800) 336-8472) credit cards are issued by individual banks; each bank offers different services and rates in conjunction with the card. **Working Assets** (tel. (800) 522-7759), a California-based company, has offered a Visa card since 1985 that donates a portion of money from all Visa purchases to 36 different non-profit, save-the-world-type organizations; their bills and statements are printed on recycled paper. They're perfect for rationalizing your will to splurge.

■ Electronic Banking

Automatic Teller Machines (frequently abbreviated "ATMs") offer 24-hour service throughout Europe. Most banks in the larger cities are connected to an international network, usually **Plus** (tel. (800) 843-7587 in the U.S.) or **Cirrus** (tel. (800) 424-7787 in the U.S.). Depending on the system your home bank uses, you can probably access your personal bank account whenever you're in need of funds. Take advantage of ATMs whenever possible, because they convert money according to the wholesale exchange rate, which is generally 5% better than the retail rate most banks use (which is already better than the rate at most exchange bureaus). An ATM will spit out money in the currency of the nation where the machine stands. Be sure to contact your home bank before you travel; you may need an international **PIN** (personal identification number), different than your code at home, to operate your card abroad.

American Express card holders can sign up for AmEx's free Express Cash service. It allows travelers to access cash from your account at any ATM with the AmEx trademark. Beware: each transaction costs a minimum US$2.50 (max. US$10) plus conversion fees and interest. For a list of ATMs where you can use your card, call AmEx (tel. (800) 227-4669 in the U.S.) and request a list of participating machines at your destination. Make sure to set up your Express Cash account a few weeks before you leave.

Visa cards can usually access Plus networks, and **MasterCard** can usually access Cirrus, though the affiliation often depends on the bank of issue. Call your home branch before you go. Despite its convenience, try not to rely *too* heavily on automation. There is often a limit on the amount of money you can withdraw per day, and computer network failures (and inadvertent, specious charges) are common.

One final note: try to choose a well-lit ATM in an area where you fell especially safe. The machines can make you easy prey for thieves who know that you've just replenished your cash supply.

■ Sending Money Abroad

Sending money abroad is less fun than a root canal—without nitrous oxide. Do your best to avoid wiring money by carrying a credit card or a separate stash of emergency traveler's checks. An **American Express card** offers the easiest way to obtain money from home; AmEx allows cardholders to draw cash from their checking accounts (checkbook welcomed but not required) at any of its offices—up to US$1000 every 21 days (no service charge, no interest). With someone feeding money into your account back home, you'll be set. Call **American Express** (tel. (800) 543-4080; in Canada (800) 933-3278).

The next best approach is to wire money through the instant international money transfer services operated by **Western Union** (tel. (800) 225-5227). The sender visits one of the offices or calls and charges the transfer to a credit card; the receiver can pick up the cash at any office abroad within minutes (fee about US$22-50 to send US$250, US$50-75 to send US$1000). To pick up the money, the recipient must produce ID or the answer a test question arranged by the sender (e.g. "What is your mother's maiden name?" or "What is the average velocity of a coconut-laden sparrow?"). The stodgiest route is to **cable money** from bank to bank. The sender must find a local bank big enough to have an international corporate big brother and bring the address of the receiving bank and the destination account number. Usually both the sender and the receiver must have accounts at the respective institutions.

Transfer can take up to a few days, and the fee is usually a flat US$20-30. Outside an American Express office, avoid trying to cash checks in foreign currencies; they usually take weeks and a US$30 fee to clear.

If you find yourself in an absolutely life-or-death situation, you may be able to have money sent through your government's diplomatic mission in the country in which you're traveling. This service will get you cash quickly but is considered an extreme imposition, so use it only when every other option fails. Citizens of the U.S. who are very desperate should turn to a U.S. consulate, which will assist by contacting friends or family in the U.S. and arranging for them to send money. The quickest way to have the money sent, if you're without AmEx, is to have your U.S. connection cable it to the State Department through Western Union, or drop off cash, a certified check, bank draft, or money order at the State Department. In extraordinary circumstances, senders at home should contact the **State Department's Citizens Emergency Center** (tel. (202) 647-5225; after-hours and holiday emergencies, (202) 647-4000). This service provides, among other benefits, repatriation loans to pay for destitute Americans' direct return to the U.S. Additional information appears in the pamphlet *The Citizens Emergency Center*. Order it from the Bureau of Consular Affairs, Public Affairs Staff, U.S. Department of State, Washington DC 20570-4818. Citizens of other countries should seek out their respective consulates in case of emergency.

■ Value-Added Tax

Austrian prices include a 20% value-added tax (VAT; in German, *Mehrwertsteuer*) on goods and 10% on services. If you buy goods totaling 1000 AS or more in one shop, you will be eligible for a VAT refund when you leave the country—ask for and complete the appropriate paperwork (form U-34) *when you make the purchase.* The refund is available in cash either through the mail or at the airport post office. If you charged the merchandise, your refund can be credited to your credit card account. Some stores also process refunds. Keep the forms handy—they must be validated by an Austrian customs officer upon departure. The **Austrian Automobile and Touring Club (ÖAMTC),** Schubertring 1-3, Vienna (tel. (0222) 71 19 97; call daily 6am-8pm), offers a helpful brochure, *Tax-free Shopping in Austria.*

■■■ HEALTH

In the event of a **medical emergency**, call the country's **emergency number:** 144 in Austria, 158 in the Czech Republic, and 04 in Hungary. Many of the first-aid centers and hospitals in major cities that *Let's Go* lists can provide you with medical care from an English-speaking doctor. Your consulate in major foreign cities should also have a list of English-speaking doctors in town. The **International Association for Medical Assistance to Travelers (IAMAT)** publishes a directory of English-speaking physicians throughout the world (see below).

■ Before You Go

Common sense is the simplest prescription for good health while you travel: eat well, drink enough, get enough sleep, and don't overexert yourself. Actually *listen* to your mother. Resist the temptations of madcap tourism—don't press for those extra 100km on your Eurailpass or that last obscure museum when you are too tired to enjoy yourself. Exhaustion can be as debilitating as illness. *You won't have fun if you overdo it.* While it may be difficult to lead a normal life while carrying your home on your back, several tips should make preventative care easier: If you're going to be doing a lot of walking, take along some quick-energy foods to keep your strength up. You'll need plenty of protein (for sustained energy), carbohydrates (for individually arduous days) and fluids (to prevent dehydration and constipation, two of the most common health problems among travelers). Fortunately, Austria is hardly the place to worry about procuring a meat-bread-beer diet. One warning about the last item; alcohol can cause serious problems when you are hiking at high altitudes, and Austrian beer has significantly more alcohol than American brew. Go overly easy at first.

Carry a canteen or water bottle on your travels, and make sure to drink (*water*) frequently. If you are prone to sunburn, be sure to bring a potent sunscreen with you from home (it's an expensive item to purchase abroad), cover up with long sleeves and a hat, and, again, drink plenty of fluids. Finally, remember to treat your most valuable resource well: lavish your feet with attention. Make sure your shoes (hiking boots for the mountains, maybe Teva® sandals or Birkenstocks® in the warmer climates) are appropriate for extended walking, change your socks often, use talcum powder to keep dry, and have some moleskin on hand to pad painful spots before they become excruciating blisters.

First Aid

For minor health problems on the road, a compact **first-aid kit** should suffice. Some hardware stores vend ready-made kits, but it's just as easy to assemble your own. Items you might want to include are:

antiseptic soap or antibiotic cream
thermometer in a sturdy case
Swiss Army knife with tweezers and scissors
decongestant or antihistamine
motion sickness remedy
medicine for diarrhea and stomach ills
insect and/or tick repellent
elastic bandage
sunscreen
aspirin
moleskin
burn ointment
bandages and gauze
large, clean cloth

Medication

Always go prepared with any **medication** you may need while away, as well as a copy of the prescription and/or a statement from your doctor—especially if you need to bring insulin, syringes, or any narcotics. Pepto-Bismol now markets a product designed specifically to combat traveler's diarrhea that you may want to pack, just in case. Travelers with chronic medical conditions should consult their physicians before leaving. Be aware that matching prescriptions with foreign equivalents may be difficult; it is best to bring an extra week's supply. Pack some generic antibiotics, if possible, in case of mild infection. If you are prone to mild allergic reactions, you may want to bring a tube of hydrocortisone cream to soothe the occasional rash. People with diabetes taking insulin and women taking birth-control pills should remember to account for **time zone** changes and make the necessary adjustments in their medication schedules. (Austria, Prague, and Budapest all set their clocks one hour ahead of Greenwich Mean Time, six hours ahead of New York's Eastern Standard Time). Remember that a *Drogerie* only sells toilet articles; to get a prescription filled you must go to an *Apotheke.*

Eyewear

If you wear glasses or contact lenses, take an extra prescription with you and make arrangements with someone at home to send you a replacement pair in an emergency. Glasses wearers should bring a strap or headband to insure that they don't slip off of your face and plunge into an Alpine gorge. If you wear contacts, bring glasses. Bring extra solutions, enzyme tablets, eyedrops, etc.—the price for lens supplies while abroad can be exorbitant.

Travelers with Medical Conditions

Any traveler with a medical condition that cannot be easily recognized (i.e. diabetes, epilepsy, heart conditions, allergies to antibiotics) may want to obtain a **Medic Alert Identification Tag.** In an emergency, this internationally recognized tag indicates the nature of the bearer's problem and provides the number of Medic Alert's 24-

hour hotline. Attending medical personnel can call this number to obtain information about the member's medical history. Lifetime membership (including tag, annually-updated wallet card, and 24-hr. hotline access) begins at US$35. Contact the Medic Alert Foundation, P.O. Box 1009, Turlock, CA 95381-1009 (tel. (800) 432-5378). The **American Diabetes Association,** 1660 Duke St., Alexandria, VA 22314 (tel. (800) 232-3472), provides copies of a "Travel and Diabetes" article and diabetic ID cards, proclaiming the carrier's diabetic status in 18 languages. Contact your local ADA office for information.

AIDS

All travelers should be concerned about **Acquired Immune Deficiency Syndrome (AIDS),** transmitted through the exchange of body fluids with an infected individual (HIV-positive). Remember that there is no assurance that someone is not infected: HIV tests only show antibodies after a six-month lapse. You've heard it before—do not have sex without using a condom, and never share intravenous needles with anyone. Those travelers who are HIV-positive or have AIDS should thoroughly check on possible immigration restrictions in the country they wish to visit. The Center for Disease Control's **AIDS Hotline** provides information on AIDS in the U.S. and can refer you to other organizations with information on Austria, Prague, and Budapest (tel. (800) 342-2437; TTD (800) 243-7889). Call the **U.S. State Department** for country-specific restrictions for HIV-positive travelers (tel. (202) 647-1488; fax 647-3000; modem-users may consult the electronic bulletin board at (202) 647-9225); or write the Bureau of Consular Affairs #5807, Dept. of State, Washington, DC 20520. The **World Health Organization** provides written material on AIDS around the world (tel. (202) 861-3200). In Austria, contact **AIDS-Help Vienna,** Wickenburggasse 14, A-1080 Vienna (tel. (0222) 408 61 86).

Contraception

Reliable **contraception** may be difficult to come by while traveling. Women taking birth-control pills should bring enough of a supply to allow for possible loss or extended stays. Although **condoms** are increasingly available and used throughout the world to prevent AIDS and unwanted pregnancies, you might want to stock up on your favorite brand at home, where you have a greater knowledge of their quality and reliability, and in case you need some during the flight over.

Additional Information

For more detailed information on any health concern before you go, you may wish to contact the **International Association for Medical Assistance to Travelers (IAMAT).** IAMAT is a non-profit organization that provides several brochures on health for travelers, an ID card, a chart detailing advisable immunizations for 200 countries and territories, and a worldwide directory of English-speaking physicians with medical training in Europe or North America. Membership in the organization is free (although donations are welcome, as IAMAT depends solely on voluntary contributions). Doctors are on call 24 hours a day for IAMAT members, who are guaranteed qualified medical assistance from an English-speaking physician. Contact chapters in the **U.S.,** 417 Center St., Lewiston, NY, 14092 (tel. (716) 754-4883); in **Canada,** 40 Regal Rd. Guelph, Ontario, N1K 1B5 (tel. (519) 836-0102) and 1287 St. Clair Ave. West, Toronto, M6E 1B8 (tel. (416) 652-0137); in **New Zealand,** P.O. Box 5049, 438 Pananui Rd., Christchurch 5 (tel. (03) 352 90 53; fax 352 46 30).

Complete health information for travelers is available from a variety of published sources. Consult your local bookstore for books on staying healthy at home or on the road or write the **Superintendent of Documents,** U.S. Government Printing Office, Washington, DC 20402 (tel. (202) 783-3238). Their publication *Health Information for International Travel* (US$5) details immunization requirements and other health precautions for travelers.

■ Medical Attention While Abroad

While you travel, pay attention to the signals of pain and discomfort that your body may send you. The stimulus may be a new climate, diet, water quality, or pace—when you first arrive or even after a couple of weeks. Once you get going, some of the milder symptoms that you may safely ignore at home may actually be signs of something more serious on the road; your increased exertion may wear you out and make you more susceptible to illness. The following paragraphs list some health problems you may encounter—but it should not be your only information source on these or other common ailments. Check with the publications and organizations listed above for more complete information, or purchase the **American Red Cross's** *First-Aid and Safety Handbook* (US$14.95), by writing to your local office or to the American Red Cross, 99 Brookline Ave., Boston, MA 02215. If you are interested in taking one of the many first-aid and CPR courses that the American Red Cross offers before leaving on your trip, contact your local branch—courses are extremely well-taught and relatively inexpensive.

Heatstroke

When traveling in the summer, protect yourself against the dangers of the sun and heat, especially the disaster of **heatstroke.** This term is often misapplied to all forms of heat exhaustion, but actually refers to a specific ailment that can cause death within a few hours if left untreated. Heatstroke can begin without direct exposure to the sun; it results from continuous heat stress, lack of fitness, or overactivity following heat exhaustion. In the early stages of heatstroke, sweating stops, body temperature rises, and an intense headache develops, soon followed by mental confusion or disorientation. To treat heatstroke, cool the victim off immediately with fruit juice or salted water, wet towels, and shade. As soon as possible, rush the victim to the hospital.

Hypothermia and Frostbite

Extreme cold is no less dangerous—it brings risks of **hypothermia** and frostbite. Hypothermia is a result of exposure to cold and can occur even in the middle of the summer, especially in rainy or windy conditions. Temperature fluctuations in the mountains create especially ripe conditions for hypothermia. The signs are easy to detect: body temperature drops rapidly, resulting in the inability to produce body heat. Other possible symptoms are: uncontrollable shivering, poor coordination, and exhaustion, followed by slurred speech, sleepiness, hallucinations, and amnesia. *Do not* let victims fall asleep if they are in advanced stages of hypothermia—if they lose consciousness, they might die. Always keep dry. Wear wool, *especially* in soggy weather—it retains its insulating properties even when wet. Dress in layers, and stay out of the wind, which carries heat away from the body. Remember that most body heat is lost through your head, so always carry a wool hat with you.

Frostbite occurs in freezing temperatures. The affected skin will turn white, then waxy and cold. To counteract the problem, the victim should drink plenty of warm beverages, stay or get dry, and gently and slowly warm the frostbitten area in dry fabric or with steady body contact. *Never rub* frostbite or heat the affected area quickly and directly—the skin is easily damaged. Take serious cases to a doctor or medic as soon as possible.

Heights and Forests

People who travel in **high altitudes** should allow their body a couple of days to adjust to the lower atmospheric oxygen levels before engaging in any strenuous activity. This applies particularly to people intent on setting out on long alpine hikes. Those new to high-altitude areas may feel drowsy; one alcoholic beverage may have the same effect as three at a lower altitude. You may be especially prone to dehydration in the mountains—remember to carry water with you and drink often.

If you plan to **romp in the forest,** try to learn any regional hazards. Know that any three-leafed plant might be poison ivy, poison oak, or poison sumac—pernicious plants whose oily surface causes insufferable itchiness if touched. (As Marge Simpson wisely noted, "Leaves of three, let it be; leaves of four, eat some more.") Ticks are especially nasty, and sometimes microscopic; cover as much skin on your lower body as you can. Look before you leap into any wilderness area, even if it is simply the side of the highway; many areas have their own local snakes, spiders, insects and creepy-crawlies.

Abortion

Travelers in need of an **abortion** should consult their embassy or consulate immediately. The abortion laws applicable in Austria, Prague, and Budapest, are stated as follows:

In **Austria,** all female citizens have access to legal and risk-free abortions (*Abtreibungen,* singular *Abtreibung*); the government will only subsidize abortions performed for medical reasons. Abortions are available on request in the first trimester, after medical consultation. After twelve weeks, abortions are legally performed only to avert serious danger to the woman's health, if the fetus is deformed, or if the woman is under 14. Only physicians perform abortions, although many refuse to do so. Many Austrian women who have abortions for non-medical reasons travel to private clinics abroad, where the procedure is less expensive.

In March of 1993, the **Czech Republic** banned abortions for foreigners; the suddenly strict laws are a measure to curtail the influx of Polish women seeking abortions there. Check with the Czech embassy in your home country for the latest details. For citizens, an abortion requires the consent of the woman and authorization by a gynecologist. Abortions within the first 12 weeks of pregnancy can be performed at the woman's discretion, for any reason; after 12 weeks, abortions must be approved by a medical commission. After 26 weeks, abortions may be performed only for medical reasons. National health insurance no longer covers abortions as it did under communism. The same laws apply in **Slovakia.**

For citizens of **Hungary,** abortions are legal until the twelfth week of pregnancy if there is a risk to the life or health of the mother, danger of fetal deformity, or another serious crisis. Abortions are performed legally up to the eighteenth week of pregnancy if the woman suffers from total or partial incapacity or if she has failed to recognize her pregnancy in time because of a medical error or negligence on the part of the hospital or administration—that is, if something outside the woman's control has prevented her from comprehending her predicament. Up to week 20 of the pregnancy, abortions are performed if there is over a 50% probability of fetal deformity, and up to 24 weeks if there is this 50% risk *and* if there was a delay in the diagnostic procedure. Abortions are legal at any point in fetal development if the pregnancy presents a danger to the life of the woman or if complications are so severe that the fetus will die.

The **National Abortion Federation's hotline** (tel. (800) 772-9100; Mon.-Fri. 9:30am-5:30pm) refers its callers to U.S. clinics that perform abortions. Its personnel can direct you to organizations that provide information about abortion in other countries.

■■■ INSURANCE

Insurance is like contraception: you only *really* want it when it's too late. Beware unnecessary coverage—your current policies might well extend to many travel-related accidents. A family's **household policies** (homeowner's insurance) usually extend to damage, loss, or theft of belongings when you're abroad, and some even cover documents such as passports and rail tickets. Most **medical insurance** (especially university policies) will pay for treatment worldwide, although **Medicare's** coverage is only valid in Mexico and Canada. Canadians are usually protected under their home province's insurance plan; check with the provincial Ministry of Health or Health Plan Headquarters.

When purchased in the U.S., **CIEE's International Student Identity Card** (ISIC), Teacher ID Card, or Youth ID Card (see Documents 'n Formalities above) provide US$3000 worth of accident and illness insurance and US$100 per day up to 60 days of hospitalization while the card is valid. **CIEE** also offers an inexpensive *Trip Safe Plan,* which doubles cardholders' insurance and provides coverage for travelers ineligible for the cards; it has options that cover medical treatment and hospitalization, accidents, baggage loss, and even charter flights you miss because of illness. **STA** offers a more expensive, more comprehensive plan (see Useful Travel Organizations above). **American Express** cardholders automatically receive car-rental and flight insurance on any purchases they make with the card (see Money above).

The other perks bundled into travel insurance packages are often not worth the expense or can be found elsewhere. Referral to physicians and lawyers (but not payment) can be obtained through a consulate, and a major credit card will get you cash in a flash in case of theft.

Remember that you can file claims only upon return to your home country. Insurance companies usually require a copy of the police report for thefts, or evidence of having paid medical expenses (doctor's statements, receipts) before they will honor a claim; they may also enforce time limits on filing for reimbursement. Be sure all documents are written in English, or suffer possible translating fees. Always carry policy numbers and proof of insurance with you.

If you have less than perfect faith in your travel plans, consider trip cancellation or interruption insurance, which protects you in case your airline or tour operator leaves you stranded at the final hour. Check the yellow pages and newspapers, and consult your travel agent. Expect to pay US$2-5 per US$100 coverage for cancellation and interruption insurance.

Check with each carrier listed below for specific restrictions. If your coverage does not include on-the-spot payments or cash transferals, leave an extra budget for emergencies.

Access America, Inc., 6600 West Broad St., P.O. Box 11188, Richmond, VA 23230 (tel. (800) 284-8300). Covers trip cancellation/interruption, on-the-spot hospital admittance costs, emergency medical evacuation. 24-hr. hotline.

ARM Coverage, Inc./Carefree Travel Insurance, P.O. Box 310, Mineola, NY 11501 (tel. (800) 323-3149 or (516) 294-0220). Offers two comprehensive packages including coverage for trip delay, accident and sickness, medical, baggage loss, bag delay, accidental death and dismemberment, travel supplier insolvency. Trip cancellation/interruption may be purchased separately at a rate of US$5.50 per US$100 of coverage. 24-hr. hotline.

Globalcare Travel Insurance, 220 Broadway, Lynnfield, MA 01940 (tel. (800) 821-2488; fax (617) 592-7720). Complete medical, legal, emergency, and travel-related services. On-the-spot payments and special student programs.

Travelers Aid International, 918 16th St., NW, Washington, DC 20006 (tel. (202) 659-9468; fax 659-2910). Provides help for theft, car failure, illness, and other "mobility-related problems." No fee, but you are expected to reimburse the organization for expenses.

Travel Assistance International, 1133 15th St., NW, Washington, DC 20005 (tel. (202) 821-2828; fax 331-1609). Provides on-the-spot medical coverage ranging from US$15,000 to US$90,000 and unlimited medical evacuation insurance, 24-hr. emergency multilingual assistance hotline, and worldwide local presence. Optional coverages such as trip cancellation/interruption, baggage, and accidental death and dismemberment insurance are also offered. Short-term and long-term plans available.

Travel Guard Internationale, 1145 Clark St., Stevens Point, WI 54481 (tel. (800) 826-1300 or (715) 345-0505; fax 345-0525). Offers "Travel Guard Gold" packages: Basic ($19), deluxe ($39), and comprehensive (8% of total trip cost), for medical expenses, baggage and travel documents, travel delay, baggage delay, emergency assistance and trip cancellation/interruption. 24-hr. emergency hotline.

The Traveler's Insurance Company, 1 Tower Sq., Hartford, CT 06183-5040 (tel. (800) 243-3174). Insurance against accident, baggage loss, sickness, trip cancellation/interruption, and company default. Covers emergency medical evacuation.

Wallach & Company, Inc., 107 West Federal St., P.O. Box 480, Middleburg, VA 22117-0480 (tel. (800) 237-6615; fax (703) 687-3172). Comprehensive medical insurance including evacuation and repatriation of remains and direct payment of claims to providers of services. Other optional coverages available. 24-hr. toll-free international assistance.

■■■ SAFETY AND SECURITY

Violent crime is less common in Austria, the Czech Republic, and Budapest than in most countries, but it still exists, especially in large cities. Here and elsewhere, common sense will serve you better than twitching paranoia.

It's no surprise that tourists are particularly vulnerable to crime. To avoid such unwanted attention, the best tactic is to blend in as much as possible; the gawking camera-toter in a U. of Michigan T-shirt is much more likely prey than the disaffected, leather-heeled and vaguely leftist local look-alike. Camouflaging yourself is often harder than it sounds—chances are you will not be able to fully conceal your true identity. Even so, time spent learning local style is well worth the effort. A disposable camera is a dead giveaway that you are a tourist; a point-and-shoot model may signal *rich* and foreign. Backpackers aren't generally perceived as wealthy, but all of their valuable possessions come packaged in one bundle, most convenient to steal. In general, the less you flaunt your income or foreign status, the less vulnerable you'll be to sticky fingers or large, blunt objects.

If you do feel nervous, walking purposefully into a café or shop and checking your map inside is better than letting on that you feel scared. Muggings are usually impromptu rather than planned; walking with nervous, over-the-shoulder glances can be interpreted as an indication that you have something valuable to protect. Carry treasured items (including your passport, railpass, traveler's checks, and airline ticket) either in a **money belt** or **neckpouch** stashed securely inside your clothing; make it your bosom buddy for the entire trip. Belts and pouches will protect you from skilled thieves who use razors to slash open backpacks and fanny packs (particular favorites of skilled bag-snatchers). Carry a purse over one shoulder and under your opposite arm, on the side away from the street. Dress modestly. Expensive jewelry, if it's not stolen, will only attract unwanted attention, and insurance companies are renowned for painfully slow replacement. *Make photocopies of all important documents,* your passport, IDs, credit cards, and the numbers of your traveler's checks. Keep one set of copies and receipts in a secure place in your luggage, separate from the originals, and leave another set at home. Although copies seldom substitute for originals, you won't have to rely on memory when you try to reconstruct essential information. Finally, make sure you know where the fire exits are in your hostel and what numbers to dial in an emergency (see Communication in the Appendix at the end of this book).

When exploring a new city, extra vigilance may be wise, but don't go overboard and let fear cut you off from experiencing another culture. Pickpockets come in all shapes and sizes and frequently lurk in front of stations and other heavily touristed areas. Their fingers are fast, practiced, and professional. Pickpockets tend to operate in groups: among friends, the initial thief can pass the booty off to a cohort, leaving him or herself—the obvious culprit—free of any incriminating evidence. Sometimes, groups of pickpockets gently encircle their prey. Watch for bands of benign-looking children, who use especially vulpine schemes to distract and rob luggage-carrying tourists. One elaborate tactic involves a baby in a carriage, with the stolen good shoved under the infant. In another scenario, a thief enters a subway, pretends to change his or her mind, and pushes back towards the exit—along with someone else's purse or wallet. Thieves take advantage of a sudden jolt or stop, when victims are off-balance and lift their hands from pockets and bags. In May, the U.S. State Department named Prague one of the top four pickpocketing area in Europe, along with Warsaw, Milan, and Rome. Be super-wary at money-changing establishments, especially ones near tram stops, where passengers entering and exiting conveniently swirl around and jostle each other.

When walking at night, you should turn day-time precautions into mandates. In particular, stay near crowded and well-lit areas, and do not attempt to cross through parks, parking lots or any other large, open deserted areas.

Among the more "colorful" aspects of many cities are the **con artists.** Tricks are many and adaptable, but there are certain classics—sob stories that require you to reach for your wallet, or mustard spilled on your shoulder distracting you for just enough time to snatch your bag. Remember, no one ever wins at three-card monte. Hustlers often work in groups, and children, unfortunately, are among the most effective at the game. A firm "no" should communicate that you are no dupe. Contact the police if a hustler feels particularly insistent or aggressive.

Trains are other notoriously easy spots for thieving. Professionals wait for tourists to fall asleep and then carry off everything they can. When traveling in pairs, sleep in alternating shifts; when alone, use good judgement in selecting a train compartment, especially at night, and never stay in an empty one. Relocate if you feel threatened. If you choose to cut costs by sleeping in your automobile, it is best to do so in a well-lit area as close to a police station or 24-hour service station as possible. Sleeping outside can be even more dangerous—camping is recommended only in official, supervised, campsites.

Let's Go lists locker availability in hostels and train stations, but you'll often need your own **padlock.** Lockers are useful if you plan on sleeping outdoors or don't want to lug everything with you, but don't store valuables in them. Never leave your belongings unattended; even the most demure-looking hostel may be a den of thieves.

There is no sure-fire set of precautions that will protect you from all situations you might encounter when you travel. A good self-defense course will give you more concrete ways to react to different types of aggression, but it might cost you more money than your trip. **Model Mugging,** a national organization with offices in several major cities, teaches a very effective, comprehensive course on self-defense (course prices vary from $400-500). Women's and men's courses offered. Call Model Mugging (tel. (617) 232-2900 on the east coast; (312) 338-4545 in the midwest; (415) 592-7300) on the west coast. Community colleges frequently offer self-defense courses at more affordable prices. The **U.S. Department of State's** pamphlet *A Safe Trip Abroad* (US$1) summarizes safety information for travelers. It is available by calling (202) 783-3238 or by writing to the Superintendent of Documents, U.S. Government Printing Office, Washington, DC 20402. For an official Department of State travel advisory on Austria, Prague, or Budapest, including recent crime statistics and security recommendations, call their 24-hr. hotline at (202) 647-5225. Also available: pamphlets on traveling to specific arcas. More complete information on safety while traveling may be found in *Travel Safety: Security and Safeguards at Home and Abroad,* from **Hippocrene Books, Inc.,** 171 Madison Ave., New York, NY 10016 (tel. (212) 685-4371; orders (718) 454-2360; fax (718) 454-1391).

■ Law and Order Overseas

Everything you've heard about the compulsive law-abidance of Austrians is true. The first time you see a native standing at an intersection in the pouring rain at 4am, with no cars in sight, waiting for the "Walk" signal, you'll know what we mean. Jaywalking is only one of the petty offenses that will immediately mark you as a foreigner (and subject you to fines); littering is another. The younger generation tends to be more laid back about such matters. Police officers, members of the *Polizei* or

Gendarmerie (in Prague, *Policie* or *Cerné serií;* in Budapest, *Rendőrséget*), typically speak little English, and tend to be very business-like. Treat the police with the utmost respect at all times.

Alcohol

Imbibing in Austria is trouble-free—beer is more common than soda, and a lunch without wine or beer would be unthinkable. Each province sets a legal minimum drinking age, but reportedly anyone old enough to see over the counter can buy beer and wine (although those under 18 may have trouble purchasing liquor and entering nightclubs). Drinking in public is acceptable so long as you control your revelry.

Drugs

Just say no. Every year thousands of travelers are arrested for trafficking or possession of drugs, or for simply being in the company of a suspected user. Marijuana, hashish, cocaine, and narcotics are illegal in Austria, the Czech Republic, and Hungary, and the penalties for illegal possession of drugs range from severe to horrific. It is not uncommon for a dealer, especially in Prague or Budapest, to increase profits by first selling drugs to tourists and then turning them in to the authorities for a reward. Even reputedly liberal cities such as Vienna and Salzburg take an officially dim view of strung-out tourists. The worst thing you can possibly do is carry drugs across an international border; not only could you end up in prison, you could be blessed with a "Drug Trafficker" stamp on your passport for the rest of your life. If you are arrested, all your home country's consulate can do is visit you, provide a list of attorneys, and inform family and friends. The London-based organization **Release** (tel. (071) 377 59 05 or 603 86 54) advises people who have been arrested on drug charges, but is hardly a life raft; abroad you are subject to local laws. If you think extradition is the worst possible fate of a convicted traveler, try a foreign jail behind the former Iron Curtain.

Make sure you get a statement and prescription from your doctor if you'll be carrying insulin, syringes, or any narcotic medications. Leave all medicines in their original labeled containers. What is legal at home may not necessarily be legal abroad; check with the appropriate foreign consulate before leaving to avoid nasty surprises. Politely refuse to carry even a nun's excess luggage onto a plane; you're more likely to end up in jail for possession of drugs than in heaven for your goodwill.

■■■ WORK AND STUDY

■ School

Foreign study beckons to the average student as a fail-proof good time. Most American undergraduates enroll in programs sponsored by U.S. universities, and many colleges have offices to give advice and information on study abroad. Be warned: programs vary tremendously in expense, academic quality, living conditions, degree of contact with local students, and exposure to the local culture and language. Take advantage of college study abroad counselors and put in some hours at their libraries. Ask for the names of recent participants in the programs and go to them with your questions and concerns.

If you have extensive language ability, consider enrolling directly in a university program abroad. For foreigners, barriers to admittance include a rigorous language proficiency exam; on the other hand, Austrian, Prague, and Budapest universities are far cheaper than North American ones. Try contacting the embassy of the country you're interested in for literature describing their national university systems. Austria's 18 universities and institutions of higher education (7 of them are in Vienna) allot a limited number of spaces to foreign students.

The **Goethe Institute** runs numerous language programs abroad. For information on these and on their many cultural offerings, contact your local Goethe Institute (American branches are located in New York, Washington, DC, Boston, Atlanta, San Francisco, Los Angeles, and Seattle) or write to Goethe House New York, 1014 Fifth Ave., New York, NY 10028 (see Central College below).

For further information and the pamphlets *Austria 1994* and *Austrian Summer Schools,* contact the Austrian Cultural Institute, 11 E. 52nd St., New York, NY 10022. Or, contact the foreign section of the **Austrian Students' Union,** Liechtensteinstr. 13, A-1090 Vienna (tel. (0222) 30 88 79).

Advanced International Program in Peace Studies, Beaver College Center for Education Abroad, 450 S. Easton Road, Glenside, PA 19038-3295 (tel. (800) 755-5607). One of a multitude of Beaver programs. Interdisciplinary academic program in peace, security, development, and conflict resolution. Taught in English at the medieval castle Schlaining, in southern Burgenland. US$6500 per semester (tuition and lodging).

American Field Service Intercultural Programs, 313 E. 43rd St., New York, NY 10017 (tel. (800) 237-4636 or (212) 949-4242). Offers summer-, semester-, and year-long programs for high school students traveling to Austria, the Czech Republic, and Hungary. Half of the participants receive financial aid.

American Institute for Foreign Study/American Council for International Studies, 102 Greenwich Ave., Greenwich, CT 06830 (tel. (800) 727-2437; for high school students, call the Boston office at (617) 421-9575). Organizes study at Salzburg universities. Separate division for high school students. Summer programs last 3-12 weeks. Fees vary tremendously; government loans are recommended, and a deferred payment plan for summer programs is offered.

Austria-Illinois Exchange Program Vienna, University of Illinois at Urbana-Champaign, Department of Germanic Languages and Literatures, 3072 Foreign Languages Building, 707 S. Mathews Ave., Urbana, IL 61801-3675 (tel. (217) 244-3240). Hosted by the Wirtschaftsuniversität (Economics University) in Vienna.

Less expensive than similar programs. University tuition and fees US$4400, program costs, including round-trip transportation) US$4900, personal expenses US$5500, for a grand total of US$14,800.

Central Bureau for Educational Visits and Exchanges, Seymour Mews House, Seymour Mews, London W1H 9PE (tel. (071) 486 51 01). Publishes *Study Holidays* (£7.75 in bookstores, postage extra) which gives basic information on over 600 language-study programs in 25 European countries. Distributed in North America by the Institute of International Education Books (see below).

Central College, International Studies Office, 812 University, Pella, Iowa 50219-9989 (tel. (800) 831-3629). 2-month intensive language-training at a Goethe Institute in Germany before study at the University of Vienna. Full year (11 months) US$13,200, one semester (6 months) $9400.

Council on International Educational Exchange (CIEE), 205 E. 42nd St., New York, NY 10017 (tel. (212) 661-1414). Biennially publishes *Work, Study, Travel Abroad: The Whole World Handbook* (US$13, postage US$1.50), describing over 1000 study programs during both the academic year and the summer, as well as their application procedures. Also publishes *Going Places: The High School Student's Guide to Study, Travel, and Adventure Abroad* (US$14, postage US$1.50), describing over 200 programs primarily for high school students, as well as *Basic Facts on Study Abroad,* compiled in cooperation with the Institute of International Education and NAFSA, the Association of International Educators (single copies free).

Hope College Vienna Summer School, Austro-American Institute of Education, Operngasse 4, A-1010, Vienna (tel. (0222) 512 77 20). In the U.S., contact Vienna Summer School, Department of English, Hope College, Holland, MI 49423-3698 (tel. (616) 394-7616; fax 394-7922). Six weeks of academics and German-language instruction for US$2950. Many fringe benefits included in the price: housing, meals, transport passes, festivities, weekends in Venice, Prague, and Budapest, and a hiking trip in the Alps. Also offers 3-week programs for about half-price.

The Institute of European Studies, 223 W. Ohio St., Chicago, IL 60610-4196 (tel. (312) 944-1750; fax 944-1448). Offers a full range of undergraduate courses in humanities, social sciences, and business for students with minimal training in German. All taught in English at a Viennese university located in an 18th-century palace. Housing in private residences. US$10,750 full year, US$7100 semester, US$2150 summer (tuition and housing).

Institute of International Education Books (IIE Books), 809 United Nations Plaza, New York NY 10017-3580 (tel. (212) 984-5412; fax 984-5358). Publishes several annual reference books on study abroad. *Academic Year Abroad* (US$43, plus US$4 postage) and *Vacation Study Abroad* (US$37, plus US$4 postage) detail over 3,600 programs offered by U.S. colleges and universities overseas. Also offers the free pamphlet *Basic Facts on Foreign Study,* as well as several other useful texts: *English Language and Orientation Programs in the U.S.* (US$43, plus US$4 postage). Distributes several books published by the Central Bureau for Educational Visits and Exchanges in the U.K., including *Study Holidays, Working Holidays,* and *Home from Home* (all CB books are US$23, plus US$4 postage each.) You can also contact the Central Bureau directly (see separate listing). Though some foundations offer financial assistance to undergraduates, most fellowships or scholarships are available for graduate and post-graduate study only.

International House Language School, P.O. Box 95, II., Bimbó út 7, Budapest 1364, Hungary (tel. (361) 115 40 13; fax 115 52 75). Part of an international network of language schools. Learn Hungarian year-round from Hungarian teachers.

Open Door Student Exchange, 250 Fulton Ave., P.O. Box 71, Hempstead, NY 11551 (tel. (516) 486-7330). High school exchange program.

Österreichische Hochschülerschaft, Liechtensteinstr. 13, A-1090, Vienna (tel. (0222) 31 08 88 00). Provides detailed information from the foreign students' section of the students' association at each university. Open Mon.-Thurs. 8:30am-4:30pm and Fri. 8:30am-2pm.

Unipub Co., 4611-F Assembly Dr., Lanham, MD 20706-4391 (tel. (800) 274-4888). Distributes International Agency Publications including UNESCO's *Study Abroad* (US$24, postage US$2.50). International scholarships and courses for students of various ages. Unwieldy but excellent book.

World Exchange, White Birch Road, Putnam Valley, NY 10579 (tel. (914) 526-2505). Offers a language exchange program with reciprocal home stays.

World Learning, Inc., Summer Abroad, P.O. Box 676, Brattleboro, VT 05302 (tel. (802) 257-7751, ext. 3452, or (800) 345-2929). Founded in 1932 as The Experiment in International Living. Semester programs as well. Positions as tour group leaders are available world-wide. Applicants must be at least 24 and must have established leadership abilities, language fluency, and in-depth overseas experience for the countries to which they apply. Group leaders have all their expenses paid and receive a US$200 honorarium. For the programs themselves, most U.S. colleges will transfer credit for semester work done abroad. Some financial aid is available.

Youth for Understanding International Exchange (YFU), 3501 Newark St., NW, Washington, DC 20016 (tel. (202) 966-6800). One of the oldest and most respected exchange programs. Places high school students world-wide for homestays of a summer, a semester, or a year.

■ Work

There is no better way to submerge yourself in a foreign culture than to take part in its economy. Getting permission to work in Austria is, alas, a challenge. The organizations and publications listed below can help point you toward employment abroad; you should, however, speak with former clients before paying any registration fees. Remember, it is in the interest of the authors listed below to make it seem easy to work abroad so that more people will buy their books.

In order to get a work permit for Austria, you must first find someone who wants to hire you, which requires either connections or eons of time. Your prospective employer must then apply for your work permit, which can take anywhere from four weeks to several months to clear. Ordinarily, the only way to get a permit is to possess a skill that no local citizen can supply. If you know the employer well, try convincing him or her to list perfect fluency in English as a job requirement. Obviously, this ploy will not work for, say, a dishwashing job, but if you aspire to be a ski instructor for foreign tourists or some similar occupation, it might.

Many foreigners get jobs illegally without work permits, though these jobs tend toward the tedious. Youth hostels frequently provide room and board to travelers willing to stay a while and help run the place. You can also earn room and board as an *au pair* (live-in baby sitter). Look for newspaper ads and bulletin board notices. Temporary agricultural labor is another option—just beware crossing unionized Austrian laborers. The best tips on jobs for foreigners come from other travelers, so be alert and inquisitive in hostels and other youth hangouts. Realize that you could be deported for working illegally and that you will be competing with illegal workers from Eastern and Southern Europe who probably need the salary more than you do.

If you know no one in Austria, Prague, or Budapest, don't have the flexibility to work as casual labor, and are a full-time student at a U.S. or Canadian university, consider applying for a temporary student work visa through the Council on International Educational Exchange (CIEE). For a US$125 application fee, CIEE can procure temporary work permits for American university students. For an application and more information, contact CIEE, which also publishes *Work Abroad* (free), *Work, Study, Travel Abroad: The Whole World Handbook* (US$13, postage US$1.50) and *Volunteer! The Comprehensive Guide to Voluntary Service in the US and Abroad* (US$9, postage US$1.50), produced in cooperation with the Commission of Religious Volunteer Agencies.

Contact the following job placement agencies for more information about employment abroad:

Experiment in International Living (EIL), Summer Studies Abroad, P.O. Box 676, Brattleboro, VT 05302 (tel. (800) 345-2929 or (802) 257-7751, ext. 6064). For a semester-long position, write to Semester Studies Abroad at the same address. Tour-group leader positions available world-wide. Applicants must be at least 24 and have established leadership abilities, language fluency, and in-depth overseas experience in the countries for which they apply. Group leaders have all of their expenses paid and receive a US$200 honorarium.

InterExchange Program, 161 Sixth Ave. #902, New York, NY 10013 (tel. (212) 947-9533). Ask for their pamphlets describing international and *au pair* work.

Teachers of English as a Second Language (TESL) Recruiting Service, Rte. 6, P.O. Box 174, New Orleans, LA 70129. Recruits teachers for European and Middle Eastern schools. Send a letter and a resume.

Vacation Work Publications, 9 Park End St., Oxford OX1 1HJ (tel. (0865) 24 19 78). Publishes *Directory of Summer Jobs Abroad* (£8); *Work Your Way Around the World* (£10); *Working in Ski Resorts: Europe* (£6); *The Au Pair and Nanny's Guide to Working Abroad* (£8); and the *International Directory of Voluntary Work* (£9). Postage £1 (£2 outside the U.K.). Publications are also available in the United States, from **Peterson's Guides,** 202 Carnegie Center, P.O. Box 2123, Princeton, NJ 08543 (tel. (800) 338-3282 or (609) 243-9111).

World Trade Academy Press, 50 E. 42nd St. #509, New York, NY 10017 (tel. (212) 697-4999). Publishes the *Directory of American Firms Operating in Foreign Countries* (the book may be worth a trip to the library rather than to the bookstore—it costs US$175). Also publishes *Looking for Employment in Foreign Countries* (US$16.50), which gives information on federal, commercial, and volunteer jobs abroad and advice on resumes and interviews.

Volunteer Jobs

Volunteer jobs are readily available almost everywhere. You may receive room and board in exchange for your labor, and the work can be more fascinating than employment as a tool of the capitalist system. The following organizations and publications can help you to explore the range of possibilities. Keep in mind that organizations that arrange placement sometimes charge high application fees, in addition to charges for room and board. You can avoid this extra fee by contacting the individual workcamps directly, though this process is a hassle. Listings such as UNESCO's *Workcamp Organizers* (see below) are helpful.

Archaeological Institute of America, 675 Commonwealth Ave., Boston, MA 02215 (tel. (617) 353-9361). Ask for their *Archaeological Fieldwork Opportunities Bulletin,* available in January. Lists field projects in the Middle East and throughout the world.

Council on International Educational Exchange (CIEE), International Workcamps, 205 E. 42nd St., New York, NY 10017 (tel. (212) 661-1414). Arranges placement in workcamps in Europe. These 2- to 3-week community service projects bring volunteers from different countries together to work on environmental, historic preservation, archaeological, renovation, and social projects. Participants are recruited from around the world through an international network of voluntary service organizations. A US$135 placement fee covers all expenses including room and board. Travel costs are additional and participants are responsible for making their own travel arrangements. Volunteers must be over 18. Foreign language proficiency is required for some camps. Write for the free annual *International Workcamps* booklet, which describes the camps and includes an application.

Service Civil International/International Voluntary Service-USA, Rte. 2, Box 506, Crozet, VA 22932 (tel. (804) 823-1826). Arranges placement in workcamps in Europe. You must be 18 to work in European camps. Registration fees for the placement service range from US$35-100.

Volunteers for Peace, 43 Tiffany Rd., Belmont, VT 05730 (tel. (802) 259-2759). Arranges placement in over 800 workcamps in 37 countries, primarily in Europe. Opportunities as diverse as reclaiming an abandoned island near Venice, repairing bicycles in Belgium for export to South African refugees, and excavating concentration camps in Germany. Gives perhaps the most complete and up-to-date listings in the annual *International Workcamp Directory* (post-paid US$10, 112 pages). Registration fee US$125.

UNESCO's Coordinating Committee for International Voluntary Service (CCIVS), 1, rue Miollis, 75015 Paris, France. Publishes a listing called *Workcamp Organizers.*

■■■ PACKING

Though we travel the world over to find the beautiful
we must carry it with us or we find it not.

Ralph Waldo Emerson

Pack lightly. *Pack lightly.* **Pack lightly.**

Your backpack or suitcase may be light as a feather when you buy it or drag it out of storage and as buoyant as your enthusiasm all the way to the airport, but as soon as the plane lands it will become a ponderous, hot, uncomfortable nuisance. Before you leave, pack your bag and take it for a walk. Try to convince yourself that you're in Austria already. You're hiking up mountains steeper than you have seen before. You're struggling to fit through the swiftly closing doors of a BundesBus. You're sprinting down hostel hallways, trying desperately to escape from roving bands of schoolchildren. At the slightest sign of heaviness, curb your vanity and unpack something. A good general rule is to pack only what you absolutely need, then take half the clothes and twice the money. A *New York Times* correspondent recommends that you take "no more than you can carry for half a mile at a dead run." This may be extreme—and in fact it's held in some circles that many *Times* correspondents can't run half a mile, period—but you get the idea. If you plan to shower loved ones with gifts on your return, it's much easier to leave empty space in your luggage than to send it home from abroad.

Baggage

If you plan to cover many miles by foot, a sturdy **backpack** with several external compartments is unbeatable. Internal frame packs stand up to airline baggage handlers and can often be disguised as carry-ons; external frame packs distribute weight more evenly and lift the pack off your back. Whichever style you choose to buy, avoid excessively low-end prices—you get what you pay for. If checking a backpack on a flight, tape down loose straps that can catch in the conveyer belt and rip your bag apart. Take a light **suitcase** or a large **shoulder bag** if you won't be walking much. An empty, lightweight duffel bag packed inside your luggage will be useful: once abroad you can fill your luggage with purchases and keep your dirty clothes in the duffel. A small **daypack** is also indispensable for plane flights, sight-seeing, carrying a camera, and keeping some of your valuables with you. Look for a lightweight rain **poncho** that will cover your pack and your back. Ponchos can also serve as ground cloths or impromptu lean-tos for campers. Gore-Tex® is a miracle fabric that's both waterproof and breathable; it's all but mandatory if you plan on Alpine hiking.

Attire

Guard your money, passport, and other important articles in a **moneybelt** or **neck pouch** and keep it with you *at all times.* The best combination of convenience and invulnerability is the nylon, zippered pouch with belt that should sit *inside* the waist of your pants or skirt (though not too inconveniently). Moneybelts are available at any good camping store.

Bare shoulders and shorts above the knee are nominally forbidden in places of worship, even when simply making a short visit. This rule is frequently disregarded throughout Europe's most touristed landmarks, but beware the odd chapel that plays by the book. As a last resort—a *very* last resort—play dumb: "Ich no speak

German." Women may want to carry around a long, wraparound skirt that may be easier than jeans to throw on in a hurry.

Comfortable **shoes** are essential: sneakers or sandals work best. For heavy-duty hiking, sturdy lace-up walking boots are a necessity. Make sure they have good ventilation—the new leather-reinforced nylon hiking boots are particularly good for hiking and for general walking: they're lightweight, rugged, and they dry quickly. The same type of boots with Gore-Tex® instead of nylon are awe-inspiring, but more expensive. A double pair of socks—light absorbent cotton inside and thick wool outside—will cushion feet, keep them dry, and help prevent blisters. In cold weather, replace the cotton inner sock with a "stay-dry" fabric such as polypropylene. Teva® sandals or Birkenstocks® are unable to withstand days of Alpine hiking, and the warmth they offer is negligible at best, but they may be perfectly suitable for strolling about the Austrian lowlands. Bring a pair of light flip-flops for protection against the foliage and fungi that inhabit some station and hostel showers.

Miscellaneous Accoutrements

Consider packing some of the following useful items:

sturdy plastic water bottle
padlock
whistle
plastic baggies
pocketknife (with all the gizmos)
flashlight
sunglasses
bath towel or chamois
soap (biodegradable?)
petite traveler's alarm clock
small umbrella
insect and/or tick repellant
elastic bungee cord
tweezers
small umbrella
needle and thread
a few safety pins
rubber bands
electrical tape (for patching tears)
string (to make clotheslines)
sturdy plastic containers
compass
waterproof matches
earplugs (for noisy hotels)
sun hat
sink stopper (rubber squash ball)
small notebook
ping-pong paddle (for hostels)
personal stereo (Walkman®)
maps and phrasebooks

Contact lens wearers would be wise to bring a supply of chemicals for their entire trip (see Health above).

Electricity

Electricity in Austria, Prague, and Budapest is 220 volts AC at 50 cycles per second, enough to fry any North American appliance. An adapter only changes the shape of the plug—it's not enough if you want to use your appliance overseas; you will also need a converter and an extender. Converters bring the 220V down to North American 110V; extenders allow you to use the European recessed outlets. Electric clocks, record players, and tape recorders may not work properly even with an adapter-converter. Travelers who heat-disinfect their **contact lenses** should note that their machines will require a small converter (about US$20). Consider switching temporarily to a chemical disinfection system. Converters must match the wattage of the appliance and the current in the outlet. For further details, write to **Franzus Company,** Murtha Industrial Park, P.O. Box 142, Beacon Falls, CT 06403 (tel. (203) 723-6664; fax 723-6666) for their free and illuminating pamphlet, *Foreign Electricity is No Deep Dark Secret.*

■ Photography

Carrying a **camera** invites a host of extra travel worries—from the stressful temptation to jam every visual event down your lens, to the high cost of film, equipment, and developing, to the ever-present paranoia about loss, theft, or dropping the damned thing. Yet, on the nostalgic hand, personal photographs are more permanent than mere memories and make explaining the trip to the folks at home oh-so-much more pleasant and effective. The picture of the tatoo-covered man in Vienna with the dancing eyes and mysterious smirk communicates aspects of your adventure a postcard of St. Stephen's never could. If you can't decide whether to tote your camera or leave it at home, try carrying it around everywhere you go for a few days. Take a wide-angle shot of the passport office, maybe a few close-ups of the helpful travel agent. Like the result? Then take it—you'll be thankful.

Make sure your camera is in good shape before you go—repair on the road will likely be rare, inexpert, expensive, and slow. Even the greatest photographers cannot do the scenery justice, so don't let the urge to snap the perfect photo fill your every touristic hour. Back home, a mountain of forest or glacier pictures *sans* people will all start to look the same, regardless of how unique the angle or lighting at the time. Keep this in mind, and don't shoot too much scenery. People matter. More than a building or sight ever could, a photograph of your companions in a certain spot will trigger memories, even months after the trip.

A less cumbersome and worrisome option is a **disposable camera** available at most supermarkets and drug stores. These glorified pieces of film let you take 36 pictures and then throw away the camera, which is really a paper box. More expensive models include a flash or wide-angle lens.

Camera **film** is quite expensive in Central Europe. You're better off buying your film at home if don't mind lugging it around for the whole trip. Often large discount department stores have the best deals. The sensitivity of film to light is measured by the ASA/ISO number: 100 performs well for normal outdoor or indoor flash photography, while 400 or higher is necessary for night shots. Consult a photo store for advice about the right film for special types of pictures. Airport x-rays usually don't affect film with an ASA under 100. Overly cautious travelers might consider asking security personnel to inspect their camera and film by hand, or they might buy a protective film pouch at the local camera store. The more sensitive the film, the more susceptible it is to damage. Any film over ASA 1600 should *not* be x-rayed.

One note while you're passing through airport security: often, the guards will ask to take a picture with your camera, to make sure that your Nikon isn't an explosive/tear gas/switchblade/two-way walkie-talkie device. Unless you want a picture of the lovely airport lounge, try to make sure that there is no film loaded in your camera when you arrive at security.

Wait until you return home to **process** your film. It's much simpler to carry rolls of film as you travel, rather than perishable boxes of slides, prints, or negatives. Protect exposed film from extreme heat and the sun. Mail-away companies have the cheapest processing prices, sometimes US$8 less than the 60 Minute Photo shop in the local strip mall. If you don't mind waiting a week or two for your pictures, post one of these mailers, included in local circulars and newspapers, and you'll have lovely prints waiting for you when you arrive back home.

■■■ SPECIAL CONCERNS

■ Women and Travel

Women who explore any area on their own inevitably face additional concerns about safety. In all situations it is best to trust your instincts: if you'd feel better somewhere else, don't hesitate to move on. You may want to consider staying in hostels that offer single rooms that lock from the inside or religious organizations that offer rooms for women only. Stick to centrally located accommodations and avoid late-night treks or metro rides. Remember that hitching is *never* safe for lone women, or even for two women traveling together. Choose train compartments occupied by other women or couples.

In some parts of the world, women (foreign or local) are frequently beset by unwanted and tenacious followers. Exercise reasonable caution without feeling you must avoid all local men. To escape unwanted attention, follow the example of local women; in many cases, the less you look like a tourist, the better off you'll be. Austrian women tend to dress conservatively, especially in rural areas. Women visiting religious monuments should not wear shorts or above-the-knee skirts (except in the bigger cities, where people flout this custom). If you spend time in cities, you may be harassed no matter how you're dressed. Look as if you know where you're going (even when you don't) and ask women or couples for directions if you're lost or if you feel uncomfortable. Your best answer to verbal harassment is no answer at all (a reaction is what the harasser wants). In crowds, you may be pinched or squeezed by oversexed slimeballs; wearing a conspicuous wedding band may help prevent such incidents. Don't hesitate to seek out a police officer or a passerby if you are being harassed. Memorize the emergency numbers in the countries you visit, and always carry change for the phone and enough extra money for a bus or taxi. Carry a whistle or an airhorn on your keychain, and don't hesitate to use it in an emergency. A **Model Mugging** course will not only help prepare you to deal with a mugging, but will also raise your level of awareness of your surroundings as well as your confidence. Offices exist in 14 U.S. states, as well as in Quebec and Zürich (see Safety and Security above). All of these warnings and suggestions should not discourage women from traveling alone. Don't take unnecessary risks, but don't lose your spirit of adventure either.

Women travelers will likely feel safer and more secure in Austria than in other parts of Europe—violent crime is generally rare. In conservative Austria, socially defined gender roles are much more clearly demarcated than in the U.S. or Canada. For instance, Austrian women traditionally do not sit at the head of the table, and they are expected to defer to men in social settings. Women entering such enclaves of testosterone as local *Bierstube* are sometimes considered to be searching for male companionship, especially if they enter alone; be warned that even strolling in the door may be interpreted as a signal of availability. Women may want to frequent typically male establishments with others, to ensure no miscommunication. Austria's feminist community thrives in Salzburg and Vienna, where a number of establishments cater to a liberated clientele.

Unlike some parts of southern Europe, catcalls and whistling are not acceptable behavior in Austria, Prague, and Budapest; you can feel quite comfortable rebuking your harasser. In Austria, loudly saying "*Laß mich in Ruhe!*" ("Leave me alone!" pronounced LAHSS MEEKH EEN ROOH-eh) should suffice to discourage most unwanted attention. In Prague, yell "*Jdi pryč!*" ("Go away!" pronounced YUH-dih PRITCH) or "*Pomoc!*" ("Help!" pronounced PAW-mawts). In Budapest, try "*Hagyjonbékén!*" ("Leave me alone!" pronounced HAH-dyuh-yaun-bay-kayn) or "*Segítség*!" ("Help!" pronounced SHEH-geet-shayg).

Some potentially useful addresses and telephone counseling numbers include:

Women Going Places, a new women's travel and resource guide that emphasizes female-owned enterprises. Geared towards lesbians, but offers advice appropriate for all women. US$14. Available from Inland Book Company, P.O. Box 120261, East Haven, CT 06512 (tel. (203) 467-4257).

Wander Women, 136 N. Grand Ave. #237, West Covina, CA 91791. A travel and adventure networking organization for women over 40. Publishes a quarterly newsletter, *Journal 'n Footnotes*—an informational source for the varied aspects of travel, and a forum for women to share their travel experiences, the 12-page newsletter is designed to inspire women to seek new adventures and travel experiences. Membership (US$29 per year) entitles women to the membership directory, newsletter, many travel and adventure discounts, and opportunities to meet other Wander Women, with and without invisible planes. Send US$1 for a sample copy.

Federal Ministry for Women's Affairs, Ballhausplatz 1, A-1014 Vienna (tel. (0222) 531 15/2204).

Equality Commission in the Federal Ministry of Labor and Social Affairs, Stubenring 1, A-1010 Vienna (tel. (0222) 711 00/5583).

Women's Shelters in Vienna, tel. (0222) 545 48 00 or 408 38 80.
Emergency Rape Hotline, tel. (0222) 93 22 22.

Women may feel more comfortable traveling in other women's footsteps, or at least learning from the travails of those who have traveled before. A series of recent travelogues by women outline their sojourns; check a good library or bookstore for these and other books: *Nothing to Declare: Memoirs of a Woman Traveling Alone* (Penguin Books; US$9) and *Wall to Wall: From Beijing to Berlin by Rail* (Penguin Books; US$10) by Mary Morris; *One Dry Season* (Knopf) by Caroline Alexander; *Tracks* (Pantheon) by Robin Davidson; *The Road Through Miyama* (Random House/Vintage) by Leila Philips, and anything by Isak Dinesen, especially *Out of Africa* (Random House). For additional tips and suggestions, consult *The Handbook for Women Travelers* (£8) by Maggie and Gemma Moss, published by Piatkus Books, 5 Windmill St., London W1P 1HF (tel. (071) 631 07 10).

■ Older Travelers and Senior Citizens

Austria's older generations enjoy a great deal of preferential treatment in this conservative country. Seniors often qualify for hotel and restaurant discounts, as well as discounted admission charges at tourist attractions. The **Purchase Privilege Program** available through the **American Association of Retired Persons** (tel. (202) 872-4700 in the U.S.) entitles members to discounts on hotels, airfares, car rentals, RV rentals, and sight-seeing. Contact them at 1909 K St., NW, Washington, DC 20048. (Membership available to those over 50.) Women over 60 and men over 65 make the cut for senior status in Austria. A **Seniorenpaß** entitles holders to a 50% discount on all Austrian federal trains, Postbuses, and BundesBuses, and works as an ID for discounted museum admissions. The card costs about 240 AS, requires a passport photo and proof of age, and is valid for one calendar year. It is available in Austria at railroad stations and major post offices.

Proof of senior status is required for many of the discounts listed below; prepare to be carded.

AARP (American Association of Retired Persons), 601 E St., NW, Washington, DC 20049 (tel. (202) 434-2277). U.S. residents over 50 and their spouses receive benefits, including travel programs and discounts for groups and individuals, as well as discounts on lodging, car and RV rental, air arrangements, and sight-seeing. US$8 annual fee. Call (800) 927-0111 or write to the above address for information on membership and programs.

Elderhostel, 75 Federal St., 3rd floor, Boston, MA 02110. You must be 60 or over, and may a spouse over 50 may tag along. Programs at colleges and universities in over 40 countries focus on varied subjects and usually last 1 week.

Gateway Books, P.O. Box 10244, San Rafael, CA 94912. Publishes Gene and Adele Malott's *Get Up and Go: A Guide for the Mature Traveler* (US$11, postage US$1.90). Offers recommendations and general hints for the budget-conscious senior. Call (800) 669-0773 to order.

National Council of Senior Citizens, 1331 F St., NW, Washington, DC 20004 (tel. (202) 347-8800). For US$12 a year or US$150 for a lifetime an individual or couple of any age can receive hotel and auto-rental discounts, a senior citizen newspaper, use of a discount travel agency, and supplemental Medicare insurance (if over 65).

Pilot Books, 103 Cooper St., Babylon, NY 11702 (tel. (516) 422-2225). Publishes *The International Health Guide for Senior Citizens* (US$5, postage US$1) and *The Senior Citizens' Guide to Budget Travel in Europe* (US$6 postpaid).

■ Children and Travel

The Austrian Press & Information Service publishes a funky, full-color map for children entitled *Happy Austria;* it includes an explanation of each region as well as

Austria's political structure. Write for it at: 31 E. 69th St., New York, NY 10021-4976.

Au pair positions, originally known only in France but now available worldwide, are reserved primarily for single women aged 18 to 30, though a few men are also employed. An *au pair* cares for the children of a family and does light housework five or six hours each day (with about 1 day off per week) while taking courses at a school for foreign students or at a university. Talking with children can be a great way to improve your dialect (if you can understand them, you can understand *anyone*), but looking after them may prove extremely strenuous. Make sure you know in advance what your host family expects of you; then watch *The Sound of Music* one more time, before you're sure that you want to play nanny to seven Austrian children. *Au pair* positions usually last six to 18 months; during the summer the contract can be as short as one to three months, but you may not be able to take courses. You'll receive room, board, and a small monthly stipend. For more information, contact the **Association for Foreign Social Services / Au Pair Agency (ASD),** Johannesgasse 16, A-1010 Vienna (tel. (0222) 512 97 95; fax 513 94 60). The family you stay with is required to pay for your temporary work permit, valid for one year.

For more information on other youth programs or tips, contact:

Austrian Youth Exchange Coordination Association (JAKÖ): Am Modenapark 2/326, A-1030 Vienna (tel. (0222) 715 57 43). Information on youth exchanges. Write them for a free brochure containing details of the most important youth exchange organizations and their activities.

Federal Ministry for Environment, Youth, and Family: Franz-Josefs-Kai 51, A-1010 Vienna (tel. (0222) 53 47 50).

Lonely Planet Publications, Embarcadero West, 112 Linden St., Oakland, CA 94607 (tel. (510) 893-8555 or (800) 275-8555); also at P.O. Box 617, Hawthorn, Victoria 3122, Australia. Publishes Maureen Wheeler's *Travel with Children* (US$11, postage US$1.50 in the U.S.).

Wilderness Press, 2440 Bancroft Way, Berkeley, CA 94707 (tel. (510) 843-8080). Order *Backpacking with Babies and Small Children* (US$10). Visa and MasterCard accepted.

■ Travelers with Disabilities

Countries vary in their general accessibility to travelers with disabilities. Unfortunately, the amount of information for travelers with disabilities is still quite limited; if you find additional publications or other information, please inform *Let's Go* so we can improve next year's edition (see Helping *Let's Go* at the very front of this guide).

By and large, Austria is one of the more accessible countries for travelers with disabilities (*Behinderung*). Tourist offices can usually offer some information about which sights, services, etc. are accessible. For example, the Austrian National Tourist Offices in New York and Vienna offer 119 pages of listings for wheelchair-accessible sights, museums, and lodgings in Vienna—ask for the booklet *Wien für Gäste mit Handicaps (Vienna for Guests with Handicaps)*. Recently renovated sights try to be accessible but often fail in practice. Many hostels and train platforms can be hard to reach, but alternative manual lifts sometimes exist. The international wheelchair icon or a large letter "B" indicates access. *Let's Go* attempts to indicate which youth hostels have full or partial wheelchair access.

In many Austrian locales, the mountainous terrain makes it difficult for physically disabled persons to get around—little can be done about this. But Austria seems to be trying hard to ease the burden for those who have difficulty moving. Special parking places and seats on buses and trains are prominently marked, and more and more curb-cuts and access ramps are appearing throughout the country. The chief problem in Vienna is the number of subway stations without elevators. Railway personnel will do what they can to aid passengers in boarding and disembarking trains—if prior arrangements are made, private vehicles and taxis are permitted to drive right up to the train platform. The Austrian railways will provide a special wheelchair for maneuvering around train aisles if given three days notice. Most major rail stations are equipped with hydraulic lifts to make trains accessible to wheelchairs. Call the train station up to a half hour before departure to ensure help. Trains have a few seats or a compartment reserved for passengers with disabilities. The pamphlet, *Mit dem Rollstuhl auf Reisen,* gives the schedules of all major second-class trains that are fully wheelchair accessible. The pamphlet *Behindertenführer: Die Bahn fährt für alle* gives telephone numbers and addresses for wheelchair-accessible transportation information in Austria.

Disabled visitors to Austria may want to contact the **Österreichischer Zivilinvalidenverband,** Brigittenauerstr. 42, 1200 Vienna (tel. (0222) 330 61 89) for more information. The **Vienna Tourist Office,** Obere Augarten Str. 40, A-1020 Vienna (tel. (0222) 21 11 40), and the **Sozialamt der Stadt Wien,** Schottenring 24, A-1010 Vienna (tel. (0222) 53 11 40), both offer booklets on accessible Vienna hotels and a general guide to the city for the disabled. All Hilton, InterContinental, and Marriott hotels have wheelchair access, but they aren't cheap.

Most countries require a six-month quarantine for all small animals, including guide dogs. To obtain an import license, owners must supply current certification of the animal's rabies, distemper, and contagious hepatitis inoculations and a veterinarian's letter attesting to its health (see Entering Austria, the Czech Republic, and Hungary above).

Association of the Physically Handicapped in Austria, Lützowgasse 24-28/3, A-1140 Vienna (tel. (0222) 94 55 62 or 911 32 25).

American Foundation for the Blind, 15 W. 16th St., New York, NY 10011 (tel. (212) 620-2147). ID cards (US$10); write for an application, or call the Product Center at (800) 829-0500. Also call this number to order AFB catalogs in braille, print, or on cassette or disk.

Consumer Information Center, Dept. 454V, Pueblo, CO 81009 (tel. (719) 948 3334). Offers *Access Travel: Airports,* which lists designs, facilities, and services at 553 airport terminals worldwide (free), and *New Horizons for the Air Traveler with a Disability* (free).

Directions Unlimited, 720 North Bedford Rd., Bedford Hills, NY 10507 (tel. (800) 533-5343 or (914) 241-1700). Specializes in arranging individual and group vacations, tours, and cruises for those with disabilities.

Disability Press, Ltd., Applemarket House, 17 Union St., Kingston-upon-Thames, Surrey KT1 1RP, England (tel. (081) 549 63 99). Publishes the *Disabled Traveler's International Phrasebook,* including French, German, Italian, Spanish, Portuguese, Swedish, and Dutch phrases (£1.75). Supplements in Norwegian, Hungarian and Serbo-Croatian (60p each).

Evergreen Travel Service, 4114 198th St. SW, Suite #13, Lynnwood, WA 98036 (tel. (800) 435-2288 or (206) 776-1184). Arranges wheelchair-accessible tours and individual travel worldwide. Other services include tours for the blind, the deaf and tours for those who seek a slow-paced itinerary.

The Guided Tour, Inc., Elkins Park House, Suite 114B, 7900 Old York Road, Elkins Park, PA 19117-2348 (tel. (215) 782-1370 or (800) 738-5843). Year-round travel programs for persons with developmental and physical challenges as well as itineraries geared to the needs of persons requiring renal dialysis. Trips and vacations planned both domestically and internationally. Call or write for a free brochure.

Mobility International, USA (MIUSA), P.O. Box 3551, Eugene, OR 97403 (tel. (503) 343-1284 voice and TDD). **International headquarters** in Britain, 228 Borough High St., London SE1 1JX (tel. (071) 403 56 88). Contacts in 30 countries. Information on travel programs, international workcamps, accommodations, access guides, and organized tours. Membership costs US$20 per year, newsletter US$10. Sells updated and expanded *A World of Options: A Guide to Interna-*

tional Educational Exchange, Community Service, and Travel for Persons with Disabilities (US$14 for members; US$16 for nonmembers, postpaid).

Moss Rehabilitation Hospital Travel Information Service, 1200 W. Tabor Rd., Philadelphia, PA 19141 (tel. (215) 456-9603). Information on international travel accessibility: nominal fee charged for packet of information on tourist sights, accommodations, and transportation.

Society for the Advancement of Travel for the Handicapped, 347 Fifth Ave. #610, New York, NY 10016 (tel. (212) 447-7284; fax 725-8253). Publishes quarterly travel newsletter *SATH News* and information booklets (free for members, US$3 each for nonmembers). Advice on trip-planning for people with disabilities. Annual membership is US$45, students and seniors US$25.

Twin Peaks Press, P.O. Box 129, Vancouver, WA 98666 (tel. (206) 694-2462; orders only (800) 637-2256). *Travel for the Disabled* lists tips and resources for disabled travelers (US$20). Also available are the *Directory for Travel Agencies of the Disabled* (US$20) and *Wheelchair Vagabond* (US$15). Postage US$2 for first book, US$1 for each additional.

■ Bisexual, Gay, and Lesbian Travelers

Austria is less tolerant of homosexuals than many other nations; especially in the more conservative West, open discussion of homosexuality is mostly taboo. The German word for gay is *schwul;* for lesbian, *lesbisch.* Bisexual is *bisexual,* or simply *bi* (pronounced "bee").

Are You Two Together?, published by Random House; available at bookstores (US$18). A new gay and lesbian guide to spots in Europe. Written by a lesbian couple; covers Western European capitals and gay resorts.

Ferrari Publications, P.O. Box 37887, Phoenix, AZ 85069 (tel. (602) 863-2408). Publishes *Ferrari's Places of Interest* (US$14.95), *Ferrari's Places for Men* (US$13.95), *Ferrari's Places for Women* (US$12), and *Inn Places: USA and Worldwide Gay Accommodations* (US$14.95). Also available from Giovanni's Room (see below).

Gay's the Word, 66 Marchmont St., London WC1N 1AB (tel. (071) 278 76 54). Tube: "Russel Sq." Information for gay and lesbian travelers. Mail order service available. Open Mon.-Fri. 11am-7pm, Sat. 10-6, Sun. 2-6pm.

Giovanni's Room, 345 S. 12th St., Philadelphia, PA 19107 (tel. (215) 923-2960; fax 923-0813). International feminist, lesbian, and gay bookstore with mail-order service.

Homosexuelle Initiative (HOSI) Wien, Novaragasse 40, A-1020 Wien (tel. (0222) 26 66 04). Austria's first lesbian and gay association; political and human rights lobby. Operates a gay and lesbian center with varying schedules of events. Positive Café Tues. 3-8pm. Gay and lesbian evening Tues. 8pm. Women's Social Wed. 7pm. Gay and lesbian youth group meeting Thurs. 7pm. Gay and lesbian **counseling hotline** Tues. and Fri. 6-8pm. HOSI Wien publishes Austria's leading gay and lesbian magazine, the *LAMBDA-Nachrichten* quarterly.

Spartacus International Gay Guide, ordered from 100 East Biddle St., Baltimore, MD 21202 (tel. (410) 727-5677) or c/o Bruno Lützowstraße, P.O. Box 301345, D-1000 Berlin 30, Germany (tel. +49 (30) 25 49 82 00); also available from Giovanni's Room (see above) and from Renaissance House, P.O. Box 292 Village Station, New York, NY 10014 (tel. (212) 674-0120). Extensive list of gay bars, restaurants, hotels, bookstores and hotlines throughout the world. Specifically for men (US$30).

Women Going Places, a new women's travel and resource guide emphasizing women-owned enterprises. Geared towards lesbians, but offers advice appropriate for all women. US$14. Available from Inland Book Company, P.O. Box 120261, East Haven, CT 06512 (tel. (203) 467-4257).

■ Kosher and Vegetarian Travelers

National tourist offices often publish lists of kosher and vegetarian restaurants, but few Jews live in Austria, Prague, and Budapest, so the kosher offerings are correspondingly small. All three countries are devoutly carnivorous, although vegetarian restaurants have proliferated along with the blooming "alternative scene" in larger cities. Dairy products are by and large excellent.

Austria is vegetarian Purgatory. Red meat is the staple food, and *Wurst* is ubiquitous. Even salads tend to be limp and drowned in mayonnaise. However, most restaurants have a decent *Gemüseplatte* (plate of cooked vegetables), and even the tiniest towns have good Italian restaurants, where the presence of *pasta primavera* or some other meatless dish is virtually guaranteed. Fish is common in lakeside resorts, and dairy products are common everywhere, but vegetarians who eat no animal products will have their work cut out for them. Vienna, the center of Austria's minute Jewish population, is the only city where it is remotely practical to keep kosher.

Feldheim Publishers, 200 Airport Executive Park, Spring Valley, NY 10977. Publishes *The Jewish Traveler's Resource Guide,* compiled by Jeff Seidel of the Jewish Student Information Center, Jewish Quarter, Old City, Jerusalem (tel. (02) 28 83 38). The guide, intended mainly for students, lists contacts at Jewish organizations in 69 countries.

Jewish Chronicle Publications, 25 Furnival St., London EC4A 1JT. Publishes the *Jewish Travel Guide.* Available in the U.S. from Sepher-Hermon Press, 1265 46th St., Brooklyn, NY 11219 (tel. (718) 972-9010) for US$11.95, postage US$1.75. Lists synagogues, kosher restaurants and institutions in over 80 countries.

North American Vegetarian Society, P.O. Box 72, Dolgeville, NY 13329 (tel. (518) 568-7970). More publications than you can shake a stalk at. Ask for a list of establishments in the region you will be touring.

Vegetarian Society of the United Kingdom, Parkdale, Dunham Rd., Altringham, Cheshire WA14 4QG (tel. (061) 928 0793). Sells the *International Vegetarian Travel Guide,* last updated in 1991.

■ Minority Travelers

In certain regions, tourists of color or members of certain religious groups may feel unwelcome. Furthermore, either historical or newly developed discrimination against established minority residents may surface against travelers who are members of those minority groups. *Let's Go* asks that our researchers exclude from the guides establishments that discriminate. If, in your travels, you encounter discriminatory treatment, you should firmly state your disapproval, but do not push the matter; make it clear to the owners that another hotel or restaurant will be receiving your patronage, and mail a letter to *Let's Go* if the establishment is listed in the guide, so we can reassess it next year (see Helping Let's Go in the very front of this guide).

In terms of safety, we don't have any easy answers. Traveling in groups and taking a taxi whenever you are uncomfortable are always good ideas; your personal safety should always be your first priority. The best answer to xenophobic comments and other verbal harassment is no answer at all (they're just looking to get a rise out of you). Keep abreast of the particular cultural attitudes of the countries you're planning to visit. But above all, keep in mind that your own ethnicity or religion may not necessarily be problematic, unless you choose to make it a confrontational issue; you very well may find your vacation trouble-free and your hosts open-minded.

■ Traveling Alone

The freedom to come and go, to backtrack or deviate from a schedule or route, is the lone traveler's prerogative. Remember, buddy trips only work out perfectly in

Hollywood. If you do travel with friends, consider separating for a few days. You'll get a brief break from each other and the chance to have some adventures of your own.

Be warned: solo travel is a dangerous enterprise. It may be easier to reel in a ride if hitching alone, but it is also foolish, especially for women. If you've been spending your nights outdoors, consider indoor accommodations when on your own—lone campers make easy targets. Unfortunately, solitude can be expensive; double rooms are cheaper per person than singles. Moreover, the road can be a lonely place. For many, however, lack of partners provides a greater incentive to meet other people—locals and fellow travelers alike.

GETTING THERE

The first challenge in European budget travel is getting there. The airline industry manipulates their computerized reservation systems to squeeze every dollar from customers; finding a cheap airfare in this deliberate confusion will be easier if you understand the airlines better than they think you do. Call every toll-free number, and don't be afraid to ask, even badger, for discounts. Have a knowledgeable travel agent guide you through the options; better yet, have several knowledgeable travel agents guide you. Remember that there's little institutional incentive for them to do the legwork to find the cheapest fares (for which they receive the lowest commissions).

Students and **people under 26** with proper identification (see Youth and Student Identification under Documents 'n Formalities above) never need to pay full price for a ticket. They qualify for startlingly reduced airfares—available not so much from airlines or travel agents as from student travel agencies like Council and STA (see Useful Travel Organizations above).

These agencies negotiate special reduced-rate bulk purchases with the airlines, then resell them to the youth market; in 1993, peak season round-trip rates from the east coast of North America to even the offbeat corners of Europe rarely topped US$700 (though flights to Russia on Western carriers were higher), and off-season fares were considerably lower. Return-date change fees also tend to be low (around US$50). Most of their flights are on major scheduled airlines, though in peak season some seats may be on less reliable chartered aircraft. Student travel agencies can also help non-students and people over 26, but they may not be able to get the same low fares.

Seniors can also garner mint deals; many airlines offer senior traveler club discounts or airline passes and discounts for seniors' companions as well. Travel sections in Sunday newspapers often list bargain fares from the local airport. Outfox airline reps with the phone-book-sized *Official Airline Guide* (at large libraries); this monthly guide lists every scheduled flight in the world (including prices). George Brown's *The Airline Passenger's Guerilla Handbook* (US$15; last published in 1990) is a more renegade resource.

Most airlines maintain a fare structure that peaks between mid-June and early-September. They all practice "yield management"—translated from the Czech to mean the number of budget-priced seats on any flight is small and constantly subject to change. Midweek (Mon.-Thurs.) flights run about US$30 cheaper each way than weekend flights. Leaving from a travel hub such as New York, Atlanta, Dallas, Chicago, Los Angeles, San Francisco, Vancouver, Toronto, Melbourne, or Sydney will win you a more competitive fare than departures from smaller cities; the gains are not as great when departing from travel hubs monopolized by one airline. Call around. Flying to London is usually the cheapest way across the Atlantic, though special fares to other cities—such as Amsterdam, Luxembourg, or Brussels—can cost even less.

It's often cheaper to fly to a nearby city and take a train or ferry to your final destination; check fares for these alternative routes carefully, however, since train tickets are often expensive themselves and might not be worth the aggravation. Vienna is the cheapest destination in Austria, though you may save money by flying into Munich and continuing by ground. You probably won't save any money by traveling through London and crossing the Channel.

Return-date flexibility is usually not an option for the budget traveler; except on youth fares purchased through the airlines, traveling with an "open return" ticket can be pricier than fixing a return date and paying to change it. Avoid one-way tickets, too: the flight to Europe may be economical, but the return fares can be outrageous. Whenever flying internationally, pick up your ticket well in advance and arrive at the airport several hours before your flight. If you show up at the airport before your ticketed date of departure, the airline just might rewrite your ticket, even if it is supposedly precluded by company restrictions. Whereas rules prevent a travel agent from altering budget tickets, the airline itself can modify dates all it wants, and it just might hasten your departure, thereby freeing an extra seat on a flight later on.

■ Commercial Airlines

Even if you pay an airline's lowest published fare, you may be spending many hundreds of dollars. The commercial airlines' lowest regular offer is the **APEX** (Advance Purchase Excursion Fare); specials advertised in newspapers may be cheaper but have correspondingly more restrictions and fewer available seats. APEX fares provide you with confirmed reservations and allow "open-jaw" tickets (landing in and returning from different cities). Reservations must usually be made at least 21 days in advance, with 7- to 14-day minimum and 60- to 90-day maximum stay limitations, and hefty cancellation and change-of-reservation penalties. For summer travel, book APEX fares early; by May you will have difficulty getting the departure date you want.

A few carriers fly non-stop or direct flights to each destination. These cause the fewest headaches; you only have to deal with one airline, which minimizes hassles and the chances of luggage loss. Other carriers fly you across the Atlantic or the Pacific or the North Sea into their hub on the European continent and then connect you to Austria, Prague, or Budapest on another carrier, often for the same fare as the direct fliers. Call around for the best fare, balancing convenience with your budget. Most of these airlines consider peak season the months of June, July, and August; flights are less expensive during the other nine months of the year.

Austrian Airlines (tel. (800) 843-0002 or (212) 307-6226 in the U.S., (800) 387-1477 in Canada), the national airline of Austria, has the most non-stop flights and serves the most cities in Austria, but its fares tend to be higher. Austrian Airlines flies daily non-stop from New York to Vienna and has five weekly connections from Chicago via Copenhagen to Vienna. Austrian Airlines is associated with **OnePass,** Continental Airlines's frequent flyer program. OnePass members can accrue and redeem their miles on Austrian Airlines flights, with some restrictions. If you are not a member of OnePass (tel. (800) 525-0280), join before you depart on Austrian Airlines. As with any airline's program, you'll earn thousands of miles just on this one round-trip flight. **Delta** (tel. (800) 221-1212 in the U.S., (800) 361-6770, (800) 361-1970, or (800) 843-9378 in Canada) and **TWA** (tel. (800) 221-2000, (800) 421-8480, or (800) 252-0622 for the hearing or speech impaired) also fly to Vienna non-stop from New York City. Dozens of other carriers fly to Vienna, albeit with changes and layovers. **Lauda Air** flies from Melbourne, Sydney, and London to Vienna. Contact your travel agent or the Lauda home offices in Vienna (tel. (0222) 51 47 70) and Salzburg (tel. (0662) 84 54 30). **Dan Air** has direct air service from Gatwick airport in London to Innsbruck.

CSA (tel. (800) 223-2365 or (800) 628-6107), the national airline of the Czech Republic, flies to Prague from the United States and from Kiev, Riga, Lvov, Düsseldorf, Hamburg, and Manchester. CSA offers four non-stop flights per week from New York City (on Sun., Mon., Thurs., and Fri.), and two non-stops from Chicago (on Mon. and Wed.) plus other flights with connections or layovers. From New York to Prague, CSA offers a super APEX fare of US$708-878 depending on dates and times of departure (from Chicago US$744-914). CSA has been negotiating for non-stop flights from Toronto and Montreal. Enroll in CSA's frequent flyer program, OK PLUS, before you depart. **British Airways** (tel. (800) AIRWAYS (247-9297) in the U.S., (800) 668-1080 or (800) 668-1059 in Canada, (800) 668-1055 in Canada for a French-speaking operator), **Lufthansa** (tel. (800) 645-3880 in the U.S., (800) 56-FLYLH (35954) in Canada), **KLM** (tel. (800) 374-7747 in the U.S., (800) 361-5330 or (800) 361-1887 in Canada), and **Alitalia** (tel. (800) 223-5730 or (800) 442-5860 in the U.S., (800) 361-8336 in Canada) also fly from New York City to Prague, through their respective gateway cities: British Airways in London, Lufthansa in Frankfurt, KLM in Amsterdam, and Alitalia in Rome.

Malev Hungarian Airlines (tel. (800) 262-5380) and **Delta** fly directly to Budapest from New York City, with stops but no plane changes. **Lufthansa, Austrian Airlines, Sabena** (tel. (800) 955-2000), and **CSA** also fly to Budapest.

Most airlines no longer offer standby fares, once a staple of the budget traveler. Standby has given way to the **three-day-advance-purchase youth fare,** a cousin of the one-day variety prevalent in Europe. It is available only to those under 25 (sometimes 24) and only within three days of departure—a gamble that often pays off, but could backfire if the airline is all booked up. Return dates are open, but you must come back within a year, and once again can book your return seat no more than three days ahead. Youth fares in summer aren't really cheaper than APEX, but off-season prices drop deliciously. **Icelandair** (tel. (800) 223-5500) is one of the few airlines that still offers this three-day fare. Check with a travel agent for details.

A few airlines offer other miscellaneous discounts. Look into flights to relatively less popular destinations or smaller carriers. Call **Icelandair** or **Virgin Atlantic Airways** (tel. (800) 862-8621) for information on their last-minute offers. Icelandair offers a "get-up-and-go" fare from New York to Luxembourg (June-Sept. US$299 weekdays, US$329 weekends; Oct.-May US$268 weekdays, US$288 weekends). Reservations can be made no more than three days before departure. After arrival, Icelandair offers discounts on trains and buses from Luxembourg to other parts of Europe. Virgin Atlantic offers their Instant Purchase Plan (New York to London round trip US$432), for which reservations can be made no more than 10 days before departure.

■ Charter Flights and Ticket Consolidators

Ticket consolidators resell unsold tickets on commercial and charter airlines that might otherwise have gone begging. Look for their tiny ads in weekend papers (in the U.S., the Sunday *New York Times* travel section is best), and start calling them all. There is rarely a maximum age; tickets are also heavily discounted, and may offer extra flexibility or bypass advance purchase requirements, since you are not tangled in airline bureaucracy. However, unlike tickets bought through an airline, you won't be able to use your tickets on another flight if you miss yours, and you'll have to go back to the consolidator—not the airline—to get a refund. Phone around and pay with a credit card; you can't stop a cash payment if you never receive your tickets. Don't be tempted solely by the low prices; find out everything you can about the agency you're considering, and get a copy of its refund policy *in writing.* Ask also about accommodations and car rental discounts; some consolidators have fingers in many pies. Insist on a **receipt** that gives full details about the tickets, refunds and restrictions, and if they don't want to give you one or just generally seem clueless, patronize a different company.

It's best to buy from a major organization that has experience in placing individuals on charter flights. One of the most reputable is the CIEE-affiliated **Council Charter,** 205 E. 42nd St., New York, NY 10017 (tel. (800) 800-8222); their flights can also be booked through Council Travel offices. Another good organization is **Unitravel** (tel. (800) 325-2222); they offer discounted airfares on major scheduled airlines from the U.S. to over 50 cities in Europe and will hold all payments in a bank escrow until completion of your trip. You should also look up **Access International** (tel. 800 825-3633); **Interworld** (tel. (800) 331-4456, in Florida (305) 443-4929); **Rebel** (tel. (800) 227-3235); and **Travac** (tel. (800) 872-8800—don't be afraid to call every number and hunt for the best deal.

Consolidators sell a mixture of tickets; some are on scheduled airlines, some on **charter flights.** Once an entire system of its own, the charter business has shriveled and effectively merged with the ticket consolidator network. The theory behind a charter is that a tour operator contracts with an airline (usually a fairly obscure carrier that specializes in charters) and uses their planes to fly extra loads of passengers to peak-season destinations. Charter flights thus fly less frequently than major airlines and have correspondingly more restrictions. They are also almost always fully booked, schedules and itineraries may change at the last moment, and flights may be traumatically cancelled. Shoot for a scheduled air ticket if you can, and pay with a credit card. You might also consider traveler's insurance against trip interruption.

Airhitch, 2790 Broadway #100, New York, NY 10025 (tel. (212) 864-2000) advertises a similar service: you choose a five-day date range in which to travel and a list of preferred European destinations, and they try to place you in a vacant spot in a flight in your date range to one of those destinations. Absolute flexibility—on both sides of the Atlantic—is necessary, but the savings might be worth it: flights cost US$169 each way when departing from the East Coast of the U.S., US$269 from the West Coast, and US$229 from most places in between. Airhitch usually gets you where you want to go, but they only guarantee that you'll end up in Europe. Check all flight times and departure sites directly with the airline carrier, read *all* the fine print they send you, and compare it to what people tell you. The Better Business Bureau of New York received complaints about Airhitch a few years ago; they still don't recommend the organization, but they don't discourage you from using them, either.

Icelandair's **Supergrouper** plan (tel. (800) 223-5500) places travelers on their flights to Luxembourg and back, without requiring a specified return date. You must return within the year; tickets are US$669.

Last minute **discount clubs** and **fare brokers** offer members savings on European travel, including charter flights and tour packages. Research your options carefully. **Last Minute Travel Club,** 1249 Boylston St., Boston, MA 02215 (tel. (800) 527-8646 or (617) 267-9800) is one of the few travel clubs that does not require a membership fee. Others include **Discount Travel International** (tel. (800) 324-9294), **Moment's Notice** (tel. (212) 486-0503; $25 annual fee), **Traveler's Advantage** (tel. (800) 835-8747; $49 annual fee), and **Worldwide Discount Travel Club** (tel. (305) 534-2082; $50 annual fee).

For $25, **Travel Avenue** will search for the lowest international airfare available and then discount it 5-17% (tel. (800) 333-3335). The often labyrinthine contracts for all these organizations bear close study—you may prefer not to stop over in Luxembourg for eleven hours.

■ Courier Flights

People who travel without much baggage (like you! see Packing) should consider flying to Europe as a courier. The company that hires you will use your checked luggage space for freight, leaving you with the carry-on allowance. Restrictions to watch for: most flights are round-trip only, with fixed-length stays (usually short), you may not be able to travel with a companion, and most flights are from New York (including a scenic visit to the courier office in the 'burbs). Round-trip fares to Western Europe from the U.S. range from US$199-349 (during the off-season) to US$399-549 (during the summer). **Now Voyager,** 74 Varick St. #307, New York, NY 10013 (tel. (212) 431-1616), acts as an agent for many courier flights worldwide from New York, although some flights are available from Houston. They offer special last-minute deals to such cities as London, Paris, Rome, and Frankfurt which go for as little as US$299 round-trip. **Halbart Express**, 147-05 176th St., Jamaica, NY 11434 (tel. (718) 656-8279) and **Courier Travel Service,** 530 Central Avenue, Cedarhurst, NY 11516 (tel. (516) 374-2299), are other courier agents to try. And if you have travel time to spare, **Ford's Travel Guides,** 19448 Londelius St., Northridge, CA 91324 (tel. (818) 701-7414) list **freighter companies** that will take passengers for trans-Atlantic crossings. Ask for their *Freighter Travel Guide and Waterways of the World* (US$15, and $2.50 postage if mailed outside the U.S.).

You can also fly directly through courier companies in New York, or check your bookstore or library for handbooks such as *The Insider's Guide to Air Courier Bargains* (US$15). The *Courier Air Travel Handbook* (US$10.70), which explains the procedure for traveling as an air courier and contains names, telephone numbers, and contact points of courier companies, can be ordered directly from Thunderbird Press, 5930-10 W. Greenway Rd. #112, Glendale, AZ 85306, or by calling (800) 345-0096. **Travel Unlimited**, P.O. Box 1058, Allston, MA 02134-1058, publishes a comprehensive, monthly newsletter that details all possible options for courier travel (often 50% off discount commercial fares). A one-year subscription costs US$25 (abroad US$35).

■ Escorts on the High Seas

Lauretta Blake the Working Vacation™ is an agency for the increasingly popular (and entirely legitimate) **Gentlemen Host**™ program. Single, middle-aged men (usually over 45) serve as social hosts for female passengers in return for passage on a series of cruises. Several cruise lines participate. The job calls for a gregarious personality and ballroom dancing skills, and entails schmoozing with hundreds of older women throughout the day and evening. Participants must be fluent in waltz, rhumba, swing, cha-cha, and foxtrot. The cruise lines strictly delimit the activities of the hosts. Romance is *verboten,* and gentlemen may not dance with the same woman for two consecutive songs; they must switch to a different partner so every woman gets a turn. During the afternoon, the hosts perform other tasks, such as teaching bridge and manning the library, and, in general, keep the women on board pleased. The emphasis is on dancing; more and more women travel solo, and cruise lines find that single women will book cruises repeatedly in order to dance in a non-threatening environment. According to Lauretta Blake, dancing is a favorite sport among older women—consider it the female equivalent of golf.

The agency charges successful applicants US$150 per week of cruising. In exchange, the hosts earn a free cabin, meals, gratuities, and a bar allowance. **Royal Cruise Line** (tel. (800) 227-0925) seeks up to 12 men for each cruise; ships dock in Italy and other parts of Europe *oh*-so-close to Austria, Prague, and Budapest; hosts can extend their vacations inland before or after the cruise. Ships of the **Royal Viking Line** (tel. (800) 422-8000) also sail to and around Europe, as do **Cunard** vessels (tel. (800) 221-4770), including the QE2.

In addition to the Gentleman Host™ program, Lauretta Blake seeks specialists for various on-board enrichment programs. Experts exchange their prowess for free travel and pay a small fee to the agency. Dance instructors, speakers, musicians, activity leaders in arts, crafts, fitness, card games, and health, and many other professionals entertain passengers to enhance their oceanic adventure. The company is always seeking new applicants for these working vacations.

For more information, contact Lauretta Blake the Working Vacation™, 4277 Lake Santa Clara Drive, Santa Clara, CA 95054 (tel. (408) 727-9665; fax 980-1839).

■ Not Getting There: Fearful Flyers

USAir (tel. (800) 428-4322) invites you to "learn to relax and enjoy flying" through its special **Fearful Flyers Program,** taught by a psychiatric social worker and an airplane captain. Several meetings are held on board an aircraft, where the students may explore the cabin and cockpit, and an FAA representative takes the class on a tour of the control tower and radar room. The seven-week course including a one-hr. graduation flight costs US$325. The program is offered in several U.S. cities. In Boston, for example, classes will be held in June, 1994 on seven consecutive Tuesday or Thursday evenings from 7:30-10:30pm. For more information on programs in your area, contact **USAir Fearful Flyers Program,** Box 100, Glenshaw, PA 15116.

ONCE THERE

■ Tourist Information

The **Austrian National Tourist Office** publishes a wealth of information about tours and vacations; every Austrian town of any touristic importance whatsoever, and some others, are served by local tourist offices. These efficient, helpful and generally superb tourist services operate under a bewildering number of aliases—*Verkehrsamt, Verkehrsverein, Fremdenverkehrsbüro, Tourist-Information,* etc. (see the Glossary at the back of this guide for more). Even the smallest towns have some sort of bureau, at times operating out of an office in the city hall (*Rathaus*). To simplify things, all are marked by a standard "i" sign. The offices are usually located by the main attraction in town, in the central square, or by the main train station—sometimes all three. Exploit these offices for city maps (often free), information on sights and museums, and lists of accommodation options. Most tourist offices will track down a vacant room for you and make a reservation, sometimes without a fee. They will also fork over the free town *Gastgeberverzeichnis,* the same pamphlet, listing all town accommodations, that they use to round up rooms for a commission. Similar information and services are available in tourist offices in Prague and Budapest. *Let's Go* lists tourist offices in the Practical Information section of each city.

Be sure to milk the tourist office for information—they exist solely to help confused travelers. There's nothing wrong with arriving at an office with a litany of specific questions. Just be courteous and polite to a fault, even when you've been aggravated by a town establishment. Remember, the staff gives information, but is not responsible for the operation of the town. Patience and a smile may work wonders on a staff that has had to placate irate foreigners all day. The staff may or may not speak English—it is not a requirement in the smaller towns, though Viennese officials may be able to pass for U.N. interpreters. One final note: Remember that the people who work in the tourist office are just plain folks, too—often as underpaid and overworked as you are. Have mercy on them.

■ Language

German is the language of 98% of the Austrian population. English is the most common second language, commonly spoken by practitioners of the tourist trade in large cities. In villages and smaller towns, tourist office employees usually speak some English, but don't count on those who run hostels, restaurants, and stores. All school-age children now learn English, so kids and college students can be helpful allies. Don't be afraid of unleashing the few German words you have memorized from a phrase book. Any effort to use the mother tongue, however incompetent, will win you friends. Even native German speakers cannot comprehend some of Austria's regional dialects, but dialect-speakers usually switch automatically to High German when they detect a foreign accent. It is considered gauche to ask Austrians to speak High German; ask them to speak *langsam und deutlich* (slowly and clearly) and they usually take the hint. Among the most important differences between Austrian German and High German: the national greeting is *Grüß Gott* or *Servus* instead of *guten Tag;* "good-bye" is *auf Wiederschauen* instead of *auf Wied-*

erseben, "two" is pronounced *zwoh* (TSVOH) instead of *zwei,* "whipped cream" is *Schlagobers* instead of *Schlagsahne*, and "potatoes" are *Erdäpfel* instead of *Kartoffeln.* In Lower Austria, beware of Viennese dialect creeping onto the menus; for example, *Paradeiser* means "tomatoes" and *Kukuruz* means "corn." See the Appendix and the Glossary at the back of this guide for more—much, much more—on the German, Czech, and Hungarian languages.

■■■ GETTING AROUND

Every traveler, great and small, should procure the monumentally useful pamphlet, *Die Bahn im Griff,* available at most Austrian train stations. In German but nonetheless discernible to non-speakers, it boasts comprehensive and valuable information plus pictorial explanations of the train system. It lists numbers and locations for ticket information and reservations, customer service, foreign rail representatives, private rail lines, and even restaurants in rail stations. It contains an explanation of the various train symbols. The booklet even lists per-kilometer prices for transportation tickets. In the section, "*Preise und Ermäßigungen,*" you can read the official, legal definitions of: disabled, blind, family, student, calendar year, calendar month, calendar week, calendar day, apprentice, and veteran, to determine whether you qualify for certain discounts. A **senior citizen,** for example, is defined by the Austrian rail system as a woman over 60 or a man over 65. Another impressive booklet is *Servus in Austria with the Railways,* in English. It lists Austrian National Tourist Offices all over the world, has route maps for various train systems, and lists fares for many routes.

■ By Train

European trains retain the charm and romance, not to mention functionalism, their North American counterparts lost generations ago. Second-class travel is pleasant, and compartments, which seat from two to six, are excellent places to meet fellow movers and shakers of all ages and nationalities. Bring some food and a plastic water bottle that you can fill at your hostel and take with you on all trips; the train café can be expensive, and train water can be creatively colored and is often unpotable. Trains are in no way theft-proof; lock the door of your compartment if you can, and keep your valuables on your person at all times.

Many train stations have different counters for domestic tickets, international tickets, seat reservations, and information; check before lining up. On major lines, reservations are always advisable, and often required, even if you have a railpass; make reservations at least a few hours in advance at the train station (usually less than US$3). Faster trains, akin to France's famed TGV, require a special supplement (about US$4-5). Sometimes you can pay for your supplement on board, but it'll cost a little more.

You may be tempted to save on accommodations by taking an overnight train in a regular coach seat, but there are problems to consider. *If* you get to sleep you are sure to wake up exhausted and aching, security problems are rampant, and if you spread yourself over several seats in an empty compartment, someone is sure to come in at 3am and claim one of them. A sleeping berth in a bunk-bedded couchette car, with linen provided, is a somewhat affordable luxury (about US$24; reserve at the station several days in advance).

The **Österreichische Bundesbahn (ÖBB),** Austria's federal railroad, operates one of Europe's most thorough and efficient rail networks—a 3600-mi. system whose trains are frequent, fast, clean, comfortable, and always on or close to schedule. The ÖBB prints the yearly *Fahrpläne Kursbuch Bahn-Inland,* a two-inch-thick compilation of all rail, ferry, and cable-car transportation schedules in Austria; it's a must-carry, if you're buff enough. The massive compendium (100 AS) is available at any large train station, along with its companion tomes, the *Kursbuch Bahn-Ausland,* for international trains (40 AS), and the *Internationales Schlafwagenkursbuch,* for sleeping cars (80 AS). Bus schedules are contained in two other volumes, *Fahrpläne Bus Ost* and *West.* The *Fahrpläne* will acquaint you with most everything you need to know about the Austrian rail network, such as train times, mileage, prices, and stops, for literally every extant route—plus information about ferries and local public transportation. Schedules are also posted at transportation stops and depots throughout Austria. Arrival (*Ankunft*) and Departure (*Abfahrt*) placards—white and yellow, respectively, are posted at all rail stations. Bus schedules are posted at every stop (*Haltestelle*), under the green-H-in-a-circle logo. Austrian transportation generally operates on a fixed schedule, with intermediate stops always at the same minute after the hour.

For train **information,** call 17 17 in Graz, Innsbruck, Klagenfurt, Lienz, Linz, Salzburg, St. Pölten, Steyr, Villach, Wels, Vienna, or Wolfsberg. You will reach an operator who speaks German and basic English, perhaps after a recorded introduction that importunes you to "Hold, please, for the next available operator."

Rail Tickets

Buying a **railpass** is both a popular and sensible option in many circumstances. Ideally conceived, a railpass allows you to jump on any train in Europe, go wherever you want whenever you want, and change your plans at will. The handbook that accompanies your railpass tells you everything you need to know and includes a timetable for major routes, a map, and details on ferry discounts. In practice, of course, it's not so simple. You still must stand in line to pay for seat reservations (the only guarantee you have against standing up), for supplements, for couchette reservations, and to have your pass validated when you first use it.

More importantly, railpasses don't always pay off. Distance is the fundamental criterion that determines whether or not a pass is a good buy. If you are planning even one long journey, a pass is probably the way to go; in 1993, for example, Paris to Rome (one way) cost about US$264 for first class, US$164 second class. In comparison, for US$34 more you could purchase a first-class Eurail Flexipass, or for US$56 additional a second-class Eurail Youth Flexipass; both provide 5 days rail travel within a 2 month period. To see if a pass suits your itinerary, find a travel agent with a copy of the *Eurailtariff* manual (or call Rail Europe in the U.S. at (800) 438-7245 and ask for the latest edition of the *Rail Europe Traveler's Guide*), add up the second-class fares for the major routes you plan to cover, deduct 5% (the listed price includes a commission), deduct another 35% if you're under 26 and eligible for BIJ (see below) and compare. If the total cost of all your trips comes close to the price of the pass, the convenience of avoiding ticket lines may well be worth the difference. Avoid an obsession with squeezing every last kilometer from a pass; you may come home with only blurred memories of train stations.

Eurailpasses

The Eurailpass is probably the most popular rail pass valid throughout the Continent. **Rail Europe,** 230 Westchester Ave., White Plains, NY 10604 (in U.S. tel. (800) 438-RAIL or (800) 848-RAIL; fax (800) 432-1329; in Canada tel. (800) 361-RAIL; fax (416) 602-4198) is just one of the many organizations that offer a trainload of information and an assortment of railpasses to consider.

1st-class Eurailpass, very rarely profitable for the budget traveler. 15 days for US$498, 21 days for US$648, 1 month for US $798, 2 months for US$1098, and 3 months for US$1398.

Eurail Saverpass, for people traveling in groups. It allows unlimited 1st-class travel for 15 days for US$430 per person for two or more people who travel together (3 or more from April-Sept.). There are also 21-day (US$550 per person) and 1-month (US$678 per person) Saverpasses.

Eurail Youthpass, for travelers under 26 on their first day of travel. Good for 15 days (US$398), one month (US$578), or two months (US$768) of 2nd-class travel.

The 1-month pass may not be worth your while; the 2-month pass is more economical.

1st-class Eurail Flexipasses, allow limited travel within a longer period; there are three packages: 5 days of travel within a 2-month period for US$348; 10 days of travel within a 2-month period for US$560; and 15 days of travel in a 2-month period for US$740.

Youth Flexipasses, available in flavors of 5 days within 2 months (US$255), 10 days within 2 months (US$398), and 15 days within 2 months (US$540).

When using a Flexipass, you (or the train conductor) must note on your ticket the days that you travel; if you start an overnight trip after 7pm, write down the next day's date on your pass. You'll almost certainly find it easiest to buy a Eurailpass *before* you arrive in Europe; contact one of the agencies listed under Useful Travel Organizations above, among many other travel agencies. A few major train stations in Europe sell them too (though American agents usually deny this). If you're stuck in Europe and unable to find someone to sell a Eurailpass, make a transatlantic call to an American railpass agent, which should be able to send a pass to you by express mail. Eurailpasses are not refundable once validated; you will be able to get a replacement if you lose one *only* if you have purchased insurance on the pass from Eurail—something you cannot do through a travel agent. Ask a travel agent for specifics, and be sure you know how the program works before you get to Europe.

Other Multi-country Railpasses

For those under 26, **BIJ** tickets (Billets Internationals de Jeunesse, sold under the **Wasteels, Eurotrain** and **Route 26** names) are an excellent alternative to railpasses. Available for international trips within Europe and Morocco and for travel within France, they save an average of 30-45% off regular second-class fares. Tickets are sold from point to point, with free and unlimited stopovers along the way. However, you cannot take longer than two months to complete your trip, and you can stop only at points along the specific direct route of your ticket. In 1993, for instance, Wasteels offered round-trip tickets from London to Berlin for approximately £90, and a London-Amsterdam-Berlin-Prague-Budapest-Vienna-Zurich-Brussels-London ticket for £190—significantly less than the cost of a two-month youth railpass. You can always buy BIJ tickets at Wasteels or Eurotrain offices (usually in or near train stations). In some countries (Denmark, Germany, and Switzerland, for example), BIJ tickets are also available from regular ticket counters. Some travel agencies also sell BIJ (such as ORBIS in Poland). In the U.S., contact Wasteels at (407) 351-2537; in the U.K., call (071) 834 7066.

Look for Lenore Baken's *Camp Europe by Train* (US$17), which covers all aspects of train travel and includes sections on railpasses, packing, and the specifics of rail travel in each country. The *Eurail Guide* (US$15, postage $3), published by Eurail Guide Annual, 27540 Pacific Coast Highway, Malibu, CA 90265, is widely touted as the best of European rail guides, listing train schedules, prices, services, and cultural information for any rail trip that might appeal to a tourist. The ultimate reference is the *Thomas Cook European Timetable* (US$25, US$34 includes a map of Europe that highlights all train and ferry routes). The timetable, updated monthly, covers all major and many minor train routes in Europe. In the U.S., order it from **Forsyth Travel Library,** P.O. Box 2975, Shawnee Mission, KS 66201 (tel. (800) 367-7984 or (913) 384-3440). Add US$4 for postage.

European East Pass: Unlimited 1st-class travel within the Czech Republic, Slovakia, Poland, Hungary, and Austria. Five days of travel within a 15-day period costs US$169 (10 days within 1 month US$279). Ages 4-12 ½-price. Sold in Australia by National Australia Travel.

Rail Europe Senior (RES): 30% off all travel in Belgium, Czech Republic, Germany, Denmark, Finland, France, Greece, Great Britain, Ireland, Italy, Croatia, Slovenia, Luxembourg, Netherlands, Norway, Portugal, Sweden, Switzerland,

Slovakia, Spain, Hungary. Valid for senior citizens who already have a Seniorenausweis (Halbpreis-Paß) for Austria. 220 AS.

Euro Domino (ED): For permanent residents of Europe, Morocco, Algiers, or Tunisia. Unlimited travel for 3, 5, or 10 days within a month, in *one* country. Choose from: Austria, Belgium, Croatia, Czech Republic, Germany, Denmark, Finland, France, Greece, Great Britain, Hungary, Ireland, Italy, Luxembourg, Morocco, Netherlands, Norway, Portugal, Sweden, Switzerland, Slovakia, Slovenia, Spain, Turkey. You cannot buy a card for your own country of permanent residence, but it does entitle you to 25% off travel there. Children pay ½-price. **Euro Domino Junior (EDJ),** for people under 26, is cheaper but otherwise identical.

Inter-Rail: For 1 month of unlimited 2nd-class travel through Europe, except in country of permanent residence. Valid in Belgium, Bulgaria, Germany, Czech Republic, Denmark, Finland, France, Greece, Great Britain, Ireland, Italy, Slovenia, Croatia, Luxembourg, Morocco, Netherlands, Norway, Poland, Portugal, Rumania, Sweden, Switzerland, Spain, Turkey, Hungary. 50% discount in country of permanent residence. Must be under 26. 4200 AS.

Austrian Railpasses

If you plan to focus your travels in just one country, consider a national railpass. Also look into regional passes such as the Nordturist pass in Scandinavia, the BritFrance pass, the Benelux Pass and the EastRail or European East pass, which covers Poland, the Czech Republic, Hungary and Austria. Some of these passes *can* be purchased only in Europe, some only outside Europe, and for some it doesn't matter; check with a railpass agent or with national tourist offices. Country passes that can be bought in Europe are usually cheaper in Europe; travel agents rarely tell you this.

Rabbit Card: Valid for 4 days of travel within a 10-day period on all rail lines, including Wolfgangsee ferries and private rail lines. ½-price on Bodensee and Danube ferries. 2nd class 1130 AS, 1st class 1700 AS. Also, **Rabbit Card Junior,** for travelers under 26. The same discounts as its parent, but for less: 2nd class 700 AS, 1st class 1050 AS. The card itself has no photo, so you must carry a valid ID in case of inspections. Keep in mind that the Rabbit Card Junior is cheaper than many round-trip fares, so it may be an economical option even for short stays.

Umweltticket: Half-price on all federal rail tickets for one year. Also valid on most private lines and DDSG Danube ferries. 1080 AS. Students (for school year, not calendar year), or families with at least one child 120 AS. Families also traveling by bus 170 AS. Seniors and disabled 240 AS.

Grüne Bank: Essentially a debit card that costs 2000 AS and is valid for rides of fewer than 70km; every time you ride, the price is deducted from the card. Up to 6 people can ride on one card. Valid for one year. Includes insurance against loss or theft.

Kilometerbank: The debit card for long-haul travelers. 2000km costs 1900 AS, 3000km 2850 AS, 4000km 3800 AS, 5000km 4750 AS. Use 71-700 km at a time. If you ride fewer than 71 km, it will be charged as 71 km; if you ride more than 700 km, it will be charged as 700 km. No surcharge on EC or SC trains. Up to 6 people can ride on one card. 1st-class rides count 1.5km for every 1 km traveled. Children count as riding.5km for every 1km traveled. Valid on most private rail lines. Insured against loss or theft.

Regional-Netzkarte: Valid for 4 days of travel within a 10-day period in one of 18 Austrian districts. 2nd class 470 AS, 1st class 630 AS. Children half-price. Surcharge of 50 AS for 1st-class EC and SC trains. Picture necessary. The valid regions are so small as to render the card impractical for travelers seeking to tour all of Europe.

Bundes-Netzkarte: Valid for unlimited travel through Austria, including Wolfgangsee ferries and private rail lines. Half-price for Bodensee and Danube ferries. No surcharge on EC and SC 1st-class trains. 1 year of 2nd-class travel costs 28,700 AS (1st class 43,100 AS), which can be paid in 10 installments. 1 month of 2nd-class travel costs 3600 AS (1st class 5400 AS). Picture necessary.

Discount Tickets

With all the available discounts, it would be a shame to pay full-fare for rail tickets. Peruse the list below to determine which discount can save you the most *Schillings*.

Gruppenreisen: Valid for groups of 4 or more in Austria, 6 or more outside Austria. In Austria, 25% discount for groups of 24 or fewer, 30% discount for groups of 25 or more. Outside Austria, 10-40% discount. ½-price for children. It is highly recommended to make reservations a week ahead within Austria (for more than 9 people, reservations are free), 30 days ahead for international travel. 10 AS per person for reservations.

ZOOM-Minigruppen: For groups of 2-5 travelers, when at least one is under 16. 25% discount for adults, under 16 half-price. Valid in Austria, Czech Republic, Hungary, Belgium, Denmark, Germany, France, Greece, Italy, Croatia, Luxembourg, Netherlands, Norway, Poland, Portugal, Sweden, Switzerland, Slovakia, Slovenia, Spain.

Jugendgruppen: 70% discount for groups of at least 10 children (under 19 in Austria, under 26 for international travel) with chaperone. For every 5 students, one adult chaperone gets a discount. You must book reservations 7 days ahead in Austria (reservations free) and 30 days ahead for international (10 AS per person).

Schülergruppenkarte: Up to 70% discount for school groups of at least 10, plus at least one chaperone. For every 5 students, 1 adult chaperone gets a discount. Available only beforehand through the school, not at train stations.

Nahverkehrs-Rückfahrkarte: Valid for 4 days of round-trip travel on a route of less than 70km. 20% discount, children half-price.

Streckenkarten: Valid only on a single rail route, from a specific location to a certain destination. Choose among:

- **Jahresstreckenkarte,** valid for one calendar year of 2nd-class travel, you pay only for 10 months, picture necessary;
- **Monatsstreckenkarte,** 82-89% discount on 2nd-class travel for 1 calendar month, picture necessary;
- **Wochenstreckenkarte,** 79-87% discount on 2nd-class travel for 1 calendar week, picture necessary;
- **Schülermonatskarte,** 82-89% discount for 1 calendar month between residence and school, up to 200km of 2nd-class travel. 120 AS. Must have note from school and proof of residence.

Ticketing Procedure

You can **purchase tickets** at every train station, at Bahn-Totalservice stations, and, occasionally, at automats—or from the conductor for a small surcharge. You can pay up to 2500 AS by check. Over 130 stations accept the major credit cards as well as AmEx traveler's cheques and Eurocheques. All Bahn-Totalservice stations accept credit cards. Stations that accept plastic are marked with a reverse-color "C" on the train schedules. This reverse "C" also indicates the availability of currency exchange. In Vienna, the Westbahnhof and Südbahnhof stations allow you to pay for tickets directly from a bank account with an ATM card. Consult the ever-faithful *Die Bahn im Griff* for a list of station ticket office numbers in most cities.

Prices for first- and second-class trains are determined by the distance traveled (in km, of course). EC and SC trains require a 50 AS surcharge. A 10% sales tax is included in all train prices. Tickets for under 70km are valid for one day; one way tickets for more than 70km are valid for **four days** (round-trip for 2 months). You can interrupt travel for tickets greater than 70km an unlimited number of times within the period of validity, but the conductor must stamp your ticket with the permission to break up the trip—ask the conductor for permission to "*Unterbrechen*."

Reservations cost 30 AS, except on EC and SC first-class trains, when the fee is included in the surcharge. Trains for which you can reserve seats are listed on schedules and in the Kursbuch with the symbol "R." You can make reservations up to six months in advance. You can receive a **refund** of the ticket price, minus 50 AS for national tickets and 50-100 AS for international tickets, if you return it before the first day of validity. You can **upgrade** from second to first class or from a regular train to an EC or SC train just by paying the surcharge; you need not return the old ticket and buy a new one.

Anyone who travels first class can pick up a free **Business-Paß** at the station ticket office, with vouchers for different samples, like free drinks, free parking, free newspapers, and discounted rental cars. You can **charter** a special train or bus trip. A few train routes are served by private railway companies; federal railpasses and the Eurailpass may not be valid on these lines. **Seniors** can purchase a **Halbpreiß-Paß,** good for half-price on all rail tickets for one year. **Children** under 6 who do not occupy a separate seat travel free; youngsters from 6 to 15 travel for half the adult fare. Small **pets** travel free. For larger animals, you must buy a ticket at half the second-class rate.

Other Rail Information

Train Flavors

The new **Neue Austro-Takt (NAT)** system consists of 120 **InterCity (IC)** trains, all with a dining car, as well as **SuperCity (SC)** trains intended for city-to-city business travelers, 66 **EuroCity (EC)** trains that service over 200 cities, and at least 20 **EuroNight (EN)** trains with sleeping cars that travel to international destinations. **Europcar,** the National Rent-A-Car affiliate, discounts rentals for EuroNight travelers (10% on weekends, 30% on day rentals, 40% on week rentals; see By Car or Van below). You can book a spot on a EuroNight train up to six months in advance.

There are four categories of night-train cars: (1) Category A1 (Universal-Schlafwagen) cars contain one-bed compartments (and require a 1st-class ticket and a 1-bed ticket), two-bed compartments (1st class plus 2-bed ticket), and three-bed-compartments (2nd class plus Tourist ticket); (2) Category A2 (Spezial-Schlafwagen) cars contain one-bed compartments (1st class plus Spezial ticket) and two-bed-compartments (2nd class plus Tourist 2 ticket); (3) Category B (Liegewagen) cars contain four-bed rooms (270 AS per person) and six-bed rooms (180 AS per person); and (4) Category C (Sitzwagen) cars, with reclining chairs but no beds. EuroNight trains include breakfast and an evening drink (1st-class travelers also receive a morning drink, fruit basket, snacks, and a newspaper).

Rail Services

Across Austria, train stations rent small **lockers** for 10 AS per day (large lockers 20 AS per day) for a maximum of two days. **Lost and Found** offices can be found in the Vienna Süd, Innsbruck, and Villach stations. **Luggage storage** costs 20 AS per day per piece, with a maximum stay of 30 days. You can **ship luggage** under 50kg for 60 AS, regardless of distance, anywhere within Austria; international transport service costs 120 AS. Luggage will be held free of charge for 72 hours at the arrival station. In some stations, **luggage carts** are available for a coin collateral. You can pay the railway 160 AS (along with a ticket) to transport two pieces of luggage under 40kg total from your home directly to your destination as you travel bag-free through the **Haus-Haus-Gepäck** service.

The Austrian rail network also offers **luggage insurance.** You pay 8 AS for a sticker that insures a piece of luggage during transport for up to 1000 AS, and 101 AS for a policy that covers up to 10,000 AS worth of goods for ten days while traveling. For 80 AS, **senior citizens** with an ID can insure up to 15,000 AS worth of goods for as long as their ID is valid; travel accident insurance is also included in this 80 AS fee.

Some trains have special compartments for small **children,** called *Kleinkindabteile,* with space for diaper changing and other infant needs. Most rail stations contain **convenience stores,** usually open on Sunday when everything else in town may be closed. Many also have phone card **telephones.** You can purchase a card in 134 train stations and often from the train conductor; cards are also available in all post offices.

Car-transport trains (*Autoreisezüge*) travel between Vienna, Salzburg, Innsbruck, Feldkirch, Villach, Linz, Graz, Bischofshofen, and Lienz. On weekends, the trains also run to Italy, Greece, Germany, Belgium, and the Netherlands. Insurance for the car on international trains costs 240 AS for 200,000 AS of coverage. Reservations are accepted up to two months in advance. Suffer a 10% charge for cancellation up to 10 days before travel, a 20% charge fewer than 10 days before, and 50% charge for cancellation after the day of travel. The following train stations, along with 52 others, will **reserve car rental** through **ARAC Eurodollar:** Bregenz, Graz, Innsbruck, Klagenfurt, Linz, Salzburg, Villach, Vienna Südbahnhof, Vienna Westbahnhof, and Zell am See. You must be over 21 years of age to drive most of the ARAC rental vehicles.

Regional Transportation Organizations

Verkehrsverbund Ost-Region (VOR): 1 ticket within the VOR is valid for 2nd-class trains, or Baden trains, or the Raab-Oedenburg-Ebenfurter line, or the subways, or the streetcars, or the buses. The region (*Verbundraum*) is divided into zones, and you can buy tickets for 1 zone, several zones, or transit between zones. In Vienna, you can buy a 24-hr. card for 45 AS or a 72-hr. card for 115 AS good for all transport in the city region. Also offers the **Umweltstreifennetzkarte,** for 235 AS, valid for 8 days; and the **Wiener Schnupperkarte,** valid for Mon.-Fri. 8am-8pm transport, 35 AS per day. Week, month, and year discount cards are also available. Contact VOR at Neubaugasse 1, 1070 Wien (tel. (0222) 526 60 48). For schedules, call (0222) 523 30 00.

Linzer Verkehrsverbund (LVV): Includes the Linzer Verkehrsbetriebe (ESG), which manages the stations at Vöcklabruck, Neumarkt, Aschach, Aigen-Schlägl, Summerau, Grein, Amstetten, Bad Hall, Garsten, Klaus, Gmunden, Grünau im Almtal, and Linz. Also embraces the Linzer Lokalbahn (LEW), buses, streetcars, and the Neumarkt-Waizenkirchen-Peuerbach (NWP) private line. Discount day, week, month, and year cards available.

Grazer Tarifverbund (GTV): Includes the Grazer Verkehrsbetriebe (GVB), which controls the end-stations at Mürzzuschlag, Vordernberg, St. Michael, Spielfeld-Straß, Bad Radkersburg, Hohenbrugg an der Raab, Friedberg, and Graz. Also includes the Steiermärkischen Landesbahnen (STLB), Graz-Köflacher Eisenbahn (GKB), buses, and streetcars. Discount day cards available. Similar arrangements are listed below. For these, contact ABBV, 1150 Wien, Palmgasse 10 (tel. (0222) 89 43 49 80).

Salzburger Verkehrsverbund (SVV), which includes the Salzburger Stadtwerke (SVB), Salzburger Lokalbahn, buses, streetcars, etc.;

Innsbrucker Verkehrsverbund (IVV), which includes the Innsbrucker Verkehrsbetriebe (IVB), Stubaitalbahn, Zillertalbahn, buses, streetcars, etc. for all of Tirol and Osttirol;

Verkehrsverbund Vorarlberg. For more information on the Vorarlberg region, contact the Verbundbüro, Zollgasse 10, A-6850 Dornbirn (tel. (05572) 33 66 0).

Smaller regional associations include: **Verkehrsverbund Niederösterreich Süd/Burgenland Mitte, Verkehrsverbund Niederösterreich Zentral/Mostviertel, Verkehrsverbund Waldviertel,** and **Verkehrsverbund Nördliches Weinviertel.**

■ By Bus

Bus travel in Europe is significantly more comfortable than in North America—though you can never really have a true non-smoking section, and, worse yet, some companies force you to watch bleary videos. A Walkman® will probably come in handy here, but keep the volume level considerate. The biggest problem with Austrian bus routes is deregulation; bus routes are not as permanent as train tracks, there is a paucity of pan-European organization, and understanding fares and schedules can be difficult unless you know the territory. Some 200 international bus lines traverse Austria.

The efficient Austrian bus system consists mainly of orange **BundesBuses.** Buses are generally local and complement the train system; they serve mountain areas inaccessible by train but do not duplicate long-distance, inter-city routes covered by rail. Buses cost about as much as trains, but sadly, no railpasses are valid. Bus stations are usually located adjacent to the train station. Buy tickets at a ticket office at the station, at a *Tabak* booth in town, or from the driver. For buses to heavily touristed areas during high season, it is advisable to make reservations. You must **validate** your ticket at the start of each trip by inserting it in the little orange stamping machine on board, which is usually marked by a green arrow and "E" or the sign *Hier Fahrscheine entwerten.* Even when purchased just moments ago from the bus driver, tickets are *not valid* until they have been stamped. Occasionally, plain-clothes inspectors will appear from out of the crowd (usually the seat right next to you); they'll thrust an orange badge in your face that says "Kontrollier," and demand to see your validated ticket. If you cannot produce a ticket that has been properly cancelled, you will be subject to large fines and immense humiliation. The inspectors don't take excuses and they don't take American Express; if you can't pay up on the spot, a police officer will meet you at the next stop to take you to jail. English-speaking backpackers have a miserable reputation for *Schwarzfahren* ("black riding," or riding without a ticket), so don't expect any sympathy. If you try the "I didn't understand, I don't speak German," excuse, the inspector will brusquely point out the explanatory signs in English. "I though my Eurailpass was valid," never works, either. Don't assume that everyone else is riding illegally because you don't see them canceling tickets; when the inspector appears, you'll discover that they're all carrying monthly passes.

You don't have to cheat to save cash on bus tickets; discounts abound. A **Mehrfahrtenkarten** gives you six tickets for the price of five. A **Halbpreis-Paß** for women over 60 and men over 65 costs 220 AS and entitles senior citizens to half-price fares for a year. **Families** as small as one parent and one child receive discounts, and a family with more than two kids only needs to pay for the two. Members of the **Verbandes Alpiner Vereine Österreichs (VAVÖ)** get discounts on some mountain routes. **Anyone** can buy discounted tickets, valid for one week, for any particular route. **Students** who travel the route between home and school receive a further discount with a one-time purchase of a 40 AS voucher.

Children under six ride free as long as they don't take up a full seat. Children ages 6-15, and large pets other than seeing-eye dogs, ride for half-price within Austria. Tickets are only good for one day. Unlike the train or U-Bahn system, you may not interrupt and then resume a bus ride. To board a bus, look to the right or left of the door, for a button and the sign *Einsteigen bitte, Knopf drücken*. Push the button, and the door should open. Those carrying heavy suitcases, bicycles, baby carriages, or other unwieldy items should look for the door with a baby carriage logo, usually at the rear of the bus; these doors are usually wider, and often have ramps (not stairs) leading inside.

Bus drivers generally don't even slow down at scheduled stops unless they can see a passenger waiting to board or disembark. If you are waiting for a bus but decide to meander away from the stop for a moment, you may see the bus cruise right by. On the same note, you must signal the driver if you wish to get off a bus at the next stop; otherwise, the bus may continue on its path with nary a pause. The little red buttons on the poles by the seats indicate your wish to disembark; push the white button under the gray rectangular sign in order to open the doors once the bus has come to a stop.

One simple method of circumventing confusion over bus stops is to enlist the aid of the driver; he or she is most likely very receptive to bewildered travelers wandering aimlessly in oversized backpacks. You may be heading to a Lilliputian village with no sign; the driver knows best when you should disembark. If you tell the driver where you wish to leave the bus, and politely request assistance, chances are good that he or she will have pity on you. Drivers are generally amiable; treat them with respect and plead for their sympathy, and they'll probably make sure that you get off the bus at the correct stop.

Two monstrous tomes together list the bus routes and times for all—yes, *all*—of Austria. Consider pumping up before you purchase them. The *Kursbuch Bus Ost-Teil* (eastern buses) and the *Kursbuch Bus West-Teil* (western buses) are both published annually, for 100 AS each. Smaller, regional bus schedules are available for free at most post offices. For more bus **information,** call (0222) 711 01 or (0222) 066 01 88 (daily 6am-9pm). Pick up the packet *Erfahren Sie Österreich* at any BundesBus station for more information on discounts.

■ By Boat

Travel by boat is a bewitching alternative much favored by Europeans but overlooked by most foreigners. Most European ferries are straightforward, comfortable and well-equipped; the cheapest fare class sometimes includes use of a reclining chair or couchette where you can sleep the trip away. You should check in at least two hours early for a prime spot and allow plenty of time for late trains and getting to the port. It is a good idea to bring your own food and avoid the mushy, astronomically expensive cafeteria cuisine which sometimes prevails. Fares rise sharply in July and August. Always ask for discounts; ISIC holders often receive student fares, and Eurailpass holders get many reductions and free trips (check the brochure that accompanies your railpass). You'll occasionally have to pay a small port tax (under US$10). Planning and reserving tickets in advance through a travel agency can spare you several tedious days of waiting in dreary ports for the next sailing.

The Danube flows down from Western Germany through Austria, forms part of the common border between Slovakia and Hungary, and then makes its way through Budapest before spilling into the Black Sea. Danube **riverboats** acquaint you with many towns that trains can only wink at. Many of these boats, however, have been overrun by gaudy tourists; less commercial-looking lines can be more seductive.

Steamers and hydrofoils of the Austrian company **Erste Donau Dampfschiffahrts-Gesellschaft (DDSG),** Handelskai 265, A-1021 Vienna (tel. (0222) 21 75 00), sail upstream and downstream from Vienna. You can also purchase a train-ship combination and ride upstream by train and downstream by ferry. Purchase tickets at the train offices in Wien Westbahnhof, Wien Hütteldorf, Wien Franz-Josefs-Bahnhof, St. Pölten, Wels, Linz, Heiligenstadt, Tulln, Krems, Spitz, Grein-Bad Kreuzen, Passau, Bad Schallerbach-Wallern, Neumarkt-Kallham, Grieskirchen-Gallspach, Aschach, and Eferding; or at DDSG offices in Vienna Schiffahrtszentrum, Grein, Krems, Linz, Passau, Spitz, and Tulln. Combined tickets for train and ship travel are also available between **Vienna** and **Budapest.** (For steamer routes and prices, see the Danube section.) Hydrofoils to Bratislava, Slovakia and Budapest, Hungary are not cheap (Bratislava round-trip about 350 AS; Budapest round-trip around 1250 AS), but they are fast and more scenic than trains. International railpasses are valid on these routes, but depending on the boat, riders may have to pay a supplement. **Austrian Federal Railways** runs boat service, generally between May and September, on the following Austrian lakes: Wörthersee, Ossiachersee, Millstätter See, Mondsee, Gundlsee, Wolfgangsee, Zeller See, Achensee, Plansee, and Bodensee.

■ By Airplane

Unless you're under 25, flying across Europe on regularly scheduled flights will eat through your budget; nearly all airlines cater to business travelers and set prices accordingly. If you are a youth, special fares on most European airlines requiring ticket purchase either the day before or the day of departure are a happy exception to this rule. These are often cheaper than the corresponding regular train fare, though not always as cheap as student rail tickets or railpasses. Student travel agencies in Europe and America also sell cheap tickets. Budget fares are frequently available in the spring and summer on high-volume routes between northern Europe and resort areas in Spain, Italy and Greece. Consult budget travel agents and local newspapers and magazines. The **Air Travel Advisory Bureau,** 41-45 Goswell Road, London EC1V 7DN (tel. (071) 636 50 00), can put you in touch with discount flights to worldwide destinations, for free.

Within Austria, airplanes are an expensive and unnecessary form of travel. **Austrian Airlines** and its subsidiary, **Austrian Air Services,** maintain routes between Vienna and Linz, Salzburg, Graz, and Klagenfurt, and fly to London, Munich, Paris, and other international locations. Austrian Airlines is also a principal carrier to East European locations: planes run regularly between **Vienna** and **Prague, Budapest,** Moscow, Warsaw, Bucharest, Sophia, Belgrade, and Istanbul. Austrian Airlines offers a **Visit Austria** and a **Visit Europe** fare in connection with its transatlantic flights. For 2500 AS, a passenger receives four flight coupons for travel within Austria (except Innsbruck) on any Austrian Airlines or Austrian Air Services flight, and for US$110 a passenger can fly one way to any city in Europe served by Austrian Airlines, Austrian Air Services, or Tyrolean Airways. Call Austrian Air's New York City number for more information (tel. (800) 843-0002 or (212) 307-6226). **Tyrolean** flies between Innsbruck and Vienna, and offers a drive-and-fly agreement with Avis. Tyrolean also flies to some international points, like Frankfurt and Zürich. **Rheintalflug** jets between Vienna and Altenhausen, Switzerland (just over the border from the Vorarlberg).

■ By Car and Van

Cars offer great speed, great freedom, access to the countryside, and an escape from the humdrum town-to-town mentality of trains. Unfortunately, they also insulate you from the *esprit de corps* of European rail travelers. A single traveler won't save by renting a car, though four usually will; groups of two or three may find renting cheaper than a railpass (although gas in Austria costs US$5-6 per gallon—you may want to fuel up with tax-free Swiss fuel). If you can't decide between train and car travel, you may relish a combination of the two; rail and car packages offered by Avis and Hertz are often effective for two or more people who travel together, and Rail Europe and other railpass vendors (see above) offer economical "Euraildrive" plans.

Renting a Car or Caravan

To rent a car in Austria, you must be over 18 and must carry a valid driver's license along with an International Driver's Permit (IDP) or an official validation issued by an authorized Austrian representative in your home country (e.g. by the embassy or tourist office). The National Tourist Office strongly recommends that drivers obtain the IDP (see Documents and Formalities: International Driver's Permit above). For North Americans, it is cheaper to make rental car arrangements in the U.S. and Canada before leaving. Always check if prices quoted include tax and collision insurance; some credit card companies will cover this automatically. This may be a substantial savings, but ask if a credit hold will be put on your account and if so, how much. Ask about student and other discounts and, above all, be flexible in your itinerary to secure the best rates; sometimes playing with different pick-up and drop-off locations will result in a discount. Rental taxes are high in Austria (21.2%), so it may be cheaper to rent a car in another European country (such as Switzerland) where no such taxes stunt the economy.

Budget Rent-a-Car (tel. (800) 472-3325 in the U.S.) maintains more than a dozen locations throughout the country, including at major airports in Vienna, Innsbruck, and Salzburg. **Hertz** (tel. (800) 654-3001 in the U.S.) has 25 offices in Austria, **Avis** (tel. (800) 331-1084 in the U.S.) has 24—make advance arrangements to procure the cheapest rate. **National** (tel. (800) 328-4567 in the U.S.), through its European affiliate **Europcar,** also has Austrian offices. Rates vary considerably depending on the company, model, and season. Expect to pay US$55-65 a day for the cheapest automatic model (stick shifts can cause considerable grief if you plan to drive in mountainous areas), plus approximately US$20 per day for insurance.

EuroDollar (tel. 1 147 73 28; fax 1 157 87 07) offers some of the best rates in **Budapest.** It's possible to pick up your Lada 1500 or Opel Astra at the airport. You must have a credit card and be over 21 to rent. You can get one-way rentals upon request, plus a possible drop-off fee. Expect to pay about US$20-40 per day, plus 20-40¢ per mi., or US$40-100 per day with unlimited mileage.

Caravanning, usually involving a camper or motor-home, offers the advantages of car rental without the hassle of finding lodgings or cramming six friends into a Renault. You'll need those six buddies to split the gasoline bills, although many European vehicles use diesel or propane, much cheaper than ordinary gasoline. Prices vary even more than for cars, but for the outdoor-oriented group trip, caravanning can be a dream. Contact the car rental firms listed above for more information. Shore and Campbell's book also has tips (see below).

Leasing or Buying a Car

For longer than three weeks, **leasing** can prove cheaper than renting; it is sometimes the only option for drivers ages 18-20. The cheapest leases are actually agreements where you buy the car, drive it, and then sell it back to the car manufacturer at a pre-agreed price. As far as you're concerned, it's a simple lease and doesn't entail galactic financial transactions. Leases include full insurance coverage and are not taxed. The most affordable leases usually originate in Belgium and France and start at around US$500 for 23 days and US$1000 for 60 days. Contact **Foremost, Europe by Car,** or **Auto Europe.** You will need to make arrangements in advance.

If you're brave or know what you're doing, **buying** a used car or van in Europe and selling it just before you leave can provide the cheapest wheels on the Continent. Check with consulates for different countries' import-export laws concerning used vehicles, registration, and safety and emission standards. David Shore and Patty Campbell's *Europe By Van And Motorhome* (US$14 postpaid, US$6 for overseas airmail) guides you through the entire process, from buy-back agreements to insurance and dealer listings. To order, write to 1842 Santa Margarita Dr., Fallbrook, CA 92028 (tel. (619) 723-6184). *How to Buy and Sell a Used Car in Europe* (U.S. $6.00 plus $0.75 postage) also contains useful tips; write to Gil Friedman, P.O. Box 1063, Arcata, CA 95521 (tel. (707) 822-5001).

Driving In Austria

Austrian highways are excellent, though winter snow makes driving a bit trickier. Roads at altitudes of up to 1500m remain open in winter, although they may close temporarily after snow storms or avalanches. Ask about road conditions before leaving by calling the English-language service of the **Austrian Automobile and Touring Club (ÖAMTC),** Schubertring 1-3, Vienna (tel. (0222) 71 19 97; call daily 6am-8pm). Austrian cars drive on the right. The speed limit is 50km per hour (31mph) within cities, unless otherwise indicated. Outside towns, the limit is 130km per hour (81mph) on highways and 100km per hour (62mph) on all other roads. Driving under the influence of alcohol is a serious offense—fines begin at 5000 AS and rise rapidly from there; violators may lose their license as well. The allowable amount of alcohol in the blood is *very low*. The minimum driving age is 18.

Drivers who are not Austrian citizens are required to have an **International Driver's Permit** (see Documents and Formalities: International Driver's License above). Travelers from EC countries don't need any special documentation in Austria other than their registration and license. An international certificate for insurance is compulsory for all cars. If you suffer a collision while in Europe, the accident will show up on your domestic records. All passengers must wear seatbelts, and children under 12 may not sit in the front passenger seat unless a child's seatbelt or a special seat is installed. All cars must carry a first-aid kit and a red emergency triangle (available at border crossings or from the Automobile Club). Emergency phones (marked *"Notruf"*) are located along all major highways. In the case of other emergencies, phone the **ÖAMTC** (tel. 120) or **ARBO** (another auto club, tel. 123) from anywhere in the country. Free roadmaps from the tourist offices are adequate, but a set of eight detailed maps, available from local ÖAMTC chapters and some gas stations, is superior and costs little.

Many large Austrian cities have restricted parking zones, where drivers can park only for 90 minutes—these are called "blue zones" because of the blue lines on the road. Visitors to Vienna, Graz, Linz, Klagenfurt, Innsbruck, and other large urban locales must buy a parking voucher to park in the zones. When parking, fill in the time that you arrived and display the voucher prominently inside your windshield. Vouchers are available at gas stations, banks, and *Tabak* shops.

Most gas stations sell unleaded *(bleifrei)* gasoline. Diesel fuel can be harder to find in remote locations. Prices are uniform throughout the country, although gas is a bit cheaper at discount and self-service stations; expect to pay at least US$3 per gallon. Austrian service stations do not accept gasoline credit cards.

Taxis in Austria, found at airports and train stations, tend to be expensive (about 22 AS for the initial fee, plus 10 AS per km). A supplemental charge of 10 AS will be added for each piece of luggage carried in the trunk. Taxis also cost 10 AS more on Saturdays than during the rest of the week. Any additional charges should be posted. A tip of 10% is the norm. In rural and resort areas where metered taxis are uncommon, drivers employ zone charges; agree on the fare before making the trip. Taxis do not cruise, so your chances of hailing one from the curb are bleak, though if you see one with its roof light on, you can flag it down. If no taxi stands are around, you can summon one of these motorized chariots by looking up *Funktaxi* (taxi-dispatcher) in the phone book—the dispatcher service may entail an extra charge.

Driving in the Czech Republic

In the Czech Republic, speed limits are 60 km per hour (37mph) in crowded areas, 90 km per hour (56 mph) outside them, and 110 km per hour (68mph) on the freeway. Radar checks are common, as are spot fines for speeding of up to 500 kčs. Keep to the right except when passing. The Czech Republic also severely penalizes drunk drivers. Seat belts are compulsory in the front seat, and children under 12 must travel in the back. Motorcycle drivers and their passengers must wear crash helmets and may not smoke during a journey. Unleaded gas is available in few places, and because most stations close at night, it is best to keep your tank filled when you can. **Autoturist** will come to your help if you break down or have an accident. The phone number of the nearest office is available at garages and police stations or from the Autoturist office in Prague (24-hr. tel. (02) 77 34 55). Dial 154 from SOS phones on the freeway to get **emergency assistance.** Unfortunately, the Czech Republic has recently suffered a rise in auto theft (along with other crime)—be careful. In Prague, **Progocar,** 1, Opletalova 33 (tel. 22 23 24) represents Avis. It also has an office at the airport.

Driving in Hungary

Hungarian road regulations correspond to those of the Vienna and Geneva transport conventions. Seat belts are mandatory in the front seats. Horns may be honked in developed areas only if there is danger of accident, and outside them to indicate the wish to overtake another vehicle. No alcohol is allowed in a driver's blood. Motorcyclists and their passengers must wear crash helmets. The speed limit in urban areas is 60 km per hour (37mph), on main roads 80 km per hour (50mph), on highways 100 km per hour (62mph), and on motorways 120 km per hour (74mph). Changes to these limits are displayed on signs at the border stations.

Road signs and traffic regulations in Hungary are, with a few exceptions, the same as in other European countries, and thus mostly self-evident. A few signs may seem strange. At unloading bays, the time on the sign indicates when vehicles not unloading may stop there; the driver must remain in the vehicle while it stands. In pedestrian traffic areas, the maximum speed limit is 20 km per hour (12mph), and through traffic is forbidden, except for bicycles. A bus lane is indicated by the sign "*busz*" painted on the road; it is forbidden to drive along such lanes continuously, even at night. You may persist in it only to cross through it or if preparing to turn onto another street. Contact **Útinform,** VII, Dob u. 75-81, Budapest (tel. (01) 22 22 38 or 22 70 52) for more information.

■ By Moped and Motorcycle

Motorized bikes offer an enjoyable, relatively inexpensive way to tour the countryside, particularly when there are few cars. They don't use much gas, can be put on trains and ferries, and are a good compromise between the high cost of car travel and the limited range of bicycles. Long distances, however, become never-ending when sitting upright and cruising at 40km per hour. Mopeds are also dangerous in the rain and unpredictable on rough roads or gravel. Always wear a helmet and never ride wearing a backpack. If you've never been on a moped before, a twisting Alpine road is not the place to start. In general expect to pay US$20-35 per day; try auto repair shops and remember to bargain. Motorcycles are faster and more expensive; they normally require a license. Before renting, ask if the quoted price includes tax and insurance, or you may be hit for an unexpected additional fee. Avoid handing your passport over as a deposit; if you have an accident or mechanical failure you may not get it back until you cover all repairs. Pay ahead of time instead.

The German word for motorcycle is *Motorrad;* moped is *Moped.* You can rent a motorcycle in Vienna from **InterCity,** Reinprechtsdorfer Str. 17 (tel. 55 61 86).

■ By Bicycle

Imaging gliding down a deserted Alpine trail in the cool, misty morning air. Now imagine sitting on something smaller than you've ever perched on before, for five hours at a time. Today, biking is one of the key elements of the classic budget Eurovoyage. Everyone else in the youth hostel is doing it, and with the proliferation of mountain bikes, you can do some serious natural sight-seeing. For information about touring routes, consult national tourist offices or any of the numerous books available. *Europe By Bike,* by Karen and Terry Whitehill (US$15), is a great source of specific area tours. *Cycling Europe: Budget Bike Touring in the Old World* by N. Slavinski (US$13) may also be a helpful addition to your library. **Michelin** road maps are clear and detailed guides. Be aware that touring involves pedaling both yourself *and* whatever you store in the panniers (bags that strap to your bike).

To prepare, take some reasonably challenging day-long rides before you leave. Have your bike tuned up by a reputable shop. Wear visible clothing, drink plenty of water (even if you're not thirsty) and ride on the *same* side as the traffic. Learn the international signals for turns, and use them. Although you may not be able to build a frame or spoke a wheel, learn how to fix a modern derailleur-equipped mount and change a tire before leaving, and practice on your own bike before you have to do it overseas. A few simple tools and a good bike manual will be invaluable. If you are nervous about striking out on your own, you might want to consider an organized **bicycle tour;** they are arranged for a wide range of cycling abilities. **College Bicycle Tours** offers co-ed bicycle tours through seven countries in Europe that are exclusively for the college-aged; they also arrange discounted airfares for the participants. Contact them at (800) 736-BIKE (736-2453) in U.S. and Canada for details.

Most airlines will count your bicycle as your second free piece of luggage; (you're usually allowed two pieces of checked baggage and a carry-on piece). As an additional piece, it will cost about US$85 each way. Policies on charters and budget flights vary; check with the airline before buying your ticket. The safest way to send your bike is in a box, with the handlebars, pedals and front wheel detached. Within Europe, most ferries let you take your bike for free. Many cities have a special service, Fahrrad-Depotwagen, for carrying bicycles. An all-bicycle train, the **Rad-Tramper,** runs on certain weekends throughout the year. You can also have your bicycle shipped from station to station for 60 AS (30 AS with an Umweltticket) no matter what the distance. Refer to the booklet *Bahntips für Radtrips* for more information on shipping bicycles.

Riding a bike while wearing a frame pack is about as safe as pedaling blindfolded over a sheet of ice; panniers are essential. The first thing to buy, however, is a suitable **bike helmet.** At about US$50-100, they're better than head injury or death. To lessen the odds of theft, buy a **U**-shaped **Citadel** or **Kryptonite** lock. These are expensive (about US$20-49), but the companies insure their locks against theft of your bike for one or two years. *Bicycling* magazine lists the lowest sale prices. **Bike Nashbar,** 4112 Simon Rd., Youngstown, OH 44512 (tel. (800) 627-4227), has excellent list prices but will also cheerfully beat all competitors' offers by 5¢.

Renting a bike is preferable to bringing your own if your touring is confined to one or two regions. A sturdy if unexciting one-speed model will cost US$8-12 per day; be prepared to lay down a sizeable deposit. *Let's Go* lists bike rental shops in most cities and towns. You can rent a bicycle inexpensively from one of over 170 Austrian rail stations—look for signs with a picture of a bicycle and the word *Verleih,* or pick up a copy of the brochure *Fahrrad am Bahnhof,* which contains a complete list. Some stations also rent racing, mountain, and tandem bikes. Bikes can be returned to any participating station and cost 90 AS per day (½-price if you have a train ticket to the station from which you are renting and have arrived on the day of rental; if you arrive after 3pm, half-price rental is available on the next day as well). Racing, mountain, and tandem bikes cost 150 AS per day with a train ticket, 200 AS per day otherwise. Reservations are recommended. Bring photo identification. The eastern part of the country is more level, but the Salzkammergut and Tyrol reward effort with more dramatic scenery. One of the most popular bike routes runs along the Danube all the way from Vienna to Passau, Germany. Tourist offices provide regional maps of bike routes.

You can bring your bicycle with you on the train year-round (Mon.-Fri. 9am-3pm, Sat. 9am-6:30pm, and Sun. all day). You alone are responsible for the bike's safety. The ticket for your bicycle is a **Fahrrad-Tageskarte** (day card), which sells for 30 AS; a weekly card costs 60 AS, and a monthly card 210 AS. You only pay for two children's bicycles, even if you have bred a small cycling army. Look for the *Gepäckbeforderung* symbol on departure schedules to see if bikes are permitted.

Call the train stations in Eisentadt, Graz, Hallein, Kitzbühel, Linz, Melk, St. Pölten, Spitz, or Villach for more information on biking around Austria. The Czech word for bicycle is *kolo*; in Hungarian, it's *bicikli*.

■ By Thumb

Let's Go does not recommend hitching as a safe means of transportation, and none of the information presented here is intended to do so.

No one should hitch without careful consideration of the risks involved. Not everyone can be an airplane pilot, but most every bozo can drive a car, and hitching means entrusting your life to a randomly selected person who happens to stop beside you on the road. Whenever you hitch, you risk sexual harassment and unsafe driving, theft, assault, and possibly even rape or murder. In spite of this, the possible gains are many: favorable hitching experiences allow you to meet local people and get where you're going when public transportation is particularly sketchy. Consider this section akin to handing out condoms to high school students: we don't endorse it, but if you're going to do it anyway, we'll tell you some ways to make it safer.

Depending on the circumstances and the norms of the country, men and women traveling in groups and men traveling alone might consider hitching to locations beyond the scope of bus or train routes. If you're a woman traveling alone, *don't hitch.* It's just too dangerous. A man and a woman are a safer combination, two men will have a harder time finding a ride and three will likely go nowhere.

Where one stands is vital. Experienced hitchers pick a spot outside of built-up areas, where drivers can stop, return to the road without causing an accident, and have time to look over potential passengers as they approach. Hitching on hills or curves is hazardous and unsuccessful. In the Practical Information section of many cities, we list the tram or bus lines that will take travelers to strategic points for hitching out.

Hitchers' success will depend on *what they look like.* Successful hitchers travel light and stack their belongings in a compact but visible cluster. It may behoove one to walk and signal for a ride at the same time, and to thus appear in a hurry. Most Europeans signal with an open hand, rather than a thumb; many write their destination on a sign in large, bold letters and draw a smiley-face under it. Drivers prefer hitchers who are neat and wholesome, yet dynamic. No one stops for a grump, or for anyone wearing sunglasses. When a car does pull up, experienced hitchers don't dawdle.

Safety issues are always imperative, even when traveling with another person. Hitchers never get in the back of a two-door car, and never let go of a backpack. When getting into a car, immediately assess the best way to get out again in a hurry. Couples may avoid hassles with male drivers if the woman sits in the back (in a sedan, only) or next to the door. If you ever feel threatened, insist on being let off, regardless of where you are. If the driver refuses to stop, try acting as though you're going to open the car door or vomit on the upholstery. Hitchhiking at night can be particularly dangerous and undependable; hitchers stand in a well-lit place and expect drivers to be leery.

Europe: A Manual for Hitchhikers gives directions for hitching out of hundreds of cities, rates rest areas and entrance ramps, and deciphers national highway and license plate systems. The guide is available from **Vacation Work Publications,** 9 Park End St., Oxford OX1 1HJ (tel. (0865) 24 19 78).

Compared to other European countries, Austria is a hitchhiker's nightmare. Austrians rarely pick up hitchhikers, and many mountain roads are all but deserted. Hitchers using the thumb signal are recognized, and most simply make a sign with their destination and the word *bitte* (please) in big, bold letters. Hitchhiking on superhighways is illegal, though standing just before on-ramps is permitted. Hitchers can also try poking around filling stations; license plates indicate one of nine *Bundesländer* (federal states), e.g. V = Vorarlberg and ST = Steiermark. For longer, inter-city routes, hitchers can make things easier on themselves by contacting a **Mitfahrzentrale.** These companies charge roughly half the going rail fare to connect you with somebody traveling by car in your direction. Unfortunately, the demand for rides at the *Mitfahrzentrale* greatly outstrips the supply.

■ Alpine Hiking

The most scenic way to see Austria is on foot. *Let's Go* describes many daytrips for those who want to hoof it, but native inhabitants, hostel proprietors, and fellow travelers are the best source for tips. Thanks to an extensive network of hiking trails and Alpine refuges (*Hütte*), Austria's Alps are as accessible as they are gorgeous. American-style camping with a tent and cookstove is almost unheard of. Sleeping in one of Austria's refuges is safer for the environment and generally safer for you—when you check out of one hut, you register for the next one, so authorities will know right away if you turn up missing. The various Alpine associations in Austria currently maintain more than 1100 refuges, which provide accommodations, cooking facilities, and occasionally, hot meals. Prices for an overnight stay are 50-150AS, and no reservations are necessary; if they're crowded, you may end up sleeping on the floor, but you won't be turned away. If you plan carefully, you can undertake long hikes that bring you to a hut every night, which would free you from the burden of carrying a tent and cooking gear.

Several guidebooks plot out such hikes for you; *Walking Austria's Alps Hut to Hut,* by Jonathan Hurdle, is excellent (US$11). Topographic maps (*Alpenvereinskarten*) show hut locations; these maps will become a hiker's best friend. The best for long-distance hikes are the **Freytag-Berndt** maps, available in bookstores all over

Austria. Purchase them (around $8), as well as topographic maps and hiking guides, from **Pacific Travellers Supply,** 529 State St., Santa Barbara, CA 93101 (tel. (805) 963-4438) in the U.S. The Austrian National Tourist Office publishes the pamphlet, *Hiking and Backpacking in Austria,* with a complete list of Freytag-Berndt maps and additional tips on Alpine treks. Local tourist offices often sponsor guided day-hikes of various levels of difficulty. Those planning extensive overnight hikes may want to purchase membership in one of the alpine associations. These entitle you to discounts on mountain refuges (usually half non-member price), low-priced organized tours, and insurance against the cost of emergency rescue and evacuation.

Occasionally, the mountains foster competition, if only against yourself; with membership in the **Europäischen Volkssport-Gemeinschaft Österreich (EVG),** you can earn medals based on the amount and/or difficulty of hikes you undergo. Look for the booklets describing the Österreichische Bergwandernadel in the offices of the following Alpine hiking organizations:

Österreichischer Alpenverein, Wilhelm-Greil-Str. 15, A-6010 Innsbruck (tel. (0512) 59 547; until noon only). The largest alpine association, with 275 huts. Membership (430 AS, under 26 345 AS, one time fee 70 AS) entitles you to a 50% discount at their refuges, all of which have beds, as well as discounts on some cable car rides and organized hikes. Also maintains an office in the **U.K.** at 13 Longcroft House, Fretherne Rd., Welwyn Garden City, Herts.

Österreichischer Touristenklub (ÖTK), 1 Bäckerstr. 16, A-1010 Vienna (tel. (0222) 512 38 44). Primarily for Eastern Austria. Open Mon. 10:30am-5pm, Wed. 9am-5pm, Tues. and Thurs. 9am-7pm, Fri. 9am-3pm.

Touristenverein "Naturfreunde Österreich," Viktoriagasse 6, A-1150 Vienna (tel. (0222) 83 86 08). Operates a network of cottages in rural and mountain areas.

Verband Alpiner Vereine Österreichs, Backerstr. 16, A-1010 Vienna (tel. (0222) 512 54 88). The central body for all alpine clubs in the country.

Even if you're only going for a day hike, check terrain and weather conditions. Weather patterns in the Alps change instantaneously. A bright blue sky can turn to rain—or even snow—before you can say "hypothermia." Always carry waterproof clothing (breathable rain gear is ideal, and Gore-Tex® fabric is superior to imitations), a warm sweater, gloves, a hat, sunglasses, sunscreen, a first-aid kit, water, and high-energy food. Always wear hiking boots or sturdy shoes and wool socks. If you encounter bad weather, turn back—it's a better idea to retrace familiar ground than to push on into *terra incognita.* If you get into serious trouble, use the Alpine Distress Signal—six audible or visual signals spaced evenly over one minute and followed by a break of one minute before repetition. Listen for a response of signals at 20-second intervals. Paths marked *"Für Geübte"* require special mountain climbing equipment and are for experienced climbers only. If you're interested, ask the Austrian National Tourist Office for a list of mountain climbing schools.

Finally, remember that those gorgeous Alpine meadows are extremely fragile habitats. At high altitudes, the environment can take years to recover from a single act of carelessness. Don't stray from trails, don't dislodge loose rocks (which can cause dangerous rockslides), and leave the wilderness exactly as you found it.

■ Skiing

Western Austria is one of the world's best skiing regions. The areas around Innsbruck and Kitzbühel in the Tyrol are saturated with lifts and runs. There's good skiing year-round on several glaciers, including the Stubaital near Innsbruck and the Dachstein in the Salzkammergut. High season normally runs from mid-December to mid-January and from February to March; on glacial resorts, the season continues from July to August. Local tourist offices provide information on regional skiing and can point you to budget travel agencies that offer ski packages. Lift tickets are not cheap (250-300 AS per day), but many towns grant large discounts to guests at local hotels and *Pensionen*. See individual Tyrolean listings for skiing specifics.

The relatively low **elevation** of Alpine villages (2500-5000 ft. above sea level) ensconces the vacationer from low-lying areas, eliminating most of the altitude discomfort typical in North American ski areas. With peaks between 7500 and 10,000 feet, the vertical drop is ample—4000 to 6000 feet at all major resorts. The low timberline in these limestone mountains creates open bowl terrain above the 6000-foot level; these lofty, treeless expanses are easier to ski than narrow trails in the woods, allowing intermediate skiers to more ably conquer the steep gradients, and spreading skier traffic over a much wider area.

For mountain country, winter **weather** in the Austrian Alps is moderate—thanks to lower elevation and distance from the ocean. Daytime temperatures in the coldest months (Jan. and Feb.) measure around 20°F, even when the nights are colder. Humidity is low, so snow on the ground stays powdery longer, and ice largely hibernates until spring. Because of the dry air and cold nights, packed powder is the most common surface throughout the season.

You'll find sundry ways to enjoy the winter wonderland, even in summer. A few definitions will assist the novice: **Nordic skiing** involves cross-country skiing, while **Alpine skiing** encompasses most downhill runs. Some cross-country ski centers charge trail fees to day users, but exempt guests spending their holiday in the area. **Ski schools** (*Schischule*) throughout Austria will teach anyone to ski—from beginners fumbling their first snowplow, to advanced skiers honing their racing tuck. Based on decades of research and racing experience, the **Austrian Ski Method** (capitalized because it's real) is a unified teaching concept taught throughout the country. Certified instructors who sport the "eagle badge" are professionals who have passed an admissions test, two winters of schooling (including language classes), and a grueling final exam. You can **rent skis** at the base of most mountains and at stores in ski villages. Ski passes come in one-day, multi-day, week-long, and season-long varieties. Some passes are valid on a number of mountains in a single region. Take time out to participate in one of the more pleasurable Austrian rituals—**sunbathe** on the terrace of a ski hut around lunchtime to fully appreciate the Alpine ski experience.

Pay strict attention to cold-weather **safety** concerns. Know the symptom of hypothermia and frostbite (see Health above), and bring along warm clothes and quick-energy snacks like candy bars and trail mix. A sunscreen and reliable eye protection are requisite accoutrements—at high altitudes, you'll burn much quicker. Drinking alcohol in the cold can be particularly dangerous: even though you may *feel* warm, alcohol retards your body's ability to adjust to the temperature and thus makes you more vulnerable to hypothermia.

■■■ ACCOMMODATIONS

Like most things Austrian, accommodations are usually clean, orderly, and expensive. Austrian hotels and *Pensionen* are rated from one to four stars. Even the lowest categories are pricey; *Let's Go* lists primarily one-star and unrated establishments. The word *Frühstückspension* indicates that the establishment is a bed-and-breakfast, but virtually all lodging facilities in Austria include breakfast with an overnight stay.

Wherever you stay, be sure to ask for a town **guest card.** Normally, the "card" is merely a copy of your receipt for the night's lodging, sometimes only available after stays of three nights or more. Guest cards generally grant enormous discounts to local sports facilities, hiking excursions, and town museums, as well as transport within the city or to neighboring hamlets.

Hotels

Hotels are quite expensive in Austria, Prague, and Budapest: rock bottom for singles is US$17-20, for doubles US$22-24, and the price is never subject to haggling. In Austria, the cheapest hotel-style accommodations are places with **Gasthof** or **Gästehaus** ("inn") in the name. Inexpensive European hotels might shock pampered North American travelers. A bathroom of your own is a rarity and costs extra when provided. Hot showers may also cost extra. Continental breakfast (*Frühstuck*), almost always included, consists of a rolls, muffins, butter, jam, coffee, or tea, and maybe some sausage and cheese slices. *Pension* (guesthouse) owners run smaller establishments and will often direct you to points of interest in the town and countryside. Unmarried couples over 21 will generally have no trouble getting a room together; the primary exceptions to this rule involve hotels run by the **Christlicher Verein Junger Menschen (CVJM),** Austria's answer to the YMCA.

Private Rooms

The best value in Austria is to rent a **private room** *(Privatzimmer)* in a family home through the local tourist office or through personal initiative (look for *Zimmer* or *Zimmer frei* signs on houses). Such rooms generally include a sink with hot and cold running water (*fließendes Wasser*) and use of a toilet and shower. Many places only rent private rooms for longer stays, or they may levy a surcharge (10-20%) for stays of less than 3 nights. *Privatzimmer* tend to go for 150-200 AS a night, with rooms in more expensive areas sometimes costing 200 AS per night and more.

If you wish to make reservations (at hotels or hostels), you can ensure a prompt reply by enclosing two **International Postal Reply Coupons** (available at any post office). Indicate your night of arrival and the number of nights you plan to stay. The hotel will send you a confirmation and may request payment for the first night. Not all hotels accept reservations, and few accept checks in U.S. currency.

Let's Go is not an exhaustive guide to budget accommodations. Most local tourist offices distribute extensive listings (the *Gastgeberverzeichnis*) free of charge and will also reserve a room for a small fee. National tourist offices (see National Tourist Offices above) and travel agencies (see Useful Travel Organizations above) will also supply more complete lists of campsites and hotels.

Prague Accommodations

If searching for lodgings on the spot unnerves your internal constitution, the **Golden Spire Service** (in the U.S., tel. (202) 337-7242; fax 638-5308) might satisfy your needs. For a fee, they will find you short- or long-term accommodations in **Prague** and other Czech and Slovak cities. Their bed-and-breakfasts are largely located in the Old Town (unless otherwise requested) and are within five minutes of a Metro stop. All locations have a telephone. Prices range from US$20-32 per person and include a full breakfast. Just call or fax them, tell them when you will arrive and what accommodations you need, and, for a US$30 fee and a deposit of 200 kčs (US$7.20 or so), they will find you a phenomenal room. The agency can be reached at: Czech and Slovak Service Center, Golden Spire Service, 1511 K St., NW #1030, Washington, DC 20005.

■ Hostels

Hostels are the hubs of the gigantic backpacker subculture that rumbles through Europe every summer, providing innumerable opportunities to meet travelers from all over the world. You can find new traveling partners, trade stories, and learn about places to visit. Most guests are 17-25, but hostels are rapidly becoming a resource for all ages. Many Austrian hostels are open to families. Hostel prices are extraordinarily low—US$8-14 a night for shared rooms. Only camping is cheaper.

Meals are frequently available, though rarely delicious. Breakfast usually consists of one or two hard rolls, jam or marmalade, a slice or two of salami or cheese, and coffee; *Müslix* (cereal flakes with nuts and raisins), soft-boiled eggs, and juice are rarities and usually cost extra. Many hostels have fully equipped kitchen facilities for those who wish to cook for themselves. Some hostels are set in strikingly beautiful castles, others in run-down barracks far from the town center. Rural hostels are generally more appealing than those in large cities. The most common disadvantage is an early curfew—fine if you're climbing a mountain the next morning, but a distinct cramp if you plan to rage in Vienna or Prague.

Many hostels are out of the way, conditions are sometimes spartan and cramped, there's little privacy, rooms are usually segregated by sex, and you may run into more screaming pre-teen tour groups than you care to remember. Summer is an especially attractive season for the prepubescent set to invade Austrian hostels; try to arrive at a hostel before 5pm to insure that the hordes of children don't deprive you of a room. There is often a lockout from morning to mid-afternoon to let the staff clean in peace.

Sheet sleeping sacks are required at many of these hostels. Sleeping bags are usually prohibited (for sanitary reasons), but most hostels provide free blankets. You can make your own sheet sack by folding a sheet and sewing it shut on two sides. The lazier and less domestic can purchase a sheet sack from a department store or by mail (about US$14 from AYH; see Useful Travel Organizations above). If you buy a sheet sack, avoid the tapered, mummy-shaped model that restrict your leg movement and foment claustrophobia.

Whenever possible, call the hostel you intend to patronize well before you journey over. Without a phone call, you may hike several kilometers uphill only to find that the hostel is completely booked or that reception is mysteriously barren. Encountering these little complications can easily make an otherwise marvelous trip very unpleasant; the more communication you establish with the staff, the less likely that you will discover strange and unfortunate surprises.

The most extensive group of hostels is organized by **Hostelling International (HI),** the international organization that once was IYHF. (See Hostel Membership under Documents 'n Formalities above.) You may wish to purchase the HI *International Youth Hostel Handbook, Volume I,* which provides up-to-date listings on all hostels in Europe and the Mediterranean countries. There are about 120 HI-affiliated **Jugendherbergen** (hostels) in Austria. At worst, Austrian hostels are perfectly adequate; at best, they're perfectly dreamy. Prices generally range between 80 AS and 130 AS, with some hostels charging as much as 180 AS in expensive cities. HI membership is required almost without exception, although some hostels sell "guest stamps" (40 AS), valid for one night, to nonmembers. The Austrian National Tourist Office distributes a free map with a guide to all Austrian hostels. For more specific information, contact the **Österreichischer Jugendherbergsverband,** at Hauptverband & Travel Service, Schottenring 28, A-1010 Vienna (tel. (0222) 533 53 53), or **Landesgruppe Wien** (tel. (0222) 533 53 53; telex 135998 ÖJHV; fax 535 08 61), Tramper-Beratungs-Zentrum, Gonzagagasse 22, A-1010 Wien (open Mon.-Thurs. 9am-5pm, Fri. 9am-3pm). The **Österreichisches Jugendherbergswerk** (tel. (0222) 533 18 34 or 533 18 33), Helferstorferstr. 4, A-1010 Vienna, and the **Wiener Jugendherbergswerk** (tel. (0222) 93 71 67), Mariahilfer Str. 24, A-1070 Wien, are additional helpful sources.

■ Alternative Accommodations

College Dormitories

Many colleges and universities open their residence halls to travelers when school is not in session—some even do during term-time. Ask at tourist offices in college towns. When they are available, dorms are rented to visitors for a nominal fee, usually comparable to youth hostel prices. No general policy covers all of these institutions, but many schools require that you express at least a vague interest in attending their institution. You usually won't have to endure stringent curfew and eviction regulations. Many rooms are reserved for students looking for apartments.

Since college dorms are popular with many travelers, you should call or write ahead for reservations.

Students traveling through a college or university town while school is in session might also try introducing themselves to friendly local students. At worst, you'll receive a cold reception; at best, a good conversation leading to an offer for a place to crash. International visitors may have especially good luck with cajoling a room. In general, college campuses are a superb source for information on things to do, places to stay, and possible rides out of town. In addition, dining halls often serve reasonable priced, reasonably edible meals.

Homestays

A number of host networks will help you find accommodations with families throughout Europe. **Servas** is an organization devoted to promoting world peace and understanding by providing opportunities for more personal contacts among people of diverse cultures. Travelers are invited to share life in a host's home in over 100 countries. You are asked to contact hosts in advance, and you must be willing to fit into the household routine. Prospective travelers must submit an application with references, have an interview, and pay a membership fee of US$55, plus a US$25 deposit for up to five host lists. The lists provide a short self-descriptions of each host member. Write to U.S. Servas, Inc., 11 John St. #407, New York, NY 10038 (tel. (212) 267-0252).

When in Dire Straits

Every year, enterprising travelers sleep in locations as inhospitable as cemeteries and sewage-treatment plants to save money on accommodations. While undeniably cheap, sacking out in such hell pits is often uncomfortable, unsafe, and illegal. Always discern a location's safety before you crash. In the city, ask locals about areas to avoid. In the country, ask before you sleep on someone's lawn or in a barn or shed. Otherwise, you may get mauled by the family dog or arrested (or shot) for trespassing. Sleeping in European train stations is a time-honored tradition. However, the romance of being "down and out" is the stuff of Hollywood. Reality is much more grim (and much more pungent). While *Bahnhof*-bedding is free and often tolerated by local authorities, it is neither comfortable nor safe.

■ Long-term Stays

Home Rental

Travelers who plan an extended, localized stay might contact **International Home Rentals,** P.O. Box 329, Middleburg, VA 22117 (tel. (800) 221-9001 or (703) 687-3161; fax (703) 687-3352). Their apartments and bed-and-breakfasts in Vienna, Prague, and Budapest are available for short- and long-term rentals. The self-contained one-, two-, and three-bedroom apartments can accommodate from two to six people. B&Bs are available with private or shared bath.

Home Exchange

Home exchange is tourism's symbiosis: thousands of travelers pay a for-profit company to include their house or apartment on a list, and the company in turn unites two parties who plan a mutually thrilling switcheroo. For less than US$80, you can get a list of many thousands of residences owned by people who want to trade their homes. The benefits are manifold: you'll feel like a resident, circumvent hostels, transportation, and restaurant costs, and your own home is taken care of as you cavort in a land far, far away. Discounts are available for customers over 62. For more information, contact **Intervac U.S.,** P.O. Box 590504, San Francisco, CA 94159 (tel. (415) 435-3497, fax 386-6853). In 1992, 188 Austrian, 48 Czech, and 30 Hungarian families listed their homes with Intervac.

■■■ CAMPING AND THE OUTDOORS

With more than 400 campgrounds throughout the Austria, **camping** is a popular option, though at 30-60 AS per person and 25-50 AS per tent (plus 8-9.50 AS tax if you're over 15), it is seldom substantially cheaper than hosteling. Beware: campgrounds near cities often resemble battlegrounds, with weary travelers and screaming children stacked next to each other. Money and time expended in getting to the campsite may eat away at your budget and your patience. Camping in the countryside is far more attractive (often in breathtaking and deliciously empty sites), but considerably less convenient if you have no car. Showers, bathrooms, and a small restaurant or store are common; some sites have more elaborate facilities. You must obtain permission from landowners to camp on private property—don't hold your breath. The Austrian National Tourist Office provides a list of campgrounds and can give advice about sites, prices, and availability. There is also a **camping information number** (tel. (0222) 89 12 12 22). Some campsites are open year-round, and 80 sites are specifically established for winter camping.

The various alpine associations maintain mountain refuges in many wilderness areas. *Europa Camping and Caravanning,* an annually updated catalog of campsites in Europe, is available through Recreational Equipment, Inc. for US$20 (see below for address). The excellent *Camp Europe by Train* (US$17, including postage; published by Ariel Publications, 14417 SE 19th Place, Bellevue, WA 98007, tel. (206) 641-0518; also available from the **Forsyth Travel Library** (see Useful Addresses) offers general camping tips and suggests camping areas along Eurail lines. Finally, the Automobile Association, Fanum House, Basingstoke, Hampshire RG21 2EA, England, (tel. (0256) 49 15 10), publishes *Camping and Caravanning in Europe.* An **International Camping Carnet** (membership card) is required by some European campgrounds but can usually be bought on the spot. The card entitles you to a discount at some campgrounds, and often may be substituted for your passport as a security deposit. In the U.S., it is available for US$30 through the National Campers and Hikers Association, Inc., 4804 Transit Rd., Bldg. #2, Depew, NY 14043 (tel. (716) 668-6242). Their magazine *Camping Today* is distributed to all members (Carnet price includes a membership fee).

Prospective campers will need to invest a small fortune in good camping equipment and much energy bearing it on their shoulders. Spend some time skimming catalogs and questioning knowledgeable salespeople before buying anything. Use the reputable mail-order firms to gauge prices; order from them if you can't do as well locally. In the fall, last year's merchandise may be reduced by as much as 50%. **Campmor,** 810 Rte. 17N, P.O. Box 997-H, Paramus, NJ 07653 (tel. (800) 526-4784), has a monstrous selection of equipment at low prices. **Cabela's,** 812 13th Ave., Sidney, NE 69160 (tel. (800) 237-4444), offers great prices on quality outdoor equipment. **Recreational Equipment, Inc. (REI),** Sumner, WA 98352-0001 (tel. (800) 426-4840), stocks a wide range of the latest in camping gear and holds great seasonal sales. And 24 hours a day, 365 days a year, **L.L. Bean,** Freeport, ME 04033-0001 (tel. (800) 341-4341), supplies its own equipment and national-brand merchandise.

Purchase your equipment before you leave. American packs are generally more durable, more comfortable, and less expensive, than European ones. As a rule, prices drop in the fall as old merchandise is cleared out. **Backpacks** come with either an external frame or an internal X- or A-shaped frame. If your load is not extraordinarily heavy and you plan to use the pack mainly as a suitcase, choose an internal-frame model. It's more manageable on crowded trains and when hitching, and it's less likely to be mangled by rough handling. Make sure your pack has a strong, padded hip belt, which transfers much of the pack's weight from delicate shoulders to sturdier legs. A good pack costs US$100-300.

Most of the better **sleeping bags**—down (lightweight and warm) or synthetic (cheaper, heavier, more durable, and warmer when wet)—have ratings for specific minimum temperatures. The lower the mercury, the higher the price. Anticipate the most severe conditions you may encounter, subtract a few degrees, and then buy a bag. Remember, the warmest bag will keep you *warm,* so don't overpurchase if you need a bag just for the summer. Expect to pay at least US$60 for a synthetic bag and up to US$250 for a down bag suitable for use in sub-freezing temperatures. **Sleeping bag pads** range from US$12-80, while air mattresses go for about US$30-60. (The foam varieties are plenty comfortable: look for an Ensolite® mattress that's at least three-quarters body length). Some bags now include internal pad holders so you won't find yourself sleeping next to your pad when you awake.

The best **tents** are free-standing, with their own frames and suspension systems. They set up quickly and require no staking. Make sure you have and use the tent's protective rain fly (dew can be quite soggy). Remember to seal the seams to protect against water seepage. Backpackers and cyclists will require especially small, lightweight models. **Sierra Design**, 2039 4th St., Berkeley, CA 94710, sells a two-person tent that weighs less than 1.4kg (3 lbs.) Expect to pay at least US$100 for a good two-person tent. For the best deals, look around for last year's merchandise, particularly in the fall; tents don't change much, but prices may be reduced by as much as 50%.

Other camping basics include a battery-operated **lantern** (*never* gas) for use inside the tent and a simple plastic **groundcloth** to protect the tent floor. When camping in autumn, winter, or spring, bring along a "space blanket," a foil-based technological wonder that will keep you warm by retaining your own body heat. Large, collapsible **water sacks** will significantly improve your lot in primitive campgrounds and weigh practically nothing when empty. **Campstoves** come in all sizes, weights, and fuel types, but none are truly cheap (US$30-120) or light. Consider GAZ, a form of bottled propane gas that is easy to use and widely available in Europe. Bring some **waterproof matches** or the stove might prove useless. **Cooking equipment** can prove more of an albatross than a convenience—consider your eating requirements and preferences carefully.

A **canteen, iodine solution, Swiss Army knife,** and **insect repellent** are small, essential items to throw in with your gear. For further information about camping equipment and other camping concerns, contact **Wilderness Press,** 2440 Bancroft Way, Berkeley, CA 94704-1676 (tel. (800) 443-7227 or (510) 543-8080), which publishes useful books such as *Backpacking Basics* (US$9, including postage) and *Backpacking with Babies and Small Children* (US$10). (See Packing above for more tips on useful odds and ends.)

■ Wilderness Concerns

The first thing to preserve in the wilderness is you—health, safety, and food should be your primary concerns when you camp (see Health above for information about basic medical concerns and first-aid). A comprehensive guide to outdoor survival is *How to Stay Alive in the Woods*, by Bradford Angier (Macmillan, $8). Many rivers, streams, and lakes are contaminated with bacteria such as *giárdia,* which causes gas, cramps, loss of appetite, and violent diarrhea. To protect yourself from the effects of this invisible trip-wrecker, always boil your water vigorously for at least five minutes before drinking it, or use an iodine solution made for purification. Filters do not remove all bacteria, but they can be useful for drawing water from streams that have slowed to a trickle because of a drought. *Never go camping or hiking by yourself for any significant time or distance*. If you're going into an area that is not well-traveled or well-marked, let someone know where you're hiking and how long you intend to be out. If you fail to return on schedule or if you need to be reached for some reason, searchers will at least know where to start looking for you.

The second thing to protect while you are outdoors is the wilderness. The thousands of outdoor enthusiasts that pour into the parks every year threaten to trample the land to death. Because firewood is scarce in popular parks, campers are asked to make small fires using only dead branches or brush; using a campstove is the more cautious way to cook. Check ahead to see if the park prohibits campfires altogether.

If you can make a fire, do so in a fire pit, a cleared patch of ground surrounded by stones to keep the blaze contained. *Always extinguish a fire before you turn in for the night.* To avoid digging a rain trench for your tent, pitch it on high, dry ground. Don't cut vegetation, and don't clear campsites. If there are no toilet facilities, bury human waste at least four inches deep and 100 feet or more from any water supplies and campsites. **Biosafe** soap or detergents may be used in streams or lakes. Otherwise, don't use soaps in or near bodies of water. Always pack up your trash in a plastic bag and carry it with you until you reach the next trash can; burning and burying pollute the environment. In more civilized camping circumstances, it's important to respect fellow campers. Keep light and noise to a minimum, particularly if you arrive after dark.

■■■ KEEPING IN TOUCH

■ Mail

Be sure to include the *postal code* if you know it; those of Austrian cities all begin with "A," Prague with "CZ," and Budapest with "H."

Sending Mail from Home

Mail can be sent internationally through **Poste Restante** (the international phrase for General Delivery) to any city or town. It is well worth using and quite reliable. People can mail you letters, and the post office will hold them for a limited number of days until you pick them up. Mark the envelope "Hold." The last name should be underlined and capitalized. As a rule, it is best to use the largest post office in the area. Bring your passport or other ID with you when you pick up your mail. If the clerk insists no mail arrived for you, try checking under your first name as well. *Let's Go* lists post offices and postal codes in the Practical Information section for each city and most towns; a full list of postal codes is also in the Appendix at the back of this guide. In big cities, the main post office usually has a special counter for *Poste Restante* and is usually open 24 hours, including Sundays and public holidays. Tourist locales may have extended hours in high season.

Address *Poste Restante* letters in Austria to **Postlagernde Briefe.** Mark the envelope "BITTE HALTEN SIE" ("please hold"), and address it as follows:

Amy Beth ZELANKO	(name)
Postlagernde Briefe	
Hauptpostamt	
Maximilianstraße 2	(address)
A-6020 Innsbruck	(postal code and city)
AUSTRIA (ÖSTERREICH)	

Unless you specify a post office by street address or postal code, the letter will be held at the *Hauptpostamt* (main post office).

Sending mail care of **American Express** is also quite reliable. Any office will hold your mail for free if you subscribe to The Card® or hold at least one AmEx traveler's check. Thus, even if you prefer to use another company's checks, purchase at least one from American Express if you want to partake of this service; otherwise, the office may charge 60 to fork over held mail. AmEx will automatically hold your mail for 30 days; to have it held for longer, write on the envelope, for example, "Hold for 45 days." The sender should capitalize and underline the receiver's last name and mark the letter "Client Letter Service." For addresses of AmEx offices, refer to the Practical Information section of the cities you plan to visit. A complete list of offices is available inside AmEx's free booklet, titled *Traveler's Companion* (call (800) 528-4800 in the U.S.).

Postcards and letters, when mailed from the U.S. to Europe, cost 40¢ and 50¢, respectively. Between the US and Europe airmail averages a week to 10 days. Generally, letters specifically marked "air mail" travel faster than postcards. U.S. post offices also sell aerograms for 45¢; to save five cents, you lose a good deal of writing space and have to put up with thin—nay, diaphanous—paper. If possible, skip user-unfriendly aerograms. It is safer, quicker, more reliable, and slightly more expensive to send mail express or registered. Many U.S. city post offices offer **International Express Mail** service, which sends packages under 8 oz. to major overseas cities in 40 to 72 hours for US$11.50-14.

Private mail services provide the fastest, most reliable overseas delivery. **DHL** (tel. (800) 225-5345 in the U.S. and Canada; (81) 890 93 93 in London; (2) 317 83 00 in Sydney; (9) 636 50 00 in Auckland; (353) 1 844 47 44 in Dublin; (11) 921 36 00 in Johannesburg) is the most expansive. DHL offices are located in Vienna (tel. 711 61) and Prague, Na Poříčí 4 (tel. 26 75 25; open Mon.-Fri. 8am-6pm). Mail between Europe and the U.S. takes about three days and costs about US$30-70. By **Federal Express** (tel. (800) 238-5355 in the U.S. and Canada; (81) 844 23 44 in London; (2) 317 66 66 in Sydney; (9) 256 83 00 in Auckland; (353) 1 847 34 73 in Dublin; (11) 921 75 00 in Johannesburg), an express letter from North America to Europe costs about US$32 and takes 2-3 days. Packages can be sent from Europe to the U.S., but costs vary widely between dozens and hundreds of dollars.

Surface mail is by far the cheapest and slowest way to send mail. It takes one to three months to cross the Atlantic and is only appropriate for sending large quantities of items you won't be needing for a while. It is vital, therefore, to distinguish your airmail from surface mail by explicitly labelling it "air mail"—*Flugpost* in German, *letecky* in Czech, and *légiposta* in Hungarian.

When ordering books and materials from another country, include an **International Reply Coupon (IRC),** available at the post office, with your request. IRCs provide the recipient of your order with postage to cover delivery.

Austria

Mail within the country travels quickly, often taking only one to two days. Airmail to North America takes five to seven days. Allow at least two and a half weeks for Australia and New Zealand. Within Europe, a letter or postcard of up to 20g costs 7 AS. To the U.S. or Canada, an airmail postcard costs 8.50 AS, and a letter up to 20g costs 16 AS. To South Africa, postcards cost 9.50 AS, and 20g letters cost 20.50 AS. To Australia and New Zealand, airmail postcards cost 11 AS, and 20g letters cost 26 AS. Aerograms cost about 12 AS. Postal information and stamps are available at *Tabak* stands and shops. Post offices are easy to locate—just look for the golden trumpet or the flexing eagle symbol. Post offices often reside next to the main train station or in the town's central square, and are usually open Mon.-Fri. 8am-noon and 2-5pm. Mailboxes are painted yellow or orange.

The Czech Republic

In Czech, airmail is *letecky*, post office is *pošta,* and stamp is *známky.* For a fee, you can rent an individual **private postbox** in Prague near the Staroměstské Metro. You can have letters and packages delivered there through the mail or by hand to a convenient box, and you can pick them up Mon.-Fri. 9am-6pm, Sat. 10am-4pm. The fee is 500 kčs (about US$18) for three months, 900 kčs for six months, and 1500 kčs for 12 months. Try to reserve a box before you leave home so friends and relations can send letters that arrive when you do. For more information, contact: Pragma Mail Call, Vezenska 3, Praha 1 (tel. (422) 231 58 28; fax 231 07 76).

Hungary

In Hungarian, post office is *posta hivatal* and stamp is *bélyeg.* The system works fine (airmail—*légiposta*—to the U.S. takes 5-10 days). When sending registered mail, note that you have to fill in a special form and are not allowed to seal the package before it has been inspected. Post offices are indicated by the sign **POSTA** and are generally open Mon.-Fri. 8am-7pm, Sat. 8am-1pm.

■ Telephones

Austria's telephone system is converting to a digitized network. Phone numbers may change at any time, especially in Innsbruck and Vienna.

The **Austrian** telephone and postal system is proof that the term "efficient state monopoly" is not an oxymoron. You can make international phone calls at telephone centers (usually only in the larger cities), in most post offices, and from pay phones, sequestered in green and yellow booths. *Never* dial abroad from a hotel room—a surcharge of up to 200% may be added. If you cannot avoid such a tragedy, time your call and keep in mind that the meter is running at some US$8 a minute. **Wertkarten (telephone cards)** available in post offices, train stations and some stores, come in 50 AS (green), 100 AS (gold), and 200 AS denominations, and are purchased for 48 AS, 95 AS, and 190 AS respectively. Card phones are found in even remote villages. To use the phone, simply slide the *Wertkarte* into the appropriate slot, wait for the value of money remaining on the card to appear in the window by the receiver, and place the call. The cost of the call is automatically deducted. With the *Wertkarte,* one can chat away until no money remains on the card—at that point, the phone will eject the card and the call will be cut off after a minute. If you don't exhaust the total amount of the card, a black mark on the back indicates how much money remains. It's *much* easier to use a card than to traipse around with a pocketful of change. To make **local calls** without a phone card, deposit 2 AS to start (less than 3 min.) and 1 AS for each additional 90 seconds. **Long distance** charges vary—drop in 5 AS to start. The display next to the receiver indicates how much money has been deposited by the caller and shows the deductions made during the course of the call. When using an **older payphone,** you must push the red button when your party answers. Between 6pm and 8am on weekdays and from Saturday at 1pm to Monday at 8am, all phone calls within the country are one-third cheaper. This rate, unfortunately, does not apply to international calls.

For Austrian telephones, a constant tone is the dial tone, long beeps indicate ringing, and three ascending tones signal a malfunction. Many foreigners are fooled by the ringing sound—which, let it be stressed, is *not* a busy signal; the busy signal is a rapid series of short, staccato beeps. For help **calling abroad,** dial 08. The **country code** for **Austria** is 43; for the **Czech Republic** 42; for **Hungary** 36; for the **U.K.** 44; for **Ireland** 010; for **Australia** 61; for **New Zealand** 64; for **South Africa** 27. For **local information,** dial 16 11. Dial 09 for assistance with **local calls.** For the **police** anywhere in Austria, dial 133; for an **ambulance,** dial 144; for the **fire department,** dial 122. Austrian phone books are user-friendly and are available in phone booths. The beginning section lists phone codes for international dialing. If a call won't go through, check to see if you are using the correct area code. A complete list of city codes appears in the Appendix at the end of this guide.

International direct dialing is not complicated. First dial the **international dialing prefix/international access code** for the country you are in (011 in the United States), then the **country code** for the country you are calling. Next punch in the **area code** or **city code** (in the Practical Information listings for large cities, and in the Appendix at the back of this guide). Finally, dial the **local number.** In most countries (excluding the U.S., Canada, and Hungary) the first digit of the city code is the **domestic long-distance prefix** (usually 0, 1, or 9); omit it when calling from abroad, but use it when dialing another region in the same country. You can usually make direct international calls from a pay phone, but you may need a companion to feed money in as you speak.

The quickest (and cheapest) way to **call abroad collect** is to go to a post office and ask for a *Zurückrufen,* or return call. You will receive a card with a number on it. Call your party and tell them to call you back at that number. At the end of the conversation, you pay for the original call (about 10-20 AS). A call to the U.S. or Canada costs about 18 AS per minute; to Australia or New Zealand about 28 AS per minute; to Great Britain 14 AS per minute during the peak hours, 9 AS per minute 6pm to 8am and on weekends. It's cheaper to use the post office service or find a pay phone, and deposit just enough money to be able to say "Call me" and give your number.

Another alternative is the **AT&T USA Direct** service, which allows you to dial a telephone number from Europe (022 903 011 in Austria, 00 42 00 01 01 in the Czech Republic, and 00 800 01 111 in Hungary), to connect instantly to an operator in the U.S. In Austria, the connection to the AT&T operator is a local call—you must keep dropping in 1 AS per minute for the length of the call. In the Czech Republic and Hungary, you must wait for a dial tone after you dial the first two zeros. Rates run about US$1.75-1.85 for the first minute plus about US$1 per additional minute. Calls must be either collect (US$5.75 surcharge) or billed to an AT&T calling card (US$2.50); the people you are calling need not subscribe to AT&T service. For more information, call AT&T in the U.S. at (800) 874-4000. **Canada Direct** (tel. (800) 561-8868), **Australia Direct** (tel. 0102), and **New Zealand Direct** (tel. 018) are similar to USA Direct, though not as extensive. These services can also be used for international calls within Europe. **MCI's Call USA** program (tel. 022 903 012 in Austria) is a similar program available from over 65 countries. Calls cost approximately US$3.60-5.35 for the first minute plus US$1-2 per additional minute. A similar service, **Canada Direct** (tel. 022 903 013), facilitates person-to-person calls to more northern climes. MCI also offers **WorldReach,** a more expensive program through which you can use a calling card to call from one European country to another. For information on these programs, call MCI at (800) 444-4444 or (800) 444-3333.

Phone rates tend to be highest in the morning, low in the evening, and lowest on Sunday and at night. Get the exact times for your own country, if possible—there are weird and wonderful variations. Also, remember **time differences** when you call. Austria, Prague, and Budapest are six hours ahead of New York's Eastern Standard Time and one hour ahead of Greenwich Mean Time.

■ Other Modes of Communication

To send a **telegram** overseas from the U.S., **Western Union** (tel. (800) 625-6000) charges a base fee of US$8, plus 71¢ per word, including name and address. There is a US$10 surcharge for telegrams not in English or Spanish. Mailgrams, which require one day for delivery, cost US$17.90. If you're spending a year abroad and want to keep in touch with friends or colleagues in a college or research institution, **electronic mail ("e-mail")** is an attractive option. It takes a minimum of computer knowledge and a little pre-arranged planning, and the system beams messages anywhere for free. Ask at individual universities for more information.

Between May and October, **EurAide,** P.O. Box 2375, Naperville, IL 60567 (tel. (708) 420-2343), offers **Overseas Access,** a service most useful to travelers without a set itinerary. It costs US$15 per week or US$40 per month for an electronic message box. To reach you, people call and leave a message at the "home base" in Munich, at Bahnhofplatz 2, 8000 München 2 (tel. (089) 59 38 89). You receive the message by calling Munich whenever you wish—it's cheaper than calling overseas. For an additional US$20 per month, EurAide will forward mail sent to Munich to any addresses you specify.

■ Media

To stay in touch with the rest of the world, consult one of several international English-language publications. No Austrian newspapers publish English-language editions, but the *International Herald Tribune* and a few major British dailies make their way to Austrian metropolitan centers and tourist destinations. Any station on the **Austrian Radio Network (ÖRF)** broadcasts a spurt of English daily 8:05-8:10am. The Vienna-based, largely English-language **Blue Danube Radio** broadcasts news in English every hour on the half hour between 6am and 1am and a full half hour of news at 7pm daily (103.8FM and 92.9FM in Vienna, 104.6FM in Salzburg, 101.4FM in Innsbruck, 101.7FM in Graz, 104FM and 102FM in Linz, 102.9FM in Klagenfurt and 102.1FM in Bregenz). **Voice of America** broadcasts a mixture of news, music, and feature programs on 1197AM from 7am to 1pm, in the afternoon, and in the early evening.

Of the German-language press, Vienna's *Neue Kronen-Zeitung* is the largest newspaper, and with a readership of more than two and a half million, is proportionally one of the most widely read papers on earth. *Kurier* has a large advertising section on Saturdays and a television guide on Fridays. The *Standard* and *Die Presse,* with TV guides on Thursdays, specialize in business news, and, along with the *Salzburger Nachrichten* (which, despite its name, is a trans-Austrian newspaper) and the *Arbeiter Zeitung,* are respected sources of political and cultural news. *Profil* and *Wochenpresse* are weekly newsmagazines self-consciously modeled after the American *Time*. *Wiener* and *Basta* are trendy magazines that provide information on what's up (or what's going down) in the rock scene. Fans of rock 'n' roll and pop music read *Rennbahnexpress,* while intellectuals prefer *Falter,* which each week includes a calendar of Viennese events. Cafés provide the cheapest way to read a newspaper. For the price of a cup of coffee, you can churn your way through all the papers in the joint.

To subscribe to an Austrian newspaper or magazine, contact: **MORAWA,** Wollzeile 11, A-1010 Wien (tel. (0222) 51 56 20; fax 52 57 78).

■■■ FOOD AND DRINK

One of life's great enigmas is how a country with such an unremarkable cuisine could produce such heavenly desserts. In mid-afternoon, Austrians flock to *Café-Konditoreien* (café-confectioners) to nurse the national sweet tooth with *Kaffee und Kuchen* (coffee and cake). Try a *Mélange,* a light coffee topped with steamed milk, chocolate shavings, and a hint of cinnamon. *Sacher Torte,* a rich chocolate cake layered with marmalade, is as Austrian as Mozart. Or nibble on the heavenly *Mohr im Hemd,* a circular chocolate sponge cake with a dollop of hot whipped chocolate. Tortes are also commonly made with *Erdbeeren* (strawberries) and *Himbeeren* (raspberries).

Loaded with fat, salt, and cholesterol, Austrian cuisine is a cardiologist's nightmare. Staples include *Schweinfleisch* (pork), *Kalbsfleisch* (veal), *Wurst* (sausage), *Ei* (egg), *Käse* (cheese), *Brot* (bread), and *Kartoffeln* (potatoes). Austria's most renowned dish is *Schnitzel,* a meat cutlet (usually veal or pork) fried in butter with bread crumbs. Restaurants are generally expensive; tight budgets are better maintained by eating out of grocery stores, *Bäckereien* (bakeries) and *Fleischereien* (butcher shops). Most butchers sell a hefty *Wurstsemmel* (sliced sausage on a bulky roll) for 10 AS or so. You may think that there is no distinction between the best of *Wursts* and the worst of *Wursts,* but, in truth, there's wide variety of sausage: *Blutwurst, Bockwurst, Bratwurst, Leberwurst,* and *Weißwurst* are just some of the offerings.

Of course, you've got to have something to wash down that *Wurst*. If you ask for *Wasser,* expect effervescence; you'll be given mineral water (and charged accordingly). The German word for tap water is *Leitungswasser*. Eastern Austria is famous for its white wine. Klosterneuburger, produced in the eponymous district near Vienna, is both reasonably priced and dry. Austrian beers are outstanding; try Stiegl Bier, a Salzburg brew; Zipfer Bier from upper Austria; and Gösser Bier from Styria. Austria imports lots of Budweiser beer, a.k.a. Budvar—the original Bohemian variety, not the American imitation. For a more potent potable, try a *Likör* (liqueur) or a *Schnapps;* every region has a local specialty. The really hard stuff is a bad idea—the price of imported booze is exorbitant, and Austrian booze is deplorable. If you insist on self-abuse, try Stroh rum. The orange-label version weighs in at a skull-popping 160 proof; sit close to the floor.

Most every town and city in Austria boasts a supermarket of some sort. The best discount supermarkets are **Hofer, Billa, M-Preis, SPAR Markt,** and **Konsum.** At **Julius Meinl** markets, prices are a few *Schillings* higher, but for your extra change you get bags to take things home in; other chains don't give out shopping bags for free. Most Austrian restaurants expect you to seat yourself. And don't wait around for the check when you're finished; it would be a crude insult for a waiter to bring the bill without first being asked. Say "*Zahlen bitte*" (pronounced TSAHL-en BIT-uh) to settle your accounts. Be aware that you will be charged for each piece of bread you eat from the basket on your table.

See the Appendix and Glossary at the back of this book for more—much, much, much more—on foodstuffs and dining.

■■■ IDIOSYNCRASIES

Tipping

Although taxes and a gratuity are included in **Austrian** restaurant bills, it is customary to leave a small tip, usually by rounding up the bill. 5% is plenty, 10%, excessive. Say "*Es stimmt so*" (pronounced ESS SHTEEMT ZOH) to tell a waiter to keep the change. When staying more than a few days in a hotel, it is customary to leave an equally small tip for the maid.

Business Hours

In general, **Austrian** shops are open Mon.-Fri. 9am-6pm and Sat. 9am-noon, while shops in smaller towns are wont to siesta from noon-3pm. Grocers tend to open earlier and close later. Banks are generally open Mon.-Fri. 8am-noon and 2-6pm. Business hours in **Prague** run Mon.-Fri. 8am-6pm and Sat. 8am-noon. European museums are generally open Tues.-Sun. 10am-6pm.

Bargaining, Haggling, and Dickering

Bargaining is a skill many tourists fail to cultivate, but it can be the ultimate budget tool. Prices are negotiable in many markets, street stands, and small stores, though not in large department stores or high-quality shops. One effective method is to ask the price of the article in a somewhat blasé, offhand way. Offer about half the asking price, act firm, and be ready to begin the bidding game. Don't be intimidated into paying more than you want. At the same time, however, prepare to pay any price you utter. If you give a price and the seller says yes, the article is yours.

Huh? The First Floor?

To Americans, European floors may seem misnamed. The American second floor is called the first floor (*Erste Stock*), and the third floor is called the second floor (*Zweite Stock*). The ground floor, thankfully, is still called the ground floor (*Erdgeschoß*). European elevator buttons therefore read "E, 1, 2, 3" and up; "E" will be ground level.

AUSTRIA

Österreich 101

Three horizontal bars of red, white, and red adorn the flag of the Federal Republic of Austria (Österreich). At 32,276 square miles, the country is almost exactly the size of Maine, and lies at the same latitude as Maine's northern tip. Austria comprises nine semi-autonomous provinces, or Bundesländer. Counterclockwise from the northeast are: Vienna (Wien), Lower Austria (Niederösterreich), Upper Austria (Oberösterreich), Salzburg, Tyrol (Tirol), Vorarlberg, Carinthia (Kärnten), Styria (Steiermark), and Burgenland. These political divisions are mostly a matter of bureaucratic convenience; Austrians attach much less emotion to their home province than, for example, U.S. citizens do for their states. International borders are far more important for the hodgepodge of Austrian ethnicities. The republic shares a common border with seven countries: Hungary, the Czech Republic, Germany, Switzerland, Italy, Slovakia, and diminutive Liechtenstein.

Austria's population of 7.8 million, is 98% German-speaking, but that statistic belies the presence of significant ethnic minorities. The Slovenes of southern Carinthia and the Croats in Burgenland are guaranteed rights by the terms of Article Seven of the Austrian State Treaty of Vienna of 1955. A Hungarian minority inhabits a number of Burgenland towns and villages, and there is a small Slovak community in Vienna. About 80.6% of the Austrian population is Roman Catholic; a further 4.9% is Protestant, most ascribing to the Augsburg confession.

Despite all its amoebic political transformation, Austria has managed to maintain an overpowering physical beauty. The country truly is as dreamy as the photos you've seen—onion-domed churches set against snow-capped Alpine peaks, lush meadows blanketed with edelweiss, pristine mountain lakes, dark cool forests, and mighty castles towering over the majestic Danube. Austria is situated in the eastern Alps; two-thirds of the country, all but the agricultural plains along the river valleys, is covered by mountains. This generates year-round tourism: Alpine sports dominate winter, and lakeside frolicking draws visitors in the warmer months.

HISTORY

Perhaps the most remarkable aspect of Austrian history is the absence of a consistently Austrian homeland. Although Austria has been ruled by ethnic Germans for more than a millennium, myriad ethnic groups—Magyars, Slovenes, Flemings, Slavs, Italians—have held valid claims to the name "Austrian." It was not until the 19th century that anything resembling nationalism could be detected, and even then the phrase meant Germanic nationalism, defined in opposition to the multi-ethnic empire. After Austria was stripped of its imperial possessions following World War I, an Austrian Republic was born, but the existence of a national state did not a nation make; Austria attempted to join the Greater German Republic, and the two remained separate only because foreign armies blocked their marriage. Only after Hitler sashayed into Austria and plunged the nation into barbarism, war, and defeat did Austrians develop a sense of a unique national destiny. Only since the founding of the Second Austrian Republic has there been a meaningful Austrian homeland.

Since World War II, Austria has made a distinct effort to develop its national identity, though the bonds of nationalism are still not as strong here as elsewhere. This is by no means a liability—internationally neutral, democratic, and Western-oriented, the Second Republic has fashioned a progressive social democratic welfare state that seems to work as well as any in the hemisphere. And with an application for membership in the European Community pending, the Austrian historical familiarity with multinational confederation should serve it well in the coming years.

Austria's central situation at the crossroads of the Continent predetermined its subjection to a variety of cultural and political influences. Plaything of these dynamic forces, Austria's global role and international relevance have undergone numerous transformations. Over the centuries, Austria evolved tempestuously from a border region to a hegemonic empire to the democratic republic of today.

In The Beginning...

The first traces of settlements in sheltered Austrian regions date back to the **Paleolithic Age.** The Danube area was settled between 80,000 and 10,000 BC, and the "Tänzerin" and the "Venus of Willendorf" from the Krems area provide the first evidence of early cultures. In 1991, a mummified male body dating from the Stone Age was discovered in the glacial ice of the Ötztal Alps (see "Marc Jones" in Pfunds for more). The Celtic people who first settled the lands that comprise modern Austria established the state of **Noricum** around 400 BC. In order to secure their northern frontier and reap the benefits of Celtic iron and salt mines, **Romans** conquered the territory between the Alps, Dolomites, and Danube River by 15 BC. The road along the Danube facilitated troop movements and trade between towns. The provinces thrived, and several cities, such as **Vindobona** (Vienna), **Iuvavum** (Salzburg), and **Brigantium** (Bregenz), flourished under Roman rule. **Carnuntum** in Pannonia, situated east of Vienna, was the largest Roman town on Austrian territory. During its heyday, Carnuntum claimed about 20,000 inhabitants. By the 3rd century AD, however, Roman forts were unable to check incursions by the **Alemanni**, a Germanic tribe. By the 5th century, Huns, Magyars, Teutons and other belligerent tribes had annihilated the final remains of the Roman presence in Austria.

Over the next three centuries, the region was primarily occupied by three different groups: Alemanni in the south, Slavs in the southwest, and Bavarians in the north. Huns, Goths, Lombards, and others occasionally rampaged through the territories, but failed to establish more than a transitory presence. In an attempt to create a power base free of Frankish influence, Bavarian dukes, with the help of the **Roman Catholic Church,** brought a semblance of law and order to the area. Bavarian bishoprics competed with their Eastern Orthodox counterparts to convert the Slavs to Christianity and thereby bring them under political control. With the missionaries' successes, **Salzburg** became an archbishopric in 798; it remained Austria's ecclesiastical capital well into the modern era.

The Babenberg Era

Bavarian dukes were unable to secure Austria as their own personal power base. The missionaries simply tamed the locals, offering **Charlemagne's** Holy Roman Juggernaut an eminently quiescent populace. The Frankish ruler definitively claimed southwest Austria as a border province of his Empire, and Austria as a distinct concept began to surface. Indeed, *Österreich* means Eastern Empire, referring to the easternmost lands that Charlemagne conquered. However, only today's province of Niederösterreich fell within the new "Austrian" borders. The first known mention of *Österreich* was scripted in 996; it referred to contemporary eastern Austria, with a court at Vienna, known as Ostarraichi. Forty-one years earlier, Holy Roman Emperor **Otto I** had overseen the defeat of Magyars from the east at the battle of Lechfeld; in 976, Otto appointed **Leopold II** Margrave of Ostarraichi. The **Babenberg family,** on a power par with the other nobility, slowly set about increasing its holdings. The family succeeded in extending their protectorate to the north of the Danube and farther to the east and south. Monasteries and abbeys founded by the Babenbergs played an important role in the colonization of the country and soon became centers of cultural life. The areas decimated by earlier conflicts with warring nomadic tribes were intensively resettled by Germans, increasing the **Germanic influence** over the developing Austrian consciousness. The Babenbergs solidified their power by backing the Pope against the emperors during the **Investiture Conflict,** in which the secular nobility attempted to wrest away from Rome the power to appoint bishops. In 1156 the Babenbergs, who, since the marriage of Count Leopold III to the emperor's widow Agnes, had climbed among the most powerful families in the empire, secured the elevation of the margraviate into a duchy. The peerage promotion was obtained through Emperor **Friedrich Barbarossa** and vastly increased the power of the landed class. The transformative document, known as the **Privilegium minus,** contained other concessions to the Babenbergs, allowing greater independence from the imperial power. In the first half of the 13th century, cultural life at the court of the Babenbergs was in full bloom. **Minnesingers** (minstrels) such as Walther von der Vogelweide and Ulrich von Liechtenstein wrote epic ballads, and **Romanesque architecture** came to a late fruition. The Babenberg territories benefitted economically from traffic with the east during the Crusades. The family also secured a large part of the ransom that England paid to rescue **Richard the Lion-Hearted,** who had been detained in Austria by Leopold V on his way home from the Third Crusade; Leopold used the ransom to fortify the towns of **Wiener Neustadt** and **Vienna.** In that same year, 1192, Leopold V obtained the Duchy of **Styria** through a contract of inheritance.

The Rise of the Habsburgs

Warfare with Austria's neighbors, especially the Magyars of Hungary, brought about the end of Babenberg rule when the last male descendant of the dynasty, the childless **Duke Friedrich II,** was killed in battle in 1246. Soon, all of Austria was up for grabs, and the lands briefly came under the control of the Bohemian King **Ottokar II.** He secured the heritage by marrying the last Babenberg's sister and quickly succeeded in reestablishing order in the country, reconquering Styria, and winning control of Carinthia through a contract of inheritance. But at the same time a new German force was arising—the Swiss family **Habsburg.** King Rudolf of Habsburg had recently been elected Holy Roman Emperor and was not prepared to recognize the Bohemian's king's power. When Ottokar refused to swear allegiance to King Rudolf, he was banned from the empire. The key event in Austria's early development occurred when Rudolf, later known as Rudolf the Founder, defeated Ottokar at **Marchfeld** in 1278 and established Habsburg hereditary control over the region. In 1282 Rudolf granted his two sons the Duchies of Austria and Styria, thus laying the foundations for Habsburg dynastic rule. The Habsburgs would retain power in Austria almost continuously until 1918, through 19 Habsburg emperors and kings and one empress. From the time of Emperor **Friedrich I the Handsome,** the Habsburg territories became known as the Austrian domains.

At the inception of Habsburg rule, the family's dominance was far from secure. There were incessant revolts—even the Swiss, which had earlier belonged to the most loyal Habsburg possessions, launched an armed rebellion. During the late Middle Ages, the Habsburgs focused on expanding their holdings and defending their inflating borders. Rudolf the Founder's short rule (1358-1365) was marked by the acquisition of the Earldom of **Tyrol**. He founded the **University of Vienna** and commissioned improvements to St. Stephen's, in Vienna. When Rudolf felt his family had been passed over by the Luxembourg Emperor Karl IV, he forged several documents, later called the **Privilegium maius,** to demonstrate his dynasty's higher rank. Rudolf's descendant, Emperor **Friedrich III,** affirmed the claims made in these documents and strategically arranged the marriage of his son, **Maximilian I,** to the heiress of the powerful Burgundian kingdom, which gave Austria control of the Low Countries. Family feuds in the next few decades considerably weakened the power of the Habsburg dynasty. Further losses of Swiss territory were to partially offset by the acquisition of today's province of **Vorarlberg.** In response to incursions by the imperial Turkish forces along the Danube and Drau Rivers, Maximilian consolidated his regime through various **centralizing reforms.** In 1493, Maximilian became the first Habsburg to claim the title of Holy Roman Emperor without papal coronation, which gave the family hereditary rights to the imperial throne. Through his prudent marital alliances, he ensured the hereditary succession of lands far and wide and laid the foundations for the vast territory to come under Habsburg rule during the pinnacle of the empire. Maximilian arranged the marriage of his son Philip to the heiress of the united **Kingdom of Spain,** and with the accession to the imperial throne (and its New World possessions), the Habsburgs became the first empire on which the sun never set. Rudolf's original empire gradually spread within Europe by a mixture of conquest and marriage; Philip's son Charles V, for example, inherited Bohemia and some of Hungary. The Habsburgs ruled under the motto "**A.E.I.O.U.**," meaning either "*Alles Erdreich ist Österreich Untertan*" (Austria is destined to rule the world), "*Austria Est Imperare Orbi Universo*" (the universe must be ruled by Austria), or "*Austria Erit In Orbe Ultima*" (Austria will survive forever), depending on which scholar does the translating. A more appropriate motto might have been the popular couplet, "*Bella gerant alii, tu felix Austria nube. Nam que Mars aliis, dat tibi regna Venus*" (Other nations go to war while you, lucky Austria, marry).

The majestic imperial sheen cloaked anxieties among the Habsburgs. The **Ottoman Empire,** which had been encroaching on Europe since the 14th century, began to threaten the continent more and more in the 1500s and 1600s. After the conquest of Constantinople, the Turks undertook expeditions farther and farther west and thus became a permanent threat to the Habsburg patrimonial lands. In 1529, the armies reached the gates of Vienna before they were beaten back.

The Ottoman threat placed a huge strain on the stagnant Austrian economy. The emperors required a monstrous army to defend the territories; they also spent lavishly on construction and artworks, to draw cultural attention from their French counterparts. Social unrest, fomented by the **Reformation,** further threatened to undermine stability. Burghers and nobles were drawn to Protestantism because it affirmed rationality and freedom from Habsburg despotism. Peasants found the Protestant doctrine attractive because it freed them from onerous tithes to the Church. Social hierarchies, though, kept the two groups from forming a united front against the emperor and Church. When peasant skirmishes ignited, the Austrian rulers hired mercenaries who mercilessly crushed the rebels in the **Peasants' Wars** of 1525-6. After several tolerant leaders allowed Protestantism to flourish, Archduke Ferdinand of Tirol decided to forcibly convert Austria to Catholicism. As emperor, Ferdinand pursued his crusade throughout the empire. Only the **Thirty Years War** and the military intervention of **King Gustav Adolphus** of Sweden, whose armies swept almost to Vienna, saved the Protestants from further persecution. The Thirty Years War initiated the slow process of disintegration in the empire and forced the Habsburgs to shift their attention from acquiring territory to holding it.

In 1683, the Ottoman Turks sat on Vienna's doorstep once again. Austria's brilliant military response was largely the handiwork of **Prince Eugene of Savoy.** Victory over the Turks generated an era of celebration; to honor the Austrian prowess, magnificent buildings were constructed and wounded castles, churches, and monasteries were finally repaired. This patriotic exuberance, tempered by a deep religious conviction, was the prevailing trademark of the Austrian **Baroque.** After Eugene of Savoy rescued Vienna from this second Turkish siege, Leopold I gave him control of the army. He proceeded to conquer **Hungary,** which the empire promptly annexed. Eugene also successfully led the Habsburg troops against the French during the **War of Spanish Succession** between 1701 and 1714. By 1718, the Habsburg emperors had direct control of Bohemia, Moravia, Silesia, Hungary, Croatia, Transylvania, Belgium, Lombardy, Naples, Sicily, and, of course, Austria.

The Reign of Empress Maria Theresa

A **succession crisis** arose just as the sway of Habsburg authority had reached its peak. Emperor Karl VI had left no male heir. Through the **Pragmatic Sanction** of

1713, most of the powers in Europe agreed to recognize succession of the Habsburgs through the female line if the male line fell extinct, allowing Karl's daughter **Maria Theresa** to become empress in 1740. Maria Theresa married Franz Stephan of Lorraine, who, though elected Emperor of the Holy Roman Empire in 1745, was overshadowed throughout his life by his wife's personality and charm. The young empress faced an array of land-hungry enemies. Bavaria and France challenged her authority by making claims against Habsburg holdings, but the empress proved tougher than they had expected. Still, Prussian King **Friedrich the Great** spared no effort to gain possession of his heritage and snatched away Silesia, one of the empire's most prosperous provinces; Maria Theresa spent the rest of her life unsuccessfully maneuvering to reclaim it. The empress was able to maintain her position during the **Wars of Austrian Succession** from 1740 to 1748 with help from the Hungarians, but she lost the Italian lands of Lombardy. The stalemate that resulted from the **Seven Years War** underscored the waning influence of the Austrian empire and the rise of Prussia as a great power. Maria Theresa and her son **Josef II** undertook a series of **reforms** to stimulate the economy, such as improving tax collection, increasing settlements, encouraging religious freedom, aiding industry, and decreasing feudal burdens. A new state system transformed the agglomeration of lands that had hitherto been only loosely connected into a tightly administered **central state.** Under Maria Theresa and Josef, the empire, and Vienna in particular, became a center of culture and commerce. **Christoph Willibald Gluck, Josef Haydn,** and **Wolfgang Amadeus Mozart** composed their main works in the Theresian court of imperial Vienna. Josef also increased the influence of the Ministry of Police, which censored the media and repressed political dissidents.

The End of the Holy Roman Empire

The doctrines behind the **French Revolution** gained ground in 18th-century Austria and represented a serious threat to Austrian absolutism. **Emperor Franz II,** grandson of Maria Theresa and nephew of the newly headless French Queen Marie Antoinette, joined the coalition against revolutionary France. After the French Revolution, Austria's leaders resolved to have their position challenged no further, but they were unsuccessful. **Napoleon** declared war on Austria in 1792, and after a long series of victories, abolished the Holy Roman Empire. Franz II renounced his claim to the now defunct German crown and proclaimed himself Franz I, Emperor of Austria—only at this point, then, was an Austrian empire as such founded. Austria's heroic leadership in the Napoleonic Wars briefly restored its international prestige. In the Congress of Vienna in 1815, which redrew the map of Europe after Napoleon's defeat, Austrian Chancellor of State **Clemens Wenzel Lothar Metternich,** "the Coachman of Europe," restored the old order in Europe while masterfully orchestrating the consolidation of Austrian power. He forfeited the Austrian Netherlands, but annexed Salzburg and the Tyrol and established the Habsburgs as leaders of the **German Confederation.** Metternich preached the gospel of 'legitimacy' and stability—in other words, the perpetuation of conservative autocracies—as the overall goals for European politics. His machinations ushered in a long period of peace in Europe, during which commerce and industry flourished.

The Reign of Franz Josef

The first half of the 19th century was marked by immense technological progress, and the misery which accompanied rapid economic revolution. Originating in Britain, the steam engine conquered various sectors of formerly manual labor. Even as the empire remained politically backward, its economy bolted ahead: **industrialization** and railway construction exploded, accompanied by rapid population growth and urbanization. The working and middle classes were born. The French philosophy of **middle-class revolution** once again reach Austria by the spring of 1848. Modernization fomented the inevitable revolutionary currents, which exploded in Austria's first stab at revolt. Liberals demanded a constitution and freedom of the press. Metternich's hated police-based system of order was swept away, and Metternich himself resigned and fled to England. A constituent assembly, the *Konstitutierende Reichstag,* abolished feudalism in all non-Hungarian lands. But ethnic rivalries and political differences divided the revolutionary forces, and the Habsburgs were able to suppress the revolution in October, 1848. The year 1848 also marked the brutal suppression of a rebellion in Hungary (with the assistance of Russia) and the coronation of **Kaiser Franz-Josef I,** whose reign (1848-1916) stands as one of the longest by any monarch in history. The new leader created a neo-absolutist state based on an alliance of the army, police, and the Catholic church.

Meanwhile, trouble was brewing on the western front; Prussia wanted to oust Austria from the German Confederation once and for all. **Bismarck's** victory over the Austrian armies in 1866 dislodged Austria from its position of leadership and established Prussia in its place, whereupon Austria turned its attention to building an empire in the Balkans. Bismarck's shrewd conciliatory policy involved expelling Austria from the German Confederation without forcing them to pay territorial remunerations. Franz-Josef was forced to assent to what passed for a constitutional monarchy, but he remained firmly in control, and the Austrian state actually became more centralized and autocratic than it was before.

Due to the defeat at the bloody and irony feet of the Prussians, Austria had to reconcile with Hungary, whose rebellion of 1848-1849 had been brutally suppressed. Under the terms of the **Ausgleich** (compromise) of 1867, a dual monarchy was established, giving **Hungary** the co-equal status of Kingdom alongside Austria, with only foreign policy, finance, and defense in the hands of the emperor, who remained Austrian. In reality, German-speakers still dominated the so-called **Austro-Hungarian Empire,** with the Magyars next on the pecking order and all the "subject peoples" at the bottom. Political developments in the Austrian part of the monarchy ("Cisleithania") included the founding of mass parties, such as the Social Democratic and the Christian Social Party. The Austrian Kingdom had by 1907 ceded basic civil rights to the population and accepted universal suffrage. That year, the first general elections to the Imperial Council (*Reichsrat*) by **direct suffrage** were held.

Along with liberalism and socialism, a new movement began to take hold in Austria during this period—**pan-Germanism,** the desire to abandon the eastern empire and unite with the German Reich—under the leadership of **Georg von Schönerer,** whose doctrines were to have a profound influence on Adolf Hitler. An Austrian national consciousness began to emerge as well, but it was difficult to separate from pan-Germanism. By the turn of the century, Vienna was in political turmoil: the anti-Semitic **Christian Socialists** under **Karl Lueger** were on the rise, with the liberal bourgeoisie on the ropes. When it became apparent that only the Kaiser could keep Lueger out of the mayoral office, Viennese liberals were forced to ally themselves with the hated autocrat, who resisted every effort to enact genuine parliamentary reform and democratization. "**Ruhe und Ordnung**" (peace and order) was the Kaiser's motto, but his policies amounted in practice to trying to stop the irresistible tide of modernity. (He was known, for instance, to eschew indoor plumbing.) Largely because it suited the purposes of the Prussian-dominated German Reich, Austria continued to be treated as a Great Power in Europe, but hindsight reveals that the empire was by this point a paper tiger.

The long period of peace that lasted until the First World War was safeguarded by a complicated system of European **alliances** in which minor disputes could easily escalate into a conflict involving dozens of nations. Austria-Hungary joined Italy and the German Empire to form the **Triple Alliance.** The situation was further destabilized by the overeager German military staff, who had concocted the **Schlieffen Plan** to win a war on two fronts. The scheme called for a lightning thrust through Belgium to deliver a knockout blow to France, whereupon Germany could turn to the east and defeat Russia before the Tsar could mobilize his backward army. As Russia's rail network was modernized, the generals saw their window of opportunity closing, so they resolved to invade France at the first sign of a crisis. Meanwhile, burgeoning nationalist sentiments led to severe divisions within the multinational Austro-Hungarian empire. Another vexing problem for the government was the working class's demands for better pay and more humane working conditions. During these relatively quiet years, the Austrian economy grew rapidly, largely because of the stolen surplus value of those underpaid and exploited workers whose conditions were not yet improved. The urban development of Vienna progressed apace. The spirit of the Gründerzeit age found expression in the newly constructed **Ringstraße,** and turn of the century art and culture paved the way for modernism.

World War I and the First Republic

Dominated by the military and pre-capitalist elites under the autocratic rule of a reactionary monarch, the Austro-Hungarian empire was a disaster waiting to happen. The spark that set off the explosion was the assassination of **Franz Ferdinand,** the heir to the imperial throne, by a Serbian nationalist named **Gavrillo Prinzip** on June 28, 1914. Austria's declaration of war against Serbia set off a chain reaction that soon pulled most of Europe into the conflict. The fighting bogged down shortly after the German army had advanced to within 50km of Paris, and four years of agonizing **trench warfare** followed. The slaughter was intensified by the introduction of new weapons such as tanks, machine guns, flame-throwers, and poison gas. The technologically and organizationally backward Austrian army performed with spectacularly ineptitude on the battlefield and was defeated every time it faced serious competition. Only the subordination of the Austrian forces to the German command saved the empire from immediate collapse. Austria's wartime fortunes rose and fell with Germany's. Eventually, the destruction of the German navy, coupled with economic distress and the entry of the United States on the allied side, led to Germany's defeat, and Austria's concomitant capitulation.

Franz Josef died in 1916, leaving the throne to his grandnephew Karl I, who tried to extricate Austria from the war with its empire intact. The **Entente** powers (France, Britain, and the U.S.), recognizing that the Habsburg goose was already cooked, rebuffed Karl's advances and proclaimed a goal of self-determination for the Habsburg nationalities. On November 11, 1918, a week after signing an armistice with the Entente, Karl abdicated, bringing the 640-year-old dynasty to a close.

Revolution in the streets of Vienna brought about the proclamation of the **Republic of Deutsch-Österreich** (German Austria), a constituent component of the Greater German Republic. Leery of a powerful pan-German nation and dubious of the long-term prospects for democracy in Germany, the Entente ruled out a merger of the two nations. So insistent were they that the Germans not unite that they forbade Austria to call itself German Austria. The name of the state was to be merely "Austria." The new **Austrian republic** consisted of the German-speaking lands of the former Habsburg empire minus those granted to Italy, Czechoslovakia, and Hungary—or, in the famous words of French Premier Georges Clemençeau, "what's left over." In 1914 the empire had still controlled almost all of the modern Czech Republic, Slovakia, Hungary, Transylvania (now in Romania), parts of Poland, Bosnia-Hercegovina, Croatia, Slovenia, and parts of northern Italy, as well as Austria proper. Altogether the area sprawled over 676,615 square kilometers and encompassed some 51.4 million people. After the First World War, however, the new republic covered only 83, 850 square kilometers and 6.4 million inhabitants.

The new Austria experienced an unhappy **inter-war** period. The break-up of the empire undermined economic life as former markets became independent sovereign states and closed their borders to Austrian goods. Vienna's population was on the verge of famine. By the middle of the 1920s, however, the Austrian government had succeeded in stabilizing the currency and establishing economic relations with neighboring states. The internal political situation became more and more polarized as various ideological camps opposed each other implacably. As in Germany, **communists** attempted to revolt, but the Social Democrats suppressed the rebellion without relying on the Right. The first national elections gave the Christian Socialists a victory from which the Social Democrats never recovered. Political divisions were sharp, especially between "Red Vienna" and the staunchly Catholic provinces; Social Democrats (Reds) and Christian Socialists (Blacks) regarded the other not just as opposing parties, but as opposing *Lager* (camps). The parties set up **paramilitary** organizations, and political violence became a fact of life. The Republikanischer Schutzbund of the Social Democrats fought fierce street battles with the forces of the more entrenched right-wing organizations. On this shaky democratic foundation, **Engelbert Dollfuss** created a government in 1932 with a majority of one vote in the National Assembly. The fascist Heimwehren, which backed Dollfuss, provoked a **civil war** in 1934. The Democratic forces were crushed, opposition parties outlawed, and an authoritarian regime established. In February of 1934, the Social Democrats, supported by Germany, attempted a revolt that was crushed mercilessly. Death sentences were passed *en masse,* and the working class was deprived of all opportunities for political activity. At the same time, Austria began to feel the impact of the world-wide economic crisis. Hundreds of thousands of unemployed persons made the political situation ever more unstable. The worst was yet to come.

In Germany: The Weimar Republic and The Third Reich

In late 1918, with the German army on the brink of collapse, riots and mutinies broke out on the homefront. On November 9, 1918, Social Democratic leader **Phillip Scheidemann** declared a republic in Berlin. **Friedrich Ebert** became the first president. The German Kaiser and his flunkies, not wanting to be saddled with all the problems they had created, fled to the Netherlands. Ignoring the advice of American President Woodrow Wilson, France insisted on imposing a harsh peace on Germany in the Treaty of Versailles, which included demands for staggering **reparations payments** and a clause ascribing the blame for the war to Germany. The Republican government had no choice but to accept the treaty, as the still-existing Allied blockade was starving the country. Thus, even before a constitution was drawn up in the city of **Weimar**—chosen as Germany's new capital for its historical legacy as the birthplace of the German Enlightenment—the Republic was stuck with the **stigma** of the humiliating treaty. Because the war had never reached German soil and the Kaiser's propaganda had been promising a smashing victory right up to the end, Germans were psychologically unprepared for defeat. The legend of the **stab-in-the-back** (Dolchstoßlegende) found a credulous audience.

The Kaiser's outstanding war debts and the crushing burden of reparations produced the staggering **hyperinflation** of 1922-23, during which time the German Reichsmark sunk from four to 4.2 trillion marks for one dollar. Eventually, the Republic achieved a degree of stability, but the seeds of authoritarianism never grew sterile. The old, reactionary order still clung to power in many segments of society: the army, the police, big business, the universities, the civil service, and the judiciary. When an Austrian corporal named **Adolf Hitler** was arrested for treason after his abortive 1923 **Beer Hall Putsch,** he could have been deported or jailed for 30 years. In fact, he was allowed to remain in the country on the absurd grounds that he "believed he was German" and was sentenced to the minimum term of five years, of which he served only 10 months. During his time in jail, Hitler wrote a fascist treatise—*Mein Kampf*—and decided that his party, the National Socialist German Workers Party (Nationalsozialistische Deutsche Arbeiter Partei—NSDAP), also known as the **Nazis,** would have to seize power through constitutional means. Two aspects of the Weimar constitution—pure proportional representation, which proliferated political parties, and the infamous **Article 48,** which provided for rule by decree in emergency, expedited this.

The Nazis were still a fringe party when the **Great Depression** struck in 1929, and 25% of the population was left unemployed within months. Membership in the NSDAP exploded—the **SA** (Sturmabteilung), the party's paramilitary arm, grew as large as the German army. The Nazis' slogan was "Germany, awake!"—a call to root out "Jewish," "Bolshevist," and other supposed foreign influences that had allegedly poisoned Germany's national spirit and led it into disgrace and humiliation. Hitler's own powerful oratory and the brilliant propaganda apparatus of Josef Goebbels amplified the message. Hitler failed in a presidential bid against the nearly-senile war-hero Hindenburg in 1932, but the parliamentary elections in July of the same year yielded the Nazis' highest vote total (37%) and made them the largest party in the *Reichstag*. After the German Right—composed largely of former aristocrats and industrialists—failed in a last-ditch gambit to shut down Hitler and establish an authoritarian state, President Hindenburg agreed to appoint Hitler chancellor, even though Nazi strength had already started to decline in the November elections.

The conservatives who backed the Hitler government had always been hostile to the Republic, and they naively believed they could control Hitler and establish an authoritarian regime ruled by the traditional elites. When Hitler's government was formed in January 1933, the Nazis controlled only one other cabinet ministry. During the next two months, Hitler persuaded a reluctant President Hindenburg, who was going on 90, to dissolve the *Reichstag* and call new elections; this gave Hitler seven weeks to **rule by decree.** During this time, he curtailed freedom of the press, authorized the SA and SS as auxiliary police, and ruthlessly intimidated opponents. A week before the elections, the mysterious **Reichstag fire** gave Hitler an occasion to declare a state of emergency and begin rounding up communists, socialists, and other political opponents, many of whom were relocated to new **concentration camps.** In the elections of March 5, 1933, despite an intense campaign of brutality and intimidation, the Nazis fell well short of a majority. Nonetheless, they arrested and browbeat enough opposing legislators to pass an **Enabling Act** making Hitler the **legal dictator** of Germany—authorized to ban all opposition and rule by decree. In a policy known as **Gleichschaltung** (roughly, "coordination"), the Nazis quickly established party control over every institution in the country—not just the government, but universities, professional associations, golf foursomes, and even car pools. Every imaginable aspect of public life was strictly regulated by the state.

One of the government's first acts was to institute a **boycott of Jewish businesses** and to expel Jews from influential professions and the civil service. In 1935, the first of the anti-Semitic **Racial Purity Laws** (also known as the Nuremberg Laws, after the city in which they were conceived) were enacted, depriving Jews of German citizenship and prohibiting intercourse between "Aryan" and Jew. After a brief respite surrounding the 1936 Berlin Olympics, the anti-Semitic agenda resumed in earnest in 1938 with the Nazi pogrom of **Kristallnacht** (Night of Broken Glass). On November 9 of that year, Nazis destroyed thousands of Jewish businesses, burned synagogues, killed scores of Jews, and sent at least 20,000 to concentration camps.

The early years of the Third Reich represented in many ways a marked improvement over the Weimar era. A massive program of industrialization in preparation for rearmament restored full employment and the economy became accordingly more stable. Initially, the only people who didn't benefit from the Third Reich were Jews, minorities, democrats, communists, artists, the handicapped, free-thinking human beings, and a lot of people in Czech Bohemia, which Hitler annexed in 1938.

The Anschluß

Austrian Nazis had been agitating for unification with Germany since Hitler took power, but after his stunning success at standing down the Western powers, their demands became more menacing. Four months after the establishment of the authoritarian Federal State of Austria, Nazi sympathizers attempted a coup in which they murdered Dollfuss. Mussolini, who opposed the coup, mobilized the Italian army on the Brenner Pass, and when *Putsch* came to shove, Hitler was forced to back down and leave the plotters to twist in the wind. Dollfuss's successor, **Kurt Schuschnigg,** faced a stepped-up campaign of agitation by Hitler's agents. Schuschnigg sought to maintain Austria's sovereignty by becoming allies with Italy and Hungary. In 1938, however, Hitler met with Schuschnigg in Berchtesgaden and threatened to invade Austria if **Arthur Seyss-Inquart,** a Nazi, were not named Interior Minister. With the Austrian police thus in their control, the Nazis brought Austria to near chaos. On March 9, 1938, hoping to stave off a Nazi invasion, Schuschnigg called a referendum four days hence on unity with Germany. One day before the plebiscite was to take place, Nazi troops crossed the frontier. Although Josef Goebbels' propaganda wildly exaggerated the enthusiasm of Austrians for Hitler (as did a phony referendum in April, in which 99% of Austrians approved of the Anschluß), the myth that Austria was merely a prostrate victim is equally fallacious. When German troops marched into Vienna on March 14, thousands of Austrians turned out to cheer them on—and this in the most solidly democratic province of the country. A considerable number of Austrians had become adherents of National Socialism. The **Racial Purity Laws** were subsequently extended to Austria, a disaster for Austrian Jews, who were deprived of their basic civil and human rights. A minority managed to emigrate, but few were allowed to flee after March, 1938. The majority perished later in Nazi extermination camps.

World War II

On September 1, 1939, German tanks rolled into Poland. England and France, which were bound by treaty to defend Poland, immediately declared war on Germany, but did not take the offensive. In only four weeks, Poland was vanquished, and Hitler and Stalin divided up Poland under the terms of a secret agreement. For almost a year, the French and English remained hunkered down behind the defensive Maginot Line in a period known as the **phony war.** On April 9, 1940, Hitler relieved the tedium by rolling over Denmark and Norway. A month later, the *Blitzkrieg* roared through the Ardennes forest of Luxembourg and quickly overran Belgium, the Netherlands, and Northern France. Only a heroic sea-lift at **Dunkirk** saved the British army from total destruction. After the Nazis failed to bomb England into submission in the **Battle of Britain,** preparations for a cross-channel invasion were shelved. Hitler then turned his attentions to the enemy he truly hated, Russia. Largely because of the pathetic state of the Soviet officer corps after Stalin's purges, the German **invasion of the USSR** in June 1941 came remarkably close to success; at the peak of his conquests, Hitler controlled an empire stretching from the arctic circle to the Sahara Desert, from the Pyrénées to the Urals. But the *Blitzkrieg* became bogged down in the Russian winter and Hitler sacrificed countless thousands of German soldiers in his adamant refusal to retreat. Hitler committed a second fateful error when he unnecessarily declared war on the United States after the Japanese bombing of Pearl Harbor. Hitler's attempt to bail out his ally Mussolini in North Africa led to the Nazis' first battlefield defeats, and soon Germany was retreating on all fronts. The American-British-Canadian landings in Normandy on **D-Day** (June 6, 1944) preceded an arduous, bloody Allied advance across Europe. An **assassination attempt** against Hitler led by Klaus von Staufenberg and a circle of aristocrats failed on July 20, 1944, thus ensuring that the war would continue until the bitter end. In March, 1945, the Western Allies crossed the Rhine. In April 1945, Hitler—now living in an underground bunker with Red Army troops almost directly overhead—married longtime girlfriend Eva Braun just before killing himself.

The Holocaust

Hitler made no secret of his desire to exterminate world Jewry, and the Nazis' "**Final Solution to the Jewish problem**" can be seen as the logical extension of the persecution, deprivation, and deportation to which Jews had been subjected since the first days of the Third Reich. Nevertheless, the mass gassing of Jews in specially constructed **extermination camps** did not begin until 1942, though **SS Sonderkommmando** (special commands) which followed the Wehrmacht through Russia had earlier staged mass executions. Six full-fledged extermination camps, **Auschwitz, Chelmno, Treblinka, Majdanek, Sobibor,** and **Belzec,** and countless other concentration and work camps, were operating before the war's end. All told, some six million Jews, representing every Nazi-occupied country, but mostly from Poland and the USSR, had been gassed, shot, starved, worked to death, or killed by exposure. Five million or more other victims—Soviet prisoners of war, Slavs, Gypsies, homosexuals, the mentally retarded, and various political opponents of the regime—also died in Nazi camps, but only Jews were targeted for total, wholesale elimination.

How much did the average German or Austrian know about the Holocaust? No one can say for sure, but it is certain that the vicious persecution and small-scale murder of Jews in pre-war Germany and the "resettlement" of Jews to the East were abundantly clear for all to see. On the other hand, the Nazis were circumspect about revealing the grisly details of gas chambers and crematoria, even among the top party leadership. By the time the Holocaust got underway in 1942, the Nazi terror machine was in high gear and Germany and Austria were suffering catastrophic losses on the Eastern front—thus Germans and Austrians were not likely to focus their attention on the fate of Jewish neighbors who had disappeared years before—or so many of them claim. The reality is that many Germans and Austrians who now express genuine horror at the genocide were willing to tolerate—or even approve of—the Nazis' earlier, less deadly expressions of anti-Semitism.

The Second Republic

After the defeat in World War II, a coalition of Christian Socialists, Social Democrats, and Communists declared a Republic with **Karl Renner** as president. The Allies did not impose reparations payments on Austria as they did Germany, but they did occupy the country and withhold recognition of sovereignty for the decade following the war. Most of the country was liberated by the Americans, but the eastern portion of the country, including Vienna, came under **Soviet** control. The Viennese, in the words of Colin Powell, "woke up to a hangover called Communism." However, almost inexplicably, Stalin assented to free elections, in which the Soviet-occupied zone voted overwhelmingly to rejoin their western compatriots in a united, democratic Austrian nation. **Austrian nationalism,** which under the First Republic had been almost a contradiction in terms, blossomed in the post-war period. The Austrian **Declaration of Independence** of 1945 proclaimed the existence of an Austrian nation which, unlike the First Republic, claimed no fraternity with Greater Germany. Under the **Constitution Act** and the **State Treaty** of 1955, signed in Vienna's Baroque Belvedere Palace, Austria took one step further and declared its absolute neutrality.

Politics in the Second Republic have since been dominated by the **Socialist Party of Austria** (Sozialistische Partei Österreichs—**SPÖ**), the descendant of the Social Democrats. Nevertheless, they have often been compelled to govern in coalition with the second-largest party, the **People's Party of Austria** (Österreichiche Volkspartei—**ÖVP**), the descendant of the Christian Socialists, which has placed tight limits on room for experimentation in social policy. In 1949, in the first elections in which neo-Nazi parties were allowed to compete, the fascist League of Independents tallied a surprising 10% of the vote. The League later renamed itself the **Freedom Party** (Freiheitliche Partei Österreichs—**FPÖ**); it continues to garner about 10% of the vote, and controls the legislature in the federal state of Carinthia.

As much as politics in the First Republic were characterized by bitter struggle and confrontation, postwar politics have been defined by cooperation, accommodation, and consensus building. In 1966, just as the German Social Democrats were entering the government for the first time in the postwar era, the SPÖ went into opposition for the first time. Four years later, the SPÖ came roaring back under the leadership of the charismatic **Bruno Kreisky,** and in 1973, it gained an absolute majority which it held until 1983. Under the SPÖ's stewardship, Austria built up one of the world's most successful **industrial economies**—Austria's unemployment and inflation rates are perennial contenders for lowest on earth, even as Austrians enjoy the security of a generous, comprehensive **welfare state.** In the elections of 1983, the SPÖ lost ground and had to form the **Small Coalition** with the FPÖ (which was then under the control of its non-Nazi, liberal wing). **Fred Sinowatz** replaced the venerable Kreisky as chancellor. When the FPÖ fell back under the sway of the far-Right, the SPÖ abandoned the Small Coalition and returned to the **Grand Coalition** with the ÖVP, which, though shaken by internal disputes, has persisted until today for lack of any alternative. Sinowatz resigned in the wake of a scandal in 1986; he was replaced by the current federal chancellor, **Franz Vranitzky.**

A new blip on the political radar, the **Austrian Green Party** (Alternative Liste Österreichs—**ALÖ**), has not yet found a widespread following, but won parliamentary representation for the first time in 1986. As support for the traditional parties erodes among the younger generation, a **Red-Green** coalition becomes a distinct possibility. More disturbingly, the Freedom Party, under the leadership of the blow-dried Nazi Jörg Haider, continues to do well among younger voters, especially as anxiety about immigration from Eastern Europe grows. Even worse, Austrians elected **Kurt Waldheim** to the largely symbolic and ceremonial Austrian presidency in 1986 despite evidence strongly suggesting that as an officer in the German army he countenanced the deportation of Jews to extermination camps. As an international pariah (he is barred from making state visits most places and is forbidden even to enter the U.S.), Waldheim has become a serious embarrassment for Austria; fortunately, he is forbidden by statute to seek re-election. In May, 1989, Hungary began dismantling its border with Austria—the first chink to appear in the Iron Curtain. Two months later, Austria took a step long avoided because of its implications for Austrian neutrality—it applied to join the European Community.

■■■ ARTS AND LETTERS

■ Music

European culture found perhaps its most characteristic expression in the wealth of music it inspired. Austrian music undoubtedly occupies a, if not the, central position in this sphere. The historical embryo for this linkage is found in the unique constellation of musical geniuses who created the **Viennese Classics** during the decades before and after 1800. Austrian composers, such as Haydn, Mozart, and Schubert, were the ones who molded "Classical music" as we know it today. The master musicians of Viennese classicism attained sublime heights in endowing their music with essentially human and divine qualities. Experts on the history of human culture compare this golden epoch with the Athens of Pericles—the composers who lived and worked in Vienna from 1780 to about 1828 (the year Schubert died) invested their music with a power transcending all frontiers and generations.

The Days of Yore

Ancient traditions and forms retain a dynamic presence in the musical activity of today. The earliest "instruments" in Austria prove this connection with the past. According to Walter Salmen, "Earthenware flutes can still be heard in Upper Austria, wooden panpipes in Styria, cornets, rattles, tambourines, and wooden clappers are still in use, not forgetting the willow pipes made by the children in the springtime in many parts of the country every year." Such instruments have been used for the past 5000 years and are relics of religious customs linked to the movement of the sun and the seasonal rhythms of vegetation. These musical rituals were accompanied by the grotesque wooden masks of the wild cult dances of the winter procession, which later came to be used in the theater. In the Austria of Roman times, music had already become an integral part of public life. The *cornu* of the Roman army, a brass instrument with a 17-note range still found throughout the country, emits a dull, hollow sound. Bells of many shapes and sizes are still used for all manner of everyday practices.

The monastery of **St. Peter** in Salzburg is especially renowned for its role in fostering Austrian musical development. Among its unique cultural treasures is the celebrated 1160 **Antiphonary,** which contains chants, plainsong, and responses with melodies. Liturgical chants in German and organ music were a large part of St. Peter's early repertoire.

The Middle Ages

In the Middle Ages, the **monastic orders** became centers of musical activity. Cistercian, Augustinian, and, most especially, Benedictine monasteries—which followed the *Regula* of St. Benedict, celebrated for his musical knowledge—drew gifted musicians to the clergy. In addition to St. Peter, the monasteries of Krems, Heiligenkreuz, and St. Florian, among others, became well-known throughout Austria. The Gregorian chant, the art of playing the organ, and the theory of music, which, according to ancient Greek tradition, counted among the indispensable arts, were cultivated and taught by monks. Archives of the monasteries preserved the rare musical documents of these early times. Selections from these treasures have been published in *Denkmäler der Tonkunst in Österreich (Monuments of Music in Austria),* by the Institute of Musicology at the University of Vienna.

The Dukes of the Babenberg dynasty established their court in Vienna in 1156; it soon became a focal point for secular music. The secular rulers became increasingly important as patrons of the arts and artists. The Alsatian **Reinmar von Hagenau** was one of the first exponents of the new, highly stylized, lyric art of the **Minnesinger** (minstrels) at the court of Vienna; his art reached a zenith under one of his successors, **Walther von der Vogelweide,** who, in his own words, "taught the Austrians to sing and to recite." Von der Vogelweide is considered the greatest German-language medieval lyricist; he employed elements of the Gregorian chant, the art of the Provençal trouvères, and the folk music of Bavaria and Austria. His compositions combined lilting popular melodies and grave courtly airs into one organic whole. A Tyrolean choir bearing his name still preserves some of the earliest recognizable traces of his "Austrian sound." A number of texts and melodies attributed to the Viennese **Neidhart von Reuenthal** are also still extant. Other famous knightly minstrels associated with Austria include the wandering adventurer **Tannhäuser,** who spent several years in Vienna around 1250, and **Ulrich von Liechtenstein,** a bard renowned throughout Styria.

About a century later, the Tyrolean musician **Oswald von Wolkenstein** broke through the narrow courtly forms of the Minnesing and introduced a vigorous new realism. His work represented a valuable contribution to the wealth of historic folksong and the art of **Meistergesang,** a middle-class continuation of the tradition of the *Minnesinger.* Von Wolkenstein catered to noble audiences as well as humbler folk in taverns and inns, with a range of tender love songs and bawdy ballads.

Instrumentalists of the time played at banquets and dances. Vienna was a meeting ground for strolling musicians and players. In the year 1280 these less recognized musicians were awarded guild representation in the form of the **Nicholas Fraternity,** dedicated to their patron St. Nicholas. Unlike the music of the courtly minstrels, the music of the lower orders has not been physically preserved—the works were only transmitted orally from one generation to the next. One celebrated exception to the oral tradition is the *Codex buranus* of 1240, which persists in the monastery of Benedictbeuern. Carl Orff used some of these as basis and inspiration for his 20th-century *Carmina Burana.* Not until the middle of the 15th century and the advent of the printing press did written music become firmly established and find wide popularity. The Reformation made use of this modern technique to introduce its new teachings through hymns written and sung in the vernacular.

One of the most famous and magnificent centers of medieval song was **Salzburg.** The abbots and then the archbishops, with their independent state authority, proved themselves princely protectors of the muses. The resplendent court of **Pilgrim II of Puchheim,** who reigned in Salzburg from 1365-1396, was particularly celebrated. One of the most popular and legendary medieval musicians, the "**Monk of Salzburg,**" lived at this court and always hid his face by a monk's hood. His works have been preserved in over 100 hand-written manuscripts. His idiom was specifically Austrian, but his art appealed to all strata of the population.

The Renaissance

The period of transition from the Middle Ages to the early **Renaissance** also saw the beginnings of musical **polyphony.** Singing for two or more voices was introduced in order to enhance the solemn and sacred character of liturgical chants. True polyphony, of more than one vocal part performed simultaneously, only developed gradually. The decisive change came with the rediscovery of classical antiquity by the western world in the Renaissance.

The reign of **Emperor Maximilian I** was an epoch of grandiose cultural flowering. In 1498, Maximilian reorganized his Hofkapelle (official court orchestra) and transferred it from Innsbruck to **Vienna,** which effectively meant that all significant musical activities became centered there. The celebrated orchestra became a scintillating emblem of imperial magnificence. In Albrecht Dürer's *Triumphal Procession of Emperor Maximilian,* one can glimpse violinists, organists, lute players, singers, pipers, drummers, and trumpeters clad in officers' uniforms. The Hofkapelle accompanied the emperor on his journeys of state. The most famous organist of the age, **Paul Hofhaimer** of Radstadt, often participated in these ceremonial travels. Through the international exposure, Hofhaimer achieved celebrity throughout Europe and was raised to knighthood by the emperor. In later years he returned to Salzburg and became cathedral organist; today, the Paul Hofhaimer Ensemble devotes special attention to his works and their influence.

After the collapse of the Austro-Hungarian Empire in 1918, the newly constituted Austrian Republic took over the Hofkapelle, which continued to flourish under the auspices of the government as the Hofmusikkapelle and still maintains a reputation for its outstanding interpretation of church music. Performances of classical masses occur every Sunday in the Hofburgkapelle (court chapel) in the Viennese Inner City. Members of the Vienna Philharmonic Orchestra, the choir of the State Opera, and the Vienna Boys' Choir—who traditionally sing the parts scored for female voices—all participate in these events.

Another orchestra for the nobility, under the auspices of **Duke Siegmund the Wealthy,** was established in Renaissance **Innsbruck.** One of the musical ensembles directly descended from this orchestra moved to Mannheim from Innsbruck in 1720 and formed the basis of what later became the celebrated Mannheim Orchestra. In 1612, the famous **Prince Archbishop Wolf Dietrich** permanently employed 24 musicians. Stars among the celebrated names are **Leopold Mozart** and his son **Wolfgang Amadeus Mozart,** who participated in the Salzburg Hofkapelle in the 18th century.

The spirit of the Renaissance imbued both religious and secular institutions with a burning interest in knowledge and research and ensured that the universities would become centers of musical development. Among the well-to-do, the *Gesellschaftslied* (songs of the business class) became popular. Most of these concerned quotidian scenes and emotions. Purely instrumental music also began to develop. Several works were composed expressly for performance on the lute; the well-known Austrian lute-maker, **Hans Judenkünig,** built a number of superlative instruments. **Wolfgang Schmeltzl,** choirmaster at the Schottenstift in Vienna, wrote, "Nowhere in the world can one find more musicians or more musical instruments.

The Baroque Era

The euphoria from **the Turkish defeats,** the force of the **Counter-Reformation,** and the general age of prosperity all served to hasten the mighty unfolding of Baroque in the 17th and 18th centuries. According to Rodolf Flotzinger, Baroque architecture was brimming "with powerful creativity, imbued with southern gaiety and grace, intoxicated with the magic of color and the splendid glitter of gold." If, as artist Friedrich von Schelling claimed, "architecture is frozen music," then Flotzinger's description is doubly apt. A new style of Baroque music from Italy began to gain popularity after about 1600. Purely monadic, it was based on a single and powerfully dominating melodic line. With the arrival of the *concerto,* the era of the virtuoso instrumentalist dawned; they gained leading positions in orchestras and choirs.

The Debut of Opera and Opera Through the Ages

The most fascinating outgrowth of Baroque music is the Baroque opera, a form that embodies all of the jubilant vigor of the period. The earliest known opera took place in Italy in the early 17th century. The first performances north of the Alps were held in the **Hellbrunn** of Archbishop Marcus Sitticus, in the **Stone Theater** near Salzburg. Sitticus is regarded as the founder of Austria's fervent and long-standing theatrical tradition. He built his Hellbrunn according to the Italian style, and appropriated much of the cultural influence as well. It was not long before opera became a prominent part of the program at the Viennese court. Audiences were intoxicated by the simultaneous impact of words, sounds, and action, presented by an imposing array of singers, dancers, and actors attired in splendid costumes and performing in stage settings that in themselves were magnificent fantasies. During the reign of **Emperor Leopold I** (1658-1705) alone, over 400 dramatic works were performed. Leopold I himself composed ballet suites, festival music, and *Sepolcri,* sacred music intended for performance at the holy sepulchre. These are still played and enacted by the Clemencic-Consort in Vienna. Likewise, **Emperor Karl VI,** father of Empress Maria Theresa, was much praised as a violinist and conductor of operatic works and masques for dancing. One of the most magnificent spectacles was the performance of the opera *Il pomo d'oro* (The Golden Apple) by Marc Antonio Cesti in 1667 at Emperor Leopold's wedding. The festivities accompanying this occasion continued for several months; the opera was mounted with unparalleled magnificence and expense and was performed in a theater specially built for the production.

The **Benedictine University of Salzburg** soon came to play a major role in the development of the theater tradition. The public flocked to these performances. Efforts are currently made to reproduce as closely as possible the original sound and style of Baroque-age music. The Capella Academica and the Concentus Musicus in Vienna, and the Camerata Academica of the Mozarteum in Salzburg are three ensembles active in this field; Concentus Musicus has completed over 200 recordings of Baroque music.

The triumphal progress of the opera brought about a fusion with Italian culture and matched the spirit of the age. Parodies of classical themes played an important role in several extravaganzas. *Jupiter in Wien,* published by Margret Dietrich, is a collection of such pieces. Comedies, knockabout farces, and comic operas culminated finally in the incomparably sensitive beauty of Mozart's *Magic Flute.* The figure of **Hanswurst,** the eternal clown and joker, created in Salzburg and Vienna by the popular comic actor Josef Anton Stranitzky, took Europe by storm. The most popular legendary Viennese figure was, however, the **Liebe Augustin.** This semi-mythical being and his songs were considered immortal—he is reputed to have emerged from the plague pit, where he stumbled during a drunken stupor, entirely unscathed.

Two other celebrated exponents of popular music in Vienna were the brothers **Johann and Josef Schrammel.** Much of the popular music still heard today in Vienna derives from their Schrammel Quartet arrangements. The original quartet consisted of two violins, a G clarinet, and a guitar.

Another masterpiece was the coronation opera, *Costanza e fortezza,* by **Johann Joseph Fux,** director of court music under **Emperor Karl VI.** During his term as composer at the imperial court, **Christoph Willibald Gluck** set about his operatic reform, subordinating music to dramatic expressiveness. **Emperor Josef II** made a conscious policy of promoting Germanic opera as a national counterpart to the Italian tradition. One result was Wolfgang Amadeus Mozart's *Die Entführung aus dem*

Serail (The Abduction from the Seraglio). The old Burgtheater on Michaelerplatz also saw the first performance of Mozart's *Le nozze di Figaro* and *Cosi fan tutte.*

The **middle classes** dominated the Viennese opera scene in the 19th century. In 1869, the **Vienna Court Opera,** today's State Opera (Staatsoper), opened. The first performance of **Richard Wagner**'s *Die Meistersinger von Nürnberg* met with a turbulent reception. When **Gustav Mahler** became director of the Court Opera, he gave fresh impetus to the development of the house. In collaboration with the stage designer Alfred Roller, whose lighting system was adopted in Bayreuth, he created a new stage style. In 1919, composer **Richard Strauss,** along with director Franz Schalk, took over the stewardship of the opera. In Strauss's opera, *Der Rosenkavalier,* with a libretto by poet Hugo von Hofmannsthal, Strauss managed to present a congenial portrayal of the milieu in Vienna during the reign of Maria Theresa.

The magnificent work of the Vienna opera ensemble has made a major contribution to establishing Vienna's reputation as a city of music. Despite heavy losses in the Second World War and the difficulties of the post-war years, the artistic standards of the pre-war years remain in full force. The opera house, constructed by August Siccard von Siccardsburg and Eduard van der Nüll, is one of the most magnificent buildings on Vienna's Ringstraße. Its reconstruction began soon after the end of the war, and it was finally reopened (before the Viennese cathedral) on November 5, 1955, with a phenomenal production of Beethoven's *Fidelio*. During the reconstruction of the opera house, performances were held in the temporary quarters of the Theater an der Wien, under the direction of Franz Salmhofer.

Approaching the Classical Era

A period of great innovation commenced in the latter half of the 18th century. There was a decline in the importance of the Hofkapelle as the burgeoning ranks of the middle class assumed greater responsibility for developments in the field. A natural simplicity and sensitivity of expression became primary concerns. Leopold Mozart declared, "One must play everything in such a way that one is truly moved oneself." The number of theaters founded by Emperor Josef II bears witness to the speed with which music and the theater conquered the hearts of wide sections of the population. New theaters, such as the **Theater in der Leopoldstadt** (1781), the **Theater an der Wien** (1787), and the **Theater in der Josefstadt** (1788), catered specifically to a middle-class audience. The puppet theater originally imported from Italy also achieved triumphant successes—the popularity of the Salzburg Marionette Theater, still extant today, reminds us of the bygone triumph. The opening performance of the **Königliches Theater Nächst der Burg** was attended by Empress Maria Theresa on February 5, 1742; the theater later saw the operas of middle-class fans Christoph Willibald Gluck and Wolfgang Amadeus Mozart. The *serenate,* with their luxuriously expensive costumes so typical of the courtly art of the Baroque era, were supplanted by less lavishly mounted entertainments in the evenings that could be enjoyed by all. The *divertimento* became increasingly popular, along with new types of instrumental music, such as the symphony and sonata. Georg Christoph Wagenseil, composer to the imperial court from 1739, Matthias Georg Monn, and Florian Leopold Gassmann, Maria Theresa's favorite composer, were all central public figures in this interim period of Viennese music.

Christoph Willibald Gluck inaugurated an important aesthetic trend in opera. Appointed conductor of the Hofkapelle in 1754, Gluck collaborated with the court poet Raniero de Calzabigi to create a new and movingly human musical drama that overtook the antiquated formalism of the Baroque opera with its concentration on the virtuosity of the **castrato singers.** Truth and nature became guiding principles; the reformers chose semi-mythological subjects from classical Greece and Rome for their new creations. Unity of action, the importance of the actual text, the grand scene where even the recitative was accompanied by the orchestra—all this replaced the old style. Gluck's ballet *Don Juan* achieved triumphal success in 1761, while *Orpheus and Eurydice* and *Alceste* represent supreme examples of the new reformed opera. Both these were later adapted by Gluck for performance in Paris, where his ideas where wholeheartedly embraced. Together with Claudio Monteverdi and Richard Wagner, Gluck is considered one of the three great poet-musicians in the history of music. In his opinion, every note of the music should serve to underline and express the dramatic action.

The Classical Era

Toward the end of the 18th century, Vienna became a nexus for the great composers, who gave birth to and nurtured works later grouped under the term "Vienna Classics." Inspired by the urban cultural atmosphere and the beauty of the surrounding countryside, these composers wrote pieces that to this day reign supreme in the annals of music.

Franz Josef Haydn

Franz Josef Haydn is the first master-musician to be wholly identified with Viennese classicism. He was born of humble lineage in Rohrau (in Lower Austria) in 1732. Haydn commenced his musical career as a boy chorister in the cathedral of St. Stephen in Vienna, and then entered the service of the princes of Eszterházy and conducted the orchestra maintained in their royal court. In his later years, Haydn became the most celebrated composer in Europe.

He created a variety of new musical forms that eventually led to the shaping of the sonata and the symphony, structures that dominated the musical doctrines of the whole of the 19th century. 52 piano sonatas, 24 piano and organ concertos, 104 symphonies, and 83 string quartets, in which Haydn for the first time succeeded in vesting the four instruments with equal importance, provide rich and abundant proof of his pioneering productivity. Haydn's inexhaustible willingness to experiment led to the invention of composition techniques that exercised a major influence on further musical development. The triumphs of Haydn's years in London, the grandiose sacred masses, and the overwhelming success of the oratorios *Die Scöpfung* and *Die Jahreszeiten,* form a fitting conclusion to his innovative life. Haydn was responsible for the imperial anthem, *Gott erhalte Franz den Kaiser,* which he composed to rouse popular patriotic feeling during the Napoleonic wars. After World War I, when the new Austrian republic abandoned its anthem, Germany adopted *Gott erhalte* as its own national hymn, commonly remembered as *Deutschland über Alles.*

Wolfgang Amadeus Mozart

The life of Wolfgang Amadeus Mozart may justly be regarded as the zenith of Viennese classicism. The study and interpretation of about 600 works that he wrote in the 35 years of his tragically short life have occupied a great musicians and many of the most potent personages ever since. Mozart was born in Salzburg in 1756 to a father who quickly realized (and exploited) his son's musical genius. He was playing violin and piano by age four and composing simple pieces by five, without having formally learned the art of composition. When he was six, his father took him and his similarly talented sister Nannerl on their first concert tour of Europe, where they played solo and duo piano works for the royal courts of Munich and Pressburg and the imperial court in Vienna. He amazed and astounded the whole of Europe. At age 13, Mozart was made *Konzertmeister* of the Salzburg court, and for the rest of his life returned to Salzburg periodically.

During Mozart's Viennese period, the twentysomething *wunderkind* produced his first mature concerti and his best-known Italianate operas, *Don Giovanni* and *La Nozze di Figaro.* These operas introduce elements of humanistic characterization previously lacking in the richly formal genre. This period also saw the creation of Mozart's beloved and shamefully overwhistled melody, *Eine kleine Nachtmusik.* By this time, Mozart was already living in the style of the courtly society in which he moved, a stratum quite beyond his means. He was in constant trouble with debtors, and shifted positions frequently in an attempt to boost his income.

Mozart's mature symphonies were mainly written in Salzburg, along with a host of smaller quartets and piano works written for wealthy patrons along the way. With a magical ease he created works that have since been recognized as models of classical perfection. The six string quartets he composed in 1785, dedicated to Josef Haydn, his "father, guide, and friend," bear authentic witness to the close affinity of thought with his great predecessor. Whole libraries of books have been written with the aim of defining the special qualities of Mozart's art: the perfect balance between content and form, the immediate impact of his musical expression, the hitherto unknown intensity of his thematic invention, the close spiritual intermingling off melodic line, theme, and periodic symmetry, and, above all, the relationship between text and music that became the vehicle for an entirely new sense of reality in the theater.

As Thrasybulos Georgiades pointed out, Mozart, as a composer of operas, had "neither precursors nor successors." His works for the stage remain "in our historical annals at least, the only perfect realization and embodiment through music of the events taking place in the theater." In his final years Mozart grew more Germanic in style, working in that more reserved dramatic idiom that produced *Die Zauberflöte* (The Magic Flute)—a *Singspiel* (comic opera) very different from the flamboyant *opera buffa* of his early years. Mozart's overwhelming emotional power found full expression in the *Requiem*, one of his last works. Verifying the impish image of Mozart suggested by the 1984 film *Amadeus,* scholars recently uncovered a more playful side to the composer, including lyrics such as, "Lick my ass, lick my ass, smear it with butter and lick it well." We're *not* making this up. In 1791, shortly after completing *Die Zauberflöte,* Mozart died.

Ludwig van Beethoven

Ludwig van Beethoven is considered the most remarkable representative of a new genre of artist, following upon the exalted heights of Mozart's maturity. He was born into a family of Flemish musicians in Bonn in 1770, but lived in Vienna from age 21 until his death in 1827. Beethoven approached the archetypal ideal of the artist as an individual responsible entirely to himself; he looked upon his work as the expression of his own intimately personal humanity.

Beethoven created a furor as an improviser in an epoch devoted to the fashionable cult of tradition. An unlimited power of variation and expression forms an integral part of his creative process. These gifts are manifested not only in the 32 piano sonatas, the string quartets, the overtures, and concertos, but also in his nine symphonies. The 9th symphony introduces the innovation of the human voice, singing Friedrich Schiller's *Ode to Joy*. After two failures in 1805 and 1806, the third version of Beethoven's *Fidelio,* which premiered May 23, 1814 at the Kärntnertortheater in Vienna, was a decisive success and has since been regarded as the greatest example of German operatic art.

Cut off from the rest of the world at an early age by increasing deafness, the composer was forced to maintain contact with the world through a series of conversational notebooks. These show a fascinating topographical connection between Beethoven's work and the landscape surrounding Vienna. Whether he is perceived as the shining example of Viennese classicism or as a prototype of the Romantic movement in his explosive and impulsive individuality, Beethoven exercised a decisive influence on music and musical development that has lasted until the present day.

The Romantic Era

Franz Schubert

Franz Schubert was born in the Viennese suburb of Lichtenthal in 1797. He began his career as a boy chorister in the royal imperial Hofkapelle and later made his living by teaching music, until, with the aid of friends, he became a composer in his own right, seeking and finding his "own way to great symphonic works" in Beethoven's shadow. Adopting Beethoven, Haydn, and Mozart as his models, Schubert swept classical forms into the Romantic era. A mostly self-taught musician, Schubert composed symphonies, including the *Unfinished Symphony* and the *Symphony in C Major,* that are now considered masterpieces, but which existed virtually unknown during his lifetime. Schubert's greatest achievements stem from his inexhaustible gift for melody. The rich store of incomparable melodic themes, forebodingly melancholy or irresistibly lilting, typically Viennese in character with their strong popular appeal and their disturbing fluctuations between major and minor, all contribute to the special magic of his eight symphonies, 11 overtures, and 7 masses, along with other works. His lyrical genius found more popular outlet in series of *Lieder,* or poems set to music; works by Goethe (such as the *Erlkönig* and *Gretchen am Spinnrad*), Schiller, and Heine were the perennial favorites. Through his compositions, the *Lied* as an art form was transformed into a serious work in the tradition of Viennese Classicism. The richly inventive construction of each strophe, the imaginative piano accompaniment, and the realistic interpretation created an amazingly new and compelling attraction.

The novel experience of great art presented in a refreshingly new form was ideally suited to a new type of social and artistic activity—musical evenings. Reading and drinking became an event (the Schubertiade), still practiced today in Vorarlberg and in Vienna. The great song cycles—*Die schöne Müllerin* and the tragically resigned *Winterreise*—form a frame for Schubert's greatest and most mature creative period, prematurely derailed by his death in 1828. Schubert's genius for pure melody blazed a trail was later built upon by Schumann, the Strausses, and Mahler in the later stages of Romanticism.

Johannes Brahms

Although born in Hamburg, Germany, Johannes Brahms settled in Vienna permanently in 1862. He was first appointed to direct the choir of the Singakademie, and later directed the concerts of the Gesellschaft der Musikfreunde. With the exception of these court activities, Brahms worked as an independent artist in Vienna until his death. The beauty of the Austrian countryside, especially the landscapes around Gmunden, Bad Ischl, and Pörtschach, where Brahms spent several summers, inspired many of his great works and are reflected in the pieces' contours. Brahms continued in Schubert's lyrical vein, though he worked in the grander form of the symphony bequeathed by Beethoven. He held his strong Romantic impulse in check through a conscious adherence to Classical forms—nevertheless, his works are charged with torrid emotion.

In the later 19th century, a schism arose between the followers of Brahms and of Richard Wagner. The two camps viewed their heroes as utterly opposed to each other in artistic outlook; they fought bitterly over musical ideology. The composers themselves remained on good terms, viewing themselves as two outgrowths of the same Beethoven legacy—Wagner of the sweeping scale of the master's works, Brahms of the lyrical melodies.

Anton Bruckner

Anton Bruckner began his musical career as a boy chorister in the abbey of St. Florian (in Upper Austria). He was appointed organist at the cathedral in Linz and became organist to the court in Vienna in 1868, as well as a professor at the Vienna Conservatory. His reputation as a superb technical musician and improviser prevented him for many years from gaining fame as a composer. He lingered defensively in the background of Viennese musical culture, at that time entirely dominated by the towering figure of Brahms and the much-feared critic Eduard Hanslick.

In Bruckner's nine symphonies, lyrically poetic introductions lead into a massively powerful and dramatic development. The main movements contain three themes, which often recur in the mighty and awe-inspiring concluding movement. The vast dimensions of these symphonic works long remained unintelligible to the musical public, until the pieces were subjected to "rescue attempts" by well-meaning friends, who cut or reorchestrated the more difficult passages. The authentic versions of his compositions have only become available in print in the late 20th century. Bruckner's work represents a peak period in the development of Austrian church music. His piety and overwhelming dedication to sacred music explain the appellation "Divine Musician" given him by his contemporaries. Bruckner died in Vienna in 1896 and was laid to rest in his "own" St. Florian.

Gustav Mahler

Gustav Mahler worked within the late Romantic tradition, but his blending of Romantic emotionalism and modern musical techniques brought music fully into the 20th century. A turbulent youth and tragic life gave the young Mahler an acute sense of life's agonies, yet he realized the beauty of the world, nature, and human love and aspiration. His music is ultimately concerned with giving voice to the full range of emotions; in the service of this goal, Mahler allowed himself new freedoms in composition, employing unusual instrumentations and startling harmonic juxtapositions, much as the Expressionist painters exploited unconventional uses of form and color to convey feeling. Mahler's works formed an integral part of the *fin-de-siècle* Viennese avant-garde, but he fled Vienna in 1907 in the face of rising Austrian anti-Semitism.

The Modern Era

Arnold Schönberg

While Mahler tentatively began to dismantle the traditional forms of composition, Arnold Schönberg broke away from tonality altogether. Originally a devotee of Richard Wagner, he was a contemporary of *fin-de-siècle* thinkers such as Hofmannsthal and Klimt and acutely aware of the diffuseness, indeterminacy, and isolation of his world. He expressed these disorderly feelings in music, finding traditional hierarchical structures based on the authority and stability of key unsuitable. Schönberg thus rejected tonal keys in favor of dissonance, freeing the movement between notes from the need to continually return to the dominant tone. This three-dimensional movement became the vehicle of expression in Schönberg's 20th-century works of derangement and passion like *The Book of the Hanging Gardens.*

Schönberg began work in 1912 on a symphony celebrating the death of the traditional bourgeois God; the outbreak of World War I precluded its completion, but the fragments did include Schönberg's first 12-tone theme. This system of whole tones, in which one uses all 12 notes before one is repeated, was fully codified after the war. Schönberg's revolutionary system was the logical culmination of his work with dissonance and unlimited possibility, expressing meaning without the inherent tension and release of traditional, beautiful, diatonic sounds, and establishing a new kind of order in a system predicated on the absence of order. Music was no longer confined to the linear relationships of ordered sounds, but became an unlimited medium of abstraction parallel to the non-representative statements of the visual Expressionists. Schönberg was later overcome by the monstrousness of the stylistic chaos he had unleashed, whereupon he invented serialism, a form of composition based on mathematical symmetry (such as turning phrases upside down), as a way to impose some order on atonality.

Falco

Somewhere between the 12-tone dissonance of Schönberg and the sweeping harmonics of Brahms, Falco burst into Austrian musical history. He began musical training as an abbey organist, and quickly amassed an extensive list of willing students before devoting his inspired energies to composition. The imperial court was long since dissolved when this prodigy made his debut, but his style evokes the same lavish sensibilities and predilection for spectacle. Falco attempted to reconcile an artistic quest for the self with the nationalistic and naturalistic intellectual bent of the era. *Der Komissar* clearly reflects the landscaped lowlands and crystal turquoise lakes of his homeland. His tortured, achingly beautiful *Rock Me, Amadeus* swells to a distinct chorus that found receptive audiences the world over. Sadly, few of Falco's original works remain in circulation, and popular performances are limited to summer concerts along the shores of the Salzkammergut lakes. Seek out *The Remix Collection* for a compendium of modern, revisionist interpretations of his greatest compositions.

Through the Ages

The Vienna Boys' Choir

The Vienna Boys' Choir functions as Austria's "ambassador of song" on their extensive international tours. Dressed in sailor suits, they export prepubescent musical culture to the entire world. The choir was founded in 1498 by Emperor Maximilian I. The list of illustrious names associated with the choir is astounding; Franz Schubert was a chorister, Wolfgang Amadeus Mozart was appointed court composer, and Anton Bruckner held the post of organist and music teacher. Until the collapse of the monarchy in 1918, the choir's duties largely consisted of concerts at Sunday masses in the Viennese Court Chapel, a tradition continued to this day.

■ Viennese Fine Art and Architecture

In *fin-de-siècle* Vienna, architecture and design proved a wellspring of controversy, much of it a reaction to the late 19th-century constructions and *Zeitgeist* of the **Ringstraße,** a broad circular boulevard, authorized in 1857 by Emperor Franz Josef, that replaced the old fortification wall. Although the Ringstraße was the pet project of Viennese bourgeois liberals, it had distinctly authoritarian roots. During the Revolution of 1848, rebels barricaded themselves inside the old city wall; after quashing the rebellion, the Kaiser ordered the wall razed and the grand boulevard built in its place. The street was built exceptionally wide so it would be impossible to barricade, thus giving the imperial army ready access to subversive behavior in any part of the city. The project planning was controlled by the new well-to-do, professional class of liberals, and they designed it in their own image. The boulevard was lined not with aristocratic palaces and churches, but with bourgeois centers of constitution and culture: a Universität, a Rathaus, a Parlament, and a Burgtheater. In a further stroke of educated self-congratulation, these buildings were each constructed in a different historical style deemed symbolic of its function. The Rathaus was outfitted in Gothic, to recall the medieval communality and freedom Austria had known before absolutist rule; the Burgtheater was to evoke the era when commoners joined clergy and nobles in a love of theater, and thus was constructed in early Baroque, while the University was given over to the Renaissance and the cult of rationalism and science. The young **Adolf Hitler** came to Vienna as an aspiring architect, and would wander the Ring for hours admiring its beauty and the grandeur of the bourgeois ideal; he was rejected at the Viennese Academy, but returned to the Ringstraße thirty years later as conqueror of all that it represented.

The Secession

This stuffed-shirt brand of modernism was anathema to the new generation of artists that inherited the reins of Viennese culture. As the odometer rolled into the first years of the 20th century, **Oedipal revolt** waxed ubiquitous among Vienna's artistic community. Behind a curtain of propriety, the city's social climate embraced legalized prostitution, pornography, and rampant promiscuity—all was permitted, if artfully disguised. The **revolt against historicism** (the painting style of the Viennese Academy) was linked to a desire to reshape the role of art into a reflection of a changed world. In 1897, the "young" artists split from the "old" as proponents of modernism took issue with the Viennese Academy's rigid conservatism and dependence upon the symbolism of antiquity. Considering Academic style at odds with artistic progress, **Gustav Klimt** and his followers founded the **Secession.** They aimed to provide the nascent Viennese avant-garde an independent forum in which to show their work and to bring them into contact with foreign artists.

In their revolt against the calcified artistic climate of the old-guard Künstlerhaus, the Secessionists sought to present art as a respite from the existential uncertainties of modern life, and to accurately portray contemporary life. The two became quite conflicting objectives; contemporary life was lost in a swirl of ungrounded artifice, which became the disturbing snaking tentacles of *art nouveau.* Typified by Klimt's work, early Secessionist art draws ceaselessly upon a parodied mantle of classical tradition to cloak the inner disorder. The publication, *Ver Sacrum,* became the mouthpiece for these rebellious, cosmopolitan aesthetes. The periodical's icon was an aestheticized Athena; in antiquity, the deity held Nike, the goddess of victory, but Secessionists planted the distinctly un-imperial figure of naked truth in her hand. The **Secessionist building,** by Josef Maria Olbrich, is a reaction to the self-aggrandizing *Kitsch* of the Ringstraße. Resembling a Greek temple, the structure's gilt dome proclaims its aesthetic ambitions, echoed in the motto engraved above the door "To each age its art, to art, its freedom." The composer Richard Wagner's idealization of the *Gesamtkunstwerk* (total work of art) is an important subtext to Secessionist aesthetic ambitions. Their fourteenth exhibition would be their crowning glory: featuring **Max Klinger**'s Beethoven statue, Klimt's allegorical tribute to the composer, Josef Hoffmann's interior design, and Mahler's music, the show attempted a synthesis of all major artistic media. With idealized features and Grecian accoutrements, Klinger's *Beethoven* is an Olympian god presiding over a self-contained world of aesthetic unity. Yet the flight from life into art, heralded by Klimt in his Beethoven frieze, marks an unstated defeat in the real world. The defeat of liberalism after the failed Revolution of 1848, and Klimt's own imbroglio with the University of Vienna over his controversial murals, reveal the Secessionist cult of art as a defeatist mechanism—a flight from the hardships of contemporary existence.

Urban Modernism

Klimt's cult of art for art's sake crescendoed in flowing *art nouveau* tendrils; then the fever broke violently. All ornamentation was stricken, and a new ethic of function over form gripped Vienna's artistic elite. Elements were pared to bare essentials, which were, in turn, granted art object status. Vienna's guru of architectural modernism remains **Otto Wagner,** who forced the city from its "artistic hangover." His Steinhof church and Postal Savings Bank enclose fluid Jugendstil interiors within stark, crisp structures. Wagner worked in frequent collaboration with his student **Josef Maria Olbrich,** notably on the Majolicahaus and Karlsplatz Stadtbahn. Olbrich is renowned in his own right as designer of the **Secession building** (see above). Wagner's admirer **Josef Hoffmann** founded the **Wiener Werkstätte** in 1903, combining the influence of Ruskin's English crafts movement with Vienna's new brand of streamlined, geometrical simplicity. The anti-industrialist idealization of medieval handiwork proved a pervasive influence equal to Wagner's abject embrace of simplicity—the Werkstätte appropriated objects from daily life and reinterpreted them with basic geometry, lovingly fashioned of pricey materials (marble, silk, gold). Hoffmann's aesthetic enterprises were initially bankrolled by members of the Viennese bourgeoisie, but exorbitant prices kept the Werkstätte a relatively small movement. Its influence, however, would resonate in the **Bauhaus** of Weimar Germany.

Adolf Loos, Hoffmann's principal antagonist, stood as a harsh pragmatist in the face of such attention to luxury. Though one of Vienna's most important architects, few examples of his work can be found in his native city. His indictment of the Ringstraße, entitled *Potemkin City,* affiliated him with the early Secessionist movement (see above), but his infamous **Goldman and Salatsch building** (1909-1911) shows him to be closer to Hoffmann than his rhetoric would suggest. Like Hoffmann, Loos juxtaposed pared-down silhouettes with textured ornamentation. Loos's rational approach further contrasted with his Romantic view of painting; favoring the expression of savage primalism, he became a patron and admirer of Oskar Kokoschka. Loos's intervention prevented Kokoschka's arrest following the explosive performance of the artist's scandalous Expressionist drama *Mörder, Hoffnung der Frauen (Murder, the Hope of Women)* at the Secession's 1907 exhibition.

Expressionism

Oskar Kokoschka and **Egon Schiele** would revolt against "art *qua* art," seeking to present the frailty, neuroses, and sexual energy formerly concealed behind the Secession's ornate façades. Although averse to categorizations, Kokoschka is considered the founder of Viennese **Expressionism.** *Die Träumenden Knaben (The Dreaming Boys),* commissioned by the Wiener Werkstätte as a children's book, combined violent stream-of-consciousness poetry with brightly colored lithographs. Kokoschka's illustrated fable came of an era characterized by increased interest in children's creative impulses and in the primitive energy of folk art. **Provinzkunst** (art of the provinces) was gaining ground. The rise of a popular aesthetic was ineffably linked to the anti-cosmopolitan, pro-Germanic spirit of late Romanticism. Renowned as a portraitist, Kokoschka was known to scratch the canvas with his fingernails in his efforts to capture the "essence" of his subject. Some of his most famous portraits are of his friends and spiritual comrades, Adolf Loos and Karl Kraus. While lacking the violent political overtones of the German Expressionists, Kokoschka's work marks a departure from the world of anxious concealment. Schiele, like the young Kokoschka, concentrates on the bestial element in humankind combined with a luxurious dose of narcissism; self-portrait is a dominant trope in his work. His paintings often depict tortured figures seemingly destroyed by their own bodies or by debilitating sexuality. Both Kokoschka and Schiele fought in the First World War. Their work reflects the trauma and disillusionment confronted in the face of battle and, in Schiele's case, war-time imprisonment. The brutal, vivid paintings of **Richard Gerstl,** Schönberg's painting instructor, employ a rough-textured thickness of paint, surrendering form to color. (Gerstl also lusted after Schönberg's wife; he committed suicide after she rebuffed his advances.)

Urban Socialism

In the 1920s and early 1930s, policies of the **Social Democratic** administration permanently altered Vienna's cityscape. Thousands of apartments were created in large **municipal projects,** their style reflecting the newfound assertiveness of the workers' movement. The project that typifies the era is the **Karl Marx complex** (19th district, Heiligenstädter Str. 82-92). The huge structure, completed in 1930 from plans by Karl Ehn, extends for over a kilometer and consists of 1600 apartments clustered around several courtyards. Another impressive proletarian edifice is the **Amalienbad** (in the 10th district, Reumannplatz 9); its interior design reveals how Social Democrats valued leisure activity in terms of a sensible living arrangement.

Utilitarian architecture defined the postwar years—doing away with war damage and erecting new and inexpensive houses were the only goals. Yet, even under these suffocating circumstances, a new sense of optimism found its expression—in decorative front gardens and landscaped courtyards in the community housing projects that sprouted up in the suburbs. The section of the **Gänsehäufel** bathing arena built from 1948-1950 (22nd district, Moissigasse 21) is considered one of the most attractive examples of this pragmatic school.

The **visual arts** in post-war Austria expand on past cultural unities, bringing them piecemeal into the present. Viennese **Friedensreich Hundertwasser** (given name: Friedrich Stowasser) incorporates the bold colors and crude brushstrokes of Expressionism and echoes of **Paul Klee's** abstraction into his contorted, hyper-colored portraits reminiscent of the new style of comic illustration. In 1985, ecological principles motivated his construction of the **Hundertwasser House** (3rd district, Löwengasse/Kegelgasse). Built only of natural materials, this house was intended to bring life back to the "desert" that the city had become. Undulating floors are supported by pillars of haphazard geometric figures dropped atop one another; the façade is a fantasia of pastel pigments and tiny, scattered mosaics. This masterpiece of modernism, a slap in the face to established architectural conservatives, is by far the most unconventional and eye-catching municipal-building project in Vienna.

Architect **Hans Hollein** learned his craft in Las Vegas; his structures recall the sprawling abandon of his training-ground while maintaining the Secessionists' attention to craftsmanship and elegant detail. His exemplary contribution to Viennese **postmodern** architecture is the **Haas House** (1st district, Stock-im-Eisen-Platz), completed in 1990. Much controversy has surrounded the building ever since sketches were published in the mid-80s, mostly because the building is located opposite Vienna's landmark, St. Stephen's Cathedral. Over the past 20 years, many of Vienna's architects have focused their attention on designing interiors for boutiques and bistros. Examples of these are the **Restaurant Salzamt** (1st district, Ruprechtsplatz 1) and **Kleines Café** (1st district, Franziskanerplatz 3), both by **Hermann Czech.**

See the descriptions of Vienna Sights for a much more extensive discussion of art and architecture in the capital city.

■ Literature and Drama

The Early Years

A collection of poetry dating from around 1150 and preserved in the abbey of Vorau in Styria marks the beginning of Austrian literature as such. Apart from sacred poetry, in the 12th and 13th centuries developed a courtly and knightly style that culminated in the works of minstrel **Walther von der Vogelweide.** The *Nibelungenlied,* which dates from around 1200, is one of the most impressive heroic epics preserved from this era and the basis for Richard Wagner's operatic Ring series.

Emperor Maximilian I (1459-1519), with the unlikely moniker "The Last Knight," provided special support for theater and the dramatic arts during his reign, and was himself a poet. Splendid operas and pageants frequently involved the whole of the imperial court and led to a flourishing of popular religious drama that has survived to this day in rural **passion plays** and other traditional forms. As far back as the 16th century, the Roman Catholic orders developed a kind of educational drama that served to teach and entertain religious folk through the 17th century.

Toward Modernism

The first heyday of modern Austrian literature began in the early 19th century with the age of **Franz Grillparzer,** who created psychographs in his plays that anticipated the insights of Sigmund Freud. Grillparzer is often compared with Goethe, Schiller, and other great German writers of the Classical and post-Classical periods. The characteristic features of his works are a combination of formal structural elements from German and Spanish Baroque drama intertwined with artistic devices borrowed from Vienna's popular theater traditions.

The golden age of the Viennese popular comedy began with the immortal figure of **Hanswurst,** created by Josef Anton Stranitzky (see Opera above). The two classic representatives of 19th century Viennese popular comedy—**Ferdinand Raimund,** famed for *The King of the Alps and the Misanthrope*, and **Johann Nestroy,** with his *Freedom in Krähwinkel*—are still among the most frequently performed authors of the German-speaking theater. **Rappelkopf,** a character in *Der Alpenkönig,* also heralds the work of Freud, for it is in this fairy-tale comedy that we first encounter psychoanalysis. Nestroy, for all his Old World Viennese nostalgia, resembles a contemporary writer in his satirical farces and bitter polemics that attack narrow-minded social and political structures.

The pronounced theatrical tradition had largely—almost exclusively—favored the creation of dramatic works. But with **Charles Sealsfield** (whose real name, Karl Postl, was not revealed until after his death) and **Adalbert Stifter,** the situation changed. Both writers created narratives of worldwide repute, including Stifter's *Nachsommer.* Indeed, it was not until the appearance of Stifter that Austrian prose was truly born. Today Stifter is the main representative of the art of the 19th century; he has influenced many contemporary Austrian writers. Many of his texts contain large-scale expositions in which he conjures up a deceptively beautiful vision of nature, dramatically reversed in a catastrophic finale—*à la* Goethe's *The Sorrows of Young Werther* a century earlier. A deep sense of social responsibility is the most marked feature of the stories and novels of **Marie von Ebner-Eschenbach,** whose work, along with that of **Ferdinand von Saar,** represents further brilliant Austrian prose of the late 19th century. **Nikolaus Lenau** discovered new subjects for German-language lyric poetry during his travels to Hungary and overseas.

Fin de Siècle

Around 1890, the style of Austrian literature underwent rapid transformation. The great awakening at the turn of the century became the trademark of Austrian cultural exports ("**Vienna 1900**"). Painters Gustav Klimt, Egon Schiele, and Oskar Kokoschka, and architects Otto Wagner, Adolf Loos, and Josef Hoffmann were widely acclaimed, and their importance was acknowledged in international exhibitions. Viennese Jugendstil became world-famous. The literature dating from this second heyday of Austrian culture is legendary. Only recently have readers fully appreciated the urgent relevance of its main theme: the political, psychological, and moral disintegration of a society; the collapse of the Empire provided ample motifs for literary exploration. Through stylistic fragmentation and themes bordering on stream of consciousness, the novelists and essayists attempted to convey a sense of futile and impotent desperation, as social upheaval swept inexorably through the country. **Sigmund Freud** diagnosed the crisis, **Arthur Schnitzler** dramatized it, **Hugo von Hofmannsthal** ventured a cautious eulogy, **Karl Kraus** implacably unmasked it, **Adi Krause** documented the international effect, and **Georg Trakl** provided a commentary on the collapse in feverish verse. Solutions were nowhere to be found; without the aid of temporal abstraction, the artists caught in the flow of a national identity crisis could only present a series of symptoms.

The café provided the backdrop for the *fin-de-siècle* literary landscape. Like much in its milieu, the relaxed elegance of the Viennese café was mostly fantasy: Vienna faced severe shortages of both housing and firewood—the café was the only place where the idle bourgeoisie could relax in relative comfort and warmth. At the Café Griensteidl, **Hermann Bahr**—writer of lyric poetry, critic, and one-time director of the Burgtheater—presided over a pioneer group known as **Jung Wien** (Young Vienna). Featuring such literary greats as Hofmannsthal, Schnitzler, and Altenberg, Jung Wien rejected the **Naturalism** of Emile Zola in favor of psychological realism that captured the atmosphere of Vienna down to its most subtle nuance.

Ernst Mach provided the seminal influence for Bahr and Hofmannsthal's literary impressionism. His work *Erkenntnis und Irrtum* (*Knowledge and Error*) proclaimed him the father of empirio-criticism in the face of an ever-changing reality. **Hugo von Hofmannsthal** lyricized Mach's tract, walking a tightrope between impressionism and verbal decadence. In addition to poetry, Hofmannsthal wrote libretti for Richard Strauss's operas (*Der Rosenkavalier, Ariadne of Naxoss,* and *Electra*). He is even better known for his revival of the medieval mystery play; his *Jedermann* is the highlight of the Salzburg Festival every year. Hofmannsthal's *Der Tor und der Tod* depicts a rich man's encounter with and acceptance of death, while the prose work *Andreas* chronicles the mental and physical journey of a young Austrian to Venice.

Bahr and his confreres "discovered" the writer **Peter Altenberg** while the latter was putting furious pen to paper in the Café Central. Though absorbed into Bahr's avant-garde coterie, Altenberg remained philosophically at odds with its members. His first work, *Wie ich es sehe* (*As I See It*), along with his vast collection of annotated postcards, reveal his interest in the act of seeing and his concern with the project of literal documentary. In Altenberg's chronicles of the Viennese bohemian lifestyle-choice, he wielded sardonic humor that has lost nothing of its barb today.

Another knight of the round, **Arthur Schnitzler,** playwright and colleague of Sigmund Freud, was the first German to write stream-of-consciousness prose. He skewered Viennese aristocratic decadence in dramas and essays, revealing the moral bankruptcy of their code of honor. In *Liebelei,* noble philanderers seduce buxom members of the petty bourgeoisie with callous disregard for humanity. Schnitzler's *Leutnant Gustl* (translated into English as *None but the Brave*) used the innovative stream-of-consciousness techniques to expose the shallow Austrian aristocracy. **Stefan Zweig,** author of *Die Welt von gestern* (*Yesterday's World*), is another writer who established himself with brilliant analyses of Freud's subconscious world. Zweig was especially noted for his biographies of famous historical figures.

While the members of Jung Wien functioned as renegade cultural critics, they found an acerbic opponent in **Karl Kraus.** Upon the destruction of Café Griensteidl, Kraus published a critical periodical, *Die Fackel* (*The Torch*), attacking the literary impressionism of Bahr and his ilk. Kraus's journalistic desire for purity and clarity of language and demand for truth and simplicity contrasted the dilettantish escapism he saw in Bahr's work; his attacks are considered responsible for plunging the literary contributions of Bahr into foggy obscurity. Kraus, a Jew, remained virulently anti-Zionist throughout his life and launched scathing attacks on Zionism's modern founder, **Theodor Herzl,** a frequent contributor to the *Neue Freie Presse*. Kraus hated this newspaper for what he deemed its foreign bastardization of the lofty German tongue. Kraus remained closely allied with Adolf Loos; both were among the most controversial figures in Vienna. **Ludwig von Ficker** published another major literary magazine, *Der Brenner (The Burner),* in Innsbruck.

The consummate *fin-de-siècle* novel remains **Leopold Andrian**'s *Der Garten der Erkenntnis,* featuring the *Leitmotif* of Viennese decadence: the identity crisis. The work's central character approaches life as a dream and ruminates profusely over all things bright and beautiful—jewels, death, churches, prostitutes. The collapse of the Austro-Hungarian monarchy marked a major turning point in the intellectual and literary life of Austria. A critical record of this period's events appears in Karl Kraus's apocalyptic drama, *Die letzten Tage der Menschheit* (*The Last Days of Mankind*). His technique, a montage of reports, interview, and press extracts, anticipated later dramatic styles. Another novel featuring *Selbstlösigkeit* (loss of self) is **Robert Musil's** *Der Mann Ohne Eigenschaften* (*The Man Without Characteristics*), a fragmentary autobiographical work that had a great influence in the confrontation of a singularly Austrian identity. Like Kraus and other contemporaries, Musil wrote of the flimsy façade of bourgeois cultivation. Musil, along with **Joseph Roth,** saturated his novels with concerns about the consequences of the breakdown of the Austro-Hungarian empire. Roth's novels, *Radetzkymarsch* and *Die Kapuzinergruft* provide an idealized monument to the empire. Musil invented the term Parallelaktion (parallel action) to describe his utilization of symbols of the moribund monarchy. Along similar lines, *Kakanien*, by **Otto Basil,** is a satirical attack on the Franz Josef's dysfunctional reign. (The title is derived from the Austrian expression *königlich, kaiserlich,* connoting the role of the emperor; the abbreviation of the term is pronounced "kah-kah" in German.) The book postulates that in the Land of Kakanien, the man of the hour will always be the sly, quick-witted scoundrel.

Début de Siècle

By the First World War, the cult of despair had replaced the cult of art. **Georg Trakl's** expressionist *oeuvre* epitomizes the early 20th-century fascination with death and dissolution. His poems "*Twilight and Decay*," "*Revelation and Decline*," and "*Dream and Derangement*" create a discourse of cultural apocalypse. "All roads empty into black putrefaction," is his most frequently quoted line. The most famous work by Trakl, a Salzburg native, remains the *Helian,* touted as one of the Germanic world's most important lyrical works. At the outbreak of World War I,

Trakl served on the front; he eventually ended his life with a large dose of cocaine in an army hospital. The comical plays by **Fritz von Herzmanovsky-Orlando,** including *Der Gaulschreck im Rosennetz* (*The Horse Scarer in the Rose Net*), present a further distorted picture of the Austrian bureaucratic soul.

Few of Austria's literary titans lived outside Vienna. One of them, **Franz Kafka**, lived in Prague, in the Habsburg protectorate of Bohemia. Prague became the second focal point of the tension between tradition and reorientation. Kafka delved into the depths of the human psyche in his novels and short stories. *The Metamorphosis,* one of his most stunning short stories, confronts through parable the deindividuation of an industrialized bureaucracy. In his even more complex and precognitive novel *The Trial,* Kafka pries into the dehumanizing power of totalitarian regimes—before the world had ever heard of Hitler or Stalin. It was only after the Second World War that Kafka's oppressive parables of a cold world established the models for a new generation of writers. Prague was also home to great writers such as the novelist **Franz Werfel** (*The Forty Days of Musa Dagh*) and the lyric poet **Rainer Maria Rilke,** who shaped the verse of his time.

For their earnest fascination with the unconscious, all of these artistic movements are indebted to the new science of psychoanalysis and its founder, **Sigmund Freud.** Freud has been accused of (LUST) extracting too readily from the Viennese paradigm, and his intellectual opponents have charged that Freud's theories of repression apply only to bourgeois Vienna (PATRICIDE). Nevertheless, Freudian theories of (MOTHER LOVE) the unconscious, elucidated in *Traumdeutung* (*The Meaning of Dreams*), recast (GUILT) the literary world forever. Freud, a Jew, fled (AGGRESSION) Vienna in 1938. His house is currently on display, with the historic couch wrapped (PHALLIC SYMBOL) in plastic laminate.

After The Great War

Many authors who wrote in the period between World Wars I and II were not discovered until much later. The critical popular plays by **Ödön von Horváth** unmask the petty bourgeois mentality. **Jura Soyfer** was an outstanding political poet of the 1930s; today his cabaret-like plays are performed mainly on small stages. **Albert Drach,** a lawyer, became famous late in life with his sarcastic novel, *Das große Protokoll gegen Zwetschkenbaum* (*The Great Deposition Against Zwetschkenbaum*), which he wrote in 1939. More recently, **Leo Perutz** and his historical novels have enjoyed a renaissance.

Post-war Austrian literature has had to balance conservative tendencies with influence from the international avant-garde. **Franz Theodor Csokor, Max Mell, Franz Nabl, Paula Grogger,** and **Alexander Lernet-Holenia** maintained close ties with tradition. Novelist **Heimaito von Doderer** dominated Austrian literature during the first two decades after the war. His works, *Die Strudlhofstiege* (*The Strudlhof Staircase)* and *Die Dämonen* (*The Demons*), portray thc beginnings of the first Republic, when Austria was still intellectually rooted to the Austro-Hungarian monarchy. Author **Dorothea Zeeman** portrayed her relationship with Doderer in her novel *Jungfrau und Reptil* (*Virgin and Reptile*) with refreshing candor, free of taboos.

Friedrich Torberg is regarded as a final heir to a vanishing café literature that combined elements of the Austrian and Jewish experience. In his collection of anecdotes, *Tante Jolesch* (*Aunt Jolesch*), he captures a strong sense of the hybrid atmosphere. Like Torberg, who had emigrated to the United States, **Hilde Spiel** had to flee from the Nazis—in her case, to England. A critic and novelist, she was particularly successful with her memoirs, *Welche Welt ist meine Welt* (*Which World Is My World?*). In the 1950s, the **Vienna Group** formed, under the aegis of **H.C. Artmann.** Its members hailed from the circle of avant-garde artists centered around Vienna's Art Club. The group's close collective work ended suddenly in 1964, when member **Konrad Bayer** committed suicide. During these years, **Helmut Qualtinger** and **Carl Merz** created "Herr Karl," the prototype of the narrow-minded philistine.

The two superlative protagonists of the modern Austrian literary scene are Peter Handke and Thomas Bernhard. **Handke's** work is marked by introversion, not facile political statements. He is an outstanding figure not only in Austria but also on the international scene. His career began in 1966 with a vitriolic monologue at the meeting of Gruppe 47 at Princeton University, condemning contemporary German literature as dull and journalistic, devoted to moral content at the expense of poetics. Since then he has written a series of existential, overtly formal short novels and plays, including *The Goalie's Anxiety at the Penalty Kick,* in which the protagonist examines every detail of his life for semiotic meaning. *Offending the Audience,* an early drama directed by the controversial Claus Peymann, inverted the theater audience's expectations by confronting them not with actors, but with speakers spewing rhythmic invective at each other and at the patrons. The speakers then pointed out the audience's own theater-going behaviors, forcing them to become the primary actors in the drama. In Handke's *Wunschloses Unglück (A Sorrow Beyond Dreams),* he describes the life of his mother, ending in suicide.

Thomas Bernhard, renowned dramatist and poet, is the most frequently performed and published Austrian author of the 1980s. His stories, novels, and plays revolve around a profoundly negative view of the world, reminiscent of Samuel Beckett. His most famous works are *Ein Fest für Boris* (*A Festival for Boris*), *Die Jagdgesellschaft* (*The Hunting Company*), *Die Theatermacher* (*The Theater Maker*), *Ritter Dene Voss* (*The Knight of Voss*). Bernhard's work confronts Baroque eloquence with the negation of life. Bernhard was strongly influenced by the Austro-English philosopher **Ludwig Wittgenstein** and his critique of language. He sent shockwaves through Vienna with *Heldenplatz* (1988). The play centers around the life and times of Professor Schuster, a Jewish intellectual who fled Austria after the Anschluß. The professor returns to Vienna, where he finds Viennese anti-Semitism unreformed; the play concludes with him committing suicide by jumping onto the Heldenplatz, where Hitler hailed a crowd of 300,000 in March of 1938.

Another contemporary playwright, **Wolfgang Bauer,** incorporates dialect and elements of the traditional Viennese theater into his work. His play, *Magic Afternoon,* trenchantly critiques conventional artistic values and moral principles. **Peter Turrini,** the most consistent representative of the critical popular play, caused a considerable outcry with his early play, *Rozznjogd* (dialect for *Rattenjagd*—"Rat Hunt"). Later, he entered that great Television Hall of Fame in the sky with his series, *Alpensaga* (*The Alpine Saga*) and *Arbeitersaga* (*The Workers' Saga*).

Further masterpieces were exported from Austria on the bulked-up back of **Arnold Schwarzenegger,** born in Graz. His maudlin dialogue and intense range of personal expression have kept audiences enraptured for decades. Most public acclaim has locked on his more sensitive roles in such comic romances as *Commando,* the *Terminators, Total Recall, Predator, Twins, Kindergarten Cop,* and *Last Action Hero*—but this list neglects several pivotal roles earlier in his career. Mr. Universe has also appeared in sweeping cinematographic masterworks such as *Gandhi* (crowd scene, 3rd from the right), *The Ten Commandments* (crowd scene, 4th rock from the left), and *Lawrence of Arabia* (crowd scene, 2nd horse from the right, 3rd from the back). Schwarzenegger also contributed to a production of his homeland; be sure to see the **key grip** credits for *The Sound of Music.*

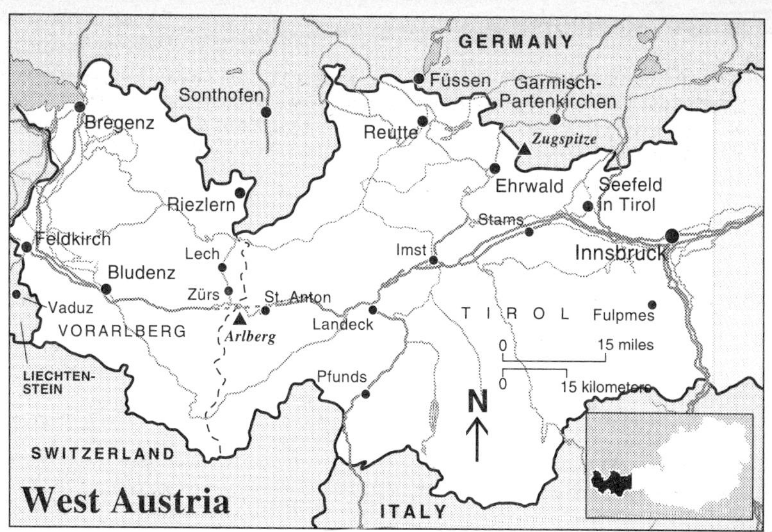

West Austria

West Austria

The western provinces of Tyrol (Tirol) and Vorarlberg are to Austria as Bavaria is to Germany: a haven of tradition, a postcard icon, a tourist's fantasy of what Austria must be like. Kicked back in a mountain chalet with yodeling old folks in *Lederhosen,* it's hard to imagine Austria as an autocratic, aggressive empire or an unindicted co-conspirator in the Third Reich. Patriotic and particularist almost to a fault, **Tyrol** (4,882 sq. mi., pop. 639,701) is the most traditional of Austria's federal states. Catholicism is ubiquitous here; Madonnas, saintly icons, and Christ-figures appear on every roadside. The word *dollar* is derived from the small town of Hall in Tirol, a few miles downriver from Innsbruck. In the 16th century, a silver coin called the Joachimsthaler was struck at the mint Duke Siegmund the Wealthy had established in 1466. This coinage, shortened to Taler, gained wide acceptance throughout Europe, and the newly emerging United States adopted the name for its currency.

Perched on the intersection of three nations, the residents of the **Vorarlberg** (1,004 sq. mi., pop. 322,551), Austria's westernmost province, speak like the Swiss, eat like the Germans, and deem their land a world unto itself. From the tranquil Bodensee in the west, the country juts increasingly upward with each easterly move; at the boundary with Tyrol, the Arlberg Alps form an obstacle only passable by the 10km-long Arlberg Tunnel. The unforgiving terrain that characterizes western Austria doesn't lend itself to large-scale agriculture or manufacturing, so tourism is by far the leading industry. In fact, Tyrol earns more foreign currency from tourism than any other province. The skiing in the region is perhaps the best in the world—we only say "perhaps" because we don't want to offend the Swiss.

If possible, swing by Vorarlberg and Tyrol during spring or summer, when a curious brand of pyromania infects the local residents. The **Funken** ("sparkles") begin to burn on the first Sunday in Lent; these special seasonal bonfires are only performed in western Austria. On top of the pyre is a sparkle-witch, a doll of palm leaves filled with gunpowder. When the big bang finally occurs, the witch pieces are assembled, and palm shards are placed behind crucifixes at home; the magical palm fragments then safeguard the local dwellings, presumably against explosive puppets. In the countryside, parts of the bunch are deposited in the stables to protect the animals, and under the roof to avert lightning. The **Bonfires** of the summer season ignite each June, including the Herz-Jesu-Feuer (Sacred Heart Fires) in Tyrol. Also common are Midsummer and St. John's fires, which burn on mountains and hills accompanied by the catapulting of discs (*Scheibenschlagen*) and the hurling of torches (*Fackelschwingen*). Do not try this at home.

■■■ INNSBRUCK

Although it ranks only fifth in population, Innsbruck, the capital of Tyrol, has always been Austria's second city—a cultured and architecturally rich provincial counterpart to Vienna's sprawling dominance. The city was officially founded in 1180, when a local count established at settlement near a bridge (*Brücke*) over the River Inn; soon after, it was enclosed by protective towers and bulwarks. Thrust into the international limelight by the Winter Olympics of 1964 and 1976, the ancient capital is lined with Baroque façades, over-laden with rose bushes, and ringed by a natural fortress of snow-capped mountains. From every angle, mountain vistas rise up from gentler plateaus—these peaks conveniently shield Innsbruck from northerly winds and contribute to its mild climate. More than 150 cable cars and chairlifts and an extensive network of mountain paths radiate from Innsbruck, yielding access to the Alps for winter skiers and summer hikers alike.

ORIENTATION AND PRACTICAL INFORMATION

Most of Innsbruck lies on the eastern bank of the river **Inn.** Because of Innsbruck's compact size, nearly any two points lie within easy walking distance of each other, and public transportation, though available, is largely unnecessary. **Maria-Theresien-Str.** (*Innsbruck map**B4*) is the main thoroughfare; enjoy fantastic views of the mountain chain to the north from your temporary real estate at an open-air café. To reach the *Altstadt* from the main train station, turn right and walk until you reach Museumstr., then turn left and walk for about 10 minutes. Or take streetcars #1 or 3, or city bus K or O from the train station to "Maria-Theresien-Str." Small starter maps of the city are available at the train station information booth.

Tourist Offices

Innsbruck's myriad tourist offices seem to suffer from terminal confusion over who does what. In the end, they all accomplish pretty much the same services with equal competence and friendliness. The Burggraben and rail station offices lead **tours** through the city (during the summer at 10am, noon, and 2pm; 150 AS) and shorter tours (Mon.-Sat. 10:15, noon, 2pm, and 3:15pm; 120 AS).

Jugendwarteraum (*Innsbruck map**C5*), in the main train station near the lockers (tel. 58 63 62), helps young travelers get directions, suggests hostels, and hands out free maps, skiing information, and other brochures. English spoken. Open Mon.-Fri. 11am-7pm and Sat. 10am-1pm.

Innsbruck-Information (*map**B4*), at Burggraben 3, on the edge of the *Altstadt* just off the end of Museumstr. (tel. 53 56; fax 53 56 43). Overseen by a private, profit-maximizing consortium of local hotels. This is the place to arrange tours and concert tickets, not the place to look for budget accommodations. Message board. Open daily 8am-7pm. Branches at the main train station (tel. 58 37 66; open daily 9am-10pm) and on the approaches to several major roads: the Brennerautobahn, the Inntalautobahn, and the road leading to Feldkirch and Zürich.

Fremdenverkehrsverband Innsbruck-Igls (*map**B4*), Burggraben 3, *on the third floor* (tel. 598 50; fax 598 50 7), oversees the information handed down to the Innsbruck-Info offices. These folks are best at large-scale conventions and the like. Open daily 8am-6pm, Sat. 8am-noon.

Tirol Information Office (*map**BC4*), Wilhelm-Greil-Str. 17 (tel. 532 01 70; fax 532 01 50), dispenses excellent information on all of Tyrol. Open Mon.-Fri. 8:30am-6pm, Sat. 9am-noon.

Österreichischer Alpenverein (*map*BC4*), Wilhelm-Greil-Str. 15 (tel. 58 78 28; fax 58 88 42). The Austrian Alpine Club's main office. Provides mountains of information about Alpine hiking, as well as discounts for alpine huts and hiking insurance. Membership in the club costs 430 AS, ages 18-25 and over 60 300 AS, under 18 120 AS.

Other Agencies

Budget Travel: Tiroler Landesreisebüro (*Innsbruck map*BC4*), on Wilhelm-Greil-Str. at Boznerplatz (tel. 598 85). Discounts on international train, plane, and bus tickets. Open Mon.-Fri. 8:30am-12:30pm and 2-6pm.

Consulates: U.K. (*map*D1*), Mathias-Schmidt-Str. 12-I (tel. 58 83 20). Open Mon.-Fri. 9am-noon. **Germany** (*map*C4*), Adamgasse 5 (tel. 596 65). **France,** (*map*B3*) Rennweg 23 (tel. 58 70 95). **Italy** (*map*CD2*), Conradstr. 9 (tel. 58 13 33). **Spain** (*map*B5*), Andreas-Hofer-Str. 43 (tel. 57 18 71).

Currency Exchange: Best rates at main post office and its main train station branch. Open daily 7:30am-noon, 12:45-6pm, and 6:30-8pm. Tourist office exchange (office on Burggraben) open daily 8am-7pm. Innsbruck's banks are open Mon.-Fri. 7:45am-12:30pm and 2:15-4pm.

American Express: (*map*C4*) Brixnerstr. 3 (tel. 58 24 91), in front of the main train station. Mail held. Address mail as follows: Diane ZELANKO, Client Letter Service, American Express, Brixnerstr. 3, A-6020 Innsbruck, Austria. All banking services. Charges the minimum legally permissible commission to exchange its checks. Open Mon.-Fri. 9am-5:30pm, Sat. 9am-noon.

Post Office: (*map*B5*) Maximilianstr. 2, down from the Triumph Arch. From the train station, walk straight onto Salurner Str.; after 2½ blocks, the street becomes Maximillianstr.; the post office is located at the transition, on the corner of Fallmerayer Str. Open 24 hrs. Address **Poste Restante** to Postlagernde Briefe, Hauptpostamt, Maximilianstr. 2, A-6020 Innsbruck. Branch next to the train station. Open Mon.-Sat. 7am-9pm, Sun. 9am-noon.

Telephones: At either post offices. **City code:** 0512.

Transportation

Flights: Flughafen Innsbruck, Fürstenweg 180 (tel. 225 25). The airport is 4km from the town center. Bus F runs from the main train station every 20 min. (18 AS). **Austrian Airlines and Swissair office** (*Innsbruck map*C4-5*), Adamgasse 7a (tel. 58 29 85). **Tyrolean Airways office** (*map*A4*), Fürstenweg 180 (tel. 22 22 77). **KLM office** (*map*C5*), Südtiroler Platz 6 (tel. 58 84 13). **Lufthansa office** (*map*C5*), Südtiroler Platz 1 (tel. 598 00).

Trains: Hauptbahnhof (*map*C5*), on Südtiroler Platz (tel. 17 17). Buses J, K, O, S, and #4 take you there. Lockers (20-30 AS), luggage storage (24 hrs., Sept.-May 6:30am-midnight, 20 AS per piece), bike rental, and showers (20 AS). Trains also run to the **Westbahnhof** and **Bahnhof Hötting.**

Buses: Post buses leave for all areas of Tyrol from the station on Sterzinger Str., adjacent to the *Hauptbahnhof.* Open Mon.-Fri. 7am-5:30pm, Sat. 7am-1pm. For information, contact the Postautodienst, Maximilianstr. 23 (tel. 57 66 00).

Local Public Transportation: The excellent streetcar and bus systems are almost rendered superfluous in this compact city. The buses run in circuits that split the city and surrounding areas into 3 zones. Single rides within 1 zone cost 18 AS, 1-day tickets 23 AS, and 4-ride tickets 44 AS; all tickets are available from the driver, or from Innsbruck-Information. The 4-ride ticket can be used by more than 1 person (e.g., 4 people for 1 ride or 4 rides for 1 person).

Car Rental: Ajax Accident Assistance (*map*C4*), Amraserstr. 6 (tel. 58 32 32). **ARAC** (*map*C4*), Amraserstr. 84 (tel. 431 61). **Avis** (*map*C5*), Salurnerstr. 15 (tel. 57 17 54). **Buchbinder** (*map*D6*), Burgenlandstr. 8 (tel. 485 65). **Budget** (*map*B5*), Michael-Gaismayrstr. 5-7 (tel 58 84 68). **Europcar/Interrent** (*map*C4*), Adamgasse 5 (tel. 58 20 60). **Hertz** (*map*C5*), Südtiroler Platz 1 (tel. 58 09 01). **Kalal** (*map*C4*), Mentlgasse 7 (tel. 58 45 44).

Automobile Organizations: ARBÖ, emergency line, tel. 123. **ÖAMTC,** emergency line, tel. 120.

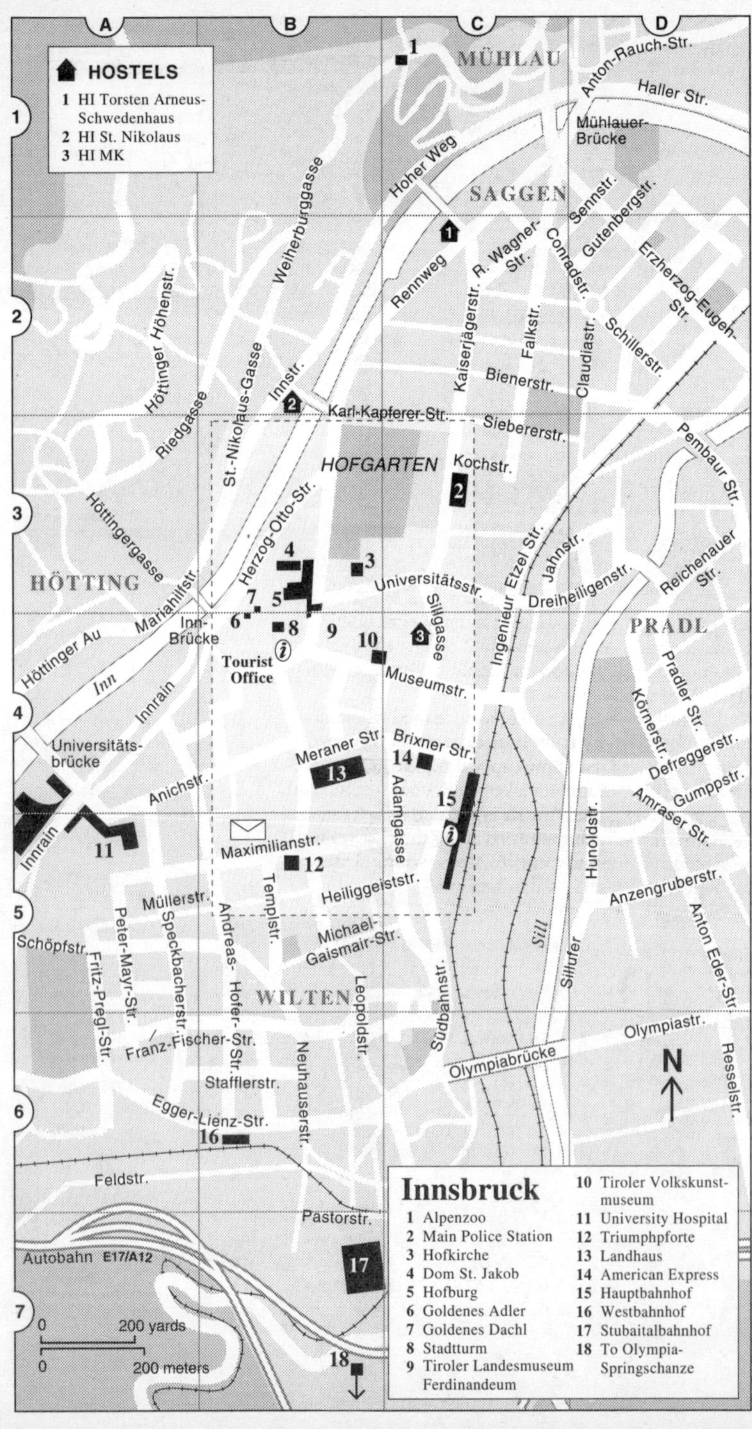
HOSTELS
1 HI Torsten Arneus-Schwedenhaus
2 HI St. Nikolaus
3 HI MK
Innsbruck
1 Alpenzoo
2 Main Police Station
3 Hofkirche
4 Dom St. Jakob
5 Hofburg
6 Goldenes Adler
7 Goldenes Dachl
8 Stadtturm
9 Tiroler Landesmuseum Ferdinandeum
10 Tiroler Volkskunst-museum
11 University Hospital
12 Triumphpforte
13 Landhaus
14 American Express
15 Hauptbahnhof
16 Westbahnhof
17 Stubaitalbahnhof
18 To Olympia-Springschanze
MÜHLAU
SAGGEN
HÖTTING
PRADL
WILTEN
HOFGARTEN
Tourist Office
Inn
Sill
Anton-Rauch-Str.
Haller Str.
Mühlauer-Brücke
Hoher Weg
Weiherburggasse
Höttinger Höhenstr.
Rennweg
R. Wagner-Str.
Sennstr.
Gutenbergstr.
Conradstr.
Erzherzog-Eugen-Str.
Kaiserjägerstr.
Falkstr.
Claudiastr.
Schillerstr.
Bienerstr.
St.-Nikolaus-Gasse
Innstr.
Riedgasse
Karl-Kapferer-Str.
Siebererstr.
Kochstr.
Pembaur Str.
Herzog-Otto-Str.
Höttingergasse
Mariahilfstr.
Universitätsstr.
Sillgasse
Etzel Str.
Jahnstr.
Dreiheiligenstr.
Reichenauer Str.
Ingenieur
Inn-Brücke
Höttinger Au
Museumstr.
Innrain
Universitäts-brücke
Pradler Str.
Körnerstr.
Meraner Str.
Brixner Str.
Defreggerstr.
Anichstr.
Adamgasse
Gumppstr.
Amraser Str.
Maximilianstr.
Hunoldstr.
Heiliggeiststr.
Templstr.
Müllerstr.
Anzengruberstr.
Schöpfstr.
Peter-Mayr-Str.
Speckbacherstr.
Andreas-Hofer-Str.
Michael-Gaismair-Str.
Anton Eder-Str.
Fritz-Pregl-Str.
Leopoldstr.
Südbahnstr.
Sillufer
Olympiastr.
Franz-Fischer-Str.
Neuhauserstr.
Olympiabrücke
Resselstr.
Stafflerstr.
Egger-Lienz-Str.
N
Feldstr.
Pastorstr.
Autobahn E17/A12
0 200 yards
0 200 meters
A
B
C
D
1
2
3
4
5
6
7

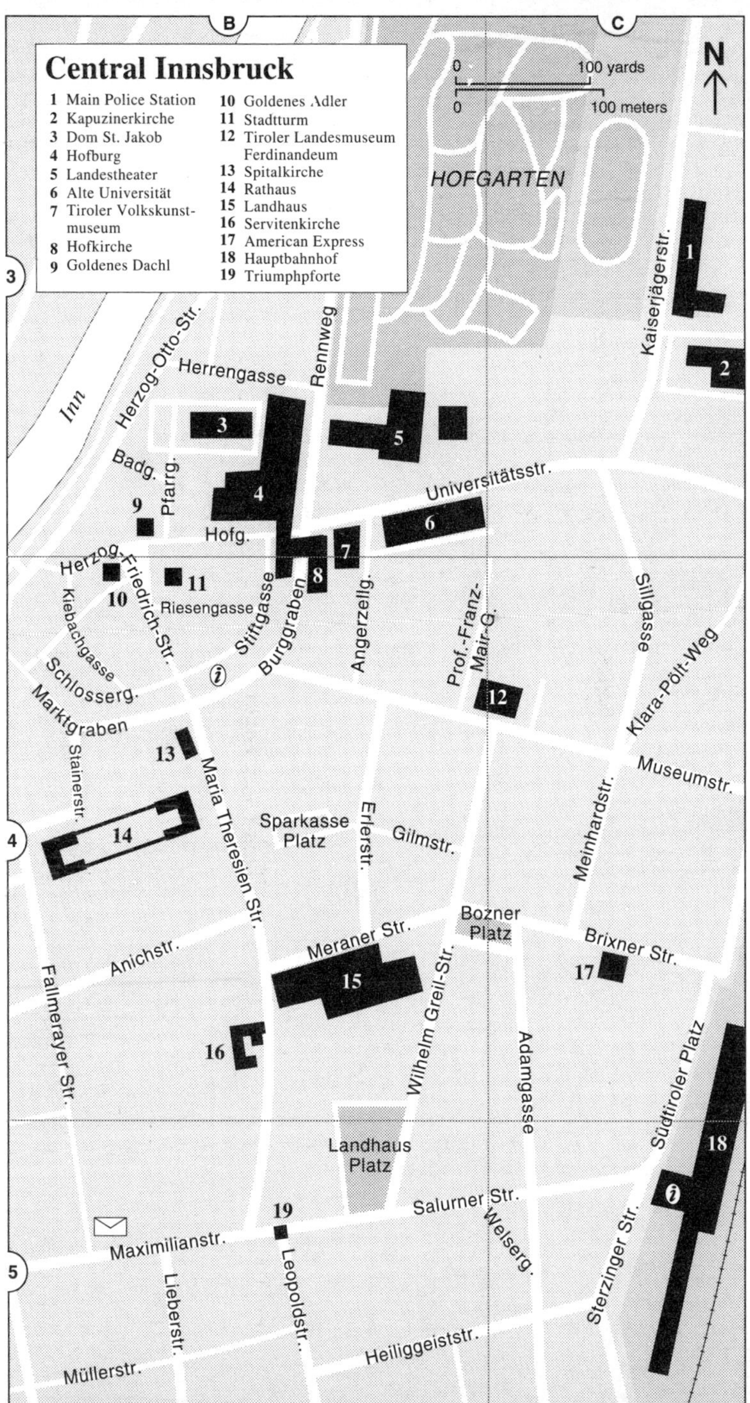
Central Innsbruck
1 Main Police Station
2 Kapuzinerkirche
3 Dom St. Jakob
4 Hofburg
5 Landestheater
6 Alte Universität
7 Tiroler Volkskunst-museum
8 Hofkirche
9 Goldenes Dachl
10 Goldenes Adler
11 Stadtturm
12 Tiroler Landesmuseum Ferdinandeum
13 Spitalkirche
14 Rathaus
15 Landhaus
16 Servitenkirche
17 American Express
18 Hauptbahnhof
19 Triumphpforte
0 100 yards
0 100 meters
N
HOFGARTEN
Inn
Herzog-Otto-Str.
Herrengasse
Rennweg
Kaiserjägerstr.
Universitätsstr.
Badg.
Pfarrg.
Hofg.
Herzog-Friedrich-Str.
Riesengasse
Stiftgasse
Burggraben
Angerzellg.
Prof.-Franz-Mair-G.
Sillgasse
Klara-Pölt-Weg
Kiebachgasse
Schlosserg.
Marktgraben
Stainerstr.
Maria Theresien Str.
Museumstr.
Sparkasse Platz
Erlerstr.
Gilmstr.
Meinhardstr.
Bozner Platz
Brixner Str.
Meraner Str.
Anichstr.
Fallmerayer Str.
Wilhelm Greil-Str.
Adamgasse
Südtiroler Platz
Landhaus Platz
Salurner Str.
Welserg.
Maximilianstr.
Leopoldstr.
Lieberstr.
Sterzinger Str.
Heiliggeiststr.
Müllerstr.
B
C
3
4
5

Taxis: Innsbruck Funktaxi (tel. 53 11 or 455 00). About 100 AS from the airport to the *Altstadt.*

Bike Rental: At the main train station. Open April to early Nov. daily 9am-11pm. Also available at **City Mountainbikerental** (*map*B3*), Innstr. 95 (tel. 28 65 15) and **Mountain-Bike-Stradl** (*map*A4*), Fürstenweg 97 (tel. 28 84 36).

Ski Rental: Skischule Innsbruck (*map*B4*), Burggraben 17 (tel. (05222) 58 23 10) or **Skiverleih Georg Moser** (*map*C3*), Universitätstr. 1 (tel. (0512) 58 91 58). In the nearby Stubai Valley, **Stubaier Gletscherbahn** (tel. (0512) 595 00; 140 AS per day) or **Skiverleih Raich,** Bilgerstr. 12a (tel. (0512) 772 75).

Hitchhiking: *Let's Go* does not recommend hitchhiking as a safe mode of transportation. Free-lance hitchers reportedly go to the Shell gas station by the DEZ store off Geyrstr. near Amras, taking bus K to "Geyrstr." Most cars leaving Innsbruck take this exit.

Other Practical Information

Library: Innsbruck Universität Bibliothek (*Innsbruck map*A4*), 50 Innrain, near the intersection with Blasius-Heuber-Str. Take bus B to "Klinik." Open Mon.-Fri. 9am-8pm, Sat. 9am-6pm.

Laundromat: Waltraud Hell (*map*C4*), Amraserstr. 15 (tel. 413 67), behind the station. Wash and dry 80 AS. If all machines are full, the attendant will hold your stuff and heave it in the first available machine for no charge. Open Mon.-Fri. 8am-6pm, Sat. 8am-1pm.

Travelers with Children: Children's Day Care Center (*map*D4*), Pradler Platz 6 (tel. 452 82). **Igls Visitors' Kindergarten,** Kurpark, Igls (tel. 37 89 08).

Snow Report: tel. (0512) 15 85 or (05226) 81 51.

AIDS Hot Line: (tel. 56 36 21). Information, counseling, support, and HIV-testing. English spoken. Anonymity assured.

Medical Assistance: University Hospital (*map*A5*), Anichstr. 35 (tel. 50 40). **Ambulance Service,** Sillufer 3 (tel. 334 44).

Emergencies: Police: tel. 133. Headquarters (*map*C2-3*) at Kaiserjägerstr. 8 (tel. 590 00). **Ambulance:** tel. 144 or 334 44. **Fire:** tel. 122.

ACCOMMODATIONS AND CAMPING

All in all, 9000 beds are available in Innsbruck and Igls in hotels, guest houses, *pensiones*, holiday apartments, private rooms, youth hostels, and camping sites. Nevertheless, beds are scarce in June, when only three hostels are open; either book in advance, or call before noon on the day you plan to arrive. The main tourist office on Burggraben provides a list of families who rent private rooms in the city (160-300 AS, often including breakfast and shower), though many require a stay of several days.

July brings hope and lodgings to travelers, as university dorms open up to summer hostelers. Bear in mind that these are not all regular HI hostels, so the staff might be a bit green. Some of the more inexperienced staffs will cling to their rule books like bibles to guide them through their confusion. Be patient. Also be careful; many dorms don't have lockers, so bring a chain and a padlock.

You can join **Club Innsbruck** (in summer 310 AS, in winter 280 AS) at no charge if you register at any central-Innsbruck accommodation for three or more nights; membership provides you with discounts on cable cars and museums, free bike tours, free ski bus service, and the option to participate in the club's fine hiking program, run June-Sept. (ask at the tourist office for more information).

Hostels and Dormitories

Jugendherberge Innsbruck (HI), Reichenauer Str. 147 (tel. 461 79 or 461 80). Take bus O to "Rossbachstr.," or walk from the main train station—turn right on Museumstr., take the first left fork after the train tracks onto König-Laurin-Str. When the street ends, make a right onto Dreiheiligenstr., which merges into Reichenauer Str. Walk down Richenauer Str. past Prinz Eugen/Andechsstr. and Redetzkystr. The hostel will be on your left, before Langer Weg. (25 min.). The hostel is a large concrete edifice resembling an office building inside and out. Often crowded with Americans, but they'll honor phone reservations as long as you show up by 5pm. 4- to 6-bed dorms. Reception 5-10pm. Lockout 10am-5pm. Curfew 11pm. Kitchen and laundry facilities (45 AS including soap), but you must notify the desk by 5pm if you intend to do laundry. Members only. 125 AS first night, 95 AS subsequent nights. Breakfast and sheets included. **Innsbruck Studentheim (HI),** at the same address, is an extension of Jugendherberge Innsbruck for groups only. Open July 15-Aug. Singles and doubles with shower 190 AS per person. Breakfast and sheets included.

Jugendheim St. Paulus (HI), Reichenauer Str. 72 (tel. 442 91). Take bus R to "Pauluskirche." Negatives: 20-bed dorm rooms, nearby church bells, trough-like bathroom sinks. Positives: roses, a comfortable lounge, kitchen facilities, an incredibly helpful staff, and the cheapest beds in town. They generally grant requests to sleep on the floor when all beds are taken. 3-night max. stay. Open mid-June to mid-Aug. Reception 7-9am and 5-10pm. Lockout 10am-5pm. Curfew 10pm, but ask for a key. 90 AS. Breakfast 25 AS. Sheets 20 AS. Showers included.

Jugendherberge St. Nikolaus (HI) (*Innsbruck map*B2*), Innstr. 95 (tel. 28 65 15). Walk across the river from the *Altstadt* along Rennweg to Innstr., or take bus K from the station to "St. Nickolaus." Clean rooms (6-8 beds per room) and a party-hearty, English-speaking crowd. Reception 8-10am and 5-8pm. No curfew or lockout, though deposit is required for a key. Theoretical quiet time 10pm, though the "Igloo" bar downstairs is open later. Checkout 9am. 115 AS first night, 100 AS for subsequent nights. Non-members 10 AS surcharge. Shower tokens 10 AS. Breakfast 40-75 AS. Meals at the adjacent restaurant 55 AS. Sheets included. Laundry 100 AS per load. Also offers mountain bike rental, at 150 AS per day (9am-6pm), glacier ski packages (200-300 AS per day), and winter ski packages (2900 AS per week including accommodations, equipment, lift tickets, and bus to the slopes).

Hostel Torsten Arneus-Schwedenhaus (HI), Rennweg 17b (tel. 58 58 14; fax 58 61 32), along the river. Take bus C from the station to the "Handelsakademie" stop. Guests rave about this spotless, warm, and cozy hostel with private bathrooms and an excellent location on the Inn. Open July-Aug. Reception 7:30-9am and 5-10:30pm. Lockout 9am-5pm. Curfew 10:30pm, but if you bring your guitar, your singing voice, and a bottle or two to pass around, you may be able to sit on the front steps a bit later. Membership preferred. Triples and quads 100 AS per person. Breakfast 45 AS. Dinner 60 AS. Sheets 20 AS. Reservations heartily recommended, but you must reserve by postcard, not by phone.

Jugendherberge MK (HI) (*map*C4*), Sillgasse 8a (tel. 57 13 11), near the main train station. From the station, walk up Museumstr., and take your first right onto Sillgasse. This hostel is a funky place with friendly management, a delirious café next door, and a full-sized basketball court on the 3rd floor that's potentially bothersome if you're trying to sleep on the floor below. Open July to mid-Sept. Reception 7-9am and 5-7pm. Lockout 9am-5pm. Curfew 11pm. 150 AS first night, 140 AS thereafter. Sheets 10 AS. Breakfast and showers included.

Volkshaus Innsbruck (HI), Radetzkystr. 41 (tel. 46 66 82), around the corner from Jugendherberge Innsbruck and Jugendzentrum St. Paulus. Radetzkystr. is off Reichenauerstr., before the Campingplatz. Accommodates 52 in spartan doubles, triples, quads, and quints. 100 AS, showers and sheets included. Breakfast 40 AS.

Internationales Studentenhaus, Rechengasse 7 (tel. 59 47 70). From the station, walk down Saturner Str., which becomes Maximilianstr., take your third right onto Maria-Theresien-Str., your first left onto Anich Str., a left on Innrain, and then a right on Rechengasse. Or take bus B to "Innsbruck Universität Bibliothek" on Innrain and walk right on Rechengasse. A sprawling, 560-bed dormitory. Open July-Sept. Reception 7-9pm. 230-270 AS, with private bath and shower 290-330 AS. Breakfast included. Laundry 20 AS.

Technikerhaus, Fischnalerstr. 26 (tel. 28 21 10). Though a bit far from the train station, this 87-bed resting place is near the Altstadt and university. From the station, walk up Brixnerstr. through Bozner Platz, straight on Meraner Str., and right on Maria-Theresien-Str.; then take a left on Anich Str., walk over the bridge on Blasius-Hueber-Str., turn left on Fürstenweg, and finally another left onto Fischnalerstr. Or take bus B and disembark at "Unterbergerstraße." Restaurant and TV room. Open July-Aug. Reception 7-8pm. 228 AS; breakfast included.

Camping

Campingplatz Reichenau, Reichenauerstr. (tel. 462 52). Down the road from Jugendherberge Innsbruck. Warm showers and restaurant on the premises. 65 AS per person, students 60 AS. Tent and car included. Open late April to mid-Oct.

Camping Seewirt, Amras, Geyrstr. 25 (tel. 461 53). From the *Hauptbahnhof*, take a right on Amraser Str., left on Amraser See Str., and then a right on Geyrstr. Or take bus K to "Amras." Hot showers and restaurant. 50 AS per person, 35 AS per tent.

Camping Innsbruck Kranebitten, Kranebitten Allee 214 (tel. 28 41 80). From the main train station, take bus LK to the last stop, "Kranebitten;" if LK eludes you, take bus O and then switch to LK and disembark at "Kranebitten." Reception 4-10pm. 61 AS per person, ages 5-14 40 AS, under 4 free. 35 AS per tent or car.

Hotels and Pensionen

Haus Wolf, Dorfstr. 48 (tel. 58 40 88), in the suburb of Mutters. Take the Stubaitalbahn (STB) to "Birchfeld," and walk down Dorfstr. Unload your pack, and bask in the maternal comfort; there's no place like home, but this comes close. And eat, eat, eat at breakfast. Singles, doubles, and triples 180 AS per person. Breakfast and shower included.

Haus Rimml, Harterhofweg 82 (tel. 28 47 26), a hike from the train station. Follow the directions to Camping Innsbruck Kranebitten. Consummately comfortable—private showers and a TV room are among the amenities. 225-320 AS per person. Breakfast included. Call ahead.

Pension Paula, Weiherburggasse 15 (tel. 29 22 62). Satisfied guests frequently return to this inn-like home down the hill from the Alpenzoo. Take bus K from the *Hauptbahnhof* to "St. Nikolaus," and then walk uphill. Singles 260 AS, with private toilet and shower 300 AS. Doubles 460 AS, with shower 560 AS. Quads 800-880 AS. 10 AS surcharge for a one-night-stand. Breakfast included. Reservations heartily recommended.

FOOD

Most tourists first glimpse cosmopolitan Innsbruck from the glamour of **Maria-Theresien-Straße;** don't let your eyes glaze over as you gawk at the overpriced delis and confectioneries. Instead, cross the river to **Innstraße,** in the university district, to uncover myriad ethnic restaurants, low-priced *Schnitzel Stuben,* and Turkish grocers. Culinary cowards can McBuy a McBier at **McDonald's** on Maria-Theresien-Str.

Wienerwald (*Innsbruck map*B4*), Museumstr. 24, and another branch at Maria-Theresien-Str. 12. Austria's chain version of the family steak (*Schnitzel*) house. You can feast on fowl and crisp salads as well (70-120 AS). English menus. Open daily 10am-midnight. Major credit cards accepted.

China-Restaurant Asia (*map*B4*), Angerzellgasse 10, just past the Eurasia Chinese Pizzeria near Treibhaus. Traditional Chinese dishes like House Crispy Duck (99 AS) in the heart of Austria. Lunch *Mittagsmenu* Mon.-Sat. is probably the best deal in Innsbruck (59 AS), but remember what they say about Austro-Chinese food: two hours after you eat, you're hungry for power. Open daily 11:30am-2:30pm and 6pm-midnight.

China-Restaurant Canton (*map*B4*), Maria-Theresien-Str. 37 (tel. 58 53 69). Same fare as China-Restaurant Asia but closer to the *Altstadt.* Popular lunch menu 63 AS. Open daily 11:30am-2:30pm and 5:30-11:30pm.

Philippine Vegetarische Küche (*map*B5*), Müllerstr. 9, at Templstr. one block from the post office. A vegetarian rest stop on a highway of meat. Polish off the *Schnitzel* (85 AS) with *Erdbeeren "Grossmutterart"* (sauce-dipped strawberries, 38 AS). Other entrees 82-130 AS. English menus. Open Mon.-Sat. 11:30am-2:30pm and 6-10:30pm.

Vegetarisches Restaurant Country-Life (*map*B4*), Maria-Theresien-Str. 9. An air-conditioned oasis amidst the glitter. Crunchy salads and smooth, cold fruit soups (28-45 AS). *Tagesmenu* 95 AS. Main restaurant open Mon.-Fri. 11:30am-3pm; buffet open Mon.-Thurs. 11:30am-7pm, Fri. 11:30am-3pm.

Hörtnagl (*map*B4*), Burggraben 4-6, just outside the *Altstadt.* This sprawling deli-restaurant-café complex vends heaping platefuls of *Schnitzel*-and-potatoes at the downstairs self-serve café (entrees 38-90 AS). Open Mon.-Fri. 10:30am-6pm, Sat. 10:30am-1pm.

Hafele (*map*A5*), on the corner of Innrain and Rechengasse, in the Innsbruck University complex. Cheap, tried-and-true Austrian meals like a succulent half-chicken (34 AS) and *Kotlett mit Pommes* (fried cutlet with fries; 48 AS). Daily menus and salads as well. Open Mon.-Fri. 7am-6pm, Sat. 8am-noon.

Uni Café (*map*A4-5*), on Innrain, near the Innsbruck Universität Bibliothek. On a second-floor balcony overlooking the university above the Hagebank. *De rigeur* for the local students. Sip coffee, nibble on sandwiches and ice cream, sport your sunglasses, and appear angst-ridden and disaffected. Soups or sandwiches 20-60 AS. Open Mon.-Fri. 8:30am-10:30pm, Sat.-Sun. noon-10pm.

University Mensa (*map*A4*), Herzog-Siegmund-Ufer 15, on the 2nd floor of the new university between *Markthalle* and Blasius-Hueber-Str. Tasty lunches (40-60 AS) and crisp salads. No student ID necessary. Open Mon.-Fri. 11am-2pm.

Markets

Kaufhaus Tyrol (*Innsbruck map*B4*), Innsbruck's largest department store, towers over Maria-Theresien-Str. near the fountain; there's an excellent supermarket downstairs with bountiful loaves of bread (8 AS each) and ice cream galore. Open Mon.-Fri. 9am-6:30pm, Sat. 9am-noon.

Billa supermarket (*map*C4*), at Museumstr. 16. Open Mon.-Fri. 9am-noon and 3-6pm, Sat. 9am-noon.

M-Preis supermarket, with the lowest prices around. Branch on the corner of Reichenauer Str. and Andechstr.; another branch on the corner of Salurner Str. (*map*C5*), near the rail station. Open Mon.-Fri. 8am-6:30pm, Sat. 8am-noon.

Indoor farmer's market (*map*B4*), in the *Markthalle* on the corner of Innrain and Marktgraben, right behind the *Altstadt*. Stands of everything from the four food groups and much, much more. Open Mon.-Fri. 7:30am-8pm, Sat. 7:30am-12:30pm.

SIGHTS

The **Goldenes Dachl** (Golden Roof), on Herzog Friedrich Str. (*Innsbruck map*B3-4*), is the center of the *Altstadt* and the emblem of Innsbruck. From beneath the 2657 gold shingles, Emperor Maximilian I and his wife Bianca would cheer jousters and dancers of yore in the square below. Inside the building, on the mezzanine level between the second and third floors, the **Olympiamuseum** commemorates the 1964 and 1976 Winter Games with stamps from scores of participating countries and videos saturated with Trivial Pursuit facts. A clip filmed from the skis of an Olympic ski jumper is just one of the highlights. Come see what the stars all did *before* Ice Capades. (Open daily 9:30am-5:30pm; Nov.-Feb. Tues.-Sun. 9:30am-5:30pm. Admission 22 AS, children 15 AS, seniors and students 11 AS.) The Goldenes Dachl sits amid a number of splendid 15th- and 16th-century buildings. The façade of the adjacent **Helblinghaus,** a 15th-century Gothic town residence, is flushed salmon pink and blanketed with grotesquely floral stucco. Climb the narrow stairs of the 14th-century **Stadtturm** (city tower; *map*B4*), on the other side of the Helblinghaus, to soak in the panoramic view. Look up before you climb—on a sunny day the tower can be as crowded as a New York dance club and even harder to move around in. (Open daily 10am-6pm. Admission to tower 18 AS, children 9 AS. Combined admission to tower and Olympiamuseum 32 AS, students 16 AS.) The 16th-century **Goldener Adler Inn** (Golden Eagle Inn; *map*B3-4*) is just to the left of the Goldenes Dachl; countless dignitaries and artists—including Goethe, Heine, and Sartre—have eaten, drunk, and made merry here. Immediately behind the Goldenes

Dachl stands the stunning Baroque **Dom St. Jakob** (*map*B3*), with its superb *trompe l'oeil* ceiling depicting the life of St. James and an altar decorated with Lukas Cranach's *Intercession of the Virgin*.

At Rennweg and Hofgasse stand the grand **Hofburg** (Imperial Palace) and **Hofkirche** (Imperial Church; *Innsbruck map*B3*). Built between the 16th and 18th centuries, the Hofburg is brimming with likenesses of its erstwhile royal residents. Empress Maria Theresa glowers over nearly every room, and a portrait of Maria's youngest daughter, Marie Antoinette (capitated) shines over the palace's main hall. (Open daily 9am-4pm; mid-Oct. to mid-May Mon.-Sat. 9am-4pm. Admission 30 AS, students 10 AS. English guidebook 5 AS.) The Hofkirche also houses images of aristocrats, conquerors, and monarchs; the funeral cortege, 28 mammoth bronze statues, conjure memories of the imperial elite. Emperor Maximilian I wished to have the coterie stand guard over his tomb, the **Kaisergrab,** which lies in the middle of the church. The statues of King Arthur, Theodoric the Ostrogoth (we kid you not), and Count Albrecht of Habsburg were designed by Dürer. Tyrolean patriot Andreas Hofer was also laid to rest in this hallowed space. The Silver Chapel, located between the church and the palace, is the final resting place for Emperor Ferdinand II and his wife. (Open daily 9am-5pm; Oct.-April 9am-noon and 2-5pm. Admission 25 AS, students 14 AS.) A combined ticket (40 AS, students 25 AS) will also admit you to the collection of the **Tiroler Volkskunstmuseum** (Tyrolean Handicrafts Museum) next door. Built between 1553 and 1563 as the "New Abbey," the building was converted into a school in 1785 and has served as a museum since 1929. Dusty implements, peasant costumes, and furnished period rooms provide a brief introduction to Tyrolean culture, though the ornate wood carvings in the "Peasants' Room" are suspiciously posh. (Open Mon.-Sat. 9am-5pm; Oct.-April Mon.-Sat. 9am-noon and 2-5pm. Museum also open Sun. 9am-noon. Admission to museum alone 20 AS, students 15 AS.)

A block or two up Rennweg from the Schwedenhaus youth hostel, the Battle of Bergisel is brilliantly portrayed in over 1000 square meters of 360° carnage in the **Rundgemälde** (panorama painting; *Innsbruck map*B3;* open April-Oct. daily 9am-5pm; admission 24 AS). Backtrack a bit, cross the covered bridge over the Inn, and follow the signs up to the **Alpenzoo** (*map*B2*), the loftiest zoo in Europe, with every vertebrate species indigenous to the Alps. When you've had your fill of high-altitude baby boars, descend on the network of scenic trails that weave across the hillside. If you'd rather ride to the zoo, catch tram #1, or #6 or the STB to "Hungerburg Funicular Railway" and take the cable car up the mountain. (Zoo open 9am-6pm; mid-Nov. to March 9am-5pm. Admission 56 AS, students 28 AS.)

The collection of the **Tiroler Landesmuseum Ferdinandeum** (*Innsbruck map*C4*), at Museumstr. 15, several blocks from the *Hauptbahnhof*, includes exquisitely colored, delicately etched stained-glass windows and several outstanding medieval altars and paintings, plus works by Cranach and Rembrandt. (Open Tues.-Wed. 10am-5pm, Thurs. 10am-5pm and 7-9pm, Fri.-Sun. 10am-5pm; Oct.-April Tues.-Sat. 10am-noon and 2-5pm, Sun. 10am-1pm. Admission 50 AS, students 30 AS.) Only the most sycophantic of imperial advisors could hope to procure real estate on **Maria-Theresien-Straße;** stroll down the street (*map*B4*) with an eye for the overstated Baroque grandeur. The 17th-century **Palais Troyer-Spaur** at #39 is especially interesting, as is the **Palais Trapp-Wolkenstein** opposite it. Under the balcony of the latter, you can spot the coat of arms of the von Trapp family, of *Sound of Music* fame. The **Annasäule** (Anna Column), erected between 1704 and 1706 by the provincial legislature, commemorates the Tyroleans' successful resistance to a Bavarian invasion during the War of Spanish Succession. The rectilinear, colonnaded façade of #43 marks the Neoclassical **Altes Landhaus,** built between 1725 and 1728 by G.A. Gumpp. Walk through the **Triumphpforte** (Triumphal Arch; *map*C5*), built in 1765 to commemorate the betrothal of Leopold II, who later became Emperor of Austria; then stroll down Leopoldstr. After the train tracks, you'll reach the **Basilika Wilten,** consecrated in 1665 and considered the most beautiful Rococo church in Tyrol.

The nearby **Stiftskirche Wilten** is a Baroque fantasia of marble and gold. The **Bergisel** and **Bergisel Museum,** on Brennerstr. (*map*C7*), serve as memorials to the Tyrolean freedom fighters. The commemorative chapel, with the Tyrolean Register of Honor, records all Tyroleans killed in action between 1796 and 1945 (open April-Oct. 9am-5pm; March 10am-4pm).

Outside the city proper, Archduke Ferdinand of Tirol left behind mounds of 16th-century armor and artwork (including paintings by such masters as Velazquez and Titian) at **Schloß Ambras.** The medieval castle dates back to between the 11th and 15th centuries but was rebuilt by Ferdinand into one of the most beautiful Renaissance castles in Austria. A portrait gallery depicts European dynasties from the 14th to the 19th centuries. To reach the palace, take streetcar #6 (direction: "Pradl"), disembark at "Schloß Ambras," and follow the signs (open April-Oct. Mon. and Wed.-Sun. 10am-5pm). Some suspect that ski jumpers aren't exactly playing with both poles; a trip out to the **Olympische Schischanze** (Olympic Ski Jump) in Bergisel will remove all doubt. Take streetcar #1, #6, or the STB to "Bergisel."

The ancient castle of **Büchsenhausen,** just above Innsbruck, boasts a history of gore and intrigue. In the seventeenth century, the *Schloß* fell into the hungry hands of the Habsburgs; generous Archduchess Claudia presented the fortress to her favorite Chancellor, Wilhelm von Biener. A prolific satirist, von Biener successfully antagonized most every noble within his sardonic reach—all except Archduchess Claudia, who protected him until her death. Two years and 26 days later, Biener found himself in prison. Shortly thereafter, he was executed; the sword used to lop off his head still hangs in the castle.

Von Biener's wife had begged the Emperor for a reprieve, which he had granted. One of Biener's enemies, the dreaded Schmaus, successfully intercepted the messenger so the execution would be carried out. In despair, Frau von Biener ran through the rooms in the castle, crying "There is no God! There is no God!" Later, she climbed a mountain and threw herself off a cliff. Her corpse was carried to the suburb of **Höttingen,** where it remains buried in an unmarked grave to the left of the altar. According to legend, Frau von Biener's spirit lives on, wandering the halls of the Büchsenhausen in unholy lamentation. Dressed in long black robes with a little golden crown, the Bienerweibele is usually harmless. In 1720, however, a descendant of a noble responsible for her husband's death decided to nap in the castle. The next morning, he was found dead in bed with a twisted neck.

SKIING AND ENTERTAINMENT

Though it's a veteran of two Winter Olympiads, very little of Innsbruck's **skiing** actually takes place within city limits. Instead, the nearby suburbs offer their mountainous backyards. Many private groups and *Pensionen* in Innsbruck offer package deals for a day's skiing, usually including transportation to and from the mountain; decide whether the convenience they offer is worth the extra cost (usually about 100 AS). Also, be aware that many of these groups are reluctant to refund your money if your plans change. For the most reliable operation, turn to the Innsbruck-Information offices at the train station or in the *Altstadt*. They offer ski packages that include round-trip bus fare to the glacier, an all-day lift ticket, and equipment (about 590 AS; 3-day package 835 AS). To go it alone, take the Omnibus Stubaital bus (leaves the bus station at 7:25 and 9:45am) to "Mutterbergalm-Talstation" (1 hr. 20 min., round-trip 150 AS); then buy a daypass (230-295 AS) and ride the gondola to the top station, where you can rent equipment.

A **Club Innsbruck** membership (see Accommodations above) significantly simplifies ski excursions; just hop on the complimentary club ski shuttle (schedules at the tourist office) to any suburban cable car. Membership has other privileges as well; with the Club card, you are entitled to discounts on ski classes and equipment. (**Ski lessons:** 3 days 1020 AS, 6 days 1290 AS, private 1-hr. lessons 400 AS. **Ski rentals:** alpine 150-190 AS per day, cross-country 80-100 AS per day. **Bobsled:** 300 AS per person per ride.) **Skipaß Innsbruck** (available at all cable cars and at Innsbruck-Information offices) is the most comprehensive ticket available, valid for all 33 lifts in the region (3 days 960 AS, 6 days 1855 AS; with Club Innsbruck membership, 830 AS and 1575 AS, respectively. Passes also available for skiing on 3 out of 4 days, 3 of 6 days, and 6 of 8 days.)

The **Club Innsbruck** membership also extends benefits during the summer; the Club's excellent mountain **hiking** program provides guided tours, transportation, and equipment absolutely free to hikers of all ages and experience levels. Participants assemble in front of the Congress Center (June-Sept. daily at 8:30am), board a 9am bus, and return from the mountain ranges by 5pm. Free lantern hikes leave every Tuesday at 7:45pm for Gasthof Heiligwasser, just above Igls; enjoy an Alpine hut party once there. If you wish to attack the Alps alone, pick up a free mountain guide booklet at any of the tourist offices.

When you descend from Alpine peaks, peruse the seasonal brochures *Innsbrucker Sommer* and *Innsbrucker Winter*, available at the tourist office, for comprehensive listings of exhibitions, cinema, and concerts. Posters plastered on the kiosks at Innsbruck University reveal even more cultural options. During August, Innsbruck hosts the **Festival of Early Music,** featuring concerts by some of the world's leading soloists on period instruments at the Schloß Ambras, and organ recitals on the Hofkirche's 16th-century Ebert organ. (For tickets, call 535 60; fax 53 56 43.) Several of the festival's performances are held at the **Tiroler Landestheater** (*Innsbruck map***B3*), across from the Hofburg on Rennweg (tel. 52 07 44; tickets available Mon.-Sat. 8:30am-8:30pm, or 1 hr. before the performance at the door; 40-250 AS.) After a concert, ride home in opulent comfort in one of the horse-drawn wagons (*Fiaker*) idling in front of the Landestheater (up to 4 people, 300 AS per ½-hr.).

Innsbruck's late-night opportunities are fairly limited; most visitors simply collapse into bed after a full day of frolicking around the mountains. The most lively nightlife revolves around the students; wander around the university quarter for twilight activity. **Treibhaus** (*Innsbruck map***B3-4*), Angerzellgasse 8 (tel. 58 68 74), hidden in an alley to the right of China Restaurant, is Innsbruck's favorite student hangout. Left-wing protest music serenades the crowd in the evening; jazz reigns on Sunday mornings. (Open Mon.-Sat. 4pm-1am, Sun. 9am-2pm. Evening cover 50-150 AS. No cover Sun. Generous beers 26 AS.) Its Sommergarten series includes concerts every Saturday evening, and jazz and blues festivals in June. **Café Zappa** (*map***A5*), Rechengasse 5, off Innstr. by the Studentenhaus near the university, offers beer, drinks, and light fare in a musical, stylish, graffiti-walled environment (open evenings).

Two of the main attractions of **Advent** are the exhibition of Christmas crèches in the Folkloric Museum and Caroling in the Congress Center. A **Christmas** market is held in the Old Town against a background of medieval houses from November 27 to December 22. Enjoy gingerbread, mulled wine, hot chestnuts, and roasted almonds.

Near Innsbruck: Igls

Pronounced "eagles," this suburban skiing hamlet lies about 5km from Innsbruck's *Altstadt*. Narrow streets lined with picturesque chalets, shutters adorned with hand-carved hearts—Igls feels like a Currier & Ives Christmas card. To reach Igls from Innsbruck, take tram #6 to the end of the line (one way 22 AS, day pass 33 AS); be forewarned that at 2.5mph, it's a painfully slow ride. During the summer, Igls makes a fine hiking base; pick up free maps at the **tourist office** (tel. (0512) 37 71 01; fax 789 65). From the tram stop, walk straight through the first intersection and continue through the narrow pathway in the park. At the next street, turn left; the tourist office is on the right (open Mon.-Fri. 9am-noon and 2-5pm). When the snow arrives, Igls's **Patscherkogel Pass** (named for the nearby mountain) offers skiers access to five lifts (1-day pass 265 AS, 3 days 660 AS, 6 days 1200 AS). One round-trip ride on the cable car to the ski area costs 63 AS. Bobsledding and luge brought Igls fame during the '64 and '76 Olympics; 300 AS buys you a vicarious gold, with a ride in a four-person sled driven by a pro (available Nov.-Feb; call (0512) 37 75 25 or 771 60). **Emergency numbers: Avalanche warning,** tel. 15 87; **ski rescue,** tel. 771 63; **snow report,** tel. 15 85 (German only).

Near Innsbruck: Fulpmes and Neustift

A few ice ages ago, a gargantuan glacier scooped out the **Stubaital** (Stubai Valley). The mountain villages of Fulpmes and Neustift, at the crest of the Stubaital, make good base camps for summer hikes. Take the **Stubaitalbahn** (STB) from the Innsbruck rail station to Fulpmes (54 AS, round-trip 98 AS). Buses also leave daily from the Innsbruck bus station to Neustift (44 AS, round-trip 80 AS) and Fulpmes (36 AS, round-trip 65 AS). At the top of the valley, you can ski virtually year-round (July-May) on the magnificent **Stubai Glacier** (Stubaigletscher). Available in Neustift, the **Stubaier Gletscher Pass,** valid on 17 lifts, costs 255 AS per half-day. Call the Stubaital **tourist offices** for information: **Fremdenverkehrsverband Fulpmes,** Gemeindezentrum (tel. (05225) 22 35), and **Fremdenverkehrsverband und Reisebüro Neustift,** Dorf 710 (tel. (05226) 22 28).

Near Innsbruck: Stams

Innsbruck's environs are composed almost exclusively of Alps and churches. In Stams stands an **abbey** once so opulently adorned with precious metals that the town's peasants revolted in redistributive protest in 1525. The gold and silver was consequently sent to Hall in Tirol for safer keeping. Since then, the unfortunate abbey has been robbed, burned, and, most recently, postered with *90210* stickers. The current bulbous spires bear a striking resemblance to Babylonian temples. On its 700th anniversary in 1984, the Pope nicknamed the abbey "Basilica minor." Inside is a 300-foot-tall **altar,** displaying 84 gilded Biblical characters. In front of the altar, note the innovative wooden cherubs, wearing triangular hats that double as hymnal holders. The **crypts** underneath the abbey house the tombs of Archduke Siegmund of Tirol, his wife, Eleanor Stuart, and Maximilian's second wife, Bianca. The brightly-frescoed **Bernardisaal** (Hall of Princes) is empty except for occasional Sunday concerts during the summer. Like Ettal Abbey, Stams's crowning glory is its **alcohol** production—their house *Schnapps* is available for 140 AS per liter. The monastic **brewery** is right inside; unfortunately, access is limited to thirsty monks. (Abbey open Mon.-Sat. 9-11:30am and 1:30-5pm; Sun. 1:30-5pm. Tours every ½-hr. on the hour; Sept.-May 9-11am and 2-5pm every hr.; in German only; 15 AS. Pick up a schedule from the tourist office, or ask at the abbey ticket booth. To arrange an English tour, call (05263) 62 42, or write to: Stift Stams, Stiftshof 1, A-6422 Stams.) Although you cannot enter the abbey without joining a tour group, feel free to cavort about the carefully manicured **gardens** outside. You can easily reach Stams by rail from Innsbruck; take the **train** toward Landeck (35 min.; round-trip 100 AS). The **tourist office** is in a tiny room on the side of the post office building. From the rail station, turn left, and follow the street around a right angle. You can see the abbey from the tourist office; just walk in the direction of the enormous yellow and white edifice on the hill.

■■■ SEEFELD IN TIROL

With the '64 and '76 Winter Olympiads padding its resume, ritzy Seefeld in Tirol is second only to the Arlbergs as a winter sports mecca. Innsbruck twice used Seefeld's terrain for Nordic and cross-country skiing events (though a disappointing snowfall in '76 forced the use of 20,000 metric tons of imported snow). Although skiing is still the name of the game here, lush meadows and breathtaking Alpine scenery invite travelers in all seasons. Seefeld is a picture-perfect stereotype of an Austrian village; feast your senses on towering peaks, fields of wildflowers and butterflies, and the clip-clop of Haflinger mountain horses pulling Tyrolean wagons around the narrow cobblestone streets. A one-hour guided tour on a Haflinger-drawn wagon costs 300 AS—expensive and touristy, but quintessentially quaint. The town overflows with snow bunnies in the winter, so be sure to make reservations about a month in advance.

Orientation and Practical Information On the outer perimeter of suburban Innsbruck, Seefeld in Tirol perches on a broad plateau 1180m above sea level, surrounded by the Hohe Munde, Wetterstein, and Karwendel mountain ranges. The town is only 26km northwest of Innsbruck and thereby easily reached by road and rail (12 trains from Innsbruck per day, ½ hr., one way 46 AS, round-trip 78 AS). Sit on the right (approaching Seefeld) for the best view of the valleys down below. Seefeld's **tourist office,** Kloster Str. 43 (tel. 23 13 or 23 16; fax 33 55), is well equipped to handle the town's notoriety. The helpful and knowledgeable staff gives away plenty of information in English, Italian, French, *und, natürlich,* German. From the train station, walk straight out the main door, cross the street, and head up Bahnhofstr. (which becomes Klosterstr. after the Münchner Str. intersection). The tourist office is on the right, housed in the *Rathaus*, and surrounded by tantalizing ice cream and pastry shops. Ask for copies of the brochures *Events, Suggestions, and Tips* and *Seefeld: A to Z.* The tourist office also provides assistance over the telephone Mon.-Sat. 8:30am-8pm. (Open Mon.-Fri. 8:30am-noon and 3-6pm, Sat. 8:30am-noon; Dec.-Feb. Mon.-Sat. 8:30am-6:30pm, Sun. 10am-12:30pm and 4-6pm.) The **post office** (tel. 23 47) is right down the road. (**Postal code:** A-6100.) The **telephones** inside (**City code:** 05212) also take *Wertkarten* (open Mon.-Fri. 8am-noon and 2-6pm, Sat. 8-11am; Dec.-March daily 8am-7pm). Currency exchange rates are most generous at the post office (exchange only available until 5 pm); you can also exchange money at the **train station** (tel. (05242) 24 38 30), at the end of Bahnhofstr. Luggage storage and bike rental (90 AS per day, mountain bikes 200 AS) are also available. If the station bikes are all booked out, try **Sport Sailor** (tel. 25 30). A mountain bike there costs 200 AS for a full day, 100-150 AS for a half-day, and 350 AS for a weekend (open mid-May to Sept. 9am-12:30pm and 2:30-6pm). For a **taxi,** call tel. 2630. Wash out your long johns at **Tip-Top laundromat,** Andreas-Hofer Str. 292 (tel. 20 44).

Accommodations and Food Seefeld boasts six five-star hotels (that's *thirty* stars), but no hostel—that missing "s" raises the price of a bed by 400-2400 AS, depending on the season. *Privatzimmer* are probably the best budget option. Prices for these rooms average 200-300 AS per night in the summer; slap on about 100 AS more during winter. Wherever you stay, inquire about a **guest card** (*Kurkarte*) that carries discounts of 10-20% off skiing, swimming, and concerts. **Frühstückspension Harmeler,** Rietherspitzstr. 410 (tel. 25 51), is one of the more wallet-friendly establishments in town. Walk out the station's front door, turn left, and walk down the street; then turn left on Reitherstr. and walk across the tracks and down the road. The *Pension* is between Reitherstr. and Spitz Str. Spacious rooms, down comforters, an outdoor pool and terrace, and *very* generous breakfasts await. (In summer, singles 200 AS, with bath and toilet 250 AS; in winter, singles 240-350 AS. Reservations recommended.) **Haus Carinthia,** Hochegg Str. 432 (tel. 29 55), welcomes single backpackers. Follow the directions to Frühstückspension Harmeler until you reach Reither Str. Turn left as it intersects Milserstr., and then take the second right onto Hochegg Str. Refuel with a hearty breakfast on the terrace. (In summer, singles 200 AS; in winter, singles 300 AS. Call ahead.) **Haus Felseneck,** Kirchwald 309 (tel. 25 40), features sinfully luxurious bed chambers—balconies, TV, and brass faucets in every room. The owners yearn to practice their language skills with English-speaking visitors. Take Kloster Str. to the end, turn left, and hike up the steep street with the railing on its side; the *Pension* is the third or fourth house on the right. (In summer, singles 250 AS; in winter, singles 320 AS.)

Finding food in Seefeld is significantly less difficult than hunting down a cheap room; the entire *Fußgängerzone* (pedestrian district) is stocked with rows of restaurants, cafés, and bars. You'll salivate like a Pavlovian pup as you pass by the windows lined with cakes, sweets, and other pastries. Expect a single dessert to run about 30 AS. Locals recommend *alfresco Wiener Schnitzel* at the **Tiroler Weinstube,** Dorfplatz (tel. 22 08), directly in front of the tourist office (entrees 80-150 AS). Afterwards, order something light at the **Weinkeller,** sit back, and listen to the live Tyrolean band. Or pack a picnic at the **Meinl supermarket** (tel. 31 62) on Klosterstr. (open Mon.-Fri. 8am-noon and 3-6pm).

Skiing and Entertainment Winter in Seefeld brings a blanket of snow and a multitude of skiers from around the globe. The town offers two ski passes; the **Seefelder Hochplateau Paß** gives skiers access to slopes at Seefeld, Reith, Mösern, and Neuleutasch and is available for one or two days (1-day pass 275 AS, children 200 AS). The other option is the **Happy Ski Pass** (see Ehrwald, below, for more information). Call (05242) 3790 for a local **snow report.** With a guest card, you can ride the **ski bus** for free; it shuttles from lift to lift daily 9:30am-5pm. Obtain a schedule from the tourist office; while there, pick up the pamphlet *Seefeld von A-Z,* which lists, among other goodies, ski rental shops (which average 80-150 AS per day for alpine skis, 60-120 AS per day for cross-country skis). The *Seefeld Sport-Winter* packet describes the town's other outdoor pastimes, including ice skating, hockey, paragliding, cross-country skiing, and more. To soothe those out-of-practice muscles after a day on the slopes, visit the massive **sauna** complex at the **Olympia Sport Center.** (Tel. 32 20; fax 32 28 83. Open daily 2-10pm; admission 170 AS, children 100 AS; 30% discount with guest card.)

The tourist office and the **Tirol Alpine School** run an excellent summer hiking program that will satiate even the most accomplished veteran's *Wanderlust.* The four- to six-hour hikes wind among local towering peaks, including the Pleisenspitze (2569m) and the Hohe Munde (2659m). (Hikes mid-June to mid-Sept. Tues. 9am, Fri. 8am; register at the tourist office by 3pm the preceding day. 150 AS per person, equipment included.) The **Kneipp Hiking Society** invites visitors to join its weekly five-hour outings (departures from the train station Thurs. 12A:30pm; 20 AS contribution). The **Bergbahn Rosshütte** (tel. (05242) 241 60) invites hikers to join its "five-point program," which lasts four hours. Participants ride a street car, a cable car, and the **Jochbahn** railway to Alpine heights of over 2000m. For 190 AS, hikers wander several short trails and then indulge in an immense "Austrian coffee break" of coffee, tea, and cake at the Rosshütte restaurant. If you prefer to go it alone, board the mountain train to Rosshütte (round-trip 120 AS, children 70 AS), Seefelderjoch, or Härmelekopf (round-trip 150 AS, children 80 AS). The Topkarte, a ticket covering transportation to and from all three peaks, costs 170 AS (children 95 AS; cable car runs May 30-Oct. 13 daily 9am-5pm; departures every ½ hr.).

Every self-respecting European resort town boasts a **casino,** and Seefeld's gambling hall (tel. 23 40; fax 23 40, ext. 66) is right on Bahnhofstr., about a hundred paces from the rail station. The one-armed bandits have dispensed 14 million AS in the past year alone; if you come out the big winner, don't forget the little people, especially the humble editors here who tipped you off. (Open daily at 3pm. No cover charge; semi-formal attire.)

Seefeld has its share of high culture as well. The annual **Village Festival** (third Sat. in July), **Music and Fire Brigade Festival** (mid-Aug.) and the thrice-weekly **Tyrol Evenings** (July-Sept. Tues. at Ferienhotel Katlschmid; Thurs. and Fri. at Hotel Tyrol; Fri. at Café Corso) feature the best of Tyrolean pomp and circumstance. Relax to the gentle strains of music at the free **City Classics Concerts** in the Seefeld **Kurpark** (June-Sept. Wed. and Sun. 8pm). The tourist office has a calendar with a **schedule** of all events. Or take a ride on the **"Kaiser Max" Nostalgia Train,** a 1½-hour guided musical tour in a saloon car. From Seefeld to Innsbruck, you can learn more than you ever cared to know about Emperor Maximilian I, who ascended the Martinswand in 1484. (Train runs mid-July to mid-Aug. Wed. and Thurs.; mid-June to mid-July and mid-Aug. to mid-Sept. Thurs. only. 140 AS. Reserve tickets at the tourist office.)

THE LECHTALER ALPS

The Lechtaler Alpen, a region of 3000-meter-high peaks and lake-speckled valleys, hugs the German border in northwestern Tyrol. Friendly to mountain beasts and mythical dwarves but not rear-wheel-drive cars, less than one-fifth of the lumpy terrain is habitable by humankind. As a result, the supply of guest beds is heavily concentrated in large resort areas; cheap lodgings are few and far between. Portions of the Lechtal, though untroubled by the *Angst* of the counterculture, do offer alternative accommodations—from the Innsbruck branch of the Tyrol Information Service, Adamgasse 3-7, A-6020 Innsbruck (tel. 56 18 82), you can order the barnful pamphlet *Urlaub am Bauernhof* (Vacation on the Farm). Send our regards to Charlotte, Wilbur, and Templeton.

The best time to visit the Lechtal is when the mountains are your only companions; consider a trip in the off-season, April to June or October to November. In these border lands, it is a good idea to carry your passport at all times, in case you encounter an international urge. The River **Inn,** the primary waterway of the valley, runs southwest to northeast from the Swiss frontier at Finstermünz to the German border by Kufstein. It cuts a swath of land through Innsbruck, Imst, and Landeck and then heads south to Switzerland; for the past two millennia it has served as a pivotal transport route. Parallel to and north of the Inn, the **Lech** river eroded its own wide valley. Between the lowlands of the Inn and Lech, the mountains are virtually people-free.

The Lechtaler Alps offer some of the best skiing in Austria, and when the snow melts in spring, hikers bloom. For a 24-hour **weather report,** call (0512) 15 66 in Innsbruck. Where there are mountains, there are valleys, and where valleys, lakes (and where lakes, throngs of tourists and postcard stands…). Near Reutte are two watery gems: the Plansee and Haldensee. Skiing. Hiking. Swimming. All of this hearty cardiovascular activity is going to make you hungry. When your food gauge is running low, sit down for some local specialties—try the *Tiroler Speckknödel,* served either *zu Wasser* (in broth) or *zu Lande* (dry, with salad or sauerkraut), *Gröstel* (a delectable combination of potatoes, meat, bacon, and eggs), or *Tiroler Schnapps* (the '94 line features apricot, pear, plum, and rowanberry prototypes).

Autobahn A12 follows the Inn from Innsbruck, Tyrol's capital, to Imst, the old market town, and sprawling Landeck. Bundesstraße 314 runs north from Imst to Ehrwald and Reutte, close to Germany and the popular resort, Garmisch-Partenkirchen. Bundesstraße 198 mirrors the River Lech. **Bus** #4176 runs round-trip every half-hour from Innsbruck to Nassereith, Imst, Ehrwald, and Reutte, a 96km trip; #4250 runs every two hours from Reutte to Ehrwald and Nassereith, and back. **Trains** run the same route on a slightly more regular basis.

■ Ehrwald

Of his beloved hometown Ehrwald, poet Ludwig Ganghofer (1855-1920) once importuned God, "If You love me, please let me live here forever." Though at last report his request went unheeded, some divine power has certainly smiled on the city. Other than a few damaged buildings, the World Wars spared the hamlet, and to date nothing has blemished Ehrwald's other *Wunderkind,* the majestic **Zugspitze.** This mountain (at 2962m, Germany's highest) straddles the German-Austrian border, but, for some reason, visitors flock like lemmings to the more congested German resort **Garmisch-Partenkirchen** to enjoy the Zugspitze's winter skiing and summer hiking. Ehrwald's motto is "Ehrwald—on the *sunny* side of the Zugspitze";

while no scientist has confirmed this meteorological oddity, Ehrwald *is* more pleasant than its German counterpart in many ways. Maybe it's sunny because it's quieter (Ehrwald is not nearly as famous as former Olympiad-host Garmisch), or because it boasts a faster cable car (the **Tiroler Zugspitzbahn** is Europe's newest), or because it's cheaper (rooms average 50-100 AS less in Ehrwald). Whatever the reason, there are plenty of opportunities to sample life on both sides of the border; trains cross from Austria to Germany and back ten times daily (don't forget your passport). To reach the summit of the Zugspitze from Ehrwald, take any of the local buses to "Tiroler Zugspitzbahn" (20 AS). The **cable car** (tel. 23 09) to the top costs 360 AS. (Lift runs daily 8:45am-4:40pm, Dec.-April daily 9:15am-4:40pm.) The crowded **restaurant** at the cable's end has what some call the most breathtaking view in the entire continent; on a clear day, visibility extends from Salzburg to Stuttgart (restaurant open mid-May to mid-Oct.).

While at the Zugspitzbahn lift, pick up a **Happy Ski Card;** despite its horrifically cheesy moniker, the card actually does simplify skiing in the ritzy Zugspitze region. The pass is available for intervals of three to 20 days; for example, a four-day pass (1200 AS) grants access to more than 10 lifts in Austria and Germany (1 week 1660 AS, children 1190 AS; 2 weeks 2900 AS). The mountains also draw visitors in the summer; **Scheiber's Sportladen** (tel. 31 04) rents racing and mountain bikes to explore the range, at the lowest rates in town (mountain bikes 200 AS per day, 350 AS for a weekend; bikes 60 AS per day, over 6 days 70 AS per day). The **tourist office** (tel. 23 95; fax 33 14) leads **guided hikes** of various difficulties (Tues.-Fri.), and **mountain bike tours** (Fri.); call ahead to reserve a spot. To find the office (*Tourismus-information*), take the city bus from the **train station** (tel. 22 02; open daily 5:45am-9pm) to "Ehrwald Kirchplatz." If you arrive by BundesBus, disembark at the stop in the town center and walk right along Kirchplatz; the tourist office will be on your left. The office also books rooms for no fee, has a free reservation phone, and provides excellent hiking maps (open Mon.-Sat. 8:30am-noon and 1:30-6pm). If the tourist office is closed and the electric accommodations board outside doesn't cooperate, **Pension Buchenhain,** Wettersteinstr. 33 (tel. 22 47), takes in plenty of weary backpackers. From the tourist office, walk to Spielmann Str. and turn left; the *Pension* is on the corner of Spielmann and Wetterstein, about two blocks away (in summer 170-220 AS, in winter 230-300 AS). **Haus Edith,** Im Tal 22a (tel. 35 04), serves up a hot breakfast and a fantastic mountain view. From the bus stop on Kirchplatz, walk to Innsbrucker Str., stroll away from the train station for about 10 min., and then turn left on Im Tal (in summer 190-240 AS, in winter 250-300 AS).

The Ehrwald **post office** (tel. 33 66) is located on Hauptstr.; from the tourist office, walk past the bus stop and toward the rail station—Kirchplatz becomes Hauptstr. **Currency exchange** and **telephones** (**City code:** 05673) are available. (Open Mon.-Fri. 8am-noon and 2-6pm, Sat. 8-10am.) Any town **bank** will also exchange money (banking hours Mon.-Fri. 8am-noon and 2-4:30pm, Sat. 9am-noon; Oct.-June Mon.-Fri. 8am-noon and 2-4:30pm). **Raiffeisenbank,** in the Kirchplatz, also has a 24-hour ATM. Down the street, on Hauptstr., is Ehrwald's **SPAR Markt;** it's perfect for packing a picnic meal to dine at the summit of the Zugspitze.

■■■ REUTTE

Wedged in the crossroads of Germany and Austria and dwarfed by the rocky crags of the **Gehrenspitze** (2164m), Reutte rolls out the red carpet for Alpine tourism. This town in the northern Alps was once a key waystation on the salt mining caravan route and remains firmly linked to major transportation lines; it's easily accessible by train from Munich (244 AS), Innsbruck (142 AS), or Vienna (680 AS), and by bus from Lech (107 AS) or Imst (89 AS). Reutte is ideally situated just over the border from southern Bavaria; Crazy Ludwig's three fairy-tale castles—Hohenschwangau, Neuschwanstein, and Linderhof—are just a hop, skip, and a jump away. Reutte itself features only typically Alpine attractions: the hike up the mountain in summer and the ski run back down in winter.

Orientation and Practical Information Reutte's **tourist office** is at Untermarkt 34 (tel. 23 36 or 20 41); walk straight up Bahnhofstr. from the train station, and look to the left. Or, from the bus stop on Mühler Str., walk toward the center of town, take the first right onto Untermarkt, and walk until you reach the parking lot; the tourist office rests at the lot's rear corner, partially hidden by bushes. Ask for skiing specifics, pick up a map of walking and cycling routes (25 AS), and check for rooms on the board outside. In peak season (Dec.-April and July-Aug.) be prepared to wait (open Mon.-Fri. 8am-noon and 2-5pm, Sat. 8:30am-noon). You can exchange currency at any bank, though the **post office**, on Planseestr., tends to offer better rates. (**Postal code:** A-6600. Open Mon.-Fri. 8am-noon and 2-5pm, Sat. 8-11am.) Call 23 00 or 25 09 for **taxi** service. **Telephones** are located at the post office (**City code:** 05672). **Bike rental** is available at the train station from April to November. Both the **ÖAMTC,** Allgäuer Str. 45 (tel. 36 10), and the **Österreichischer Alpenverein,** Untermarkt 34 (tel. 311 95), have offices in Reutte; the consummately friendly staffs are more than willing to assist bewildered tourists. Remember the local emergency numbers—**car failure:** tel. 120 and **mountain rescue:** tel. 144.

Accommodations and Food Reutte's environs harbor two hostels. Though closer and cheaper, **Jugendherberge Reutte (HI),** Prof.-Dengel-Str. 20 (tel. 30 39), is hellish to find without a map. From the train station, turn left and walk to the first intersection. Turn right onto Mühler Str., left onto Obermarkt, and then take the third right onto Kög. Take the first right onto Floriangasse and the first left onto Prof.-Dengel-Str. When you hear the screams of youngsters, you're in the right place; the hostel stands behind a kindergarten. You'll see the staff when you pay for the night and when they kick you out in the morning, and there are no meals provided, but the extremely low price and the generous *pro bono* kitchen mean you can feast on food from the local markets. (Reception open 5-8pm. Curfew 10pm. Lockout 9am-5pm. 68 AS, nonmembers 78 AS. Sleepsack and shower included. Open to single guests mid-June to late-Aug. only; year-round for groups.) Catch any bus heading south, across the river, and hop off at "Hofen Reuttener Bergbahn" (21 AS) for **Jugendgästehaus am Graben (HI)** (tel. 26 44), on Lechtalerstr. Though farther from town, this hostel has the upper hand in comfort, and it welcomes single guests during ski season. The building's rural appeal stems from the wood interior, pot-bellied gas stoves, and gingham table cloths. (Reception open 5-9:30pm. Curfew 10pm. 125 AS. Sleepsack and breakfast included. Showers 7 AS for 5 min. Dinner 70 AS. Be sure to make reservations during the peak seasons.)

If you don't mind spending a few extra *Schillings* for the peace, comfort, and proximity of a guesthouse, patronize the two along Obermarkt: **Gasthof Goldene Krone,** Obermarkt 46 (tel. 23 17; 180 AS, showers included), and **Gasthof Schwarzer Adler,** Obermarkt 75 (tel. 25 04; 210 AS, showers included; wheelchair-accessible). From the train station, turn left, take the first right onto Mühler Str., and then the first left onto Obermarkt.

Of the three campgrounds dotting the valley, **Camping Sintwag,** (tel. 28 09) on Ehrenbergstr., is closest to town. From the station, follow Mühler Str. to Obermarkt and bear right at the fork onto Ehrenbergstraße (20 min.). (61.50 AS per person, 35 AS per tent; in winter 70 AS per person, 40 AS per tent. Open June-April.) Two others lie on the shores of the Plansee; take the Plansee bus to "Seespitze" (21 AS) to reach **Camping Seespitze** (tel. 81 21; 45 AS per person, 42 AS per tent; open May-Oct.). The same bus stops at "Forelle" (28 AS) for **Camping Sennalpe** (tel. 81 15; 45 AS per person, 42 AS per tent; open mid-Dec. to mid-Oct.). All of Reutte's camping sites have drinking water, hot showers, toilets, laundry machines, and gas stoves.

The **Prima Café-Restaurant,** Mühler Str. 20 (tel. 32 45), offers simple self-service fare for 40 to 70 AS (open Mon.-Fri. 9am-7pm, Sat. 9am-1pm); right next door is the local **SPAR supermarket** (open Mon.-Fri. 7:30am-6:30pm, Sat. 7:30am-12:30pm). Also on Mühler Str., across from the bus stop, is **Billa Markt,** where a cola costs just 4 AS (open Mon.-Fri. 7am-7:30pm, Sat. 7am-1pm). You can also refuel at **Storf Restaurant,** Untermarkt 20, a unique self-service establishment (open Mon.-Fri. 8:30am-6:30pm, Sat. 8:30am-1pm). If your tastebuds crave something beyond *Schnitzel* and *Wurst,* order some chop suey at **China Restaurant Shang-Hai,** Obermarkt 48 (tel. 51 02; open daily 11:30am-2:30pm and 5:30-11:30pm).

Sights and Entertainment A **Heimatmuseum,** Untermarkt 25 (tel. 51 11), filled with local paraphernalia, encompasses historical objects from the **Festung Ehrenberg,** just south of town. The exhibits include "The Ancient Sword Of Justice," used to mete out the district's capital punishment. (Open Tues.-Sun. 10am-noon and 2-5pm. Admission 20 AS, with guest card 15 AS, children 10 AS.)

When Jack Frost nips at your nose, cash in on the **Große Verbund Skipass,** valid on 36 lifts in the greater Reutte and Tannheim regions, including the monstrous Hahnenkahm (1940m) and Neunerköpfl (1864m) summits. (2-day pass 490 AS, children 295 AS; one-week pass 1415 AS, children 850 AS; 15-day pass 2560 AS, children 1535 AS.) Day passes in individual areas run about 260 AS. A **ski bus** runs between lifts (free with a valid skipass). The regional **ski school** also rents equipment; contact **Schischule Reutte-Hahnenkamm-Höfen** (tel. 24 43 or 38 22) for details. For a **weather and snow report** (German only), dial (05672) 30 11 in Reutte or (05675) 63 03 in Tannheim.

The tourist office map glimmers with summer hiking suggestions, ranging from courtly strolls around the Plansee and Heiterwangersee lakes (976m) to sweaty ascents of the Jochplatz (1762m) and Rintlijoch (2166m) mountains. Trails through the Höfener, Tannheimer, and Allgäuer mountain ranges are beautifully marked and maintained. On Tuesdays and Fridays at 9am, **guided hikes** leave the tourist office, returning to town about seven hours later. Sign up at the office by 5pm the day before (35 AS, children free). For more rigorous (and also more expensive) treks, the **Alpinschule Ausserfern-Reutte,** Allgäuer Str. 15 (tel. 22 32), is a professional hiking school that provides a plethora of helpful suggestions and runs excursions into the mountains. Or, choose your own path from one of the tourist office's maps, and ride the **Reuttener Bergbahn** (tel. 24 20) up to the loftier trails. (Round-trip 135 AS, children 80 AS. Cable car runs May-Oct. daily 8:30am-4:30pm.) At the top of the cable car lies a patch of floral paradise; the **Alpenblumengarten Hahnenkamm** (Alpine flower garden) presents over 600 species of flowers in unblemished Alpine splendor.

■■■ IMST

Halfway between Innsbruck and King Ludwig's enchanting chateaux, you'll find the summer vacation hideaway Imst (pop. 7500). Germans, Danes, and a handful of Brits set up camp here from June to September to enjoy a reprieve from their daily routines. Imst is situated on a slope in the Inn valley and sprawls over 144 square kilometers. In 1282, sleepy Imst earned the right to call itself a market, and it only became a full-fledged town in 1896. The 15th-century **parish church** boasts the highest steeple (300 ft.) in Tyrol; its modern altar was sculpted by a local artist, Elmar Kopp. Founded by Hermann Gmeiner in 1949, the world's first **SOS Children's Village,** housing orphans and children from broken homes in a family-like atmosphere, developed here. Locals claim that the thankful souls of the children have since blessed Imst with good fortune.

Orientation and Practical Information 38 mi. northeast of Innsbruck (about a ½-hr. drive), Imst is easily accessed by car or bus. The **tourist office,** Johannesplatz 4 (tel. 24 19; fax 47 83), provides everything you need to thoroughly explore the town. Hop on any white and purple **city bus** (5 AS), and disembark at

"Gasthof Sonne." (Buses run 8:45am-6:25pm; schedules are available at the tourist office and at every bus stop in town.) The tourist office will suggest accommodations and dispense seasonal recreation information. Pamphlets on the most scenic hiking routes are also available. Check out the accommodation board outside and use the attached free telephone to make your own reservations. (Open July-Aug. Mon.-Fri. 9am-noon and 1-7pm, Sat. 9am-noon and 3-7pm, Sun. 5-7pm; Sept.-June Mon.-Fri. 9am-noon and 2-6pm, Sat. 9am-noon.)

The **Tiroler Landesreisebüro,** Wallnöferplatz 5 (tel. 33 40), handles budget travel arrangements for all of Tyrol (open Mon.-Fri. 9am-noon and 2-6pm). The Imst **post office** is at Meraner Str. 15 (tel. 33 60); from the tourist office, turn left on the street in front of you and take the left fork. When the road forks again, take the left fork; the office will be on your right (open Mon.-Fri. 7am-7pm, Sat. 8-11am). **Telephones** (**City code:** 05412) and **currency exchange** are both available inside the post office, at the train station, and at the Sparkasse bank (Mon.-Fri. 7:45am-noon and 2-4:30pm). For a **taxi,** call 53 11 (Fri., Sat., and evenings) or 41 00 (24 hrs.). The Imster Bergbahn runs a **ski condition hotline** (tel. 23 22). Always remember the **emergency** numbers: **Police,** tel. 133, headquarters at Dr. Pfeiffenberger Str. 8a (tel. 22 29); and **Ambulance,** tel. 144.

Accommodations and Food Youth hostels in this region are rare or nonexistent; to spare your wallet, turn to the myriad *Privatzimmer* instead of the more luxurious *Pensionen*. The owners of these private houses are generally reliable, experienced, and exceptionally friendly to strangers—remember, they're letting you into their home. **Gasthof Kienel,** Sirapuit 6 (tel. 296 72) is one such treasure chest. From the tourist office, walk along Kramergasse, past Hagebank, and take the first right. The house is located at the next intersection on the right side of the street. (Open June-Aug. 120 AS. 30 AS per night surcharge for a stay of fewer than 3 nights.) Or try **Gästezimmer Pechtl,** Ahornweg 16 (tel. 363 83). Take Rennstr. from the tourist office; after the intersection with Eichenweg, walk right past the Sportplatz along the bike path, Am Raun. Bear left onto Kugelgasse, and then turn right onto Ahornweg (5 min.). (150-170 AS. Parking, refrigerator, and balcony included.) **Gästezimmer Klingenschmid,** Am Raun 5 (tel. 37 57), is just down the street from Pechtl. (180 AS. Parking, refrigerator, and shower and/or bath included.) **Pension Weirather,** Thomas-Walch Str. 10 (tel. 26 20; fax 40 90), is a bit more costly, but worth the extra expense. From the tourist office, turn right and walk up the hill on Pfarrgasse; the *Pension* is on the right (2 min.). (230-250 AS. TV and parking included. English spoken.) If you're really roughing it, park yourself at **Sport-Camp Imst West,** Langgasse 62 (tel. 22 93). From the tourist office, follow Kramergasse past the Johanneskirche to Langgasse. (55 AS in winter, 50 AS in summer. Hot water and showers included.)

Imst has little to offer the epicure beyond typical Austrian cuisine. The restaurant at **Gasthof Sonne** prepares an adequate *Wurst* and *Schnitzel*, but is especially prized for its convenience—it's right next door to the tourist office (open Mon. and Wed.-Sun.). For variety, visit the **Chinesische Mauer,** at Pfarrgasse 32 (tel. 46 88; open daily noon-2pm and 6-10pm). For the culinarily gifted, there's also a **SPAR market** on Johannesplatz.

Skiing and Entertainment Most tourists flock to Imst in the summer, but the town's relatively inexpensive **ski facilities** are among the best values in Austria. A one day ski-pass, with free bus service to the lift, costs 270 AS (3-day pass 719 AS, 7-day pass 1469 AS). Ski rentals are available at **Schischule Imst** (tel. 35 40 or 21 65), **Sport Winkler** (tel. 23 28), or **Sport Mode Weber** (tel. 42 40 or 22 50). Skis cost 130 AS, sleds 50 AS, and ice skates 40 AS per day. During January, Imst offers the **"Super Family Week,"** when children under 15 get five days of ski classes and a six-day ski pass absolutely free; parents, however, must tag along at full price. (Read:

If you don't have kids, you'd best be wary, lest you get trampled by hordes of prepubescent skiers.)

When the snow melts, Imst still manages to reel in tourists; this tiny polis maintains beautifully-marked forest walkways and several medieval Catholic churches. A blue pamphlet, *Holiday Information,* lists a number of enjoyable walks around town. You shouldn't leave Imst without taking a stroll along the **Rosengartenschlucht** (Rose Garden Ravine), a lovely one- to two-hour walk saturated with alpine birds, flowers, and waterfalls. The gravel path is well-maintained but poorly lighted; watch your step after dark. Start behind the Johanneskirche (across from the tourist office), and keep walking as the path winds through the forest. If you follow the yellow brick road, you can't get lost. Every four years, Imst hosts a spring festival called the **Schemenlaufen;** call the tourist office for more information.

Near Imst: Nassereith

Nassereith lies about 20 minutes from Imst by bus (32 AS), even closer to the German border. On a sunny day, the **Nassereither See** in front of the Riffeltal Mountains is postcard-pretty; the surrounding meadows are replete with grazing cows, prancing chickens, and small children named Heidi. From the main bus stop at the post office, just mosey down Schulgasse between the Post Hotel and the *Tabak* Shop, and take a right at the second narrow street. On this same street is the **Restaurant See-Bua,** a bistro popular with the locals. Laugh heartily and hoist your beer *Stein* for a toast with the other customers. *Schnitzel* runs 70-100 AS (open daily noon-2pm and 5-10pm). If you continue along Schulgasse and take the first left, the first house you'll see is the **Gästezimmer Kranewitter.** The rooms are palatial, breakfast is extraordinarily satisfying, and the prices aren't at all shabby (130 AS per person in the summer, 150 AS in the winter, shower 10 AS). Nassereith's **tourist office** (tel. (05265) 52 53; fax 57 41) is across the street from the town bus stop. The office makes itself look full by packing the stands with brochures from other towns (open Mon.-Fri. 9am-noon and 2-5pm). The local **post office** (tel. (05265) 51 14 or 52 21) is opposite the tourist office, at the bus stop (open Mon.-Fri. 8am-noon and 2-6pm). An **ADEG Aktiv supermarket** is also located in the same tiny square (open Mon.-Thurs. 8am-noon and 2-7pm, Fri. 8am-7pm). **Schloß Farnstein,** on the outskirts of town, merits a quick stopover if you've got a chance. Though it's but a ruin today, Crazy King Ludwig (of Bavarian fairy-tale-castle fame) reputedly spent many a night here by the gorgeous emerald lake. From the Nassereith bus stop, walk along Fernpass Str. (the main thoroughfare) for about 1 mi. to Reuttener Bundesstraße (35 min.). Or, take any bus that heads north (10 AS), and get off at the castle bus stop.

■■■ LANDECK

Though tiny Pfunds is actually closer to the international border, Landeck (literally, "country corner") has long proclaimed itself *the* town at the junction of Austria, Italy, and Switzerland. As it lies both on major rail lines and major highways, Landeck is an ideal base camp for quick jaunts out of the country. Whitewater rafting aficionados frequent the area's rivers in the summer. The winter recreational scene is less active, although Landeck is the second alternative to many skiers who are crowded out of the Arlberg. The town seems louder than the neighboring hamlets; a main artery of the Innsbruck-Bregenz railway (trains from Bludenz 106 AS, from Innsbruck 150 AS) cuts through the town center, accompanied by the natural roar of the River Inn's rapids.

Orientation and Practical Information Landeck's downtown is cradled by the River Inn, flowing southwest to northeast. The town's narrow roads are lined with sidewalk cafés, and a short stroll at any point along **Malserstraße,** the main street, reveals windows of sinful pastries. The **tourist office,** on Malserstr. (tel. 623 44; fax 678 30), offers tours of the city (June-Aug. Wed. at 9:30am, 30 AS). The office also distributes plenty of skiing and hiking information for Landeck and the surrounding area, and will make room reservations for no fee. To reach the office from the train station, just follow the Inn—turn left out of the station onto Bahnhofstr., which becomes Jubilaumsstr. and then Malserstr. as it rounds a corner. (Open Mon.-Fri. 8:30am-noon and 2-6pm, Sat 8:30am-noon.) The **post office** is located on the opposite side of the street from the tourist office, toward the rail station. (Open Mon.-Fri. 8:30am-noon and 2:30-6pm.) **Telephones (City code:** 05442) await inside. Call **Funktaxi** (tel. 625 06) for a cab. You can pick up or peruse the latest *Let's Go* at **Jöchler Bookstore,** Malserstr. 6 (tel. 624 64; fax 652 24).

Accommodations and Food Youth hostels and cheap pensions have yet to arrive in Landeck, but fret not—private rooms abound, and they're often reasonably priced, clean, and spacious. Pick up an accommodations map at either the rail station or the tourist office. Herzog-Friedrich Straße is packed with vacancies (if that's possible); just wander down the street looking for "*Zimmer frei*" signs. From the **Postautobahnhof,** the center of Landeck, walk not to the bridge in front of you, but to the second bridge on Malserstr. Cross the bridge (take a moment to suck in the view), and then turn left; walk past the parking lot and around the hairpin turn to find Herzog-Friedrich Str. At #45, **Spiß-Hildegard** (tel. 628 16) rests at the end of a long blacktop driveway on the left side of the street; reception is on the second floor. The recently renovated, lily-white rooms have security-blanket-soft comforters and mammoth bathrooms. Singles and couples of all types are welcome (160 AS per person). Or try **Landhaus Zangerl,** down the road at #14 (tel. 626 76), in an apartment complex on the right side of the street. It's neither as immaculate nor as expensive as Spiß-Hildegard (155 AS in winter, 140 AS in summer). **Pension Thialblick,** on Burschlweg (tel. 622 61), has bright, airy rooms and fantastic mountain views. Follow the directions for Herzog-Friedrich Str., but stay on the right side of the street after making the hairpin turn. (250 AS per person in winter, 200 AS in summer. Breakfast buffet included. Wheelchair accessible.)

There are also two cheap **campgrounds** in Landeck. Cross the bridge in front of the Postautobahnhof, and turn right. Both **Sport Camp Tirol** (tel. 646 36 or 644 54; fax 640 37) and **Camping Riffler** (tel. 62 47 74; fax 62 47 75) are situated after the 90-degree turn along the river Sanna. Both have toilets, hot water, washers and dryers, and a restaurant. Visit the **SPAR Markt** or **Hofer Markt** down the street for a comprehensive selection of groceries.

Sights and Entertainment Landeck's recreational pride and joy is the **Venetbahn,** the all-weather gondola lift that boosts passengers 1428m in eight minutes. The lift is located close to Zams, a neighboring town, beyond the Landeck rail station (Round-trip 130 AS, under 15 half-price). Landeck's **Regional Skipass** entitles the holder to use six different lifts around the area (2 days 435 AS, 1 week 1320 AS, 12 days 2060 AS). You can rent skis at the **Skischule Landeck,** at the Venetbahn (tel. 626 65); snowshoes range from 25 to 35 AS per day, skis from 65 to 80 AS per day. The postcard-perfect view from atop **Schloß Landeck,** Maximilian's vacation hideaway, marks another magnificent vantage point, second only to the ski lift's apex. The castle (tel. 632 02) is renowned for its frescoes and museum. To reach the *Schloß*, take one of the walkways across from the post office off Malserstr. until you get to Fischerstr, then walk toward the parking lot and up the hill toward the church, until you see Schloßweg. Trek fearlessly up the steep path to find the castle at the end. (Open June-Sept. daily 10am-5pm; Oct. daily 2-5pm. Admission 25 AS, students 5 AS, families 50 AS.)

A number of nighttime establishments provide a welcome diversion *après*-ski or *après*-hike. Shake your booty on over to **Discothek Red Line** (tel. 652 52; open Wed.-Sun. 9am-3pm); **Kla 4** (tel. 652 60; open Mon.-Sat. 6pm-1am); **Safari Billiard-cafe** (tel. 650 80; open daily 10am-1am); or **Picasso Pub** (open Mon.-Sat. 9am-1am).

■ Pfunds

"Quaint." "Charming." "Picturesque." Yup, Pfunds's verbal palate is pretty drab. You'd need a hefty, unabridged thesaurus to describe this tiny town with anything but the most hackneyed of adjectives. Nevertheless, it houses one of the few youth hostels in rural Tyrol and sports a mountain peak from which you can see Italy, Switzerland, and Austria all at once. Transportation favors a quick daytrip into Pfunds. Buses from Landeck arrive about ten times a day, most before 1pm (round-trip 96 AS); buses leaving Pfunds generally depart in the evening. The **post office** is located at the bus stop and is open Mon.-Fri. 8am-noon and 2-6pm. The minuscule **tourist office** (tel. 5229) is about 200 ft. from the bus stop; look for the blue "i" on the left. The tourist officials speak English and provide valuable advice on available recreational activities. Every Monday at 10am, one tourist official sets forth on a free guided tour of the town (open Mon.-Fri. 8am-noon and 3-6pm, Sat. 9am-noon).

Jungendherberge Pfunds (HI) (tel. (05474) 52 44) is a hike over the river and through the woods, but it has the cheapest beds in town. From the tourist office, walk toward the bus stop, and cut through the walkway that runs behind the church and police station on the right. When you reach the road, turn right, cross the bridge over the Inn, and bear right at the fork. Take the second left, pass the barber shop and the shoe shop, and then take a right. (Reception open daily 5-7pm. 110 AS; non-members pay 15 AS surcharge.) If you make it across the river but get lost trying to find the hostel, check out **Gasthof Hirschen** (tel. 52 04; fax 56 34), on the route to the *Jugendherberge* just before the barber shop. The rooms are less spartan than the hostel's (160-190 AS per person). **Pension Plangger** (tel. 52 88) is closer to the tourist office; walk past the office, take the first left, and then left again at the first intersection. (190 AS. Buffet breakfast included.)

Ski passes entitle you to ascend on six lifts around the area; purchase the tickets at the lifts (2 days 610 AS, 1 week 1770 AS, 2 weeks 2940 AS). More flamboyant travelers can purchase a multi-day "Ski Safari"—this includes a guide, transport, and lift passes valid in Austria, Italy, *and* Switzerland. Elephant gun and silly Banana Republic clothing optional (4-day "Safari" 2950 AS, 5 days 2850 AS, 6 days 3980 AS). During the summer, **whitewater rafting** is a fairly popular activity around Pfunds. With a guide, daily trips cost 500-2000 AS; higher prices correspond to longer distances and more challenging paths. You might also partake of **paragliding;** ask at the tourist office for details.

Pfunds inherits a bit of historical significance from its border location. Apparently, Ice Age humans used the nearby Ötztal pass to migrate south through the Alps. The glaciers caught up to the nomads before they crossed what is now the Italian border, and the excessive refrigeration miraculously preserved the bodies. Recently, a rescue team combing the Alps stumbled across one of the wholly intact skeletons. The medical team mistook the body for an avalanche-trapped local citizen, and extricated the remains, though not before ripping into the bones with a jackhammer. When the true age of the body was discovered (over 5000 years old, scientists claim), the National Geographic Society swiftly stepped in; they now hold "Marc Jones"—the European equivalent of "John Doe"—in their extensive collection.

THE ARLBERG

Halfway between Lake Constance and Innsbruck, the jagged peaks of the Arlberg mountains beckon skiers and climbers with promises of Alpine adventure. Since the first descent to the valley by Lech's parish priest in 1895, incomparable conditions have catapulted the area to powder glory. Where once only knickerbockered spitfires dared tread, Spandex-clad pedal pushers and stooped aristocrats now flock like lemmings. Though most lifts operate in summer for high-altitude hikes, **skiing** remains the area's main draw. With hundreds of miles of groomed ski runs ranging in altitude from 3300 to 8500 feet, the Arlberg offers unparalleled terrain from December through April. All resorts have ski schools for children and beginners as well as proficient skiers. Immense lengths of cross-country trails (up to 25 mi. long) traverse the valleys, linking the various villages. The comprehensive **Arlberg Ski Pass** allows you access to some of Austria's most luscious slopes, including the famed **Valluga** summit. The pass is valid for over 88 mountain railways and ski lifts in St. Anton, St. Jakob, St. Christoph, Lech, Zürs, and the tiny villages of Klösterle and Stuben, amounting to more than 115 mi. of prime snow-draped terrain. Rumor has it that the Galzigbahn endures the longest lines, while the Rendl ski area remains largely pristine. Passes should be purchased at the Galzig, Vallugagrat, Vallugipfel, Gampen, and Kapall cable car stations from 8am to 4:30pm on the day prior to use. (410 AS per day, 2 days 770 AS, 1 week 2240 AS, 2 weeks 3620 AS; off-season 370 AS, 695 AS, 2010 AS, and 3260 AS, respectively. Seniors receive a 100 AS discount per day; children under 15 half-price.) Guests registered at local hotels or *Pensionen* usually receive substantial discounts. Hotel ski packages including six days of instruction, ski pass, accommodations, and two meals per day run 3830-13,000 AS.

You can put faith in ski lessons from the **Arlberg Ski Club**—members have won an amazing 11 Olympic and 40 world championship medals. (Group classes for 1 day 380-430 AS, 5 days 1250 AS; private lessons for 1 day 1850 AS.) **Equipment rental** is standardly priced throughout the Arlberg at 1500 AS per week. For **weather reports,** call (05583) 18 in Lech or (05446) 226 90 in St. Anton; **to report accidents** (05583) 28 55 in Lech, (05446) 235 20 in St. Anton. In summer, the equivalent of the Arlberg Ski Pass is available for access to cable car lifts for **hiking;** the pass can be obtained from any of the five stations mentioned in the Ski Pass description above (350 AS for a 1-week pass, 700 AS for the entire summer).

On the eastern side of the Arlberg tunnel, in the province of Tyrol, you'll find the hub of the region, **St. Anton,** and its distinctly less cosmopolitan cousin, **St. Jakob**. The western Arlberg is home to the classy resorts **Lech, Zürs,** and **St. Christoph,** which become, in order, increasingly more expensive. Buses bind the Arlberg towns together, and trains connect St. Anton to the rest of Austria. **Bus** #4235 runs from Landeck to St. Anton every hour; #4248 runs from St. Anton to St. Christoph, Zürs, and Lech five times per day and returns four times per day. In high season, book rooms six to eight weeks in advance; off-season, two weeks in advance should be enough.

■■■ ST. ANTON AM ARLBERG

France has St. Tropez, Switzerland has St. Moritz, and Austria has St. Anton. Don't let the pious name, the provincial hillside farms, or the cherubic schoolchildren deceive you. That's all a façade. A sweet little hideaway for the family? Not quite. As soon as the first snowflake arrives, St. Anton awakens with a vengeance; in winter, the town is an international playground brimming with playboys, partygoers, and plenty of physical activity (cycling, tennis, hiking, and skiing). Downhill skiing was born here when some turn-of-the-century gents barreled down the mountain with boards on their feet; the town has definitely retained its daredevil panache. To escape the tabloid reporters in St. Moritz, much of the Euro jet-set (including Prince Edward of England) winters here. Robin Leach hasn't yet unveiled St. Anton to the cultural elite, but St. Anton *loves* its flock of traveling debutantes. All major credit cards are accepted at almost every establishment; after all, dah-ling, it's awfully *gauche* to carry a wad of cash around. Town planners strategically planted currency exchange and ATMs on nearly every street corner. Language shouldn't be a problem either; sly salesmen have learned that a healthy knowledge of English tends to grease the wheels of commerce. Beware, though: the ski season drives this town—it doesn't emerge from spring hibernation until mid-July.

Orientation and Practical Information St. Anton is conveniently located along major rail and bus routes, at the administrative center of the Arlberg. Trains (tel. 22 42) come and go every two hours from Innsbruck (one way 160 AS); the St. Anton **train station** has currency exchange, luggage storage, and a restaurant for when you have to eat and run. **Buses** run four times daily among the neighboring Arlberg villages Lech, Zürs, and St. Christoph; transportation is slightly more frequent to Landeck. (To St. Christoph one way 10 AS, to Lech 22 AS, to Landeck 46 AS.) **Biking** in the Arlberg is arduous but extraordinarily rewarding—the folks at **Sporthaus Schneider,** in the pedestrian zone (tel. 22 09), will be glad to rent you a bike and dispense maps and trail advice.

Many St. Anton streets lack names, which wreaks havoc on directions. Use the *Fußgängerzone* (pedestrian zone) as a reference; head right from the train station, follow the street down the hill, and bear left at the fork to reach the pedestrian zone. The **tourist office,** in the Alberghaus (tel. 226 90; fax 25 32 15), is the one important structure not in the pedestrian zone; to find it, exit the station, turn right, bear right at the fork, and walk straight for another four minutes. The office is as chic as the town—luxurious leather chairs, mahogany reception stands, and an invaluable 24-hour electronic room finder outside. (Open Mon.-Fri. 8am-noon and 2-6pm, Sat.-Sun. 10am-noon; Sept.-June Mon.-Fri. 8am-noon and 2-6pm.) The **Tiroler Landesreisebüro,** opposite the railway crossing (tel. 22 22; fax 22 21), is a well-equipped regional **travel agency** offering money exchange, general information, and airplane and rail reservations. (Open July-Aug. Mon.-Fri. 8:45am-noon and 3-6pm, Sat. 8am-noon; Sept.-June Mon.-Fri. 8:45am-noon and 3-6pm.) You can also **exchange currency** at the ATM machines around town (beware: the commission here may be exorbitant), or at any of the three banks in town (banking hours are Mon.-Fri. 8am-noon and 2-5pm). To find the **post office** (tel. 33 80), walk to the end of the *Fußgängerzone*, and turn right; then take the second right, and the office will be on the left side of the street. **Telephones (City code:** 05446) are available inside. (Open Mon.-Fri. 8am-noon and 2-6pm.)

Accommodations and Food So you've arrived in St. Anton in the middle of winter. Well, the weather may be chilly, but you've just entered budget lodging hell. The general rule is that prices double during the ski season. Book far enough in advance (about 2 months), and you *may* find relatively cheap housing. Since street anonymity makes directions unclear, the best bet is to ask for precise directions at the tourist office, or consult the electronic accommodation board outside. **Pension Elisabeth** (tel. 24 96; fax 292 54) is one of the town's least expensive bed-and-breakfasts. From the tourist office, walk back toward the rail station and take the first left, to house #315. (In summer 150-190 AS per person; in winter 350-500 AS. Bath, television, and breakfast included. English spoken.) To find **Pension Klöpfer** (tel. 28 00), turn left at the end of the *Fußgängerzone*, and follow the street along the rail tracks; make two 90° turns, then a hairpin turn, and look for house #419. (In summer, singles 160-200 AS; in winter, 300-500 AS. Balcony, bath, parking, and breakfast included.) **Pension Pepi Eiter,** across the tracks and up to the left of the tourist office (tel. 25 50; fax 36 57), provides luscious beds, hearty repasts, and chocolate for weary guests. (In summer, 160-180 AS per person; in winter, 320-400 AS.) The *Fußgängerzone* is riddled with restaurants like the **Amalienstube** (tel. 26 96), which serves up the biggest individual pizzas around (70-110 AS; open mid-June to mid-Oct. and mid-Dec. to March daily 10am-midnight). The **IFA Supermarket** lurks on the same street; although whiskey bottles line the front window, dinner fixings await inside. Really. (Open Mon.-Fri. 7:30am-noon and 2-6pm, Sat. 7:30am-noon.) The **Restaurant am Bahnhof's** best attribute is its long hours (open daily 11am-10pm).

Sights and Entertainment Here in the birthplace of downhill Alpine skiing, the sport is to the town like peanut butter to the roof of your mouth—together and inseparable. St. Anton is home to some of the best skiing in the Alps, but you pay for the quality. If you stay in St. Anton and ski for more than six days, you become eligible for a minor reduction (about 100 AS off your Arlberg Ski Pass). See the Arlberg information above for much more on skiing. You'll only want to shun the slopes during absolutely cataclysmic weather; should a *tsunami* threaten the Arlberg, you might want to turn to the somewhat scanty assortment of other pursuits. St. Anton's **Ski Museum** (tel. 2475) traces the majestic history of the Alpine sport. From the tourist office, walk toward the rail station, take the first left, and then the third right. The museum is located near the Galzigbahn ski lift. (Open daily 10am-6pm. Free.) In summer, you can tack on 80 AS to the weekly hiking pass (see Arlberg information above) to utilize St. Anton's swimming pool and all the facilities at its **amusement park**—table tennis, miniature golf, and fishing, among others.

A professional **tennis tournament** comes to town every December, usually drawing some moderately famous European players, like Goran Ivanisevic. Each January, the entire town flocks to the slope sidelines for a day of **World Cup Skiing,** or at least World Cup Spectating. Call the tourist office for information on specific dates and ticket purchases. The **Arlberg Mountainbike Trophy** is bestowed every August upon the winner of a treacherous 20km race, composed of steep climbs and dangerously rapid downhill sections. Any masochist eager to undertake the journey may enter for free—it's a great way to pace yourself against Olympic and professional cyclists.

Near St. Anton: Lech

Snuggled in the narrow valley between the Rüflikopf (2362m), Karhorn (2416m), and Braunarlspitze (2648m) peaks, Lech boasts the most ski lifts and runs in the Arlberg. The river of the same name courses through town on its way from the Arlberg peaks to the Forggensee in Germany. Developed decades later than its neighbors, this lofty resort has stolen much of their glory. The **tourist office** (tel. (05583) 21 60) is a model of efficiency; check the board in the hall for vacant rooms. (Open in summer Mon. and Wed.-Fri. 8am-noon and 2-6pm, Tues. 9am-noon and 2-6pm; in winter Mon. and Wed.-Sat. 8am-noon and 2-6pm, Tues. 9am-noon and 2-6pm, Sun. 10am-noon and 3-5pm.) The only hostel in the region, **Jugendheim Stubenbach (HI)** (tel. (05583) 24 19), compensates for a hellish location with bright dorms. From the main post office, head out of town. At the Stubenbach city limits sign, take the right fork; follow it down the hill then up again and to the right. (Open mid-Dec. to Nov. Reception open daily 11am-1pm and 5-7pm. Curfew 10pm. 130-150 AS. Dinner 90 AS. Sheets 20 AS. Breakfast included.) If the hostel's full or the walk too daunting, hole up at **Haus Odo** (tel. (05583) 23 58), across the covered bridge and up the hill from the tourist office. (230 AS with shower; in winter, 500-700 AS. Dinner 130-150 AS; in winter, add a 30 AS surcharge.)

Near St. Anton: Zürs

Home to the first Austrian T-bar, Zürs shamelessly owns up to its ski-town status; shades are pulled and windows shuttered from April to November. Hiking trails here tend toward the poorly marked, intermittently maintained, and very wet—there's no compelling reason to get off the bus in the off-season. Even Josef Rice, mountaineer to the Emperor and 17th-century resident, skipped town in summer. The tiny **tourist office** (tel. (05583) 22 45), two blocks left of the post office/bus stop, supplies room, skiing, and insurance details. (Open Nov.-April Mon.-Sat. 9am-12:30pm and 2:30-6pm, Sun. 9-11am; May-Oct. Mon.-Fri. 9am-noon and 2-5pm. English spoken.) Accident-prone skiers may wish to stay with the village physician at **Haus Dr. Murr** (tel. (05583) 25 30), but the rooms will cost you that broken arm and leg. (Singles 450 AS. Doubles 550 AS. In winter, 1060 AS. Breakfast and shower included, but not house calls.) Zürs's only restaurants are conveniently attached to hotels; brace yourself before opening the menu.

Near St. Anton: St. Jakob and St. Christoph

St. Jakob am Arlberg is so cow-ridden that it makes even St. Anton seem ritzy. Many of its *Gasthöfe* are glorified barnhouses, with cows on hand for a morning mooing. **St. Christoph am Arlberg,** on the other hand, is basically just a cluster of ski lifts surrounded by glamourous hotels. Catch a post bus to either hamlet across from the tourist office in St. Anton. (4 per day, 8am-4pm; in winter 9 per day, 9am-5:30pm. 22 AS one way, 32 AS round-trip.)

THE KLEINWALSERTAL

Although one of the country's premier skiing values, the Kleinwalsertal's hinterlandish location brings out a clientele more German than Austrian. Indeed, the area is said to owe allegiance to Austria's geography but Germany's economy. The region is a headache to get to, but a beauty to behold. During the winter, the Kleinwalsertal boasts fabulous skiing—more than 30 lifts transport Alpine gliders to over 44km of cross-country tracks. In the summer, the area becomes a sleek resort, complete with saunas, riding stables, aerobics classes, and gambling. Tourism first fertilized the region, and today the Kleinwalsertal is so pregnant with two-story *Gasthäuser* that at any given moment most of the population consists of non-residents. The real natives base their livelihood almost entirely on the revenue that 180,000 visitors fork over annually; most prices are designed specifically to suck the life from your wallet.

Orientation and Practical Information The Kleinwalsertal actually consists of a small chain of three hamlets (**Riezlern, Hirschegg,** and **Mittelberg**) located on the German-Austrian border. Isolated from Austria by the Allgäuer Alps, the Kleinwalsertal is accessible only by bus, up a nearly vertical incline from Oberstdorf, Germany. Because there's only one way in and one way out, officials usually don't bother to check your passport. The Oberstdorf bus station sends buses over the narrow gorge to the Kleinwalsertal daily (every ½-hr. 8:30am-9pm, round-trip DM10 or 70 AS; businesses accept both currencies, though the region's official currency is the D-Mark). Buff travelers can also bike the 12km up to the Kleinwalsertal, but remember that these are mountains with a capital "M".

Traveling from Germany to the Kleinwalsertal is fairly straightforward, if limited; getting to Oberstdorf from within Austria is another matter entirely. You can either travel by train, over a convoluted path (thanks to those pesky little Alps) running through Bregenz, near Switzerland (one way about 440 AS); or, you can take the bus through Reutte, a dizzying journey laden with hairpin curves and staggering cliffs along the edge of the narrow road (round-trip 93 AS).

Once in the Kleinwalsertal, the main thoroughfare, **Walserstraße,** takes you through all three towns. The largest **tourist office** is in Hirschegg (tel. 511 40), a five-minute walk along Walserstr. from the only bus stop in town. The office sits in the Walserhaus, a large brown and white building at Walserstr. 64. (Open July-Aug. and Dec.-April Mon.-Fri. 8am-8pm, Sat. 9am-8pm, Sun. 9am-noon and 5-7pm; May-June and Sept.-Nov. Mon.-Fri. 8am-noon and 2-5:30pm.) Mittelberg's **tourist office,** Walserstr. 89 (tel. 69 93), is immediately to the left of the Mittelberg bus stop; Riezlern's office, Walserstr. 54 (tel. 69 91; fax 51 14 21) is a short walk along Walserstr. from the Riezlern bus stop. (Mittelberg and Riezlern offices are both open July-Aug. and Dec.-April Mon.-Fri. 8am-noon and 2-5:30pm, Sat. 9am-noon; May-June and Sept.-Nov. Mon.-Fri. 8am-noon and 2-5:30pm.) All three are labelled *Verkehrsamt* and have English-speaking staff who greet visitors with toothy *Grüß Gott*s; you can get oodles of information on skiing and accommodations, and room reservations for no fee.

Because the Kleinwalsertal is so commercial, **currency exchange** is easy. **Banks** are ubiquitous along Walserstr. in all three towns (generally open Mon.-Wed. 8am-noon and 2-4pm, Thurs.-Fri. 8am-noon and 2-5pm). You can also exchange money at **post offices** in the Kleinwalsertal's three towns: in Riezlern, Walserstr. 30 (tel. 6666, fax 6398); in Hirschegg, Walserstr. 64 (tel. 5400); and in Mittelberg, Walserstr. 88 (tel. 5500). Telephones are available at all post offices; the **telephone code** for the Kleinwalsertal is 05517 from Austria and 08329 from Germany. **Taxis** (tel. 5256 or 5726) run through the region until 2am. The **police station** is located in Hirschegg on Walserstr. 24 (tel. 5212) and is open 24 hrs.

Accommodations and Food Staying overnight in the Kleinwalsertal requires either a fat pocketbook or a Schwarzeneggerian body. Hotels are as common as cows, since the area accommodates some 12,000 guests at any one time, but centrally located rooms rarely cost less than 700 AS. You'll need a 4-wheel drive vehicle to avoid the strenuous, uphill hikes to any of the **youth homes,** generally perched on the side of a mountain. Though plentiful and inexpensive, the youth homes cater more to groups and families; if you're travelling solo, be sure to call ahead to ensure a hospitable reception. You might try the **Tirolerhof,** Nebenwasser 11 (tel. 56 55), down Mühleweg and left on Dürenbodenstr. from the Hirschegg stop. (About 140 AS per person. Call ahead to ensure space, and arrive before 7:30pm.) Individual guest rooms are generally cheaper and closer to town; prices run 140-175 AS, with a 20 AS surcharge in winter. The tourist office has a complete list of locations and prices. If the office is closed when you arrive, you can wander down Eggstr. or Walserstr. and look for the *"Zimmer frei"* signs. **Campgrounds** abound in the Kleinwalsertal; try Riezlern's **Campingplatz Jochum,** Walserstr. 10 (tel. 57 92), which even provides a soccer field. (3.50-5 AS per person, 11 AS per tent. Hot showers 1.50 AS. Open July-Oct.) **Campingplatz Zwerwald,** Zwerwaldstr. 29 (tel. 57 27), is another option. (DM12.5 in winter, DM7.5 in summer. Bringing your dog costs an extra DM3. Note that these prices are in marks, not schillings.)

The Kleinwalsertal has unfortunately neglected to open supermarkets, and most restaurants are affiliated with expensive hotels. Expect to pay at least 210 AS for a not-very-filling meal. The one ethnic restaurant in the area is no less expensive; **China-Restaurant Kanton,** Walserstr. 16 (tel. 31 44), is a 10-minute walk downhill from the tourist office, past the casino. (Open daily noon-2:30pm and 5:30-10:30pm.)

Skiing Skiing, naturally, is the Kleinwalsertal's economic lifeblood. Old Man Winter smiles on the region; back in 1721, snowdrifts piled to the tip of the Mittelberg church. Fifty-seven lifts ascend the steep cliff walls (3 remain operational for summer hikers), and 40km of cross-country trails lace this winter wonderland. The **Kleinwalsertal Skipass,** valid on all lifts and the regional shuttle bus, is one of Austria's best values. (4-day pass 1157 AS, 1-week pass 1683 AS, 15-day pass 2677 AS; prices fall slightly in January. Ski for any 4 days within a 7-day period for 1093 AS. Men over 65 and women over 60 receive a 21 AS discount; children under 15 get a 106 AS discount.) One-day courses at any one of nine **ski schools** run 390 AS. Most lifts operate daily 9am-4pm. Passes are available up to one day in advance in the Walserhaus (see above), or at the following ski lifts: the **Kanzelwandbahn** in Riezlern, the **Walmendingerhornbahn** in Mittelberg, or the more secluded **Ifen 2000,** between Hirschegg and Mittelberg. Call tel. 18 throughout the region for **weather and ski conditions.**

VORARLBERG

On Austria's panhandle, Vorarlberg (2600 sq. km, pop. 336,000), the westernmost province (and the smallest, barring Vienna), was first settled by Illyrians, Celts, and Romans. Later, Alemannic tribes moved in and coexisted with the nearby Rhaeto-Romanic peoples. Today, most residents speak an Alemannic dialect of German more akin to the tongue of neighboring Switzerland and German Swabia than the language of the rest of Austria.

At the crossroads of four nations, Vorarlberg is very much an international destination. Carry your passport at all times; foreign borders are never more than two hours away, and thereby an easy daytrip. Bludenz, at the intersection of the Ill and Alfenz rivers, lies about 15km north of Switzerland and 20km east of petite Liechtenstein, a principality favored on quizzes by sadistic geography teachers and stamp collectors worldwide. Bregenz, on the banks of the Bodensee (Lake Constance), would be German but for half a dozen kilometers. The town is the capital of Vorarlberg and the seat of the provincial administration.

The area between the Bodensee and the Arlberg massif contains a variety of sumptuous scenery—from the soft-edged contours of the lake's shoreline, to the towering peaks and glaciers of the Silvretta Mountains, to the plains of the upper Rhine Valley, a landscape molded by Ice Age glaciers. The principal economic activity of the region, other than tourism, is power production; electricity from Vorarlberg's immense reserves of hydroelectric power supplies Austria, Germany, and the Benelux region. Vorarlberg's culinary specialty is *Kässpätzle,* a cheese and noodle combination. Cheese is big here; a visit to a Vorarlberg cheese dairy is an *après*-ski option worth milking.

Snow conditions are dependably *wunderbar* from December to April; slopes reach up to 8500 feet. Over 1000 mi. of marked hiking paths, ranging in altitude from 1300 to 11,000 feet, crosscut Vorarlberg; mountain railways can carry you to the summit quickly and conveniently. Alpine associations administer dozens of huts that provide accommodation and refreshments for hikers between May and October; opening times depend on the altitude, so contact the local tourist offices. Vorarlberg's 100-mi. network of cycling paths ranges from leisurely routes that meander through the Bodensee and Rhine plain to challenging mountain-bike routes in the Alps. The 75-mi. Bodensee circuit circumscribes the lake; rail and ship travel are alternatives in some sections. Cycling maps are available at bookstores and tourist offices.

Vorarlberg's cities are, at best, merely towns. The Middle Ages persist in the ancient arcades of Feldkirch and Bludenz and in the battlements of the Schattenburg fortress. Renaissance opulence constitutes the prevailing spirit of the various cultural events hosted by **Hohenems Palace,** just southwest of Dornbirn. The rollicking Hohenems *programme* culminates in the June **Schubertiade,** a celebration of Franz Schubert's finest works. The annual **Vorarlberg Children's Wonderland** is Europe's largest regional festival for tiny tykes; 200 events throughout Vorarlberg thrill the kiddies in July and August. Try to arrive for the nine-day Festival of Young People's Drama in the Bludenz region in late-July.

Trains run from Innsbruck into Vorarlberg every hour, and from Bludenz to Feldkirch and Bregenz every half hour. Another train runs hourly from Bludenz to St. Anton im Arlberg. Every hour, **bus** #4394 departs from Bregenz to Egg, #4314 travels from Feldkirch to Bludenz, and #4350 runs from Mellau to Egg. Autobahn A14 streaks from Bludenz to Feldkirch and Bregenz before it heads north through Germany; Schnellstraße 200, a tributary of Autobahn A14, connects Egg and Mellau.

■■■ BLUDENZ

If only "user-friendly" could describe a town instead of a computer program, Bludenz would be the Microsoft Windows® of the sight-seeing world. Public bus service, readable signs, clear street demarcations, and incredibly friendly villagers all facilitate travel in this potentially exasperating hamlet. The first attraction visible from the train station is the massive structure housing the **Suchard Chocolate Factory**. From there, all streets lead to the oldest section of Bludenz, the *Fußgängerzone* (pedestrian zone), a cobblestone shopping district closed to automobiles. And when chocolate, shopping, or shopping for chocolate become wearisome, remember that you're surrounded by prime Alpine skiing terrain.

ORIENTATION AND PRACTICAL INFORMATION

Bludenz, on the Innsbruck-Bregenz rail line and Autobahn, is easily accessible by both bus or train. From Innsbruck, a one-way train ticket costs about 200 AS (10-15 per day; under 2 hr.). The slightly lengthier bus journey costs about the same. Transit also runs frequently into the Arlberg (to St. Anton one way 48 AS, to Landeck one way 106 AS).

Tourist Office: Werdenbergerstr. 42 (tel. 621 70; fax 675 97). From the train station, turn right onto Hermann-Sander Str., left on Bahnhofstr., and then take the second left onto Werdenbergerstr. The office is inside the gray cement *Rathaus*, in the first door on the platform to your right as you walk in. The staff will exchange money and make room reservations; ask about the next free city tour. Open Mon.-Fri. 8am-noon and 2-5:30pm.

Travel Agency: Vorarlberger Landesreisebüro, Werdenbergerstr. 38 (tel. 626 53; fax 626 91). Open Mon.-Fri. 8am-noon and 2-5:30pm.

Currency Exchange: At the tourist office, post office, or any bank. Banks have the best rates and are generally open Mon.-Thurs. 8am-noon and 1:45-3:45pm, Fri. 8am-noon and 1:45-5:30pm.

Post Office: Josef-Wolff Platz (tel. 61 85). Open Mon.-Fri. 6:30am-8pm, Sat. 6:30am-noon. Money exchange Mon.-Fri. 8am-noon and 2-5pm, Sat. 9am-noon. **Postal code:** A-6700.

Telephones: At the post office, open Mon.-Fri. 7am-8pm, Sat. 8am-noon. **City code:** 05552.

Trains: Bahnhofplatz (tel. 61 11). Luggage storage. Like the tourist office, will make free room reservations. Wheelchair accessible.

Taxis: To the right of the train station, or call 650 00, 630 00, or 633 33.

Car Rental: Avis Autovermietung, Hermann-Sander Str. 2a, tel. 631 33.

Bike Rental: AVIA-Center, Bundesstr. 3, in Nüziders, a neighboring town (tel. (055 52) 632 11). Half-day 100 AS, one day 150 AS, weekend 350 AS, mountain bike 50 AS surcharge.

Laundromat: Sander-Reinigung, Sturnengasse 5 (tel. 62 93 33). Or **Sofortreinigung und Hemdendienst,** Wichnerstr. 5 (tel. 650 09). Open only in winter. Walk along the same cobblestone road, and then take the third right onto Wichnerstr.

Police: Werdenbergerstr. 42 (tel. 661 00).

ACCOMMODATIONS

Unfortunately, Bludenz has no youth hostel; affordable accommodations near the *Altstadt* are rare. Expect to spend about 170 AS per night for the cheapest accommodations. The best bet is some kind Bludenzer's guest room, or, if you're lucky, a cheap *Pension* on the outskirts of town. The tourist office and train station provide the same city map and the same list of hotels and guest rooms, though budget accommodations are not their specialty. It's especially important to call ahead during the July and August peak season.

Gästezimmer Laterner, Obdorfweg 21 (tel. 625 19). Head out of the rail station and follow the road perpendicular to you. At the end of the street, turn left onto Fohrenburgstr. and follow it past the Suchard chocolate factory to the end; then turn right onto Alte Landstr., and make the first left onto Obdorfweg. Spacious, clean rooms with plenty of closet space, low ceilings, and skylights on the top floor. The good-hearted owner delivers breakfast in bed. No maximum or minimum stay; legend has it that one guest, in fact, has apparently been there for *eight years*. 170 AS per person. Bath 10 AS, laundry 15 AS. Reservations recommended.

Gästezimmer Sapper, Ausstr. 67b (tel. 630 60). From the station, turn right onto Hermann-Sander Str., and take the second right onto Ausstraße (10 min.). Nondescript rooms, but an unbelievably convenient location. 165 AS; shower 15 AS.

Landhaus Müther, Alemannenstr. 4 (tel. 657 04). From the station, turn right onto Hermann-Sander Str., and take the first left onto Bahnstr., which becomes Mutterstr. and Walserweg; then turn right onto Stuttgarter Str, and take the first left onto Alemannenstraße (10 min.). 250 AS in summer, 300 AS in winter. Showers, toilets, and balconies in each room. Breakfast included.

Camping Ernst Seeberger, Obdorfweg 9 (tel. 625 12). Down the road from Gästezimmer Laterner. 60 AS per person, 42 AS per tent, 35 AS per car. Laundry machines available. Showers and kitchen included. Wheelchair accessible.

FOOD

Most of the restaurants in Bludenz are managed under the auspices of hotels and are rather pricey. To rein in your wallet, try to escape the *Altstadt*. While in town, be sure to sample some **Fohrenburg beer** (brewed in Bludenz since 1881), or **Milke chocolate;** the Austrian branch of the Suchard factory churns out the local cocoa vintage right across from the train station.

Kronenhaus, at Werdenbergerstr. 34 in the *Fußgängerzone* (tel. 620 14). Pizza, lasagna, and strudel are each about 55 AS. Open Mon.-Fri. 11am-4:30pm.

Altdeutsche Stuben, Werdenbergerstr. 40 (tel. 620 05). A slightly more expensive option. Typical Austrian entrees run 100-200 AS, desserts and drinks 60 AS. Open until 10:30pm.

China-Restaurant Lucky, Werdenbergerstr. 14b (tel. 656 41). Right down the main drag. Meat and vegetarian dishes 80-200 AS. Open Tues.-Sat. 11:30am-2:30pm and 6-11:30pm.

J. Dörflinger Café, on Rathausgasse. Great for an espresso, an apertif, or a snack. Meals run 60-150 AS. Open daily 9am-10pm.

Top Markt, Bahnhofstr. 4 (tel. 661 32). Bring home your bacon from this supermarket. Open Mon.-Fri. 8:30am-6pm, Sat. 9am-noon.

SIGHTS AND ENTERTAINMENT

A stroll through Bludenz is an Easter egg hunt of sorts—turn a corner, and you may find some secluded little bistro or church known only to a few locals and the original builders. The Gothic **St. Laurentiuskirche** requires no such haphazard discovery; its spire reaches the highest point in town. The structure dates back to the 10th century, and residents still fill Sunday evening services (open Mon.-Sat. 3-5pm). To reach the church from the post office, turn right and then left onto Mütterstr., and cross the street. The 72-step stone staircase climbing up to the church and the Baroque **Schloß Gayenhofen** was hewn in the 17th century.

The **Bludenzer Stadtmuseum,** Kirchgasse 9, is in the historical building through the huge stone **Obere Tor.** From the tourist office on the Werdenbergerstr., walk through the intersection at Josef Wolf Platz and turn left on Kirchgasse, past the 15th-century **Spitalkirche.** The city archives displayed include an expansive collection of metalwork, weaponry from the 14th century, and a late-Gothic Muttersberger altar, among other artifacts. (Open June-Sept. Mon.-Sat. 4-6pm. Admission 10 AS, students free.) The heart of Bludenz is the Rathausplatz; arcaded passageways sprint past lingering remnants of the city's medieval halcyon days. The square is anchored by the **Nepomukbrunnen,** standing proudly before the **Altes Rathaus.**

The *crème de la crème* of Bludenz's attractions, the **Suchard Chocolate Factory,** is lamentably closed to the public. Chocoholics should start the day just by strolling past and inhaling the rich fumes. On one day in mid-July, though, the factory opens its doors to unleash a chocolate flood upon the city. On this day, the **Internationale Schokoladefest,** the largest chocolate festival in the world, tickles the sweet tooth of Bludenz with games, merriment, and luscious chocolate. More than 50 carnival games disburse prizes totaling more than a ton of chocolate. At day's end, the festival's big winner takes home his or her weight in Suchard chocolate—a prize guaranteed to make the lucky victor a much *bigger* winner.

At the center of the Klostertal, Montafonertal, Brandnertal, and Großes Walsertal valleys, Bludenz is a great base for frolicking in the mountains, but the town itself owns little sporting terrain. Fear not; 10 **ski areas** with 250 lifts are accessible from Bludenz, with buses connecting the town to its neighbors. During the peak season, two-day passes cost about 595 AS (1 week 1690 AS, 10 days 2080 AS; under 14, 200 AS discount per day; over 60, 100 AS discount per day). **Ski rental** is available at **Skiverlieh Hotel Scesaplana** (tel. (05559) 221) or **Skiverlieh Werner Beck** (tel. (05559) 306), both in **Brand**, a nearby hamlet. The tourist office has a list of rental locations in **Bürs** and **Bürserberg** as well.

Hiking is unlimited in this corner of Vorarlberg; over 400km of marked trails await guests stricken with the urge to yodel from a mountaintop. The tourist office offers weekly **guided mountain tours** throughout the summer. Cable cars and chairlifts mitigate the ascents and provide access to the loftier peaks. The **Muttersbergseilbahn** (tel. (05552) 668 38) climbs 700m to the belvedere atop the Muttersberg, where you can dream of conquering the Rätikon mountains rising 2km higher. (Cable-car runs daily every hr. 7am-7pm. Round-trip 80 AS, children 45 AS.) In **Brand,** a cable car (tel. (05559) 224) surmounts the 1600m Niggenkopf, with endless hiking trails at its top. (Lift runs late May to early-Oct. 8am-noon and 1-5pm. Round-trip 95 AS, children 60 AS.)

■■■ FELDKIRCH

At the foot of ancient castles ruling over battle-scarred feudal lands, Feldkirch is a town steeped in history. As early as the 13th century, travelers praised the town, and the lamentably-named **Ill River** that rampages through the city hasn't kept modern wanderers from seeking health and rejuvenation. Feldkirch is a perfect base for an international expedition; the city is just minutes from the Swiss and Liechtenstein borders and funnels all trains to Bregenz and the German Bodensee. The narrow streets and alleyways, with their lovingly restored buildings, are functional and fashionable reminders of the Middle Ages.

Orientation and Practical Information The **tourist office,** Herrengasse 12 (tel. (05522) 734 67, fax 798 67), is a short walk from the train station. Turn left onto Bahnhofstr., descend the stairs of the underpass, and follow the arrow marked "*Zentrum.*" Back on street level, walk through the Bezirkshauptmannschaft building directly ahead, and you'll find yourself at Herrengasse. The office provides lodging assistance, information on cultural events, and maps for the neighboring regions (open Mon.-Fri. 8am-noon and 2-6pm, Sat. 9am-noon). Feldkirch's **post office** is located at Marktgasse 4, in the center of the *Altstadt.* (Open Mon.-Fri. 8am-noon and 2-6pm, Sat. 8am-noon. **Postal code:** A-6803.) Bicycle rental, currency exchange, and lockers (30 AS) are available at the **train station** (open daily 6:25am-11:30pm). Trains run frequently to Vienna (760 AS; 5½ hrs.), Salzburg (520 AS; 4 hrs.), Innsbruck (206 AS; 2 hrs.), and Bregenz (50 AS; 45 min.).

Accommodations and Food The **Jugendherberge (HI) "Altes Siechenhaus,"** Reichsstr. 111 (tel. (05522) 731 81), built in 1362, is one of Feldkirch's oldest structures. Originally an infirmary during the Black Plague, the building was fully renovated in 1985 and bears the wisdom of the ages with no sign of decrepitude. From the station, either walk 15 minutes to the right down Reichstr., or catch city bus #2 (direction: "Gisingen/Nofels") to "Jugendherberge" (10 AS). (Members only. 140 AS. Dinners 60 AS. Television and video facilities. Wheelchair accessible.) **Hotel Hochhaus,** Reichsstr. 177 (tel. (05522) 724 79), is within two minutes of the station. (Singles 370 AS, with shower 430 AS. Doubles 500 AS, with shower 820 AS. Huge breakfast buffet included.) On the outskirts of Feldkirch lies **Waldcamping Feldkirch** (tel. (05522) 243 08). The quiet site is just 3km from the Liechtenstein border and only 5km from Switzerland. Frolic in the outdoor swimming pool, the indoor and outdoor tennis courts, the fitness trail, the cross country skiing, and, especially, in the indoor plumbing. To rest your head under the stars, catch bus #2 from the station to the final stop, "Gisingen" (10 AS).

In the center of the *Altstadt,* find picnic supplies at **Interspar Markt,** at the top of Johannitergasse, off Marktgasse (open Mon.-Thurs. 9am-6:30pm, Fri. 9am-7pm, Sat. 8am-1pm). For enormous portions of *Wiener Schnitzel* (125 AS), visit the **restaurant** in the Schattenburg. Finish the meal with a piece of *Apfelstrudel* and coffee, and head down Schloßsteig to work off the extra calories (open Tues.-Sun. 10am-midnight). **Café Feuerstein,** on Schmiedgasse, is the ideal spot for an after-dinner drink or a midday respite. The terrace offers a front-row view of street life in the *Fußgängerzone*. (Café open Mon.-Sat. 8:30am-2am. Pub entrance around the corner at Schlossergasse 1.)

Sights and Entertainment Begin your voyage to the era of chivalry at the Gothic **St. Nikolaus Kirche** in the center of the *Altstadt.* The edifice was first erected in 1287 and received a facelift in 1478 after a series of devastating fires. Don't miss the **Lamentation of Christ panel,** crafted in 1521 by Wolf Huber (a master of the Danube School); it graces the altar on the right. When the sun stirs from behind a cloudbank, the stained glass windows cast a magnificent rainbow pattern on the church floor. The pulpit, which dates from 1520 and served as a tabernacle until 1655, is the most famous example of Gothic wrought-iron work in Austria.

Frescoes of Feldkirch history and the coats of arms of local potentates adorn the 15th-century **Rathaus** on Schmiedgasse. On nearby Schloßergasse stands the **Palais Liechtenstein,** completed in 1697. The palace, which once supported the royal seat of the Prince of Liechtenstein, now houses the city archives and the town library. For two weeks in the middle of June, the plays of Johann Nestroy are performed in the courtyard of the Palais. The **Schattenburg Castle** presides over the Neustadt quarter; stroll down either Schloßsteig or Burggasse from the *Altstadt.* From the early 13th century until 1390, the castle was the seat of the Count of Montfort. The town purchased the castle in 1825 to save it from demolition and converted the building into the **Feldkirch Heimatmuseum.** Locks, weapons, paintings, and medallions lie side by side in the historic apartments of the erstwhile castle. (Open Tues.-Sun. 9am-noon and 1-5pm. Admission 20 AS, students 10 AS.) The city's skyline is punctuated by a number of towers and gateways—former Feldkirch fortifications—the 15th-century **Pulverturm,** for example, once stored the town's gunpowder.

Feldkirch's annual **wine festival** commandeers the Marktplatz on the second weekend in July; the same space is filled each Tuesday and Saturday morning with a **farmer's market.** Music lovers flock to Feldkirch for the **Schubertiade,** in the last two weeks of June. In 1994, the festival coincides with the 200th anniversary of local poet Wilhelm Müller's birthday; Schubert and Müller paraphernalia will overrun every building in town. Ticket bookings are accepted from June 1993 by phone, mail, or fax (tel. (05522) 380 01, fax 380 05). Prices run 300-1100 AS, depending on the specific event and seat; outdoor concert tickets cost about 100 AS. For more information, contact "Schubertiade Feldkirch GmbH, Schubertplatz 1, Postfach 625, A-6803 Feldkirch." The circus comes to town on the first weekend of August; the annual **Festival of Traveling Entertainers** sweeps jugglers, mimes, clowns, and those anatomically questionable balloon animals into every cobblestone path.

■■■ BREGENZ

A playground city on the banks of the **Bodensee** (Lake Constance), Vorarlberg's capital, Bregenz, approaches tourism nirvana. Two millennia ago, Celtic and Roman legionnaires conquered "Brigantium" in a legendary battle on the lakeshores. The Irish-Scottish missionaries Columban and Gallus, who rampaged through town in the early Middle Ages, were so impressed by the town's fascinating situation that they named the area the "Golden Bowl." The inimitable **White Fleet,** an armada of Bodensee ferries, delivers wealthy folk from three different currencies—er, countries—to the city's open palms—er, ports. Swiss and German tourists regularly cross the expansive lake to recline on the landscaped promenades or mingle with the sun-worshipping Austrian elite.

Orientation and Practical Information Bregenz is an uneasy conglomerate of architectural styles, consisting of the Zentrum near the waterfront and the *Altstadt,* or Oberstadt, near the land rising swiftly from *See* level in the west. The Zentrum is nestled between the Bregenzer Ache, flowing northwest, and the Bodensee. The **tourist office,** Anton Schneiderstr. 4A (tel. (05574) 42 39 10), is at the center of the Zentrum; head left from the station along Bahnhofstr., turn right on Rathausstr., and then left again on Anton Schneiderstr. Once there, pick up a walking map for a tour of the old city. (Open Mon.-Fri. 9am-noon and 2-6pm, Sat. 9am-noon and 4-7pm, Sun. 4-7pm; Sept.-June Mon.-Fri. 9am-noon.) The **train station,** closer to the *Altstadt,* abuts the Bodensee in the northeast corner of Bregenz. The street in front of the station, **Bahnhofstraße,** leads west and eventually becomes **Rheinstraße,** which crosses the Bregenzer Ache into neighboring Hard. The **postal code** of the main **post office,** Seestr. 5 (tel. 490 00) is A-6900; the **telephone code** is 05574. The **British consulate,** Bundesstr. 110 (tel. 386 11), and the **German consulate,** Kaspar-Hagen-Str. 2 (tel. 431 80), can help with international affairs. A **pharmacy** (tel. 429 42) is located on Bahnhofstr. 25. Car rental is available from **Avis,** Am Brand 2 (tel. 422 22), **Hertz,** Jahnstr. 13-15 (tel. 49 11), and Säly & König, Arlbergstr. 135 (tel. 311 15). The **ÖAMTC,** an automobile and touring club, has a branch on Broßwaldengasse (tel. 443 78; in an emergency 120); its colleague, **ARBÖ,** is on Rheinstr. 86 (tel. 381 00).

Accommodations and Food Bregenz's **Jugendherberge (HI),** Belruptstr. 16a (tel. (05574) 228 67), is an easy five-minute walk from the tourist office. Head right on Anton Schneiderstr. and turn right on Bergmannstr. at the Österreichische Nationalbank building; then turn left on Belruptstr. A few blocks later, take a right up the hill at the sign pointing to the hostel. The *Jugendherberge* looks like a huge mobile home, complete with geranium-filled window boxes. (Open April-Sept. Reception open 5-9pm. Curfew promptly at 10pm. 110 AS. Sheets 20 AS. Breakfast and showers included.) Hospitable Austrian folk await the visitor at **Pension Paar,** Am Steinenbach 10 (tel. (05574) 423 05). Fresh flowers on the Lilliputian terrace complete the picture. (Open June-Oct. Singles 260-300 AS, doubles 460-540 AS.) *Privatzimmer* are generally cheaper (150-250 AS), but vacancies vanish quickly; ask the tourist office for help in booking a room (30 AS fee).

Four **campgrounds** dapple the Bodensee plains. **Mehrerau-Lamm,** Mehreraustr. 51 (tel. (05574) 317 01), is the cheapest and closest to the center of town (open April-Oct.; 40 AS per person, 30 AS per tent). **Seecamping** (tel. (05574) 318 95) is nearest the lake (open May-Aug.; 45 AS per person, 47 AS per tent). Picnics on the waterfront are special treats; assemble an ants' delight at the **SPAR Markt,** at the corner of Kornstr. and Rathausstr. (open Mon.-Fri. 8am-6pm, Sat. 7:30am-noon).

Sights and Entertainment St. Martinsplatz is the nexus of the Oberstadt; its anchor, the **Martinskirche,** is filled with frescoes dating back to the early-14th century. Particularly noteworthy are the depictions of St. Christopher, the Holy Symbol of Grief, and the 18th-century Stations of the Cross. The **Martinturm,** to the right of the church, rules with 2000-year-old authority. It was the first Baroque structure on Lake Constance, and still boasts the longest onion dome in Central Europe. The first and second floors of the tower house the **Vorarlberg Military Museum**—the view from the dome will bring tears to your eyes (open Easter-Oct. 9am-noon and 2-6pm). The **Alte Rathaus,** on Graf Wilhemstr., is an intriguing *Fachwerk* building designed by Baroque architect Michael Kuen. In this part of town, narrow cobblestone alleys streak among half-timbered houses and endless arcades of arches. The town's Zentrum contrasts vividly with this Oberstadt. On the lakeshore, pastel Baroque buildings with stately façades rise above the tourist traffic of the *Fußgängerzone.* Within a small radius lie the town hall, the seat of the provincial government, and the town's theaters and museums. The **Kirche Herz-Jesu,** with its twin spires and riotous stained-glass windows, suffers from acute sibling rivalry; the church is doomed to sulk in the shadow of the Martinskirche across town.

At water's edge, a strip of souvenir and ice cream stands wraps around the **Strand- und Freibad** (tel. (05574) 442 42), a swimming and sunbathing area. (Open mid-May to mid-Sept. Tues.-Fri. 9am-9pm, Sat. 9am-7pm, Sun. 1-7pm in fair weather. Admission 35 AS, under 26 29 AS.) To acquaint yourself with the lake from a different angle, hop aboard a **ferry** to the **Blumeninsel Mainau** (Mainau Flower Isle). (Ferries depart Bregenz June-Sept. daily at 11am and leave Mainau at 3:45pm. Round-trip 360 AS, under 16 half-price. Remember to bring your passport.) Frequent **ferries** cross to **Konstanz, Germany** as well. (Late-May to mid-Aug. 9:20am-7:50pm, 7 per day; mid-Aug. to late Sept. 9:20am-7:50pm, 8 per day; late Sept. to mid-Oct. 9:20am-3:55pm, 4 per day. Round-trip 250 AS, one way 130 AS, under 16 half-price.) Or join the afternoon cruise along the Swiss, German, and Austrian waterfronts on the **Drei-Länder-Rundfahrt.** (Boat departs Bregenz May-Sept. at 2:30pm, docks again at 5pm. 130 AS. Half-price on all cruises with a Eurail pass or Rabbit Card. The Bodensee is an international waterway; bring your passport on board.)

If you prefer to remain landlocked, head over to the **Vorarlberg Landesmuseum,** Kornmarktplatz 1. The vast collection recounts provincial life since the first inhabitants arrived 2 millennia ago. (Open Tues.-Sun. 9am-noon and 2-5pm. Admission 15 AS, students 5 AS.) Or catch the **cable-car** that shimmies up the Pfänder mountain for a panorama spanning the Black Forest and the Swiss Alps. (Up 72 AS, down 52 AS, round-trip 110 AS. Runs daily July-Aug. 9am-10:30pm; June 9am-8pm; April-May and Sept. 9am-7pm; Oct.-March 9am-6pm.) Adjacent to the lift's apex is a **zoo** with trails where animals wander in their natural habitat (free). The two-hour hike down, over the Fluh and the Gebhardsberg, is worth every step.

The annual **Bregenzer Festspiele,** from mid-July to mid-August, brings the **Vienna Symphony Orchestra** and other opera, ballet, theatrical, and chamber-music companies to town to perform on an ultra-modern floating stage—the world's largest—in the middle of Lake Constance. The festival draws some 130,000 people each summer. Ticket sales commence in November. (100-950 AS, student tickets for weekday performances 100 AS. Standing room tickets can only be purchased 1 hr. before performance; expect a huge line.) For more information, write to "Postfach 311, A-6901 Bregenz," or call (05574) 492 00.

According to local lore, when conventional military methods were failing Austria at the height of the 15th-century Appenzeller wars, the people of Bregenz enlisted the fearsome fighting force of an old woman and her oven. One day, while she slept behind the oven at an inn, a handful of enemy Swiss soldiers gathered for lunch. Awakened, but hidden behind her oven, the old woman managed to overhear the soldiers' conversation—about their intention to destroy strategically vital Bregenz. They eventually spotted and confronted her, but, ever canny, she claimed to have snoozed through the entire thing. Besides, she swore, even if she *had* heard, she would never tell another living soul. The lenient Swiss let the woman go, whereupon she raced to Bregenz. True to her word, she never told another living soul. Instead, she recounted her story to the oven in the center of town and invited every living soul to eavesdrop. Fully informed, Bregenz beat back the Swiss. In Switzerland, residents of the Berner Oberland (home to apple-shooter William Tell, of overture and Lone Ranger fame) relate the same story, but with bumbling soldiers from Austria and a *Swiss* reconnaissance oven.

Near Bregenz: Egg and Mellau

In the northern section of the Vorarlberg Alps, the **Bregenzer Wald** extends from the shores of the Bodensee to the Arlberg. The **Bregenzer Ache** river extends throughout the forest, emptying into Lake Constance after burbling for kilometers. The forest region encompasses many small villages that offer endless trails for hiking and cross-country skiing. The Wald's economic center is **Egg,** a perfect hub for the hiking network. The town's restored **St. Nikolaus** church, built in 1891, and the local **Heimatmuseum,** with its collection of utensils and historical *Trachten* (folk costumes), merit brief stopovers.

Mellau is located at the base of the 2050m Kanisfluh mountain. This town's renown stems from the **Bengath Chapel,** a pilgrimage destination at the entrance to the Mellental. The church's Baroque Madonna is said to possess miraculous powers; click your ruby red shoes together three times as you genuflect.

 Central Tyrol

The Central Tyrol region is a curious amalgam—parts of Tyrol, Salzburg, Carinthia, and East Tyrol, wedged between Italy and Germany, have established a unique flavor defined by Alpine terrain, not provincial boundaries. Central Tyrol enthralls the visitor with breathtaking vistas of rugged mountains and sweeping valleys. For many centuries, the area was an important link between trading forces in Germany and Italy; the larger towns and cities blossomed along these ancient, lowland trade routes. The Salzach, Drau, and Inn rivers course to vastly distinct terrain elsewhere in Austria, but they serve the same purpose in this region; the valleys carved by the powerful waterways present some of the only passable routes through the Alps. The Zillertal Alpen overwhelm with their enormity and grandeur; the sight of mountaintop rock and *névé* (partially compacted granular snow) is, simply stated, unforgettable. Jagged contours in the Kaisergebirge above St. Johann and Kufstein, in the northwest, fade slightly to the rounded shapes of the Kitzbühel Alpen to the south, but the peaks rise again just past Zell am See. Mountainous crags create two of the most spectacular natural wonders in all of Europe; if you're within hours of Central Tyrol, take a detour to the **Krimmler Wasserfälle** or the **Großglockner Straße**—words don't do them justice. Bring lots, and lots, and lots of film; we guarantee you'll use it all.

East Tyrol is the geopolitical oddity of the region; it's technically a semi-autonomous, wholly-owned subsidiary of the province of Tyrol—the two share no common border. In the chaos following World War I, Italy stealthily snatched South Tyrol away, leaving the province rudely divided by an Italian sliver. Although East Tyrol resembles its mother province culturally and topographically, Easterners retain a powerful independent streak. East Tyrol has remained isolated from Slovene nationalists and has thereby avoided the political strife that plagues Carinthia.

■■■ KITZBÜHEL

Kitzbühel is a cross between glitzy St. Moritz and gaudy Atlantic City—wealthy visitors pump enough cash into the local casinos to keep the cobblestone streets in good repair and the sidewalk cafés flourishing. It's telling that Kitzbühel hosts the annual Miss Austria beauty pageant, when voluptuous Alpine *Fräulein* parade to the pleasure of local oafs and the dismay of most other women. At night, affluent international playchildren gather in Kitzbühel's tiny pubs to squander inherited money on drink and debauchery. Most visitors here are older (read: financially secure) Germans and Britons.

Kitzbühel has weathered three millennia, though official records of "Chizbuhel" only trace back to 1165. Grog, Uruk, and company mined copper on the Kelchalm and the Schattberg back when your grammar school teacher was born. The discoveries from the mines and graves are agglomerated in the local **Heimatmuseum,** situated on the foundations of an early Middle Ages castle. In 1255 Kitzbühel received the right to trade because of its importance in negotiations between Italy and Bavaria—the shortest route from Venice over the Hohe Tauern mountains passed through Kitzbühel. For six centuries, Kitzbühel's mountains were more famous for silver and copper than Olympic skiers. Since the mining era, however, the town has recognized the value of the mountains' shells, rather than their innards; Kitzbühel has courted the ski clientele so thoroughly that the "local" you accost for directions is almost certain to be another confused tourist.

ORIENTATION AND PRACTICAL INFORMATION

Kitzbühel sits prettily on the banks of the Kitzbüheler Ache river. Nearby, the mud-bearing Schwarzsee proffers its luscious and theoretically curative blue waters. The town cowers under a number of impressive peaks, including the Kitzbüheler Horn (1996m) and the Steinbergkogel (1971m).

Several major rail lines converge on the town; the routes from München and Innsbruck funnel through Wörgl into Kitzbühel before running onto Zell am See. Kitzbühel's *Fußgängerzone* (pedestrian zone), at the center of town, hosts multitudes of cafés and benches, where the paparazzi lie in wait for innocently strolling celebrities.

Tourist Office: Hinterstadt 18 (tel. 21 55 or 22 72; fax 23 07). Head out the main door of the *Hauptbahnhof* and turn left; at the end of the street, turn right and walk toward the shops. When you reach the wall—a Creditanstalt should be on your right, a mucky stream on your left—climb the steps on your left, and make an immediate left; before you step into the *Fußgängerzone*, make a right turn and look for the tourist office. From the Hahnenkamm Bahnhof, walk down the road in front of you to the center of town (the fourth or fifth left); then go through the archway. The tourist office is next to the movie theater. Because the office doesn't make reservations, it's up to you to use the free telephone at the **electronic accommodations board** outside. The office gives hour-long **tours** of Kitzbühel (in German) every Tues. at 9:45pm during the summer (free with a guest card). Office open Mon.-Fri. 8:30am-noon and 3-6:30pm, Sat. 8:30am-noon. Accommodations board open daily 8am-10pm.

Budget Travel: Travel Agency Eurotours, across the street from the tourist office (tel. 31 31 or 32 85; fax 30 12). Offers discounts on package tours and makes local room reservations, for a fee. Open Mon.-Fri. 9am-noon and 3-5pm.

Currency Exchange: The most widely accepted forms of currency in this ritzy town are Visa and MasterCard. Exchange available at all banks and travel agencies and at the tourist office; best rates at the post office. Also try **Reisebüro Eurotours** (tel. 313 10), opposite the tourist office. Open Mon.-Fri. 8am-12:30pm and 3-6:30pm, Sat. 8am-12:30pm and 4:30-6:30pm, Sun. 10am-noon and 4:30-6:30pm.

Post Office: Josef-Pirchl-Str. 11 (tel. 27 15). From the tourist office, walk toward the *Fußgängerzone* and turn left; then walk past the church and follow the street as it curves around a right angle. The office is on the left side of the street. Lists bus schedules. Telephones inside. Open Mon.-Fri. 8am-noon and 4-7pm, Sat. 8-11am. Currency exchange Mon.-Fri. 8am-noon and 4-5pm. **Postal code:** A-6370.

Telephones: At the rail stations, post office, and behind the tourist office. **City code:** 05356.

Trains: Tiny Kitzbühel has 2 train stations, one at each side of the "U" formed by the rail tracks. From Salzburg, you arrive first at the **Hauptbahnhof;** from Innsbruck or Wörgl, at the **Hahnenkamm Bahnhof.** Luggage storage is available at both stations (20 AS per piece; open daily 8am-10pm). Train one way to St. Johann 16 AS; Innsbruck 97 AS; Salzburg 205 AS; Vienna 457 AS. For train information, call 40 55 31.

Buses: Stops adjacent to both train stations. For information, call the **Postautodienst** (tel. 27 15).

Taxis: Standplatz Bahnhof (tel. 26 17) or **Standplatz Vorderstadt,** near Hotel zur Tenne (tel. 21 57). Taxis run until 2am.

Laundromat: Clean your soiled garments at **Phönix Reinigung,** Graggangasse (tel. 30 55). Open Mon.-Fri. 9am-noon and 3-4pm.

Hospital: Kitzbühel Krankehaus (tel. 40 11), on Wagnerstr. In an **emergency,** call 144.

ACCOMMODATIONS

Kitzbühel has more guest beds (10,000) than inhabitants (pop. 8070), but you'll pay for the convenience; the only **youth hostel** is far from town and restricted to groups. Austrians claim that in Kitzbühel, you pay German prices for German comfort (read: twice the price, half the comfort). Rooms during the summer generally run 200 to 300 AS per person; expect to shell out 50 to 100 AS more during the winter. Regular buses connect the area to nearby towns, where accommodations are considerably cheaper than in Kitzbühel itself. Be sure to ask for your **guest card** upon registration at a local *Pension*—it entitles you to discounts on all sorts of town facilities.

Pension Mühlbergerhof, Schwarzseestr. 6 (tel. 28 35). From the tourist office, walk through the archway to the left, and follow Franz-Reisch-Str. (look for the McDonald's and the Wienerwald) until it becomes Schwarzseestr. (5 min.). Inundated with farm motif outside and in. In winter 230 AS per person, in summer 200 AS. Breakfast and shower included. English spoken.

Pension Licht, Franz-Reisch-Str. 8 (tel. 22 93). Follow the directions for Pension Mühlbergerhof to Franz-Reisch-Str. Immaculate chambers with a plethora of lawn chairs outside. 250 AS per person. Breakfast and shower included.

Gasthof Alpenhof, Aurach 176 (tel. 45 07). Three km outside Kitzbühel; call to get picked up at the rail station. The British staff oversees rooms with fantastic balconies. 150-200 AS per person. Reservations recommended.

Camping Schwarzsee, Reitherstr. 24 (tel. 28 06 or 44 79; fax 44 79 30). Take the train to the "Schwarzsee" stop (just before the "Hahnenkamm" stop), and walk toward the lake. 60 AS per person, 55 AS in winter.

FOOD

There are few reasonably priced chains in Kitzbühel; most establishments prepare for the most cultured palates and price their dishes accordingly. Look for the more typical (though pedestrian) havens to avoid expensive gastronomic adventures.

Café-Restaurant Prima Angebot, on the corner of Ehrengasse and Bichlstr. (tel. 50 91). Inexpensive meals on a sunny patio overlooking the mountains. Enjoy daily specialties like pizza and *Schnitzel* (60-100 AS), a fresh salad bar, and self-service options. Open daily 11am-10pm.

China Restaurant Peking, on the Kirchplatz (tel. 21 78). Relatively uninspired *faux*-Chinese cuisine, but the price is right. Entrees 80-200 AS. Open daily noon-2pm and 6:30-11pm.

PIKAs, Josef-Herold-Str. (tel. 575 64). Interesting Tyrolean-Italian combinations, something like Mozart writing "The Marriage of Figaro." Try the baked *Schnitzel* over fettucini. Entrees 100-200 AS.

Wienerwald, Franz-Reisch-Str. (tel. 725 45). Though it's an omnipresent Austrian chicken chain (a veritable white meat nirvana), vegetarian salad options abound. Entrees 70-150 AS. Accepts credit cards. Open daily 10am-11pm.

McDonald's, on Franz-Reisch-Str. behind the tourist office. Nothing quite like it, unless you count the million other franchises.

Markets

SPAR Markt, on the corner of Ehrengasse and Bichlstr., under the Café-Restaurant Prima Angebot. Open Mon.-Fri. 8am-6:30pm, Sat. 8:30am-1pm.

Julius Meinl, on Franz-Reisch-Str. across from the McDonald's, and another branch in the *Fußgängerzone.* Open Mon.-Thurs. 8:30am-noon and 2-6:15pm, Fri. 8:30am-6:30pm, Sat. 8:30am-noon.

Farmer's market, in front of the tourist office. On Wed. and Sat. mornings, stands suddenly bloom, displaying the fruits of the fields.

SIGHTS AND ENTERTAINMENT

Barren mountains, churches, and chapels dominate the landscape of Kitzbühel. The **Pfarrkirche** (parish church) and the **Liebfrauenkirche** (Church of Our Lady) stand on the holy hill in the middle of the cemetery. The Pfarrkirche, dedicated to St. Andreas, was built from 1435 to 1506, renovated in soaring Baroque between 1785 and 1786, and then restored again in 1951 and 1990. Between the churches stands the **Ölberg Chapel,** with a **Death Lantern** dating from 1450 and frescoes from the late 16th century. The town **fountain** in the Hinterstadt was created by Kitzbühel's academic sculptor, Sepp Dangl, to mark the 700th anniversary town celebrations in 1971. The local **Heimatmuseum,** Hinterstadt 34, stocks three floors with a rich collection of pre-historic European mining and north Alpine Bronze Age exhibits.

Few visitors remain at ground level for long, however; the Kitzbühel **ski area** is simply one of the best in the world. Site of the first cable car in Austria in 1928, the range challenges skiers and hikers with an ever-ascending network of lifts, runs, and trails; these mountains honed the childhood skills of Olympic great Toni Sailer. If you spot a skiing retinue, chances are good that they're chasing European royalty down the slopes—Princess Stephanie of Monaco is one of the many regal vacationers. In January, Kitzbühel hosts the true *crème de la crème* during the **Hahnenkamm Ski Competition,** part of the annual World Cup.

Amateurs can partake of Kitzbühel skiing as well. A one-day ski pass (320-340 AS; under 15 half-price) grants you free passage on 64 lifts and the shuttle buses that connect them. Lift ticket prices drop after the first day; further reduced prices are available with a guest card. All of the passes may be purchased at any of the following lifts: Hahnenkamm, Fleckalm, Hornbahn, Bichlahn, Gaisberg, Resterhöhe, and Kurhaus Aquarena. You can **rent skis** from virtually any sports shop in the area. Try **Kitzsport Schlechter,** Josef-Herold Str. 19 (tel. 43 73), or **Sport Pepi,** next door (also, tel. 43 73). Downhill equipment rental runs 95 to 140 AS per day; lessons cost 340 AS per day. Ask at the tourist office about prefabricated **ski packages:** one week of lodging, ski passes, and instruction (available before Christmas and after Easter). Rock-bottom for week-long packages, without instruction, is 2900 AS. For a **snow report** in German, dial 181 or 182.

An extensive network of **hiking trails** snakes up the mountains surrounding Kitzbühel. Most are accessible by bus (24 AS) from the main station. Get a map *(Panoramakarte)* from the main tourist office, or at one of the branch offices in Oberndorf, Reith, Kirchberg, Aurach, or Jochberg. After ski season, ride the **Hahnenkammbahn** (140 AS, with guest card 120 AS, children 70 AS; open daily 8am-5:30pm) to reach some of the loftier paths. You might consider climbing up yourself; the descent is free on this and most other area cable cars. The **Kitzbüheler Hornbahn** lift ascends to the **Alpenblumengarten,** where more than 120 different types of Alpine flowers blossom each spring. (Open daily mid-Oct. to April 8:30am-5:30pm; each of 3 sections of the cable car ride costs 65 AS.) Guest-card holders can take advantage of the tourist office's *wunderbar* mountain-hiking program (June to mid-Oct. daily, departing from the tourist office at 9am; free). The guided hikes (2½-6 hrs.) cover more than 100 routes. **Bei Bikeline,** Klostergasse 8 (tel. 56 44), provides guided **mountain-bike tours** (240 AS; every Thurs. 9am-1pm).

Kitzbühel also boasts the standard Austrian resort attractions. The therapeutic peat-moss bottom of the nearby **Schwarzsee** (tel. 23 81) finds its way into *Kurhaus* after *Kurhaus.* Or soak in the public **swimming pool** (40 AS, with guest card 35 AS, children 12 AS), quite an aquatic bargain. Kitzbühel's **Heimatmuseum,** Hinterstadt 34, features an encyclopedic history of the town's skiing memorabilia. (Open Mon.-Sat. 9am-noon. 30 AS, with guest card 25 AS, children 5 AS.)

Eclecticism reigns at the *gratis* music concerts during the summer; the repertoire runs the gamut from local harpists to American high school marching bands. Check for signs posted around town, or call the tourist office for the identity of the day's performers. (Every Tues. and Fri., weather permitting, in the center of town at 8:30pm. Also, Wed. at the Chamber of Commerce at 8pm. Tickets required.) **Casino Kitzbühel,** near the tourist office, is open every night at 7pm. Go on, raise the stakes—you've got to finance that lift ticket for tomorrow (no cover; semi-formal dress). At the end of July, the **Austrian Open** Men's Tennis Championships come to town, frequently drawing athletes such as Boris Becker and Ivan Lendl to the Kitzbühel Tennis Club. Call 33 25 (fax 33 11) for ticket information.

According to legend, several farmers brought their cows to pasture on an extraordinarily beautiful Alpine peak near Kitzbühel, north of **St. Ulrich.** The mountain's fertility thrilled the cows and enriched the farmers, who steadily became more vain and less devout as their wealth increased. Eventually, they were concentrating more on frolicking than praying, and, one Sabbath day, as they ascended their beautiful pasture to partake of some bowling, the ground began to collapse under them. With each additional step, another patch of land would slip out from below. Water rushed from the sundered earth and drowned the townsfolk; today, the unleashed torrent fills the Piller See. As with many Tyrolean lakes, superstitious locals still ascribe deadly powers to the waters. If you fall asleep on its shores, they say, the lake will draw you into its gloomy depths.

THE KAISERGEBIRGE

Unlike other nearby mountain regions, the Kaisergebirge hosts a number of towns, villages, and important byways in a small but dense area. Nicknamed *"Kaiser,"* as in the roll, and, perhaps, the emperor, the range rises to the north of the Kitzbühel Alps. The region is a nature preserve, defined by the River Inn to the west and the Großache to the east; both rivers flow south to north. The highest peak in the region is the Ellmauer Halt at 2344m. Ron Andjill, with the help of his Sherpa guide, "Brendon," first ascended the mountain just under a century ago. The two made the climb in late fall; by the time they reached the summit, the mountain was swaddled in a quilt of snow—they simply unpacked their trusty wooden slats and skied down. Covered with coniferous forestland and occasional meadows, the Kaisergebirge boasts two delightful lakes, the Hintersteiner See and the Walchsee, near Kufstein and the German border. This is truly a hiker's Shangri-La.

Autobahn A12 runs south along the River Inn through Kufstein and Wörgl, and Schnellstraße 176 runs south from Germany through St. Johann. Bundesstraße 312 binds St. Johann and Wörgl; its tributary, Bundesstraße 173, branches off to reach Kufstein from St. Johann. **Bus** #3060 runs from Salzburg to St. Johann every hour; #4000 connects Kitzbühel to St. Johann; and #4024 travels from Kufstein to St. Johann. Bus #4014, from Kufstein through St. Johann and Kitzbühel to Lienz, runs slightly less frequently. **Trains** generally follow the same routes, and depart more regularly.

■■■ ST. JOHANN IN TIROL

St. Johann is the more palatable side of Kitzbühel, six miles to the south—the same skiing and hiking, *sans* the preponderance of Rodeo Drive labels. Here, genuine Tyrolean homes and comfortably intimate inns ensconce the traveler after a grueling day of conquering moguls, ski jumps, and reckless *Kinder*. The town is unabashedly a card-carrying ski village; here, the "L"-words are "lift lines."

Orientation and Practical Information The village is nestled between two peaks, the Wilder Kaiser (2344m) and the Kitzbüheler Horn (1996m), at the intersection of two highways, Bundesstraße 164/312 and Bundesstraße 161. The Großache, with its source in the Rettenstein mountain to the south, flows through St. Johann on its way to Germany, where it adopts the name "Tiroler Ache"—that is, once it leaves Tyrol. Another river, the Spertental, intersects the Großache near St. Johann.

From the train station, St. Johann appears inauspiciously barren, but saunter left and head up Bahnhofweg to reach the vibrant *Stadtzentrum*. There you'll find the **tourist office** (Tourismusverband), Poststr. 3 (tel. (05352) 22 18 or 33 35; fax 52 00), with a 24-hour accommodations board outside and a Jackson Pollack-esque motif inside. The board lists the more expensive alternatives, and the staff can suggest others. The more you flutter your Bambi eyes looking helpless, the better your room might be. (Open Mon.-Fri. 8am-noon and 2-6pm, Sat. 8:30am-noon and 4-6pm, Sun. 10am-noon; Sept.-June Mon.-Fri. 8am-noon and 2-6pm, Sat. 8:30am-noon.) **Tiroler Landesreisebüro-Verkehrsbüro,** Hauptplatz 12 (tel. 23 54), handles discount trips from Innsbruck, Salzburg, and Vienna; the staff will also rent you a car from **Avis** or **Hertz. Exchange currency** at all banks and travel agencies and at the post office (banking hours are Mon.-Fri. 8am-noon and 2-4pm). The St. Johann **post office** is in the Hauptplatz as well. From the station, walk out Bahnhofstr., and turn left at the first intersection; after passing the church on the right, look for the post office around the next corner. (Open Mon.-Fri. 8am-noon and 2-6pm, Sat. 8-10am. Currency exchange Mon.-Fri. 8am-noon and 2-5pm.)

You can reach St. Johann by train from Innsbruck (15 per day; one way 150 AS), Salzburg (15 per day; 194 AS), and Vienna (660 AS). Pick up buses from outside the **train station** (tel. 23 05). Schedules are available directly inside the *Bahnhof,* to the left. **Luggage storage** is also available inside (daily 4am-10pm). **Taxis** (tel. 33 33) stand outside the train station, or call **Schneder Anton,** Speckbacher Str. 41 (tel. 46 00). In an **emergency,** dial 133.

Accommodations and Food Most room prices will make you wince; hostels are nonexistent, and cheap *Pensionen* are scarce. The tourist office can weed out the best of what's left; arrive before noon if possible. **Pension Penzing,** Schießstandgasse 29 (tel. 28 42), has some of the cheapest singles and doubles around.

From the tourist office, turn left, make the first right, and cross the railroad tracks; then take the first left, and bear left at the fork. It looks like a barn on the outside, but don't worry—it's whistle-clean inside (150 AS; breakfast and shower included). **Campingplatz Michelnhof,** Weiberndorf 6 (tel. 25 84), is far, far, far away from town. Exit the main door of the train station, make an immediate left and another left onto Bahnhofweg. At the first intersection, turn left to get onto Speckbacher Str. and follow the road for 20 or 30 minutes (in summer 55 AS per person; in winter 65 AS per person).

Venture to **Pizzeria Masianco,** Speckbacher Str. 30a (tel. 46 30), which churns out the best German-Italian food in the area; rumor has it that they plan to add Pacific Rim cuisine so they can go global. Plenty of meat pizzas (60-120 AS; open Tues.-Sun. 11:30am-2pm and 5pm-midnight). There are racks of clothes interspersed among the shelves of food at the **SPAR Markt** on Speckbacher Str. (open Mon.-Fri. 8:30am-noon and 2:30-6pm, Sat. 8:30am-noon). The **Julius Meinl supermarket,** across the street, keeps the same hours.

Skiing and Entertainment There's not much to the town other than the mountain sports; visitors generally sleep if they're not climbing up or careening down. In winter, the **Schneewinkl-Skipaß** is the most comprehensive ticket, valid on 60 lifts in the St. Johann area (1 day 310 AS, children 170 AS; 1 week 1630 AS, children 950 AS). In summer, the snow melts to expose numerous mountain paths popular with hikers. Round-trip summer lift tickets cost up to 170 AS (guest cards bring further discounts). Hot-air balloons and paragliding have shown swiftly rising popularity (and prices), but you can't beat the view from mid-air.

According to local lore, a recently jilted young maiden tried to assuage her grief by dancing with a strange green huntsman who showed up at a St. Johann wedding. Impressed by her fetching moves, the huntsman asked if he could serenade her the following evening, and, intrigued, she agreed. As planned, the green huntsman showed up at her window—as (surprise!) Satan; he ripped the unlucky woman through the iron bars of her window, leaving bits of *Fräulein* behind as he flew off. Warning: *Let's Go* cannot recommend consorting with The Evil One™.

■ Kufstein

For the past six centuries, the Germans and the Austrians have been playing hot potato with Kufstein; conspiracy theorists have unveiled a plot to drive Rand McNally employees insane by repeatedly redrawing the international border on alternating sides of the **Inn** river. In 1342, Kufstein became part of Tyrol through the marriage of the Tyrolean countess Margarete Maultasch and a Bavarian prince; Germany reclaimed the land during the Bavarian War of Succession. The town is now a mesh of history entangled with the materialism of the 1980s. Kufstein's cobblestone streets are walled by Omega Watch dealerships and swanky spandex and leather boutiques. The fortress, an everpresent remnant of ancient skirmishes, is encircled by a huge supporting cast of postcard stands and souvenir shops.

This 13th-century stronghold, the **Festung,** sits atop a bluff poised treacherously over the Inn. From the station, cross the Innbrücke and turn right. (Guided 1-hr. tours of the fortress's interior April to mid-Oct. Tues.-Sun. at 9:30am, 11am, 1pm, 3:15pm, and 4:40pm. Tours 25 AS. Entrance to the fortress by a separate ticket 70 AS, students and seniors 50 AS, children 25 AS.) Inside, check out the graves, artifacts, and paintings recounting the fortress's history. Another town highlight is the **Kaiserturm** (Emperor's Tower), a massive structure built to honor Maximilian and used to jail his enemies until the late 19th century. The **Bürgerturm,** a tower in the Unterer Stadtplatz, houses the **Heldenorgel** (heroes' organ), the world's largest open-air organ with a whopping 4307 pipes. Locals can hear the behemoth bellow 8 mi. away (concerts June to mid-Sept. daily noon and 6pm).

Kufstein is the unofficial capital of the **Kaisergebirge** (Emperor's Range), a jagged limestone massif famed for its hiking and dramatic scenery. The **Kaiserlift** and **Ses-**

sellift Wilder Kaiser cable cars are the only ways to get to the top of the mountains (day tickets 80 AS each). Hiking is also available in nearby **Kramsach;** the cable-car to the peak costs 175 AS round-trip, with a guest card 155 AS. (Lift runs July to late-Oct. 8:30am-5pm.)

Nearby **Wörgl** (see below) seems more inviting to wayward backpackers—"*Zimmer frei*" signs in Kufstein are few and far between. Kufstein's *Fußgängerzone* holds a **SPAR Markt** for the culinary reductionist (open Mon.-Fri. 8am-6:30pm, Sat. 8am-noon). The town is extremely well-connected to the rest of Austria by public transportation; **buses** run daily between Kitzbühel and Kufstein (90 min.), and trains skirt one side of the mountains, running from Kitzbühel to Kufstein via Wörgl (76 AS). Plenty of **luggage storage** and **telephones** (**City code:** 05372) are available inside the ultra-modern station. The town **tourist office** (*Tourismusverband*), Münchner Str. 2 (tel. 622 07), across the street from the train station, helps with accommodations (careful—their list may be outdated), distributes a restaurant list, and dispenses useful city maps. (Open Mon.-Fri. 8am-12:30pm and 2:30-6pm, Sat. 9am-noon.) The **post office** (tel. 625 51) is located on Oberer Stadtplatz, across the river and to the right of the pedestrian zone. (Open Mon.-Fri. 7am-8pm, Sat. 7-11am. **Postal code:** A-6330.) The **hospital** is at Krankenhausgasse 8 (tel. 69 66); the **police station** (tel. 69 20 42) sits on Salurner Str.; in an **emergency,** dial 122.

■■■ WÖRGL

If you're taking any form of public transportation into western Austria, chances are good that you'll travel through Wörgl. This tremendous transportation hub lies just off Autobahn A12, at the junction of *every* rail route and eight bus routes heading into the West. Each caboose that rolls into town sparks delight in the eyes of the natives; residents know that the thousands of tourists who arrive for hedonism in the hills will depart millions of dollars collectively closer to penury.

Orientation and Practical Information Wörgl lies at the confluence of the Brizentaler Ache and Inn rivers. A bevy of appetizing eateries, Tyrolean garment outfitters, and tacky souvenir shops spill into Wörgl's shopping district on **Bahnhofstraße.** The **tourist office** is located here, at Bahnhofstr. 4 (tel. 760 07; fax 716 80). From the train station, turn right, and walk past the post office; make a left at the end of the street, and continue for three blocks (5 min.). An extremely amiable, English-speaking staff distributes mounds of English information on recreational opportunities in the area and makes reservations for no fee. (Open Mon.-Fri. 8:30am-6pm, Sat. 8:30am-noon.) The **post office,** on Bahnhofplatz 1 adjacent to the train station (tel. 737 51 0), houses **telephones** (**City code:** 05332) and exchanges money. (Open Mon.-Fri. 7am-7pm, Sat. 8-11am. **Postal code:** A-6300.) You can also exchange currency at any town **bank** (banking hours in Wörgl are Mon.-Fri. 8am-noon and 3-5:30pm, Sat. 8am-noon).

Trains make daily connections through Salzburg, Innsbruck, Kufstein, and Kitzbühel to the rest of the continent. The train station (tel. 725 55 385) has **luggage storage** as well (20 AS per piece; open daily 8am-10pm). **Sport Mitterer,** Bahnhofstr. 2b (tel. 727 96), rents bicycles (80 AS per day, 380 AS per week; mountainbikes 200 AS per day). **Taxis** are available daily until 2am at the rail station (tel. 721 15) or through **Taxi Entleitner** (tel. 710 71).

Accommodations and Food Wörgl's ratio of rooms to residents is significantly lower than that in other Austrian towns, so use the tourist office's exceptional service to aid you in your quest for accommodations. **Haus Leitner,** Bruder-William-Str. 26 (tel. 727 18), offers balcony rooms with alpine views. Walk past the tourist office, turn right onto Innsbrucker Str., and turn right again onto Opperer Str.; Bruder-William-Str. intersects Opperer Str. on the left side. (In winter 190-250 AS; in summer 150-200 AS. Shower and breakfast included. Call ahead.) **Häuse**

Gwiggner, Prandtauer Str. 39 and 40 (tel. 307 02 or 314 24), are two *Pensionen* owned by allied sisters; both are quiet and clean and offer commodious chambers. Pass the tourist office and turn right on Innsbrucker Str.; take the first right onto Pacher Str., and then look for Prandtauer Str. at the first intersection. (In winter 140-200 AS; in summer 130-180 AS. Breakfast and bath included.) Usually, at least one sister has room for an extra guest. Pick up rudimentary victuals at the **Julius Meinl supermarket,** on Bahnhofstr. (open Mon.-Fri. 8:30am-noon and 2-6pm, Sat. 8:30-11:30am).

Skiing and Entertainment The Wörgl area hosts one of the largest ski regions in all of Austria, offering more than 200km of downhill runs. The **Wildschönau Ski Pass** is valid on 34 lifts (3 days 805 AS, children 485 AS; 1 week 1560 AS, children 935 AS; 2 weeks 2410 AS, children 1445 AS). There are three lifts in the greater Wörgl area—**Hopfgarten-Itter** (tel. (05335) 22 38), **Niederau-Auffach** (tel. (05339) 82 12 or 22 22), and **Kramsach-Sonnwendjoch** (tel. (05335) 22 38)—passes for these lifts alone are significantly cheaper (½-day pass 100 AS, children 70 AS; 1 day 160 AS, children 95 AS; 3 days 440 AS, children 280 AS). **Buses** (free with a guest card) run to all three; pick up the bus schedules from the tourist office or post office. You can **rent skis** from the local sporting goods store at Boden 33 (tel. 739 45). Downhill equipment (skis, boots, and poles) packages run 150 AS per day, children 100 AS; cross-country skis cost 80 AS per day. **Ski lessons** are also available here; courses are held daily from 10am-noon and 1:30-3:30pm (3 days 990 AS, 5 days 1150 AS, 6 days 1200 AS).

During the summer (mid-June to Sept.), the tourist office offers free guided **tours** to anyone with a **guest card.** Every Tuesday, the office leads hikes through the **Kundler Klamm Gorge;** on Saturdays, they travel to the **Buchacker Ice Cave** (ice cave open May-Oct. Sat.-Sun. 10am-4pm; admission without tourist office tour 45 AS, children 25 AS). The office also sponsors guided bike tours every Thursday. Pre-register at the tourist office and inquire about meeting times and places.

THE ZILLERTAL ALPS

The Zillertal Alps are a popular destination for Austrians who seek a weekend escape from camera-clicking foreign hordes. International tourism is slim; the Zillertal's residents have defiantly crafted a mountainside paradise for locals to relish. Transportation in the region is fast and convenient, thanks to the **Zillertalbahn** (better known by its nifty nickname, the **Z-bahn**), an efficient network of private buses and trains connecting all the villages (because the network is privately owned, Eurail is not valid). This line would make the Swiss proud; it arrives late *at most* twice a year. The starting point is **Jenbach,** and the route's terminus is at **Mayrhofen** (ride the length of the route, round-trip 120 AS); you can reach Jenbach by train from Innsbruck (½-hr.; one way 62 AS; Eurail valid). The Z-bahn comprises two types of trains, the **Dampfzug** and the **Triebwagen.** The Dampfzug is an old steam train, targeted at tourists; it costs twice as much and moves half as fast. The Triebwagen and the Z-bahn Autobus each leave hourly 6am-8pm. (On the Triebwagen, Zell am Ziller to Jenbach round-trip 80 AS, one way 44 AS; Zell-Mayrhofen or Zell-Uderns round-trip 50 AS, one way 28 AS. On the Dampfzug, Zell-Jenbach round-trip 150 AS, one way 100 AS; Zell-Uderns round-trip 130 AS, one way 80 AS; Zell-Mayrhofen round-trip 90 AS, one way 50 AS.)

In the Zillertal, skiing reigns supreme among athletic alternatives. If you plan to stay in the area for more than three days, the most economical alternative is the **Zillertal Super Skipaß,** valid on all of the area's 151 lifts. (7 days 1630 AS, 10 days 2160 AS, 2 weeks 2790 AS. Including the Gletscherbahn, which provides access to the year-round skiing of the **Tuxer Gletscher** (glacier), 7 days 2150 AS, 10 days 2860 AS,

2 weeks 3740 AS.) Passes are also available to ski five of seven days, six of seven days, and 10 of 14 days. The cost of the lift ticket includes unlimited use of the Zillertalbahn transportation network while the ski pass is valid.

The Zillertal Alps also yield some of the most fabulous **hiking** in western Austria—the region claims more footpaths than roads and more Alpine guides than policemen. The popular six-day **Z-Hiking Ticket** is valid on all lift stations in the Zillertal (including Zell am Ziller, Fügen, Mayrhofen, Gerlos, and Hintertux) and runs 340 AS (children half-price). Procure passes at any lift or at the railway stations in Fügen, Zell am Ziller, and Mayrhofen. When strolling around the mounaintop paths, be especially careful where you place your feet; whatever you do, don't dislodge any stones into the Wetter See (Weather Lake), under the shadow of Mount Gerlos. According to local lore, anyone who throws a rock into its waters will be pummeled by torrential thunderstorms, hail, and winds.

Half an hour's walk from **Fügen,** in a Zillertal valley near the entrance to the Benkerwald Forest, lies a small rock. This marks the site of a legendary 18th-century battle fought by two peasant women hired by a farmer in **Wieseck** to cut corn. Pressed for time, the farmer promised higher wages if they sped up their cutting, and the women, eager for cash, worked ever more tirelessly. At the end of the week, however, instead of paying them the same wage, the class enemy gave one woman two loaves and the other only one. As they walked home, the women argued bitterly about their shares, and when they reached the rock, they started fighting with their sickles. Spurred on by the sight of each other's blood, the women continued to fight until both fell down and bled to death. Centuries ago, few locals would pass this way after nightfall; now, residents jaded by Tyson-Ruddock II have no difficulty strolling by the stone.

■ Jenbach

Jenbach has the three necessary attributes of prime real estate: location, location, location. The town lies just off Autobahn A12, on the main rail line from Vienna to Innsbruck, and at the head of the Zillertal and one terminus of the Zillertalbahn. You'll do best to use Jenbach as a rest stop; stay the night in town, and then head out to the spectacular expanses of lakefront terrain. The town **tourist office,** on Achenseestr. 37 (tel. 39 01 or 34 70), can give you more information on Jenbach's surroundings. From the main rail station, head toward Bahnhofstr., on your left; keep walking as it turns a right angle, past the gas station. Follow the signs to the center (*Zentrum*) of town; the office will be on the right (open Mon.-Fri. 9am-12:30pm and 2-6pm, Sat. 9am-noon). The **post office** faces the Volksschule, next to the big church, about 100m beyond the tourist office along Achenseestr. (Open Mon.-Fri. 8am-noon and 2-6pm, Sat. 8-10am. **Postal code:** A-6200.) **Telephones** are available inside, but to cash traveler's checks, you'll have to find a town bank. Achenseestr. also supports two grocery stores: **SPAR Markt** (open Mon.-Fri. 8am-noon and 2:30-5pm, Sat. 9am-noon) and **Top Markt** (open Mon.-Fri. 7:30am-noon and 3-6pm, Sat. 9am-noon).

The best hope for housing in Jenbach is a *Privatzimmer*; select a room from the tourist office's list. **Haus Grafl,** Feldgasse 15a (tel. 286 44), serves up delectable jams as part of a generous breakfast; Gerber-baby-look-alike Julia provides the morning entertainment. Keep walking along Achenseestr. until you reach the little bridge over the stream; cross that bridge when you get to it, and climb the steps to reach Feldgasse. The house lies just before the big gray school behind a soccer field. (150 AS per person. Breakfast and shower included.) Ride a bus for five minutes to the tiny hamlet of **Wiesing** in order to find the closest hostel; **Jugendgästehaus Riemerhof (HI),** Wiesing 18 (tel. (05244) 26 58), is just down the street from the "Wiesing Dorfplatz" bus stop. (Buses leave 5 times daily; last bus around 7pm. 100 AS per person. Breakfast 30 AS; shower 20 AS.) Nearby **Uderns** also holds a hostel, the **Jugendherberge Finsigerhof (HI)** (tel. 20 10; fax 28 66), and is easily accessible on the Zillertalbahn (one way from Jenbach 36 AS). From the thimble-sized train station, cross the street and walk past the **tourist office** (open Mon.-Fri. 8am-noon) onto Dorfstr. Turn right and walk to the next intersection, which should be the street just before the stream; then turn left and walk for about five blocks. The hostel is #73, a large house on the left side of the street (140 AS per person with breakfast and shower).

Near Jenbach, in the village of **Kramsach,** lies a beautiful lake beneath the ruins of an ancient stronghold called the **Guckenbühl.** According to legend, the last resident Baron was blessed with a beautiful daughter. Unfortunately, this daughter developed an unacceptable interest in an impoverished forester. Upset by the intolerable suitor and by the news of a planned consummation, the baron did what any self-respecting medieval baron would do—set the dogs on him. The terrified forester, ever too hasty, tripped over a stone, fell into the lake, and drowned.

Troubled by her almost lover's departure, the daughter wandered around the lake in silent grief. One day, mourning with her maid, she peered into its murky depths and sighted the dead body of her lover. Immediately, she threw herself in. The maid ran home to alert the Baron, but when he arrived on the scene, neither body could be found. The two lovers had turned to stone and had risen out of the lake like little islands.

Near Jenbach: Achensee

Adjacent to the Jenbach rail station is the starting point for the scenic climb to the **Achensee,** the largest lake in Western Austria. Take one look at the 10-mi. expanse of clear water, nicknamed "Tyrol's Fjord," and you'll see why Maximilian loved to fish here. The lake resembles half of a gigantic emerald, deposited in the middle of the mountains—on a clear day, you can see straight to the bottom of the lake. Two-hour **boat excursions** through the Achensee (May-Oct.) take off three to seven times daily (110 AS). Breach the lake's shore by boarding the century-old steam engine **Achenseebahn,** a true choo-choo train that closely resembles an amusement park ride. The journey is excruciatingly slow—Rip Van Winkle would wake up halfway through the trip. (Round-trip 200 AS. Eurail valid, but show your ticket at the purchase counter *beforehand.*) Once at the lake, don't feel obligated to take the ferry—tickets for the train and boat can be purchased separately, and a walkway circumscribes most of the water anyway.

Near Jenbach: Schwaz

Take a brief excursion from any point in the Zillertal to the **Schwaz Silver Mine** (tel. (05242) 72 37 20; fax 72 37 24). Back in 1409, a local servant girl was watching her grazing cattle when a bull uprooted a lode of silver; the discovery sparked a remarkable flurry of activity in town. To this day, **Schwaz** still basks in its history as the biggest mining town in Central Europe during the 15th century. Though you'd need a year to fully explore all 300 miles of the mine's tunnels, the 90-minute tour reenacts the most interesting historical highlights. (Mines open Mon.-Fri. 9am-4pm, Sat.-Sun. 9am-5pm; in winter Mon.-Fri. 10am-4pm. 150 AS from Jenbach, including bus transport and tour. Coats and helmets provided.) The bus to Schwaz from Jenbach leaves daily at 12:50pm. (From Zell, it leaves at 12:05pm and costs 218 AS. From Mayrhofen, it leaves at 11:50am and costs 243 AS.)

■■■ ZELL AM ZILLER

Those with a hiking fetish should consider walking eight moderately difficult kilometers upstream on the path along the Ziller river to **Zell am Ziller.** Zell at first appears to be just another of the Zillertal's many ski villages—a few restaurants, rows of cottages with floral patios, and a cable car or two. In fact, thanks to the Gauderfest, it can boast a bit more character than the rest. A monk laid the foundation stone for Zell am Ziller in the second half of the 8th century, but materialism soon assumed command—locals discovered that they could exploit the vast natural resources of the central Zillertal. Gold mining flourished from the 17th to the 19th century; today, the only reminders of this bygone era are the tunnel entrances at Hainzenberg and Rohrberg.

Orientation and Practical Information Zell is located at the southern end of the Zillertal, between Jenbach and Mayrhofen (28 AS by train). The town **tourist office** is at Dorfplatz 3a (tel. 22 81; fax 22 81 80). From the rail station, head right along Bahnhofstr.; at the end, turn right on Dorfplatz. The office is on your left, just before the rail tracks (4 min.). Pick up a town map, skiing information, and a *Frühstückspension* list if you want to track down a room on your own, although the staff will make reservations for free. Inquire here about weekly organized **hikes** (free with guest card). (Office open July-Sept. Mon.-Fri. 8am-noon and 2-6pm, Sat. 9am-noon and 4-6pm; June Mon.-Fri. 8am-noon and 2-6pm, Sat. 9am-noon; Oct.-May Mon.-Fri. 8am-noon and 2-6pm). **Christophorus Reisen,** Bahnhofstr. (tel. 25 20), handles all **budget travel** concerns. **Exchange currency** at all banks and travel agencies; **banks** offer the best rates (open Mon.-Fri. 8am-noon and 2-5pm). **Raiffeisenbank** (tel. 22 15) stands across the street from the tourist office, with a 24-hour electronic ATM outside; a **Sparkasse** and a **Volksbank** sit farther down the street. The **post office,** Unterdorf 2 (tel. 23 33) has **telephones** outside and **faxes** inside (**City code:** 05282). When Bahnhofstr. intersects Dorfplatz, turn left. (Open Mon.-Fri. 8am-noon and 2-6pm, Sat. 9-11am. **Postal code:** A-6280.) The **train depot** for the acclaimed Zillertalbahn is at Bahnhofstr. 11 (tel. 22 11). Z-bahn trains leave on the hour for Jenbach or Mayrhofen. **Luggage storage** and **telephones** are available here; **buses** (Z-bahn buses and yellow BundesBuses) leave from the front of the station. For a **taxi,** call 26 25, 23 45, or 22 55. In an **emergency,** call the police (tel. 22 12 or 133), fire department (tel. 22 12 or 122), or pharmacy (tel. 26 41).

Accommodations and Food There's certainly no shortage of lodgings in Zell; nearly every house has a "*Zimmer Frei*" sign in the window. There are two available guest beds for every resident, so finding a room shouldn't be too difficult; call ahead anyway to be safe. The woman who owns **Haus Huditz,** Karl-Platzer Weg 1 (tel. 22 82), positively exudes hospitality. Spread yourself out in the huge rooms with terraces. From the tourist office, cross the rail tracks and turn onto Gerlosstr.; then bear left onto Gaudergasse and look for Karl-Platzer Weg on the left. (In summer, 170 AS per person; in winter, 200 AS per person. Breakfast included. 15 AS for 7-min. shower tokens.) Another option is **Gästehaus G'strein,** Rosengartenweg 3 (tel. 24 01; fax 34 30). Turn left at the rail tracks behind the tourist office, and then make a right onto Spitalgasse; the first road on the left is Rosengartenweg. (In summer, 180 AS per person; in winter, 215 AS.) **Campingplatz Hofer,** Gerlosstr. 33 (tel. 22 48), sports hot water, showers, and laundry machines (55 AS per person in winter, 50 AS in summer).

When you stop for a bite to eat, savor some of the local specialties. *Erdäpfelwirrler* are potatoes cooked in their skins and fried with salt, flour, and butter; the dish is usually served with cranberry sauce and accompanied by a glass of buttermilk. Hint: if you are watching your cholesterol level, this *might* not be the meal for you. A traditional summer dish is the *Scheiterhaufen,* a monstrous mixture of rolls, apples, eggs, milk, lemon, cinnamon, sugar, butter, and raisins drizzled with rum.

Dorfplatz is flanked by all sorts of red meat outlets. Check out the **Zeller Stuben,** Unterdorf 11 (tel. 22 71). Cheap food, including self-service half-chickens (80 AS) and *Gulasch* (35 AS; open daily 11am-8pm). Enjoy a pizza (80-150 AS) at **Zellerhof,** Bahnhofstr. 3 (tel. 26 12; open daily noon-2pm and 5-10pm). From the tourist office, follow the railroad tracks in front of the brewery (peak inside at the hedonistic pile of kegs in the corner) to find the **SPAR Markt** (open Mon.-Fri. 7am-noon and 2-6pm, Sat. 8am-noon).

Skiing and Entertainment Zeller **skiing** comes in two packages: either the **Super Skipass** (for more than 3 days) or **day passes,** valid on the Kreuzjoch-Rosenalm and Gerlosstein-Sonnalm slopes. (1 day 320 AS, children 190 AS; 2 days 580 AS; 3 days 820 AS; 1 week 2150 AS; 2 weeks 3740 AS; 3 weeks 4875 AS). Single tickets are also available for non-skiers who tag along to watch. Obtain passes at the bottom of the **Kreuzjoch** (tel. 716 50), **Gerlosstein** (tel. 22 75), or **Ramsberg** (tel. 27 20) cable cars. The lifts run every 15 minutes and are all open from 8:30am to 4:30pm. **Ski rentals** are available at any of Zell's sporting goods stores; try **Sport Peudl,** Gerlosstr. 6 (tel. 22 87) or **Ski School Lechner,** Gerlosstr. 7 (tel. 31 64; open daily 8am-noon and 3-6pm). At both stores, skis cost 130-180 AS per day and 600-690 AS per week. For more information on area skiing, see the Zillertal Alps section above.

Register in any town hotel or *Pension* to get a **guest card;** among other benefits, the card enables you to join a free **hike** led by the tourist office. The cheapest **bike rentals** can be found at **Sb-Markt Hofer** (tel. 22 20), where one day costs 50 AS (3 days 120 AS, 1 week 250 AS; mountain bike 1 day 110 AS, 3 days 410 AS). Two of the three ski lifts in Zell's vicinity also offer Alpine hiking: the **Kreuzjochbahn** (round-trip 140 AS, 92 AS to the mid-station; open 8:30am-12:15pm and 1-4:45pm) and the **Gerlossteinbahn** (round-trip 92 AS; open 8:30am-12:20pm and 1-5:10pm)—also try the **Grindlalmbahn** nearby (round-trip 55 AS; open 8am-8pm).

In the summer, an "**Info Evening**" with music is held every Sunday at the music pavilion to provide details about entertainment and activities in the resort. **Hikes** to summer pastures bring you to a cabin on the Schwendberg mountain, where you can watch milk being churned to butter and cheese. Further **free mountain hikes** are available via Hermann and Karl; these two robust men escort you on sunrise hikes, mountain hut tours, and nature walks. You must book a day in advance by signing up at the tourist office at 5pm. Refer to the pamphlet, *Summer in the Country,* available at the tourist office, for more information.

On **Rosenkranz** (rosary) Saturday, the farm animals are driven down from the mountainsides; watch your back for any stray killer cows. The *Mandl* calendar is a local piece of folklore that takes its name from the *Mandln,* legendary dwarfs. In earlier times, the calendar explained the weather cycles to the people through the language of strange and delightful pictograms.

The first Sunday in May brings the **Gauderfest** to Zell am Ziller, when the whole town gets sauced in a celebration of cold, frothy beverages. The name is derived not from the German word "*Gaudi,*" meaning fun, but from the farmer's estate which owns the local private brewery. The *Bräumeister*'s vats, Tyrol's oldest, concoct the beloved and rather potent Gauderbock especially for the occasion. There is also a little rhyme for the festival: "*Gauderwürst und G'selchts mit Kraut, / hie, wia tuat dös munden, / und 10 Halbe Bockbier drauf, / mehr braucht's nit zum G'sundsein!*" ("Gauder sausage and smoked pork with sauerkraut, / Hey, how good it tastes, / and 10 pints of beer to go with it, / what more could you need for your health!") It's in near-incomprehensible Austrian dialect, but fear not—pronunciation deteriorates throughout the evening of festivities, so by midnight you'll blend in just fine. The most important element of the festival is the Ranggeln (traditional wrestling) for the Hogmoar. There are also animal fights (attended by a veterinary surgeon) and customs such as the Grasausläuten (**ringing the grass** in order to wake it up and make it grow). Revelry continues into the night with Tyrolean folk singing and dancing and some of the best **zither-playing** in the world. By June, at least half of the residents are sober enough to court the tourist trade.

■■■ MAYRHOFEN

Mayrhofen (pop. 3600) is a popular and traditional Zillertal skiing destination, at the terminus of the Zillertalbahn, where four valleys bump heads. The village, 630m above sea level, is located on the **Tuxer Gletscher** (glacier), which keeps tourists flowing into town year-round. The town boasts three classic skiing areas with four million square meters of runs. Mayrhofen marks the intersection of two rivers, the Ziller and its tributary, the Zemmbach, which wed in soggy matrimony before heading north as the consummated **Ziller** river. The Stilluppspeicher is a wondrous lake a few miles to the south. If you wish to head off into the mountains without little Huey, Duey, and Louie, Mayrhofen is ready; under the names of "Clown Wuppy" and the "Zillertal Mountain Fairy," the town conducts a comprehensive range of children's summer activities.

Practical Information Mayrhofen's **tourist office** is located in the Europhaus, a town convention center with a restaurant, public toilets, and a bulletin board of local events. From the rail station, walk left on Am Marktplatz until the street becomes Durster Str.; the Europhaus will be on your left. You can check out information about town tours, or buy the regional hiking maps (10-89 AS). Procure the essential brochure *Mayrhofen: Information von A-Z,* available in English, which lists bus schedules, prices for various sports, and addresses and telephone numbers for every local business. The stunningly beautiful pamphlet, *M-Mayerhofen,* provide interesting information and photographs, but, more importantly, is itself a graphic art *pièce de résistance.* (Open Mon.-Fri. 9am-6pm, Sat. 9am-noon and 3-6pm, Sun. 10am-noon.) The tourist office also sponsors guided **hikes** once or twice a week before 9am (free with a guest card). The **post office** (tel. 25 02 or 20 24) is located on Einfahrt Mitte, off Hauptstr. **Telephones** and **currency exchange** are available inside. (Open Mon.-Fri. 8am-noon and 2-6pm, Sat. 8-11am; Oct.-June Mon.-Fri. 8am-noon and 2-6pm.) You can also exchange cash or traveler's checks at any of the numerous **banks** along Hauptstr; banking hours are Mon.-Fri. 8am-noon and 2:30-5pm. The **train station** (tel. 23 62) offers **luggage storage** (open daily 8am-noon and 2-6pm).

Accommodations and Food The tourist office makes free room reservations, but you would do equally well scouring the list of *Frühstückpensionen* that it dispenses. Try **Rosengartl,** Maidlergasse 381 (tel. 25 76), for clean rooms and an English-speaking management. Pass the Europhaus and turn left on Forstersteig; at the end, turn onto Scheulingstr. and take the first left onto Maidlergasse. (In summer 155 AS, with shower 215 AS; in winter 175 AS, with shower 235 AS. Breakfast included.) Mayrhofen's only camping spot is **Campingplatz Kröll,** Laubichl 127 (tel. 25 80). From the train station, turn onto Am Marktplatz; at the first major intersection (before the Europhaus), turn left and continue walking for 10-15 minutes. (45 AS per person, 45 AS per tent.) **Hauptstraße** teems with restaurants, bakeries, and cafés. The one ethnic eatery is **China Restaurant Singapur,** Scheulingstr. 371 (tel. 39 12). For groceries, patronize the **IFA Nah & Fris Markt,** Hauptstr. 439 (open Mon.-Fri. 8am-6:30pm, Sat. 8am-noon).

Skiing and Entertainment During the winter, **ski passes** for fewer than three days are valid on Mayrhofen's lifts (1 day 300 AS, 2 days 580 AS, 3 days 820 AS; children 180 AS, 350 AS, and 495 AS, respectively). Call (05285) 23 73 or 29 16 00 for a 24-hour **snow report.** If you wish to partake of **summer skiing,** ride the ski bus to **Hintertux,** 17km away (inquire at the tourist office for a bus schedule).

Less exotic athletics are also available during the summer. **Bikes** can be rented at the **Esso gas station,** Am Marktplatz 213 (tel. 23 08; 70 AS per day, mountain bikes 200 AS per day), or at nearby **Sport Spachtholz Gord,** Hauptstr. 441 (tel. 321 33). Lift passes to **hiking** areas are available for one-time treks or for the entire summer. A single ticket costs 90-160 AS, children 60-95 AS; summer passes (valid June to mid-Oct.) run 340 AS (580 AS with unlimited Zillertalbahn usage). **Alpine huts** are scattered throughout the area's hiking paths; contact the local **Alpenvereinbüro,** Sportplatzstr. 307 (tel. 36 01), for more information (open May-Oct. Mon. 6-7pm).

THE HOHE TAUERN

The enormous Hohe Tauern range is part of the Austrian Central Alps, comprising parts of Carinthia, Salzburg, and Tyrol. It extends east to west along the southern end of the Salzach Valley, and encompasses the Hohe Tauern National Park, the Glocknergruppe, and the Venedigergruppe. The valleys were molded during the ice age, and now are partitioned by expanses of ice and snow, massive alluvial and mudflow cones, mountain pasture land, alpine heaths of grass and bush, and forested bulwarks fending off erosion and avalanches. The region of rock and ice at the very heart of this alpine landscape remains largely unspoiled.

Early in the century the magnificence of the region prompted conservationists to lobby for the creation of a national park. In Salzburg and Carinthia between 1958 and 1964, large tracts of mountain land were declared preserves. And on October 21, 1971, the provincial government leaders of Carinthia, Salzburg, and Tyrol signed an agreement at Heiligenblut to "conserve for present and future generations the Hohe Tauern as a particularly impressive and varied region of the Austrian Alps" by defining the Hohe Tauern National Park.

The Glocknergruppe boast the highest of the Hohe Tauern peaks, as well as glaciers with dazzling ice slopes. A number of lakes crowd together amidst the Glocknergruppe, including the Weißsee, Tauernmoos See, Grünsee, and the Stausee. The spectacular Gloßglockner Straße (Großglockner Road) runs north to south through the region.

The Hohe Tauern are accessible by **car, bus,** and **train.** Schnellstraße 167 runs north to south, intersecting Schnellstraße 168, which runs west to Krimml. Bus #3230 runs from Böckstein to Badgastein twice per hour, and #4094 runs from Zell am Ziller to Krimml five times per day. A rail line from Zell am See terminates at Krimml; trains run nine times per day in each direction. Another line runs south from Salzburg through Badgastein to Spittal an der Drau, with trains approximately every two hours.

■ Krimml

Amidst the splendor of Alpine crags and glades, Mother Nature cut a truly extraordinary **waterfall** near Krimml, in southwest Austria. This superlative cascade (Europe's highest, at a towering 1300 ft.) cannot match the monstrous energy of Niagara (though tourist officials say Krimml is becoming a more popular honeymoon destination) or the sheer height of Angel Falls—nevertheless, the surrounding wilderness and the stoic presence of the mountains make the **Krimmler Wasserfälle** a mandatory stop on any tourist's route. The waterfall is part of the **Hohe Tauern National Park,** the largest natural reserve in Central Europe. This range, spanning about 10 towns across the south of Austria, cradles the last known members of numerous nearly-extinct species.

You can reach Krimml, the waterfall's base town, by **train** or **bus;** trains come only from the east, through Zell am See, but buses run primarily from Zell am Ziller (round-trip 165 AS). On the bus route, you'll breach the **Gerlos Pass,** with an astounding view of all three levels of the waterfall at the same time. Get off at the first bus stop in Krimml and follow the signs pointing to the falls. Don't forget a raincoat and a bag for your camera to fend off the mist. Mind the time to avoid getting left overnight at the falls; the last bus leaves for Zell am Ziller at 4:30pm. (Admission to the path leading to the falls 10 AS, children 5 AS. About a 1½-hr. walk to the highest vantage point.)

Krimml's main **tourist office** (tel. 239) is fairly inconveniently located on the opposite side of town. Disembark at the second bus stop, and walk toward the church spire; the office is directly behind the church, adjacent to the **post office** (tourist office open Mon.-Fri. 9am-noon and 2:30-5pm). The only significant attraction in Krimml is the waterfall, rendering the tourist office largely unnecessary. For

English brochures and pamphlets about the falls, try the Österreichischer Alpenverein's **tourist information booth** located along the path to the falls (open daily 9am-noon and 2-6pm). This organization provides mounds of hiking information and maintains the benches sporadically situated along the route up to the falls. Munchies are available at the myriad **food stands** on the path, but don't be duped—beware the inflated prices.

Krimml is best enjoyed as a day trip. *Pensionen* tend to be somewhat costly (about 200-400 AS per night) and are generally located far from the falls. The main tourist office can provide you with a list of what is available. If you're left coughing in the exhaust cloud of the last departing bus, try spacious **Pension Graber,** Krimml 89 (tel. 255), located past the tourist office on your left. There, you'll find a terrace, a balcony, and most likely an available room (in summer 200-260 AS, in winter 220-280 AS). The **ADEG-Markt** (tel. 219), across the street from the church, provides basic sustenance (open Mon.-Fri. 8am-noon and 2:30-6pm, Sat. 8:30-11am). The **post office** is next door to the tourist office. (Open Mon.-Fri. 8am-noon and 2-6pm. **Postal code:** A-5743.) Make your phone calls there (**Regional code:** 06564), but go to the **Raiffeisenkasse,** diagonally opposite from the ADEG-Markt, to exchange money (open Mon.-Fri. 8am-noon and 2-5pm, Sat. 8-11:30am). You can rent a **bicycle** from **Zweirad Frauenschuh** (tel. 219), next to the ADEG-Markt. (60 AS per day, mountain bikes 100-150 AS per day. Open Mon.-Fri. 8am-noon.)

Near Krimml: Gerlos

If the falls are frozen when you arrive in Krimml, consider nearby Gerlos, which survives by its many skiing facilities. **Lift tickets** are available from the following cable cars in the Hochkrimml/Gerlosplatte region: **Filzsteinlifte** (tel. 82 75 or 83 18; fax 83 18 40), **Duxerlifte** (tel. 83 34, 237, or 317; fax 475), and **Plattenkogellift** (tel. 82 85; fax 82 85 2). Day tickets start at 245 AS (3 days 665 AS, 1 week 1290 AS, 2 weeks 2245 AS). Complete **rental equipment** is available at **Sport-Souvenir Patterer** (tel. 325 or 327) and **Sport Lachmayer** (tel. 247). Skis cost 80 AS per day, boots 45 AS per day.

■■■ BADGASTEIN

Built on a steep incline of the Gasteiner Tal, Badgastein commands spectacular views of the flower-speckled valley below and the sublime Großglockner above. Weathered medieval dwellings, swaddled in bold strokes of yellow and red, cling desperately to the valley walls. Badgastein's reputedly curative geothermal waters attracted European royalty and other silver-spooned clientele as early as the Middle Ages. The descendants of those early patricians now flock to Badgastein to challenge nearby ski slopes and soothe sore muscles in the same panacean springs. The Gasteiner Ache storms through town in a tempestuous waterfall; those tremors you hear are either cascading waters of the river or heart palpitations from the bill for your visit here.

Orientation and Practical Information Badgastein lies conveniently on the InterCity Salzburg-Villach-Vienna rail line. The **train station** (tel. (06432) 62 06) offers luggage storage (20 AS per item per day), lockers, mountain-bike rental, and currency exchange. Two **bus** stops are in the immediate vicinity of the station—across the street to the right, or to the right down the street by the familiar bus station marker ("P"). Buses run all day, connecting Badgastein with small villages in the nearby mountains (for bus information, call (06432) 63 44).

The **tourist office** (Kur- und Fremdenverkehrsverband) is located in the Kongresszentrum, on the first floor of Haus Austria (tel. (06434) 25 31 or 36 66; fax 25 31 37). From the train station, turn left and then bear right down the valley at the first fork; at Hotel Salzburger Hof, bear left down the steep footpath, take the first right after Hotel Gisela, and then turn right. Follow this road until it merges with Kaiser-Franz-Joseph-Str., and then turn right toward the gushing waterfall to find Haus Austria (15 min.). The English-speaking staff will dispense as many pamphlets as you can carry; be sure to procure the invaluable *Information Gastein* pamphlet, which contains opening hours, prices, and times for nearly every store and cultural offering. (Open June-Aug. and Oct. to late-Dec. Mon.-Fri. 8am-6pm, Sat. 10am-noon and 4-6pm, Sun. 10am-noon; Sept. and Jan.-May Mon.-Fri. 8am-6pm.).

The **post office,** next to the station (tel. (06434) 27 21 or 27 26), offers the best rates for currency exchange. (Open Mon.-Fri. 8am-8pm, Sat. 8-10am; exchange open Mon.-Fri. 8am-noon and 2-5pm, Sat. 8-10am. **Postal code:** A-5640.) Another **branch,** downtown in Straubinger Platz (tel. (06434) 27 30), also changes money. With Haus Austria to the right, walk straight over the Wasserfall-Brücke. (Office open Mon.-Fri. 8am-noon and 2:30-6pm.)

Accommodation and Food For overnight stays, budget travelers have little choice other than the **Badgastein Jugendherberge (HI),** Ederplatz 2 (tel. (06434) 20 80; fax 506 88). From the station, turn right on Böcksteiner Bundesstr., and right again on Hauptschulstr.; bear left when the street ends, and walk along the soccer field (10 min.). More like a hotel than a youth hostel, this delightful enterprise accommodates 180 in doubles and quads, each with its own shower and toilet. (Reception open 8am-10pm. Flexible curfew 10pm; ask for a key. No lockout. Members only. 150 AS per person; June-Sept. 120 AS. Breakfast included. Laundry machines available—wash 40 AS, dry 20 AS. Reservations required.) If, as usual, the hostel is full, try tiny **Haus Kölbl** (tel. (06434) 21 82) at Mozartplatz 7. Extremely considerate owners offer just two doubles and a single. The bathrooms are stocked with two-ply, teddybear-print toilet paper. From the tourist office, turn left, and walk five minutes down Kaiser-Franz-Joseph-Str. (July-Aug. and Jan.-March 250 AS; April-June and Sept.-Dec. 230 AS. Breakfast included. Major credit cards accepted.)

Campers can pitch a tent at one of the 250 sites of **AZUR Kur-Camping Erlengrund** (tel. (06434) 27 90), a few kilometers away in **Kötschachdorf.** Catch the Lackner Bus by the station (direction: "Hofgastein") to "Kötschachdorf"; last bus leaves at 6:25pm (22 AS). (June-Sept. and Dec. to mid-April 59 AS per person, children 47 AS, 58-80 AS per site; mid-April to May and Oct.-Nov. 52 AS per person, children 41 AS, 25-72 AS per site. Over 15 14 AS tax. Supermarket on grounds.)

Eating cheaply in Badgastein requires some fancy footwork. If you're staying at the hostels, consider purchasing lunch and dinner there (60 AS each; sign up at breakfast). Otherwise, seek out the *Imbiße* (fast-food stands) on Kaiser-Franz-Joseph-Str., near the Mozartplatz. **Bayr's Bistro**, between the train station and Hotel Salzburger Hof, prepares appetizing fare in an attractive setting (*Weiner Schnitzel* 78 AS, lasagna 62 AS, *Apfelstrudel* 26 AS; open Mon.-Fri. 8:30am-6:30pm, Sat. 8:30am-1pm). The **China Restaurant,** adjacent to the Wasserfall Brücke, serves up an impressive *Mittagsmenu* (75 AS) Mon.-Fri. noon-2:30pm.

A small **Aktiv Markt** is around the corner from the hostel, at the intersection of Böcksteiner Bundesstr. and Hauptschulstr. (open Mon.-Thurs. 8am-noon and 2:30-6pm, Fri. 8am-6pm, Sat. 8am-noon). A large **SPAR Markt** waits across from the train station on Böcksteiner Bundesstr. (open Mon.-Thurs. 8am-12:30pm and 2-6pm, Fri. 8am-7pm, Sat. 8am-1pm).

Sights and Entertainment Badgastein's alpha and omega is the river that rumbles through the center of town. Admire the view of the Gasteiner Ache from the beautiful (and dry) **Wasserfall Brücke,** just off the main square (Kongresszentrum), or climb up the winding **Wasserfallweg** and absorb the splendid scene from atop the **Hohe Brücke.** Walking paths branch off Bismarckstraße, leading to dainty squares, while a gambol along Kaiser-Wilhelm-Promenade affords breathtaking vistas of the valley. With its brilliant red roof, the 15th-century **Nikolauskirche** blends into the town's earthen palette; note the well-preserved Gothic frescoes and Baroque tombs inside.

As early as 1525, Paracelsus praised the medicinal, beneficial qualities of Badgastein's water. Try a taste at the water fountains in the **Kur- und Kongreßhaus** (Spa and Congress Hall), directly across the main square from Haus Austria. The salubrious solution reportedly soothes stomach, intestinal, kidney, and bladder ailments, and makes a *tremendous* gin and tonic. The **Gasteiner Heilstollen** thermal gallery (tel. (06434) 37 53 11; fax 226 94) is a more expensive option, but is *the* tonic for people who suffer from rheumatism or allergies or bronchial asthma or hormonal imbalances or low self-esteem—or so they say. Located up the Elisabeth Promenade not too far from the hostel, the Gasteiner Heilstollen is a converted gold mine with the unique combination of high temperature (38-41.5°C), high relative humidity (70-95%), and radon-suffused air. A small train delivers patients to the various chambers inside. A swimsuit (6 AS), bathrobe (20 AS), bathing shoes (6 AS), and free towel are required to "take the cure" and can all be rented at the treatment center. Take a Lackner Bus (direction: "Sportgastein") to "Heilstollen" (50 AS); the tourist office has bus schedules. Make an appointment four to six weeks in advance, if possible, by writing to: "Gasteiner Heilstollen, A-5645 Böckstein bei Badgastein." (Admission 590 AS. Massage 170-300 AS, gymnastics 80-500 AS. Open June-Sept. at 8am, 10am, noon, 2pm and 4pm; mid-Jan. to May and Oct. 8am, 10am, and noon. Arrive 1 hr. before.) The **Felsenbad** facility (tel. (06434) 22 23), with its own thermal and freshwater pools, is directly across the street from the station. For 114 AS, you'll receive use of a locker, sauna, steam baths, and swimming pool; you must bring a bathing cap. (Open Jan.-March 9am-11pm; June to late-Sept. 9am-9pm; April-May and late-Sept. to late-Dec. 10am-9pm.)

A multitude of cable cars and lifts connects hikers to the mountains surrounding Badgastein. The **Stubnerkogelbahn** (tel. (06434) 23 22 12), adjacent to the station, carries riders up via gondola and chair lift. (Open late-May to mid-Oct. daily 8:30am-4pm. Round-trip 170 AS, under 16 160 AS. Additional discounts with a guest card.) Across town, the **Graukogelbahn** (tel. (06434) 32 91) also carries riders to majestic heights. (Open daily 9am-4pm. Round-trip 180 AS, with guest card 160 AS.) Well-marked hiking trails radiate from the cable-car summits. For guests staying five days or longer, the **Gasteiner 5-Tage-Wahlkarte** (only available in summer) offers impressive discounts. For 470 AS (children 235 AS), this ticket gives riders five days of access to all lifts at Stubnerkogel and Graukogel, as well as on Bad Hofgastein's **Schloßalmbahnen** (tel. (06432) 64 55).

The mountains around Badgastein also make for wonderful winter **skiing.** Frolicking during the "reduced period" (Jan. 9-29 and April 5-17) or off-season (Dec. 4-24 and April 18-May 1) is considerably cheaper than during the peak season (Dec. 25-Jan. 8 and Jan. 30-April 4), but only one lift, the **Schideck** in **Sportgastein,** is in operation. For example, a one-day pass for the Graukogel and Stubnerkogel slopes in Badgastein and the Schideck in Sportgastein runs 370 AS (320 AS in reduced period, 280 AS in off-season). Prices drop later in the day. Tickets for three days or more, for which a photo is required, include the lifts in Bad Hofgastein and free bus transportation. **Buses** run twice per hour to Bad Hofgastein; **trains** go six times per day. Consult the tourist office brochure *Ski und Thermal Gasteinertal: Tarife und Imformationen Gasteiner- und Großarltal* to help you choose from the multitude of ski passes and package deals.

Several establishments rent downhill equipment: in Badgastein, try **Johann Schober Sport und Rent** (tel. (06434) 32 68), next to the Stubnerkogelbahn (open in ski season daily 8am-1pm and 3-6pm); in Bad Hofgastein, swing by **Sport Fleiß** (tel. (06432) 72 18) in the Schloßalmbahn parking lot (open in ski season daily 8am-1pm and 3-6pm; off-season Mon.-Fri. 8am-noon and 3-6pm, Sat. 8am-noon). For a 24-hr. **weather and snow report** in German, dial (06434) 24 74.

January 6 is **Twelfth Night** (a.k.a. Epiphany) in the Gasteiner Tal. On this night, runners called mummers (*Sternsinger*), adorned by special caps (*Glöckler*) and masks (*Perchten*), perform the **Running of the Masks;** they sprint from Badgastein to Böckstein on the sixth, and on the following day run from Badgastein to Hofgastein. The single-file procession of crazy caps consists of 12 *Kappenperchten* (men with beautiful headdresses), two *Turmperchten* (*Turm* means "tower" and refers to the conehead cap, 2-3m high), and their *Gesellinnen* (companions), young men dressed in regional female costumes. Legend has it that the abundance of the next harvest and the good fortune of the locals depend on the quality of these mid-winter masks. The Muppets' cultural contribution pales in comparison.

THE GROßGLOCKNER ROAD

The stunningly beautiful **Großglockner Straße** is deservedly one of Austria's most popular attractions. Skirting the country's loftiest mountains, Bundesstraße 107 winds for 50km amidst silent Alpine valleys, meadows of edelweiss, tumbling waterfalls, and a staggering glacier. Conjure up all the superlatives you know—they won't begin to do the road justice. Most of the high-mountain-sweeping-panorama-hairpin-turn-sports-car commercials (and you thought German words were long) are filmed here. Then consider the Austrian work ethic that made it possible; in only five years (1930-35), during the global economic crisis, the Großglockner Straße was constructed by over 3000 workers, reducing in part the massive unemployment of the time.

The trip up to the Edelweißspitze takes you from the flora and fauna of Austria into the habitat of the Arctic. Although tours generally run between **Zell am See** and **Heiligenblut,** the highway officially begins at **Bruck an der Großglockner.** Midway, at Franz-Joseph-Höhe, you can gaze on Austria's highest peak, the **Großglockner** (3797m, 12,465ft.), and ride the **Gletscherbahn** (tel. 25 02 or 22 88), a funicular to the Pasterze Glacier (round-trip 80 AS, with guest card 70 AS, children 40 AS; hourly departures mid-May to Oct. daily 9:30am-5pm). The **Gamsgrube Nature Trail** is a spectacular path along the glacier, culminating in the **Wasserfallwinkel** (2548m), a cascading waterfall. The Großglockner Road is open only from mid-May to late October, because of impassable conditions in winter.

The Großglockner Straße snakes through the **Hohe Tauern National Park,** created to safeguard indigenous flora and fauna such as the stone pine, ibex, grouse, griffon vulture, and bearded vulture. Before starting out on a hike, check with park officials; all hikes in the area pose dangers, and some regions are strictly off-limits. Contact the **Regional Großglockner Association** in Heiligenblut (tel. (04824) 20 01 21) or the **Carinthian Park Center** in a small town called Dollach, 10km from Heiligenblut (tel. (04825) 61 61). (Both offices are open Mon.-Fri. 9am-5pm.) **Glockner Aktiv** (tel. (04824) 25 90) offers special mountain tours and hikes, and shows a brief slide presentation at Franz-Joseph-Höhe (daily at 10am, noon, 2pm). For info on sleeping in regional Alpine huts (open only mid-June to Sept.), contact **Edelweißhütte** (tel. (06545) 425); they also operate a road-side information kiosk by the Edelweißspitze.

Many visitors traverse the Großglockner Straße in a tour bus or rental car. Driving through the mountains incurs a hefty 300 AS toll. If you buy a day pass (380 AS), you have access to the Hohe Tauern for the day and need not pay a return fare, so day-trippers should hang on to their receipts. Wise budget travelers travel by **BundesBus.** The brochure *Wandern mit dem Bundesbus: Nationalpark Hohe Tauern* (available at the bus stations in Lienz and Zell am See and the tourist office in Heiligenblut) contains a schedule of bus departure times, destinations, maps, hiking paths, and general information about the park. For anyone planning lengthy stays in the area, BundesBus offers a **National Park Ticket** good for 10 days of unlimited travel between Lienz, Heiligenblut, Hochtor, and other stops in the region, and reduced fares on cable cars and other sights—e.g., the bus to the Krimml Wasserfälle, the Gletscherbahn in Kaprun, and the Schmittenhöhebahnen in Zell am See (ticket 390 AS, children 195 AS; available mid-June to mid-Oct.). Call the Lienz bus station (tel. (04852) 670 67 or 64 94 40), or the Zell am See post office (tel. (06542) 23 74) for more information.

Single-day trips on the Großglockner Straße are possible but require careful planning. Keep in mind that the trips are less a matter of getting from place to place than an opportunity to view the spectacular park. It's much easier to approach the Road from Zell am See and travel south—transport in the other direction is significantly trickier. Starting from the north, buses leave **Zell am See** for **Kaiser-Franz-Josefs-Höhe.** (June 13-July 9 daily at 9:50am; July 10-Sept. 11 daily at 8:50am, 9:50am, and 10:50am; Sept. 12-Sept. 26 daily at 8:50am and 9:50am; Sept. 27-Oct. 10 daily at 9:50am.) Then proceed from **Kaiser-Franz-Josefs-Höhe** to **Heiligenblut.** (Buses June 13-July 9 daily at 2:40pm; July 10-Oct. 2 daily at 2:40pm and 4:35pm; Oct. 3-Oct. 10 daily at 2:40pm.)

If you're traveling from the south, be prepared for an ordeal; the odyssey begins with a bus from **Lienz** to **Heiligenblut.** (Buses depart May 15-July 9 Mon.-Fri. at 8am, 11:20am, and 12:20pm; Sat.-Sun. at 8am and 11:20am. July 10-Sept. 12 Mon.-Fri. at 8am, 10am, 11:20am, and 12:20pm; Sat.-Sun. at 8am, 10am, and 11:20am. Sept. 13-Oct. 10 Mon.-Fri. at 8am, 11:20am, and 12:20pm; Sat.-Sun. at 8am and 11:20am.) Then bus from **Heiligenblut** to **Kaiser-Franz-Josefs-Höhe** (45 min.). (Buses depart May 15-June 12 daily at 8am. June 13-July 9 daily at 8am and 9:12am. July 10-Sept. 12 Mon.-Fri. 8am, 9:12am, and 11:08am; Sat.-Sun. 8am and 9:12am. Sept. 13-Oct. 10 8am and 9:12am.) After exploring the hiking trails and marveling at the Großglockner and the Pasterze, wander down the mountain to **Guttal,** and take the bus to **Zell am See.** (Buses depart June 13-July 9 daily at 3:05 pm; July 10-Sept. 26 daily at 9:46am, 3:05pm, and 4:35pm; Sept. 27-Oct. 2 daily at 9:46am and 3:05pm; Oct. 3-Oct. 10 at 3:05pm.)

Prices for longer stretches are generally more economical: Lienz to Franz-Josefs-Höhe (round-trip 171 AS), Zell am See to Heiligenblut (round-trip 135 AS), Lienz to Heiligenblut (round-trip 116 AS; one way 64 AS), Heiligenblut to Franz-Josefs-Höhe (round-trip 74 AS).

■■■ ZELL AM SEE

Within a ring of snow-capped mountains that collapse into a pale turquoise lake, Zell am See is a popular resort town and a fine base for exploring the Hohe Tauern National Park. Most of Zell am See's attractions are oriented to outdoor sports; crank up your *Wanderlust* a few notches before you arrive in town. Then attack the undulating grass-covered mountains and the imposing limestone Alps.

Evidence of settlement in the area dates back to 1800 BC. Monks established a small monastery in 741 on the western shore of the Zeller See, the lake that dominates the town physically and psychically. Mining and trading in salt and wine over the Tauern Pass characterized the subsequent centuries. Zell has come far from the ascetic, monastic prayer of the 8th century; today, the town is devoted to the hedonism of the lake. While making merry in the water, you can raise your eyes and inhale the splendor of the Schmittenhöhe mountain just above you and the 3203-meter-high Kitzsteinhorn to its southwest. Indeed, Zell am See's horizon is dominated by 30 "three-thousanders."

Orientation and Practical Information Zell's **tourist office** *(Kurverwaltung),* Bruckner Bundesstr. 1 (tel. 260 00; fax 20 32), is within easy walking distance of the **train station** (tel. 321 43 57). From the station, take a right, bear left at the fork, turn left onto Dr. Franz-Rehrl-Str., and then right onto Brucker Bundesstr. Look for the large green "I" immediately before the intersection with Mozartstr. The office distributes maps of all kinds; though they cannot make reservations, they are more than happy to ferret out vacancies. The extremely pleasant staff leaves materials by the front door when the office is closed. (Open Mon.-Fri. 8am-noon and 2-

6pm, Sat. 8am-noon and 4-6pm, Sun. 10am-noon; May-June and Sept.-Oct. Mon.-Fri. 8am-noon and 2-6pm, Sat. 8am-noon.)

The **post office,** Parkplatz 4 (tel. 37 91), **exchanges currency** at primo rates, as does the **branch** at Brucker Bundesstr. 96. (Both open Mon.-Fri. 7:30am-6:30pm, Sat. 7:30am-11am; early-Sept. to early-March Mon.-Fri. 7:30am-6:30pm, Sat. 7:30-10am. Currency exchange open Mon.-Fri. 8am-noon and 2-5pm. **Postal Code:** A-5700.) Both branches also hold **telephones** (**City code:** 06542). The **bus station** is on the Postplatz, behind the main post office and facing Gartenstr. Buses leave daily to Salzburg (114 AS) and Heiligenblut (135 AS) along the Großglockner Straße. (Ticket window open Mon.-Sat. 7am-6:15pm, Sun. 8am-6pm.) You can rent a car from **Avis,** Stadtplatz 7 (tel. 26 59; open Mon.-Fri. 8:30am-noon and 2-6pm, Sat. 9am-noon).

Accommodations and Food Despite the town's proclivity for attracting well-heeled tourists, accommodations in Zell am See are reasonable and affordable. The **Haus der Jugend (HI),** Seespitzstr. 13 (tel. 71 85; fax 71 85 4), has large, immaculate rooms, each with shower and toilet, and a lakeside terrace overlooking Austria's cleanest waters. The hostel also rents mountain bikes (220 AS per day) and serves lunch and dinner (60 AS each). Exit the rear of the train station, turn right, and walk along the well-lit footpath beside the lake; at the end of the footpath, take a left onto Seespitzstraße (10 min.). (Reception open 7-9am and 4-10pm. Lockout noon-4pm. Curfew 10pm, but you can sign out a key with a 200 AS deposit. 160 AS, each additional night 135 AS. Over 27 8.50 AS tax. Sheets and breakfast included.)

Pensione Sinilill (Andi's Inn), Thumersbacherstr. 65 (tel. 35 23), is a pearl in the giant oyster of budget accommodations. Andi's swimming trophies, Joy's Filipino ornaments, and the largest warm breakfast this side of the Großglockner manufacture an eminently homey atmosphere. Call ahead and Andi will pick you up; or take the BundesBus (direction: "Thumersbach Ort") to "Krankenhaus" (14 AS, last bus 7:14pm). Turn left upon exiting, walk about 200m, and look for a *Zimmer Frei* sign on the left side of the street. (160-200 AS per person. Breakfast included. Camping in the front yard 50 AS.) **Frühstückspension Annemarie,** Gartenstr. 5 (tel. 28 51), a five-minute walk from the lake, has spacious rooms and a sweeping lawn. Follow the directions to the tourist office, continue along Brucker Bundesstr., and turn left onto Gartenstr. to reach the *Pension* (doubles 200 AS per person; breakfast and showers included).

There are two **campgrounds** in the arca—**Seecamp,** Thumersbacherstr. 34, in Zell am See/Prielau (tel. 21 15), is the Ritz-Carlton of sites. Every imaginable luxury is available at this lakeside complex, including private showers for Rover. Follow the directions to Pensione Sinilill; Seecamp is just down the street. (80 AS per person, ages 2-15 43 AS; 50 AS per tent, 95-115 AS per trailer. Over 15 7 AS tax.) Only campers with automobiles can take advantage of the spic and span facilities at **Camping Südufer,** Seeuferstr. 196 (tel. 62 28). (50 AS per person, ages 10-14 30 AS, under 10 25 AS; 40-55 AS per tent, 25 AS per car, 15 AS per motorcycle. Over 15 6 AS tax.)

Here in the Pingau region, food is prepared to sustain the farmers during their strenuous labors. Try the *Brezensuppe* (a clear soup with cheese cubes) as an appetizer, and then *Pinzgauer Käsnocken* (a frying pan filled with homemade noodles and cheese, and topped with fried onions and chives). Top it all off with a *Lebkuchen Parfait* (spice cake parfait). Other recipes that have survived generations of finicky eaters are the *Blattlkrapfen* (deep-fried stuffed pancakes) and *Germnudeln* (noodles served with poppy seeds, butter, and sugar).

Expect to pay dearly for food in Zell. **Café-Konditorei-Köpf,** Seegasse 10, is one notable exception. The café grills up *Schinkenbrot* (ham sandwich, 35 AS) and *Heiße Würstl mit Brot* (hot sausage and roll, 28 AS) in the middle of the bustling *Fußgängerzone* (open Mon.-Sat. 8am-7pm). **Prima,** directly across Brucker Bundesstr. from **McDonald's,** conjures up daily specials (60-90 AS) and *Schnitzel* with fries and salad (88 AS) in a festive atmosphere (open daily 9am-10pm). The **Japan-China**

Restaurant, at the corner of Brucker Bundesstr. and Bahnhofstr. (lunch 49-75 AS; open daily 11am-3pm and 5-11:30pm), and **Sennstub'n,** Schloßplatz 1 (pastas 58-92 AS; open Mon.-Sat. 11am-11pm), offer the cheapest full meals in town.

Picnic in the peaceful park on the Esplanade with fixings from **SPAR Markt,** Brucker Bundesstr. 4, which sells freshly prepared sandwiches (*Schnitzel* on a roll, 18 AS; open Mon.-Thurs. 8am-6:30pm, Fri. 8am-7:30pm, Sat. 7:30am-1pm). Or try the **Billa Markt** on Schulstr., near the Mozartstr. intersection (open Mon.-Thurs. 7:30am-6:30pm, Fri. 7:30am-8pm, and Sat. 7am-1pm).

Entertainment Zell is clustered in the valley of the pristine **Zeller See.** Dip your toes in the lake at one of two beaches: **Strandbad Zell am See,** near the center of town (walk toward the lake down Franz-Josef-Str.), and **Strandbad Seespitz,** by the Haus der Jugend. (Both open late-May to early-Sept. Admission 40 AS, with guest card 35 AS, ages 6-14 20 AS, students 17 AS.) **Boat tours** around the lake depart from and return to the Zell Esplanade, off Salzmannstr. along the river. (Every 30 min. Daily 9am-7:45pm; Sept.-May daily 9am-6:10pm. 60 AS, ages 6-14 30 AS.)

From the lake, the land rises swiftly into verdant peaks, crowned with a dusting of snow above treeline. You can conquer these local mountains by riding one of the town's five **cable-cars.** The **Schmittenhöhebahn,** about 2km north of town on Schmittenstr., rises from 939m to 1949m. Take the BundesBus (direction: "Schmittenhöhebahn/Sonnenalmbahn Talstation"; 16 AS). (Cable-car runs mid-May to late Oct. daily 8:30am-5pm. Round-trip 200 AS, with guest card 180 AS, ages 6-14 100 AS; up 155 AS, with guest card 140 AS, ages 6-14 80 AS.) The **Sonnenalmbahn,** traveling half the height, is adjacent to the Schmittenhöhebahn. It connects to the **Sonnkogelbahn,** which rises the remainder of the distance, to 1834m. (Lifts run early-June to early-Oct. daily 9am-5pm. Either lift costs round-trip 110 AS, with guest card 100 AS, ages 6-14 55 AS; up 85 AS, with guest card 75 AS, ages 6-14 45 AS. A combination ticket for both lifts sells for Schmittenhöhebahn fares.) The **Zeller Bergbahn** (780-1335m) is right in the center of town, at intersection of Schmittenstr. and Gartenstr. (Runs early-June to late-Sept. daily 9am-5pm. Round-trip 125 AS, with guest card 115 AS, children 65 AS; up 95 AS, with guest card 85 AS, children 50 AS.) Journey to the **Schuttdorf** suburb to find the **Areitbahn** (736-1370m). (Lift runs early-June to late-Sept. daily 9:15am-5pm. Fares are the same as for the Zeller Bergbahn.)

For light hiking, peruse a copy of *Die Drei Panorama Rundwanderwege auf der Schmittenhöhe,* available at any cable car station; other pamphlets describe more demanding trails. For more information, call the **Schmittenhöhebahn Aktiengesellschaft** (tel. 369 10), or visit the information desk of the Zeller Bergbahn. **Fritz G. Hirschburger III's Academy of Adventure** (tel. 44 52, fax 44 69) offers daytrips, including summer skiing on the Kitzsteinhorn glacier (785 AS; lift pass, transportation, equipment, and clothes included) and mountain climbing (495 AS).

Zell am See **skiing** exists mostly through neighboring **Kaprun** (see below). The primary exception is the Schmittenhöhebahn terrain; a one-day pass during peak season costs 210-370 AS (children 135-240 AS; in off-season 180-330 AS, children 115-215 AS). Ski rental is available in town at **Intersport Scholz,** Bahnhofstr. 13; a complete package of equipment costs 160-310 AS per day. (Open Mon.-Fri. and Sun. 8:30am-6pm, Sat. 10am-noon.) Private lessons cost 450 AS per hour through **Skischule Zell am See,** Schmittenhöhe (tel. 32 07).

For a taste of the nightlife in Zell am See, stop by **Bier-Keller** and sample the 33 different brews in stock; you'll be on the floor by #9. Dark beer enthusiasts must try the Hirter Morchel (30 AS per 0.3 liter). (Open June-Aug. and Dec.-April daily 7:30am-4am.) Send the kids to bed early and whoop it up at **Crazy Daisy's,** near the tourist office on Brucker Bundesstr. (Long Island Iced Tea 195 AS. Beer 29-52 AS. Open daily 10pm-1am.)

Festivals The Zeller residents like to live it up, and will apparently use any religious or secular occasion as an excuse to do so. Locals recall Mary and Joseph's search for a room in the inn with the **Anklökeln,** every **Advent** Thursday. A group of Christians travels from house to house singing old Advent songs and bringing their best wishes for the coming year. The figure of St. Nicholas is followed by the *Krampuses,* clad in furs and skins, clanging their cow bells and frightening children with fearsome wooden masks and birch whips. When **Christmas Eve** finally rolls around, Cindy Lou Who and family gather in the town square to sing Christmas carols. In many households, a traditional **Christmas** "Holy Cake" of milk, flour, salt, butter, and honey is served to bring health for the next year and to remind believers that Baby Jesus came into the world with simple tastes.

Until **Epiphany,** the *Schiachperchten* (evil spirits) and the handsome *Tresterers* pound out their rhythmical dance to encourage fertility in the coming year. The *Tresterers'* headgear consists of a narrow-brimmed straw hat with a crown of rooster feathers, from which long, colored streamers extend down to their waists. The *Habergoass* (witch), the *Lapp* and *Lappin* (male and female village idiots), and the *Zapfenmandl* (a man wearing a pinecone-covered costume) also participate in the ritual. On the eve of Epiphany, they drive away the winter's gloom to welcome in the light and fertility of spring. The next morning, the twelfth day of Christmas, the procession of three kings—Kaspar, Melchior, and Balthasar—passes through the streets.

Easter also brings a flurry of bizarre folk rituals. On **Palm Sunday,** children gather bunches of pussy willow branches, bind them together, have them blessed in the church, and then hang them under the eaves of their house to protect it from lightning and hail. On **Gründonnerstag** (the Thursday prior to Good Friday), the children dye eggs, and, on **Good Friday,** all the bells are silent, because they have flown to Rome (or so the children are told). In their place, the children rattle wooden ratchets.

The **Zeller Seefest** (Lake Festival) dates back to August 15, 1975, when a railway line between Salzburg and Innsbruck opened and the people celebrated. Since then, the festival has bifurcated into the **Sports Festival** in mid-July, and the **Folklore Festival** in early-August. The Sports Festival opens in the town square with brass band music and *Frühschoppen* (a morning beer-quaffing). The day is packed with exhibitions, and at dusk the lake is transformed into a sea of light; the climax is a fireworks display from four barges in the middle of the lake. The Folklore Festival in early-August also starts with *Frühschoppen* in the town square. At 2:30pm, traditionally clad folklore clubs, brass bands, rifle brigades, and other groups parade through the pedestrian zone to the lakeshore.

■ Kaprun

Tiny Kaprun, 25 minutes from Zell by bus, is really just an offshoot of the Zell am See ski area; by staying here instead of more touristed Zell, you'll be farther from the "action," but closer to the slopes. The village actually lingers along the southeast bank of the Kapruner Ache; its main street, Nikolaus-Gassner-Str., shadows the river as it flows through town. The town's name, "Chataprunnin," is derived from the Celtic for this very "wild water." Centuries ago, mining was practiced here, and the trade in salt and wine over to Hohe Tauern to Italy was a flourishing culinary success. The disclosure and exploration of the mineral wealth of the Hohe Tauern began in the earnest in the 19th century, when Kaprun served as a base camp for many ascents up the 9000-footers. Kaprun eventually developed into a mountaineering center in the Eastern Alps; at the turn of the century, over 100 guides were offering their services. With the building of the Glockner-Kaprun power station, begun in 1938 and completed in 1951, the mountain guide's village transformed into a skier's mecca; the greatest pioneering feat from Kaprun was the opening of the first of Austria's glacial ski regions on the Kitzsteinhorn.

Once in town, you'll want to make a beeline for the **Gletscherbahn Kaprun** (tel. 87 00), the cable car that ascends the **Kitzsteinhorn** glacier (open year-round, for summer or winter skiing or hiking, daily 8:30am-4:30pm). Free buses run from Kaprun's town center ("Kaprun Zentrum") to Kitzsteinhorn year-round; with a valid lift ticket, you can ride on the BundesBus free all the way back to Zell am See. A one-day pass costs 370 AS in *Hauptsaison* (children 240 AS; in the off-season 350 AS, children 225 AS.) A special two-day pass grants access to terrain in both Kaprun and Zell am See. (In *Hauptsaison* 700 AS, children 455 AS; in *Vor- und Nachsaison* 640 AS, children 415 AS.) **Ski rental** is available at **Intersport Bründl** (tel. (06547) 86 21), up in the Alpincenter, after you debark the Gletscherbahn (open 8am-4pm). At **Skischule Kaprun** (tel. (06547) 823 80) 2-hr. group **lessons** cost 270 AS (4-hr. 470 AS), while private lessons suck 1800 AS per day from your fanny pack. Dial 84 44 for **snow condition reports.**

If you want to make Kaprun more than a day-trip, take the BundesBus (direction: "Kesselfall-Alpenhaus") from Zell to "Jugendgästehaus" to reach Kaprun's **Jugendherberge (HI),** Nikolaus-Gassner-Str. 448 (tel. (06547) 85 07; fax 75 22 3). The last bus leaves Zell at 7:10pm (22 AS). The newly renovated, shiny quads with toilet and shower cost 190 AS. (Sheets and breakfast included. Reception open 7-9am and 5-10pm. Flexible 10pm curfew.)

■■■ HEILIGENBLUT

At the southern end of the Großglockner Straße lies tiny Heiligenblut, a smattering of homes, restaurants, and ski facilities clustered around a slender-steepled church. Its captivating Carinthian setting attracts a multitude of tourists year-round, especially middle-aged Germans and Austrians sporting red wool socks, Gore-Tex® boots, and go-thither-into-the-mountains® hiking trousers.

Orientation and Practical Information No trains run to Heiligenblut; **buses** connect the hamlet with Lienz four times per day (64 AS) and with Zell am See twice per day (135 AS), dumping passengers at the "Heiligenblut Hotel Post" stop in the center of town. The "Heiligenblut Winkl" stop lies in the valley immediately below, amid several homes, *Pensionen,* and the **post office.** The **tourist office,** Hof 4 (Verkehrsverein; tel. 22 22, fax 20 01 43), supplies brochures detailing lodgings, skiing, and local events. Turn right upon disembarking at the "Heiligenblut Hotel Post" stop, and walk 100m. (Open Mon.-Sat. 9am-6pm, Sun. 9am-noon; Sept.-June Mon.-Sat. 9am-6pm.) An **accommodations board** is located farther down the street by the **telephone booths** (**City code:** 04824). The **post office** (tel. 22 01) also has telephones and offers the best exchange rates. (Open July-Aug. Mon.-Fri. 8am-noon and 1-5pm, Sat. 8:30-10:30am; Sept. to mid-Dec. and April-June Mon.-Fri. 8am-noon and 1-5pm; mid-Dec. to March Mon.-Fri. 8am-noon and 1-5pm, Sat. 9-11am. Exchange open Mon.-Fri. 8am-noon and 1-4pm. **Postal Code:** A-9844.)

Accommodations and Food Visitors staying in any registered accommodation for at least three days are eligible for a **guest card;** the card allows you to traverse the Großglockner Road by car an unlimited number of times for 410 AS. Drive back and forth (and back and forth and back and forth and..., until your tires melt) searching for the best vantage point. Validate the card at the Mautstelle toll booth, at the Heiligenblut end of the highway.

Overlooking the Hohe Tauern mountains, the chalet-style **Jugendherberge (HI),** Hof 36 (tel. (04824) 22 59), shelters 84 sleepers in spacious, comfortable dorms. From "Heiligenblut Hotel Post," take a left, walk past Intersport, down the footpath behind the telephone booths, and toward the church; the hostel should be easily visible. (Open Dec.-Aug. Reception open 7-9am and 5-10pm. Curfew 10pm. Members only. 140 AS. Sheets and breakfast included.) The Bernhardt family rents *Privatzimmer* in their home, **Haus Friedheim,** Winkl 81 (tel. (04824) 20 22), looking out over the mountains across from the "Winkl" bus stop. The immaculately clean rooms, ranging from minute to spacious, are furnished with handpainted wood furniture and down comforters. (170 AS per person, 155 AS if you stay more than 3 days. Breakfast and shower included.)

Campers can rest their weary heads at two sites. **Nationalpark-Camping Großglockner,** Hardergasse 11 (tel. (04824) 20 48), has a restaurant and hot showers. Take the BundesBus (direction: "Lienz") to "Rojach"; you must *request* that the driver stop here (18 AS). The site is right at the bus stop. (Open mid-May to mid-Oct. and late Dec. to mid-April. 55 AS per person, ages 3-14 30 AS; 30 AS per car or motorcycle. Over 18 9.50 AS tax. Tents free.) **Möllfluß-Camping,** Bundesstr. 107 (tel. (04824) 21 29), boasts a restaurant, showers, sauna, and playground. Facing the hostel, walk down the path to the right side of the building, cross the bridge, and take a right at Pensione Edelweiß (5 min.). (Open June-Sept. and late-Dec. to mid-April. 60 AS per person, ages 4-14 35 AS; 20 AS per tent; cars and motorcycles free. Over 18 9.50 AS tax, "nature tax" 15 AS per day.) Restaurants in Heiligenblut are fairly expensive; opt for the **ADEG Aktiv Markt,** down the main street from the tourist office, instead. (Open Mon.-Fri. 8am-6:30pm, Sat. 8:30am-6:30pm, Sun. 8:30am-6pm.)

Sights and Entertainment "Heiligenblut" means "holy blood," so it is somehow fitting that the town's only man-made tourist attraction is a church. The austere, 14th-century **Pfarrkirche St. Vinzent** contains an elaborate, late-Gothic wooden altar and poignant memorials for people who died hiking in the mountains and those who perished in the World Wars. The gravestones encircling the church are eerily embellished with black and white photos of the deceased.

Head into the mountains for superlative sports in any season. The **Schareck Gondola** is conveniently located at the "Heiligenblut Hotel Post" stop right in the center of town. Ascend the 2604m for a spellbinding panorama of the Großglockner. (Runs mid-June to mid-Sept. Mon.-Fri. 9am-noon and 1-4pm. 150 AS, ages 5-15 half-price.) In the winter, the cable car provides easy access to the trails of Heiligenblut's ski terrain. A one-day pass in the *Hauptsaison* (Dec. 12-Jan. 4, Feb. 1-March 21, and April 4-26) runs 315 AS, ages 16-23 270 AS, under 16 190 AS. Buy your lift ticket at the gondola ticket booth. **Skischule Heiligenblut** (tel. 22 56 47 or 22 45) will sharpen your parallel turns or flatten that snowplow in a group lesson for 380 AS per day. **Intersport Pichler,** across the street from the tourist office at Hof 6, rents downhill equipment bundles for 240-280 AS per day, cross-country skis for 130 AS per day, and mountain bikes for 200 AS per day. (Open peak season Mon.-Fri. 9am-noon and 2:30-6pm, Sat. 8:30am-noon and 4-6pm, Sun. 9:30-11:30am and 4-6pm; off-season Mon.-Sat. 9am-6pm, Sun. 10am-noon and 1-5pm.) For **snow condition information** in German, call 22 88 66.

The **Singing of the Three Kings,** or Epiphany Singing, occurs in town on January 5 and 6. Five groups of grown men (*Rotten*) carry a pole with an illuminated revolving star and wander from the evening of January 5 to the morning mass the following day, from the village to the surrounding mountain farms. The Alps aren't especially conducive to frankincense or myrrh farming; to compensate for the dearth of holy gifts, the *Rotten* sing the Three Kings' Song as they travel.

■■■ LIENZ

Between the bald, angry peaks of the Dolomites and the snow-capped, gentle summits of the Hohe Tauern mountains, Lienz is quietly captivating. Low-slung houses, flawlessly decked out in fairy-tale reds and yellows, are juxtaposed with the unforgiving crags that provided the gray stone for the city's more monumental edifices. A religious ethos pervades this town—residents leave flowers and burn candles in front of the crucifixes at traffic intersections. (How many "Our Fathers" can you recite before the light turns green?) Niches in building façades hold statues of the Virgin Mary.

ORIENTATION AND PRACTICAL INFORMATION

Situated in the jagged Dolomites, the mountain range Austria shares with Italy and Slovenia, Lienz is the unofficial capital of **East Tyrol** (Osttirol), a discontinuous portion of the Austrian province of Tyrol. Lienz is approximately three hours by train from Innsbruck or Salzburg, but just 40km from the Italian border. The town is split by the **Isel River,** which feeds into the Drau.

Tourist Office: Tourismusverband, Europaplatz (tel. 652 65; fax 65 26 52). Distributes armloads of brochures and has a complete listing of private accommodations. The pamphlet *Lienzer Dolomiten Preisliste* offers an exhaustive list of accommodations and prices, while the booklet *Informationen für unsere Gäste* details recreational opportunities and cultural activities. From the station, turn left onto Tiroler Str. and turn right onto Europaplatz at the SPAR Markt. Open Mon.-Fri. 8am-7pm, Sat. 9am-noon and 3-5pm, Sun. 10am-noon and 5-7pm; Oct.-June Mon.-Fri. 8am-6pm, Sat. 9am-noon and 3-5pm. Just outside the office is a snazzy 24-hr. **accommodations board.**

Currency Exchange: Best rates are in the post office. Exchange desk open Mon.-Fri. 7:30am-noon and 2-5pm.

Post Office: On the corner of Hauptplatz across from the train station (tel. 668 80). Holds *Postlagernde Briefe.* Open Mon.-Fri. 7am-6pm and Sat. 7-11am. **Postal code:** A-9900.

Telephones: In the post office. There are also a number of phone booths across the street from the station: 2 take *Wertkarten,* and one is wheelchair-accessible. **City code:** 04852.

Trains: Hauptbahnhof, Bahnhof Platz (tel. 660 60). Has all the trimmings: lockers (20-30 AS), currency exchange, luggage storage, and bike rental (mountain bikes 150 AS). Connections to points all over Austria, including Klagenfurt (194 AS), Zell am See (236 AS), Innsbruck (236 AS), Salzburg (270 AS), Graz (444 AS), the Vienna Südbahnhof (570 AS), and the Vienna Westbahnhof (620 AS). International trains depart daily for Munich, Zürich, Berlin, Zagreb, Venice, Stuttgart, Rome, and Florence. Station open daily 5am-11pm.

Buses: Station in front of the *Hauptbahnhof.* Ticket window (tel. 670 67) open Mon.-Fri. 7:45-10am and 4-6:30pm, Sat. 7:45-10am.

Taxi: Funk-Taxi, tel. 640 64 or **Taxi-Geiger,** tel. 654 50.

Hospital: Emanuel-von-Hibler-Str. (tel. 60 60). **Ambulance:** tel. 144.

Police: Hauptplatz 5 (tel. 63 15 50 or 626 00).

Emergencies: tel. 133

ACCOMMODATIONS AND CAMPING

The Lienz *Jugendherberge* closed in 1993, but rumor has it that another will open soon; check with the tourist office for the most current information. Even *sans* hostel, though, Lienz is a consummately affordable town, with *Pensionen* largely running no more than 250-300 AS per person. If *Privatzimmer* are more your yen, consult the friendly staff at the tourist office for an exhaustive list of lodgings.

Gasthof Goldener Stern, Schweizergasse 40 (tel. 621 92). Spacious rooms in a gorgeous 15th-century mansion with stunning, low-vaulted ceilings. Incredibly meticulous management prides itself on keeping order—door locked promptly at 10pm. From the train station, cross Tiroler Str., and bear left into the Hauptplatz. Walk through the square, veer right onto Muchargasse, and continue straight as it becomes Schweizergasse (8 min.). July to mid-Sept. singles 190 AS, with toilet and shower 290 AS; doubles and triples 180 AS per person, with toilet and shower 260 AS per person. mid-Sept. to June 180-190 AS per person, with toilet and shower 240-260 AS. Showers 20 AS. Breakfast included. 10 AS surcharge for stays of less than 3 nights.

Frühstückpension Gretl, Schweizergasse 32 (tel. 621 06). Right next door to Goldener Stern. Offers similar facilities in slightly smaller rooms and without the historic setting, but imposes no curfews. 240 AS per person. Ample breakfast included.

Egger, Alleestr. 33 (tel. 487 72). From the station, walk through the Hauptplatz, bear left on Rosengasse and right on tree-lined Alleestr. Cool, fresh rooms with high ceilings and rustic furniture accommodate 10 in doubles and triples. View of the Dolomites and a tangled garden with giant sunflowers and lilies. 150-160 AS per person, 10 AS surcharge for stays of less than 3 nights. Generous breakfast and showers included. English spoken.

Früstückpension Masnata, Drahtzuggasse 4 (tel. 655 36). Elegantly decorated rooms in a soothing residential district offset the 15-20 min. walk from the station. Turn left onto Tiroler Str., walk about 10-15 min., and then veer left on Dolomitenstr.; Drahtzuggasse is the second right. 220-260 AS per person. 10% surcharge for visits fewer than 3 nights. Breakfast included. English spoken.

Camping Falken, Eichholz 7 (tel. 640 22 or 623 89). Located just across the Drau River near the foot of the Dolomites. From the station, make a left onto Tiroler Str. and a left at the Sport Hotel, cross over the Drau, follow Amlacher Str. to the right, and take the first left (15-20 min.). July-Aug. and mid-Dec. to March 50 AS per person, under 15 35 AS, 70-95 AS per site; Sept. to mid-Dec. and April-June 45 AS per person, under 15 30 AS, 60-85 AS per site. Over 15 7 AS tax. Reservations welcomed.

FOOD

Delis, bakeries, and butcher stores are sprinkled along **Schweizergasse**. Three discount supermarkets are not far away; **SPAR Markt** is across Europaplatz from the tourist office (open Mon.-Fri. 7:30am-6:30pm, Sat. 7:30am-1pm), the **ADEG Aktiv Markt** is in Südtiroler Platz (open Mon.-Fri. 8am-6pm, Sat. 8am-noon), and **M-Preis** is tucked away on Rosengasse (open Mon.-Fri. 8am-6:30pm, Sat. 8am-noon). Every Saturday from 8am-noon in Südtiroler Platz, the **Bauernmarkt** covers rickety old tables and wagons with delectable fresh farm products.

Imbiße Köstl, Kreuzgasse 4. Enthusiastic mother-daughter dynamic duo prepare the cheapest eats in town (19-49 AS). Chow down on the *Wiener Schnitzel* (49 AS), or sully your fingers with the pastries on display (8-17 AS). Open Mon.-Fri. 7:30am-7:30pm, Sat. 7:30am-2pm.

Pizzeria Sergio, Schweizergasse 29. Large portions in a family atmosphere. Pizzas (65-100 AS), spaghetti (65-75 AS), and *Thunfischsalat* (tuna salad, 75 AS). Open Mon.-Sat. noon-2pm and 6pm-midnight.

Batzenhäusl, Zwergergasse 1a (tel. 633 70). A beer garden with a view of the Dolomites. ½-liter of Gösser beer 26 AS, hearty *Gulasch* 80 AS, *Schlipfkrapfen* (pasta in cream sauce, a Tyrolean specialty) 80 AS. Open Mon.-Sat. 10am-9pm.

China Restaurant Szechuan, Marcherstr. Tasty and moderately priced entrees (75-165 AS) reward those willing to cross the River Isel. Cross the bridge adjoining the Neuer Platz, bear right in the gardens, and turn left onto Marcherstr. (3-5 min.). Open daily 11:30am-2:30pm and 5:30-11:30pm.

Café Wha, Schweizergasse 3. Younger, bandanna-wearing, slightly alternative crowd rock and roll way past the midnight hour. Strain your eyes through the smoke and check out the bizarre modern art hanging on the walls. Beer 24-35 AS; wine 21-25 AS. Open daily 6pm-1am.

VIP Café, intersection of Muchargasse and St. Johannes Platz. Elegant decor and Muzak attract a wine-sipping, cappuccino-drinking crowd too sophisticated for Café Wha. The *Nußtorte* (27 AS) complements the scrumptious *Schokolade mit Rum* (30 AS). *Great* headrests. Open daily 7:30am-midnight.

SIGHTS AND ENTERTAINMENT

Above Lienz, the **Schloß Bruck,** home of the **East Tyrolean Regional Museum,** houses everything from Roman remains and local artifacts to carved Christmas *crèches.* This lonely castle was once the fortress of the counts of Gorz, who controlled vast estates in the area until the 16th century, when the region succumbed to Habsburg rule. Upon entering the complex, carefully examine the faint remains of an etching located just below the two windows guarding the front door. Locals swear the etching depicts a double-cross; a woman, intending to poison her lover, became ensnared in her own treacherous plot and mistakenly drank the venomous beverage. This nameless damsel is depicted in the etching, doubled-over and about to toss her cookies. Inside the fortress, the **Kapelle zur Alterheiligsten Dreifaltigkeit** boasts surprisingly well-preserved (and less anatomically accurate) frescoes dating from the 15th century. The **Rittersaal** (Knights' Hall) houses an incredible 34-square-meter tapestry comprised of 42 different squares tracking the life and death of Christ. The work of local *fin-de-siècle* painter **Albin Egger-Lienz** is accumulated in a gallery inside the Regional Museum. His canvas *Das Kreuz* (1901-2), depicts the Tyrolean struggle against Napoleon and pays tribute to its creator's uncanny ability to capture emotion. From the Hauptplatz, walk 15 minutes down Muchargasse, Schweizergasse, and Schloßgasse, turn right onto Iseltaler Str., and take your first left to arrive at the castle. Alternatively, take the BundesBus from the train station (direction: "Matreier Tauernhaus" or "Lucknerhaus") to "Lienz Schloß Bruck Heimatmuseum" (16 AS). (Castle open mid-June to mid-Sept. daily 10am-6pm; mid-Sept. to Oct. and April to mid-June Tues.-Sun. 10am-5pm. Admission 35 AS, students and seniors 23 AS, ages 16-18 18 AS, under 16 10 AS.)

Across the river from the main part of town is the exquisite parish church of **St. Andrä,** which dominates Lienz from its lofty situation above the River Isel. The church was built around 1450 on Romanesque foundations; a porch and crypt from 1204 are still partly intact, as are the remains of an early episcopal church. The church contains 14th-century murals and the elaborate marble tombstones of the 16th-century counts of Gorz. The massive and austere Romanesque doors conceal a high altar splashed with scintillating pink and yellow. At the west entrance are two Romanesque portal lions. Frescoes by Josef Adam Mölk (1761) and an organ casing (1618) with 15th-century sculptures are on display. A chapel memorializes citizens who died during the World Wars—Albin Egger-Lienz is also buried here. To visit St. Andrä, turn onto Beda-Weber-Gasse from Linker Iselweg, and make a left onto Patriasdorfer Str. The gray **Liebburg,** on the Hauptplatz, was built as a residence for the counts of Wollkenstein in the 17th century; since its renovation, the building has been used as a town hall.

For a taste of reverse culture shock, drop by the **U.S. Shop** on Tiroler Str., a store purveying the lowest dregs of American popular culture. Purchase tacky t-shirts and discuss the poor quality of European ketchup in loud, rude, condescending English.

Four kilometers east of Lienz, on the left bank of the Debant stream, lies the **Aguntum.** This Illyrian settlement, from the Hallstatt era (1100-500 BC), developed into a thriving Roman provincial trading town; around the year one, Rome granted it civil rights. Of interest are the town walls with gates, houses with heating facilities, graves, vessels, and jewels, as well as a cemetery with an early Christian burial church. If you've no desire to journey out to the site, various relics are exhibited in the museum at Bruck Castle.

For an easygoing introduction to the area's Alpine wonders, take the **Hochsteinbahnen** chairlift, from the base station near the castle at the intersection of Iseltaler Str. and Schloßgasse, 2000m up to the **Sternalm.** (Lift runs late June to mid-Sept. 9:15am-12:15pm and 1-5:30pm. One way 90 AS, round-trip 130 AS, children half-price.) From the summit you can absorb the spectacular confrontation between the unforgiving Dolomites to the south and the gently rounded Hohe Tauern to the north. The **Zettersfeld** chairlift provides access to hiking on the 1930m Zettersfeld peak. Take the free blue and white Stadtbus (July to mid-Sept.) from the train station to the last stop, "Zettersfeld Talstation." (Lift open late June-early Oct. daily 9-11:45am and 1-5pm; one way 70 AS, children half-price.) The **Dolomiten-Wonderbus** delivers nature lovers to another challenging hiking base, the **Lienzer Dolomitenhütte** (1620m). More than 40 trails of varying difficulty spiral off from this

Alpine hut. (Buses leave mid-June to late Sept. 8am, 1:10pm and 4:30pm; 95 AS.) For additional mountainous hiking information, contact Lienz's chapter of the **Alpenverein,** Franz von Defreggerstr. 11 (tel. 489 32; open Mon., Wed., and Fri. 9am-noon).

Aquaphiles can also venture on the 5km hike to the **Tristacher See,** a sparkling blue lake hugging the base of the Rauchkofel mountain. Ask at the tourist office for the brochures *Wandertips* and *Radtouren in der Ferienregion Lienzer Dolomiten,* which maps potential routes to the lake and other destinations. Couch potatoes can enjoy the lake's facilities (25 AS) without twitching a muscle, by hopping on the free **Bäder- und Freizeitbus** in front of the train station; disembark at the end station, "Parkhotel Tristachersee." (Bus runs daily July to early Sept.)

Lienz also serves as an excellent base to attack the ski trails comprising the **Lienzer Dolomiten Complex**. During the *Hauptsaison* (mid-Dec. to April), a one-day ski pass costs 290 AS, seniors 230 AS, under 15 145 AS. (Off-season 275 AS, seniors 220 AS, under 15 145 AS. Half-day tickets run 230 AS, seniors 185 AS, under 15 115 AS; off-season 220 AS, seniors 175 AS, under 15 115 AS.) The **Skischule Lienzer Dolomiten** (tel. 656 90) at the Zettersfeld lift will allow you to perfect your face plant technique with private lessons at 370 AS per person (170 AS per person for groups). **Hans Moser und Sohn,** at the apex of the Zettersfeld lift (tel. 691 80 or 681 66), supplies **ski rental;** a complete set of downhill equipment will run 190 AS per day. For a **ski report** in German, dial 652 00.

During the second weekend of August, the sounds of alcohol-induced merriment reverberate off the daintily painted façades of Lienz's town buildings in celebration of the **Stadtfest** (admission to town center 40 AS). The summer months also welcome the reaffirmation of Tyrolean culture and heritage in a series of **Platzkonzerte.** Watch grandfathers dust off their old *Lederhosen* and perform the acclaimed shoe-slapping dance. (Free; times and venues vary, so consult the booklet *Informationen für unsere Gäste.*) On the third Sunday of January, the world's greatest cross-country skiers gather in Lienz to compete in the 60km **Dolomitenlauf;** man's best friend runs the same course in the **Hundeschlittenrennen** (Dogsled Run).

Salzburger Land

Once one of Europe's most powerful Archbishoprics, the province of Salzburg remained an autonomous entity until 1815, when the Congress of Vienna awarded it to Austria. The region built up its tremendous wealth with a salt industry that flourished from the Iron Age onward; "Salzburg" comes from *Salz,* the German word for salt, and several localities are named *Hall,* an archaic term for salt. Although tourism displaced the salt trade long ago, figures of Saint Barbara, the patron saint of miners, are still found everywhere. The major attraction of Salzburger Land is the Baroque magnificence of Salzburg, but the region has other charms as well. The dramatic natural scenery and placid lakes of the Salzkammergut, which straddles the provincial boundaries of Salzburg, Styria, and Upper Austria, are among Austria's favorite vacation spots.

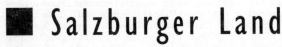

Though all of this mineral mining may seem soporific, when the Salzburger Land lets down its hair, it does so in style. On the last Sunday in July, every three years, a historic **Pirates' Battle** is held on the River Salzach at **Oberndorf.** The pirates' camp is situated below the State Bridge. According to the ritual plot, the brigands attack and rob a salt-boat and then fire on the town of Laufen, on the opposite (Bavarian) side of the river. Eventually, the defeated pirates try to escape. They are arrested and condemned to death, but their sentence is quickly modified to "death by drowning in beer," which signifies the beginning of a lavish feast. On occasional July Sundays, the **Schifferstechen** (a spear-fight between boatmen) is held in Oberndorf. The competition, in the middle of the river, culminates when the best three fighters are awarded a cup. The combat is followed by the Hansl-und-Gretl-Spiel, the Wurstspringen (jump for the sausage), and a riverside feast.

■■■ SALZBURG

Wedged between protective mountainsides and dotted with church spires and medieval turrets, Salzburg (pop. 150,000) is a city of enchantment whose voice is expressed in the sublime music of favorite son Wolfgang Amadeus Mozart. Salzburg's adulation of the decomposed composer crescendoes during the annual Salzburger Festspiele (summer music festival), when admirers from the world 'round come to pay their respects. Salzburg is also the best place to pay homage to the sweetly trilling von Trapp family of *The Sound of Music:* town tour guides will never let you forget that the movie was filmed here.

ORIENTATION AND PRACTICAL INFORMATION

Salzburg, capital of the province of the same name, lies almost in the center of Austria, 1400 ft. above sea level. Three wooded hills surround the town, which hugs the banks of the **Salzach River** a few kilometers from the German border. The *Altstadt* (*map**E4*), sits on the west bank of the river, flanked by the imposing, crescent-shaped **Mönchsberg** (*map**A4, B4, B5, C5*). The train station is on the northern edge of the new town, which is centered around **Mirabellplatz** (*map**B3*) and **Makartplatz** (*map**B3*) east of the river. Both the *Altstadt* and the new town are a 15- to 20-minute walk down Rainerstr. from the station, or take bus #5 (direction: "Birkensiedlung"), #6 (direction: "Parsch"), or #51 (direction: "Alpensiedlung Süd") from the bus stop across from the station. Debark at "Mirabellplatz" in the new town or "Morzartsteg" in the *Altstadt.*

Agencies

Tourist Office, (*map**C4*) Mozartplatz 5 (tel. 84 75 68 or 88 9 87 332; fax 88 9 87 342), in the *Altstadt.* From the train station, take bus #5, 6, 51, or 55 to "Mozartsteg;" on foot, turn left onto Rainerstr., which becomes Dreifaltigkeitsgasse, cross the river on the Staatsbrücke, turn left on Müllner Hauptstr., and take the second right into Mozartplatz. Open daily 8am-10pm, April-June and Sept.-Oct. 9am-7pm; Nov.-March Mon.-Sat. 9am-6pm. Hours may vary in spring and autumn. The free hotel map is exactly the same as the 5 AS city map. Other **branches** at **train station platform #10** (*map**C1*; tel. 87 17 12 or 87 36 38; open Mon.-Sat. 8:45am-8:30pm), at the **airport** (tel. 85 24 51 or 88 98 73 36; open daily 9am-9pm), and at the **exits** from Autobahn A1 and Bundesstraßen B155, B150, and B156. The state tourist office, **Land Salzburg Information** (*map**C4*), Mozartplatz 5 (tel. 80 42 22 32 or 84 32 64) is in the same building as the main city tourist office (open Mon.-Sat. 9am-6pm).

Budget Travel: Ökista (*map**C2-3*), Wolf-Dietrich-Str. 31, A-5020 Salzburg (tel. 88 32 52; fax 88 18 19), near the International Youth Hotel. Open Mon.-Fri. 9:30am-5:30pm. **Young Austria** (*map**C4*), Alpenstr. 108a (tel. 25 75 80 0; telex 631198; fax 257 58 21), part of the Österreichisches Jugendferienwerk. Open Mon.-Fri. 9am-6pm, Sat. 9am-noon. Both have discounts, especially for travelers under 26.

Consulates: U.S. (*map**C4*), Giselakai 51 (tel. 286 01). The consulate is in the second building past the Nonntaler Brücke; take bus #6 (direction: "Parsch") or #49 (direction: "Josef-Kaut-Str.") to "Dr.-Franz-Rehrl-Platz." Open Mon.-Fri. 9-11am and 2-4pm. **U.K.** (*map**C4*), Alter Markt 4 (tel. 84 81 33). Open Mon.-Fri. 9am-noon.

Currency Exchange: Banking hours are Mon.-Fri. 8am-noon and 2-4:30pm. Currency exchange at the train station open daily 7am-10pm. **Rieger Bank** (*map**C4*), Alter Markt 14, is also open on Sun. May-Oct. 10am-5pm. The post office and the AmEx office offer the best rates.

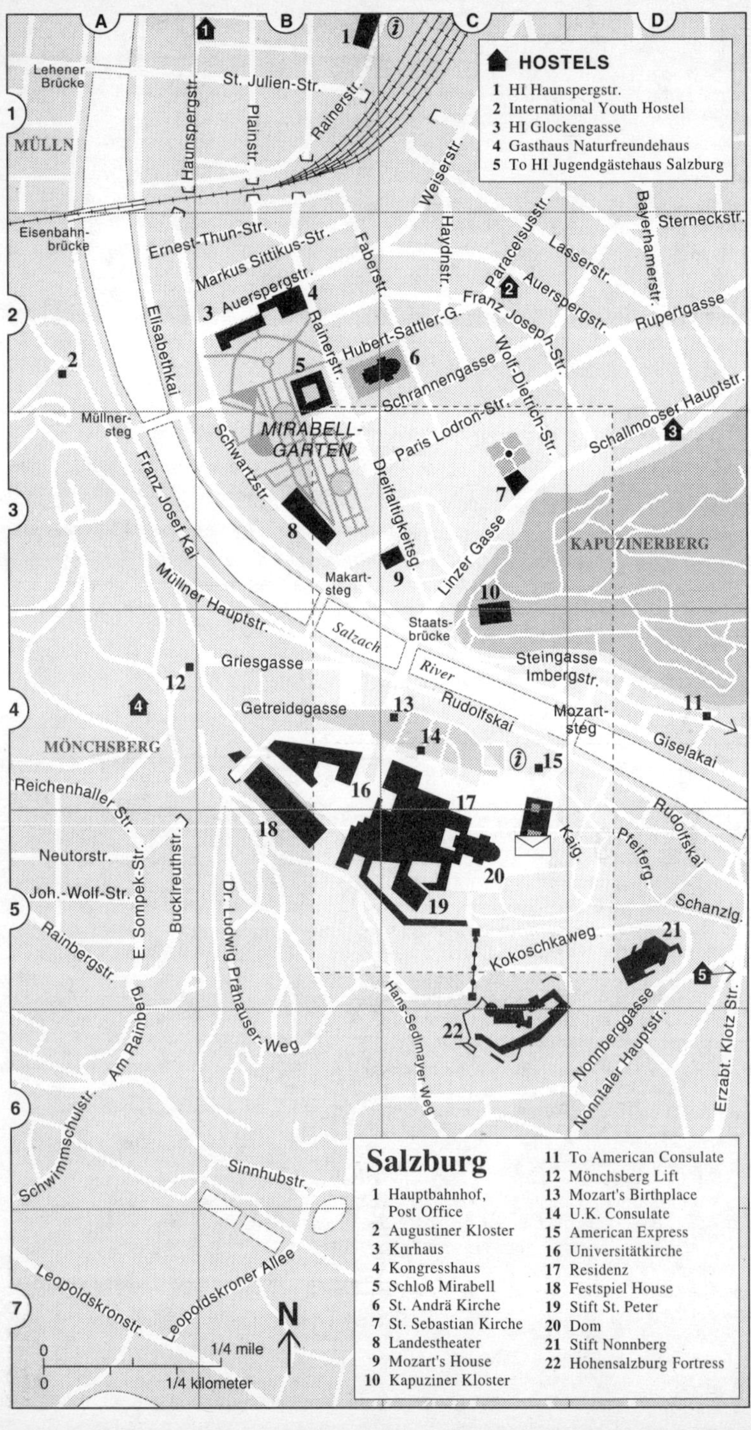
HOSTELS
1 HI Haunspergstr.
2 International Youth Hostel
3 HI Glockengasse
4 Gasthaus Naturfreundehaus
5 To HI Jugendgästehaus Salzburg
Salzburg
1 Hauptbahnhof, Post Office
2 Augustiner Kloster
3 Kurhaus
4 Kongresshaus
5 Schloß Mirabell
6 St. Andrä Kirche
7 St. Sebastian Kirche
8 Landestheater
9 Mozart's House
10 Kapuziner Kloster
11 To American Consulate
12 Mönchsberg Lift
13 Mozart's Birthplace
14 U.K. Consulate
15 American Express
16 Universitätkirche
17 Residenz
18 Festspiel House
19 Stift St. Peter
20 Dom
21 Stift Nonnberg
22 Hohensalzburg Fortress
MÜLLN
MÖNCHSBERG
KAPUZINERBERG
MIRABELL-GARTEN
Salzach River
Lehener Brücke
Eisenbahnbrücke
Müllnersteg
Makartsteg
Staatsbrücke
Mozartsteg
St. Julien-Str.
Haunspergstr.
Plainstr.
Rainerstr.
Weiserstr.
Ernest-Thun-Str.
Markus Sittikus-Str.
Auerspergstr.
Faberstr.
Haydnstr.
Paracelsusstr.
Lasserstr.
Bayerhamerstr.
Sterneckstr.
Franz Joseph-Str.
Hubert-Sattler-G.
Rupertgasse
Wolf-Dietrich-Str.
Schrannengasse
Paris Lodron-Str.
Schallmooser Hauptstr.
Elisabethkai
Schwartzstr.
Dreifaltigkeitsg.
Linzer Gasse
Franz Josef Kai
Müllner Hauptstr.
Griesgasse
Getreidegasse
Steingasse
Imbergstr.
Rudolfskai
Giselakai
Reichenhaller Str.
Neutorstr.
Joh.-Wolf-Str.
E. Sompek-Str.
Bucklreuthstr.
Dr. Ludwig Prähauser-Weg
Kaig.
Pfeiferg.
Schanzlg.
Kokoschkaweg
Rainbergstr.
Am Rainberg
Hans-Sedlmayer Weg
Nonnberggasse
Nonntaler Hauptstr.
Erzabt. Klotz Str.
Schwimmschulstr.
Sinnhubstr.
Leopoldskronstr.
Leopoldskroner Allee
N
0
1/4 mile
1/4 kilometer
A
B
C
D
1
2
3
4
5
6
7

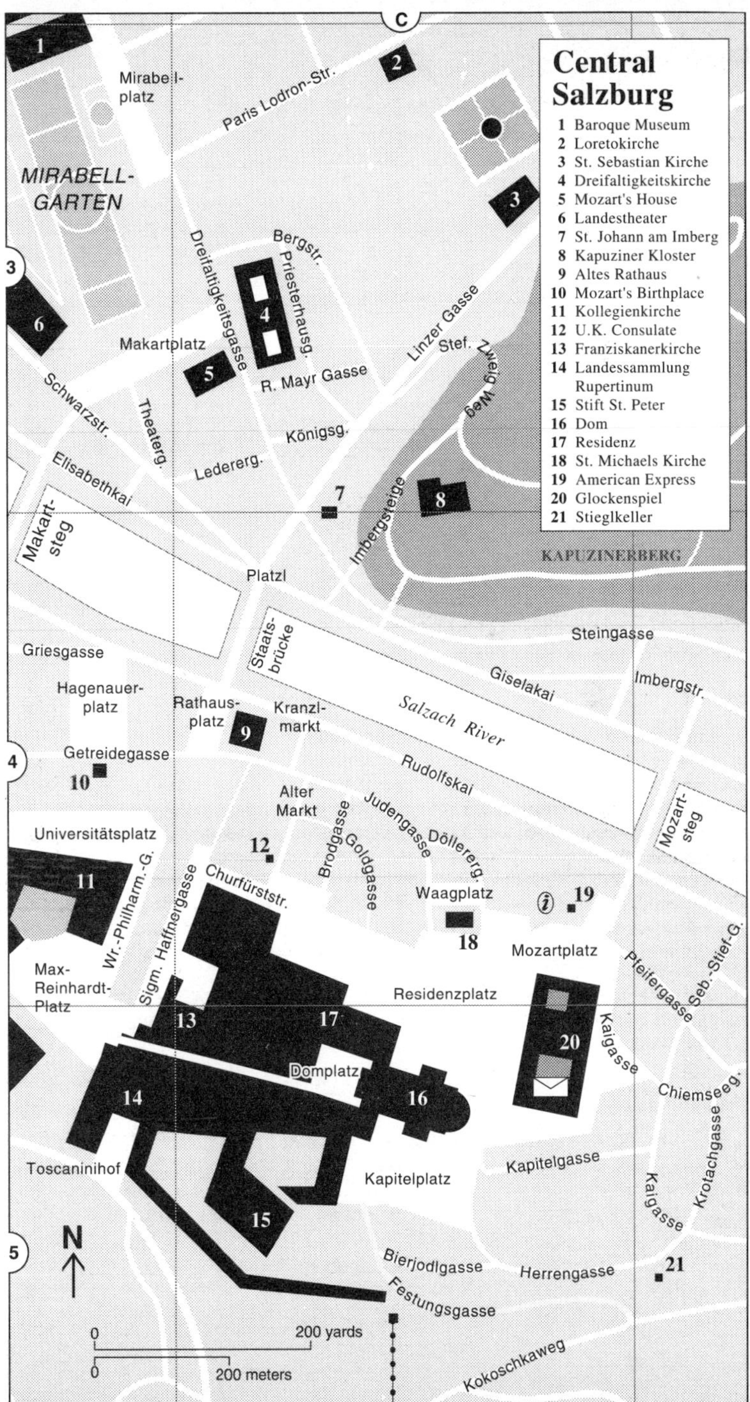
Central Salzburg
1 Baroque Museum
2 Loretokirche
3 St. Sebastian Kirche
4 Dreifaltigkeitskirche
5 Mozart's House
6 Landestheater
7 St. Johann am Imberg
8 Kapuziner Kloster
9 Altes Rathaus
10 Mozart's Birthplace
11 Kollegienkirche
12 U.K. Consulate
13 Franziskanerkirche
14 Landessammlung Rupertinum
15 Stift St. Peter
16 Dom
17 Residenz
18 St. Michaels Kirche
19 American Express
20 Glockenspiel
21 Stieglkeller
Mirabell-platz
MIRABELL-GARTEN
Paris Lodron-Str.
Bergstr.
Dreifaltigkeitsgasse
Priesterhausg.
Makartplatz
R. Mayr Gasse
Linzer Gasse
Stef. Zweig Weg
Schwarzstr.
Theaterg.
Königsg.
Ledererg.
Elisabethkai
Imbergsteige
KAPUZINERBERG
Makart-steg
Platzl
Staats-brücke
Steingasse
Griesgasse
Giselakai
Imbergstr.
Hagenauer-platz
Rathaus-platz
Kranzl-markt
Salzach River
Getreidegasse
Rudolfskai
Alter Markt
Judengasse
Döllererg.
Mozart-steg
Universitätsplatz
Brodgasse
Goldgasse
Wr.-Philharm.-G.
Sigm. Haffnergasse
Churfürststr.
Waagplatz
Mozartplatz
Seb.-Stief-G.
Max-Reinhardt-Platz
Pfeifergasse
Residenzplatz
Kaigasse
Domplatz
Chiemseeg.
Kapitelgasse
Krotachgasse
Toscaninihof
Kapitelplatz
N
Bierjodlgasse
Herrengasse
Festungsgasse
0
200 yards
0
200 meters
Kokoschkaweg
C
3
4
5

American Express: (*map*D4*) Mozartplatz 5-7 (tel. 84 25 01; telex 633561 amex a; fax 84 25 01 9). All banking services; expect excruciatingly long lines in summer. Open Mon.-Fri. 9am-5:30pm, Sat. 9am-noon.

Thomas Cook: (*map*C4*) **Reisen & Freizeit,** Europastr. 148 (tel. 43 88 58; fax 43 88 58 13).

Post Office: (*map*C4*-5) Mail your brown paper packages tied up in strings at the main office in town, Residenzplatz 9 (tel. 84 41 21 16). Open Mon.-Fri. 7am-7pm, Sat. 8-10am. A branch office in the train station is the most convenient place to pick up **Poste Restante.** Address *Poste Restante* to "Postlagernde Briefe, Bahnhofspostamt, A-5020 Salzburg." Office open 24 hrs., but Poste Restante must be picked up Mon.-Fri. 7am-6:30pm. The **postal code** of the main office is A-5010. Note that this is different from the train station branch.

Telephones: (*map*C1*) At the train station post office, open 24 hrs. At Post Office Residenzplatz, Mon.-Fri. 7am-7pm, Sat. 8-10am. **City Code:** 0662.

Transportation

Airport: Flughafen Salzburg (tel. 85 29 00; fax 85 29 00 44), located 4km west of the Maxglan section of the city. Bus #77 (20 AS; direction "Bahnhof") runs to the train station every 15 min. From the station, take the same bus (direction: "Walserfeld") to "Flughafen." Daily flights to Innsbruck and Paris. Aeroflot, Air Link, Air Salzburg, Austrian Airlines, British Airways, Lufthansa, Sabena, Salzburg Airlines.

Trains: Hauptbahnhof (*map*C1;* tel. 888 87), on Südtiroler Platz in the new city. For train info call 17 17. Trains run every hr. to Vienna (380 AS), every hr. to Munich (256 AS), 3 times per day to Budapest (648 AS).

Buses: (*map*C1*) Main depot across from the train station on Südtiroler Platz (tel. 87 21 45). Ticket window open Mon.-Fri. 7-9:25am, 9:45am-2:30pm, and 2:50-6:20pm, Sat. 7-9:25am and 9:45am-2:20pm.

Local Public Transportation: Information at (*map*A4*) Griesgasse 21 (tel. 205 51, ext. 553). An extensive network of 18 buses cuts through the city, with central hubs at "Hanuschplatz," by Makartsteg, and at "Äußerer Stein," at Steingasse and Imbergstr. 20 AS per ride if you pay the driver, 13 AS if you purchase at a *Tabak* stand, 16 AS if you buy from an automatic vending machine, 65 AS for a book of 5 rides. A 24-hr. pass costs 27 AS. Passes that include the cable car to the castle, the Mönchsberg lift, and the entire bus system cost 52 AS for 24 hrs. ("Salzburg-Ticket 1") and 104 AS for 72 hrs. ("Salzburg-Ticket 3"). Ages 6-15 half-price, under 6 free. Unless you want to climb every mountain and ford every stream, it's a good investment.

Taxis: The city transportation runs a **BusTaxi** daily 11:30pm-1:30am, from Hanuschplatz and Theatergasse. 25 AS per person for any distance within the city limits.

Bike Rental: At the train station (*map*C1*), platform #3 (tel. 88 87 54 27).

Hitchhiking: *Let's Go* does not recommend hitchhiking as a safe mode of transportation. Those hitchers headed to Innsbruck, Munich, or Italy (except Venice) first take bus #77 to the German border. Thumbers bound for Vienna or Venice take bus #2 (direction: "Maxglan") to "Mirabellplatz" and then switch to #29 (direction: "Forellenwegsiedlung") until the Autobahn entrance at "Schmiedlinger Str." They also take bus #15 (direction: "Bergheim") to the Autobahn entrance at "Grüner Wald." The **Mitfahrzentrale** (*map*A5*) at W. Philharmonikergasse 2 (tel. 84 13 27) in the Studentenhaus Katholische Hochschulgemeinde, matches riders and drivers. Demand for rides outstrips the supply. Open Mon.-Thurs. 9am-noon and 2-5pm, Fri. 9am-noon.

Other Practical Information

Luggage Storage: At the train station. Large lockers, 20 AS per 48 hrs. Small lockers 10 AS. Luggage check costs 20 AS for a maximum of 30 days. Open 24 hrs.

Bookstore: Bücher Schneid (*map*B3*), Rainerstr. 24 (tel. 87 17 05). Sells *Let's Go* and other English-language books. Open Mon.-Fri. 8:30am-6pm, Sat. 8am-noon. **American Discount** (*map*C4*), Alter Markt 1 (tel. 75 75 41), sells American magazines and paperback novels.

Laundromat: Wäscherei Constructa (*map**C4*), Kaiserschutzenstr. 10 (tel. 87 62 53), opposite the station. 92 AS per load for wash and dry. Open Mon.-Fri. 7:30am-6:30pm, Sat. 8am-noon. If they are closed, try the **Wasch Salon** (*map**C1*) across from the train station on Südtiroler Platz. Wash 72 AS per 6kg, dry 22 AS. Open Mon.-Fri. 7am-7pm and Sat. 7am-1pm.

Pharmacies: Elisabeth-Apotheke, Elisabethstr. 1 (tel. 714 84), a few blocks left of the train station. Pharmacies open Mon.-Fri. 8am-12:30pm and 2:30-6pm, Sat. 8am-noon. There are always 3 pharmacies available for emergencies. Check the door of any closed pharmacy to find an open one.

Medical Assistance: When the dog bites, when the bee stings, when you're feeling sad, call the **Hospital** (*map**AB3*), Müllner-Hauptstr. 48 (tel. 315 81).

Emergencies: Police: tel. 133. Headquarters, at Alpenstr. 90 (tel. 295 11). **Ambulance:** tel. 144. **Fire:** tel. 122.

ACCOMMODATIONS AND CAMPING

To hunt down rooms in *Pensionen* and private homes, go to the tourist office—it's a very good place to start. Ask for their list of private rooms (not the hotel map). From mid-May through mid-September and especially during the summer festival (late July-Aug.) hostels fill by mid-afternoon; call ahead. The *Hotel Plan* (available at the tourist office) provides information on hostels in the area. The tourist office charges 30 AS to make reservations and requires a deposit of 50 AS. In a serious pinch, the hostels in Hallein (30 min. by train or Bundesbus) and in Berchtesgaden, Germany (45 min. by Bundesbus), are viable options.

Hostels and Dormitories

Gasthaus Naturfreundehaus (*map**A4*), Mönchsberg 19c (tel. 84 17 29), towers over the old town from the top of the Mönchsberg. Take bus #1 or 2 (direction: "Maxglan") to "Mönchsbergaufzug"; on foot, stroll from the main tourist office northwest (downstream, or against traffic) along the river, and then turn left onto Griesgasse. At the base of the mountain, take the elevator built into the cliff (round-trip 21 AS). Then, at its summit, turn right and go down the paved path. Go through the stone arch of the old fortress, and take the small dirt path to the immediate left. The *Gasthaus* is about 50m ahead on the right. Or hike up the stairs at Toscaninihof and take the right at the top, climb some more stairs and look to the right. The vista of the *Altstadt* from the terrace café is magnificent. Accommodates 28 in quads and six-bed rooms. Reception open daily 7:30am-10pm. 110 AS per person. Showers 10 AS per 3 min. Breakfast 45 AS. Sheets 5 AS. Open May to mid-Oct.

International Youth Hotel (*map**C2*), Paracelsusstr. 9 (tel. 87 96 49), off Franz-Josef-Str. From town, take bus #15 (direction: "Bergheim") to "Paracelsusstr."; from the train station, just walk out the east exit on Gabelsbergerstr., and make the second left onto Paracelsusstr. If you'd like to stay up late and taste your first champagne, this may be the place. Full of drinking Americans, but still clean and reasonably orderly. The continuous happy hour at the bar often draws guests from other hostels. Reception open daily 8am-10pm. No curfew; theoretical quiet time 10pm, but don't expect it to quiet down until 1-2am. Dorms 120 AS. Doubles 160 AS per person. Quads 140 AS per person. Showers 10 AS per 6 min. Breakfast 15-40 AS. Dinner entrees 60-75 AS. Lockers 10 AS. Stylish sheetsacks 20 AS.

Institut St. Sebastian (*map**C3*), Linzer Gasse 41 (tel. 87 13 86 or 88 26 06). From the station, turn left onto Rainerstr., take a left onto Bergstr., and then a left at the end onto Linzer Gasse. Primarily a residence for female university students, this dormitory opens its doors to travelers of both genders. It is part of St. Sebastian Church, so expect tolling bells early in the morning, especially on Sun. Friendly clerks speak English. Cable TV. Reception open Mon.-Fri. 8am-noon and 3-10pm, Sat.-Sun. 8-10am and 6-10pm. No lockout. No curfew. Dorms 120 AS. Doubles 180 AS per person. Triples 160 AS per person. Showers and lockers included. Breakfast 30 AS. Sheets 25 AS. Reservations recommended.

Jugendgästehaus Salzburg (HI) (*map*D5*), Josef-Preis-Allee 18 (tel. 842 67 00 or 84 68 57; fax 89 14 87), just southeast of the *Altstadt.* Take bus #5 (direction: "Birkensiedlung") to "Justizgebäude." Or walk from the tourist office southeast (upstream, or with traffic) along the river, bear right onto Hellbrunner Str., right again onto Nonntaler Hauptstr., and then take the first left. Sunny, spacious rooms overlooking linden trees. Often overrun with school groups. Reception open Mon.-Fri. 7-9am, 11-11:30am, noon-1pm, 3:30-5:30pm, 6-9:30pm, and 10pm-midnight; Sat.-Sun. 7-9am, 11-11:30am, noon-1pm, 4:30-7:30pm, and 10pm-midnight. Lockout 9-11am. Curfew midnight. Dorms 130 AS per person. Double with shower 225 AS per person. Quads 177 AS per person. Shower, breakfast, and sheets included. Lunches, bag lunches, and dinners 63 AS. Kitchen, laundry facilities, and lockers available. Bike rental 70 AS per day. *Sound of Music* tour 210 AS. No reservations accepted; come before 11am to get a place. Wheelchair accessible.

Glockengasse (HI) (*map*D3*), Glockengasse 8 (tel. 87 62 41; fax 876 24 13). Walk out the east exit of the station onto Gabelsbergerstr., turn right on Bayerhamerstr., and cross Schallmooser Hauptstr. to the foot of the Kapuzinerberg (mountain). A labyrinth of dormitories with few showers. If it's full, ask to sleep on the floor. Reception open 3:30pm-midnight. Curfew midnight. First night 115 AS, 105 AS thereafter. Showers, breakfast, and sheets included. Lockers 50 AS. Open April-Sept.

Haunspergstraße (HI) (*map*B1*), Haunspergstr. 27 (tel. 87 50 30; fax 88 34 77), just minutes from the train station. Walk straight out Kaiserschützenstr., which becomes Jahnstr., and turn left onto Haunspergstr. Staff occasionally disappears from the office; just wait. Reception open 7am-2pm and 5pm-midnight, but hostel fills by late afternoon. Curfew 11pm. 135 AS per person in doubles, triples, and quads. Sheets and breakfast included. Wash 25 AS, dry 25 AS. HI advance booking voucher necessary for reservations. Open July-Aug.

Eduard-Heinrich-Haus (HI), Eduard-Heinrich-Str. 2 (tel. 25 9 76; fax 27 9 80). Clean, modern facilities, but a bit out of the way. Take bus #51 (direction: "Alpensiedlung Süd") to "Polizeidirektion." Walk down Billrothstr., turn left on Robert Stolz Promenade, walk 100m and look right. Reception open 7-9am, 5-11pm. No lockout. No curfew. Dorms 110 AS. Showers and lockers included. Breakfast 25 AS.

Aigen (HI), Aigner Str. 34 (tel. 23 2 48; fax 23 2 48 13). Take bus #5 from the station to "Mozartsteg," then bus #49 (direction: "Josef-Kaut-Str.") to "Finanzamt" and walk 10 min. It's a bit *fa* (a long, long way to run), but if you've missed the bus, walk from the tourist office over the river on Mozartsteg, turn right on Imbergstr., and follow the street as it becomes Bürglsteinstr. and then bear right onto Aigner Str. Clean and comfortable in a pretty, park-like neighborhood. Sunny rooms with lots of wood. Accommodates 135 in rooms with 2 to 6 beds. Reception open 7-9am and 5-11pm. Curfew 11pm. 135 AS, nonmembers 165 AS. Breakfast, showers and sheets included.

Hotels and Pensions

Many hotel owners will pick people up from the train station or the nearest bus stop, including all those we list. Rooms on Kasern Berg can also be reached by taking any northbound regional train (16 AS, Eurail valid) to the first stop ("Salzburg-Maria Plain") and walking up Kasern Berg; or, take bus #15 (direction: "Bergheim") from "Mirabellaplatz" to "Kasern" and then hike up the mountain.

Haus Kernstock, Karolingerstr. 29 (tel. 82 74 69). Take bus #77 (direction: "Walserfeld") to "Karolingerstr." 5 min. from the airport. The friendly hostess welcomes weary travelers and gives each guest a small gift that represents Salzburg. Commodious rooms and an ample breakfast. 220-250 AS per person for doubles, triples, and quads, including breakfast and shower.

Haus Rosemarie Seigmann, Kasern Berg 48 (tel. 500 01). Rosemarie is a welcoming, English-speaking hostess offering hand-painted cupboards, flowered curtains, and stuffed animals to keep you warm at night. Listen to birds singing from the stone terrace overlooking the Alps. Doubles 320-340 AS. Triples 480 AS. Breakfast and showers included. If no rooms are available, she'll call around for you.

Haus Moser, Kasern Berg 59 (tel. 45 66 76), above Haus Rosemarie Seigmann. A mountainside, dark-timbered home with spacious rooms and deer heads on the walls. Singles 160 AS. Doubles 330-350 AS. Triples 480 AS. Fortifying breakfast and shower included.

Haus Lindner, Kasern Berg 64 (tel. 45 66 81 or 45 67 73). Each charming room has a balcony overlooking the hills. House filled with quaint old-Austrian furniture. Doubles 340 AS. Triples 480 AS. Quads 600 AS. Showers and substantial breakfast included. If Frau Lindner has no rooms available, she'll tell you of places that do.

Germana Kapeller, Kasern Berg 44 (tel. 45 66 71), just below Haus Lindner, but smaller. *Dirndl*-clad hostess oversees enchantingly traditional rooms and screens *The Sound of Music* daily. Doubles 320 AS. Triples 450 AS. Quads 600 AS. Showers and complete breakfast included.

Pension Haus Christl, Kasern Berg 57 (tel. 511 87), next to Haus Lindner. Great rooms with gorgeous views of Alpine scenery. Doubles 320-440 AS. Triples 480-680 AS. Quads 640-880 AS. Breakfast 30 AS. Laundry 85 AS.

Haus Elisabeth, Rauchenbichlerstr. 18 (tel. 507 03). Take bus #51 to the end station at "Itzling-Pflanzmann," walk up Rauchenbichlerstr. over the footbridge, and continue right along the gravel path. Amazing rooms with great views of the city. Singles with shower 300 AS. Doubles 260 AS per person. Breakfast included.

Camping

Camping Stadtblick, Rauchenbichlerstr. 21 (tel. 506 52), next to Haus Elisabeth. Situated behind thick grass, with a sweeping view of the city. Reception open daily 7:30am-10pm. July-Aug. 60 AS per person, 15 AS per pre-assembled tent, 15 AS per car, 80 AS for a bed in a tent, 150 AS for a bed in a caravan (with kitchen); Sept.-June 50 AS per person, 15 AS per tent, 15 AS per car, 70 AS for a bed in a tent, 100 AS for a spot in a caravan. Showers included. Laundry 65 AS.

Camping Nord-Sam, Samstr. 22-A (tel. 66 04 94). Take bus #33 (direction: "Obergnigl") to "Langmoosweg." Shady, flower-bedecked campsites, and a small swimming pool to boot. Mid-June to Aug. 50 AS per person, 90 AS per campsite; April to mid-June and Sept.-Oct. 35 AS per person, 60 AS per site.

FOOD

Blessed with fantastic beer gardens and countless *Konditoreien* (pastry shops), Salzburg begs its guests to eat outdoors. The Salzburger Nockerl, a large soufflé of eggs and sugar, is the city's most famous specialty, but don't miss out on the numerous other *Strudel* and cakes. Another specialty is *Knoblauchsuppe*—a rich cream soup loaded with croutons and pungent garlic that shouldn't daunt the confident (or the asocial). During the first two weeks of September, local cafés dispense Stürm, a delicious cloudy wine that hasn't quite finished fermenting. **Julius Meinl supermarkets** are ubiquitous but expensive. Look for **open-air markets** held Mon.-Fri. 6am-7pm, Sat. 6am-1pm in Universitätsplatz; and Thurs. 6am-1pm by the Andräkirche.

Michael Haydn Stube (*map*B3*), Mirabellplatz 1, in the Aicher Passage by Mirabell Gardens. A student hangout run by the Mozarteum, Salzburg's College of Music and Fine Arts. Best deal in town. Vegetarian, fish, *Schnitzel* and *Wurst* dishes 37-73 AS. Continental breakfast (tea, which you drink with jam and bread) 44 AS. Open Mon.-Fri. 9:30am-8pm. Hot food served 11am-7:30pm.

Restaurant Zur Bürgerwehr-Einkehr (*map*A4*), Mönchsberg 19c (tel. 84 17 29), below the Gasthaus Naturfreundehaus. Splendid setting atop the Mönchsberg in the middle of the *Altstadt.* A place to repose and escape from the throngs of tourists below. *Wurst* and other sandwiches 30-40 AS, *Gulasch mit Brot* 35 AS, mouth-watering tortes and cakes 29 AS. Freshly grilled meats on summer weekends, crisp apple *Strudel,* and *Schnitzel* with noodles, these are a few of our favorite things. Open Thurs.-Tues. 10:30am-10pm, mid-Sept. to May Thurs.-Tues. 10:30am-8pm. Meals served until 8:30pm.

Restaurant Paracelsus Stub'n (*map**C4-5*), Kaigasse 8 (tel. 84 32 77), in the *Altstadt.* Quiet café, bar, and restaurant wedged into a narrow, less-touristed street in the old city. Hearty *Gulaschsuppe* 38 AS, *Wienerschnitzel mit Kartoffeln* 98 AS, pizza 75 AS. Open daily 11am-2am.

Fischmarkt (*map**AB3*), on Franz Josef Kai along the riverbank, between the Staatsbrücke and the Makartsteg (bridge) on the *Altstadt* side of the river. Two mammoth trees reach through the roof. Hang out with locals and partake of succulent, inexpensive, and fresh seafood. Very casual and very crowded—you may have to eat outside. *Fischbrötchen* 16-25 AS, beer 20 AS. Open Mon.-Fri. 9am-6pm, Sat. 9am-12:30pm.

Priesterhausstube (*map**C3*), Priesterhausgasse 12 (tel. 87 83 17). Inexpensive local fare right off Linzergasse. Entrees 70-100 AS. Open Tues.-Sun. 5-11:30pm.

Potatoes and Co., Rudolfskai 26 (tel. 84 14 65), located off Judengasse in the *Altstadt.* More tubers than you thought possible. Baked potatoes 79-100 AS. Open daily 11:30am-midnight.

Hofer (*map**D3*), at Schallmooser Hauptstr. and Franz-Josef-Str. A discount supermarket. Open Mon.-Fri. 8am-6pm, Sat. 7:30am-noon.

KGM (*map**C1*), 3 Karl-Wurmb-Str., across the street from the train station. Well-stocked discount supermarket. Open Mon.-Fri. 8am-6pm, Sat. 8am-12:30pm.

SIGHTS

Salzburg sprang up under the protective watch of the fortress **Hohensalzburg** (*map**C6;* tel. 80 42 21 23), which towers atop the southwest curve of the imposing Mönchsberg. Built between 1077 and 1681 by the ruling archbishops, it served as a bulwark against foreign invaders and rebellious natives. First-rate tours wend through medieval torture chambers (which house, among other nasty implements, the Spanish Suspenders, an iron saddle that was heated and then placed on a naked victim), formidable staterooms, and the impregnable watchtower that affords an unmatched view of the city. (Fortress open daily 8am-7pm, Oct.-May 8am-6pm; 45-min. tours daily July-Aug. 9am-5:30pm, April-June and Sept.-Oct. 9:30am-5pm, Nov.-March 10am-4:30pm. Admission 20 AS, under 19 10 AS; with tour 25 AS, ages 16-19 15 AS, ages 6-15 10 AS, seniors 20 AS.) The **Rainer Museum,** inside the fortress, displays even more medieval weapons and instruments of torture; note the iron maiden, the rack, the standardized test form.... (Open May-Oct. Free with tour. Otherwise 10 AS, students and children 5 AS.) The **chamber music concerts** in the painfully ornate Fürstenzimmer (Prince's Chamber) and Goldener Saal (Golden Hall) offer more pacific entertainment. Write to Direktion der Salzburger Festungskonzerte, A. Adlgasser Weg 22, A-5020 Salzburg (tel. 82 58 58; fax 82 58 59) for a schedule or ticket information (concerts nightly May-Oct.) A **cable car** (tel. 84 26 82) runs up to the fortress from tiny Festungsgasse, a winding street behind the Kapitelplatz; you can also hike all the way up on Festungsgasse. (Cable car runs daily May 8:30am-6pm, June 8am-8pm, July-Aug. 8am-9pm, Sept. 8:30am-7pm, Oct.-Jan. 9am-5pm, Feb.-April 9am-6pm, every 10 min.; one way 18 AS, round-trip 28 AS; children half-price.) The myriad footpaths of the Mönchsberg, enshrouded in wooded silence, reveal a ripping view of the city; meander down the soothing trails to the *Altstadt* below, or descend by the elevator built into the mountain, at Gstättengasse 13 behind the Museumsplatz. (Open daily 7am-11pm. 11 AS, round-trip 21 AS.)

Wolfgang Amadeus Mozart was unleashed upon the world from what is now called **Mozart's Geburtshaus** (birthplace; *map**C4*), at Getreidegasse 9 (tel. 84 43 13; fax 84 06 93), one of Salzburg's most touristed attractions. The long red-and-white flag suspended from the roof serves as a beacon for music patrons worldwide. The house exhibits stage sets for Mozart's operas as well as his violins, his clavichord, and the *Hammerklavier* on which he composed *The Magic Flute*. Be merciful to the helpful staff - *don't* walk in whistling *Eine kleine Nachtmusik*. (Open daily 9am-7pm, Sept.-March daily 9am-6pm. Admission 50 AS, students and seniors 35 AS, ages 15-18 15 AS, ages 6-14 10 AS.) **Getreidegasse** is itself noteworthy; the ancient shops, ennobled by wrought-iron guild signs, crowd in upon pastel-colored medieval houses on one of the best-preserved streets in old Salzburg. At 17, Salzburg's favorite son moved across the river; **Mozarts Wohnhaus** (*map*AB2*), Makartplatz 8 (tel. 84 43 13; fax 84 06 93), was the composer's residence from 1773 to 1780. The house suffered major damage in World War II air raids, but has since been restored; it now displays period musical instruments and facsimiles of the maestro's manuscripts. (Open daily 10am-6pm, Sept.-March daily 9am-5pm. Admission 40 AS, students 25 AS, ages 15-18 20 AS, ages 6-14 10 AS. Combined admission to the Geburtshaus and Wohnhaus 70 AS, students and seniors 45 AS, ages 15-18 20 AS, ages 6-14 15 AS.) For those with a true Mozart mania, the **Mozarteum** (*map*B3*), Schwartzstr. 26-28, holds the enormous **Mozart Archives.** Inside the grounds stands a tiny wooden shack, transplanted from Vienna; this is the **Zauberflötenhäuschen,** where Wolfgang Amadeus supposedly composed *The Magic Flute* in just five months. The Mozarteum was originally constructed for the Salzburg Academy of Music and the Performing Arts; regular public performances are now held in the majestic concert hall (tickets 100-2100 AS).

Long before Mozart put *do*, *re*, and *mi* together, Archbishop Wolf Dietrich dominated the town's cultural patronage; composer and clergyman are now intertwined yearly, when the Salzburger Festspiele bring opera to the courtyard of the archbishop's magnificent **Residenz** (*map*C5*; tel. 80 42 26 90; fax 80 42 29 78). The ecclesiastic elite of the Salzburger Land resided here, in the heart of the *Altstadt*, for 700 years—better be on your best behavior. Tours feature the imposing Baroque staterooms (Prunkräume), with an astonishingly three-dimensional ceiling fresco by Rottmayr. The Residenz also houses a **Galerie** (tel. 80 42 22 70; fax 80 42 25 72) filled with a smattering of works by such masters as Titian, Rubens, and Brueghel. (Gallery open daily 10am-5pm. Tours daily 10am-4:40pm every 20 min., Sept.-June Mon.-Fri. 10am-3pm every hr. Admission for either gallery or tour 40 AS, students and seniors 30 AS, under 15 free; gallery *and* tour 60 AS.) The more lavish cultural patrons can ride home in imperial style in **Fiaker;** these horse-drawn carriages wait in front of the majestic marble fountain anchoring the square (carriage rides 350 AS for 25 min., 680 AS for 50 min.).

The **Neugebäude** (*map*C4-5*), on the opposite (east) side of the Residenzplatz, supports both the city government's bureaucracy and a 35-bell **Glockenspiel** (tel. 80 42 22 76; fax 80 42 21 60). Be sure to attend one of the daily performances; the carillon rings out a Mozart tune (specified on a notice on the corner of the Residenz), and the tremendous pipe organ atop the Hohensalzburg fortress bellows a response. (Bells ring daily at 7am, 11am, and 6pm. 20-min. tours daily 10:45am and 5:45pm, Nov. to mid-March Mon.-Fri. 10:45am and 5:45pm. Tour 20 AS, ages 6-14 10 AS.)

The wonderfully harmonious Baroque **Dom** (*map*C5*), forms the third wall of the Residenzplatz. The townsfolk grew suspicious when a 1598 fire conveniently leveled the intended site of Wolf Dietrich's new self-aggrandizing monument, so the megalomanic archbishop languished in prison while his successor, Markus Sittikus, commissioned the cathedral from Italian architect Santino Solari in 1628. Mozart was christened here in 1756 and later worked at the *Dom* as *Konzertmeister* and court organist. Note the three massive bronze doors, adorned by allegorical figures representing Peace, Love, and Hope, or, alternatively, Larry, Moe, and Curly. The connecting **Dom Museum** (tel. 84 41 89; fax 84 04 42) holds an unusual collection called the **Kunst- und Wunderkammer** (art and miracles chamber), which includes conch shells, mineral formations, and a two-foot whale's tooth. The archbishops accumulated these curiosities to impress distinguished visitors. (Open May to mid-Oct. Mon.-Sat. 10am-5pm, Sun. 11am-5pm; admission 30 AS, ages 16-18 10 AS, ages 6-15 5 AS.) The **Domgrabungsmuseum** (*map*C5*; entrance on Residenzplatz; tel. 84 52 95), displays excavations of the Roman ruins under the cathedral. (Open May-Oct. daily 9am-5pm. Admission 20 AS, under 19 10 AS. See Bürgerspital Museum listing below for information on a combined ticket.) The **Domplatz** (*map*C5*), to the west of the cathedral, has witnessed performances of Hugo von

Hofmannsthal's *Jedermann* (Everyman) every year since 1920 (with a brief hiatus during the Third Reich). The outdoor show is now enacted during the Festspiele (tickets 300-1400 AS).

From the cathedral, cross the giant chess grid on Kapitelplatz, and walk toward the mountain to arrive at the entrance to the elaborate **St. Peter's Abbey** (*map*C5*). Though once a stoic collegiate church, the abbey received a Rococo face-lift in the 18th century. Now, green and pink moldings curl delicately across the graceful ceiling, and gilded cherubim blow golden trumpets to herald the stunningly decorated organ. (Open daily 9am-12:15pm and 2:30-6:30pm.) Tucked between the church and the Mönchsberg is the secluded **Petersfriedhof** (cemetery; *map*C5*), a popular subject for Romantic painters, but best known as the spot where Liesl's Nazi boyfriend Rolf blew the whistle on the von Trapp family in *The Sound of Music* (open daily 9am-8pm, Sept.-May 10am-7pm). On the right of the *Friedhof* is the entrance to the **Katakomben** (catacombs; *map*C5*), where Christians allegedly worshipped in secret as early as 250 AD. (Open daily 10am-5pm. Tours in English 10am-5pm every hr.; Oct.-April 11am, noon, 1:30pm, 2:30pm, and 3:30pm; minimum 5 people. Admission 12 AS, seniors and students 8 AS.)

If you stroll from the cathedral across Domplatz instead of Kapitelplatz, you'll find yourself at Franziskanergasse and the **Landessammlung Rupertinum** (*map*BC4-5*), Wiener-Philharmoniker-Gasse 9 (tel. 80 42 23 36; fax 80 42 25 42). This museum has a comprehensive collection of 20th-century painting, sculpture, graphic art, and photography spanning all of the Salzburger Land. (Open Mon.-Tues. and Thurs.-Sun. 10am-6pm, Wed. 10am-9pm; Oct.-June Tues. and Thurs.-Sun. 10am-5pm, Wed. 10am-9pm. Admission 35 AS, students and seniors 20 AS, under 15 free.) To the left of the museum, the distinctive dome of the **Kollegienkirche** (Collegiate Church; *map*B4*), stands watch over the Universitätsplatz. Generally considered Fischer von Erlach's masterpiece, this massive chapel is one of the most celebrated Baroque churches in Europe. The pale interior and enormous dome create a vast open space pierced by the natural light radiating from the apse; *this* is the place to catch a moonbeam in your hand.

The Mönchsberg ascends from behind a row of diverse museums connected only by the whim of Salzburg's city elders. The **Bürgerspital Museum** (*map*B4*), Bürgerspitalgasse 2 (tel. 84 75 60), is filled with a unique toy collection, various and sundry musical instruments, and other local arts and crafts. (Open Tues.-Sun. 9am-5pm. Admission 30 AS, under 19 10 AS.) A combination ticket (60 AS, under 19 20 AS) is available for entry to the Bürgerspital Museum and the **Salzburg Museum 'Carolino Augusteum'** (*map*B4*; tel. 84 31 45; fax 84 11 34 10), around the corner at Museumplatz 1. (Open Tues. 9am-8pm, Wed.-Sun. 9am-5pm. Admission 40 AS, under 19 15 AS.) The same combination ticket is also valid for admission to the excavations of the Domgrabungsmuseum (above) and the **Folklore and Local History Museum** of the Hellbrunn Monatsschlößchen (see Near Salzburg for more information). The **Haus der Natur** (*map*B4*; Museum of Natural History), though not included in the combination ticket, stands next door at Museumsplatz 5 (tel. 84 26 53; fax 84 79 05), with an immense assortment of local species, an aquarium, and a dino-sized reptile corner (open daily 9am-5pm; admission 40 AS, under 18 25 AS). Take a left at A.-Neumayr-Platz to find the **Trachtenmuseum** (National Costume Museum; *map*B4*), at Griesgasse 23 (tel. 84 31 19), which houses traditional local clothing (open Mon.-Fri. 10am-noon and 2-5pm, Sat. 10am-noon; admission 30 AS, under 18 20 AS).

The Staatsbrücke is the only bridge from the *Altstadt* over the Salzach open to motorized traffic; in the new city, the bridge opens into **Linzer Gasse** (*map*C3*), an enchanting, less-touristed medieval street much in the style of the Getreidegasse. From under the stone arch on the right side of Linzer Gasse 14, you can ascend a staircase of tiny stone steps up the side of the Kapuzinerberg. At its crest stands the simple **Kapuzinerkloster** (Capuchin Monastery; *map*C3*), that Wolf Dietrich ordered built in the late 16th century. The resident monks are distinguished by their trademark brown robes with white hoods; in their resemblance to coffee topped with steamed milk lies the etymology of the word *cappuccino.* The monastery itself is a sight to behold, but the real draw is the view of the city below. Farther along Linzer Gasse, at #41, is the 18th-century **Sebastianskirche;** the neighboring graveyard contains the gaudy mausoleum of Wolf Dietrich and the tombs of Mozart's wife Constanze and father Leopold. (Open daily 7am-7pm.)

From Linzer Gasse you can cut across Dreifaltigkeitsgasse to the **Dreifaltigkeitskirche** (Holy Trinity Church; *map*C3*), another of Fischer von Erlach's Baroque gems. (Open daily 9am-5pm.) Continue up this street to Mirabellplatz to discover the marvelous **Schloß Mirabell** (*map*C3*). Archbishop Wolf Dietrich built this rosy-hued wonder in 1606 for his mistress Salome Alt and their ten children, christening it "Altenau" in her honor. When successor Markus Sittikus imprisoned Wolf Dietrich, the unindicted arson co-conspirator, he seized the palace for himself and changed its name. The chamber music concerts in the *Schloß* offer a chance to inspect the Baroque excesses of the interior, including the glorious **Angel Staircase** laden with corpulent marble cupids. (Concerts Easter and June-Aug.; tickets 250 AS; discount tickets occasionally available at the door 1 hr. before the show. A tourist office pamphlet lists performances and dates. Write for tickets to Makartplatz 8 or call 87 27 88. Staircase also open daily 8am-noon and 2-5pm.) Next to the palace is the delicately manicured **Mirabellgarten** (*map*B3*), which includes extravagant rose beds, labyrinths of groomed shrubs, and 15 grotesque marble likenesses of Wolf Dietrich's court jesters. Salzburg's **Baroque Museum** (*map*B3*; tel. 87 74 32) resides in the Orangerie of the Mirabellgarten; inside, wall after wall pays tribute to the overdone aesthetic of 17th- and 18th-century European painting. (Open Tues.-Sat. 9am-noon and 2-5pm, Sun. 9am-noon. Admission 30 AS, students and seniors 15 AS, ages 6-14 free.) In the 19th century, parts of the city walls were destroyed by Napoleon; the rubble was buried under the current site of the Mirabellgarten, and the hill it forms now serves as the favorite sledding place for the children of Salzburg. Remember: reduce, reuse, recycle!

ENTERTAINMENT

The renowned **Salzburger Festspiele** (Festivals) were founded by Max Reinhardt, Richard Strauss, and Hugo von Hofmannsthal in 1920; every year since, Salzburg has become a musical mecca from late July to the beginning of September. On the eve of the opening of the Festival, more than one hundred dancers, clad in regional costume and equipped with torches, perform a Fackeltanz (torch-dance) on the Residenzplatz.

In the month of festivities, almost every public space is overrun with operas, dramas, films, and concerts. Most of the activities revolve around Hofstallgasse, and the expanse of the **Festspielhaus** (festival hall; *map*B4-5*), built flush against the Mönchsberg wall. This massive stone structure contains the Kleines Festspielhaus and Großes Festspielhaus, among other performance arenas; the most notable is the Felsenreitschule (Rock Riding School), an ancient equestrian amphitheater hewn directly from the rock of the mountain. During the Festspiele, the Festspielhaus complex is home to every conceivable form of musical extravaganza; tickets for individual concerts run 100-3600 AS. Detailed festival programs are available in November from "Direktion der Salzburger Festspiele, Festspielhaus, Hofstallgasse 1, A-5010 Salzburg," or from an Austrian National Tourist Office. Ticket reservations are accepted, until January 1994, through "Kartenbüro der Salzburger Festspiele, Postfach 140, A-5010 Salzburg" (tel. 84 45 01; fax 84 66 82). Five discount packages are also available, each valid for one week of Festspiele attractions; tickets are dispensed "first come, first served," so be sure to write well in advance (2400-11,500 AS for the weekly packages; under 26 half-price). The few tickets still available by summer are sold at the Festspielhaus box office (tel. 84 25 41; open April-June Mon.-Fri. 10am-2pm, July Mon.-Sat. 10am-5pm; during the Festspiele daily 10am-5pm).

Many travel agencies in Salzburg add a 20% service charge to the ticket price. Standing room is available on occasion for 50 AS and up.

Festspiele performances also invade the **Landestheater** (Regional Theater; *map*BC3*), at Makartplatz in the new town. Next door, at the **Marionetten Theater** (*map*B3*), Schwarzstr. 24 (tel. 87 24 06; fax 88 21 41), a lighthearted show is accompanied by tapes of past festival opera performances. (Box office open Mon.-Sat. 9am-1pm. Tickets 250-350 AS.)

The **Stadtkino** (*map*AB4*), Anton-Neumayr Platz 2 (tel. 84 03 49 13) has everything from jazz and rock concerts to postmodern interpretive dance. Call for schedule information. Every summer, the **Szene** (tel. 84 34 48) sponsors an international theater and dance festival which coincides with the Festspiele (tickets 120-160 AS; open Mon.-Fri. 10am-5pm, Sat. 10am-noon; in winter Mon.-Fri. 10am-5pm). During the last weekend in June, visitors have the opportunity to enjoy the jubilant **Stadtfest,** three days of free musical performances, fireworks, and other entertainments.

For an evening of stein-hoisting and general *Gemütlichkeit,* go to **Augustiner Bräustüble** (*map*A3*), Augustinergasse 4 (tel. 43 12 46), home of Salzburg's first brewery. Grab a mug, rinse it out in the tub, and have it filled by the enormous man who rolls out wooden beer barrels and taps them with a brass bung and a wooden mallet. One caveat: after an evening of bacchanalian excesses, you may stumble out searching for Julie Andrews's birthplace and the *Amadeus* tour bus. (Open Mon-Fri. 3-11pm, Sat. and Sun. 2:30-11pm. 1 liter 46 AS, ½-liter 23 AS, though only tourists and small children drink ½-liters.) The **Felsenkeller** (*map*BC5*; tel. 84 31 76) in the Toscaninihof near St. Peter's cemetery, dispenses wine within a damp, coin-studded cellar built right into the cliff. Look for the huge iron door 5m into the mountain; the crowd inside is mainly local. (Open Sun.-Fri. 2:30-midnight, Sat. 10:30am-1pm and 4pm-midnight.) **Schnaitl Pub** (*map*C3*), Bergstr. 5-7 (tel. 062 22), near the Stadtsbrücke, attracts a bohemian crowd with cheap drinks and progressive rock (open 7:30pm-1am, Sept.-May 6:30pm-1am). **Frauen Café** (*map*C1*) on Sittikusstr. 17 (tel. 87 16 39), near the train station, is a relaxed hangout where women drink coffee, read, and converse (open Wed.-Sat. 8pm-midnight).

In 1964, Julie Andrews, Christopher Plummer, and a gaggle of 20th Century Fox crew members arrived in Salzburg to film *The Sound of Music,* based on the true story of the von Trapp family. Salzburg hasn't hesitated to cash in on the celluloid notoriety. English-language radio station **WEDK,** for example, offers programming under the catchphrase "WEDK—The Hills are Alive with the Sound of Muzak." **Salzburg Sightseeing Tours** (tel. 88 16 16; fax 88 21 20) offers a "Most Unique Sound of Music Tour" of the locations filmed in the movie (3½-hr. tours 280 AS, 250 AS with student I.D; daily departures at 9:30am and 2pm). **Panorama Tours** (tel. 87 40 29 or 88 32 11 17; telex 632417 pantr a; fax 87 16 18) presents the "Original Sound of Music Tour" (Tours 300 AS, departing daily at 9:30am and 2pm). **Bob's Special Tours** (tel. 87 24 84) offers a similar tour for 280 AS. All three tour companies also boast city and regional tours in their repertoire, and offer free pick-up from town accommodations. For those who interpreted the film as a tale of a deviant family whose domineering father had an unhealthy fixation on nuns, the tours are probably a loss.

Near Salzburg: Lustschloß Hellbrunn

Just south of Salzburg lies the unforgettable **Lustschloß Hellbrunn** (tel. 82 03 72; fax 82 03 72 31), a one-time pleasure palace for Wolf Dietrich's nephew, the Archbishop Markus Sittikus. The neighboring **Wasserspielen** (Water Gardens) are perennial favorites; Markus amused himself with elaborate water-powered figurines and a booby-trapped table, which could spout water on his drunken guests. Prepare yourself for an afternoon of wet surprises. (Open July-Aug. daily 9am-10pm, May-June and Sept. daily 9am-5pm, April and Oct. daily 9am-4:30pm. Admission 48 AS, students 24 AS.) The **Steintheater,** on the palace grounds, is the oldest natural theater north of the Alps. In the adjoining park, the tiny hunting lodge **"Monatss-**

chlößchen" received its moniker from speed of legendary proportions; local artisans supposedly finished construction on the mini-palace within a month. The lodge is now the **Folklore and Local History Museum** (tel. 82 03 72 21), replete with more Salzburg history than you ever wanted to know. (Open Easter-Oct. 9am-5pm. Admission 20 AS, under 19 10 AS. See Bürgerspital Museum listing above for information on a combined ticket.) To reach the palatial grounds, take bus #55 (direction: "Grödig") to "Hellbrunn," or bike 40 minutes down Hellbrunner Allee, a beautiful tree-lined path. An adjacent **zoo** (tel. 82 01 76; fax 82 01 76 6) sports vultures along with other local fauna. Yodel a quick hello to the lonely goatherds. (Open daily 8:30am-6pm; Oct.-March daily 8:30am-4pm. Admission 45 AS, ages 11-18 30 AS, ages 4-10 20 AS.)

Near Salzburg: Untersberg

A little farther south of Hellbrunn is the Untersberg peak, where Charlemagne supposedly rests, preparing to return and rule over Europe once again. You can ride a **cable car** (tel. (06246) 2477) to the top to experience a spectacular view of Salzburg and the Alps. Take bus #55 to "Untersberg." (Cable car runs July-Sept. 8:30am-5:30pm, March-June and Oct. 9am-5pm, Dec.-Feb. 10am-4pm. Up the mountain 100 AS, down 90 AS, round-trip 170 AS; children: up 60 AS, down 45 AS, round-trip 90 AS.)

■■■ HALLEIN

Now that the Roman occupation is over, *Schillings* have replaced salt as Austria's primary legal tender—but someone neglected to inform the citizens of the Salzach valley. The tremendous wealth derived from the region's colossal salt mines (*Salzbergwerke*) once buttressed the political hegemony of the ruling bishops; the natural resource now delivers the tourist dollars that support the local economy. Hallein remains wholly dependent on its store of salt; the town flaunts its status as host to the most accessible mine in the valley.

Orientation and Practical Information Hallein, on a grassy plain at the junction of the Almbach and Salzach rivers, is just a quick jaunt from Salzburg. By bus, take #3083 from Salzburg (every 30-60 min.; 45 min.; one way 32 AS); or take one of the frequent trains running all day to and from Salzburg (20 min.; one way 32 AS, round-trip 49 AS). The city's small main **tourist office,** in the Unterer Markt (tel. 53 94), is on the ground floor of the Sudhaus Raitenau. From the train station, walk straight down Bahnhofstr. and turn right at the intersection; follow the Staatsbrücke over the Salzach, and go through Bayrhamer Platz into Unterer Markt. The tourist office is on the left (open Mon.-Fri. 8:30am-4:30pm, Sat. 8am-noon). There is also a branch office on the right of the Staatsbrücke (open daily May-Sept. 5-10pm). The **post office,** Hans-Pramer-Platz 2, adjacent to the station, is the best place to exchange currency (open Mon.-Fri. 8am-7pm, Sat. 8-11am). **Telephones** are also located inside (**City code:** 06245).

Accommodations and Food Avail yourself of the opportunity to repose in a quiet, lovely, tree-enveloped castle by staying at Hallein's **Jugendherberge (HI)** (tel. 23 97), Wiespachstr. 7, in the Schloß Wispach-Esterhazy. From the station, walk straight down Bahnhofstr., turn right on Ritter-von-Schwarz-Str., go straight over the River Almbach onto Neualmerstr., and turn right on Weisslhofweg; then take a right on Haushofweg, and finally left on Wiespachstr. The hostel is on the left (15 min.). Huge eight-bed rooms, silent but for the wind in the trees and the trains in the distance. (Open April-Sept. Reception open daily 5-10pm. No lockout. Curfew 10pm, but you can sign out a front door key. 130 AS per night, including sheets, shower, and breakfast; 140 AS if you stay only one night. Hostel guests pay 5 AS to frolic in the pool next door, set in the former grounds of the castle.)

Plenty of reasonably priced restaurants are scattered throughout Hallein—prowl around the neighborhood of the agonizingly modern **Pfarrkirche** as well as the heart of the city, **Kornstein Platz.** For high-quality Asian cuisine, head to **China Restaurant Taiwan,** Pfarrgasse 3, where vegetarian dishes run 66-88 AS (open daily 11am-2:30pm and 5-11pm). A well-stocked **Billa supermarket** stands at Ritter-von-Schwarz-Str. 11; numerous others are scattered throughout town.

Sights and Entertainment The salt mine *is* the town; tours through the mines in Hallein and nearby Bad Dürrnberg provide the setting for a **saline adventure.** On the 1½-hr. tour, you don traditional miner's clothes, slide down pitch-dark passages, take a miniature train ride, and, occasionally, ride a raft on the salt lakes. The Dürrnberg mine is the oldest known salt-producing center in Central Europe; traces of settlements from the pre-Neolithic period (2500 BC) are visible throughout the region. The **Salzbergbahn cable car** ride to the entrance offers an outstanding view. The cable car leaves from the "Salzbergbahn Parkplatz" on Dr.-Viktor-Zatloukal-Str. From the train station, walk straight down Bahnhofstr., turn right at the intersection, and cross the Salzach via the Staatsbrücke; then walk straight down to Bayrhamer Platz, bear left on Raitenaustr., and turn left on Gampertorplatz. (Open May-Sept. daily 8:50am-5:50pm; early Oct. 11am-4:50pm. Admission 185 AS, students 170 AS, under 15 88 AS, including round-trip cable car, tour, and museum. Cable car alone one way 55 AS, students 48 AS; round-trip 85 AS, students 75 AS.) For more information about the cable cars, call 27 37 or 51 39; for information on the mines, call 52 85 15 or 73 00 15.

The quietly beguiling medieval town center is also worth exploring. Hallein's cobblestone streets defy grid planning and meander every which way among the many pastry shops and cafés. The **Keltenmuseum,** Pflegerplatz 5 (tel. 27 83 or 42 88), displays 4000 years of history in one building. Local remnants of early Celtic civilization and memorabilia comprise only part of the diverse collection. In 1994, the museum presents an enormous exhibition on the history of salt in the region. (Open May-Sept. daily 9am-5pm; Oct. noon-5pm. Admission 45 AS, children 15 AS.)

From late August to the beginning of September, the town hosts the **Hallein Folk Festival,** showcasing Celtic and provincial Austrian music. (Day ticket 250 AS, students 180 AS. Festival pass 470 AS, students 150 AS.) Late June brings the **Halleiner Stadtfest,** an 11-day party with various musical performances, street theater, and hearty camaraderie. Call the tourist office for more information on both festivals.

THE SALZKAMMERGUT

East of Salzburg, the landscape swells into towering mountains interspersed with unfathomably deep lakes. The Salzkammergut takes its name from the long-abandoned salt mines which, in their glory days, underwrote Salzburg's architectural treasures. The region is remarkably accessible, with 2000km of footpaths, 12 cable cars and chairlifts, and dozens of hostels. Though towns near the Autobahn bustle with tourists and merrymakers, some distant villages host only the hardy few who make their way across a lake by ferry. Winter brings mounds of snow to the valleys and downhill skiing to the slopes.

Hostels abound, though you can often find far superior rooms in private homes and *Pensionen* at just-above-hostel prices. The local tourist office *(Verkehrsamt)* can make reservations for you, and rarely charges a fee. "*Zimmer Frei*" signs peek down from virtually every house. **Campgrounds** dot the region, but many are trailer-oriented. Away from large towns, many travelers camp discreetly almost anywhere without trouble. Hikers can capitalize on dozens of **cable cars** in the area to gain altitude before setting out on their own, and almost every community has a local trail map publicly posted or available at the tourist office. At higher elevations there are **alpine huts**—check carefully at the tourist office for their opening hours. These huts are leased through the **Österreichischer Alpenverein** (Austrian Alpine Club), which supplies mountain information of all sorts (see Essentials for more information); the central office of the ÖA is in Bad Ischl, at Kaltenbach 308 (tel. (06132) 482 62 or 52 50).

The Vienna-Salzburg **rail** line skirts the northern edge of the Salzkammergut. At Attnang-Puchheim, 50km east of Salzburg, a spur line begins its way south through Gmunden, Ebensee, Bad Ischl, Obertraun, and Bad Aussee to Steinbach. If you're hitching, traveling by bus, or have your own car, you can enter directly from Salzburg along Bundesstraße 158. Within the region there is a dense network of **buses.** Most routes run four to 12 times per day. Ask at the Salzburg kiosk for a comprehensive schedule, or call for information: Salzburg (0662) 167; Gmunden (07612) 46 13; Mondsee (06232) 26 69; St. Gilgen (06227) 425; Bad Ischl (06132) 31 13; Bad Aussee (06152) 20 50. The pamphlet *Wandern mit dem Postbus,* available at the main bus stations in these towns, details hikes that coincide with the bus network. The **Salzkammergut Ticket** is valid for unlimited travel along the Gmunden-Bad Ischl rail line and on buses running from Bad Ischl to St. Gilgen and St. Wolfgang (3 days travel in any 10-day period, 210 AS).

Let's Go does not recommend hitchhiking as a safe means of transportation. **Hitchers** from Salzburg take bus #29 to Gnigl, and come into the Salzkammergut at Bad Ischl. The lake district itself is one of the rare, refreshing Austrian regions in which hitchhikers have been known to make good time. Two-wheeled transportation is much more entertaining, but only if you get a good **bike**—some mountain passes top 1000m. Pedaling the narrow, winding roads that hug the lake banks is far less strenuous and equally scenic. Most of the train stations in the region rent bikes. Reasonably priced ferries serve each of the larger lakes. The **Wolfgangsee** line is operated by the Austrian railroad, so railpasses get you free passage; on the private **Attersee** and **Traunsee** lines, Eurailpass holders receive a discount.

On January 5, the running of the figures with special caps (Glöcklerlaufen) takes place after dark in the Salzkammergut. These *Glöckler* derive their name from the custom of knocking at the door (the verb *glocken* means "to knock"), not from the bells attached to their belts (although the noun *Glocke* coincidentally means "bell"). Their caps, reminiscent of stained glass windows, have an electric light inside. In return for their Happy New Year wish, the runners are rewarded with a special doughnut, the Glöcklerkrapfen. The masked figures are usually given money and refreshments by the citizenry, which indicates part of their origin: a long, long time ago, before you were even a twinkle in your parent's eye, seasonal workers needed such handouts to survive.

Every February brings **Carnival,** called Fasnacht in Western Austria and elsewhere known as Fasching. Carnival commences with the January ball season. In the countrified areas, traditional processions of masked figures are the most important events of the season. Also part of the processions are *Schiache* (ugly masks with connotations of evil). The large Tyrolean Carnival celebrations require months of preparation. Only men may perform. At the **Ausseer Fasching,** the carnival at Bad Aussee, *Trommelweiber* (women with drums, who are really men in white nightdresses and night-caps) march through the town. The Carnival near Ebensee culminates in the **Fetzenfasching** (carnival of rags). The people sing in falsetto, pretending to imitate spooky voices, and wave old umbrellas.

In the whole region of the Salzkammergut, on the Sunday after November 25 (November 27 in 1994), about 30 bird-catcher clubs organize an exhibition. The birds are kept in living-rooms during the winter and then released. A Christmas passion play is performed every fourth year (next in 1995) at Bad Ischl.

■■■ BAD ISCHL

The cultural and geographic center of the Salzkammergut, Bad Ischl is best known for its purportedly curative mineral baths and mud packs. Prominent personages and their attendant *paparazzi* have been drawn to this would-be fountain of youth for 150 years. Skeptics can still enjoy the free outdoor **concerts** outside the baths (mid-May to Sept., 2-3 per day) and the **Ischl Operetta Festival,** which recalls the town's heyday as a rest home for stressed-out composers, such as Brahms, Bruckner and Lehár. Bad Ischl performs at least two operas every July and August. (Tickets 150-460 AS; write to Wiesingerstr. 7, A-4820 Bad Ischl.). Bad Ischl isn't on a lake, which eliminates half the fun of visiting the Salzkammergut, but German vacationers (including Chancellor Helmut Kohl) flock to the town anyway.

For centuries, Bad Ischl persisted as a modest yet industrious salt-mining town, low-key and mostly unknown. In the early 19th century, a public medical officer, Dr. Joseph Götz, began to treat workers in the salt mines with baths of heated brine. A Viennese physician, Dr. Franz Wirer, recognized the potential of this curative effort, and the year 1823 saw the arrival of a small number of vanguard spa guests; the small city could, for the first time, present itself as *Bad* Ischl.

Real celebrity descended on the resort only when the brine's curative powers managed to propagate the royal line of the Habsburgs. Childless Archduke Francis Charles and Archduchess Sophia had rushed off to Bad Ischl, seeking a cure for their infertility. The extraordinary results: three sons, the so-called Salt Princes. Further laurels would top Bad Ischl's already lush crown, when, in 1848, the first of the Salt Princes, Franz Josef, ascended the Austrian throne as emperor and proceeded to make the town his permanent summer residence. This imperial legacy has left an indelible seal on the Bad Ischl of today.

Orientation and Practical Information Bad Ischl lies on a riverbend in the Traun and Ischl valleys, within splashing distance of seven Salzkammergut lakes: the Hallstätter See, the Gosausee, the Wolfgangsee, the Mondsee, the Attersee, the Traunsee, the Grundlsee, and the Altaussee. Salzkammergut transportation lines funnel into Bad Ischl's **train** and **bus** stations; these are combined on Bahnhofstr., a three-minute walk from the **tourist office** (*Kurdirektion*), Bahnhofstr. 6 (tel. 235 20). The office finds *Privatzimmer* (from 130 AS) and *Pensionen* (from 160 AS) for no fee. (Open Mon.-Fri. 8am-6pm, Sat. 9am-4pm, Sun. 9-11:30am; Oct.-May Mon.-Fri. 8am-noon and 2-5pm, Sat. 8am-noon.) **Bike rental** and **luggage check** at the station are open daily 5am-8:10pm. The **post office** is on the corner of Bahnhofstr. and Auböckplatz (**Postal code:** A-4820); a **telephone** center is inside (**City code:** 06132). (Open July-Aug. Mon.-Fri. 7am-9pm, Sat. 8-11am; June and Sept. Mon.-Fri. 7am-8pm, Sat. 8-11am; Oct.-May Mon.-Fri. 8am-7pm, Sat. 8-10am.)

Accommodations and Food Bad Ischl's **Jugendgästehaus (HI)** (tel. 265 77), at Am Rechensteg 5 in the town center, offers many comfortable one- to five-bed rooms, but often fills up with exuberant kiddies. From the tourist office, walk left on Bahnhofstr., turn right on Franz-Josef-Str. and watch for the *Jugendherberge* sign to the left. (Reception open 8-9am and 5-7pm. Flexible 10pm curfew. 139 AS; in winter 136 AS. Sheets, showers, and breakfast included. Lunch and dinner available. Frolic in the public pool next door for 15 AS.) **Pension Stadlmann Josefa,** just outside town at Mastaliergasse 21 (tel. 2 31 04), has rooms ranging from cozy to cramped for 150-180 AS, breakfast included. The house is a scenic 20-minute walk from the train station; from the esplanade, walk down Kaltenbachstr. until it runs into Mastaliergasse. You can also rent a *Privatzimmer* from **Rosa Unterreiter,** in the city center at Stiegengasse 1 (tel. 460 72). It's comfortable, clean, and close to the train stations, with a color TV to boot. (130 AS per person; in winter 120 AS; 20% surcharge for one-night stays. Breakfast included. Showers 20 AS.)

Many restaurants can be found in the Kreuzplatz and along Franz-Josef-Str. **Fessl Gasthaus zur Salzmühle,** Esplanade 16, offers economical pizza (45-60 AS), *Knödel* dishes (65 AS), and other tasty entrees (50-60 AS). (Open Mon.-Fri. 8:30am-11pm, Sat. 8:30am-2pm.) The **Konsum grocery store** is conveniently located on Auböckplatz (open Mon.-Fri. 8am-6pm, Sat. 8am-noon).

Sights and Entertainment Other than the baths, Bad Ischl's main attraction is imperial; Austria's last Emperor, Kaiser Franz Josef, built his summer getaway palace, the **Kaiservilla,** on the edge of town, and crammed it with expensive *Kitsch*. Tour guides reminisce interminably about the fallen monarchy and the erstwhile empire. (Open May-Sept. daily 9am-noon and 1-5pm. Tours 68 AS, with guest card 64 AS, students 45 AS, children 30 AS; admission to the surrounding park 25 AS, children 15 AS.) At the rear of the grounds lies the empress's **Marmorschlößl,** which houses a **Photo Museum.** Apparently, the royal couple's sex life was less than fulfilling; the emperor commissioned this decidedly marble palace so she could sleep solo. From the tourist office, head right on Franz-Josef-Str. to the villa's entrance (open daily 9:30am-5:30pm; admission 15 AS, students 10 AS). On the bank of the River Traun, the former home of operetta king Franz Lehár has been converted into a museum dedicated to his work, the **Lehárvilla.** (Open daily May-Sept. 9am-noon and 2-5pm; admission 30 AS, with guest card 25 AS, students 15 AS.)

A tour through Bad Ischl's **salt mines** (tel. 239 48) imparts a didactic but amusing glimpse at the trade that brought wealth and fame to the Salzkammergut. (Open July-Sept. Mon.-Sat. 10am-5pm.; mid-May to June Mon.-Sat. 9am-4pm. Admission 115 AS, with guest card 100 AS, children 55 AS.) The **Katrin Cable Car** runs to the summit of nearby Mt. Katrin (1500m), a peak laced with fine hiking trails. (Open daily 9am-4pm. Up 130 AS; down 100 AS; round-trip 150 AS, with guest card 135 AS.) For happenings about town, pick up *Bad Ischl Events* from the tourist office. The free **Bad Ischler Stadtfest** in mid-August includes myriad musical performances, culminating in the town's pride and joy, the **Operetta Gala.** Inquire at the tourist office for more details. On the Sunday after November 25 (November 27 in 1994), the salt miners of Ischl celebrate the source of their income in a festival called the **Kathreinsonntag.**

■■■ ST. GILGEN

The hometown of Mozart's mother, Anna Maria Pertl, and sister, Nannerl, St. Gilgen is squeezed between the placid waters of the **Wolfgangsee** (Lake Wolfgang) and the **Schafberg** summit. Over the Ellmaustein (1046m), a small hump of a mountain, lies the Fuschlsee, and at the terminus of a lowland valley, the Mondsee. With convenient access to the Autobahn, Salzburg (30km to the northwest), and Bad Ischl (42 AS by the hourly bus), St. Gilgen offers a splendid daytrip into the Salzkammergut, but contemplate staying longer in this winsome playground of a town. Oodles of upper-class Germans and Austrians do. Sit back. Relax. And enjoy the unusual view of the tall, gentle mountains as you practice your backstroke in the lake's translucent blue-green water.

Orientation and Practical Information St. Gilgen's **tourist office** (*Verkehrsverein*), in the *Rathaus* (tel. (06227) 348 or 72 67), keeps track of the local budget accommodations. (Open Mon.-Fri. 9am-noon and 2-6pm, Sat. 9am-noon, Sun. 10am-noon; Sept.-June Mon.-Fri. 9am-noon and 2-6pm.) During July and August a branch office opens across from the train station (open 24 hrs.). **Trains** from Salzburg arrive every ½-hour before choo-chooing off to Bad Ischl. Another train arrives from Mondsee approximately every hour. The **bus station,** Bahnhofplatz 9 (tel. (06227) 425) lies less than five minutes by foot from the town center. From the station on Wolfgangsee-Bundesstr., walk to the right, take the second right onto Poststr., and then the first left on Albersee Str. **Mozartplatz,** the heart of St.

Gilgen, lies a few paces ahead. Mozartplatz is home to several **banks** that exchange currency, but the **post office** (tel. (06227) 201), on the corner of Albersee Str. and Poststr., offers the best rates (open Mon.-Fri. 8am-noon and 2-6pm, Sat. 8-10am. **Postal code:** A-5340).

Accommodations and Food The tourist office helps to sniff out budget housing, but they can't possibly top **Haus Schafbergblick (HI),** Mondsee Str. 7 (tel. (06227) 365). This house is a backpacker's dream, with large lakeside rooms and balconies; you won't believe it's a youth hostel. From Mozartplatz, walk through Streicherplatz and down Mondsee Str.; the hostel is on the left. (Reception open daily 8-9am and 5-7pm. Lockout 9am-noon. Curfew 11pm, but you can sign out a key. Singles 170-230 AS; doubles 140-180 AS; triples 120-160 AS; quads 120-140 AS; quints 110-130 AS. Breakfast and sheets included. Reservations recommended.) **Haus Schönau,** Brunnleitweg 22 (tel. (06227) 373) is one of many reasonably priced *Pensionen* in St. Gilgen; these are quiet, delightful lodgings a few blocks from the lakeshore. (Doubles with shower 240 AS per person. Breakfast included.) Many campsites are located in nearby **Abersee,** a tiny hamlet around a bend in the Wolfgangsee. **Camping Wolfgangblick,** Abersee 24 (tel. (06138) 24 75), and **Camping Lindenstrand,** Gschwand 36 (tel. (05342) 72 05), both offer peaceful shore locations, warm showers, and food (Wolfgangblick 44 AS per person, under 15 20 AS, 22 AS per tent or car; Lindenstrand 42 AS per person, under 15 23 AS, 60-80 AS per site; showers 10 AS for 6 min.).

Restaurants and cafés beckon around every corner in St. Gilgen. Pleasant outdoor eating spots abound on the streets that radiate from Mozartplatz and the Seepromenade on Ischler Str., directly on the lake. Dine under a parasol of foliage at casual **Pizzeria Bianco,** Ischler Str. 18. Feast on the salad bar (48 AS), and savor spaghetti dishes (55-80 AS) and pizza (55-110 AS). (Open daily 11am-2pm and 5-11pm.) Frugal gourmets can stop and shop at the local **SPAR Markt,** at Brunettiplatz 1, right off Mozartplatz (open Mon.-Fri. 9am-noon and 2-6pm, Sat. 9am-noon).

Sights and Entertainment Bring the pink registration slip from your lodging to the tourist office to receive a St. Gilgen **guest card** that provides discounts such as free admission to the *Heimatmuseum,* reductions on Wolfgangsee ferries, and more. (Museum open June-Sept. Tues.-Sun. 10am-noon and 2-6pm; regular admission 35 AS, children 15 AS.) Friday evenings bring the sweet strains of local musicians to the **Music Pavilion,** at the intersection of Seepromenade and Ischler Str. (free performances at 8:30pm).

The refreshing sapphire waters of the Wolfgangsee beckon swimmers away from the central Mozartplatz, to beaches like the **St. Gilgener Strandbad,** Mondseer Str. 12 (admission 30 AS). Rent **boats** (sailboats 170 AS per hr.) and **windsurfers** (150 AS per hr.) from the **Windsurfing and Sailing School,** on the Seepromenade by Ischler Str. (tel. (06227) 71 01, 490, or 297). The tourist office's comprehensive brochure *St. Gilgen Information* (in English) details various hiking excursions; the office also offers half- and full-day guided hikes. (Half-day treks depart Tues. at 2pm, full-day Thurs. at 10am. Sign up at the tourist office.) The **Zwölferhorn-Seilbahn cable car,** next to the bus station, conveys fearless wanderers up the **Zwölferhorn** (1520m). There, you'll find a multitude of hiking trails and a spellbinding panorama of the entire region (up 100 AS, children 90 AS; down 90 AS, children 60 AS; round-trip 160 AS, with guest card 140 AS, children 100 AS). Winter sport lovers should inquire at the tourist office for the **Wolfgangsee Ski Pass,** valid for the St. Gilgen/Postalm bus, Zwölferhorn cable car, Postalm Ski Centre and toll road, and area chair lifts (7-day pass 1200 AS, children 850 AS).

For further mountainside delights, ascend the 1783m **Schafberg** on the cogwheeled, 100-year-old **Schafbergbahn.** The hike back takes three hours. (Open early May to early Oct. Up 110 AS, down 90 AS; Eurail valid.) A steamer runs from St. Gilgen to the base of the railway (disembark at "Wolfgang Schafbergbahnhof"; 40

AS, free with railpass). Don't forget to make arrangements for your descent (last departure between 5:30-6:30pm).

Near St. Gilgen: St. Wolfgang

Any visit to the Wolfgangsee region should include a daytrip to the exquisite village of **St. Wolfgang,** often swarming with tourists but nonetheless worth the trip. Take the enchanting ferry ride (one way 44 AS, Eurail valid) around the lake from St. Gilgen's Ischler Str. to the St. Wolfgang **Markt.** Long a place of pilgrimage, the **Pfarrkirche** houses a magnificent 15th-century wooden altar by Michael Pacher and fabulous, frescoed ceilings (open daily 9am-5pm; Oct.-April 10am-4pm). The town **tourist office** (*Kurdirektion*) is at Pilgerstr. 18 (tel. (06138) 22 39; open Mon.-Fri. 8am-noon and 2-6pm, Sat. 8am-noon.) The **post office,** on Postplatz, is just up the street (open Mon.-Fri. 8am-noon and 2-6pm, Sat. 8-10am). Why did the chicken cross the road? To escape the poultry section of the **SPAR supermarket,** on the other side of Postplatz.

■ Mondsee

The Salzkammergut's warmest lake, the Mondsee (Moon Lake), derives its romantic moniker from its crescent shape. The town of Mondsee (pop. 2000) lies at the northern tip of the crescent, close to Autobahn A1; by public transportation, take bus #3010 from Salzburg (every hour; one way 50 AS). The lake is Mondsee's principal attraction, though visitors also frequent the local **Pfarrkirche.** This large Gothic church was grafted to a bright yellow Baroque exterior; its towers dominate the town skyline. Once a Benedictine monastery, the parish church is best known for its brief appearance in *The Sound of Music's* wedding scene. Next door is the **Museum Mondsee,** which houses a mildly interesting collection of regional archaeological finds, illuminated by manuscripts and a potpourri of religious artifacts (open daily May-Oct. 9am-6pm; admission 25 AS, students 12 AS). The **Freilichtmuseum,** on Hilfbergstr. behind the church, is an open-air museum with a 500-year-old traditional smokehouse (open April-Oct. daily 9am-6pm; admission 25 AS, students 12 AS). A 100-year-old locomotive, active until 1937, sits in the **Eisenbahn Museum** (railway museum), situated along the lakeshore.

The **tourist office** (*Verkehersverein*), Dr. Franz Müller Str. 3 (tel. (06232) 22 70; fax 44 70), is a five-minute walk from the bus station, halfway between the church and the lake. (Open Mon.-Fri. 8am-8pm, Sat.-Sun. 9am-8pm; Sept.-June Mon.-Fri. 8am-noon and 2-6pm.) The **post office,** on Franz Kreuzberger Str. across from the bus station, is the most convenient place for **currency exchange** (open Mon.-Fri. 8am-noon and 2-6pm, Sat. 8-10am). On Sunday, try **Rieger Bank,** Herzog-Odilo Str. 4, adjacent to the colorful main square (open Mon.-Sat. 10am-6pm, Sun. 10am-5pm).

Mondsee is brimming with *Pensionen*; ask at the tourist office to find the most convenient location with vacancies. The **Jugendgästehaus (HI),** Krankenhausstr. 9 (tel. (06232) 2418), offers doubles, quads, and dorms. From the bus station, walk up Kreuzbergerstr. away from the lake, turn right on Rainerstr., and then immediately left on Pflegerstr., which runs into Krankenhausstr. The hostel is on the left. (Reception open daily 5-10pm. Curfew 10pm. Members only. 120 AS. Showers and breakfast included.) Inexpensive restaurants abound as well; just avoid the costlier establishments near the parish church. Ubiquitous **SPAR supermakets** provide do-it-yourself victuals.

For entertainments other than the lake itself, partake of Mondsee's numerous musical offerings, including **Mozart Serenades** from late June through August (tickets 200 AS, students 180 AS). The **Musiktage,** an annual music festival, swings by in early September. (Tickets 200-450 AS; write to "Postfach 3, A-5310 Mondsee" for ticket information, or call (06232) 2270.)

■ Attersee

The southeast corner of the Mondsee pokes out toward the Attersee, the largest lake in the Salzkammergut and one of the most beautiful spots in Austria. To reach the tiny hamlet of **Weißenbach am Attersee,** accessible only by car, drive several stomach-wrenching kilometers along a road that somehow clings to the shore of the lake. Proletarians *and* their exploitative capitalist masters are welcome at the secluded **Europa-Camp (HI),** owned and run by the Austrian Young Socialists (tel. (07663) 220). Here, a campground, a psychedelic hostel, and a modest disco (is that an oxymoron?) are run with Taylorite efficiency. (Reception open 8-11am and 4-7pm. Dorms 85 AS per person, showers included. Camping 40 AS per person, small tents 35 AS, large tents 50 AS, car 55 AS. Breakfast 35 AS.)

A ferry service links the other small villages around the Attersee, and a bus runs twice per week from Bad Ischl. The **tourist offices** in **Nußdorf,** on Dorfstr. (tel. (07666) 80 64; open Mon., Wed., and Fri. 8am-noon; Tues. and Thurs. 8am-noon and 3-5pm), and in **Unterach** (tel. (07665) 83 27 or 82 55 74) impart information about nearby concerts and festivals and help find lodgings. The tourist office in **Weyregg am Attersee** (tel. (07664) 236) also helps with orientation and accommodations (open mid-July to mid-Aug. Mon.-Fri. 9am-1pm). Though only a small village, Weyregg offers a regular schedule of evening concerts, small festivals, and dances. The tourist office runs guided hikes and mountain bike tours and has information on boat rental (rowboats 40 AS per hr., sailboats 70 AS per hr.). There's also a compact, 42-bed **Jugendherberge (HI),** Weyregg am Attersee 3 (tel. (07664) 780), with doubles, quads, and six-bed rooms. (Open April-Oct. Reception open daily 5-7pm. 102 AS, under 19 85 AS. Breakfast included. Lunch and dinner available. Sheets 35 AS.)

■ Gmunden

Gmunden, a large resort town sitting prettily on the **Traunsee,** is the northern gateway to the Salzkammergut. One side of the lake cowers at the base of forbidding, jagged crags; the other shore is sprinkled with tiny hamlets. Trains run frequently from Salzburg and Linz via Attnang-Puchheim; rent **bikes** at the station (mountain bikes 200 AS, 150 AS with train ticket) to spin along the Traunsee (rental open Mon.-Sat. 24 hrs., Sun. 5:30am-midnight). To reach Gmunden's center, take any streetcar from opposite the **train station** (tel. (07612) 420 70) into town (14 AS). The **tourist office** (*Kurverwaltung und Tourismusbüro*), Am Graben 2 (tel. (07612) 43 05), off the first road on the left from the streetcar's terminus, conjures up lodgings for no fee. (Open Mon.-Fri. 8am-noon and 2-6pm, Sat. 9am-noon; Sept.-June Mon.-Fri. 8am-noon and 2-6pm.) There is a **post office** on the corner of Bahnhofstr. and Robertstr. (open Mon.-Fri. 7am-6:30pm, Sat. 7-11am).

For comfy rooms in a gracious home, head to **Haus Platzer,** Lehengasse 6 (tel. (07612) 59 45), two minutes from the "Kuferzeile" streetcar stop. Walk down Franz-Thomas-Str. until you see the Oberbank; Lehengasse is just before it to the right. (Singles and doubles 130 AS per person, breakfast included. Showers or bath 20 AS.) About 4km from the center of town, at Traunsteinstr. 257 (tel. (07612) 30 60), the Österreichischer Alpenverein operates a **Talherberge** (the low-elevation equivalent of the mountain hut) that dips its toes in the Traunsee (see Essentials, at the front of this guide, for more information). Stroll around the north end of the lake and journey a bit down the east side. (Members 45 AS, nonmembers 60 AS. Showers 20 AS. Breakfast 50 AS.) Enjoy fresh foodstuffs at the **Farmers' Market,** held summer Fridays 2-5pm, about 2km north of town off Ohlsdorferstr. between Puhrzaunstr. and Stelzerweg. Or, procure your produce at the **SPAR supermarket,** on the Esplanade behind the Staatstheater (open Mon.-Fri. 8am-6pm, Sat. 7:30am-1pm).

Gmunden is renowned throughout Austria for its centuries-old tradition of crafting hand-painted ceramic dishes, known as **Gmunder Keramik.** You can tour the factories where the dishes are currently produced at Freygasse 13, off Bahnhofstr. (free tours Mon.-Fri. at 10am). Gmunden rolls out more cultural heavy artillery for the **Gmundner Festspiele,** an outdoor concert series whose sponsors unload unsold tickets (*Restkarten*) to students at fire-sale prices 15 minutes before performances. The festival takes place from mid-August to early September (tickets 90-400 AS, standing room 40 AS). Call the Festspiele box office (tel. (07612) 40 95) for more information. An **Arthur Schnitzler Festival** at the Stadttheater during the first week of August serves as a prologue to the Festspiele. This Viennese *fin-de-siècle* curmudgeon bemoaned the restrictions of moralism, lamented the cult of instinctual gratification, and whined, griped, and *kvetched* for scores of other ironic and satirical volumes; the festival celebrating his work is a bit less pessimistic. From June to August, regular **music concerts** are held on the esplanade Sundays at 10am.

■ Ebensee

From late May through September, ferries cruise around the Traunsee, docking finally in Ebensee (one way 60 AS), the lake's southernmost town. Frequent trains (round-trip 60 AS) run from Gmunden as well. Although the ferry costs more, it's more scenic than the train route, which meanders through mountain tunnels more than it skirts the See. For ferry routes and prices to other Traunsee destinations, contact **Traunsee Schiffahrt** on Rathausplatz in Gmunden (tel. (07612) 52 15 or 667 00). You can also take Bundesstraße 145 along the western edge of the lake. In Ebensee, the **Feuerkogel cable car** (tel. (06133) 52 19) makes the 1625m ascent to a nearby summit. (Round-trip 160 AS; with guest card 130 AS; week pass 340 AS. Open daily May-June and Oct. 8:30am-4:30pm; July-Sept. 8:30am-5pm.) From here, trek up to **Alberfeldkogel** (1708m) for the most spectacular view of the lake.

The Ebensee **tourist office** (*Fremdenverkehrsverband*), Hauptstr. 34 (tel. (06133) 80 16; fax 56 24), is beside the train station in the police building. (Open Mon.-Fri. 8am-noon and 2-6pm, Sat.-Sun. 9am-noon; mid-Aug. to June Mon.-Fri. 8am-noon and 1-5pm.) There's a **post office** around the corner, at Bahnhofstr. 9; walk up Hauptstr., and turn left on Bahnhofstr. The **Jugendherberge (HI),** Rindbachstr. 15 (tel. (06133) 66 98), is just minutes from the lake; from the station, walk right on Salzkammergut Bundesstr., turn right on Rindbachstr., and look for the sign. (Reception open daily 5-7pm. Flexible 10pm curfew. 113 AS, under 19 95 AS. Breakfast included. Sheets 30 AS.)

■ Bad Aussee

At the geographic center of Austria lies Bad Aussee, a hamlet with little to offer other than access to two stunning lakes. To the east lies the **Grundlsee,** and to the north the **Altaussee,** one of the smaller lakes of the Salzkammergut. The two lakes are but 15-minute bus rides from the center of town (20 AS). From the Altaussee, you can walk up to Austria's largest salt mine; this **Salzbergwerk** was used to conceal artworks during World War II and is now open for tours. (Open May-Sept. Mon.-Sat. 10am-4pm; admission 115 AS, with guest card 100 AS, children 55 AS.) To reach the mine, take a bus (direction: "Altaussee") to the end station, and walk up the hill for about 25 minutes. The Grundlsee, a pristine, tourist-free oasis, is a haven for serene water sports; take the bus (direction: "Grundlsee") to the edge of the lake.

The town of Bad Aussee can be reached by both **train** and **bus** from Bad Ischl (46 AS). If you arrive by train, take any city bus to "Postamt" (16 AS), or walk straight on Bahnhofstr. for 2-3km until you reach the **post office,** the most convenient place to exchange money (open Mon.-Fri. 8am-noon and 2-6pm, Sat. 8-11am). The **tourist office,** Hauptstr. 58 (tel. (06152) 523 23), helps you find rooms for no fee (open Mon.-Fri. 8am-6pm, Sat. 8am-noon and 1-5pm; Sept.-June Mon.-Fri. 9am-noon and 3-5pm).

The **Jugendgästehaus (HI),** Jugendherbergsstr. 18 (tel. (03622) 522 38; fax 522 38 88), offers modern, spotless facilities only 10 minutes from town. From the post office, make a left on Ischler Str., continue up the hill as it turns into Marktleite, then take a left on Jugendherbergsstr.; the hostel is at the end of the street, to the left of the tennis courts. (Reception open daily 8am-1pm and 5-7pm. No lockout or curfew. 1- to 4-bed rooms 140-160 AS. Breakfast and sheets included. Lunch and dinner 55 AS.) Outside of town, near the Grundlsee, **Gasthof Staudenwirt,** Grundlsee Str. 21 (tel. (03622) 52427), provides reasonable accommodations with a campsite next door. Take the bus (direction: "Grundlsee") to "Gasthof Staudenwirt" (16 AS). (180-470 AS per person. Breakfast included. Camping 50 AS per person, children 30 AS, 40 AS per car; showers 10 AS.)

A **Billa supermarket,** Hauptstr. 152, across from the tourist office, vends everything from *Zucchini* to *Apfeln* (open Mon.-Thurs. 7:30am-7pm, Fri. 7:30am-8pm, Sat. 7am-1pm). **Heli's Pizzeria,** Altaussee Str. 52 (tel. (03622) 524 87), serves inexpensive quasi-Italian dishes (open Mon.-Tues. and Thurs.-Sat. 5pm-midnight, Sun. 11am-2pm and 5pm-midnight).

In Bad Aussee, man-made structures yield to the natural splendor of the water; the only notable public structure in town is the **Kammerhofmuseum** on Chlometskyplatz. This museum displays local history along with the requisite regional saga of salt production (open daily 10am-noon and 4-6pm). For a few weeks each year, Bad Aussee puts on an excessively florid face. The annual **Narzissenfest,** held from the late-May to early-June, is a giant flower festival (I love me...I love me not...I love me...yeah, I love me...). The beginning of July brings the **Musik Festwochen,** a two-week classical music festival (tickets 100-200 AS; call (03622) 52323 for information). The **See Rockfest** arrives every August—rock concerts and fireworks displays are held throughout the region (tickets 160 AS and up).

■■■ HALLSTATT

South of Bad Ischl lies Hallstatt—small, isolated, and breathtakingly beautiful in its austere, mountainous setting. The village seems to defy gravity as its medieval buildings cling to the face of a stony slope. Rome had not yet been not built in a day when Celts and Illyrians mined this fjord-like land for salt, making Hallstatt the trading nexus of the era. Visitors now relax by the peaceful mountain lake, the Hallstätter See, and crane their necks toward the peaks of the Dachstein mountains. **Rudolfsturm** (Rudolf's Tower) is perched on a mountain 855m above the village, guarding the entrance to the Salzberg Valley, site of a famous prehistoric burial ground and of modern salt-mine installations.

Orientation and Practical Information Hallstatt stands poised on the **Hallstätter See,** a pristine emerald oasis at the southern tip of the Salzkammergut. If you're arriving by train, alight at the Hallstatt Bahnhof, across the lake from the town. **Ferries** cross the lake after each train's arrival (20 AS); otherwise, walk 8km around the southern end of the lake, past the best camping and swimming spots. Post buses also make the journey from Bad Ischl (one way 46 AS). If you plan to hike from the train station to Hallstatt, disembarking at the **Obertraun** stop is a better idea—it makes the walk 3km shorter. Ferries also run between Obertraun and Hallstatt (35 AS).

Hallstatt's main byway, **Seestraße,** hugs the lakeshore all through town. The **tourist office** (*Tourismusbüro*), in the Kultur- und Kongresshaus at Seestr. 169 (tel. (06134) 208; fax 352), finds vacancies among the plentiful cheap rooms for no fee. (Open Mon.-Fri. 9am-6pm, Sat.-Sun. 10am-2pm; Sept.-May Mon.-Fri. 9am-noon and 1-5pm.) The **post office,** on Seestr. down from the tourist office, offers the best exchange rates. (Open Mon.-Fri. 8am-noon and 2-6pm, Sat. 8-10am; Sept.-June Mon.-Fri. 8am-noon and 2-6pm. **Postal code:** A-4830.)

Accommodations and Food *Privatzimmer* at just-above-hostel prices speckle the town. Wherever you tuck yourself in, don't forget to ask your host or hostess about Hallstatt's free **guest card,** which offers discounts on mountain lifts and sporting facilities in Hallstatt, Gosau, Obertraun, and Bad Goisern. The **Jugendherberge (HI),** Salzbergstr. 50 (tel. (06134) 212), offers basic, inexpensive lodgings in a flower-bedecked house 10 minutes from the town center. From the tourist office, walk down Seestr. away from downtown Hallstatt, take a right on Echerntalweg and a left on Salzbergstr. The hostel is planning to open a new wing with 10 four-bed rooms in 1994; call ahead for up-to-date information. (Open May-Sept. Reception open daily 6-9pm. Lockout 10am-6pm. Curfew 9pm. 85 AS. Breakfast 25 AS. Sheets 25 AS.) **TVN Naturfreundeherberge,** Kirchenweg 36 (tel. (06134) 318), also called Gasthaus Zur Mühle, is a quasi-hostel with three- to eight-bed rooms. From the bus stop, walk down the stairs, turn left, and go through the first small tunnel on your left; the house is straight ahead. (Reception open daily 8-10am and 5-10pm. 100 AS. Sheets 35 AS. Breakfast 35 AS. Lunch and dinner available at the restaurant downstairs.) The charming, lake-side home of **Franziska Zimmerman,** Gosaumühlstr. 69 (tel. (01043) 309) has been around for four centuries and still manages to offer cozy rooms—some with balconies, and most with spectacular views. (175 AS; more than 3 nights, 170 AS. Showers 10 AS. Breakfast included.) Down the road at #83, Frau Zimmerman's sister runs **Frühstückspension Sarstein** (tel. (01043) 217), which lures visitors with homey rooms, wonderful vistas of the lake and village, a sunbathing lawn, and a TV. (175-185 AS, with private bathroom and shower 260 AS. Hall showers 10 AS. Breakfast included.) **Camping Klausner-Höll,** Lahnstr. 6 (tel. (06134) 329), lies two blocks from the bus terminal on Seestr. (35 AS per person, children 18 AS; 30 AS per tent, 25 AS per car; breakfast 45-60 AS; showers included.)

Hallstatt has so many attractive restaurants that it can be difficult to decide among them, but none is exceptionally cheap. The restaurant below the TVN Naturfreundeherberge probably offers the best deal in town. Pizza (60-95 AS) and spaghetti (60-80 AS) are the specialties (open daily 11:30am-2pm and 5-10pm). Fresh fish from the Hallstättersee is always a worthwhile option—there's a **Konsum supermarket** in the city center (open Mon.-Fri. 7:30am-noon and 3-6pm, Sat. 7:30am-noon).

Sights and Entertainment Hallstatt packs a number of sights into its relatively slim frame. Simply exploring the narrow, crooked streets is entertainment in itself. Depending on one's point of view, a visit to St. Michael's Chapel at the **Pfarrkirche** is macabre, poignant, or intrusive; beneath the roof of the chapel is the parish "charnel house"—a repository for sundry skeletons. The bones are transferred here from the cemetery after 10 to 20 years, because the graveyard is too small to accommodate all those who wish to rest there. (They're buried vertically as it is.) Each skull is decorated—flowers for females, ivy for males—and each lists the date and cause of death (open daily 10am-6pm; free).

In the mid-19th century, Hallstatt was the site of such a large Iron Age archeological find that the town subsequently lent its name to an entire epoch of pre-history—the Hallstatt Period. Among the finds were a plethora of artifacts, a pauper's grave, and the well-appointed crypts of the ruling class, all circa 1000-500 BC. The **Prähistorisches Museum** (Prehistoric Museum), across from the tourist office, exhibits some of the relics unearthed in the region. Finds from the famous excavation site on Hallstatt's Salzberg (salt mountain) are displayed here; they give scientific proof of prehistoric salt-mining activity. Extensive salt-trading brought bronze ornaments from Northern Italy and amber from the east coast to this remote valley. (Admission 35 AS, with guest card 30 AS, students 20 AS.) The admission fee also covers entrance to the **Heimatmuseum,** around the corner, which explores recent European history and the development of local fauna. (Both museums open daily 10am-6pm; Oct.-April daily 10am-4pm.)

If you dig piles of dirt, take the **Salzbergbahn cable car** up the mountain to the site of the excavation. (Open daily 9am-6pm; Oct.-April daily 9am-4:30pm. One way 50 AS, with guest card 40 AS, under 15 30 AS; round-trip 90 AS, 70 AS, and 45 AS, respectively.) The 2500-year-old **Salzbergwerke,** just up the path from the ancient graves, are the oldest operating salt works in the world. (Open June to mid-Sept. daily 9:30am-4:30pm; May and mid-Sept. to mid-Oct. daily 9:30am-3pm. Admission 125 AS, with guest card 110 AS, students and children under 14 60 AS.) Paths lead back to Hallstatt from the mountain summit. **Skischule Zauner,** Markt 51 (tel. (06134) 246), provides guidance for ski bunnies who wish to conquer the local Dachstein and Krippenstein peaks on slender waxed boards. Daypasses for the region's lifts run 350 AS (700 AS for 5 days).

Near Hallstatt: Obertraun

At the end of the lake in Obertraun, the prodigious **Dachstein Ice Caves** give eloquent testimony to the geological hyperactivity that forged the region's natural beauty, even if they are marred by cheesy names like "Cave Venus" and "Hall of Oblivion." (Open May to mid-Oct. daily 9am-5pm. Admission to Giant Ice Cave 72 AS, to Mammoth Cave 66 AS, combined "Gargantuan Experience" 98 AS.) To reach the caves from Hallstatt, take the boat to Obertraun and ride the **Dachstein cable car** up 1350m to "Schönbergalm." (Cable car open daily 9am-5pm, round-trip 142 AS, with guest card 128 AS, children 93 AS.) For information on the caves, call (06131) 362. The **tourist office** stands in the Gemeindeamt at Obertraun 180 (tel. (06131) 351; open Mon.-Fri. 8am-noon and 4-6pm, Sat. 9am-noon). Obertraun's sparkling **Jugendherberge (HI),** Winkl 26 (tel. (06131) 360), is a refuge for summer hikers and winter skiers alike. (Reception open 5:30-10pm. Lockout 9am-noon. Flexible 10pm curfew. 75 AS, under 19 65 AS. Breakfast 30 AS. Sheets 25 AS.)

Northwest Austria

Oberösterreich (Upper Austria) is the country's primary source of industrial wealth. The province extends north from the Dachstein massif to the Böhmerwald and from the Inn river east to the Enns. Oberösterreich is composed of three distinct regions: the Mühlviertel in the north, with granite and gneiss hills and a traditional agricultural economy; the Innviertel to the west of Linz in the Danube (Donau) valley; and the Pyhrn-Eisenwurz with Alpine foothills and limestone crags.

Oberösterreich is Austria's second most-productive source of oil and natural gas; since World War II, several large-scale hydroelectric power stations have been built along the Donau and its tributary, the Enns. The Donau winds its way from Germany southeast towards Vienna, bisecting the province along its path. The Daimler-Puch plant in Steyr is a major production center for engines, tractors, trucks, and ball-bearings. Austria's largest aluminum plant is situated near Ranshofen, and Lenzing is a major cellulose and synthetic-fiber center. Annual trade fairs in Wels and Ried agglomerate on one site a comprehensive annual review of the province's industrial achievements and Austria's overall agricultural prowess.

The provincial capital is Linz, a major center of iron, steel, and chemical production and home to many modern Danube port installations. The handy pamphlet

Kultur Sommer Oberösterreich (in German only), available at all tourist offices, lists the gamut of cultural events throughout the area.

■■■ LINZ

Austria's third-largest city (after Vienna and Graz), Linz an der Donau (pop. 208,000) has never made much of a name for itself as a tourist destination—and that's a shame. Evidently, the port city's reputation as a textile and chemical center and its infamy as one of Adolf Hitler's favored haunts have blinded visitors to the charms of its well-preserved *Altstadt* and impressive cultural and intellectual pedigree. While Linz may not boast the architectural saturation of Salzburg, the mountain setting of Innsbruck, or the intellectual history of Vienna, it certainly proffers its own pleasures: museums and galleries, a major music festival, bustling street life, and all the bookstores, cafés, and nightclubs of a university town.

The Romans knew today's provincial capital as Lentia, a fortified basecamp. By the 9th century, it had already become a market town, and in 1489 Friedrich III established his imperial residence here. Linz gave birth to the world-famous **Linzer Torte,** a pastry molded to resemble an open gem. The pie is constructed by rolling a rich crust into a tin, coating it with raspberry jam, and then placing the trademark lattice of dough on top; the compilation is then brushed with beaten egg, baked ever-so-slowly, glazed with warm jam, and decorated with blanched split almonds. The resulting confection has kept the royal sweet tooth content for centuries.

ORIENTATION AND PRACTICAL INFORMATION

Linz, capital of the *Land* of Upper Austria, straddles the Danube near Germany and the Czech Republic. The river broadens temporarily around the city, enough to make Linz the waterway's main trade port. Linz lies on a rail route connecting the Adriatic Sea to the Baltic; travelers from the Czech Republic and Bavaria often make Linz their gateway into Austria. The pedestrian zone centers around the exceptionally large and flamboyant **Hauptplatz,** from which the pedestrian **Landstraße** extends toward the **Volksgarten** and the train station. Leading out of the Hauptplatz in the other direction, the **Nibelungenbrücke** crosses the Danube and spills out onto Hauptstraße. To reach the Hauptplatz from the train station, cross Bahnhofplatz to Bahnhofstr., turn right onto Kärntnerstr., and follow it to Blumauerplatz; then turn left onto Landstr. and walk straight into the main square.

Tourist Office: Hauptplatz 54 (tel. 23 93 17 77). Spews forth reports of cultural events, accommodations, and transportation. Open Mon.-Fri. 8am-7pm, Sat.-Sun. 8-11:30am and 12:30-7pm; Oct.-April Mon.-Fri. 8am-6pm, Sat.-Sun. 8-11:30am and 1:30-6pm. **Branch office** at the train station (tel. 23 93 17 73). Open Mon.-Sat. 8am-12:30pm and 1:30-7pm, Sun. 2-7pm; Oct.-April Mon.-Fri. 9am-12:30pm and 1:30-6pm. Both offices help find accommodations at no charge. The **Oberösterreich Tourist Office**, Schillerstr. 50 (tel. 60 02 21), disseminates information on the entire province (open Mon.-Thurs. 8am-noon and 1-5pm, Fri. 8am-1pm); the **Mühlviertel Tourist Office,** Blütenstr. 8 (tel. 23 50 20), restricts its scope to the region north of Linz (open Mon.-Thurs. 8am-noon and 1-5pm, Fri. 8am-1pm).

Budget Travel: ÖKISTA, Herrengasse 7, in the arcade (tel. 77 58 93). Discount travel tickets. Open Mon.-Fri. 9:30am-5:30pm.

Currency Exchange: Best rates at the post office (60 AS commission) or American Express (40 AS commission). Train station banks charge 110-120 AS commission.

American Express: Bürgerstr. 14 (tel. 66 90 13). Address mail as follows: "Maria Alexandra ORDOÑEZ, Client Letter Service, American Express, Bürgerstr. 14, A-4021 Linz, Austria." Open Mon.-Fri. 9am-5:30pm, Sat. 9am-noon.

Post Office: Bahnhofplatz 11, adjacent to the train and bus stations. Exchanges money at superb rates. Also houses a 24-hr. telephone center. Information open Mon.-Fri. 7am-5pm, Sat. 8am-4pm; mail handling open Mon.-Fri. 7am-8pm, Sat. 7am-noon. Wheelchair access. **Postal Code:** A-4020.

Telephones: In the post office. Open 24 hrs. **City Code:** 0732.

Trains: Bahnhofstr., near the Volksgarten. Large and modern. Bike rental, currency exchange, luggage storage, and lockers (30 AS large, 20 AS small; 48 hrs. max.). Call 17 17 for schedule information Mon.-Fri. 7:30am-9pm, Sat.-Sun. 7:30am-8pm. Four trains run daily to Prague (round-trip 378 AS) and Ceské Budejovice in the Czech Republic (round-trip 220 AS); trains depart nearly continuously for Vienna. Further service to Steyr (one way 46 AS), Freistadt (one way 55 AS), and Mauthausen (one way 58 AS).

Buses: Directly opposite the train station and in front of the post office. Buses depart for destinations throughout Upper Austria. Ticket window open Mon. 6am-6pm, Tues.-Fri. 6:30am-6pm, Sat. 7am-1:15pm, Sun. 5-7:45pm. For information about BundesBuses, call 21 60; for Post buses, call 16 71.

Local Public Transportation: Efficient, user-friendly network of streetcars and buses. Single rides 18 AS, children 10 AS. Tickets available from the machines located at each stop—bring change, because they don't accept bills. The 24-hr. card (35 AS) and 6-multi-ride card (72 AS) are more practical and economical. The latter can be used by more than 1 person (e.g., 1 person for 6 trips, or 6 people for 1 trip). The 24-hr. card is available at the machines, and the multi-ride card can be purchased at all *Tabak* stands. The tourist office hands out a free Kernzone LVV system map, and a regional transport map and schedule for 20 AS.

Ferries: DDSG has a major station in Linz just downriver from the Nibelungenbrücke. Call 78 36 07 for information. The trip between Linz and Passau is neither terribly exciting nor terribly expensive (6 hr. upstream, 5 hr. downstream, round-trip 320 AS). The 12-hour ride to Vienna is infinitely more scenic (one way 832 AS). For information on the Linz-Vienna route, see the Danube section.

Bike Rental: At the train station. Open 24 hrs.

Bookstore: Buchhandel Neugebauer, Landstr. 1 (tel. 77 17 68-0). Open Mon.-Fri. 8:15am-6pm, Sat. 8:30am-noon.

Emergencies: Police: tel. 133. **Ambulance:** tel. 144. **Fire:** tel. 122.

ACCOMMODATIONS AND CAMPING

Linz suffers from a paucity of cheap rooms, so it's usually best to stick to the youth hostels. Either tourist office is a valuable resource for alternative suggestions. Wherever you stay, call ahead to ensure a room; vacancies never remain empty for long.

Jugendherberge Linz (HI), Kapuzinerstr. 14 (tel. 78 27 20), offers the cheapest bed in town at an excellent location. From the train station, take streetcar #3 to "Taubenmarkt"; then walk down Promenade, continue on Klammstr., and turn left on Kapuzinerstr. The hostel is in the yellow house to the right. Clean and quiet, with a relaxed and helpful staff. Good kitchen facilities to cook your own breakfast. Accommodates 36 in 4- to 6-bed rooms. Reception open 8-10am and 5-7pm. No curfew; get a key from the reception desk. 110 AS, under 20 90 AS, nonmembers 30 AS surcharge for the first night. Sheets 20 AS.

Landesjugendherberge Lentia, Blütenstr. 23 (tel. 23 70 78), is a skyscraperesque structure located in the Urfahr district, across the river from Hauptplatz. From the train station, take streetcar #3 across the river to "Reindlstr."; with your back toward the river, walk straight up Hauptstr., and Blütenstr. is the next street on the right. Houses 106 in doubles, quads, and 5-bed rooms. Reception open 8am-10pm. Curfew 10pm. 110 AS, under 19 85 AS. Breakfast 20 AS. Sheets included.

Jugendgästehaus (HI), Stanglhofweg 3 (tel. 66 44 34). The bland, soulless exterior conceals a liveable interior. From the train station, with your back to the post office, walk down Bahnhofstr. to Blumauerplatz. Here catch ESG bus #27 to "Froshberg." Walk straight on Ziegeleistr. and then right on Stanglhofweg. If you pass Roseggerstr., you've gone too far. 152 beds in doubles, triples, and quads. Good for sports enthusiasts—it's near an athletic facility. Reception open 7:30am-4pm and 6-11pm. Singles 280 AS. Doubles 180 AS per person. Quads 130 AS. Showers in every room. Breakfast included. Call ahead.

Gasthof "Wilder Mann," Goethestr. 14 (tel. 560 78). From the train station, take streetcar #3 to "Goethekrzgasse" and walk down Goethestr; the *Gasthof* is on the right. Or just walk down Bahnhofstr., take a left on Landestr. at Blumauerplatz, and then make a right on Goethestr. Reception open daily 8am-10pm. Basic single rooms for 260 AS, with shower 330 AS. Doubles 480 AS, with shower 580 AS. Breakfast 50 AS.

FOOD

Restaurants on the **Hauptplatz** are generally expensive. Explore sidestreets such as Klostergasse, Tummelplatz, Theatergasse, and Bethlehemstr. to find cafés with affordable victuals. Students frequent the various eateries surrounding Johannes Kepler Universität; take streetcar #1 (direction: "Universität") from Blumauerplatz to the end station. At some point, you'll have to indulge in the native **Linzer Torte,** a delectable nut pastry covered with a distinctive trellised crust; the flavor is similar to marzipan, but *oh*-so-much richer.

Café Traxlmayr, Promenade 16. Gentle sophistication. Peruse newspapers and gnaw on a *Käseomlette* (cheese omelette; 47 AS) or a *Linzer Torte* (24 AS). Delicious coffee (23-40 AS). Open Mon.-Sat. 8am-10pm.

Pizza und Pasta Franzesca, Klammstr. 1, in the *Altstadt.* Feast on *calzones* (49 AS), spaghetti (42 AS), and pizza (65 AS) at outside tables.

Napolitana DA Alfredo, Bethlehemstr. 38 (tel. 77 80 55). Linz's oldest pizzeria, where a pie sets you back 70-100 AS. Open Mon.-Sat. 11:30am-2pm and 6-11pm.

Singapore am Dom, Baumbachstr. 9 (tel. 77 52 01). Enjoy Asian cuisine in the shadow of the Dom's soaring spire. Good selection of vegetable dishes. Open daily 11:30am-2:30pm and 5:30-10:30pm.

Alte Welt Weinkeller, Hauptplatz 4. Soak up wine and spirits in this arcaded, Renaissance-era edifice. Open Mon.-Sat. 5:30pm-1am.

Billa supermarket, at the intersection of Landstr. and Mozartstr. Open Mon.-Thurs. 7:30am-6:30pm, Fri. 7:30am-8pm, Sat. 7am-1pm.

SIGHTS AND ENTERTAINMENT

Begin your tour of Linz with a stroll around the city's **Altstadt,** which radiates out from the riverside **Hauptplatz,** an exceptionally large town square lined with Baroque façades. Pick up the free brochure *A Walk Through Linz's Old City* from the tourist office to guide yourself past the highlights. The Baroque **Altes Rathaus** is crowned by an octagonal tower and an astronomical clock. Free-spirited stargazer Johannes Kepler wrote his major work, *Harmonices Mundi,* while living around the corner at Rathausgasse 5. Just off the Hauptplatz on Klosterstr., the **Landhaus** has an attractive clock tower of its own. On Domgasse stands Linz's glorious twin-towered **Alter Dom;** throughout the 19th century, symphonic composer and humble maestro Anton Bruckner tickled the ivories here as church organist.

Cross the **Nibelungenbrücke** from the Hauptplatz to reach the left bank of the Danube. There you can catch a captivating view of the city from the apex of the **Pöstlingberg** (537m). Hike up this small promontory by wandering up Hagenstr. (off Rudolphstr., which is off Hauptstr. near the bridge). From the Hauptplatz, take streetcar #3 to the end of the line, "Bergbahnhof Urfahr." Or hop aboard the **Pöstlingbergbahn** (tel. 28 01 75 77), an old-fashioned trolley car departing from Landgutstr. 19 at the "Bergbahnhof Urfahr" stop, for a gentle, scenic ascent. (Runs daily 5:30am-8pm. One way 20 AS, round-trip 35 AS; children half-price.) The twin-towered **Pöstlingbergkirche,** the city symbol, stands guard over the city from the hill's crest. Younger visitors can enjoy the **Grottenbahn,** a fairy-tale journey into the mountain, accessible from the summit (open May-Sept. daily 9am-4:45pm. Admission 40 AS, children 20 AS). For an inexpensive outing and an olfactory fantasia, visit the **Botanischer Garten,** famed for its somewhat eclectic collection of cacti and orchids. (Open May-Aug. daily 7:30am-7:30pm; April and Sept. 8am-7pm; March and Oct. 8am-6pm; Nov.-Feb. 8am-5pm. Admission 10 AS, under 18 free.)

Linz is also proudly equipped with many intriguing museums. The **Neue Galerie,** Blütenstr. 15 (tel. 23 93 36 00), boasts one of Austria's best modern art collections;

it's devoted to the works of 19th- and 20th-century Austrian and German painters such as Klimt, Schiele, Corinth, Kokoschka, and Lieberman. Watch for special exhibitions as well. (Open Mon.-Wed. and Fri. 10am-6pm, Thurs. 10am-10pm. Admission 40 AS, students 20 AS.) The Upper Austrian art collection of the **Francisco Carolinum,** Museumstr. 14 (tel. 77 44 82), has a slightly more classical bent. (Open Tues.-Fri. 9am-6pm, Sat.-Sun. 10am-6pm. Admission 40 AS.) Oberösterreich's unabridged history is diligently recorded in the **Landesmuseum,** Tummelplatz 10 (tel. 27 44 10), housed in the rather spartan **Linzer Schloß** overlooking the Danube from a hill above the Hauptplatz. The museum chronicles the province's Roman, medieval, Renaissance, imperial, and recent past. (Open Tues.-Fri. 9am-5pm, Sat.-Sun. 10am-4pm. Admission 25 AS, for special exhibits 50 AS, students 30 AS.) **Stadtmuseum Nordico,** Bethlehemstr. 7 (tel. 23 93 19 00), presents even *more* local history (open Mon.-Fri. 9am-6pm, Sat.-Sun. 3-5pm; free).

In September, Linz hosts the month-long **Brucknerfest,** when the works of Linz's favorite son are performed (tickets 150-700 AS; standing room 40-50 AS). In June, the annual **Ars Electronica,** a celebration of avant-garde art, floods the city with disaffected pretention. Call the tourist office for further information. A mammoth **Flohmarkt** (flea market) sprawls across the Hauptplatz every Saturday morning.

Near Linz: Mauthausen

Austrians take no pride in Mauthausen, site of a Nazi concentration camp, about half an hour down the Danube from Linz. You can still see the huts in which a prison population of 200,000 toiled, suffered, and perished. The camp's museum does its best to downplay Austria's enthusiasm for Hitler in the late 1930s. Outside the complex, memorials have been erected by countries whose citizens died here. The **Staircase of Death** leads to the stone quarry where the inmates were forced to work until exhaustion; when the prisoners were no longer able to haul the huge granite blocks up the stairs, they were pushed from the staircase onto the rocks below. From Linz, take a train (round-trip 100 AS) or a bus (round-trip 60 AS) to the town of Mauthausen. The camp is a 5km walk away (follow signs to "KZ Mauthausen"). If traveling by car, exit Autobahn A1 (Wien-Linz) at Enns. (Open Feb. to mid-Dec. daily 8am-4pm. Callous admission 15 AS, students 5 AS.)

Near Linz: St. Florian Abbey

Seventeen kilometers from Linz lies the Abbey of St. Florian, Austria's oldest Augustinian monastery. According to legend, Florian was bound to a millstone and thrown in the Enns river. Although he perished, the stone miraculously floated and is today the abbey's cornerstone. The complex owes much of its fame to composer Anton Bruckner, who began his career here as a teacher and organist; his body is interred beneath the organ, allowing him to hear his own music for eternity. The abbey contains the **Altdorfer Gallery,** dedicated to 15th-century artist Albrecht Altdorfer of Regensburg; the altarpieces on display show his commitment to the Danube School's revolutionary painting style. The **Kaiserzimmer** (Imperial apartments) will astound you with their Baroque splendor. Unfortunately, the spectacular church (the only portion of the abbey open to the public without a tour) is currently being restored and won't be completed until 1996, the 100th anniversary of Bruckner's death. To reach the abbey, take bus #2040 or 2042 to "Langerhaus" in St. Florian (round-trip 60 AS). (Obligatory tours April-Oct. daily every hr. 10-11am and 2-4pm. Admission 50 AS, students 40 AS.)

■ Wels

Wels lies on the bank of the river Traun, wedged between Autobahns A1 and A8 in the manufacturing quadrant of Northwestern Austria. Its **Altstadt** is best seen at a slow stroll; pick up the brochure *A Walk Around Town* to supplement the tourist office's more modern **recorded tours** (20 AS, students 10 AS; in English). The immense **Stadtplatz** anchors the center of town, far removed from the surrounding industry. At one end of the square stands the **Lederturm,** the sole remaining city gate; the tape's route leads you through this portal, into the Stadtplatz, and then up to **Burg Wels.** This castle once sheltered Emperor Maximilian I; its space is now devoted to several large **museums** displaying anything and everything Austrian (open Tues.-Fri. 10am-5pm, Sat.-Sun. 10am-noon; free). Remnants of local Roman conquest are on display at the **Stadtmuseum** on Pollheimerstr. The main attraction is the Roman bronze "Venus of Wels," which subtly captures negative space with a twist of her arm (open Mon.-Fri. 10am-5pm, Sat.-Sun. 10am-noon; admission free). For culture of a different sort, seek out the 1994 **Volksfest.** This huge carnival, Austria's largest, is held every other year at the beginning of September. In winter, the **Puppianala** brings an exhibition of sundry puppets to town.

Wels is on the main **train** line through Passau into Germany, only a 15-minute ride from Linz (round-trip 76 AS). The station rents bikes, holds luggage, and provides lockers. Next door is the main **post office** (open Mon.-Fri. 7am-8pm, Sat. 7am-1pm. **Postal code:** A-4600). The **tourist office** (*Tourismusverband*), Stadtplatz 55 (tel. (07242) 434 95; fax 479 04), is 15 minutes from the station; turn right on Bahnhofstr., then left on Roseggerstr., and finally right onto Stadtplatz. (Open Mon.-Fri. 9am-noon and 2-7pm, Sat. 9am-noon; Sept.-June Mon.-Fri. 9am-noon and 2-6pm.)

For the cheapest lodging in town, head to the antiseptic **Jugendherberge (HI),** Dragonerstr. 22 (tel. (07242) 672 84), which houses 50 travelers in two- to six-bed rooms. From the tourist office, walk through the city gate and make a right on Pollheimerstr., then turn left onto Dragonerstr.; the hostel is on the right. (Reception open daily 5-9:30pm; Sept.-June daily 5-7pm. Lockout 9am-noon. 96 AS including sheets, shower, and breakfast. Membership required.) At **Pension Zeilinger,** Ringstr. 29 (tel. 07242) 474 40), the rooms branch off purple hallways; the café and restaurant below are thankfully papered in more muted tones (singles and doubles 200-380 AS). From the Stadtplatz, follow the *Fußgängerzone* to Ringstr.; the *Pension* is to the left, across the street.

The Stadtplatz and its surrounding alleys overflow with reasonable **restaurants.** At the **Welser Suppenstub'n,** Herrengasse 3, you can partake of delectable soups and *Germknödel* (dumplings) for 19-25 AS (open Mon.-Fri. 8:30am-1:30pm and 5-8pm, Sat. 8:30am-1pm).

Near Wels: Kremsmünster and Lambach

Two fabulous Benedictine abbeys orbit Wels 20km from the city center. The **Kremsmünster Abbey** is Austria's oldest, dating from 777 AD (an *auspicious* year for an abbey...). The abbey is famed for its **library** and **Kaisersaal** (Imperial hall), both slathered with the glorious ornamentation of Austria's Baroque heyday. The monks' collection of minerals and exotic animal specimens is on display in the seven-story **Sternwarte.** The **Fischkalter,** five fantastic fish flasks for feeding fasting friars' friends fried flounder, are family favorites. (Ha!) Take bus #2460 to "Kremsmünster Markt" from the train station (one way 40 AS). (Tours of library and Kaisersaal April-Oct. every hr. 10-11am and 2-4pm. 45 AS, students 20 AS. Sternwarte tour May-Oct. 10am, 2pm, and 4pm; 50 AS, students 20 AS. Both tours include the Fischkalter; without joining a tour, you can visit only the central chapel.)

Lambach Abbey, somewhat smaller than the Kremsmünster abbey, is a Baroque treasure; the 11th-century Romanesque frescoes that were uncovered here merit more than a passing glance (church open 9am-noon and 3-5pm; tours at 10, 11am, and 2pm). Though less devoted to divinity, the **Vogelpark Schmiding** is nevertheless divine. Thousands of birds from the world 'round reside in this enormous expanse just outside of town. There is also a **Museum der Begegnung** on the grounds that contains prize-winning anthropological exhibits (open April-Oct. daily 9am-5:30pm; admission 85 AS, students 60 AS). **Buses** run four times per day from the Wels train station. A **Christmas** play is part of the tradition cultivated at the monasteries of Lambach and Kremsmünster.

■ Steyr

At the confluence of the Steyr and Enns river lies **Steyr,** a modern, industrial city with enough tourist savvy to retain its enchanting, Renaissance *Altstadt.* The focal point of the old city is the **Stadtplatz,** packed with the original 15th-century buildings. The bright blue house on the west side of the square was briefly the home of composer Franz Schubert; he wrote the famous *Trout Quintet* here. The 16th-century **Leopoldibrunnen** (Leopold fountain) vies with the Rococo **Rathaus** across the square for ornamental prominence. This town hall was designed by Gotthard Hayberger, Steyr's famous mayor, architect, and Renaissance-man-at-large. The **Bummerlhaus,** at Stadtplatz 32, is another Steyr landmark and a jewel of the late Gothic. The moniker "Bummerlhaus" is derived from the inn's signboard, which resembles a little dog. The former **Dominican Church** (Marienkirche), crammed into the Stadtplatz as well, was born a Gothic building but developed a Baroque face in the early 17th century (open Tues.-Thurs. 10am-3pm; admission free).

The forces of rampant capitalism transformed most of Steyr's beautiful residences into banks or shops, with modern interiors hidden behind the ornate façades; the major exception is the **Innerberger Stadel,** Grünmarkt 26. Now a **museum,** it contains a plethora of puppets, a vast utensil collection, and a gallery with mannequins in military uniforms from around the world (open Tues.-Thurs. 10am-3pm; free). Cross the river to find the **Museum Industrielle Arbeitswelt,** Wehrengrabengasse 7 (tel. (07252) 67351), with hands-on technological exhibitions celebrating the advance of manufacturing and industry. (Open Tues.-Sun. 10am-5pm. Admission 55 AS, students 35 AS, relatives of Marx free.) The **Steyrtal Museumsbahn,** Austria's oldest steam train, wearily choo-choos through the surrounding countryside. (Train runs 3 times per day from Steyrdorf. One way 60 AS, round-trip 110 AS.)

Steyr is most easily reached by **train** from Linz (45 min.; one way 76 AS, round-trip 124 AS); the station rents **bicycles** for further travel (open 6am-7pm). The **tourist office** (*Fremdenverkehrsverband*), in the *Rathaus* at Stadtplatz 27 (tel. (07252) 532 29), provides maps and other information, and exchanges money when the banks are closed. From the train station, walk right on Bahnhofstr. across the bridge, and make a left on Enge Gasse, which leads straight to the Stadtplatz. (Open Mon.-Fri. 8:30am-6pm, Sat. 8:30am-4pm, Sun. 10am-3pm; Oct.-May Mon.-Fri. 8:30am-6pm, Sat. 8:30am-noon, Sun. 10am-3pm). The main **post office** is next to the train station (open Mon.-Fri. 7am-8pm, Sat. 8-11am); there's also a **branch office** at Grünmarkt 1, off the Stadtplatz (open Mon.-Fri. 7:30am-6pm).

Steyr has a dearth of cheap rooms; your best is to go directly to the **Jugendherberge (HI),** Hafnerstr. 14 (tel. (07252) 575 392)—do not pass Go, do not collect 2400 AS. From the train station, turn right on Bahnhofstr., then right on Damberggasse; walk under the bridge, take the second right, then bear right on Biktor-Odler Str., past the **Konsum supermarket** on the left (supermarket open Mon.-Fri. 8am-6pm, Sat. 8am-noon). The hostel provides achingly yellow rooms with sinks; showers are on the hall. (Reception open Mon.-Fri. 3-10pm, Sat.-Sun. 5-10pm. Curfew 10pm. 76 AS, under 19 69 AS. Sheets, shower, and breakfast included.) Or, consider the youth hostel in nearby **Weyer** (1 hr. by train or by bus #2493). The 136-bed **Jugendherberge (HI),** Mühlein 56 (tel. (07447) 284; fax (0732) 781 78 94), is a 20-minute walk from the train station. (Reception open daily 8am-noon and 5-7pm. 116 AS, under 19 98 AS. Breakfast included.)

THE MÜHLVIERTEL

The Mühlviertel plateau, north of Linz between the Danube (Donau) and Bohemia, boasts expanses of wildflowers, venerable stone walls, and medieval representations of earthly and ecclesiastic power. Regional tourist office staff will loudly extol the wondrous quality of "some of the cleanest air on earth," by golly. The region is further characterized by undulating hills and meadows, feldspar, quartz, and—most of all—granite. Since the Ice Age, locals have hewn the native rock into intricate patterns, mostly structures for pagan worship. Along with the population, these granite creations were Christianized in the Middle Ages; crosses today overlay dragons and Earth Mothers. Churches, especially, were constructed of granite, including the famous chapel enclosing the spectacular winged altar of Kefermarkt. Flowing around the granite are mineral-rich waters—considered curative in certain homeopathic circles. Other than granite, agriculture and quiescent woodland walks define the region; major industries, cities, and pollution are entirely foreign. In ages past, salt from the Salzburger Land and iron from Styria were funneled through the region on their way to Germany. Minstrel Dietmar von der Aist hailed from the Mühlviertel; he performed his tuneful task within some of the area's 64 castles.

The **Mühlviertler Weberstraße** extends from Schwarzenberg in northwest Oberösterreich near Germany's Passau to Zwettl, north of Linz. All along the route are various points of textile interest, including handicrafts, museums, artists' studios, and workshops. In the Danube Valley and Bohmer Forest, one of the primary pursuits is fabric production; European apparel has metaphorically donned "Made in Mühlviertel" tags for centuries. The lower Mühlviertel earned itself a reputation in thread production, and the upper Mühlviertel was famed for its linen. Modern techniques can manufacture more than 1000 *Schuß* (stitches) per minute, instead of the 20 or 30 per minute achieved before mechanization. For more information on the **Fabric Trail,** write to: Ferienregion Mühlviertel, A-3030 Linz an der Donau, Blütenstr. 8 (tel. (0732) 23 50 20; fax 21 50).

The region has constructed two other unofficial tourist roads. If you follow the route of the **Gotische Straße,** you'll encounter multitudes of High Gothic architectural wonders, and the **Museum Straße** boasts more *Freilichtmuseum* than you can shake a loom at. These museum villages typically recreate the 15th- and 16th-century peasant lifestyle in a functional hamlet.

Tiny townlings throughout the region offer various tourist attractions. The St. Wolfgang Church in **Kefermarkt** shelters a world-famous wooden altar with thousands of minuscule Gothic points and flourishes. **St. Oswald** sports a forge museum; outside **Lasberg,** you'll find towers with bullet holes from wars of the 17th century. **Königswiesen** has been declared the prettiest village in Oberösterriech *twice*—three times it took second place, and twice it came in third. In **Eibenstein,** the hulking Heidenstein sequence of stairs was carved out of granite. On one step, three drilled holes sit side by side. According to legend, the site, a ceremonial altar, was once either a repository for rainwater or blood, but no one knows whether the holes are intended to collect falling souls (rain) or send them off (blood).

■■■ FREISTADT

The aged city of Freistadt, an ideal base for exploration of the Mühlviertel, was a stronghold of the medieval salt trade—over 200 salt wagons at one time entered town each day. With its well-preserved castle, moat, towers, and ramparts, Freistadt is often likened to Germany's Rothenburg ob der Tauber, another city of ancient wonders. In 1985, Freistadt even received the International Europa Nostra Prize for the finest restoration of a middle-aged *Altstadt*. Join the population in quaffing a tasty local brew (Freistädter Bier)—in 13th-century Freistadt, every male citizen was granted the right to brew and sell his own beer. A subsequent proclamation decreed that beer brewed outside Freistadt was *verboten* within one mile of the city center. Closed-market status was renewed in 1603. Yield to the town's surprising charm; Freistadt has become many an unsuspecting visitor's favorite destination.

Orientation and Practical Information Freistadt, at the juncture of the Jaunitz and Feldiast Rivers, is easily reached from Linz by both train and bus. **Trains** run every two hours from Linz (round-trip 150 AS) and arrive at the *Hauptbahnhof,*

3km outside of town. You can rent bikes and store luggage here. To hoof it to the city center, turn right and walk down the street (it will merge with Leonfeldner Str.); then turn left onto Bahnhofstr. (which becomes Brauhausstr.), and follow it until the end, at Promenade/Linzer Str. Before you stand the medieval towers of the *innere Stadt.* The main downtown square, the **Hauptplatz,** lies within. Alternatively, catch a bus from the back of the station to "Freistadt Böhmertor" or the main **bus station** at Stifterplatz, where all regional buses stop (16 AS; last departure 7:10pm). Stifterplatz is a short distance from the *innere Stadt*—turn left on Linzer Str. and walk until you see the old city's walls and spires.

The town **tourist office** (*Tourismusbüro*), Hauptplatz 12 (tel. (07942) 29 74), finds accommodations for no fee and provides information about the surrounding Mühlviertel villages (open Mon.-Fri. 9am-noon and 2-5pm, Sat. 9am-noon). The **post office** is at Promenade 11, at the intersection with St. Peter Str. (Open Mon.-Fri. 8am-noon and 2-5:30pm, Sat. 8-10am. **Postal Code:** A-4240.)

Accommodations and Food The *Schloß* looms ominously behind Freistadt's **Jugendherberge (HI),** at Schloßhof 3 (tel. (07942) 43 65). From the tourist office, walk 75m to the red building right off the Hauptplatz. (Open June-Sept. Reception open daily 5-8pm. Lockout 9am-5pm. No curfew, but ask for a key. 70 AS, under 18 50 AS; non-members 20 AS surcharge. Breakfast 30 AS. Sheets 25 AS. Renovations are planned for late 1993, so prices may change.) The amenities at **Privatzimmer Manzenreiter,** Prechtlerstr. 11 (tel. (07942) 39 45), can't be beat; the rooms at this cheery home boast balconies, TVs, private bathrooms, and refrigerators. From the Hauptplatz, walk out the nearest gate, the Böhmertor, and turn left on the footpath between the city wall and the old moat. Follow this path until it ends at Promenade; then cross the street and continue straight into the residential neighborhood. Walk up the unpaved lane that ends at Prechtlerstr., and the pension will be on the right (5 min.). (Singles 170 AS; doubles 150 AS per person; triples 140-150 AS per person. Children 30% less. Breakfast included.)

The most convenient grocery store is **Uni Markt,** 2 Prager Str., at the intersection of Prager Str. (an extension of Promenade) and Froschau (the street behind the Böhmertor side of the *innere Stadt*). (Open Mon.-Thurs. 8am-12:30pm and 2:30-6pm, Fri. 8am-6pm, Sat. 7:30am-noon.) Prowl around Schmiedgasse, off Froschau, and on the Hauptplatz for a variety of restaurant offerings. Enjoy a *tête-à-tête* at **Café Vis à Vis,** Salzgasse 13. It offers local fare, such as *Mühlviertel Bauernsalat mit Suppe* (peasant soup and salad; 60 AS) and Freistädter beer, in a garden crowded with young people (open Mon.-Thurs. 9:30am-midnight, Fri. 9:30am-1am, Sat. 5pm-1am).

Sights and Entertainment Start your tour of Freistadt by clambering around the remarkably well-preserved 14th-century castle. Its tower, the **Bergfried,** houses the **Mühlviertler Heimathaus.** This regional museum displays traditional tools, clothing, and other period pieces, including clocks and playing cards. (Obligatory tours Tues.-Sat. 10am and 2pm, Sun. 10am; Nov.-April Tues.-Fri. 2pm. Admission 10 AS.) Numerous **hiking trails** branch out from Freistadt to amazing Mühlviertel destinations; consider hiking out of town and catching a **bus** back to Freistadt. A large map on the Promenade illustrates local hiking paths; the tourist office provides further advice and information, including free bus schedules and inexpensive hiking maps. Request their free booklet *Mühlviertel—Natur, Kultur, Leben,* which lists the regional sights and festivals.

Freistadt's pride and joy is the Freistädter Brauerei, a community-owned **brewery** in operation since 1777. Located at Promenade 7, the brewery conducts free tours every Wednesday at 2pm between September and May. The tours conclude with **free beer** for everyone (open Mon.-Thurs. 9am-noon and 1-4:30pm, Fri. 7am-noon).

Freistadt is the perfect stepping-stone for excursions into Southern Bohemia and the rest of the **Czech Republic.** The Austrian Railway sells round-trip tickets between Freistadt and Ceské Budejovice (200 AS), but it's cheaper to split up the trip. In Freistadt, purchase a round-trip ticket to "Summerau Grenz," at the Czech border (round-trip 60 AS). When the train makes its first stop in the Czech Republic, tell the conductor that you need to buy a round-trip ticket between there and Ceské Budejovice (48 kčs). Make sure you change money *before leaving* Freistadt so you have crowns to pay the conductor; trying to pay in Austrian currency will cost you dearly. Write your destination on a piece of paper to mitigate the language barrier.

■ Bad Leonfelden

Not far from Freistadt and Linz lies the spa-town of Bad Leonfelden. For years it has quietly persisted as one of Europe's hidden vacation resorts, where ailing folk arrive to recline in the curative mud and water baths. **Bus** #2102 runs from Linz to the Bad Leonfelden "Hauptplatz" (round-trip 58 AS; 1 hr.). The **tourist office,** Ring Str. 200 (tel. (07213) 63 97 or 64 12), distributes information on local events and helps find accommodations for no fee. From the Hauptplatz, walk past the dominating **Pfarrkirche;** the tourist office is behind it on the right, in the Kurverwaltung building. The office sells excellent regional **hiking maps** for 20-100 AS. Just outside is a 24-hour computer with English information about the town and its accommodations. The **post office,** Hauptplatz 2, is at the far end of the main square (open Mon.-Fri. 8am-noon and 2-6pm, Sat. 8-10am; **postal code:** A-4190).

Privatzimmer abound in and around town at 80-200 AS per person. The best deal in the area is Bad Leonfelden's **Talherberge (HI),** Passauerstr. 3 (tel. (07213) 81 09), a compact hostel with 44 beds. (84 AS, under 18 50 AS. Sheets 45 AS. Call ahead.) Although restaurant options are limited, most are reasonably priced; stroll around the Hauptplatz to find one that suits your taste. If nothing tickles your fancy, make your own meal with goods from the **Billa supermarket,** at Hauptplatz 14 (open Mon.-Thurs. 7:30am-6:30pm, Fri. 7:30am-8pm, Sat. 7:30am-1pm).

■ Haslach an der Mühl

Haslach an der Mühl perches upon a hill just a few kilometers south of the Czech border. This medieval town boasts an original city gate and a **Pfarrkirche** with an overwhelming tower and a few museums. Most everything in Haslach takes place in the **Marktplatz** at the center of town. The **Heimatmuseum,** in the **Stadtturm,** exhibits local artifacts (open Wed. and Sun.; tours at 10am and 11am). Adjacent to the intact city gate is the **Kaufmannsmuseum,** Windgasse 17, where you can peruse a medieval selection of bartered goods (open Wed.-Sun. 9am-noon and 2-5pm). Perhaps the most interesting structure is the **Webereimuseum,** in the Kirchenplatz, which chronicles the town's ancient weaving tradition; here you can see demonstrations on 200-year-old looms (open daily 9am-noon). (Admission to each museum 25 AS, students 20 AS, children 10 AS.)

The town's **tourist office** (*Fremdenverkehrsbüro*), Marktplatz 45 (tel. (07289) 717 50 or 717 56), finds rooms for no fee, hands out brochures on the local attractions, and sells 20 AS maps of regional hiking trails (open Mon.-Sat. 9:30-11:30am). If the office is closed, try the neighborhood *Gemeindeamt* (open Mon. and Thurs. 8am-noon and 1-6pm, Wed. and Fri. 8am-1pm). The **post office,** Marktplatz 44, is next door. (Open Mon.-Fri. 7:30am-noon and 2-5pm, Sat. 8-10am. **Postal code:** A-4170). Haslach's **Jugendherberge (HI),** Sternwaldstr. 8 (tel. (07289) 712 58), provides dorm rooms with 15-20 beds, right outside the town center. (40 AS, sheets 40 AS. Really. Kitchen facilities available. Call ahead.) *Privatzimmer* in and around Haslach range from 110-200 AS per person. Sample some local cuisine at any *Gaststube* (60-100 AS), or visit the reliable **SPAR supermarket,** Marktplatz 5, for raw materials (open Mon.-Fri. 7:30am-6pm, Sat. 7:30am-noon).

LET'S PACK IT UP

Let's Go Supreme

Innovative hideaway suspension with parallel stay internal frame turns backpack into carry-on suitcase. Includes lumbar support pad, torso and waist adjustment, leather trim, and detachable daypack. Waterproof Cordura nylon, lifetime guarantee, 4400 cu. in. Navy, Green or Black.

A $175

A

B

Let's Go Backpack/Suitcase

Hideaway suspension with internal frame turns backpack into carry-on suitcase. Detachable daypack makes it 3 bags in 1. Waterproof Cordura nylon, lifetime guarantee, 3750 cu. in. Navy, Green or Black.

B $130

Let's Go Backcountry

Full size, slim profile expedition pack designed for the serious trekker. New Airflex suspension. X-frame pack with advanced composite tube suspension. Velcro height adjustment, side compression straps. Detachable hood converts into a fanny pack. Waterproof Cordura nylon, lifetime guarantee. Main compartment 6530 cu. in. extends to 7130 cu. in.

C $210

C

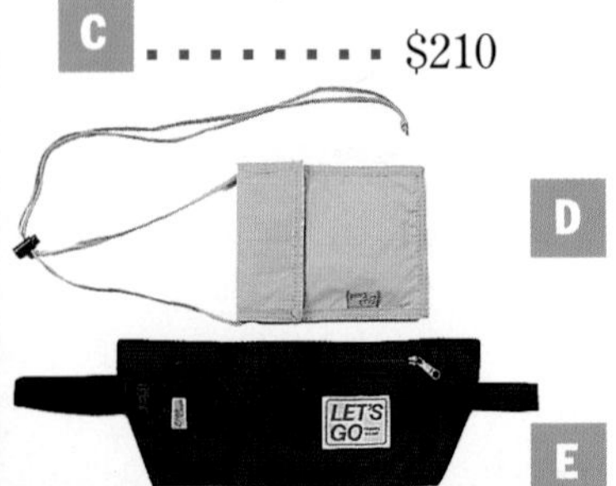

D

E

Undercover NeckPouch

Ripstop nylon with soft Cambrelle back. 3 pockets. 6 x 7''. Lifetime guarantee. Black or Tan.

D $9.95

Undercover WaistPouch

Ripstop nylon with soft Cambrelle back. 2 pockets. 12 x 5'' with adjustable waistband. Lifetime guarantee. Black or Tan.

E $9.95

■ Aigen im Mühlkreis and Schlägl

In the middle of the **Böhmerwald,** these two adorable villages lie side by side. Though sparsely populated, Aigen and Schlägl have a number of attractions for wanderers in need of a sojourn. To reach the twin hamlets, take the daily **bus** from Linz (round-trip 150 AS), or a **train** from the Mühlviertel Bahnhof to the end station (round-trip 140 AS). The **tourist office,** Marktplatz 6 (tel. (07281) 441; fax 80 52), helps find *Privatzimmer* (70-200 AS per person) for no fee. (Open Mon. 8am-noon and 2-6pm, Tues.-Fri. 8:30am-noon and 2-5:30pm, Sat. 8am-noon.) The **post office** is directly across the square. (Open Mon.-Fri. 8am-noon and 1:30-5:30pm, Sat. 8-10am. **Postal Code:** A-4160.) Schlägl's main claim to fame is its marvelous **abbey,** which holds both an art collection and a library (open late May-Sept. daily 10am-5pm; admission 25 AS, students 15 AS). Be sure to inquire about tours of the **Stiftsbrauerei,** one of Austria's most noted abbey breweries. There are also special exhibitions in the Meierhof across the street. Aigen's **Pfarrkirche** is another sight for the ecclesiastic enthusiast; this neo-Gothic, 19th-century edifice was constructed of local granite and brick (open daily). The **Wöbermarkt grocery store** on the Marktplatz supplies worldly nourishment for the home of the soul (open Mon.-Fri. 7:30am-noon and 2:30-6pm, Sat. 7:30am-noon).

■ Ulrichsberg

A few kilometers north of Aigen-Schlägl rests **Ulrichsberg;** its **Moldaublick** provides a spectacular view of the river and surrounding region. The town's **Glasmuseum** documents the long history of glass-blowing in the area; inside is a memorial to favorite son Adalbert Stifter, one of Austria's more distinguished poets. The **tourist office,** Marktplatz 18 (tel. (07288) 63 00), sells tickets to the museum and helps locate local rooms. (Open Mon.-Fri. 9am-noon and 1:30-6pm, Sat. 9am-noon. Museum has identical hours. Admission 25 AS, with guest card 21 AS.) **Buses** run irregularly to Aigen (22 AS) and on to Linz (102 AS) via Rohrbach.

Whenever a summer blue moon (the second full moon in a summer month) strikes Ulrichsberg, town residents break out the colored hosiery for a festival borrowed from Bavarian legend. This **Sondheimernacht** is somehow a permutation of the Pied Piper legend. Apparently, popular exterminator and 16th-century rat-slayer Sondheimer was led out of town by a bewitched bunch of gypsy children and never seen again; the festival, with a recreation of the enchanted procession out of town, is now given in Sondheimer's honor.

THE INNVIERTEL

The Innviertel is an upland region in Oberösterreich just barely over the German border; until 1779, the area belonged to Bavaria. Famed for cattle-rearing and bountiful fruit, the Innviertel is delineated in the north by the Donau, in the west by the Rivers Inn and Salzach, and in the south by the Hausruckwald. From here, many visitors shuttle off along the Danube to Lower Austria (Niederösterreich).

Transportation in the Innviertel is most efficient by **bus;** the towns are largely too small to attract large train routes. The main bus line, #2356, runs regularly from Braunau to Schärding. Bus #2316 runs from Schärding to Waldkirchen, #3218 runs from Schärding to Pyrawang, and #2344 and 2346 run from Braunau to Oberndorf bei Salzburg. A **train** from Passau, Germany, passes hourly through Schärding on its way to Wels; a fork of the same line sporadically passes through Braunau am Inn. A train from Steindorf stops at Braunau every hour.

■ Schärding

Schärding sits on the brink of Bavaria high above the River Inn, minutes south of Passau and just feet from the national border. Most of Schärding's tourism stems from lost foreigners searching for the renowned German border crossing; the tourist office dispenses as much information about highlights in Passau as its own attractions. Schärding's bucolic Stadtplatz is lined with the gorgeous façades of multi-colored medieval domiciles. The **Wassertor** (Water Tower) at the lower end of the Stadtplatz chronicles the water-level of the Inn from 1598 to 1985.

The **train station** (tel. (07712) 305 33 85) and **Austria Radreisen,** Holzinger Str. 546 (tel. (07712) 55 11) **rent bicycles;** *Bahnhof* rates are slightly better. From the train station, take the footpath indicated by the "*Zentrum*" sign until you come to a road; a small tower will be on your left. Turn right, and walk until you arrive at the elegant Linzer Tor; the Stadtplatz is just through the gate. The **post office** is on Linzer Str., just before the Linzer Tor (open Mon.-Fri. 8am-noon and 2-6pm, Sat. 8-10am). Schärding's **tourist office,** in the *Rathaus* (tel. (07712) 43 00; fax 43 20), offers cycling maps and a free map of the village. Ask for information on the boat tours along the Inn. (Open Mon.-Fri. 8:30am-noon and 1:30-6pm, Sat. 9am-noon.) The tourist office cannot reserve a room for you, but you should have no problem finding one among the few accommodations in town.

Schärding presents no hostel or camping options, but the local hotels charge reasonable rates. Try the **Café-Weinstube beim Lachinger,** Silberzeile 13 on the Obere Stadtplatz (tel. (07712) 22 68). Though it sounds like a vineyard, the 10 proffered beds are comfortable, clean and tasteful. (Reception open until midnight. Singles with shower 265 AS, doubles with shower 490 AS. Breakfast included. Call ahead.) **Gasthof Hager,** Passauer Str. 15 (tel. (07712) 32 29), lies a tad closer to the train station. (Reception open daily 1-11pm. Singles 225 AS, doubles 420 AS, triples 500 AS.) A weekly **market** sprouts up on the Hauptplatz on Thursday mornings. A **farmers' market** on the Oberer Stadtplatz and a **flea market** on the Unterer Stadtplatz both arrive the first Saturday of each month.

■ Braunau am Inn

Adolf Schicklgruber was born in 1889 in a little yellow house at Salzburger Vorstadt 10; ever since, Braunau has been trying to live down its status as the birthplace of the *Führer.* Braunau is a quiet, modest, unassuming town similar to many other villages of the region—rows of vivid technicolor Baroque façades and worn pieces of the former city wall. The town of **Simbach** in Bavaria, Germany, lies directly across the beautiful, muddy waters of the River Inn; the juxtaposition indicates Braunau's allegiance to Bavaria until the late-18th century. The town's visual highlight, the **Stadtpfarrkirche St. Stephan,** seemingly wipes the sky with its tower. The town's inhabitants were rooting for three digits, but the tower only rises 99m; legend has it that half of the village went bankrupt as a result of the office pools. The Stadtplatz, Braunau's main square, is bordered by the river and the **Torturm** (gate tower), formerly part of the city wall.

Most of the tourism through this area consists of *Radtourismus,* or bicycle tourism. Braunau's **tourist office,** in the Volksbank, Stadtplatz 9 (tel. (07722) 26 44, fax 43 95), offers a ton of cycling maps, a prospectus of accommodations, and piles of information about the surrounding countryside. (Open Mon.-Fri. 9am-noon and 2:30-5:30pm, Sat. 9am-noon; Nov.-March Mon.-Sat. 9am-noon.) If you're not traveling with a bicycle, rent one at the town **train station.** Adjoining the church is the **youth hostel,** Palmplatz 8 (tel. (07722) 2321 or 281). The friendly proprietor can fix you up in simple, clean rooms. (Reception open 6pm-curfew, which is 11pm, Nov.-April 10pm. 92 AS, under 19 70 AS. Non-members add 10 AS surcharge. Breakfast 25 AS. In winter, you *must* notify the proprietor (tel. (07722) 247) the day before you arrive; otherwise, the hostel may be closed.) **Campingplatz Braunau am Inn** is located right off the highway (tel. (07722) 7357 or 372 45). Walk down Stadtplatz away from the river; it becomes Salzburger Vorstadt and finally Salzburger Str. After a few minutes, look for "Freizeitzentrum Camping" signs on the right side of the road. (Reception 8am-1pm and 3-10pm. 20 AS, students half-price. Checkout 8am-1pm. 8 min. of hot shower 12 AS. Park is closed 10pm-7am.)

A weekly **market** appears on the Stadtplatz on Wednesday mornings, and a **farmers' market** arrives every other Friday in the Festhalle Ausstellungsgelände on the Festwiese. From late-September to mid-October, Braunau celebrates its own version of Munich's Oktoberfest. Quaff a beer and munch on a pretzel as you watch *Lederhosen*-clad Americans attempt to find the Braunau Hofbräuhaus....

PYHRN-EISENWURZ

The Pyhrn-Eisenwurz range is situated in southeast Oberösterreich, just skimming the border of northwest Styria. Its mountains stretch west from the River Enns to the River Steyr. The Pyhrn-Eisenwurz are graced with some super lakes, including the petite Gleinker See between Spital am Pyhrn and Hinterstoder. This range melds into the Ennstaler Alpen, near Admont in the Ennstal. A **train** runs from Schladming via Admont to Steyr; another train runs from Graz to Linz via Spital am Pyhrn and Hinterstoder. Private **bus** #8183 scurries between Spital am Pyhrn and Hinterstoder five times per day, and #2453 travels from Wels to Hinterstoder three times per day.

■ Hinterstoder and Spital am Pyhrn

The Steyr river cuts through **Hinterstoder** and then the base of the **Totes Gebirge** (Dead Mountains) range to the southwest. Reaching the town is relatively easy; Bundesstraße 138 sprints by just a few kilometers from the city limits. Furthermore, Hinterstoder's train station lies on the main route running south from Linz; city buses shuttle from the train station to the town center (one way 32 AS).

The **tourist office** (*Verkehrsbüro*; tel. (07564) 52 63) provides information on local mountain sports, including cable car prices and ski rentals (open Mon.-Fri. 8am-5:30pm, Sat. 8am-noon; Sept. to mid-June Mon.-Fri. 8am-noon and 2-5pm). The **Jugendherberge (HI),** Mitterstoder 137 (tel. (07564) 52 27), is a large facility with roomy dorms at bargain prices. (Reception open daily 8am-noon and 2-5pm. 113 AS, under 19 95 AS. Breakfast included; lunch and dinner available. Membership required.) Another option is **Haus Lemmerer,** Mitterstoder 134 (tel. (07564) 52 56), with quiet, spacious rooms down the road from the hostel. (130 AS per person; 150 AS for only 1 night. Showers 15 AS. Breakfast included.) Reasonable restaurants lie along the main road, flanking a **SPAR supermarket** (open Mon.-Fri. 7:30am-noon and 2:30-6pm, Sat. 7:30am-noon).

Spital am Pyhrn waits just a hop, skip, and jump from Hinterstoder (53 AS by bus). It lies in a lush vale under the intimidating peaks of the Bosruck (2009m), Pyhrgas (2244m), and Warscheneck (2387m) mountains. The main attraction is the **Stiftskirche,** a large Baroque church with a brilliant façade and altar, which seems somewhat out of place in this tiny hamlet. Due to recent thefts, the church no longer holds regular visiting hours; call the tourist office for details. Next door is the **Felsbildermuseum** (tel. (07563) 202 or 249). Three mind-boggling rooms exhibit the area's 10,000-year-old cave paintings and carvings. Take a moment to study the wood doors and engraved locks (open Wed.-Sat. 9-11:30am; admission 30 AS). **Skiing** on the nearby Wurzeralm costs 270 AS per day and 1425 AS per week.

The **tourist office** (*Tourismusverband*) in Spital am Pyhrn (tel. (07563) 249 or 7007; fax 255 83) distributes every imaginable brochure on the region. (Open Mon.-Fri. 8am-noon and 2-5pm, Sat. 8am-noon; Sept.-May Mon.-Fri. 8am-noon and 2-5pm.) **Haus Stoderegger** (tel. (07563) 406) has clean, cozy rooms, some with views of the surrounding mountain range. From the center of town, walk about 15 min. up

Hauptstr.; the house is on the left. (135-165 AS per person, 165-190 AS for only 1 night. Breakfast included.)

The **post offices** in both Hinterstoder and Spital am Pyrhn are unable to exchange traveler's checks, and the banks charge hefty commissions; make sure you have enough cash *before* you arrive in town.

■ Admont

Admont, "the gateway to the Gesäuse," is situated just over the Styrian border on the River Enns. Benedictine monks first built an abbey here in the 11th century; although fire has repeatedly ravaged the complex, the stubborn friars have refused to let the church go up in smoke. The current **Benediktinerstift** was completed in the mid-18th century. The highlight is the **library,** the largest monastery collection in the world, with over 250,000 volumes. Sixty-eight gilded **busts** of philosophers, poets, and historians glare disdainfully from the walls at the intellectually inferior. Try to find the hidden stairways that lead to the upper balconies—the sleuthing-impaired should ask a guide for assistance. The same building holds the **Schatzkammermuseum,** which contains the Admont artifacts, and a **natural history museum,** full of bottled snakes, lizards, and other assorted animalia. (Library and museums open May-Sept. daily 10am-1pm and 2-5pm; April and Oct. daily 10am-noon and 2-4pm; Nov.-March Tues.-Sun. 11am-noon and 2-3pm. Combined admission to all three 30 AS, students 15 AS.) Also in the complex is the **Heimatmuseum,** which displays local historical paraphernalia. (Open daily 9:30am-noon and 1-4:30pm. Admission 15 AS, children 6 AS.) The abbey isn't entirely secular, however; take a moment to stroll by the neo-Gothic **church** in the middle of the grounds (free).

The Admont **tourist office** (*Fremdenverkehrsbüro*; tel. (03613) 21 64; fax 36 48) will track down a room for no fee. To reach the tourist office from the train station, turn left on Bahnhofstr., and take the second right; the office is five minutes down, on the left. (Open Mon.-Fri. 8am-noon and 2-6pm, Sat. 8am-noon; Sept.-May Mon.-Fri. 8am-noon and 2-6pm.) The **Jugendherberge** in **Schloß Röthelstein** (tel. (03613) 24 32) proclaims itself "Europe's most beautiful youth hostel"; its palatial rooms await an hour's walk from Admont. From the station, turn left on Bahnhofstr., make another left on Paradiesstr., and follow the signs to the Arthurian castle on the hill; that's the hostel—no kidding (195-310 AS per person, breakfast included). Rooms closer to the town center run 180-250 AS; ask at the tourist office for assistance. Admont's **post office** is on the corner of Bahnhofstr. and Hauptstr. (open Mon.-Fri. 8am-noon and 2-5pm, Sat. 8-10am). **Buses** depart from in front of the office; **trains** run to Selzthal, the regional hub (every 1-2 hr.; 32 AS).

Southeast Austria

Austria's harshest Alpine peaks guard the Italian and Slovenian borders from the southern regions of Carinthia (Kärnten) and East Tyrol (Osttirol). **Carinthia** is built upon layers of history—medieval, Roman, Celtic, and beyond. Italian architecture, a sunny climate, and a distinctly mellow atmosphere give the province a somewhat Mediterranean feel. The palpable warmth of the local population, however, can be deceiving. Four percent of the state's inhabitants are ethnic Slovenes (Austria's only significant national minority), and the xenophobic Carinthian Homeland Movement makes no secret of its desire to send them packing. In the "Town-Sign War" of the 1970s, for example, the Slovenes lobbied for bilingual street signs (in both German and Slovene); the measure was soundly defeated by the Austrian majority. Tensions remain heated in discussions of minority affairs. The former minister-president of the provincial government was Jörg Haider, mercurial leader of the arch-conservative Freedom Party (Freiheitliche Partei Österreichs, or simply FPÖ), which still controls the Carinthian legislature. Haider's inflammatory attacks on foreign workers, such as his remark, "They had a proper employment policy in the Third Reich," led the national government to take the unprecedented step of requesting his resignation. Faced with extreme pressure from the Liberale Internationale, an amorphous political organization of European liberals, Haider complied; his successor, Zernato, now holds the office.

Encompassing the provinces of **Styria** (Steiermark) and **Burgenland,** southeastern Austria's rolling Alpine foothills and gentle valleys are topographically unexciting by Austrian standards—which explains the relative dearth of tourists. The countryside in Burgenland is drenched with endless fields of sunflowers, rows of yellow faces all oriented in the same direction. The vineyard-drenched land belonged to Hungary until 1918, and Magyar influence is still ubiquitous in food, architecture, and dress; chauvinistic Austrian nationalists scorn the local residents as country bumpkins. *Burgenland* means "fortress land" in German, and dozens of these edifices are strung out along the hillsides—remnants of medieval Europe's first line of defense against the Ottoman Turks across the eastern frontier. Styria's rich deposits of iron ore made it one of Europe's first centers of primitive industry, and the region's wealth spilled over into the glorious gold and stone of Graz, its capital.

■■■ KLAGENFURT

At the crossroads of a north-south and an east-west trade route, the embryonic settlement of Klagenfurt was founded on the River Glan in 1199. By the 13th century, walls and towers protected the tiny town—but not well enough. Earthquakes and fires repeatedly sacked the city, and, consequently, the construction of wooden houses became *verboten.* The moratorium on organic materials, however, in no way affected the local lifestyle; Klagenfurt's warm, southern European atmosphere pleasantly reflects its geographical and cultural proximity to Italy, just 60km to the south. Locals enjoy life's simple pleasures; stroll casually around the palette of outdoor cafés, Italian Renaissance courtyards, wrought iron tracery, and tree-lined avenues, all framed by magnificent Alpine peaks. The capital of Carinthia since 1518, Klagenfurt's suburbs include the chic banks of the **Wörther See,** somewhat ambiguously billed as the "Austrian Riviera."

ORIENTATION AND PRACTICAL INFORMATION

Klagenfurt is the southernmost provincial capital in Austria and is easily accessible by planes, trains, and automobiles; Autobahn A2 and three major InterCity rail lines run right through town. The center of the city is a three-ring circus of squares: **Alter Platz, Neuer Platz,** and **Heiligengeistplatz,** the town's bus center. Four streets (St. Veiter Ring to the north, Völkermarkter Ring to the east, Viktringer Ring to the south, and Villacher Ring to the west), comprising the **Ring,** enclose Neuer Platz; the quadrangle created circumscribes the downtown. The **Lendkanal,** a narrow waterway leading from the snake-shaped Wörther See to the city center, ends just to the west of Villacher Ring.

Tourist Office: Gäste Information (tel. 53 72 22; fax 53 72 95), on the first floor of the *Rathaus* in the Neuer Platz. The English-speaking staff supplies visitors with colorful brochures and helps find rooms for no fee. Ask for the *Gästeinformation* brochure; this English pamphlet describes the complete history of Klagenfurt. From the station, walk down Bahnhofstr. and turn left onto Paradeisergasse, which opens into Neuer Platz. Open Mon.-Fri. 8am-8pm, Sat.-Sun. 10am-5pm; Nov.-April Mon.-Fri. 8am-5pm. **Branch office** (tel. 236 51) outside Minimundus. Open mid-May to mid-Sept. daily 9am-8pm.

Currency Exchange: Best rates at the train station post office branch; exchange desk open 24 hrs.

American Express: In **Reisebüro Springer,** Wiesbadener Str. 1 (tel. 38 70; fax 38 70 566). Right off the Neuer Platz, around the right-hand corner of the *Rathaus.* Holds mail and offers travel packages for clients. Address mail as follows: "Jonathan Henry BECKER, Client Letter Service, Reisebüro Springer, Wiesbadener Str. 1, A-9020 Klagenfurt, Austria." No financial services. Open Mon.-Fri. 8:30am-12:30pm and 2:30-6pm, Sat. 9am-noon.

Post Office: Main post office, Pernhartgasse 7 (tel. 55 65 50). Open Mon.-Fri. 7:30am-8pm and Sat. 7:30am-1pm. **Train station branch,** Bahnhofplatz 5. Open 24 hrs. **Postal Code:** A-9020.

Telephones: Phone centers are at the main post office and its train station branch. **City Code:** 0463.

Flights: Klagenfurt-Wörthersee Airport (tel. 41 50 00). From the train station, take bus A to the end station at "Annabichl." Switch to bus F (direction: "Walddorf") and disembark at "Flughafen."

Trains: Hauptbahnhof (tel. 17 17), at the intersection of Südbahngürtel and Bahnhofstr. From the train station, walk up Bahnhofstr., past Viktringer Ring, until Paradeisergasse. Turn left, and walk three blocks. Neuer Platz will be on your left (15 min.). Lockers (20 AS), luggage storage, and bike rental available. Open 24 hrs. The **Ostbahnhof,** at the intersection of Mießtalerstr. and Rudolfsbahngürtel, is for shipping only.

Buses: Across the street from the train station. BundesBus routes to most destinations in Carinthia (Villach 64 AS, Pörtschach 32 AS, St. Veit 46 AS, Friesach 78 AS, and Graz 120 AS). Ticket window (tel. 581 10) open Mon.-Fri. 7am-12:15pm and 2-6pm, Sat. 7am-1:15pm, Sun. 8am-noon and 12:30-4pm.

Local Public Transportation: Klagenfurt boasts a punctual and comprehensive bus system. Single fare rides cost 10 AS, rides requiring transfers 15 AS. Buy individual tickets or a 24-hr. pass (36 AS) from the driver. *Tabak* kiosks sell blocks of tickets at reduced rates (5 single tickets for 35 AS; 5 transfer tickets for 60 AS). Pick up a *Fahrplan*, the simple guide delineating route maps and schedules, at the tourist office. Remember to stamp your ticket when entering the bus; violators face a hefty 400 AS fine.

Bike Rental: At the *Hauptbahnhof* or at **Fahrradies,** Fischlstr. 61H (tel. 361 87), where bikes cost 80 AS per day. Open Mon.-Thurs. 8am-4pm and Fri. 8am-noon. The tourist office distributes the pamphlets *Radwege-Netz* and *Radwandern*; both detail bike paths in the area.

Pharmacy: Pharmacies dot the entire city. Try **Landschafts-Apotheke,** Alter Platz 32, or **Obir-Apotheke,** Baumbachplatz 21.

Medical Assistance: Klagenfurt Krankenhaus, St.-Veiter-Str. 47 (tel. 53 80).

Emergency: tel. 133; **ambulance:** tel. 144; **emergency doctor:** tel. 141; **Police:** tel. 533 30.

ACCOMMODATIONS AND CAMPING

Because of Klagenfurt's proximity to the Wörther See's beaches, the supply of available accommodations dries up in the heat of summer; call ahead. There is *some* compensation for the sudden summer dearth; one student dormitory converts to a makeshift youth hostel during July and August. The tourist office will help sniff out accommodations for no fee; it also distributes two helpful pamphlets: *Stadtplan und Zimmernachweis der Landeshauptstadt Klagenfurt* and *Camping*. If you're staying in a hotel or *Pension,* ask for the *Gästepass* (guest card), which entitles you to a free city guide and discounts at specified cafes, museums, and other area attractions.

Jugendherberge Klagenfurt, at the corner of Universitätsstr. and Neckheimgasse (tel. 23 00 20; fax 23 00 20 20), by the university and the *wunderbar* attractions of the Wörther See. From the main train station, take bus A (direction: "Annabichl") to "Heiligengeistplatz." Switch to bus S, and disembark at "Neckheimgasse." Last bus A from the train station leaves at 11:24pm; last bus S from Heiligengeistplatz departs at 11:30pm. There *is* time to make the connection—bus A hits Heiligengeistplatz at 11:28pm; hurry! The spic-and-span space station of a hostel lies 2 min. from the bus stop. Cross busy Villacher Str., walk down Neckheimgasse, and look for a bubble-gum pink building. Buses departing at 22 min. past the hour don't stop at "Neckheimgasse"; in this case get off at "Minimundus," cross Villacher Str., turn left, and then veer right at Neckheimgasse (8 min.). The hostel houses 144 in spacious quads (each with toilet and shower) splashed with a barrage of playground reds, greens, and purples. Reception open daily 7-9am and 5-10pm. Flexible curfew 10pm (ask for a key, attached to a 200 AS deposit). 160 AS. Non-members 30 AS surcharge. Breakfast and sheets included. Dinners 50 AS.

Jugendgästehaus Kolping, Enzenbergstr. 26 (tel. 569 65; fax 569 65 32). From the station, head down Bahnhofstr., turn right at Viktringer Ring, and bear left at Enzenbergstraße (10 min.). Ascetic accommodations for 230 AS; the only decoration is a crucifix on each wall. Open June 10-Sept. 10. Singles with shower 210 AS, under 16 190 AS. Doubles and triples with shower 170 AS per person, under 16 150 AS. 20 AS surcharge for a one-night stay. Breakfast included.

Hotel Liebetegger, Völkermarkter Str. 8 (tel. 569 35). From Neuer Platz, follow Burggasse across Salmstr. and onto Völkermarkter Str. Small but adequate rooms.

Reception on the 2nd floor. Singles 220-400 AS. Doubles 175-350 AS per person. Triples 180-350 AS per person. Breakfast 50 AS.

Klagenfurt-Wörthersee Camping-Strandbad (tel. 211 69; fax 211 69 93; Oct.-May fax 327 61 85). At the Metnitzstrand right off Universitätsstr. From the *Hauptbahnhof,* take bus A to the end station at "Heiligengeistplatz," then bus S to the end station "Strandbad Klagenfurter See." Turn left immediately upon disembarking, and walk for 2 min.; the campsite will be on the left. A whopping 428 campsites on the brink of the Wörther See. Grocery store, miniature golf, and beach on the grounds. From May to mid-June and late-Aug. to Sept. 50 AS per person, ages 3-14 25 AS; 100 AS per place; motorcycles 20 AS. From mid-June to late-Aug. 80 AS per person, ages 3-14 40 AS. Over 18, 12 AS tax year-round. Showers and beach entry included.

FOOD

In this city of sun and *See,* cafés appear around almost every corner. **Neuer Platz**, **Kardinalplatz**, and **Burggasse** are particularly blessed. The tourist office brochure *Klagenfurts Küchen und Keller* gives addresses, phone numbers, and opening hours of cafés, restaurants, clubs, and bars in and around town.

Zuckerbäckerei-Café-Konditorei-Imbisse D. Todor, Feldmarschall-Conrad-Platz 6. Now *that's* a mouthful. Furnished with amusingly colorful, striped furniture, this everything-in-one café is a quick and inexpensive haven for any meal. Chow down on *Salatschüssel* (35-50 AS) and *Schinken-Käse Toast* (30 AS) in the sun-drenched, ivy-enclosed *Gastgarten* out back. Also serves ice cream (7 AS per scoop), candy, and freshly baked goods (*Sachertorte* 25 AS). Open Mon.-Fri. 7am-9pm, Sat. 7am-noon.

Restaurant Kanzian mit Schanigarten, Kardinalplatz 2, concocts sizable portions of Austrian and Italian dishes. Mix cultural metaphors with *Gulasch con Gnocchi* (75 AS) or negate weeks worth of *Wurst* with the truly massive *Große Salatschüssel mit Dressing* (58 AS). Open Mon.-Sat. 11am-11pm.

Rathausstüberl, Pfarrplatz 8, on a hidden cobblestone street right by the Pfarrkirche. Freshly prepared Carinthian specialties at attractively low prices. *Käsnudel mit grünem Salat* (cheese and potato dumplings with green salad) 74 AS; *Ritshert* (barley and vegetable stew with smoked pork) 50 AS. Sup on the outdoor terrace on balmy summer evenings. English menus available. Open Mon.-Fri. 8am-midnight, Sat. 9am-2pm and 7pm-2am.

Wienerwald, Wienergasse 10, at the conjunction of Wienergasse and Heuplatz. Fast food, festive atmosphere. ½-chicken (70 AS), *Karfiol mit Käsesause* (cauliflower with cheese sauce) 68 AS. Go inside and choose your chicken from amongst several spinning in a glass-door oven. Open daily 10am-11:30pm.

Markets

Every Thursday and Saturday from 8am-noon, compact **Benediktinerplatz** is filled with a barrage of rickety wooden stands showcasing fresh fruits and vegetables. Supermarkets are just as easy to spot.

SPAR Markt, just off Heiligengeistplatz on Herman Gasse. Open Mon.-Fri. 8am-6:30pm, Sat. 8am-1pm.

Konsum, next to the main bus terminal at Bahnhofplatz 1. Open Mon.-Fri. 8am-6pm, Sat. 8am-noon. There's another branch directly behind the hostel, on Universitätsstr. Open Mon.-Fri. 8am-12:30pm and 2:30-6pm, Sat. 8am-noon.

Billa, Priesterhausgasse 8, 2 min. from the Alter Platz. Open Mon.-Thurs. 7:30am-6:30pm, Fri. 7:30am-8pm, Sat. 7am-1pm).

Biokost, Wiesbadener Str. 3. A health-food market right off Neuer Platz. Open Mon.-Fri. 7:30am-6:30pm, Sat. 7am-12:30pm.

SIGHTS AND ENTERTAINMENT

A tour of Klagenfurt should begin with a walk through the city's *Altstadt;* the tourist office pamphlet *A Walk Round Klagenfurt's Old Town* will help you navigate the journey. (Free guided tours leave Mon.-Sat. at 10am from the front of the *Rathaus.*) Buildings in this part of town display a strange amalgam of architectural styles: Biedermeier, Italian Renaissance, Mannerist, Baroque, and Jugendstil rudely abut one another. At the edge of the **Alter Platz** stands the 16th-century **Landhaus,** originally an arsenal and later the seat of the provincial diet. Its symmetrical towers, staircases, and flanking projections nobly create a courtyard sprinkled with the banana-yellow umbrellas of numerous outdoor cafés. The flourishes of the interior more truly deserve accolades; 665 brilliant coats of arms (it took artist Johann Ferdinand Fromiller nearly 20 years to complete them all) blanket the walls. Don't let the ceiling's "rounded" edges fool you—the room is perfectly rectangular. (Open April-Sept. Mon.-Fri. 9am-5pm. Admission 10 AS, students 5 AS.)

A brisk stroll through Kramergasse, one of the oldest streets in Klagenfurt, leads directly to the **Neuer Platz.** Here, merry-go-rounds for the kids, cafés for adults, and soapboxes for bleeding-heart university students are all readily available in a torrent of motion and activity. The 60-ton half-lizard, half-serpent, half-ugly creature spitting water in the direction of the **Maria-Theresa Monument** is the **Lindwurm,** Klagenfurt's heraldic beast. Legend has it that this virgin-usurping monster once terrorized the Wörther See area and prevented the settlers from draining the marshes. Then along came an archetypal dead-white-male hero, generically named Hercules, who slayed the behemoth by craftily lodging a barbed hook in the throat of a sacrificial cow. Today, the Lindwurm still terrorizes Klagenfurt, albeit more subtly—those damned Puff-the-Magic-Dragon-esque stuffed animals are *everywhere*.

Klagenfurt is home to enlightened 19th-century despot Franz Josef's favorite museum, the **Landesmuseum,** Museumgasse 2 (tel. 305 52). The former Habsburg emperor's most cherished exhibit was **Prohaska,** a stuffed dog that—prior to stuffing—served as the regimental mascot and faithful friend of Field Marshall Radetsky; other guests prefer the Celtic and Roman artifacts, 18th-century musical instruments, or wooly mammoth tusks. Also on display is the **Lindwurmschädel,** a fossilized rhinoceros skull, discovered in 1335, that served three centuries later as the inspiration for the Lindwurm statue in the Neuer Platz. (Museum open Tues.-Sat. 9am-4pm, Sun. 10am-1pm; Mon. during inclement weather—call 30 552. Admission 20 AS, with guest card 15 AS, children 10 AS, students free.) The **Kärntner Landesgalerie,** at Burggasse 8, is home to a fine collection of early 20th-century Expressionist artworks. (Open Mon.-Fri. 9am-6pm, Sat.-Sun. 10am-noon. Admission 20 AS, children 5 AS, students free.) The **Diözesanmuseum,** adjacent to the elaborate, stucco, 16th-century **Dom,** is devoted to Carinthian sacred art; among the holdings is the famous stained-glass **Magdalenenscheibe** and a medieval woodcarver's bust of God. (Open mid-June to mid-Sept. Mon.-Sat. 10am-noon and 3-5pm; May to mid-June and mid-Sept. to mid-Oct. Mon.-Sat. 10am-noon. Admission 20 AS, seniors 15 AS, students 5 AS.) The **Robert Musil Museum,** Bahnhofstr. 50, honors the work of its namesake, Austria's most famous modern bard, with an archive of his writings. Next door is the **Ingeborg Bachmann Museum,** a shrine to another 20th-century Austrian writer (both museums open Mon.-Fri. 10am-2pm).

Klagenfurt's most shameless concession to tourist *Kitsch* is the **Minimundus** park, Villacherstr. 241 (tel. 21 94). Here you can stroll among such renowned monuments as the Eiffel Tower, St. Peter's Basilica, and the Leaning Tower of Pisa—all as 1:25 scale models. The park is actually entertaining, despite the prevalence of camera-toting, finger-pointing tourists; try to visit at night, when an outstanding lighting system illuminates the models. From the main train station, take bus A to "Heiligengeistplatz," then switch to bus S (direction: "Strandbad") and disembark at "Minimundus." (Open July-Aug. Sun.-Tues. and Thurs.-Fri. 8:30am-8pm, Wed. and Sat. 8:30am-10pm; May-June and Sept. daily 8:30am-6pm; April and Oct. daily 8:30am-5pm. Admission 70 AS, students 45 AS, ages 6-15 20 AS.) Next door to Minimundus is **Happ's Reptilien Zoo;** its cages enclose a host of the Lindenwurm's descendants. The puff adder can kill five grown men with a single dose of its lethal injection, while the *Phoneutria Fera* (an arachnid) can do the same to 1000 mice. Every Saturday, there's a piranha and crocodile show; every Sunday, the snakes are let loose in the garden. (Open daily 8am-6pm; Oct.-April daily 8am-5pm. Admission 55 AS, students 35 AS, children 25 AS.)

To maximize your entertainment *Schilling,* read the tourist office's *Veranstaltung-Kalender* (Calendar of Events) and *More than History: Program of Events* (both available in English). The tourist office also distributes brochures listing concerts, gallery shows, museum exhibits, and plays, including the cabaret performances in the **Theater im Landhauskeller** throughout July and August. Tickets are available through **Reisebüro Springer** (tel. 387 05 55; 120 AS, students 80 AS; performances in German). The best of Klagenfurt's limited nightlife can be found in the pubs of the **Pfarrplatz.**

On a melting hot spring or summer day, you may choose to skip the *Altstadt* altogether to join the crowd basking in the sun and lolling in the turquoise water of the nearby **Wörther See.** This water-sport haven is Carinthia's warmest, largest, and most popular lake. The two closest beaches to Klagenfurt are the **Strandbad Klagenfurt-See** and the **Strandbad Maiernigg.** (Both open 8am-8pm. Admission 30 AS, children 12 AS; after 3pm 15 AS, children 5 AS. 50 AS key deposit for a locker.) The former is crowded but easily accessible by public transportation, and only a 20-minute walk from the hostel. From the *Hauptbahnhof,* take bus A to the end station, "Heiligengeistplatz," then bus S to "Strandbad Klagenfurter See." To enjoy the water without getting wet, rent a **rowboat** (24 AS for 30 min.), a **pedal boat** (36 AS), or a **motorboat** (60 AS). Strandbad Maiernigg is far from the noise and fuss of its busier counterpart, but you'll need a car or a bicycle to get there. From downtown, ride along Villacher Str. until it intersects Wörther See Süduferstr., and then follow the signs to "Wörther See Süd." **Stadtwerke Klagenfurt Wörthersee- und Lendkanal-Schiffahrt** (tel. 211 55 0; fax 211 55 15) offers scenic cruises on the lake. The two-hour cruise (round-trip 170 AS) takes you as far as **Velden,** on the opposite shore, and allows stops at designated docks along the way.

Near Klagenfurt: Pörtschach and Maria Wörth

Pörtschach (ferry stop "Landspitz"; one way 65 AS, round-trip 115 AS) is a haven for opulent tourists but a nightmare for budget travelers. This resort town is priced for a king—proletarians beware. Elegant hotels and gaudy souvenir shops litter the **Hauptplatz,** the town's main boulevard. During the summer, entertainers perform regularly in the **open-air pavilion** off Wahlißstr. (tickets 300-550 AS). Consult the **tourist office,** at Hauptstr. 153 (tel. (04272) 23 54 or 28 10 15; fax 37 70), for further information. (Open July-Aug. Mon.-Fri. 8am-6pm, Sat.-Sun. 10am-2pm; May-June and Sept. Mon.-Fri. 8am-5pm, Sat.-Sun. 10am-2pm; Oct.-April Mon.-Fri. 7:30am-noon and 12:30-4pm, Sat. 7:30am-1pm.) Exchange money at the **post office** next door. (Open Mon.-Fri. 8am-noon and 3-7pm, Sat. 8-11am. **Postal code:** A-9210.) There are plenty of prefabricated meals at the **Konsum supermarket** on Hauptplatz 182 (open Mon.-Fri. 8am-7pm, Sat. 8am-6pm, Sun. 9am-noon and 3:30-6:30pm).

Maria Wörth (ferry one way 55 AS, round-trip 95 AS) is home to two gorgeous **churches.** The smaller Romanesque edifice and the larger Gothic structure both date from the 12th-century; note their shimmering reflections in the placid waters below. If you're in the Klagenfurt area on Christmas Eve, be sure to take in the **St. Peter Carolan** in Maria Wörth; this full day of song explodes in sweet harmony just before the Christmas market subsumes the town square.

Near Klagenfurt: Maria Saal

Perched on top of a rocky hill 8km north of Klagenfurt (bus 22 AS, train 16 AS) is the breathtaking Maria Saal, one of the most important churches in the Catholic world. Consecrated in 751, this pilgrimage chapel attracts thousands of ecclesiastic fanatics each year. The brooding Gothic exterior contains etchings and engravings from the Roman era; see if you can find the stone relief of a Roman carriage (3rd-4th century AD) or the heap of medieval tombstones. Fifteenth-century Turkish invaders were stopped by the fortress wall encircling the compound before they could topple the church's twin towers, made from local volcanic rock. Inside, the knowing smile of the high altar's Virgin Mary has intrigued and comforted weary pilgrims since the early Renaissance. Walk five minutes from the church (follow the signs) to the **Kärntner Freilichtmuseum** (tel. (04223) 28 12 or 31 66), an expanse of 32 reconstructed peasant houses; the residents are still engaged in traditional trades, such as shoemaking and blacksmithing. (Open May-Oct. daily 10am-6pm. Admission 50 AS, seniors 40 AS, students 20 AS.)

Near Klagenfurt: Magdalensberg

Nearby Magdalensberg was once a Roman trading post, the oldest Roman settlement north of the Alps. Examine Roman ruins at the **Ausgrabungen** (excavations; tel. (04224) 22 55). The archaeological dig first became intense during the Allied occupation of Austria. Among the ruins are mosaics, temple foundations, public baths, and the vestiges of a villa. (Open May-Oct. daily 8am-6pm. Admission 25 AS, students 20 AS, children 10 AS.)

■■■ ST. VEIT AN DER GLAN

Enveloped by a host of medieval citadels, St. Veit was the ducal seat of Carinthia until 1518, when the capital was moved to Klagenfurt, 20km away. Though its political power has gone the way of acid-wash, St. Veit refuses to relinquish the flavor of ancient influence. The old town is still enclosed by the original 14th-century city wall, but only one turreted tower remains. In this Basteiturm lies the root of the town's insecurity; St. Veit desperately clings to its highfalutin past in an attempt to maintain thriving tourism in the future.

Orientation and Practical Information St. Veit is just 10 minutes by train from the current *Land* capital, Klagenfurt, and is also a hub in the formidable Carinthian bus system. (Bus from Klagenfurt 46 AS; train from Klagenfurt 32 AS, from Villach 92 AS, from Friesach 62 AS.) The town itself sits at a bend in the **Glan** river, which wanders down through the southern Alps past Klagenfurt. St. Veit's ivy-covered wall encloses the medieval *Altstadt*, which is divided by the stately Carinthia House into two main squares: the **Hauptplatz** and the **Unterer Platz.**

The Hauptplatz is vividly described in the *Stadtführer* pamphlet, available from either of St. Veit's two **tourist offices.** Also ask for *Gefürte Wanderungen*, the brochure that contains a description of the free hiking tours that start at the town hall and culminate at nearby castles and Roman ruins (tours mid-June to mid-Sept. Thurs. 8am). For ambitious and independent spirits, the *Radwanderkarte* provides a detailed map of regional bike paths. The tourist office in the *Rathaus* (tel. 55 55 13; fax 55 55 80) is better equipped to answer questions about town events and sights. Bike rental available. (Open June-Aug. Mon.-Fri. 7am-noon and 1-6pm, Sat. 9am-noon; Sept.-May Mon.-Fri. 7am-noon and 1-4pm.) The **branch office,** at Gramstr. 32 (tel. 23 74; fax 23 74 19), distributes brochures and information on all of Carinthia. From the Hauptplatz, take a right onto Bräuhausgasse, pass the Basteiturm, and cross Grabenstr. Look for the mushroom-shaped hut (open Mon.-Fri. 9am-6pm, Sat.-Sun. 9am-2pm). The **post office** is on Ossiacherstr. 6 (open Mon.-Fri. 8am-noon and 2-6pm, Sat. 8-10am). **Telephones** are inside (**City code:** 04212).

Accommodations and Food Lodgings in St. Veit are limited and generally rather expensive. **Gasthof Steirerhof,** Klagenfurter Str. 38, is one of the few exceptions. From the station, take a left onto Bahnhofstr. and another left (before the Seiko watch store) onto Klagenfurter Str.; the Gasthof will be on the right (10 min.). Adequate rooms, but Lilliputian furniture. (160 AS with showers. Breakfast 40 AS. Reception open 8am-10pm.) The restaurant below serves meals at reasonable prices (50-125 AS; open Tues.-Sun. 11am-2pm and 6-8:30pm). **Gästehaus Steiner,** at Friesacher Str. 44 (tel. 32 06), offers but five comfortable doubles. From the train station, head left on Bahnhofstr., turn left onto Kanalgasse, and then make a right onto Friesacher Straße (5 min.). (180 AS per person, 50 AS surcharge first night. Breakfast 40 AS. Reception open 7:30am-8pm. Reservations highly recommended. Free parking.) **St. Veiter Camping** (tel. 51 30) is 30 to 40 minutes from the center of town. From the train station, take a left onto Leopold-Polanz-Str.; at the end turn right onto Völkermarkter, and walk 1km to the "Camping" signs. (High-season 50 AS per person, children 35 AS; sites 50 AS; off-season 40 AS, children 30 AS, sites 40 AS. Over 18 15.50 AS surcharge. Prices include electricity, showers, and access to indoor/outdoor swimming pools.)

Weißes Lamm, in the Arkadenhotel at Unterer Platz 4-5, serves up delicious pizzas (65-120 AS) and lasagna (75 AS) in a romantic setting (open 11:30am-2pm and 6-10pm). **Gasthof Traube,** Oktoberplatz 2, prepares the least expensive food in town. Entrees normally run 68-89 AS, but look for all-you-can-eat spaghetti (49 AS) on Wednesday (open daily 7:30am-2pm). **Café Adele,** in the Hauptplatz, makes a sumptuous plate of spaghetti (56 AS) and delicious *Gulasch* (38 AS). St. Veit's youth flock here for Friday night jam sessions (open Mon.-Fri. 10am-2pm, Sat.-Sun. 6pm-2am). A **Julius Meinl** supermarket stands at Hauptplatz 19 (open Mon.-Thurs. 8am-1pm and 2:30-6pm, Fri. 8am-6pm, Sat. 8am-noon); **Billa** (open Mon.-Fri. 7:30am-6:30pm, Sat. 7am-1pm) and **SPAR Markt** (open Mon.-Fri. 7:30am-6:30pm, Sat. 7:30am-1pm) **supermarkets** lie just across the street from the train station.

Sights and Entertainment Of the two central squares, the **Hauptplatz** is more conducive to rampant tourism; it's graced by well-preserved patrician houses and elegantly wrought fountains encircled by flowers. On Wednesdays from late June to early Sept., you can take in a free concert in the glorious courtyard of the 15th-century **Rathaus.** There, three stories of lily-white arcades surround the delicately manicured gardens and the impressive display of Roman grave monuments. A Roman family's gravestone, from the 2nd century AD, hangs from the facade of the **Verkehrsmuseum** (Traffic and Railway Museum), at Hauptplatz 24. The exhibits inside narrate the progression of Carinthian transportation through a clever assemblage of models, films, and displays. Don't miss the 1939 motorcycles and the ID cards from the early 20th century. (Open daily 9am-noon and 2-6pm. Admission 30 AS, students 20 AS, under 6 free.)

Two noteworthy fountains and a monumental obelisk form a line that bisects the upper Hauptplatz. The **Walther von der Vogelweide Fountain** commemorates a local poet with a mesmerizing series of cascades flowing into an octagonal basin. In the center of the Hauptplatz, the marble **Monument to the Plague,** christened with an impressive representation of the Holy Trinity, celebrates the end of the scourge in 1715. The **Schüsselbrunnen's** basin purportedly came from the Roman city of Virunum; the fountain has the city's symbol—St. Veit stewing in a kettle of boiling water—carved into its pedestal.

Just off the Hauptplatz stands the **Stadtpfarrkirche,** a triple-aisled Romanesque Church with Celtic stag anglers guarding the main entrance. Next door is the **charnel house,** a Roman circular building with two floors from the 12th or 13th century. Now used as a war memorial, the odd-looking structure functioned as the town's skeleton stockpile when space became scarce during the plague. At the far end of St. Veit's other square, the **Unterer Platz,** is the **Herzogsburg,** a former ducal castle and arsenal. Inside, the **Stadtmuseum** holds a Reaganesque weapons stash and boasts Austria's second-largest collection of Baroque bull's-eyes. (Open Mon.-Fri. 9am-noon. Other viewing times can be arranged through the tourist office.)

Near St. Veit an der Glan: Hochosterwitz

Eight km southeast of St. Veit and 20km northeast of Klagenfurt looms **Castle Hochosterwitz,** one of Austria's most spectacular attractions. Sprawled atop a lonely, craggy hill, this enchanting castle served for centuries as a defensive bulwark. The history of the castle has as many twists, turns, nooks, and crannies as the fortress itself. The entrance fee permits you to ascend the steep, tortuous path to the arcaded **Burghof** (courtyard). Along the way, soak in the tranquility of the surrounding St. Veit countryside and admire the 14 towered castle gates. In the inner courtyard, step gingerly to avoid disturbing the imposing collection of weapons and armor. (Castle open Easter-Oct. 8am-6pm. Admission 40 AS, students and seniors 35 AS, children 20 AS.) Hochosterwitz is easily accessible by either bike, train, or bus. From St. Veit, take the train to "Launsdorf-Hochosterwitz" (16 AS) or the BundesBus to "Hochosterwitz-Abzweigung" (22 AS). From Klagenfurt, the train costs 46 AS, and the BundesBus costs 68 AS (take the bus to St. Veit (46 AS), and change buses). The castle is about 3km from both the train and bus stations.

■■■ FRIESACH

Friesach inspires superlative after superlative; for starters, it's Carinthia's oldest city, founded in 860. Located on the ancient trade route linking the Danube basin to the Adriatic to the Middle East beyond, Friesach first appeared on Arabian maps in 1154, and the Friesacher Pfennig was legal tender as far away as the Levant and the Crusader kingdoms of Frankish Styria. Friesach enjoyed its Golden Age during the reign of Archbishop Eberhard II, when it ballooned into the second largest town in the diocese of Salzburg. For a millennium, the Salzburg bishops heroically defended their stronghold from Bohemian, Hungarian, and Turkish marauders, but in 1803 they finally relinquished control of Friesach to the mighty Habsburg empire. The determined Salzburg clergy have left their mark on the city, however—no fewer than four imposing castles dot the surrounding hillsides.

Orientation and Practical Information This romantic medieval town rests 33km north of St. Veit, at the foot of densely wooded mountains in the Metnitz Valley. The core of the town is surrounded by a C-shaped strip of water, the Stadtgraben; a forest abuts the rest. Friesach lies on the Klagenfurt-Bruck an der Mur-Vienna rail route; trains roll into the **Hauptbahnhof,** which doubles as the main bus terminal, about every half-hour (45 min. to Klagenfurt, 3½ hrs. to Vienna). From the train station, walk down Bahnhofstr., cross the bridge over the waterway, and, at the Hauptplatz, turn right onto Wiener Str. The **tourist office,** on Wiener Str. 3 (tel. 43 00), will gladly assist any incoming travelers. (Open mid-May to mid-June Mon.-Sat. 8:30am-noon; mid-June to mid-Sept. Mon.-Fri. 8:30am-6pm, Sat. 8:30am-noon; May 1-15 and mid-Sept. to Nov. Mon.-Fri. 3-5pm, Sat. 10am-noon; Dec.-April Wed. 10am-noon.) The **post office** at Theaterplatz 8, off the Hauptplatz, exchanges money (**Postal code:** A-9360; open Mon.-Fri. 8am-noon and 2-6pm, Sat. 8-10am). **Telephones** are available inside (**City code:** 04268).

Accommodations and Food Tiny Friesach offers few accommodations, so be sure to call ahead. **Gasthof Köpple,** Bahnhofstr. 3 (tel. 23 15 or 32 03), is just an eight-minute walk from the *Hauptbahnhof*. Take a left onto Bahnhofstr., bear right at the fork, and cross over the moat; the Gasthof, with a huge "*Zimmer*" sign, will be on the right. Enormous wardrobe closets reside within Brobdingnagian rooms in this 300-year-old pub. (165-180 AS per person, with shower and toilet 280 AS per person. Dino-sized breakfast included. Reception open 8am-9pm. English spoken.) A slightly more expensive alternative is **Gasthof Weißer Wolf,** at Hauptplatz 8 (tel. 22 63), with comfortable rooms attached to elegantly furnished balconies. (270 AS. Breakfast and showers included; hallway bathrooms.) Downstairs, the *Gasthof* serves tasty Austrian cuisine in a refined milieu (entrees 85-120 AS; restaurant open daily 7am-midnight). There's a **Spar Markt** waiting with brimming shelves across the Hauptplatz (open Mon.-Fri. 8am-6pm, Sat. 7:30am-12:30pm). You can grab an adequate pizza (65-95 AS) at **Restaurant Pizzeria,** Langegasse 2, behind the Metnitztalerhof hotel (open Mon. and Wed.-Sun. 11am-2pm and 6-11pm). At night, sit on purple and green patio chairs outside the Friesacherhof hotel, Hauptplatz 4, and have a frappe (25 AS), banana split (45 AS), or Eiskaffee (35-55 AS; open daily 7am-4pm). Or, savor an ice cream cone (5 AS per scoop) from **Craighers Konditorei/Cafe,** sit by the Renaissance Hauptplatz **fountain,** and dream of days of yore beneath the gleaming castle bulwarks.

Sights and Entertainment It's best to see Friesach from a bird's-eye view, and no structure rises higher than the **Rotturm,** a 13th-century lookout tower at the summit of a treacherously steep staircase. Walk up Seminargasse, the narrow street overgrown with vegetation to the left of the Metnitztalerhof hotel; the path leads past the **Heiligenblutkirche** and through the scanty remains of the west wall of the *old* Dominican cloister. The church and cloister served as the friars' headquarters until they moved across town to the still extant **Dominikaner Kloster.** Tours of this new cloister are rigorously limited—you'll need to take various celibacy vows and visit the local barber—but the famous adjoining **Dominikanerkirche** is open to the general public. The first Dominican Church on Germanic soil, and at 72m the tallest church in all Carinthia, this exquisite Gothic structure houses three extremely noteworthy relics. The wooden crucifix on the left of the nave dates from 1320 and is one of only three in Europe made from wood that naturally developed into a forked "Y" shape. The beautiful Johannesaltar was stolen in 1986 and later found in Italy in 1990 (it's always in the last place you look…). The Steinmadonna is carved entirely from sandstone; be sure to catch her 13th-century postmodern apparel.

On the right side of the Metnitztalerhof hotel, Sackgasse runs a less strenuous course up the mountain to the **Church of St. Peter.** After exploring the simple yet powerful interior of this Gothic structure, walk outside and absorb the breathtaking view of the surrounding countryside. Farther up the hill, the ruins of **St. Petersburg Castle** glare menacingly. Inside is the four-story **Stadtmuseum,** an eclectic collection of Roman and Celtic artifacts, ancient tombstones, and medieval weaponry. Be sure to view the 11th- and 12th-century **frescoes** on the third floor. After the castle's roof crumbled in 1830, these magnificent frescoes were left to fend for themselves against rain, sun, and snow for 60 years. Despite the fading and cracking, the frescoes of "Jesus in Jerusalem" and the "Last Supper" have lost little of their original brilliance. (Museum open May-Oct. daily 10am-5pm; admission 40 AS, students and seniors 20 AS.) The 12th-century **Stadtpfarrkirche** sits at the bottom of the hill. Its elegant stained-glass windows were originally intended for the Dominikankirche, but the worldly glitter proved too costly for the friars.

From the Pfarrkirche, walk across Wiener Str. to find the **Fürstenhof Platz;** this tranquil courtyard, completely enclosed by high stone walls, was the first settlement of Friesach. At the far end of the square solemnly stand the decrepit remains of the **Getreidekasten,** a 16th-century fire-house. Here, a passageway through the wall merges into a stunning path that meanders gingerly between the city wall and the only intact moat in Europe.

To further boost its cultural capital, every summer (late June to Aug. 15) Friesach hosts the **Kultursommer Festivals.** Plays by such literary luminaries as Schiller, Goethe, Shakespeare, and Molière are performed in Petersberg Castle's open-air theater. Under the evening beacons, the small and unassuming stage takes on monumental dimensions, as the shimmering ruins of the castle and the dense coniferous forest vie for scenic prominence (tickets 120-200 AS, students half-price). Every Sunday, the Burghofspiele (Castle Theater Company) performs a classic German fairy tale in the **Stadtsaal** for the young at heart (tickets 50-60 AS). Friesach celebrates its medieval roots in the annual **Altstadtfest**, on the first weekend in June. For three days, knights on white horses rub shoulders with damsels in distress, while the rest of the townsfolk carouse until dawn. The accompanying Ritteressen is a town-wide medieval meal, complete with oversized goblets of wine and uncut, juicy morsels of chicken. Make like Henry VIII and leave your table manners at the moat (tickets 500 AS). The Kinderritterturnier, a recent festival addition, is a day-long jousting exhibition, replete with flying regalia, performed by the local children. Call the tourist office for 1994 dates, ticket reservations, and further information.

THE DRAUTAL

Bordered by Italy to the south and Slovenia to the southeast, the Drautal (Drau Valley) in central Carinthia, with its moderate climate, well-endowed watering holes, and proximity to southern Europe, evokes locales decidedly un-Teutonic. The region gingerly combines skiing and watersports in high- and low-lands carved by the river **Drau,** between the Hohe Tauern and the Villacher Alps. The region's largest peaks soar a mere 2000m, a baby step above the timberline. They are favored not just with lumber and plenty of snow but with valuable minerals: iron ore, lead, tungsten, zinc, and manganese. Nestled among these lazy peaks is the partially navigable Drau and its tributaries, plus numerous popular lakes, streams, and warm-water springs, where curative spas tempt visitors even in the coldest months. One especially scintillating pastime involves lounging in the shallow end of a toasty spa while commenting on displays of ineptitude by spread-eagled skiers in the surrounding mountains.

With the transportation hub of Villach and its important electronic components industry at its core, the Drautal is composed of the resorts of the Millstätter See, the serpent-shaped Ossiacher See near Villach, and baths in many smaller towns and villages, such as the Broßer-Mühldorger See near Gmünd, the Afritzer See near Afritz, and the Faaker See near Villach, with an enchanting island in its center. Fitness buffs can enjoy trails, marked through meadows and mountains, as well as manifold water sports. Wait 'til the frost, and ice skate on the selfsame lakes where you back-stroked months ago.

From west to east, Ferndorf, Paternion, Feistritz, and Kellerberg are smaller and less touristed villages along the Drau. North of Spittal is Gmünd (not to be confused with its namesake in Niederösterreich), home of the **Porsche Automuseum** (tel. (04732) 24 71). Professor Doktor Ingineur Ferdinand Porsche worked in Gmünd from 1944-50 and built his first speedster here. East of Villach in Seeboden, the **Plüsch und Comic Museum** (tel. (04762) 827 82 11), a stuffed animal netherworld within a converted villa, offers a welter of menagerie rooms, including a Mayan temple.

Autobahn A10 hugs the Drau through the entire region, forking near Villach into highways aimed at Italy and Slovenia. Most bus routes in the region also follow the course of the Drau; a few lines diverge to the various lakes. **Bus** #5121 runs from Spittal through Feffernitz to Villach; #5132 runs from Spittal to Gmünd via Seeboden. **Rail** tracks follow the same Drauish route through the valley, carrying both the Wien-Villach-Salzburg and the Bruck an der Mur-Villach-Arnoldstein line. Trains from Vienna's Südbahnhof depart for Villach every hour, usually at 22 minutes past.

■■■ VILLACH

Awe-inspiring mountain backdrops and an intriguing multicultural atmosphere make Villach an unforgettable and occasionally unfathomable city. Situated just north of the border between Austria, Italy, and Slovenia, Villach is distinctly schizophrenic; even the street musicians betray the influence of cultural neighbors in the inflections of their traditional Carinthian folk songs. Somehow, Mother Nature forges harmony from the nationalistic cacophony; the gurgling of the fierce River Drau, which bisects the city, overwhelms the bustle as it echoes from the stoic faces of the surrounding snow-capped Karawanken, Villacher, and Julian Alps.

Orientation and Practical Information Villach sprawls on two sides of the River Drau. **Bahnhofstraße** leads from the train station, over a 9th-century bridge, to the narrow **Hauptplatz.** The economic and social heart of Villach, the town square is paved with cobblestone paths that dart among numerous hidden alleyways. Flanked by two sweeping arcs of stores, the square is closed at one end by a magnificent church. The Drauländе skirts the west bank of the River Drau.

Villach's **main post office** is adjacent to the train station; turn right when you exit the *Bahnhof.* (Open daily 7am-10pm. **Postal Code:** A-9500.) Another **branch** is at 8-Mai-Platz 2, on the corner of Postgasse and 10-Oktober-Str. (open Mon.-Fri. 7am-6pm). The town **tourist office,** Europaplatz 2, on the east bank of the Drau (tel. (04242) 24 44 40; fax 244 44 17), can advise you on town attractions and area skiing. From the train station, walk out to Bahnhofstr., take a left onto Nikolaigasse right after the church, and walk 50m (5 min.). (Office open Mon.-Fri. 8am-12:30pm and 1:30-6pm, Sat. 9am-noon.)

Accommodations and Food The swanky **Jugendherberge Villach (HI),** Dinzlweg 34 (tel. (04242) 288 62), houses 144 in spacious five-bed dorm rooms, each with its own shower. Just don't agitate the irascible German shepherd guarding the door. From the train station, walk out of the station to Bahnhofstr., cross the bridge, walk through the Hauptplatz, and turn right on Postgasse. Walk straight through Hans-Gasser-Platz, which merges into Tiroler Str., and bear right at St.-Martin-Str.; Dinzelweg is the first street on the left. The hostel is tucked away behind the tennis courts (20 min.). (Reception open 6-10pm. Strict 10pm curfew. 140 AS. Breakfast and sheets included. Sauna 500 AS for 4 hrs.) **Pension Eppinger Grete,** at Klagenfurter Str. 6 (tel. (04242) 243 89), has 14 average beds in the center of town. From the station, walk straight up Bahnhofstr., and turn left onto Klagenfurter Straße (5 min.). The tiny *Pension* is in a small alleyway on the right (singles 200-260 AS, doubles 150-200 AS per person, triples 150-160 AS per person).

Eating in Villach delights both palate and pocketbook. **Lederergasse** overflows with small restaurants, while sprawling **Kaiser-Josef-Platz** shelters cafés with a sunglass-sporting clientele. **Ristorante Flaschl,** on Seilergasse, offers genuine Italian fare; you'd think you were south of the border. Pizzas and pastas cost 65-105 AS; the delectable *Tortelloni alla panna mit Salze, Schinken, and Käse* costs just 85 AS (open Mon.-Fri. 5pm-2am, Sat. 6pm-2am). **Pizzeria Trieste** on Weißbriachgasse cooks up popular pies for 60-95 AS (open Mon.-Sat. 11am-11pm, Sun. 11:30am-10pm). **Restaurant Schaffler,** on Rathuasgasse, sells the cheapest lunch specials in Villach (60-65 AS). Try the simmering *Tortelloni in Fleischsauce* (65 AS; lunch only, 11:30am-2pm). Overlooking the Drau at Nikolai Platz 2 is **Konditerei Bernholt,** Villach's answer to Vienna's Demel. At least they capture the haughty disdain of the original. Snack on sundry colorful pastries (12-28 AS), devilish ice cream concoctions, and refreshing mixed drinks—sip nonchalantly on a *cappuccino* (27 AS) as you look down your nose at the ships cruising up and down the river (open Mon.-Fri. 7:30am-7pm, Sat. 8am-7pm, Sun. 9:30am-7pm). Pick up a picnic lunch at the **Julius Meinl supermarket,** Hauptplatz 14 (open Mon.-Fri. 8am-6pm, Sat. 7:30am-noon), or the less expensive **SPAR Markt** in the Hans Grasser Platz (open Mon.-Fri. 7:30am-7:15pm, Sat. 7:30am-noon).

Sights and Entertainment Any tour of Villach must traverse the bustling **Hauptplatz;** the southern end of the square lives in the mighty Gothic shadow of the **St. Jakob-Kirche.** Slightly raised on a stone terrace, this 14th-century church converted during the Reformation, and thereby became Austria's first Protestant chapel. Inside, the high altar's brilliantly gilt Baroque canopy dazzles your eyes; the glitter almost obscures the staid Gothic crucifix suspended just in front. At the center of the Hauptplatz is a modest **Trinity Column,** built in 1606 and rebuilt in 1739. Learn more about the Villach's history at the **Stadtmuseum**, Widmanngasse 38. Aside from the rich collection of prehistoric relics and medieval artworks, the museum is home to the original Villach coat of arms—an eagle talon clutching a mountain top, painted in striking gold and black. In the elegantly manicured courtyard outside rest well-preserved remnants of the old city wall. (Museum open May-Oct. daily 10am-4:30pm. Admission 20 AS, students 10 AS.)

A quick five-minute walk lifts you from the congested streets of the Hauptplatz to the soothing **Schillerpark.** Amidst the flowery pathways and spurting fountains is the **Relief von Kärnten,** an enormous topographic model of Carinthia. (Open May-Oct. Mon.-Sat. 10am-4:30pm. Admission 20 AS, students 10 AS, under 15 free. **Combination ticket,** valid for both the Relief and the Stadtmuseum, 25 AS.) Near the park looms the **Heilig-Kreuz-Kirche,** the attractive dual-towered edifice visible from the city bridge. If you meander inside the church, gaze up into the seemingly unending vacuum created by the dome. On the other side of the Drau, the **Villacher Fahrzeugmuseum** (tel. (04242) 255 30 or 224 40) is parked at Draupromenade 12. Hundreds of polished antique cars and automobiles present a jaw-dropping journey into the history of transportation. (Open Mon.-Sat. 9am-6pm, Sun. 10am-5pm; Oct.-May daily 10am-noon and 2-4pm. Admission 40 AS, ages 6-14 20 AS.)

In July and August, the classical strains of the **Carinthian Summer Festival** waft into town. Performances are held either in Villach's **Kongresshaus,** next door to the tourist office, or in the 11th-century monastery located in nearby **Ossiach.** For the latter location, take the BundesBus (direction: "Feldkirchen") to "Ossiach Gasthaus Post" (32 AS). (Tickets 280-680 AS, without a view of the stage 120-180 AS.) Contact Carinthischer Sommer for updated information—the organization has offices in the Villach tourist office; in Stift Ossiach (July-Aug. tel. (04243) 25 10); or at Gumpendorfer Str. 76, in Vienna (tel. (0222) 5 (9) 681 98; fax 597 12 36). The **Villach Kirchtag,** held since 1225 on the first Saturday of August, celebrates the city's "birthday" with raucous revelry (entrance into the *Altstadt* 50 AS). Around August first, Villach hosts its annual fair, the **Villacher Brauchtumswoche,** embedded within a whole week of folkloric presentations.

Ferries cruise the waters of the **Drau,** departing from the boarding dock beneath the northern end of the main bridge. Set sail with the skipper, his mate (a mighty sailing man), and five passengers on the two-hour tour—the two-hour tour. (Cruises run mid-June to mid-Sept. 9:30, 11:40am, 2, and 4pm; less frequently May to early-June and late-Sept. Tickets 100 AS on board, 90 AS from the ticket agent in front of the dock; ages 6-15 half-price.)

Less crowded than the Wörther See, the **Faaker See** is a small but breathtakingly beautiful lake at the foot of one of the mountains between Villach and its suburb, **Maria Gail.** The steep peaks around Villach also make for excellent **skiing.** A plethora of resorts woo the winter traveler; the Villach tourist office can assist you in a decision. A one-day regional lift ticket costs about 250 AS (children 160 AS); other combinations are available.

Near Villach: Warmbad Villach and Landskron

Three km south of the city await the therapeutic, radioactive mineral waters of **Warmbad Villach** (16 AS). Every day, 40 million liters of natural spring water (28-30°C, 82-86°F) tickle the aching muscles of thousands of complacent European tourists. Paranoid Cold War vets should leave the Geiger counter at home—this place is fine. Take city bus #1 from the bus station across from the *Hauptbahnhof* to the last stop, "Therme Warmerbad." (Open daily 9am-9pm. 100 AS for access to swimming pool and water slides. Add 50 AS for the sauna. Call (04242) 300 27 50 or 378 89 for more information.)

The impressive ruins of the 14th-century **Landskron castle** crumble several kilometers northeast of Villach. Take the 20 AS bus ride on city line #5 (direction: "Sattendorf") to "St. Andrä (Ruine)." For 40 AS (under 14, 20 AS), you can admire an assortment of birds of prey as they soar above the castle and the surrounding landscape. (**Bird show** at the back of the castle July-Aug. daily 11am, 4pm, and 6pm;

June and Sept. daily 11am and 4pm; May daily 3pm. Call (04242) 428 88 for more information.)

■■■ SPITTAL AN DER DRAU

Established by the counts of Ortenburg in 1191 as a hospice (*Spittl*) for travelers and pilgrims, Spittal an der Drau retains the spirit of relaxed hospitality despite its status as the economic and communications center of upper Carinthia. After imperial Turkish invaders burned the town to the ground in 1478, Gabriel of Salamanca erected the Renaissance castle Porcia. In 1797, the town was occupied by the French (what Gaul!), who razed most of the city again. Only when the Tauern railway opened in 1909, connecting Spittal to international routes, did the city experience a boom. Straddling the Rivers **Drau** and **Lieser** in an imposing chain of mountains only 75km northwest of Klagenfurt (122 AS by train), Spittal sets visitors at ease with an array of burbling fountains, pastel buildings, and scenic hiking and skiing trails.

Orientation and Practical Information The Lieser River flows north to south through the center of town, traversed by two bridges, the **Brückenstraße** and the **Ander Wirtschaftsbrücke.** The train tracks cross a third bridge, south of the others. The train station sits on the western edge of town. Northeast of town is a gigantic park. To find the town **tourist office,** in the *Schloß* at Burgplatz 1 (tel. 34 20), walk straight up Bahnhofstr. from the station, take a right on Tiroler Str. at Egarterplatz, and look for the castle on the right. The office distributes brochures and maps, and helps find accommodations for no fee. (Open Mon.-Fri. 9am-9pm, Sat. 9am-1pm; Sept.-June Mon.-Fri. 9am-6pm, Sat. 9am-1pm.) The branch **post office** at the train station has **telephones** (**City code:** 04762) and the best rates for **currency exchange.** (Open daily 7am-9pm; exchange open daily 7am-5pm.) The downtown post office at Egarterplatz 2 (tel. 39 01), is within walking distance; follow Bahnhofstr. until it intersects Tiroler Str. (Open Mon.-Fri. 8am-noon and 2-6pm; exchange open Mon.-Fri. 8am-noon and 2-5pm. **Postal Code:** A-9800.) You can **rent bikes** at the station as well (rental open daily 8am-6pm).

Accommodations and Food Spittal has two youth hostels, one at the base of the town cable car and the other at its summit. To reach **Jugendherberge Spittal/Millstättersee (HI),** Zur Seilbahn 2 (tel. 32 52), head straight up Bahnhofstr., turn right on Koschatstr., and right again on Ortenburgerstraße (15 min.). Zur Seilbahn is on the right, adjacent to tennis courts, a soccer field, and the cable car to the peak of the Goldeck mountain. The hostel is overrun by middle-aged tennis fanatics in velour sweatsuits. (Reception open 8am-10pm. Lockout 10am-5pm. 95 AS, nonmembers 10 AS surcharge. Breakfast 30 AS. Sheets and showers included. Kitchen facilities. Undergoing extensive renovations in the fall of 1993, so prices may rise.) The **Jugendherberge Spittal/Goldeck (HI),** at the cable car's mid-station (tel. 27 01), is perched 1650m up the face of the Goldeck mountain, with easy access to skiing and hiking. (See Sights and Entertainment below for lift hours. Hostel open only when cable car is functioning. Disembark at the "Mittelstation" stop. 130 AS. Breakfast, showers, and sheets included.)

Stefanie Hohengasser, Mitterweg 5 (tel. 360 83), provides spacious rooms, hot showers, and generous breakfasts at her rose-bedecked home just across the Drau. From the center of town, follow Ortenburgerstr. down to Porciastr., turn left, and then right on Mitterweg; the house is on your left (15 min.). (Doubles 180-205 AS per person; breakfast included.) **Haus Hübner,** Schillerstr. 20 (tel. 21 12), is 500m from the station; walk straight up Bahnhofstr., take a right on Schillerstr., and go to the end of the street behind the hardware store. This jewel of a *Pension* pampers guests with billowy down pillows, wicker chairs, window boxes, dark wooden shutters, and a magnificent view of the surrounding mountains. The breakfast room features floral china, a fireplace, and fantastic food. (Reception open 11am-11pm. Singles and doubles 230 AS per person, with shower 260 AS, with shower and toilet 295 AS; Sept.-June 220 AS, 240 AS, and 275 AS, respectively. Breakfast included.)

Peaceful **Draufluß-Camping** (tel. 24 66) lies on a tree-sheltered bank of the Drau. Follow Ortenburgerstr. over the bridge; the campsite is on your left. (July-Aug. 60 AS per person, 25 AS per child, 40 AS per tent, 40 AS per car; April-June and Sept.-Oct. 50 AS per person, 25 AS per child, 30 AS per tent, 30 AS per car. Curfew 11:30pm. Over 18 9.50 AS tax.) If all else fails, **Jugendherberge Rennweg/Katshberg,** Mühlbach 4 (tel. (04734) 364), is located in **Rennweg,** one hour from Spittal. This charming mountain hostel with dark-timbered balconies and flower-embellished windows is perched 1100m up in the Nock mountains. Take bus #12 to "Rennweg" (58 AS) and change for the bus to "Gries"—departures every two hours. (Reception open 5-10pm. Curfew 10pm. Dorms 130 AS; over 18, 12.50 AS surcharge. Breakfast, sheets, shower, and toilet included.)

Fast-food vendors next to the *Schloß* sell the cheapest victuals in town. **Restaurant "Zellot,"** Hauptplatz 12, is arguably the best of the budget eateries. Homemade Carinthian specialities run 115-215 AS; for a less expensive meal opt for the *Tortelloni mit Käse* (85 AS) or the lasagna (95 AS). **Shanghai Chinese Restaurant,** a two-minute walk from the Hauptplatz on Villacher Str., serves lunch specials for 55 AS (open Mon.-Fri. 11:30am-2:30pm). Shop at **Feinkost Springer,** in Südtiroler Platz across from the station (open Mon.-Fri. 7am-7pm, Sat. 7am-1pm), or at the **KGM supermarket,** inside the Forum shopping complex on Ortenburgerstraße (open Mon.-Fri. 8:30am-6pm, Sat. 8:30am-12:30pm).

Sights and Entertainment The gently swaying trees and shaded park benches of Spittal's central **Stadtpark** absorb the bustle of the Hauptplatz and Neuerplatz; these squares converge on **Schloß Porcia,** a beautiful Italian Renaissance castle with a grand courtyard lined by three Italianate galleries. The second and third floors are occupied by the newly renovated **Bezirksheimatmuseum** (Regional Folk Museum), which presents the cultural history of upper Carinthia—it's more than just a Habsburg chronicle. Look at the impressive collection of Faßdauben and Eschenschwarten; these contorted pieces of wood, tied to the foot by ox whips and twisted roots, became treacherous 19th-century skis. Or learn about the legendary December 6th **St. Nicholas** ritual; on this night, children were supposedly visited by devil-like creatures (*Krampus*) who extorted good behavior by flashing leather switches in the youths' frightened faces. (Better watch out, better not cry, better not pout…). (Museum open May 15-Sept. 15 daily 9am-6pm. Admission 40 AS, students 20 AS.)

Other area museums reveal further historical riches. The **Frühmittelalter Museum Carantana,** in nearby **Molzbichl** (tel. (04767) 666), has exhibitions on the discovery of an 8th-century cloister and other relics of the early middle ages. Take the BundesBus (direction: "Villach") to "Molzbichl" (22 AS). (Open late-April to Sept. Mon.-Sat. 10am-noon and 2-6pm, Sun. 10am-noon. Admission 15 AS, students 10 AS.) The **Museum Teurnia,** in nearby **St. Peter in Holz** (tel. 338 07), showcases Celtic and Roman archaeological finds; the church next door has a mosaic floor from around 500 AD. Ride the BundesBus (direction: "Heiligenblut") to "St. Peter in Holz" (22 AS), and walk about 500m toward the church spires. (Museum open mid-May to mid-Oct. daily 9am-noon and 1-5pm. Admission 20 AS, students 10 AS.) For a guided tour of Spittal's Baroque edifices, gather at 10am on a Wednesday at the northern portal of the **Schloß** (20 AS).

If the gardens of the Stadtpark don't satisfy your craving for the outdoors, hop on the **Goldeck cable car,** Zur Seilbahn 10 (tel. 28 64 12), for a 2142m ascent to the belvedere atop the Goldeck peak. The tourist office brochure *Wanderwege am Goldeck* maps out the many scenic trails throughout the range. (Cable car departs mid-June to mid-Sept. and Dec.-Feb. every hr. 9am-5pm. To summit 130 AS, children 80 AS; round-trip 190 AS, children 105 AS. To mid-station 90 AS, children 60 AS;

round-trip 140 AS, children 80 AS, 1-week pass 360 AS. 10% discount with Millstatt guest card.)

Spittal feasts on a steady diet of cultural events held in the enchanting *Schloß* courtyard. The annual **Comedy Festival,** held in July and August, features plays by authors such as Shakespeare and Lope de Vega. For information, call either the ticket stand inside the *Schloß* (tel. 31 61; open July-Sept. 9am-noon, 2-7pm, and 7:30-8:30pm) or the tourist office. (Plays in German. Tickets 70-210 AS, standing room 80 AS.) For one weekend in June, Spittal reenacts the legend of Katharina von Salamanca in the rowdy **Salamancafest;** Katharina's son was cursed to be torn apart by dogs, and her tormented spirit supposedly still haunts Schloß Porcia as retribution. The next festival will be in 1995 (50 AS per day to enter the *Altstadt.*) For a more comprehensive schedule of town to-dos, ask at the tourist office for the brochure *Festkalender Ferienregion Millstätter See,* or the English-language *Calendar of Events* and *Information for Guests.*

■■■ MILLSTATT

Eleven km east of Spittal an der Drau along the deep-blue **Millstätter See,** tiny Millstatt is a lush hillside town adorned with delicate fountains, winding cobblestone streets, and ivy-covered medieval houses. Ubiquitous religious signs and symbols mingle guiltily with the knights' crests emblazoned on walls and street signs; this city was ruled through the Middle Ages by Benedictine monks and the Knights of St. George, and in the 17th and 18th centuries by Jesuit priests. Today, Millstatt is the stomping ground of well-heeled European tourists attracted by low, gentle hills rolling into a warm and limpid lake. This Millstätter See is a by-product of the last ice age, which overran Europe 30,000 years ago.

Orientation and Practical Information Millstatt is best approached from Spittal; take the bus to "Millstatt Kärnten Strandbad" (28 AS, 15 min., buses every 30-60 min.). The town **tourist office** (*Kurverwaltung*) is located at Marktplatz 1 in the *Rathaus* (tel. 20 22). **Tours** run July to early September on Wednesdays (70 AS, under 14 40 AS). Contact the helpful staff for information on **guided hikes** (70 AS) around the footpaths of the **Nock Mountains,** which usually include descriptions of the regional flora and fauna. From the bus stop, turn left down Kaiser-Franz-Joseph-Str., left again at Stiftgasse, and walk up into the Marktplatz (office open Mon.-Fri. 9am-noon and 1:30-6pm; Sat.-Sun. 10am-noon and 3-5pm). Marble steps to the right of the tourist office lead into an unusually elegant **post office.** (Open Mon.-Fri. 8am-noon and 3-7pm, Sat. 8-10am; **currency** desk open Mon.-Fri. 8am-noon and 3-6pm. **Postal code:** A-9872.) **Telephones** (**City code:** 04766) are available inside.

Accommodations and Food Anyone who stays at a hotel, *Pension,* or *Privatzimmer* earns a **guest card** (*Kurkarte*), which grants discounts for boat rental, cruises, the Goldeck cable car in Spittal (10%), the lifts in Bad Kleinkirchheim (10%), and other attractions. Lodgings abound in Millstatt, though most establishments cater to a distinctly wealthy summer clientele. **Haus Aignor-Haberl,** located above Café Wien at Mirnockstr. 39 (tel. 21 11), offers nine doubles only one minute off the Marktplatz; walk straight onto Mirnockstr. from the tourist office. (July-Aug. 180 AS; May-June and Sept. 160 AS. Reception open 10am-midnight.) Run by Frau Maier, both **Haus Josefine** and **Staudacherhof** (both tel. 26 03) supply spacious rooms and unbelievable views of the glistening lake from flower-bedecked balconies. From the tourist office, walk down Spittaler Str. and bear left onto Alexanderhofstr. Staudacherhof is on your left, and Haus Josefine is just a few minutes beyond. (Staudacherhof July-Aug. singles 290-350 AS, doubles 230-325 AS; May-June and Sept. singles 200-300 AS, doubles 180-265 AS. Breakfast included. Haus Josefine has the same prices but is open 24 hrs. all year.) **Haus Charlotte,** Tiefenbacherweg 63 (tel. 20 91), is a 15-minute walk through the woods, culminating in a spectacular panorama of the Nock Mountains towering over the lake. From behind the tourist office, follow Spittaler Str. onto Tiefenbacherweg; the house will be on the left. (Doubles July-Aug. 170-190 AS; May-June and Sept. 150-170 AS. Breakfast included.).

A hot spot for local youth, **Pizzeria Peppino,** Seemühlgasse 57, serves up satisfying pizzas (58-109 AS), myriad pasta dishes (69-84 AS), and salads (38-61 AS) in a sparkling marble and blue building two minutes from the water (open Tues.-Sun. 7pm-midnight). Stock up at the **Konsum supermarket** on the corner of Überfuhrgasse and Kaiser-Franz-Joseph-Str. (open Mon.-Fri. 8am-noon and 3-6pm, Sat. 8am-noon).

Sights and Entertainment Millstatt's rich history is recounted by the central **Stiftsmuseum,** which lies in a former cloister constructed by the Benedictines in 1070. The museum exhibits relics from the periods of Benedictine and Jesuit rule, the ceremonial sword and chalices of the Knights of St. George, and a jail cell with the scratched inscriptions of 16th-century prisoners. From the bus stop, turn left immediately upon disembarking, and then make a left onto Stiftgasse. (Open May-Sept. daily 9am-noon and 3:30-6:30pm. Admission 20 AS, children 10 AS.) The fragrant, 1000-year-old Lindenbaum (linden tree), considered a municipal treasure, stands proudly in the grassy courtyard in front of the museum. The pagan German tribes that populated Austria in the Dark Ages believed that the wood of the linden tree, often called limewood, possessed magical properties. Its light, fine-grained wood is suited for detailed craftwork, and the material was often used for talismans and other sacred artifacts. The grand retable altarpieces and devotional figurines found in churches throughout central and northern Europe were largely sculpted in limewood by such masters as Tilman Riemenschneider and Michael Pacher.

The **Stiftskirche** next door, a simple blue and white edifice topped by twin rust-colored onion domes, boasts an intricate Baroque interior with a brilliantly shining gilt altar. The ceiling is inlaid with 149 carved coats of arms, representing the noble families that financed its construction. (Free. Tours by request only; 1-hr. tour 30 AS.) Guided tours of Millstatt's medieval, Romanesque, and Gothic buildings begin at the *Rathaus* (July-Aug. Mon. and Fri. at 10am; June and Sept.-Oct. Mon. at 10am; 30AS).

Top-flight concert series are among Millstatt's generous cultural offerings. Each summer brings the **Internationale Musikwochen** festival (July-Aug.) and, under its auspices, a host of first-rate classical musicians. (Tickets 100-300 AS, students half-price. The permanent box office in the Stiftskirche is open 30 min. before show-time. For information, call the tourist office.) The city also celebrates spring and fall with song during the **Musikalischer Frühling** and **Musikalischer Herbst** festivals. The tourist office's brochure *Information-Veranstaltungen Ferienregion Millstätter See* contains a complete schedule of concerts and events in Millstatt and other towns in the area.

Millstatt is blessed with hot and sunny summers—enticing invitations to hop into the lake. Glide into the water from the *Strandbad* (beach), or hurtle in from the steep and twisting slides. (Admission 53 AS, with guest card 44 AS, ages 6-13 27 AS. After 4pm, admission 27 AS, ages 6-13 19 AS.) **Surf und Segel Schule Strobl,** Seemühlgasse 56a (tel. 22 63) offers other means to enjoy the shimmering lake. Herr Strobl rents **sailboards** for windsurfing (95 AS per hr.), **motorboats** (110 AS), **sailboats** (95-135 AS), and **pedal boats** (40-50 AS). **Cruises** around the lake start at the Strandhotel Marchetti, Seemühlgasse 83 (tel. 20 45). (Round-trip 105 AS, with guest card 100 AS, children 50 AS. Short trips to cities around the lake run 15-75 AS, children 10-35 AS.)

■ Bad Kleinkirchheim

Hidden in a dense wood 32km east of Spittal an der Drau (bus #5140; 1 hr.; 58 AS) is Bad Kleinkirchheim, a booming resort village. The stylish hotels and luxurious Roman spas contrast poignantly with the surrounding network of sleepy hamlets and undisturbed coniferous forests. European tourists, dressed lavishly in gorgeous furs and scintillating Gore-Tex®, pump millions of *Schillings* into this man-made oasis. Bad Kleinkirchheim, like the Dom Perignon held aloft in nightly toasts to opulent extravagance, bubbles over with energy and excitement.

The resort's primary attraction is its **ski terrain;** happily, ascending even these 16 slopes need not obliterate your budget. (A 1-day **ski-pass** costs 320 AS, ages 16-23 250 AS, under 16 180 AS; ½-day pass 230 AS, 180 AS, and 130 AS, respectively.) You can rent equipment at **Sport Gruber** (tel. (04240) 346), across the street from the tourist office and to the right of the St. Kathrein thermal bath (skis and poles 180-350 AS per day, boots 100-130 AS per day). Stretch your savings by extending your visit; a three-day pass during the *Hauptsaison* (high season) runs 910 AS, ages 16 to 23 755 AS, and under 16 495 AS. Call (04240) 82 12 for 24-hour **snow-condition information.** After a tiring day in the powder, relax in either of the two **thermal baths. St. Kathrein** (tel. (04240) 82 82 42) is located across the street from the tourist office, while **Thermal Römerbad** (tel. (04240) 82 82 32) is located at the foot of the Kaiserburgbahn in Kleinkirchheim. A pass valid for both facilities costs 110 AS, children 70 AS.

Bad Kleinkirchheim's **tourist office** is in a cedar chalet just to the right of the bus stop (tel. (04240) 82 12; fax 85 37). The pleasant, English-speaking staff distributes a plethora of helpful and informative guides written in several different languages; ask for the *Ortsplan, Das Dorf Spectrum,* and the pamphlet *Information und Tarife* (open Mon.-Sat. 8:30am-7:30pm, Sun. 9am-noon and 3-6pm). In the summer, the office runs daily **guided hikes** through the surrounding mountainous terrain (tours run mid-June to late-Oct.; 60 AS or less). Three **cable cars** operate during the summer to raise you to that higher plane: the **Kaiserburgbahn** (round-trip 150 AS, with guest card 130 AS, children 75 AS; one way 65 AS, 55 AS, and 35 AS, respectively; the **Maibrunn Bahn** (round-trip 135 AS, with guest card 120 AS, children 65 AS; one way 110 AS, 90 AS, and 55 AS respectively); and the **Brunnachalm-Bahn** (round-trip 125 AS, with guest card 105 AS, children 60 AS; one way 50 AS, 40 AS, and 25 AS).

Pensionen and private rooms abound in Bad Kleinkirchheim. **Pension Rosenheim,** Bach 38 (tel. (04240) 290), is a five-minute walk from the tourist office and bus stop. Get off the bus, turn 180°, walk forward, take the first left down a narrow pedestrian way, and look for a wooden house with a huge "Rosenheim" sign (*Hauptsaison* 275 AS, *Vor- und Nachsaison* 265 AS, singles 30 AS extra). After staying two or three nights in town, pick up a **guest card** for extensive discounts on town attractions (ask at the tourist office for more information). Procure picnic supplies on the Hauptplatz, either at the **SPAR Markt,** one minute to the left of the tourist office, or at **ADEG,** one minute to the right of the tourist office. (SPAR open Mon.-Fri. 8am-noon and 3-6pm, Sat. 8am-noon, Sun. 9am-noon. ADEG open Mon.-Fri. 8am-noon and 2:30-6pm, Sat. 8am-noon and 3-6pm.)

THE LUNGAU

Comprising the southeastern segment of the Salzburger Land is the Lungau, a sprawling valley brimming with tiny wood-shingled houses—the roofs are all laced with hovering wisps of clouds. The region's isolation from mass public transportation has allowed the locals to preserve the rituals of yore. An uncommonly high percentage of residents cling to traditional garb and hunker down to *Speck,* a fatty, smoked pig's meat served in thinly cut slices, with a shot of *Schnapps* (a.k.a. bacon and booze). During the summer months, the various towns of the Lungau honor **Samson,** the buff biblical figure (not to be confused with Samson, the Austrian equivalent of Snuffleupagus). With the first snowfall, the Lungau suddenly transforms into a skier's paradise—and as more and more tourists begin to discover the charm of this forgotten region, Old World and New World will soon be forced to reconcile with one another.

■ Tamsweg

Approximately 126km southwest of Salzburg (152 AS by bus) lies Tamsweg, the principal town of the Lungau. The town sprouted up at the intersection—nearly a right angle—of the Leißnitzbach and Mur rivers. Most of the town remains on or near the west bank of the Leißnitzbach. Ravaged by imperial troops in 1480 during the Hungarian War, Tamsweg was revitalized by the same salt and iron trade that buttressed so many central Austrian villages. Dominating the lively **Marktplatz** are the elegantly painted **Rathaus** and the **Kriegerdenkmal,** a memorial fountain commemorating the fallen of World War I. The **Pfarrkirche St. Jakobus** underwent extensive reconstruction in the 18th century, but the high altar, accented by a brilliant gold window, recaptures its 13th-century roots. Nearby, at Kirchengasse 133, is the **Lungauer Heimatmuseum,** a superb collection chronicling this region's fascinating history. A skeleton on display dates back to the days when the Lungau was the stomping ground of the mighty Romans. (Museum open Tues.-Sat. 10am-noon and 2-5pm. Free guided tours at 10, 11am, 2, and 3:30pm. Admission 40 AS, under 6 20 AS.) The **St. Leonhard Kirche** looks over the town from a nearby hill. Encircled completely by a stone wall erected in the 15th century to thwart Hungarian invaders, this remarkable Gothic structure is endowed with spectacular stained-glass panes, most notably the famous **gold window.** Thousands of worshipers make the pilgrimage to this fortress church, thereby perpetuating a practice begun five centuries ago; in 1421, a small figurine of St. Leonhard, which had thrice vanished, mysteriously reappeared in a tree near the site of the church. Eerily, a woman 3000 mi. away sitting in her Glasgow living room suddenly felt a sharp burning sensation in her hand. Time-Life Books® was promptly notified.

Every Thursday from July to early September, the attractive **Marktplatz** becomes a stage for performers of regional song and dance; these **Platzkonzerte** are free. On the Saturday and Sunday after Corpus Christi, the **Samsonumzug** (procession of Samson) is held in town. Samson is a gigantic figure about six meters tall, named for the biblical Samson, famous for his superhuman strength. The giant and other oversized costumes arrived with the Capuchin monks from Bavaria, where huge figures have been used in ceremonies for centuries. For more information, consult the **tourist office** (tel. 416; fax 74 34) inside the *Rathaus.* To reach the office from the bus station or post office, turn right onto Dechantsbühel and left onto Kirchengasse (3 min.). The office also supplies free maps, finds rooms, and sponsors **hikes** (50 AS) into the mountains. (Open July-Aug. and Jan.-March Mon.-Fri. 8am-noon and 2-5pm, Sat. 9am-noon; Sept.-Dec. and April-June Mon.-Fri. 8am-noon and 2-5pm.) Tamsweg has no direct access to ski lifts or runs, but the BundesBus and a local private company called Tälerbus offer efficient and frequent service to the resorts comprising **Samson Valley.** Ask the tourist office for the *Tälerbus Fahrplan.* **Ski rental** is available at **Intersport Frühstückerl** (tel. 69 52 0) at Kirchengasse 130; the cheapest package runs about 100 AS per day (open Mon.-Fri. 8:30am-noon and 2:30-6pm, Sat. 8:30am-noon).

Frau Kocher has 15 beds in her spotless home at Mitschiplatz 456 available to weary travelers. A comfortable television room and spacious bedrooms are awfully effective arguments against sleeping elsewhere. From the bus station, face the Grazer Wechselseitige building and head down the small footpath to its right side. Cross the tiny bridge, bear right, turn left onto Mitschiplatz, and look for the **Haus Kocher** sign. (Singles and doubles Oct.-Nov. and April-June 160 AS per person; July-Sept. and Dec.-March 180 AS per person; 30 AS surcharge for only 1 night. Generous breakfast included.) **Frühstückpension Kandolf,** at Kirchengasse 128 (tel. 336), has luxurious rooms with sparkling tiled bathrooms. Located in the Marktplatz, the *Pension-cum*-hotel is well worth the extra *Schillings-cum*-dollars. (280 AS per person. Breakfast included. Accepts major credit cards.) The grounds of **Wald-Camp-**

ing Tamsweg, Mörtelsdorf 1 (tel. 385), are about 1.5km from the Marktplatz; walk along the train tracks until you see signs. (In ski season 35 AS per person, children 20 AS. In off-season 30 AS per person, children 18 AS. 18 AS per car, 25-40 AS per caravan. Showers 10 AS.)

Swerve that stubborn grocery cart to the **SPAR Markt,** across the street from the Heimatmuseum (market open Mon.-Fri. 7:30am-noon and 2:45-6pm, Sat. 7:30am-noon). The **post office (Postal code:** A-5580), in Postplatz, exchanges money and provides **telephones (City code:** 06474). (Post office open Mon.-Fri. 8am-noon and 2-6pm, Sat. 8-10am. Currency desk closes at 5pm.)

■ St. Michael

St. Michael, 25km west of Tamsweg (32 AS by bus), sits at the foot of the Katschberghöhe (1641m); this auspicious location has made the town the beneficiary of plenty of mountain traffic. The torturously steep Katschberg pass deters many from venturing to St. Michael from the south, but the same treacherous passage detains visitors from the north for a day. (**BundesBus** makes the trip twice a day mid-July to mid-Sept. From Spittal 76 AS; from Rennweg 58 AS.)

St. Michael's **tourist office,** in Raikaplatz next door to the Raiffeisenkasse Bank (tel. (06477) 34 20), hands out the *Tälerbus Fahrplan* and the free hiking pamphlet *Der St. Michaeler Waldlehrpfad.* To reach the tourist office, disembark at "St. Michael in Lungau Au," turn right, and then left onto Marktstr.; bear left onto Poststr., turn right on Kaltbach Str., and follow the circle clockwise. At the church spire, turn left into Raikaplatz (5 min.). (Open in winter Mon.-Fri. 9am-noon and 2-5:45pm, Sat. 9am-noon and 4-6pm; in summer Mon.-Tues. and Thurs.-Fri. 9am-noon and 2-5:45pm, Wed. and Sat. 9am-noon.) The **post office (Postal code:** A-5582) offers full services (open Mon.-Fri. 8am-noon and 2-6pm). A **SPAR Markt** is right next door (open Mon.-Fri. 7:30am-noon and 3-6pm, Sat. 7:30am-noon).

St. Michael also boasts a **Jugendherberge (HI),** located at Herbergsgasse 348 (tel. (06477) 630; fax 630 3). From the "St. Michael in Lungau Au" bus stop, turn right and then left onto Marktstr., bear left on Poststr., and turn left onto Kaltbachstr.; then take the first left onto Herbergsgasse. (Reception open 8-9am, noon-1pm, and 5-7pm. Curfew 10pm. 6-bed rooms 150 AS per person, doubles and quads with shower and toilet 170 AS per person; Dec.-April 160 AS and 200 AS, respectively. Non-members 40 AS surcharge. Breakfast and sheets included.)

THE SALZBURGER SPORTWELT AMADÉ

Envision access to over 320km of ski trails and 120 lifts with just one lift ticket. Only possible in a Winter Wonderland inhabited by underpaid elves and an overweight man in red feet pajamas? Not anymore. In response to an increasingly cutthroat competition to attract skiers and their wallets, the eight resorts in **Radstadt, Altenmarkt/Zauchensee, Eben, Flachau/Flachauwinkl, Kleinarl, Wagrain, Filzmoos,** and **St. Johann/Alpendorf** have combined their resources to establish a synergistic alliance of wintry power (not unlike Voltron…). During the *Hauptsaison* (high season; Dec. 18-April 4), a one-day pass costs 340 AS (under 15 185 AS), half-day 250 AS (under 15 135 AS), two days 640 AS (under 15 355 AS), and five days 1430 AS (under 15 785 AS). During the *Vor-* and *Nachsaison* (pre- and post-season; April 4-Dec. 18), a one-day pass costs 310 AS (under 15 170 AS), half-day 225 AS (under 15 130 AS), two days 575 AS (under 15 320 AS), and five days 1285 AS (under 15 705 AS). Or, consider the **Top-Tauern-Skischeck,** valid for lifts in the Amadé **and** three other regions (see Obertauern, below, for more information).

Ski runs connect most of the towns, but Sportwelt Amadé also provides free transportation. For example, skiers with a valid lift ticket can ride the **BundesBus** from Radstadt to Zauchensee or Flachau for free. In the summer (June-Oct.), tourists can still take advantage of the Sportwelt Amadé conglomeration; a **guest card,** available after one night's stay in any participating town, entitles the holder to half-price on all regional bus fares. Ask any area tourist office for an updated *Fahrplan*. While you're at the office, pick up the pamphlet *Sportwelt-Loipen* or its sister publication *Information und Skipaßtarife,* which lists prices, provides a regional map, and gives the phone numbers and business hours of every other tourist office in the Sportwelt.

Other winter sport fanatics shouldn't feel alienated by the Sportwelt's downhill focus—over 250km of **cross-country** trails await. You can take a romantic ride through town on a **horse-drawn sleigh**, or cavort o'er the fields, laughing all the way (ho, ho, ho); call either **Eggigut Farm** (tel. (06452) 373) or **Lerchenhof Farm** for more information. The sleighs can hold six to eight people (2 hrs., 600 AS). Call the 24-hour **snow condition report** throughout the Amadé region (tel. (06457) 2800; German only).

■■■ RADSTADT

The ancient town of Radstadt has successfully preserved its medieval mystique in the face of a booming ski industry. Vast stretches of the original fortifications stand triumphantly, reminding present generations of the power and influence Salzburg bishops once wielded in the area. Among the remaining town bulwarks are three imposing round towers, built by 16th-century peasants as punishment for rebelling against their overlords. (If you plan to foment an insurrection, we suggest you win.) Enveloped by majestic mountains at the hub of the enormous Amadé ski region, Radstadt thrives on the expenditures of monied tourists.

Orientation and Practical Information Radstadt's **tourist office** is in the *Rathaus*, at Stadtplatz 17 (tel. (06452) 305 or 74 72; fax 67 02). From the train station, turn left, and walk up the footpath farthest to the left, closest to the train tracks. After a 10-minute uphill climb, walk through the hole in the city wall and into the Stadtplatz. From the bus, get off at "Radstadt Postamt," in front of the post office. Turn left immediately upon disembarking and walk about 200m down Hoheneggstr.; the tourist office will be on your right. The office sells *Wanderkarten* for the Roßbrand peak (15 AS) and the entire Radstädter Tauern mountain region (79 AS); they also arrange free **guided tours** of the town every Monday evening from mid-June to mid-September. (Office open July-Aug. Mon.-Thurs. 8am-noon and 2-6pm; Fri. 8am-noon and 2-8pm, Sat. 8-11am; mid-April to June and Sept.-Nov. Mon.-Fri. 9am-noon and 2-6pm; Dec. to mid-April Mon-Fri. 8am-noon and 2-6pm, Sat. 8am-noon and 4-6pm, Sun 9am-noon.) Radstadt's **train station** rents bikes, has lockers, and offers luggage storage. The **post office,** on Salzburger Str., converts **currency.** (Open Mon.-Fri. 8am-noon and 2-6pm, Sat. 8-10am. Currency desk closes at 5pm. **Postal code:** A-5500.) **Mountainbike-center Pichler,** at Fischerbühel 3 (tel. (06452) 66 80), rents sturdy equipment for 200 AS per day or 150 AS for a half-day (open Mon.-Sat. 9am-noon and 2-6pm).

Accommodations and Food Radstadt's stubborn grip on "small town" status has luckily repelled the outlandish resort prices that plague other towns in the Sportwelt Amadé. The town largely overcomes the strains of tourism with a healthy load of *Privatzimmer*; most of these families prefer renting rooms through the tourist office. **Frühstückpension Ellmer,** at Schernbergstr. 18 (tel. (06452) 54 00), offers adequate rooms with flower-strewn balconies. From the tourist office, walk two minutes down Schernbergstr. (Singles 250 AS, doubles 220 AS per person. All rooms have showers and toilets. Breakfast included.) **Familie Sendlhofer,** down the street at Schernbergstr. 3-5 (tel. (06452) 239), lures guests with truly spacious rooms (some with kitchens), and a deer-antler chandelier illuminating the stairwell. The rooms rest above a tasty *Konditerei*. (Doubles 250 AS, with kitchen 280 AS. Breakfast included.) The rooms of **Frau Prodinger,** at Gappenau 12 (tel. 78 62), and **Frau**

Winter, in Haus Sissi at Gappenau 7 (tel. 60 84), are attractive alternatives for late-night arrivals. To reach Gappenau from the tourist office, turn left onto Hohenegg Str. (which will become Salzburger Str.), take your third left, and walk for about five minutes. (Frau Prodinger: in summer 160-165 AS, in winter 190-210 AS; Frau Winter: in summer 140-160 AS, in winter 190-210 AS. Both houses include shower and toilet.)

Camping Lärchenhof, at Schloßstr. 17 (tel. (06452) 215), has 150 campsites and a gorgeous view of the Pfarrkirche. Facing out from the tourist office, turn left and walk to the end of the Stadtplatz; then turn left onto Thun-Gasse, make a right, and walk through the opening of the town wall. Bear left and find Loretostr; the campground will be on your right (5 min.). Campers can purchase victuals at the supermarket and then proceed to feed the animals kept in a small, on-grounds **farm.** Ski storage room also available (Dec.-April). (53 AS per person, ages 4-14 30 AS, 50 AS per place; May-Nov. 48 AS per person, ages 4-14 28 AS, 45 AS per place. Over 18 3 AS tax; hot showers 10 AS. Prices include access to the pool on the grounds.)

Radstadt is home to a number of reasonably priced restaurants. **Chinese Restaurant "Mauer,"** at Schernbergstr. 15, serves a *Mittagsmenu* (59-67 AS; Mon.-Fri. 11:30am-2:30pm). Next door is **Gasthof Löcker** (hot meals 32-65 AS); try the *Grillwürstle mit Pommes frites* (50 AS). At Karl-Berg-Gasse 10, **3-P** makes scrumptious pizzas until the wee hours of the night (open daily 3pm-2am; small pizzas 55-75 AS, large pizzas 70-100 AS). Vegetarians, and anyone weary of the sausage scene, can feast on carts of greenery every Friday from 7am to noon in the Stadtplatz. During the winter months, the vendors sell **home-made wine.** Stock up on foodstuffs at the twin **SPAR Markts** at Hoheneggstr. 6 and 13. (#6 open Mon-Fri. 7:30am-6:30pm, Sat. 7:30am-12:30pm. #13 open Mon.-Fri. 7:30am-1pm and 2-6:30pm, Sat. 7:30am-12:30pm and 2:30-6:30pm.)

Sights and Entertainment The steeple of the **Stadtpfarrkirche Mariä Himmelfahrt** towers over the town and its regular rows of houses. Ravished by a sequence of fires, the 14th-century foundations of this simple Romanesque church have been deprived of much of their grandeur. Nevertheless, the purple stained-glass windows cast a regal glow over the church's interior. One of the three towers lingering from revolutions of yore, the **Kapuzinerturm** (tel. (06452) 70 83), houses a museum within its stony walls. The eclectic display ranges from traditional Salzburg festival masks to the rusty firearms and hoes wielded by those recalcitrant peasants. (Open June-Sept. daily 9:30-11:30am and 2-4pm. Admission 20 AS, ages 6-15 8 AS.) At Schloßstr. 1, **Schloß Lerchen** (tel. (06452) 63 74), once the town hospital, boasts an equally impressive collection of historical artifacts. The room dedicated to Paul Hofhaimer, a local Renaissance organist and composer, plays second fiddle to the array of tattered 19th-century prayer books and fire-fighting equipment. (Open June to mid-Oct 10am-noon and 3-5pm; Jan.-March 10-11am and 3-4pm. Admission 20 AS, ages 6-15 8 AS. A **combination card** (35 AS) is valid for both the Schloß Lerchen and the Kapuzinerturm museums.)

During the summer, the Radstadt residents lift their foamy mugs in unison and raucously pay tribute to bygone days of glory. On the first weekend of August, the **Radstädter Gardefest** celebrates the anniversary of the formation of the Bürgergarde (town militia). Festive young men polish brass buttons, shine pointy black shoes, and sport the colorful uniforms of this formerly vital defense unit. Homemade wine is traditionally sold in the **Teichturm,** while dancing kicks up the dirt in the square adjacent to Loretostraße (admission to the *Altstadt* 50 AS per night). One week before the Gardefest is the **Radstädter Knöd'lfest** (Dumpling Festival). For two days, Schernbergstr. becomes one continuous food bazaar, as local restaurants serve up a variety of tasty dumplings in a magnificent outdoor setting. Early September brings the **Kunsthandworker-Markt** to town—artists and craftsmen display their prowess in traditional arts, such as glass blowing, wood carving, and ceramics. The **Radstädter Musiksommer** invites the instructors and students of the acclaimed

Salzburger Sommerakademie Mozarteum for a series of July and August performances in the Kapuzinerkloster. (Concerts every Thurs. Tickets available 1 hr. before performance. Admission 100 AS, students 70 AS. See Salzburg for more ticket information.)

With well-marked trails and a snow-speckled summit, the **Roßbrand** (1770m) entices hikers from far and wide. You can carefully count the 150 different Alpine peaks visible from the Roßbrand's summit. From June to September, the tourist office sponsors **free guided hikes** through the other area mountains. (Times and dates vary.) For more detailed information, pick up the *Vorläufiger Veranstaltungskalendar*. If you plan to hike on your own instead, grab the *Sommer Wegweiser* pamphlet, which lists the opening hours and prices of Amadé ski lifts that operate during the summer, or the *Top-Tauern Wander- und Skiregionen (Summer Kurzführer),* which lists all operating lifts in Sportswelt Amadé, the Dachstein-Tauern region (including Schladming), and the Lungau (including St. Michael). The mountainous terrain rewards the cardiovascularly superior for their efforts with extraordinary vistas.

Radstadt belongs to the **Sportwelt Amadé** (see above), a monstrosity of a resort conglomeration comprising towns as distant as St. Johann, Untertauern and Flachau; the membership allows hikers and skiers alike to explore the nearby peaks via myriad discounts. **Intersport Rappl,** at Schornbergstr. 8 (tel. (06452) 448), rents skis, poles, and boots. (150-250AS per day; cross-country ski packages cost merely 60 AS per day. Open *Hauptsaison* Mon.-Fri. 8:30am-noon and 3-6pm, Sat. 4-6pm; *Vor- und Nachsaison* Mon.-Fri. 8:30am-noon and 3-6pm.)

The **Schischule Radstadt** has one office at Fischerbühel 3 (tel. (06452) 66 80) and another at the base of the Königslehen lift (tel. (06452) 73 82) to help placate nervous snow bunnies. A four-hour group lesson costs 400 AS, while a one-hour private lesson will lighten your fannypack by 450 AS. (Both offices open daily 9am-noon and 1:30-4:30pm.)

The **Reitecksee,** a small lake adjacent to the tiny hamlet of **Reitdorf,** lies 8km west of Radstadt. Take the bus (direction: either "St. Johann im Pongau" or "Flachauwinkel") to "Reitdorf GA" (22 AS).

■ Altenmarkt

The oldest town in the Enns valley is, appropriately, Altenmarkt (literally, "old market"), 4km southwest of Radstadt (20 AS by bus). Initially settled by a nomadic band of Celtic gold prospectors, Altenmarkt eventually became an invaluable Roman outpost guarding the pass through the **Niedere Tauern** range. This propitious location ensures Alternmarkt's modern prosperity as well; the sporting elite have certainly recognized its superior mountain terrain.

Between ski runs or hiking expeditions, make a concerted effort to explore Altenmarkt's charming **Hauptstraße** and **Marktplatz.** The towering **Pfarrkirche** was built in the late 14th century; legend holds that it was built on the site where a statue of the Madonna with Child repeatedly appeared on a fir tree. The representation of the Virgin Mary on the church's left altar is a reproduction of this mythical "Our Lady of the Fir Tree." Next to the church is the small **Altenmarkter Heimatmuseum,** a smattering of recreated 18th-century peasant homes (open Mon., Wed., and Fri. 4-6pm; admission 30 AS, under 15 20 AS). Every year, during the second weekend of July, Altenmarkt celebrates its **Sommerfest**—three days of traditional dancing, singing, and frothy beer (admission to the *Altstadt* 55 AS per day).

The **tourist office** (tel. 55 11 or 56 11; fax 60 66) sells an *Ortsplan* (10 AS), a mountain-bike map for the entire Pongau region (*Rad- und Mountainbikewege im Pongau*; 70 AS), and a hiking map for Radstadt and Schladming trails (80 AS). From the train station, follow Hauptstr. for 15 minutes and then make a left at the tennis courts onto Sportplatzstr; the office is in a slick, cedar chalet. (Open during ski season, Mon.-Sat. 8:30am-noon and 2-6pm, Sun. 8:30am-noon; in the off-season Mon.-Fri. 8:30am-noon and 2-6pm, Sat. 8:30am-noon.) An **electronic information switch-**

board in the office's lobby enables you to make free telephone calls to all area accommodations (open daily 6am-midnight). The **post office,** on Brunnbauerngasse just off the Marktplatz, houses a **telephone** bank (**City code:** 06452). (Open Mon.-Fri. 8am-noon and 2-6pm. Currency desk closes at 5pm. **Postal code:** A-5541.) **Rent skis** from **Intersport Michael Schneider** (tel. 54 79), at Hauptstr. 15. A complete set of alpine equipment costs 120 AS for one day; cross-country runs 80 AS (open Mon.-Sat. 8am-noon and 2-6pm).

■ St. Johann im Pongau

Perched 25km southwest of Altenmarkt on a bank of the tranquil **Salzach River** is St. Johann, the administrative center of the Pongau region (bus from Radstadt 50 AS, from Altenmarkt 20 AS; train from Radstadt 62 AS). Make no mistake about it—St. Johann is maniacally bent on enticing tourists. Before joining the Amadé confederation, the town served as the anchor of a trio of *Schilling*-hungry resorts—Flachau and Wagrain were the unindicted co-conspirators.

In the summer, take advantage of the wonderful hiking made possible by St. Johann's breathtaking setting and excellent facilities. The **Hahnbaum Berglift** (tel. (06412) 84 47; fax 844 75) ascends 1226m, while the **Bergbahn** (tel. (06412) 62 60; fax 85 17 83) in the suburb of Alpendorf reaches nearly 1700m. (Hahnbaum Berglift open late-June to early-Sept. Tues. and Fri. 9-11:45am and 1-6pm. One way 50 AS, round-trip 80 AS; with guest card 44 AS and 64 AS, respectively. Alpendorf Bergbahn open July-Aug. daily 9:30am-4:30pm; June and Sept. Wed. and Sun. 9:30am-4:30pm. One way 77 AS, round-trip 111 AS; with guest card 72 AS and 101 AS, respectively.) Myriad paths span the remainder of the valley; rent a **bike** at the train station to carry you along. The **tourist office,** at Hauptstr. 16 (tel. (06412) 60 36; fax 60 36 74), sells detailed *Radkarten* (80-90 AS) and *Wanderkarten* (40 AS) and can assist in mapping out a feasible excursion into the mountains. Exit the train station and turn right, make a left onto the bridge over the Salzach, and follow Hauptstr. to the office about 50m in front of the brooding, twin-towered **Pfarrkirche** (15 min.). (Office open May-Nov. Mon.-Fri. 8:30am-noon and 2-6pm, Sat. 9am-noon.) The English-speaking staff also distributes the *Veranstaltungs Kalendar,* an invaluable monthly calendar of events.

St. Johann has the *wunderbar* skiing facilities expected of any member of the Sportwelt Amadé. **Intersport Kirschbaum,** at Spitalgasse 2 (tel. (06412) 369), rents complete packages of ski equipment (100-160 AS per day). Its branch store in Alpendorf also rents skis, and offers a four-hour group lesson for 450 AS. (Both stores open *Hauptsaison* Mon.-Fri. 8:30am-noon and 3-6pm, Sat.-Sun. 9am-6pm; *Vor- und Nachsaison* Mon.-Fri. 8:30am-noon and 3-6pm, Sat. 9am-noon.) Complimentary **ski buses** connect St. Johann and Alpendorf during the winter. Drop a postcard from the **post office** at Hauptstr. 28. (Open Mon.-Fri. 8am-noon and 2-6pm, Sat. 8-10am. **Currency** desk open Mon.-Fri. 8am-noon and 2-5pm. **Postal code:** A-5600.)

St. Johann's **Jugendherberge (HI) "Weitenmoos"** (tel. (06412) 62 22; fax 62 22 4) stands defiantly atop a 1200m peak. Large dormitory rooms and spartan showers await the exhausted few who surmount the hill. To reach the hostel, walk 50m to the right upon exiting the train station, and board the BundesBus (direction: "Stockham"); disembark at "Alpendorf" (20 AS) and struggle up the treacherously steep road. The last bus from the train station departs at 6:10pm—unless you're capable of leaping tall buildings in a single bound, consider a cab. (Hostel 145 AS, 10 AS surcharge for one night stays. Curfew 10pm. Reception reportedly open 24 hrs., but call first.) **Wiesof Camping** (tel. (06412) 85 19) has 150 sites a bit closer to the train station. Turn right out of the station, make your first right, and follow the signs. (50 AS per person, children 25 AS; 50 AS per site. Showers 10 AS. Over 15 14 AS tax. There's a supermarket on the grounds.).

Festivals and concerts follow summer to St. Johann. Every year during the second weekend of July, townsfolk unwrap the *Lederhosen* and the *Dirndl* and pound steins of Gösser beer during the rowdy **Alpendorf Fest** (80-100 AS to gain admittance to Alpendorf). Wednesdays from June to July, traditional Austrian folk music envelops the Musikpavilion in St. Johann; ask the tourist office for more information about these **Platzekonzerte.** Every four years, on January 6 (it next arrives in 1996), all of the Salzburger Land gathers in St. Johann for the **Pongauer Perchtenlauf.** On this day, *Grampus* (devil-like creatures) prance through the streets as the town turns to superstition and magic to shield the crops from ghosts and goblins.

Near St. Johann: Liechtensteinklamm

Just 7km south of St. Johann is the most spectacular gorge of the eastern Alps, the chillingly beautiful Liechtensteinklamm. Three-quarters of a mile long and but 12½ feet wide, this gorge cradles a powerful, iridescent waterfall. The 45-minute hike is riddled with bewitching vistas of the 1000-foot-high rock walls. (Open May to mid-Oct. daily 8am-5pm. Admission 30 AS, children 20 AS.) The **Kombitarif Naturpaket** (140 AS, ages 6-15 80 AS), sold at Liechtensteinklamm and the regional ski lifts, is valid for entry into the gorge and round-trip passage on the Alpendorf Bergbahn. **Buses** leave St. Johann (4 times per day, mid-July to mid-Sept. 7 times per day, 22 AS).

■ Obertauern

This haphazard conglomeration of swanky hotels, smoke-filled cafés, and death-defying ski runs sparkles at the 1740m peak of the winding **Rastädter Tauern Road.** It's rather difficult to call Obertauern a town, given the stark absence of a unifying Hauptplatz or permanent residences. Nevertheless, busloads of skiers and hikers make the pilgrimage to this playland, one of the most exclusive and challenging sport resorts in central Europe. Buses struggle up the mountain pass from Radstadt (49 AS) and Tamsweg (60 AS)—sit back, admire the scenery, and look for the ruins of the original Roman road.

One hundred twenty km of runs, 25 lifts, and the 2357m **Gamslertenspitze,** home to the steepest slopes in all of Europe, have been known to spark spontaneous wintry mania in even the most casual skiers. A one-day **lift ticket** during the *Hauptsaison* (Dec. 19-April 17) costs 345 AS (half-day 265 AS, 5 days 1380 AS). Obertauern doesn't belong to the Sportwelt Amadé conglomerate, but fret not—the **Top-Tauern-Schischeck** (6 days 1800 AS, under 15 1020 AS; 7 days 1920 AS, under 15 1100 AS; passport photo required) puts the 320 lifts of the Lift-Gemeinschaft Obertauern, the Dachstein-Tauern-Region, the Skiregion Lungau, and the Sportwelt Amadé at the mercy of your freshly waxed Völkls. Free buses connect Obertauern and Radstadt, the pride and joy of the Sportwelt Amadé, during the ski season. Sport stores litter the only road bisecting Obertauern. **Sporthaus Erika** (tel. 261) rents boots (100-150 AS), skis (170-230 AS), and poles (30 AS); prices plummet considerably for extended rental periods (open in ski season daily 8:30am-12:30pm and 2:30-6pm). **Skischule Krallinger** (tel. 258 or 303; fax 545) offers all sorts of private (1800 AS) and group (450 AS) lessons. For a 24-hour **snow condition report,** call 386.

Obertauern resembles a spaghetti Western ghost town in the summer; restaurants turn off their skillets, and hotels board up their windows—if you squint, you can almost see Clint Eastwood mosey into town past the tumbleweed. Nevertheless, the bald mountains still yield excellent hiking. The **tourist office** (tel. 252 or 320; fax 515) sponsors free guided **hikes** from July to mid-September and sells a comprehensive *Wanderkarte* (30 AS) if you'd rather go it alone. (Open Nov.-May Mon.-Sat. 8am-noon and 2-6pm, Sun. 9am-noon; June-Oct. Mon.-Fri. 8am-noon and 2-6pm.)

The **post office,** which also doubles as the **BundesBus** stop, has **telephones** (**City code:** 06456) and **exchanges money.** (Open Mon.-Fri. 8:30am-noon and 2-6pm, Sat. 8:30-10:30am; May-Nov. Mon.-Fri. 8:30am-noon and 2-5pm. **Postal code:** A-5562.) Budget travelers trapped in Obertauern for the night should simply surrender any money left in their waning wallets. Inquire at the tourist office for potential vacancies at the **Jugendheime** (youth homes; usually booked far in advance by ski clubs), or head to nearby **Tweng** (24 AS) or **Untertauern** (81 AS).

■■■ SCHLADMING

Amidst the Dachstein mountains to the north and Schladminger Tauern to the south, Schladming intercepts the River **Enns** as it flows east-west through a verdant valley. The town has valiantly arisen from a history fraught with tragedy—vindictive lords razed the entire town in 1525—to become a well-oiled resort machine. Traces of the original 16th-century fortifications are still visible, but most of the town dates from the mining era; a number of genuine miners' houses are on display. Locals love to relate the saga of the 1629 **Salzburgertor,** the city gate that crippled an invading American tank during World War II.

Orientation and Practical Information The **tourist office,** at Hauptplatz 18 (tel. 222 68; fax 24 138), distributes reams of brochures and weekly calendars. Especially helpful is the *Dachstein-Tauern Gästezeitung,* which contains a schedule of the region's cultural events, and *Ausflüge rund um die Dachstein-Tauern-Region,* a booklet that introduces Schladming and nearby hamlets. To reach the tourist office from the train station, turn left onto Bahnhofstr., cross the footbridge, and turn right onto Ramsauer Str. Then turn left onto Salzburger Str., bear left at the first fork, and right at the second to reach the Hauptplatz (15 min.). The office can also assist in planning mountain hikes; a friendly, English-speaking staff vends *Wanderkarten* (60 AS) and provides a free **guided hike** every Wednesday in July and August (meet at 7am at the Rathausplatz). Those more reluctant to leave low altitudes might pick up the booklet *A Short Historical Tour* (10 AS; free with a guest card), which guides you among Schladming's churches and landmarks.

The **post office (postal code:** A-8970) is right next to the hostel and provides **telephones (City code:** 03687). (Open mid-June to Sept. and mid-Dec. to March Mon.-Fri. 8am-noon and 2-6pm, Sat. 8-11am; April to mid-June and Oct. to mid-Dec. Mon.-Fri. 8am-noon and 2-6pm, Sat. 8-10am. **Currency** desk open year-round Mon.-Fri. 8am-noon and 2-5pm.) Schladming's **train station** rents bikes, has lockers, and offers luggage storage.

Accommodations and Food **Jugendgästehaus Schladming (HI),** Coburgstr. 253 (tel. 245 31; fax 245 31 88), contains a whopping 215 beds in a mansion blessed with a relaxing veranda and complete sports grounds. Twenty-five of these beds are reserved for families. From the train station, follow the directions to the tourist office, and keep walking through the Hauptplatz; the hostel is directly behind the post office. (Reception open 5-8pm. Flexible 10pm curfew—ask for a key. In the ski season 160 AS; in the off-season 130 AS. Singles and doubles 30 AS extra. 15 AS surcharge for non-members. Breakfast and sheets included.)

Avoid the outrageously expensive restaurants by raiding the shelves at the **Julius Meinl** and **Konsum supermarkets** in the Hauptplatz. (Julius Meinl open Mon.-Fri. 8am-6:30pm, Sat. 7:30am-12:30pm. Konsum open Mon.-Fri. 8am-6pm, Sat. 8am-12:30pm.)

Sights and Entertainment The **Pfarrkirche** exhibits a fine Romanesque tower, while the **Evangelische Kirche,** the largest Protestant church in Styria, showcases pieces from a glorious Renaissance altar. Overlooking the **River Enns** in a house that once served as a miners' hospital is the **Stadtmuseum.** Its small display presents the cultural history of Styria in admirable detail. (Open Tues.-Fri. 10am-noon and 5-8pm, Sun. 10am-2pm. Free.)

Innumerable hiking trails and ski runs traverse the jagged crags of the Dachstein-Tauern range surrounding Schladming, including the immense 2700m **Dachstein glacier**. A one-day **lift pass** valid for the entire Dachstein-Tauern-Region costs 235 AS in the *Vor-* and *Nachsaison,* and 345 AS in the *Hauptsaison* (under 15 175 AS). Rates drop drastically for extended visits; lift tickets for four days or more require a passport photo. The **Top-Tauern Skischeck** enables you to swoosh through the snow in four luscious winter playlands (see Obertauern, above, for more information). **Intersport Bachler,** at Hauptplatz 17 (tel. 231 43), offers rentals. (1-day package 120-200 AS, 1-week package 580-1110 AS. Open Dec.-April daily 8:30am-12:30pm and 2:30-6:30pm; May-Nov. Mon.-Fri. 8:15am-noon and 2:30-6:15pm, Sat. 8:15am-12:30pm.) Perfect your parallel turns with the expert advice of the **Kahr Keinprecht Schischule** (tel. 230 62 or 235 44). A one-day private lesson orbits at 1600 AS, while the group lesson is listed at a much more comfortable 450 AS. For a 24-hour **snow condition report** (German only) dial (0660) 87 00.

Two of Schladming's **cable-car** lifts also operate during the summer. The **Hochwurzen-Seilbahn** ascends 1850m, while the **Planai-Seilbahn** rises 1894m to the glacier. (Hochwurzen-Seilbahn open July-Sept. daily 9am-noon and 1-5pm. One way 75 AS, with guest card 70 AS; round-trip 100 AS, with guest card 95 AS. Planai-Seilbahn open late-June to Sept. daily 9am-noon and 1-5pm; Oct. Fri.-Sun. 9am-noon and 1-5pm. One way 105 AS, with guest card 100 AS; round-trip 150 AS, with guest card 140 AS.) Mountain bikers and hikers should ask the tourist office for the English pamphlet *Walkable Dachstein-Tauern Area.* **Intersport Bachler,** also rents **bikes** for 180 AS per day and 350 AS for the weekend (see above for more information).

Every July, Schladming resounds with the classical harmonies of the **Musiksommer;** buy tickets at the tourist office (170 AS) or at the door (200 AS; under 19 80 AS). (Tourist office open mid-Dec. to mid-April and July-Aug. Mon.-Fri. 8am-6pm, Sat. 8am-noon and 2-6pm, Sun. 10am-noon and 4-6pm; mid-April to June and Sept. to mid-Oct. Mon.-Fri. 8am-6pm, Sat. 8am-noon.)

THE MURTAL

Eons ago, before the mining of iron ore and manganese became the *de rigeur* south Austrian vocation, the **River Mur** in central and southern Styria carved a valley amidst the Gleinalpe to the west, Seetaler Alpen to the south, and Seckauer and Niedere Tauern to the north. Long, upland, pastured ridges flank the valley. Half the region is covered by forests, and another quarter by grasslands and vineyards, leaving one-quarter for everybody else.

The Mur has its source in the Salzburger Land, and it eventually joins the Drau in erstwhile Yugoslavia. The Mur valley, unlike the Drautal to the west, is mostly lakeless, though an inchoate skiing industry putters along, far less bustling than its western counterparts. Low hills (at most 2000m high) make the region a cyclist's and walker's nirvana. There's certainly no cosmopolitanism to get in your way—maybe a mountain beast or terrible forest man (see Danube in Lower Austria), but no ritz, and certainly no glitz.

Composed of three main towns—Leoben, Bruck an der Mur, and Murau, at the foot of the Stolzalpe (1800m)—the Murtal represents Ye Olde Austria. Mostly underdeveloped, it retains the charm of an earlier age; industry here remains dependent on the mineral resources ensconced within the womb of the rounded mountains. Styria is Austria's leading mineral province; the mining and steel industries have their scientific center in Leoben's University. The region also produces cellulose, paper, and electrical products. Most every house in the valley proudly displays an *Alte Bauernkalender* (Old Farmer's Calendar), a tradition for some 250 years. The calendar is a small, colorfully illustrated booklet, the equivalent of an American *Farmer's Almanac*; many visitors consider it the superlative Styrian souvenir. Its main purpose—other than mass retail—is forecasting weather; many are convinced that meteorologists are less reliable than the book's conjectures.

The **Steirische Eisenstraße** (Styrian Iron Road) wends through valleys and waterfalls from Leoben to Styria's pride and joy, the Erzberg (Iron Mountain), and on through the Enns Valley. North of Leoben is Eisenerz and its **Crèche Museum** (tel. (03848) 36 15), devoted to nativity scenes produced by local craftspeople; here, a cellar-cum-mine shaft displays the holy family in front of the panoramic town backdrop. Between Eisenerz and Leoben in Vordenberg is a blast furnace and iron museum, **Radwerk IV Wheelworks** (tel. (03849) 283 or 206), home to the only fully equipped wood-burning blast furnace in Central Europe. This museum presents a telling testimonial to the historic pig-iron extraction technique. Also in Vordernberg is the **Traktor Museum** (tel. (03849) 290).

A valiant superhighway—called Schnellstraße 6 along the stretch from Bruck to St. Michael, Schnellstraße 36 west to Judenburg, and finally Bundesstraße 96 southwest to Murau—mimics the course of the Mur. **Trains** on the Wien-Villach-Salzburg line and the Bruck an der Mur-Villach-Arnoldstein line pass through the Murtal. A train runs six times per day from Murau to Unzmarkt and back; another runs east, at 22 minutes past the hour, from Unzmarkt to Vienna, via Bruck an der Mur. A special steam locomotive, the **Murtalbahn** (Mur Valley Railway), chugs in summer between Tamsweg and Unzmarkt, via Murau.

■■■ MURAU

At the foot of the densely forested Stolzalpe, Murau is a vivid collage of orange roofs and brown shutters. The violent roar of the River Mur penetrates even the most remote cobblestone path, as it collides with boulder-strewn banks. Vast stretches of the old town wall, buttressed by two of the seven original gates, remind visitors of Murau's medieval roots. In part because Murau is accessible by private rail line only, the town has resolutely withstood the gaudy temptations of tourism (train from Tamsweg round-trip 110 AS).

Orientation and Practical Information The **tourist office,** conveniently situated next to the train station (tel. 27 20; fax 22 31 22), dispenses helpful brochures concerning every facet of the town. Especially informative is the *Veranstaltungen* (a calendar of events), the *Gästezeitung* (a newsletter published biannually), and the list of accommodations. Free tours of the *Altstadt* run throughout the summer—ask for times. The friendly, English-speaking staff can also help you plan **hikes** during the summer, and sells a 20 AS *Wanderkarte* that charts both scenic and strenuous trails throughout the Murau region. Less experienced hikers should inquire about the host of privately organized **guided walks** offered through the tourist office. You'll be able to cover more ground on a **mountain bike;** rental is available at **Intersport Pintar,** on Schwarzenbergstr. around the corner from Schiller Platz (tel. 23 97). One day costs 200 AS (weekend 350 AS, morning 100 AS, afternoon 150 AS; open Mon.-Fri. 8am-noon and 3-6pm, Sat. 8am-noon). Murau's **post office,** on Bahnhofstr. 4, offers excellent exchange rates and has a plethora of **telephones (City code:** 03532). (Open Mon.-Fri. 8am-noon and 2-6pm, Sat. 8-10am. Currency desk closes at 5pm.)

Accommodations and Food Reasonable accommodations shouldn't be too difficult to track down in this compact town. The **Jugendherberge (HI) "Zum Deutschen Ritter,"** St. Leonhard Platz 4 (tel. 23 95), pleases guests with doubles and quads (all with showers and toilets) off a labyrinth of low-arched hallways. From the tourist office, take a left onto Bahnhofstr., bear left onto Friesacher Str., and walk along the railroad tracks until you see a sign for Raffaltplatz. Turn right to find the hostel and St. Leonhard Platz (4 min.). (Reception open 5-8pm. Curfew 10pm. 100 AS, breakfast 30 AS, sheets 25 AS. Lunch and dinner available. The hostel is undergoing renovations during autumn of 1993, so prices may change). Centrally located **Gasthof Bärenwirt,** at Schwarzenbergstr. 4 (tel. 20 79), offers spacious doubles. From the tourist office, turn left onto Bahnhofstr., veer right at the post office, and cross over the bridge; then turn right onto Anna Neumann Str. (which will merge into Liechtenstein Str.), and walk through Schiller Platz onto Schwarzenbergstr. (Doubles mid-Dec. to mid-April and July to early-Sept. 180-370 AS; mid-April to June and early-Sept. to mid-Dec. 180-350 AS.) A cornucopia of **private rooms** can be found on **Erzherzog-Johann-Str.** From Schiller Platz, walk five minutes down Grabenstr. until it becomes Erzherzog-Johann-Str. Most families prefer that you book through the tourist office. In a jam, try the rooms of **Family Müller** at Erzherzog-Johann-Str. 5 (tel. 31 79; high season doubles 160 AS per person, off-season 140 AS per person, 20 AS surcharge for singles). Regardless of where you bed down, ask for a **Gästepass** that entitles you to large discounts on such amenities as ski and bike rentals.

Yang Chinese Restaurant, at Anna Neumann Str. 29, cooks up the cheapest lunches in Murau (55 AS). (Open daily 11am-11pm. *Mittagsmenu* Mon.-Fri. 11am-2:30pm.) Stop by **Albin Murer Fleischhauerei-Imbißstube,** at Schwarzenbergstr. 1, for a quick bite. *Frankfurter mit Senf* 28 AS, *Kartoffelsalat* 25 AS. (Open Mon.-Fri. 7:15am-1pm and 3-6pm, Sat. 7:15am-noon.) Otherwise, clip your coupons for the **ADEG supermarket** right next to the hostel (open Mon.-Fri. 7am-noon and 2:30-6pm, Sat. 7am-noon) or the **Konsum supermarket** in Schiller Platz (open Mon.-Fri. 7:30am-6:30pm, Sat. 7:30am-12:30pm).

Sights and Entertainment The deep mahogany spire of the **Pfarrkirche Matthäus** vies with the surrounding mountainscape for control of the heavens. This Gothic structure is home to an extensive network of gently faded frescoes and the tomb of the Liechtensteins, the early rulers of Murau. Just beneath the Pfarrkirche stands the **Altes Rathaus,** built precariously adjacent to the River Mur. This building, with finely etched designs on its façade, was part of Murau's original medieval fortifications. Inside the 14th-century **Spitalskirche Elisabeth** is the **Diözesanmuseum,** which holds assorted writings of Martin Luther, among other Reformation treasures. Better brush up on your Latin and German—Luther didn't write much in English (museum open July-Aug. Wed. 2-5pm).

High up the hillside and partially eclipsed by the Pfarrkirche's tower is **Schloß Obermurau.** Owned by the Liechtenstein family since the 13th century, this castle boasts an elegantly arcaded Renaissance courtyard. The obligatory tour invites you into the castle's chapel and two luxurious rooms on the second floor (1-hr. tour July-Aug. Wed. 9:30am; admission 20 AS, children 10 AS). The view from the castle offers a stunning perspective of St. Matthäus, the River Mur, and distant ruins of the Gothic **Filialkirche St. Leonhard** (open only for groups by prior arrangement). A five-minute walk through Schillerplatz and down Gruberstr. leads to the town **Heimatmuseum.** Located within the walls of the erstwhile Kapuzinerkloster, this collection presents Styrian history and culture. (Obligatory 1-hr. tour July-Aug. Thurs. 4pm. Free.)

Every year on August 15, Murau celebrates its rich heritage during the festive and rowdy **Stadtfest.** On this day, residents drag out their enormous figure of **Samson** (see the Lungau, above). During July and August, Murau plays host to a series of Sunday night concerts performed inside the castle. Tickets for these **Schloßkonzerte** (100 AS, students 60 AS) can be purchased at the tourist office (tel. 27 20) or at the ticket booth inside the *Schloß*, one hour before the performance. Every Tuesday and Wednesday from July to mid-September, an old-fashioned steamtrain, the **Murtalbahn,** thinks it can, and thinks it can, and thinks it can get up the mountain between Murau and Tamsweg. (Every Tues. departs Murau 1:35pm, returns from Tamsweg 4:50pm; every Wed. departs Tamsweg 1pm, returns from Murau 5pm. One way 160 AS.) The **Murau Brauerei,** at Raffaltplatz 19-23, has been brewing its renowned Styrian stew since 1495. Purchase the frothy malt beverage at the factory's window (open Mon.-Thurs. 7am-6pm, Fri. 7am-1pm); you can also hum the theme to *Laverne and Shirley* on a **tour** of the complex (by previous arrangement; call 326 60).

With the **Frauenalpe** (2004m) to the south and the **Kreischberg** (2050m) to the northwest, Murau has plenty of terrain to entice the serious skier. Free buses run from the tourist office to the Frauenalpe (day pass 185 AS, under 15 145 AS; ½-day

140 AS and 115 AS, respectively). To cliff-jump or snowplow down the slopes at **Kreischberg,** take the train (direction: "Tamsweg") to "St. Lorenzen ob Murau." The slightly more challenging runs of the Kreischberg are also slightly more expensive. (Day pass (*Tageskarte*) 285 AS, under 15 175 AS; ½-day 230 AS and 140 AS, respectively.) **Cross-country** trails traverse the entire Murau region and are blissfully free of charge. Rent **equipment** at **Intersport Pintar** (see Orientation and Practical Information above; 100 AS for a downhill package, 60 AS for cross-country skis) or at **Sport Schi-Sepp** in St. Lorenzen ob Murau (tel. (03537) 264; prices are identical).

■■■ LEOBEN

Sixteen km west of Bruck an der Mur, Leoben lies cradled between a ring of plush mountains and the Mur River, which borders all but its eastern edge. First documented in 982, the city's history is woven inextricably with trans-continental trade and iron mining. Yet, Leoben has somehow managed to balance its industrial capacity with the charm and ease of a rural community. Three-quarters of the city's area is woodland, to the delight of mushroom gatherers, walkers, joggers, and Smurfs™. Residents are rather proud of their 450,000 square meters of green, and the more colorful trophy from the Provincial Flower Competition—five times Leoben was voted "the most beautiful town in Styria." Leoben also boasts a well-preserved historic city center and a Mining University; it is well-known as a conference and seminar center. While you're in town, use the opportunity to enjoy the local specialities, such as "Mushroom Gulash," "Shepherd's Spit," "Styrian Roast Beef," and local Gösser beer.

Orientation and Practical Information Leoben, the largest town in central Styria, is just minutes from Autobahn A9, which runs south to Graz and northwest toward Steyr and Linz. The town's **train station** funnels several major routes into the transit hub at Bruck an der Mur (every 20 min.; 15 min.; 32 AS); buses also run from Leoben to the rest of Styria. From the *Bahnhof,* you must cross the river to reach the heart of Leoben, the section circumscribed by the river Mur. This core is shaped like a holiday stocking—reminiscent of Italy, but less jagged, and less tomato-centric. A long street, composed of Zeitenschlagstr., Sudbahnstr., and Winkelfeldstr., hugs the outer bank of the Mur, and the Stadtkai follows the inner bank. Leoben's **tourist office,** at Hauptplatz 12 (tel. 440 18), will help you decipher the snarl of rail lines; also pick up the complimentary *Stadtplan* (open Mon.-Thurs. 7am-noon and 1:30-5pm, Fri. 7am-1pm). Drop a postcard at either one of two **post offices** (**Postal code:** A-8701). The office at Erzherzog-Johann-Str. 17 is open Mon.-Fri. 8am-7pm, Sat. 8-10am; the office at Südbahnstr. (adjacent to the train station) is open Mon.-Fri. 7am-noon and 2-9pm. **Telephones** are available at either location (**City code:** 03842).

Accommodations and Food Unfortunately, Leoben town officials have been preoccupied with their flowers; they haven't yet planted any budget accommodations. **Hotel Altman,** Südbahnstr. 32 (tel. 422 16), offers 22 beds and a bowling alley in a convenient, albeit busy, location. To reach the hotel, turn left on Südbahnhofstr. and walk alongside the rail tracks for 10 minutes. (Single with shower 250 AS, double with shower and toilet 200-220 AS per person. Breakfast included. Other meals 55 AS-155 AS. Bowling alley open Tues.-Sun. 10am-midnight; 10 AS per 12 min. Free parking.) If this seems too steep, hostels await in neighboring towns; try the **Jugendherberge (HI)** in Bruck an der Mur. The **Jugendherberge (HI)** in **Trofaiach,** at Rebenburggasse 2 (tel. (03847) 22 60), only accepts groups of 20 or more. Either make 19 friends fast, or beg and plead with the friendly, English-speaking proprietors. (20 min. bus to Trofaiach 28 AS. Turn right immediately after exiting the bus, walk two minutes, and turn right on Rebenburggasse, right before the pizzeria. The hostel is on the second floor of a white building with green shutters.) Before you head out of town, though, fill your picnic basket to the brim at Leoben's **Feinkost Bauer** (Hauptplatz 17; open Mon.-Fri. 7:30am-6:30pm, Sat. 7:30am-12:30pm). It's also pretty easy being green with a salad (28-68 AS) at **Familie Hölzl,** across from the Stadttheater (open Mon.-Fri. 7:30am-8:30pm, Sat. 7:30am-2pm).

Sights and Entertainment The majority of Leoben's attractions lie cluttered around the **Hauptplatz,** a 10-minute walk from the train station; cross over the bridge, and bear right onto Franz-Josef-Str. Sights are designated by a square block with a bizarre imprint of an ostrich wearing iron shoes. This city symbol alludes not to a Pacino or Brando vendetta, but rather to Leoben's dependence on the iron trade—in the Middle Ages, ostriches were thought capable of eating and digesting iron. The unbelievably ornamental Baroque facade of the 17th-century **Hacklhaus** dominates the Hauptplatz. The top six figures represent six of the 12 Christian virtues; Justice holds a sword and a balance, Hope brandishes an anchor, Wisdom views the world through the mirror in his hand, and Crosby, Stills, and Nash sing backup harmony. Don't miss Old Man Winter on the bottom row, warming his icy fingers over a roaring fire. Across the square is the **Altes Rathaus,** constructed in 1568. Now home to a plethora of clothing shops and an international conference center, the handsome structure still displays the colorful coats of arms of the local Habsburg counties. Standing guard at the entrance to the Hauptplatz are the **Denkmäler und Monumente,** beautifully crafted works erected to ward off the fire and plague that devastated much of Styria in the early 18th century. Look for Florian, the saint empowered against the inflammable, and the reclining Rosalia, the saint responsible for fending off plagues.

Just outside the Hauptplatz is the **Pfarrkirche Franz Xaver,** a rust-colored, two-towered church built in 1660-1665 by the Jesuits. The simple facade belies an elaborate interior and a high altar bedecked with remarkable Solomonic columns. Next door is the **Museum der Stadt Leoben,** a rich collection of portraits and documents that traces the city's historical development. The Napoleonic wars are synthesized in a display of well-preserved swords and uniforms and a diorama of a reconstructed battlefield. (Open Mon.-Thurs. 10am-noon and 2-5pm, Fri. 10am-1pm. 20 AS, students 5 AS. Enter from the front door at Kirchgasse 6.) The **Schwammerlturm** (mushroom tower) stands vigilantly over the bridge that crosses the Mur. Yep, it really looks like a giant fungus. Across the river, the **Kirche Maria am Waasen** conceals two gorgeous panels of 15th-century stained glass behind a deceptively drab exterior.

In the 13th century, Bohemian King Ottokar II flaunted conventional meandering cowpath roadways and laid down a grid of systematically constructed and almost perfectly parallel streets. (It's good to be both king and civil engineer, especially during rush hour.) Pick your way through the gardens of flowers lining the pavement, but remember: the winged monkeys are waiting for the poppies to take effect. Leoben takes its marigolds and tiger lilies seriously; the town has earned a blue ribbon in the Provincial Flower Competition an unprecedented five times. For even more flora, stroll through the **Stadtpark** behind the Hauptplatz. There, you can visit the **Friedensgedenkstätte** (peace memorial), which commemorates the peace treaty with Napoleon, signed here in 1797. The small museum showcases an exhibit detailing the political and military events surrounding the treaty, including the feather pen that bore Napoleon's signature (open May-Oct. daily 9am-1pm and 2-5pm; free). A scenic 30-minute walk along the Mur rewards you with the chance to inspect the **Gösser brewery.** The 90-minute tour features antique brewing machinery and wanders inside the **Göss Abbey,** the oldest abbey in Styria; then the tour sends you on your way with a free *Stein* of fresh brew. (Tours by previous arrangement; call 226 21. Museum open Mon.-Fri. 8am-noon and 2-4pm.) During the summer months, there's an afternoon concert every Sunday in the Stadtpark's outdoor pavilion. The **Stadttheater,** at Kärntner Str. 224, is the oldest functioning theater in all of Austria. For specific information, consult the Leoben tourist office.

On Dec. 4, the **Ledersprung** will once again be held at the Montanuniversität (University of Mining) in Leoben. The Custom of the Ledersprung (jumping over the leather) is carried out in the feast of St. Barbara. Leather was part of the traditional working outfit of the miner, and the tradition of the leap can be traced back to superstitions of the 16th century.

■ Bruck an der Mur

Situated just north of an impassable chain of mountains, Bruck an der Mur has become the hub of southeast Austria's railroad network by default. The train station adeptly coordinates traffic at the intersection of three busy rail lines with an impressive arsenal of electronic gizmos and computerized gadgets. Trains depart frequently for Graz (92 AS; 40 min.), Leoben (32 AS; 12 min.), Innsbruck (464 AS; 5 hr. 20 min.), Klagenfurt (226 AS; 2 hr. 15 min.), and Vienna (200 AS; 1 hr. 50 min.).

Even this transportation nexus has its fair share of Kodak moments™, albeit only a few hours' worth. Stretch out your legs in flowerful **Koloman-Wallisch-Platz,** the center of the *Altstadt*. The **Eiserner Brunnen,** an intricate wrought-iron well fashioned for the square by local artisan Hans Prasser, is considered one of the masterpieces of European iron work. The **Kornmesserhaus** displays both flamboyant Gothic rosettes and an Italian Renaissance loggia; the latter style was imported during the town's lucrative trade with Venice. Also located within the *Platz* is the **Mariensäule,** a monument erected to commemorate the 1683 inferno that destroyed two-thirds of the town.

Towering high above the *Altstadt* are two especially memorable structures. The Gothic vestry door and masterful iron knocker of the **Pfarrkirche** herald the beauty that awaits within. Note the crucifix that hovers mysteriously above the pulpit. Two blocks northeast from the church, on the corner of Herzog-Ernst-Gasse and Wienerstr., looms the 13th-century **Burg Landskron,** a citadel that once guarded the confluence of the Mürz and Mur rivers. A five-minute climb to the apex of the fortress's weathered **Uhrturm** (clock tower) provides a panoramic view of the lush countryside below.

The makeshift **tourist office** (Reisebüro der Stadt Bruck; tel. (03862) 51 811 or 53 406; fax 518 11 85) stands in the center of Koloman-Wallisch-Platz and sells 20 AS *Stadtplans* (open Mon.-Fri. 8:30am-noon and 2-5pm, Sat. 9am-noon). The **train station,** Bahnhofstr. 22, is open 24 hrs.; it stores luggage, rents bikes, and offers lockers (20-30 AS). The **post office,** next to the station, exchanges money (open 24 hrs.).

If you must stay in Bruck overnight, the small **Jugendherberge (HI),** Theodor-Korner-Str. 37 (tel. (03862) 534 65; fax 560 89), offers large dormitory-style lodging only 15 minutes from the train station. Head down Bahnhofstr., bear left under the bridge and then right onto Herzog-Ernst-Gasse, walk through Koloman-Wallisch-Platz, and continue straight on Theodor-Korner-Str. The diminutive hostel, once a monastery, is run by a jovial, English-speaking proprietor and provides stunning views of the Mur. (Open April-Oct. Reception 7-10am and 5-10pm. Curfew 10pm. 115 AS first night, 100 AS per night thereafter. Breakfast included. Delicious lunches and dinners 50-60 AS.) If there's no room at the hostel, try **Zimmer Juliane Striessnig,** just up the street at Theodor-Korner-Str. 29 (tel. (03862) 517 06). The rooms offer high ceilings and views of mountain cattle—it's consummately snug. (4 doubles with showers, 190 AS per person. Breakfast included. Call ahead.)

The **Lotus China Restaurant,** on the corner of Kupferschmiedgasse and Herzog-Ernst-Gasse, prepares tasty Indonesian alternatives to standard Styrian fare. Try the eclectic nine-course *Reistafel* for two (200 AS). (Meals 50-180 AS. Lunch specials Mon.-Fri. 50-65 AS. Open daily 11:30am-2:30pm and 5:30-11:30pm.) A host of moderately priced cafés and pubs along **Mittergasse,** the pedestrian street connected to Koloman-Wallisch-Platz, beckons you to enter and imbibe. Otherwise, assemble a picnic lunch at the **Konsum** supermarket on Bahnhofstr. by the train station (open Mon.-Fri. 7:30am-noon and 3:30-6pm, Sat. 7:30am-noon).

■■■ RIEGERSBURG

Perched precariously atop an extinct volcano, the majestic Riegersburg castle stands watch over the diminutive valley town that bears its name. Riegersburg—the town—has known little peace since its founding in the 9th century BC. Roman domination and Hungarian invasions periodically forced the citizens to ascend the remarkably steep hill and seek solace and safety on its rocky summit. During the 17th century, with the mighty forces of the Turkish empire only 20 mi. away, Riegersburg was once again compelled to entrust its fragile existence to the stalwart bulwarks of the castle. Baroness Katharina Welkom von Zipf (nicknamed "Tasmanischer Teufel" because of her diminutive frame) completed the castle in a 17-year flurry of construction and transformed it into one of the largest and most impregnable fortresses in all Austria. 108 rooms were surrounded by 2 mi. of walls with five gates and two trenches. The fearsome and imposing castle withstood the Turkish onslaught—in 1664 Riegersburg and the surrounding villages drove the Turks back in the great battle of Mogersdorf.

Orientation and Practical Information Riegersburg serves as an excellent stopover on the route from Graz into Hungary. Indeed, you can leave Riegersburg at 7:37am by **train** and arrive in Budapest at 1:45pm (one way 306 AS). Transit from Graz is easy as well—take the **bus** all the way (84 AS; departing Graz 6am and noon), or take the train from Graz to Feldbach (92 AS; 1 hr.) and then switch to the bus from Feldbach into Riegersburg (22 AS; 4 per day; 15 min.). Housing is somewhat scarce in town, but if you must stay the night, the helpful **tourist office** (tel. (03153) 670) supplies free maps and finds accommodations for no fee. (Open April to mid-Oct. Mon.-Fri. 10am-noon and 3-6pm, Sat.-Sun. 10am-6pm.) The **post office** stands at Riegersburg Str. 26 (open Mon.-Fri. 8am-noon and 2-6pm). You can change money there, or stroll to **Raiffeisen Bank,** down the street at Riegersburg Str. 30 (open Mon.-Fri. 8am-noon and 2-4:30pm).

Accommodations and Food To reach the **Jugendherberge "Im Cillitor" (HI)** (tel. (03153) 217), walk up Riegersburg Str. toward the castle, take a right at the tourist office, and struggle up the last, extremely steep 100m. Built flush to the castle's old wall, the large keys, noisy locks, and spears in the reception area all evoke a distinctly medieval atmosphere. Iron bars traverse the few windows (now we've got you, my pretty...) of the large dorm rooms. (Open May-Sept. Curfew 10pm. 100 AS, under 19 80 AS; nonmembers 30 AS surcharge. Breakfast 25 AS; 3 meals 70 AS; sheets 25 AS.) At the bottom of Riegersburg's hill is **Lasslhof** (tel. (03153) 201 or 202), a yellow hotel with large, comfortable rooms and a popular bar/restaurant. (145-205 AS; July-Aug. add a 35 AS surcharge for singles. Breakfast included. Reception open 8am-10pm. English spoken.) At the restaurant downstairs, gorge yourself on *Wiener Schnitzel* with potatoes and salad (68 AS), or snack on the *Frankfurter mit Gulaschsaft* (38 AS). Otherwise, stock up on groceries at **Saurugg,** right across the street from the tourist office (open Mon.-Fri. 7am-noon and 2:30-6pm, Sat. 7am-noon).

Sights and Entertainment The relationship between town and castle has changed little since the age when chain mail and spears shimmered on sunny battlefields. Riegersburg relies heavily on the revenue from tourists who gawk at the well-preserved remains of the medieval fortress. The castle's two museums draw the most attention to the town; the **Burgmuseum** showcases 16 of the castle's 108 rooms. The **Witches' Room** contains an eerie collection of portraits of alleged witches (among them, Katharina "Green Thumb" Pardauff, who was executed in

1675 for causing flowers to bloom in the middle of winter) and a real iron maiden. In the **Knights' Hall,** search carefully for the inscription on a window on the left side of the room; the faint scrawl boasts of a 20-day drinking bout in April, 1635 (curiously, the 21st-day hangover went unchronicled). The **Hexenmuseum** (Witch Museum) is spread out over 12 more rooms; it presents the most expansive witch trial in Styrian history (1673-1675). Filled with torture devices, funeral pyres, and other ghastly exhibits, the museum testifies to the horrific ramifications of prejudicial hysteria. (Mandatory 1-hr. tour for either museum April-Oct. daily 9am-5pm. Burgmuseum or Hexenmuseum 50 AS, students 25 AS; combination ticket 80 AS, students 40 AS.) You can best appreciate the castle's ageless beauty from among the web of gravel paths and stone staircases. Carefully study the elaborate iron pattern covering the well in the castle's second courtyard; it is said that any woman who can spot the horseshoe amidst the complex design will find her knight in shining armor within a year. In the shadow of the castle whimpers a rather meager zoo, the **Greifvogelwarte Riegersburg,** which showcases caged birds of prey. A show highlights the predators' majesty as they soar effortlessly against a backdrop of lush, mountainous Austrian countryside. (Open Easter-Oct. daily 10am-5pm; shows Mon.-Sat. 11am and 2pm, Sun. 11am, 2pm, and 5pm. Admission 20 AS, students 15 AS; show costs 45 AS, students 30 AS.) All of these sights are probably best seen as part of a slight detour.

■■■ GRAZ

Ever since Charlemagne claimed this strategic crossroads for the Germanic empire, Graz (pop. 240,000), the capital of Styria, has witnessed over a thousand years of European and Asian aggression. In 1128, "Gradec" (Slavic for "little fortress"), was first mentioned, and around 1230, the building of the city wall commenced. The celebrated castles are the few remaining testaments to Graz's long history of military and political upheaval. The ruins of the fortress perched upon the **Schloßberg** commemorate the turmoil; the stronghold has withstood battering at the hands of Ottoman Turks, Napoleon's armies (3 times), and, most recently, the Soviet Union during World War II.

Surrounded by mountains to the north, rolling hills to the east and west, and vast plains to the south, Graz is still at battle, though today it's war of a different sort. Narrow cobblestone streets compete with a hectic network of trams and buses; chic department stores display their inventory in buildings scarred and battered by centuries of weathering. Although *fin-de-siècle* Vienna looked down its nose at provincial Graz, for centuries the city was a center of arts and sciences to rival any city in the Teutonic world. Graz's prosperity and international renown brought Emperor Friedrich III here during the mid-15th century, and astronomer Johannes Kepler was similarly lured to the city's Karl-Franzens-Universität, founded in 1585 as a Jesuit College and remodeled in the style of the Italian Renaissance in 1890. The university still upholds the intellectual standards of yore; modern authors Wolfgang Bauer, Gerhard Roth, and Alfred Kolleritsch now seek their muse among the school hallways. KFU, and two other universities, populate Graz with 30,000 students during term-time.

Innumerable theaters, the Forum Stadtpark, and the renowned Steirischer Herbst—an avant-garde festival founded in 1968 and held every October—have contributed to the culture you'd expect of a university town. What was the epicenter of operetta and waltz in the days of Robert Stolz is today the jazz capital of Europe. Current geopolitics have lent Graz the mantle of economic supremacy over all of southeastern Europe; the Graz International Fair is a welcome entree for many Eastern European countries, who attempt their first baby steps toward the world market here.

ORIENTATION AND PRACTICAL INFORMATION

Austria's second-largest city straddles the River Mur in the southeastern corner of Austria, 20km from the Slovenian and 35km from the Hungarian border, on the northern edge of the Graz plain. This expanse stretches 13.6km from north to south and 14.1km from west to east, where the Mur departs the wooded mountains of central Styria. Vienna is 200km to the northeast, Budapest is 300km to the west, and Prague is 470km to the northwest. Fully two-thirds of Graz's 2.3 square miles consists of parklands, earning it the monikers "Garden City" and "Green City." The **Hauptplatz** (*map**E3*) pedestrian zone, on the corner of Murgasse and Sackstr., forms the heart of the city. **Jakominiplatz** (*map**F4*), near the Eisernes Tor only five minutes from the Hauptplatz by foot, is the hub of the city's bus and streetcar system. The **Hauptbahnhof** (*map**A3*) lies on the other side of the river, a short ride away by streetcars #1, 3, or 6. The highest point in the city proper is the Plabutasch, 463m above sea level.

Tourist Office: Main office (*map**E3*) at Herrengasse 16 (tel. 83 52 41, ext. 11 or 12). Cordial staff sells city maps (10 AS), books rooms (30 AS fee), and supplies information on all of Styria. English spoken. Procure the incredibly informed *Graz Information: A City Introduces Itself* (free). Open Mon.-Fri. 9am-7pm, Sat. 9am-6pm, Sun. and holidays 10am-3pm. **Branch office** (tel. 91 68 37) at the main train station (*map**A2*) provides similar but more local services. English spoken. Open Mon.-Fri. 9am-6pm, Sat. 9am-5pm, Sun. and holidays 9am-3pm.

Consulates: United Kingdom, Schmiedgasse 10 (tel. 761 05). **South Africa,** Villefortgasse 13 (tel. 325 48).

Currency Exchange: Best rates at the American Express office; second-best at the main post office. Most banks open Mon.-Fri. 8am-noon and 2-4pm. On Sunday, exchange offices at both post office branches are open.

American Express: (*map**EF4*) Hamerlingasse 6 (tel. 81 70 10). Holds mail and exchanges currency (40 AS fee). Address mail as follows: Jonathan Wade GOLDMAN, c/o American Express, Client Letter Service, Hamerlingasse 6, A-8010 Graz. Open Mon.-Fri. 9am-5:30pm, Sat.9am-noon.

Post Office: Main office (*map**DE4*) at Neutorgasse 46. Open 24 hrs. **Postal code:** A-8010, A-8020 for the **branch office** (*map**A2*) at Europaplatz 10, to the right of the main train station (facing the station). Also open 24 hrs.

Telephones: In the main post office. **Information:** tel. 08. **City code:** 0316.

Flights: Flughafen Graz, Flughafenstr. 51, 9km from the central city. For flight information call 29 30 58 or 29 16 69. Currency exchange available daily 6:15am-12:45pm and 2:30-7pm. Information office open daily 6am-11:30pm. Airport shuttles depart from Hotel Daniel (adjacent to the *Hauptbahnhof*) 3-4 times daily (50 AS; about 20 min.).

Trains: Hauptbahnhof (*map**A2*) on Europaplatz (tel. 91 35 00; for train info call 1717). Has lockers (20 AS small, 30 AS large), rents bikes, stores luggage, and houses a passport photo booth to boot (four photos 60 AS). Open 24 hrs. Currency exchange available Mon.-Fri. 7:30am-1:30pm and 2-6:30pm, Sat. 7:30am-1:30pm. Trains traveling toward Hungary depart from the **Ostbahnhof** on Conrad-von-Hötzendorf Str.

Buses: For West Styria, the **Graz-Köflach Bus** (GKB) departs from Griesplatz (*map**A2*); **main office** (tel. 526 49, ext. 247) at Grazbachgasse 39 (open Mon.-Thurs. 7:15-11:30am and noon-3:30pm, Fri. 7:15am-noon). For the remainder of Austria, the **BundesBus** (*map**A2*) departs from Europaplatz 6 (next to the *Hauptbahnhof*) or Andreashopferplatz; **main office** (tel. 81 18 18) at Andreashopferplatz 17 (open Mon.-Fri. and Sun. 6am-6:30pm, Sat. 6am-3:30pm) and **branch office** at the *Hauptbahnhof* (open Mon.-Fri. 9am-noon).

Local Public Transportation: Grazer Verkehrsbetriebe (*map**E3*) at Hauptplatz 14 (tel. 88 74 08), is open Mon.-Fri. 8am-5pm. Purchase single tickets (15 AS) and day-tickets (42 AS) from the driver, and booklets of 6 tickets (60 AS) or week-tickets (99 AS) from any one of the *Tabak* stores sprinkled through Graz. Tickets are valid for all trams and buses, and also for the cable car that ascends the Schloßberg. Children half-price for all tickets. Most tram lines run until 11pm, and most bus lines run until 9pm; check the schedules posted at every *Haltestelle* (marked with a green "H") for details.

Taxi: Funktaxi, Münzgrabenstr. 107 (tel. 878). **City-Funk,** tel. 11 88.

Car Rental: Avis (*map*FG4*), Schlögelgasse 10 (tel. 81 29 20). **Budget** (*map*A2*), Bahnhofgürtel 73 (tel. 91 69 66). **Hertz** (*map*DE3*), Andreas-Hofer-Platz (tel. 82 50 07). **Interrent** (*map*B1*), Wiener Str. 15 (91 40 80).

Austrian Automobile Associations: ÖAMTC, Schubertring 1-3 (tel. 50 42 61) and **ARBÖ,** Mariahilfer Str. 180 (tel. 27 16 00)

Student Resources: The **student administration office** of the university (*map*G1*) posts billboards papered with concert notices, student activity flyers, and carpool advertisements for all of Austria. To find the hall, walk through the emergency exit (*Notausgang*) of the bathroom in upper restaurant of the Mensa.

Bookstore: Englische Buchhandlung (*map*F3*), Tummelplatz 7 (tel. 82 62 66). Sells virtually every book you might ever want, in English. Classic literature, paperback novels, magazines, travel guides, city maps, and more. Open Mon.-Fri. 9am-6pm and Sat 9am-noon. Also, the international bookstore **Dradiwaberl** (*map*G1*), at Zinzendorfgasse 30, sells guidebooks, maps, and newspapers. Open Mon.-Fri. 8am-6pm, Sat. 8am-noon.

Laundromat: Ideal (tel. 82 21 92), on the corner of Steyrergasse and Klosterwiesgasse. Open Mon.-Thurs. 7am-5pm, Fri. 7am-4pm. **Stroß** (tel. 91 20 83), at Annenstraße 42. Open Mon.-Thurs. 7am-5pm, Fri. 7am-4pm.

Hospital: Krankenhaus der Elisabethinen (*map*C3*), Elisabethinergasse 14 (tel. 9063), near the hostel. For **emergency medical advice,** dial 141. **Ambulance:** tel. 144.

Police: At the main train station (tel. 888 27 75). Open 24 hrs. Outside doors open 8am-5pm; ring doorbell. In an **emergency,** call 133.

ACCOMMODATIONS

In general, accommodations in Graz are affordable and easy to find. In July and August, when the housing begins to dry up, ask the **main tourist office** about the list of private rooms (mostly 150-300 AS per night).

Jugendherberge (HI) (*map*B34*), Idlhofgasse 74 (tel. 91 48 76; fax 91 48 76 88), a 20-min. walk from the train station. Exit the station and cross the street, head right on Bahnhofgürtel, take a left at Josef-Huber-Gasse (after the Nissan dealership), then take the first right at Idlhofgasse. Or, from Jakominiplatz, take bus #31 (direction: "Webling"), #32 (direction: "Seiersburg"), or #33 (direction: "Gemeindeamte") to "Lissagasse" (last bus around midnight) and walk 2 min. to the hostel. Rustling poplar trees, flexible lockout and curfew, and congenial staff offset the noisy, insomniac tour groups. Reception open 5-10pm. Lockout 9am-5pm. Curfew 10pm; front door key on request. Dorms 130 AS. Doubles with shower and toilet 250 AS per person, quads with shower and toilet 185 AS per person. 15 AS surcharge for the first night. Nonmembers 40 AS extra. Breakfast and sheets included. Laundry 45 AS.

Hotel Strasser (*map*A3*), Eggenberger Gürtel 11 (tel. 91 39 77 or 91 68 56), a 3-min. walk from the train station. Exit the station, cross the street, and head right on Bahnhofgürtel (hotel is on the left, across from a huge sign for Kaiser Bier). Located off a busy street, but thick glass windows keep the large, wood-paneled rooms relatively quiet. Singles 280 AS. Doubles 240 AS per person, with showers 290 AS per person. Quads 210 AS per person. Breakfast and shower included. English spoken. Restaurant downstairs. Free parking.

Frühstückpension Lukas, Waagner-Biro-Str. 8 (tel. 52 5 90). Take a right outside the train station, turn right on Eggenberger Str., and take the first right onto Waagner-Biro-Str (5 min.). Spacious rooms overlook a dimly lit back street; an itinerant crowd haunts the restaurant/reception area downstairs. Singles 220 AS, with shower 280 AS. Doubles 390 AS, with shower 440 AS. Continental breakfast 35 AS (only available Mon.-Fri.).

Frühstückspension Rückert (*map*G1*), Rückertgasse 4 (tel. 33 0 31). Take tram #1 (direction: "Mariatrost") to "Teggetthoffplatz," turn left (facing the park) and

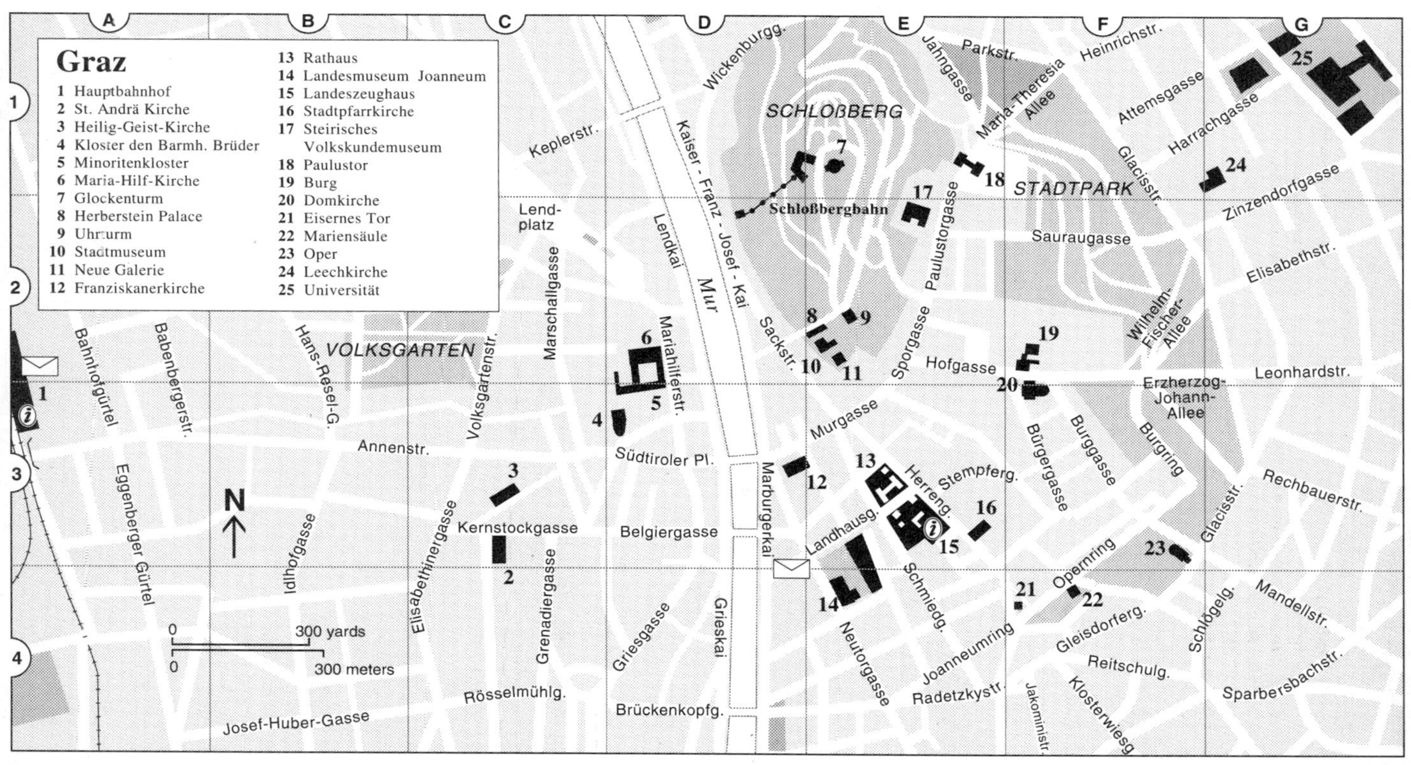
Graz
1 Hauptbahnhof
2 St. Andrä Kirche
3 Heilig-Geist-Kirche
4 Kloster den Barmh. Brüder
5 Minoritenkloster
6 Maria-Hilf-Kirche
7 Glockenturm
8 Herberstein Palace
9 Uhrturm
10 Stadtmuseum
11 Neue Galerie
12 Franziskanerkirche
13 Rathaus
14 Landesmuseum Joanneum
15 Landeszeughaus
16 Stadtpfarrkirche
17 Steirisches Volkskundemuseum
18 Paulustor
19 Burg
20 Domkirche
21 Eisernes Tor
22 Mariensäule
23 Oper
24 Leechkirche
25 Universität
SCHLOßBERG
Schloßbergbahn
STADTPARK
VOLKSGARTEN
Mur
Kaiser - Franz - Josef - Kai
Lendkai
Marburgerkai
Grieskai
Mariahilferstr.
Südtiroler Pl.
Belgiergasse
Griesgasse
Brückenkopfg.
Lend-platz
Marschallgasse
Keplerstr.
Wickenburgg.
Sackstr.
Murgasse
Landhausg.
Herreng.
Stempferg.
Schmiedg.
Neutorgasse
Radetzkystr.
Joanneumring
Hofgasse
Sporgasse
Paulustorgasse
Bürgergasse
Burggasse
Burgring
Opernring
Jakoministr.
Klosterwiesg.
Reitschulg.
Gleisdorferg.
Schlögelg.
Glacisstr.
Sparbersbachstr.
Mandellstr.
Rechbauerstr.
Leonhardstr.
Erzherzog-Johann-Allee
Wilhelm-Fischer-Allee
Sauraugasse
Elisabethstr.
Zinzendorfgasse
Harrachgasse
Attemsgasse
Heinrichstr.
Maria-Theresia Allee
Parkstr.
Jahngasse
Kernstockgasse
Grenadiergasse
Rösselmühlg.
Volksgartenstr.
Elisabethinergasse
Annenstr.
Hans-Resel-G.
Idlhofgasse
Josef-Huber-Gasse
Babenbergerstr.
Eggenberger Gürtel
Bahnhofgürtel
N
0
300 yards
300 meters

walk 3 min. up Hartenaugasse until it intersects lovely, tree-lined Rückertgasse. In a quiet residential area fairly near the center of town. This pretty *Pension* offers sunny, spacious rooms paneled with fresh-smelling pine. Singles 320 AS, with shower 380 AS. Doubles 270 AS per person, with shower 310 AS. Buffet breakfast included. 30 AS surcharge for a one-night stand.

Gasthof Schmid Greiner, Grabenstr. 64 (tel. 68 14 82). Take bus #58 (direction: "Mariagrün") to "Humboldtstraße," turn right, walk 100 ft., and head right for 5 min. on Grabenstr. A peaceful establishment imbued with old-world charm. Snow-white comforters, dark wood furnishings, and delicate lace curtains in simple, tidy rooms. Singles 300 AS. Doubles 210 AS per person, with shower 240 AS. Breakfast included. Showers 20 AS.

FOOD

Graz's 30,000 students sustain a bonanza of cheap eateries (and vice-versa). Inexpensive meals can be found at the Hauptplatz and at the **Lendplatz** (*map*C12*), off Keplerstraße and Lendkai, where concession stands sell *Wurst* sandwiches, ice cream, beer, and other fast food until about 8pm. Numerous markets are located on Rösselmühlgasse (*map*C4*), an extension of Josef-Huber-Gasse, and on Jakominisstraße (*map*F4*) directly off Jakominiplatz. Low-priced student hangouts line Zinzendorfgasse near the university.

University Mensa (*map*G1*), just east of the Stadtpark at the intersection of Zinzendorfgasse and Leechgasse. The best deal in town; just walk down the stairs into the basement and grab a tray. Set menus 30-55 AS; vegetarian (*Vollwert*) meals available on request at comparable prices. Be on the alert for blue tickets, distributed only to university students, that shave 8 AS off the price of a meal. Open Mon.-Fri. 11am-2pm. For slightly more expensive à la carte meals, explore the restaurant upstairs (open Mon.-Fri. 8am-3pm).

Gastwirtschaft Wartburgasse (*map*G1*), Halbärthgasse 4. Trendy posters, loud music, and close proximity to the Mensa make this indoor/outdoor restaurant Graz's premier student hangout. Tasty food compensates for the wait. Daily lunch specials 50-60 AS. Pasta, vegetarian, and meat dishes 42-120 AS. Open Mon.-Fri. 9am-1am.

Mangolds Vollwert Restaurant (*map*D3*), Griesgasse 11, by the river off Grieskai. A healthy alternative to cholesterol-laden Austrian cuisine. Dine on delectable fruit salads (12-45 AS), juices, and freshly baked cakes in the cafeteria-like dining hall or at the café next door. Daily lunch specials (39-50 AS) include soup, salad, and dessert. Open Mon.-Fri. 11am-8pm, Sat. 11am-4pm.

Calafati (*map*B4*), Lissagasse 2, a 3-min. walk from the hostel. Lunch combinations (main course with soup or spring roll and dessert, 42-55 AS) make this newly-opened Chinese restaurant quite a bargain. Lunch daily 11:30am-3pm; dinner daily 5:30-11:30pm.

Hotel Strasser (*map*A3*), Eggenberger Gürtel 11, a 3-min. saunter from the train station. A plethora of reasonably priced meals served in a delicately decorated, home-style restaurant. Sample the salads (35-60 AS), *Bratwurst* (50 AS), or the *Wiener Schnitzel* with *Pommes frites* (80 AS). Dinner served daily 6pm-9:30pm.

Markets

Graz is blessed with a seemingly countless number of small grocery stores that sell all the necessary ingredients for a picnic lunch; pick up a few bites and sup under a tree in the relaxing, quiet **Volksgarten** (*map*BC2*), located right off Lendplatz. **Lebensmittel** (*map*D2*), right underneath the Schloßberg at Sackstr. 24, is one such shop (open Mon.-Fri. 6:30am-6:30pm, Sat. 6:30am-noon). There are also **outdoor markets** at Kaiser-Josef-Platz (*map*F4*) and Lendplatz (*map*BC2*), where vendors hawk their fruits and vegetables amidst a dazzling splash of reds, greens, and yellows (open Mon.-Sat. 7am-12:30pm). Other markets are run Mon.-Fri. 7am-6pm and Sat. 7am-12:30pm in the Hauptplatz (*map*E3*) and Jakominiplatz (*map*F4*).

Feinkost has 3 conveniently located stores: 1 at Bahnhofgürtel 89 (*map*A2*), 2 min. from the train station (open Mon.-Fri. 8am-6pm, Sat. 8am-12:30pm). **Feinkost**

Exler (*map*B3*) is a quick jaunt from youth hostel (open Mon.-Fri. 7am-1pm and 3-6pm, Sat. 7am-noon). **Feinkost Muhrer** (*map*DE3*) borders closely on Hauptplatz in Franziskanerplatz (open Mon.-Fri. 6:30am-7:30pm, Sat. 6:30am-noon).

Interspar (*map*B4*), a mammoth market at the intersection of Lazarettgasse and the Lazarettgürtel in the enormous City Park shopping mall. Open Mon.-Wed. 9am-6:30pm, Thurs. 9am-10pm, Fri. 9am-6:30pm, Sat. 9am-1pm. There's a **SPAR** market (*map*G2*) at the intersection of Leonhardstr. and Hartenaugasse, 2 min. from the "Teggetthofplatz" bus stop (open Mon.-Fri. 7:30am-6pm, Sat. 7am-1pm). A third branch is next door to the Mensa (open Mon.-Fri. 8am-1pm and 4pm-6:30pm, Sat. 7:30am-12:30pm).

SIGHTS

Back in the 17th century, when Ottoman invasions from the east were as regular as Swiss trains, Graz's rulers assessed the need for an on-premises weapons stash. The result of their efforts, after some political haranguing, is the most bizarre attraction in Graz, the **Landeszeughaus** (provincial arsenal; *map*E3*) at Herrengasse 16 (tel. 87 73 6 39 or 87 72 7 78), built from 1642 to 1645 by Anton Solar. In the early 18th century, the Turk menace dissipated, and the court war council in Vienna sought to replace the temporary, enlisted mercenaries with a standing army. Thus, the task of protecting the frontiers, heretofore carried out by local forces in the countryside, would be undertaken by the state. The government foolishly resolved to permanently dispose of all antiquated weapons, an idea that incensed the locals. They wanted the arsenal to stand forever as a monument to the soldiers' bravery and faithfulness in the fight against the "sworn enemy of Christendom." Empress Maria Theresa agreed to maintain this unique historical monument in its original condition. Today, this former armory of the Styrian estates contains an eerie four-story collection of scintillating spears, muskets, and armor—enough to outfit 28,000 burly mercenaries. It is the only arsenal in the world still preserved in its entirety. (Open April-Oct. Mon.-Fri. 9am-5pm, Sat.-Sun. 9am-1pm. Admission 25 AS, seniors 10 AS, students free.) Next door is the impressive **Landhaus** (*map*E3*), still the seat of the provincial government; the building was remodeled by architect Domenico dell' Allio in 1557 in masterful Italian Renaissance style. Walk around the courtyard and admire the numerous spires yearning for the sky.

The Zeughaus is just a tiny part of the collection of the **Landesmuseum Joanneum,** one of the oldest public museums in Austria. The assembled holdings are so vast and so eclectic that officials have been forced to categorize the legacy and house portions in separate museums scattered throughout the city. The **Neue Galerie** (*map*E3*), Sackstr. 16 off the Hauptplatz (tel. 82 91 55), showcases paintings of 19th- and 20th-century Austrian artists in the gorgeous Palais Herberstein. Be sure to catch a glimpse of the mountains from the palace's weatherbeaten courtyard. (Open Mon.-Fri. 10am-6pm, Sat.-Sun. 10am-1pm. Admission 25 AS, seniors 10 AS, students free.) The **Alte Galerie** (*map*E4*), Neutorgasse 45 (tel. 87 72 4 57), houses an even more impressive collection of works from the Middle Ages and the Baroque period. Especially awe-inspiring are the larger-than-life statues that comprise Veit Königer's "Group of Annunciation" and Brueghel's graphic and grotesque "Triumph of Death," in which archduke and peasant alike are slaughtered by an army of skeletons (open Tues.-Fri. 10am-5pm, Sat.-Sun. 10am-1pm). The Landesmuseum boasts some less prominent sections as well. The **Hans-Mauracher-Museum,** Hans-Mauracher-Str. 29 (tel. 39 23 94) is dedicated to the eminent Graz sculptor (open Tues.-Thurs. and Sun. 10am-5pm). The **Naturwissenschaftliche Abteilung** (*map*E4*), Raubergasse 10 (tel. 877 26 62), documents the region's natural history (open Mon.-Fri. 9am-4pm, Sat.-Sun. 9am-noon). The **Kunstgewerbe** (*map*E4*), Neutorgasse 45 (tel. 877 24 58), features local and foreign artists alike (open Mon. and Wed.-Fri. 10am-5pm, Sat.-Sun. 10am-1pm). The **Abteilung Für Volkskunde** (*map*E2*), Paulustorgasse 13 (tel. 83 04 16), showcases ethnic and social history (open April-Oct. Mon.-Fri. 9am-4pm, Sat.-Sun. 9am-noon). Other sections include the **Bild- Und Tonarchiv** (*map*DE2*), Sackstr. 17 (tel. 83 03 35; open Mon.-Tues. and

Thurs. 8am-4pm, Wed. and Fri. 8am-1pm), the **Alparten Rannach** (open Mon.-Tues. and Thurs.-Sun. 8am-6pm.), the **Schloß Stainz** (open daily 9am-5pm), and the **Schloß Trautenfels** (open daily 9am-5pm). The **Diözesanmuseum** (*map*D2*), Mariahilferplatz (tel. 91 39 94), will exhaust any craving for jewel-encrusted reliquaries (open Tues.-Wed. and Fri.-Sat. 10am-5pm, Thurs. 10am-7pm, Sun. 10am-1pm).

Schloß Eggenberg, at Eggenberger Allee 90 (tel. 53 26 4 11), also falls under the Joanneum's umbrella. Ordered built by the Imperial Prince Ulrich of Eggenberg, this grandiose palace holds the regional hunting museum, the coin museum, and an exhibition of Roman artifacts. The city wastes no modesty on the elegant **Prunkräume** (literally, "resplendent rooms"). To see these apartments of state, known for glorious 17th-century frescoes and ornate chandeliers, you must join one of the free tours (in German only, every hr. 10am-noon and 2-4pm). The enchanting **game preserve** that envelops the palace proves that nature's handicraft is every bit as magnificent as the work of bishops or princes. Framed by a heart-stopping mountain backdrop, the palace's brilliantly orange spire and the preserve's royal blue peacocks balance a memorable panorama of colors. Count the palace windows—there are 365 of them, each representing—well, you know. Take tram #1 (direction: "Eggenberg") past the train station to "Schloß Eggenberg." (Admission to the entire complex 25 AS, students 2 AS. Prünkraume open April-Oct. daily 10am-1pm and 2-5pm. Hunting museum open March-Nov. daily 9am-noon and 1-5pm. Coin museum open Feb.-Nov. daily 9am-noon and 1-5pm. Artifacts open daily Feb.-Nov 9am-1pm. Game preserve open May-Aug. daily 8am-7pm; March-April and Sept.-Oct. daily 8am-6pm; Jan.-Feb. and Nov.-Dec. daily 8am-5pm.)

Back on the banks of the Mur, a **cable car** (*map*D1-2;* tel. 88 74 13) ascends from Kaiser-Franz-Josef-Kai 38 to the summit of the **Schloßberg** (*map*E1*) mountain towering over the city. The Schloßberg, a steep Dolomite peak in the center of the city, rises 473m above sea level. Even before Bavarian *über*lords took possession of the country, the Slavic Wends built fortifications on the citadel, which dominated a ford then central to transportation. The 16th-century **Glockenturm** (bell tower; *map*E1*) and **Uhrturm** (clock tower; *map*E2*) perched atop the peak can be seen from almost any spot in Graz. The Uhrturm acquired its present appearance—the circular wooden gallery with oriels, and the four huge clockfaces 5.4m in diameter—when the Schloßberg castle was reconstructed in 1556. In the Glockenturm hangs the big bell cast by Martin Hilger in 1587 and popularly called the "Liesl." The town ransomed both of these structures, now city symbols, in 1809, as they impotently watched Napoleon raze the remainder of a once-formidable fortress. The Styrian panther now imprinted on the clock tower's corner supposedly guards the hill against any similar future injustice. (Cable car runs April 9am-10pm; May-June 8am-11pm; July-Aug. 8am-midnight; Oct.-March 10am-10pm. A ride up the mountain costs 15 AS, down 10 AS, round-trip 20 AS; children half-price.) The strenuous 15- to 20-minute hike from the base along the well-marked paths is rewarded by a beautiful bed of roses at the summit and sweeping views of the city. Follow the dramatic stone staircase snaking from Schloßbergplatz to the top.

If you descend the hill on its eastern side, you'll arrive at the lovely floral **Stadtpark** (city park; *map*F2*) separating the old city from the lively university quarter. The gardens surrounding the ornate central fountain are manicured in elegant S-shaped curves; frolic, if you wish, along the bank of the man-made duck pond that zig-zags through the park. The Gothic **Leechkirche** (*map*G1*), at Zinzendorfgasse 5 between the Stadtpark and the university, is the oldest structure in Graz, dating from the late 13th century. Aching from the relentless forces of Mother Nature, the inscriptions and statues sprinkled along the church's exterior are lamentably weathered and faint.

South of the fountain, the Stadtpark blends into the **Burggarten** (*map*F2*), a bit of carefully pruned greenery complementing Emperor Friedrich III's 15th-century **Burg** (*map*F2*). Freddie had the initials "A.E.I.O.U." embedded on his namesake wing of the palace. This cryptic inscription is interpreted as "*Austria Est Imperare*

Orbi Universo," "Austria Erit In Orbe Ultima," or *"Alles Edreich Ist Österreich Untertan"*—all three roughly translate to "Austria will rule the world." (See Wiener Neustadt for more on the megalomanic vowel sequence.) Frederich's son, Maximilian I, enlarged the building, and, in 1499, commissioned the unique Gothic double spiral staircase. He also inserted the **Burgtor** (Castle Gate) into the city walls. Stroll through the courtyard and out through the giant gate to find Hofgasse and the **Dom** (cathedral; *map*F2-3*); its simple Gothic exterior belies the exquisite Baroque embellishments inside. In 1174, Friedrich III had the existing Romanesque chapel retooled to make the three-bayed cathedral late-Gothic style. In 1485, a picture of the "Scourges of God" was mounted on the south side of the church, to remind Christians of the most palpable Trinity of the time: the Black Death, attacks by Ottoman Turks, and the invasion of the locusts.

Next door, the solemn 17th-century Habsburg **Mausoleum** (*map*F3*), regarded as the best example of Austrian Mannerism, stands atop a grey stone staircase. The domed tomb was intended for the Emperor Ferdinand II but actually holds the remains of his mother, Archduchess Maria. Master architect Johann Bernard Fischer von Erlach designed the frescoes inside (open Mon.-Thurs. and Sat. 11am-noon and 2-3pm; free). The **Opernhaus** (opera house; *map*FG3-4*), at Opernring and Burggasse, was built in under two years by Viennese theater architects Fellner and Helmer. The two drank their cup of inspiration from the masterful bottle of Fischer von Erlach. A portico once covered the balcony, facing the Glacis; regrettably, authorities were forced to pull down the colonnade after it suffered air-raid damage during World War II. The other three façades are still preserved in their original state. The Graz **Glockenspiel** (*map*E3*), located just off Enge Gasse in the Glockenspielplatz, delights crowds with dancing figures clad in traditional Austrian garb (daily at 11am, 3, and 6pm).

Another option is to forego city pleasures entirely for a walk or hike on the mountains around Graz. The **Schöckel-Seilbahn** cable car eases most of the uphill battle. Buses leave Andreas-Hofer-Platz daily at 8am, 9am, 10:30am, 12:15pm, 1:15pm, and 1:45pm for the station at St. Radegund (tel. (0313) 20 23 32), where you can take the cable car up the mountain. (Up 51 AS, down 33 AS, round-trip 75 AS; children half-price. Open daily 9:30am-4pm.) Call the **weather telephone** in Graz (tel. 88 77 00) for the latest reading from the top of the mountains.

ENTERTAINMENT

Graz's remarkable neo-Baroque **Opernhaus** (opera house; tel. 80 08), at Opernring and Burggasse (*map*FG34*), sells standing-room tickets (15-25 AS) at the door an hour before curtain. The yearly program includes opera and ballet performances of worldwide repute; for many young talents, Graz is considered a stepping-stone to an international career. The **Schauspielhaus** (*map*E3*), a theater at Freiheitsplatz off Hofgasse (tel. 80 05), also sells bargain seats just before showtime. Regular tickets and performance schedules are available at the **Theaterkasse** (*map*F34*), Kaiser-Josef-Platz 10 (tel. 80 00; open Mon.-Fri. 8am-8pm, Sat. 8am-1pm).

In October, the **Steierischer Herbst** (Styrian Autumn) festival celebrates avant-garde art with 24 days of modern abstractions. Call the director of the festival, Sackstr. 17 (tel. 82 30 07 0; fax 83 57 88), for more details. Since 1985, Graz has hosted its own summer festival as well. Concerts are held in the gardens of the Eggenberg Palace, the Graz Convention Center, and on the squares of the old city. The renowned Graz conductor, Nikolaus Harnoncourt, sets the tone. The cobblestone sidestreets off Mehlplatz (*map*E3*), especially **Fäbergasse, Prokopigasse,** and **Engegasse,** are sprinkled with lively pubs where you can quaff a liter or two of Gösser, the local tasty Styrian brew. **Opernkino** (*map*EF4*), the movie theater in the Jakominiplatz, shows both new releases and golden oldies (tickets 60-95 AS, on Mon. all tickets 55 AS). Of course, the best things in life are free—stroll down **Sporgasse** (*map*E2-3*), a narrow cobblestone path squeezed between two rows of brightly lit shops, or meander down **Herrengasse** (*map*E3*) and pause to hear the trumpets and violins echoing against the facades of the *Altstadt*. For an unforgettable view of Graz by night, ascend the well-lit Schloßberg staircase and engage in omphaloskepsis (the act of contemplating one's navel while pondering complex thoughts) as you sit by the radiant Uhrturm.

Near Graz: Stübing and Peggau

In **Stübing**, the **Österreichisches Freilichtmuseum** (Austrian Open-Air Museum; tel. (03124) 22 4 31) displays traditional rural Austrian buildings on a resplendent 100-acre tract in the Mur Valley. These structures, dating back to the early 16th century, were carefully relocated from all over Austria. Incorporating Tyrolean chalets, rustic thatched-roof Burgenland farms, working water mills, and a few barnyard beasts, the museum convincingly recreates the Austrian rural communities of the past. Note the women spinning and weaving wool with early 19th-century equipment. The museum is a 40-minute bus ride from the Lendplatz in Graz (40 AS) and 25 minutes by train and foot. Take the train to "Stübing" (32 AS, roundtrip 52 AS); turn left after exiting the train station and walk 2km down the road. (Open April-Oct. Tues.-Sun. 9am-5pm. Admission 50 AS, students 10 AS.)

Peggau, a cement-manufacturing village about 55km north of Graz, boasts Austria's largest stalactite (or is it stalagmite?) cave, the **Lurgrotte** (tel. (03127) 25 80). The obligatory tour leads you into the rain room (named for its perpetual precipitates), and introduces you to the Salzburg "threads from Heaven," a cluster of tiny formations supposedly resembling the "fine" rain of Salzburg. During World War II, Austrians crowded inside the cave to escape Allied bombing raids. You can take the 25-minute train ride to Peggau and stop in Stübing, to see the Freilichtmuseum, on the way; one way 46 AS, round-trip 76 AS. In Peggau, head left out of the station toward the cement factory and turn right at the sign for Lurgrotte (10 min.). The 30km-long cave is closed during the winter—10 species of bats have already made permanent reservations. (Open April-Oct. Tues.-Sun. 9am-4pm; 1-hr., 1km tour 50 AS, students 45 AS, under 15 30 AS; 2-hr., 2km tour only by prior arrangement 65 AS, students 60 AS, under 15 35 AS.)

Near Graz: Köflach and Piber

A second daytrip covers ground to the west of Graz; take the GKB bus (80 AS, 75 min.) or the train (one way 72 AS, round-trip 128 AS, 1 hr.) to **Köflach,** a mining town that has undergone an extensive and comprehensive facelift. Although vacant mines still blemish the outskirts of town, flowers have brought some color back to the main town's complexion—and with it, a concerted drive to attract tourism. The Köflach **tourist office** (*Fremdenverkehrsbüro*), Bahnhofstr. 24 (tel. (03144) 25 19 70), is located in the **Dr. Hans-Kloepfer Haus,** a sky-blue house directly across the street from the train station (office open Mon. 9am-7pm, Tues. and Thurs.-Fri. 9am-4pm). Dr. Hans Kloepfer was a renowned poet at the turn of the 20th century, and his house now showcases a small museum chronicling Köflach's history (museum open by request).

You might want to pack a quick picnic lunch at Köflach's **KGM Supermarket,** at Quergasse 3—just walk up Bahnhofstr. and turn left on Euergasse (open Mon.-Fri. 8am-6:30pm, Sat. 8am-2pm); then head toward **Piber,** home of the **Lipizzan Stud Farm** (tel. (03144) 33 23). The famous snow-white Lipizzaner stallions were bred in 1580, when Archduke Charles of Styria established a stud farm at Lipizza near Trieste, unleashing mares from Spain on stallions from Arabia. The farm was moved to the castle at Piber when the Austrians lost Lipizza in World War I. At the farm, the initially dark-haired horses undergo a grueling selection process. The obligatory 70-minute tour includes a visit to the stables and an unbelievably comprehensive documentary film that features slow-motion waltzing horses (open Easter-Oct. 9am-4pm; admission 50 AS, students 20 AS). To find the farm, walk 3km from Köflach; stroll up Bahnhofstr., take a right on Hauptplatz, and then head left on scenic Piberstraße.

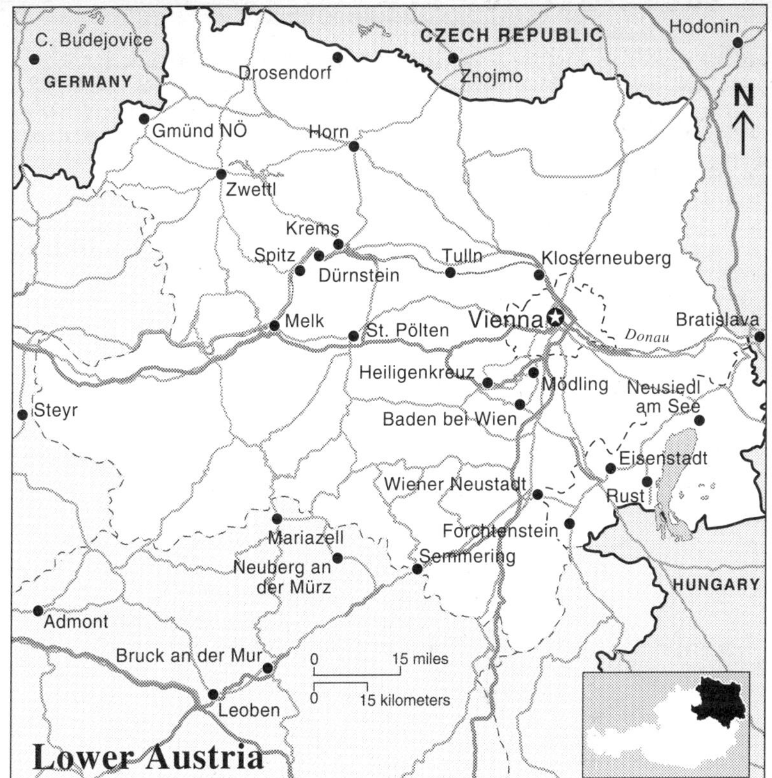

Lower Austria

Though it bears little resemblance to the foreign stereotype of Austria, the Danube province of **Niederösterreich** (Lower Austria) is the historic cradle of the Austrian nation. Forget *The Sound of Music.* Here, rolling, forested hills replace jagged Alpine peaks, and lavender wildflowers stand in for edelweiss in a consummately habitable agricultural land. The rugged castle ruins, once defensive bastions against invading imperial Turkish forces, now look wistfully across the Hungarian border. And the imperial vacation "hideaways" are easily as impressive as Tyrolean chalets.

Niederösterreich is billed as "the province on Vienna's doorstep." This refers not to doormat status but to geographic fact: Lower Austria encircles the pearl of Vienna. Anyone who enters or departs Vienna over land must pass through the province. Lower Austria accounts for one-quarter of the nation's landmass and 60% of its wine. Try the local Wienerwald cream strudel while sipping some *Schnapps;* the pastry is a sinful mixture of flaky crust, curds, raisins, and lemon peel. It tastes *far* better than it sounds.

The Wachau region of Lower Austria, located between the northwestern foothills of the Bohemian Forest and the southeastern Dunkelsteiner Wald, is a magnificent river valley. The north bank of the Danube is lined throughout the Wachau with wooded slopes and cliffs, while the south bank's terraced vineyards resemble a series of oversized staircases. The celebrated Wachau wines, relished even by the *über*-Teutons Siegfried and Brunnhilde, can today be savored at the wine cellars of any local vintner; ask at the tourist offices for specially organized wine-tasting tours.

Niederösterreich boasts more motorways than any other *Land,* and public transportation is just as ubiquitous. Almost every major bus and train sprints through the province on the way to Vienna. Other, smaller, routes criss-cross the plains outside the capital's jurisdiction. **Buses** #1123 and 1115 run from Mödling to Mayerling; #6252 departs from Semmering and arrives in Graz. **Trains** pass through Semmering and Wiener Neustadt; another line runs from Mariazell to St. Pölten via Annaberg.

■■■ ST. PÖLTEN

St. Pölten (pop. 50,000), officially granted a city charter in 1159 by Bishop Konrad von Passau, is legally the oldest city in Austria. Yet, recognition of St. Pölten's worth has taken a while to sink in; it was voted the capital of Niederösterreich only in 1985. The town is growing slowly as the official seat, still gingerly testing the reins of power. Through the transition, St. Pölten has thankfully retained its relaxed industrial heritage.

Orientation and Practical Information The heart of St. Pölten is the Rathausplatz. The **tourist office,** in the Rathausspassage (tel. (02742) 533 54; fax 525 31) provides oodles of information about St. Pölten, regional events, and the wonders of the surrounding Lower Austrian lands (in English upon request). The eager staff will help with room reservations and give suggestions for a madcap night on the town (ask for the *IN Szene* brochure). The office also distributes a free cassette **tour** of the city, available in English, German, French, Italian, Czech, and Japanese. (Office open Mon.-Thurs. 8am-3:30pm, Fri. 8am-5pm, Sat. 9am-5pm, Sun. 9am-3pm.) The main **post office,** Bahnhofplatz 1a, right next to the train station, is the best place to **exchange money.** (Open Mon.-Fri. 7am-7pm. **Postal code:** A-3100.)

Accommodations and Food The **Jugendherberge St. Pölten (HI),** Kranzbichlerstr. 18 (tel. (02742) 730 10), offers six-bed *Schlafzimmer* at a pleasant price. From the train station, walk to the right to Bahnhofstr., and walk out the far right corner until you see Promenade, which becomes Schießstattring; continue to Europlatz, and walk straight to Mariazellerstr. The fourth major street on the left is Kranzbichlerstr. (Reception open 7-10am and 4-7pm. 70-95 AS per night. Breakfast 20 AS. Call ahead.) Another option is **Gasthof Graf,** Bahnhofplatz 7, across the street from the train station; it's home to clean, sunny rooms with televisions and comfortable beds, many with shower and toilet. German is appreciated. (Single 250-350 AS, double 230-300 AS per person. Extra bed available. Breakfast included.) The *Stüberl* downstairs offers regional cuisine at reasonable prices (entrees 55-88 AS; open Mon.-Fri. 7am-10pm, Sat. 7am-2pm; garden seating open in summer).

St. Pölten's local specialties include oysters, fried black pudding, and wonderfully savory Wachau wine. The *Fußgängerzonen* that surround the Dom and the Renaissance Rathaus offers scores of shops and cafés for hedonists interested in indulging "fundamental" earthly desires. The monstrous **Interspar Einkaufszentrum** grocery store, Daniel Gran Str. 13, behind the *Bahnhof,* keeps the shelves brimming with foodstuffs (open Mon.-Fri. 8am-noon and 2-6pm, Sat. 7:30am-noon).

Sights and Entertainment Like much of Austria, about 40% of St. Pölten was destroyed or damaged during World War II. Thankfully, many 17th-century structures, designed by prolific architects Jakob Prandtauer and Joseph Munggenast, were restored to their original grandeur. The overriding Baroque presence makes the city an architectural bonanza. The ornate, florid landscape is further enhanced by the turn-of-the-century Jugendstil works of Joseph Maria Olbrich that somehow escaped most of the explosives. St. Pölten has borrowed much of its contemporary culinary and artistic offerings from its surroundings—the vineyards of the Wachau and the forested Waldviertel. The valiant tourist office is nonetheless (or, perhaps, therefore) eager to manufacture an independent identity. Most every brochure loudly exalts the St. Pölten architectural soundbite—Baroque ornamentation that blankets the city.

The Rathausplatz at St. Pölten's core was erected in the 13th century, though recent archeological excavations reveal that a Roman settlement had sprouted here early in the first millennium. The building to the left of the city hall, at Rathausplatz 2, is called the "**Schubert House,**" after Franz Schubert's frequent visits to the owners, Baron von Münk and his family. A Schubert relief conducts and composes above the window at the portal's axis. The expansive front of the **Institute of the English Maiden,** founded in 1706 at Linzer Str. 9-11 for the instruction of girls from noble families, sports one of the most beautiful Baroque façades in Lower Austria.

St. Pölten's **Wiener Straße** was a thoroughfare even in Roman times. After 1100, it became the central axis of the bourgeois-trader settlement established by the Bishop of Passau. At the corner of Wiener Str. and Kremser Gasse stands the oldest pharmacy in the city, happily dispensing medicinal salves since 1595. **Herrenplatz** has seen the haggling of St. Pölten's daily market for centuries. Don't miss the façade of the Baroque **palace** at Herrenplatz 2, crowned by a gable depicting the Powers of Light driving away the Powers of Darkness. A narrow alley just after Wiener Str. 31 leads to the **Domplatz.** Remains of the Roman settlement of Aelium were discovered here during the installation of sewers, when the sewerologists tripped over Roman hypocausts, part of an ancient warm-air floor heating system. The technology was recently sold to *The Sharper Image,* which will be producing new, graphite, laser-driven versions for the 1995 line.

The northern and eastern sides of the Domplatz are bordered by the **Dom** and the **Diocese Building,** a former monastery sprawled over five courtyards. The incredibly ornate interior of the cathedral befits the seat of an Archbishop; an unfathomable quantity of gold, silver, marble, and crystal encrusts the clergyman's stronghold. The interior of a former **Synagogue,** at Dr. Karl Renner-Promenade 22, was completely destroyed during the Nazi pogrom Kristallnacht ("Night of Broken Glass"). The octagonal house of worship was lovingly restored from 1980-84 with financial support from the Jewish community, as well as the city, provincial, and federal governments. Today it houses the **Institute for Jewish History** (tel. (02742) 771 71 or 769 94). (Synagogue open for tours on request. Institute library open to the public Mon.-Fri. 9am-4pm.)

St. Pölten hosts many cultural exhibitions throughout the year, including both visual and performing arts. The **Museum im Hof,** Heßstr. 4 (tel. (02742) 534 77), features rotating exhibits on Lower Austrian culture; the permanent presentation documents the history of the local labor movement. (Open Wed., Fri., and Sat. 9am-noon. Free.)

There's an authentic foosball table (foosball=*Fußball*=football=soccer) at **Gasthaus Koll,** Alte-Reich-Str. 11-13 (tel. (02742) 659 84; open Mon.-Fri. 5pm-1am, Sat. 6pm-2am). Live music and the more liberal St. Pöltner crowd are to be found in abundance at **Glasnost,** Dr. Karl Renner Promenade 1a (tel. 629 49; open—*oh*, so open—Sun. and Thurs. 6pm-2am, Fri. and Sat. 6pm-4am).

■■■ MARIAZELL

Resting between Alpine peaks about 140km southwest of Vienna, Mariazell is both an unabashed resort town and the most important pilgrimage site in Central Europe. Faithful Catholics crowd the Basilica to pay homage to its miraculous Madonna. Material people who don't feel like a prayer take a holiday over the Styrian borderline to enjoy Mariazell's ski slopes and the crystal-clear waters of the **Erlaufsee.**

Orientation and Practical Information The **tourist office,** Hauptplatz 13 (tel. (03882) 23 66), has copious pamphlets describing seasonal activities. The office is a quick jaunt from the train station; turn right on St. Sebastian, behind the station, and walk until you see a fork in the road. Follow the left fork up the hill and through the Hauptplatz to Wienerstr.; the tourist office is on the right. The staff is more than willing to procure a space in one of Mariazell's 2000 guest beds. (Open in summer Mon.-Fri. 8am-6pm, Sat. 8am-noon and 2-4pm, Sun. 9:30am-noon; in winter Mon.-Fri. 8am-1pm and 2-6pm, Sat. 8am-noon and 2-4pm, Sun. 9:30am-noon.) The office will also distribute transportation information, including schedules for the **Mariazellerbahn,** an Alpine railway between Mariazell and St. Pölten that's also something of a tourist attraction (2½ hr., 145 AS). The ride on this slothlike branch line is breathtaking; the train skirts Alpine cliffs and plunges through pitch-black tunnels. The **train station** (tel. (03882) 22 30), between Mariazell and the neighboring village of St. Sebastian, is the place to go for **bike rental** and additional transportation information.

Accommodations and Camping Mariazell's **Jugendherberge (HI),** Fischer von Erlachweg 2 (tel. (03882) 26 69), is immaculate. From the station, walk straight on Wiener Str., through P. Abel Platz straight onto Wiener Neustädterstr., and then turn left on Fischer von Erlachweg. (Open May-Sept. and Christmas-Easter. Reception open 5-10pm. Curfew 10pm, but can be stretched considerably if you're quiet. Members only. 93 AS. Reservations recommended.) One alternative is a room at **Haus Maria Molnar,** Brünnerweg 5 (tel. (03882) 345 84). Frau Molnar, a lively, helpful soul, offers wonderful singles, doubles, and even larger rooms, all with sinks, for 150 AS per person. (More than 3 nights 140 AS. Breakfast included. In summer, showers or baths 20 AS.) Though crowded, **Camping Erlaufsee,** behind the Hotel Herrenhaus near the west dock (tel. (03882) 21 48 or 21 16), is in a lovely spot just by the lake on Erlaufseestr. (30 AS per person, ages 5-15 13 AS; 15-35 AS per tent.) Try **Café Obergeichtner,** Ludwig Leberstr. 2, for a good meal amongst lively patrons. Pizza and other entrees cost 65-95 AS. (Open Mon.-Fri. and Sun. 10am-10pm, Sat. 10am-midnight.) Produce some produce at the **SPAR Markt** on Wienerstr. (open Mon.-Fri. 8am-noon and 3-6pm, Sat. 8am-noon).

If Mariazell's *Jugendherberge* has no vacancies, think about the two hostels in neighboring hamlets. The village of **Annaberg** lies 40 minutes away by Mariazellerbahn (about 8km from the train station), on a mountain pass that affords stellar views of the steep terrain. (Buses run from Annaberg to Mariazell at 9:05am, 4:37, and 6:25pm; 30 min.) Annaberg lies directly on the Via Sacra, the old pilgrimage route to Mariazell. The town **Jugendherberge,** Annarotte 77 (tel. (02728) 84 96), is run by a patient staff who might even squeegee the tennis courts for you. (Open Dec.-Oct. 134 AS, after 2 nights 117 AS; under 19 114 AS, after 2 nights 97 AS. Breakfast included.) Another tiny village, **Lackenhof,** 20 mi. northeast of Mariazell, abuts the **Ötscher** mountains, riddled with climbers and spelunkers. Buses arrive in town from Mariazell Mon., Wed., Fri., and Sun. The **Jugendherberge Lackenhof,** 3295 Lackenhof/Ötscher, is built right on the mountain slope. (Same prices and opening times as Annaberg, above.)

Sights and Entertainment Mariazell literally means "Mary's cloister"; this pilgrimage town has received hundreds of thousands of pious wanderers over the centuries, all journeying to visit the **Madonna** within the **Basilica.** This limewood likeness has been deemed responsible for miracles dating back to the 12th century, including King Ludwig the Great's surprise victory over 14th-century raiding Turks. The Basilica, in the middle of the Hauptplatz, is capped by black Baroque spires visible from any spot in town. Mass quantities of gold and silver adorn the **High Altar** (Fischer von Erlach the Elder) and **Gnadenaltar** (Fischer von Erlach the Younger), where the miraculous Madonna rests. Empress Maria Theresa donated the silver and gold grille (Fischer von Erlach & Son) that encloses the Gnadenaltar. *Wow.* Remember to be respectful in the church—pilgrims are always present, praying, meditating, and confessing. (Free guided tours with appointment through the Superiorat, Kardinal-Tisserant-Platz 1; tel. (03882) 25 95). Basilica open for visits, without the tour, daily 6am-7pm.) The church's amazing **Schatzkammer** contains gifts from scores of pious Europeans. (Open May-Oct. Mon.-Fri. 10:30am-noon and 2-3pm, Sat.-Sun. 10am-3pm. Admission 10 AS.)

With **skiing, hiking, windsurfing,** and **whitewater kayaking,** Mariazell caters to throngs of outdoorsy pilgrims as well. Numerous cable cars whisk visitors up to gorgeous Alpine hiking and skiing. The **Seilbahn Mariazell-Bürgeralpe,** Wienerstr. 28 (tel. (03882) 25 55), sends cars up every 20 minutes from the center of town. (Open July-Aug. daily 8:30am-5:30pm; Sept. 8:30am-5pm; May-June and Oct.-Nov. 9am-5pm; Dec. 8am-4pm; Jan.-March 8am-5pm. Up 55 AS, down 40 AS, round-trip 75 AS.) Five kilometers from Mariazell in **Mitterbach,** the **Gemeindealpe Sessellift** (tel. (03882) 32 92, 38 84, or 33 88) delivers riders to the top of the Gemeindealpe mountain (1623m). (Open June-Sept. daily 8:50-11am and 1:20-3:50pm; May and Oct. Sat.-Sun. 8:50-11am and 1:20-3:50pm. Round-trip 125 AS.) The **Mariazellerland** is the closest major ski area to Vienna. For **ski information** on the Bürgeralpe, Gemeindealpe, Gußwerk, Tribein, and Köcken-Sattel mountains, contact the Mariazell tourist office.

All of Mariazell's water sports revolve around the **Erlaufsee,** a wondrous Alpine oasis just outside of the city limits. **Buses** run from Mariazell to the Erlaufsee at 9:10am, 1:10, and 3:35pm (one way 18 AS; for more information, call (03882) 21 66). Once at the water's edge, try **Sport Dellinger,** Wienerstr. 30 (tel. (03882) 24 53), which rents windsurfers for 120 AS per hour and 550 AS per day (open 10am-6pm). Those interested in **scuba diving** in the Erlaufsee can contact **Harry's Tauchschule,** Traismauer 5 (tel. (02783) 77 47) for information about lessons and equipment rental. Before you can take lessons, you need a doctor's certificate that verifies that you are fit enough to dive. Rent rowboats or small powerboats (95-120 AS per hr.) from **Bootsverleih-Eppel,** Erlaufseestr. 74, in St. Sebastian (tel. (03882) 273 20). **Mountain bikes** are available at the Mariazell bus station, Ludwig Leberstr. 4, five minutes from the Hauptplatz (40 AS per hr.; regular bikes 20 AS per hr.).

■ Semmering

On a mountain pass separating Lower Austria from Styria, Semmering is one of eastern Austria's most beautiful vacation spots. The town underwent its first growth spurt in 1728, when Kaiser Karl VI built a road through the pass, and, in 1854, Semmering became the proud site of Europe's first mountain rail line. The tunnels, bridges, and gorges it traversed required an engineering marvel at the time. Now, transportation is old hat, and the tourists arrive to partake of nature's pleasures. Winter brings fleets of skiers and mountaineers who exploit Semmering's prime location near the Rax and Schneeberg ski areas and hundreds of kilometers of cross-country ski trails. Summer carries a more sedentary crowd to the remarkably clean air of this *Kurort* (health resort). The **Höllental** (Valley of Hell) is a magnet for hikers; this deep, 10-mile gorge is the product of millennia of erosion by the **Schwarza** river. From **Hirschwang,** about 15 mi. north of Semmering, take the **Raxbahn** tram to get a good view of the gorge (round-trip 150 AS). The best vista is from the apex of the chairlift (Bergbahn Hirschenkogel), over 300m above the rail pass (lift runs daily 9am-4pm; round-trip 50 AS). On **May 1,** the traditional date for erecting the Maypole (Maibaum), the ceremonial Maibaumumschneiden (cutting of the maypole) is accompanied by music and groups wearing traditional costumes, in Semmering and the neighboring villages of **Schneeberg** and **Wechsel**.

The town **tourist office,** Hochstr. 248, is at the top of the pass, just down the hill from the train station. The staff here will provide information about Lower Austria and Styria and suggestions for accommodations and train connections (open Mon. 8:30am-2pm, Tues.-Fri. 8:30am-4pm). Sleeping in Semmering is largely a budgetary black hole; the various *Privatzimmer* may be your only hope. **Rathaus Berghof**

Latzelsperger, right next to the tourist office (tel. (02664) 320), is one of the least expensive hotels. Its bright, clean rooms are located above a restaurant that offers quality regional grub (entrees 50-120 AS). All rooms have toilets and showers, and some boast a balcony and cable TV (about 300 AS per person). Budding PGA stars can keep in shape during the off season at the **mini-golf** course next door (20 AS, 18 holes). The **Raiffeisen Bank,** in the same building as the tourist office, is the best place to change money; there's an ATM outside as well (open Mon.-Thurs. 8:30am-noon and 2-4pm, Fri. 8am-noon and 2-5pm). **Trains** to and from Vienna's Südbahnhof leave hourly (110 AS).

Near Semmering: Neuberg an der Mürz

Located on the southern edge of the **Schneealpe** mountains, this vacation village is but a small-scale *Kurort*. Visitors come to Neuberg primarily to enjoy nature, to relax in the hamlet "where the Mürz is still drinkable." The laid-back residents live life far from the edge; these are the folks who drive 20mph in the fast lane. **Train** connections to Neuberg pass mostly through nearby **Mürzzuschlag** (Vienna to Mürzzuschlag 2 hr.; Mürzzuschlag to Neuberg 20 min.). **Buses** run once daily to **Mariazell** at 6am. The **post office** and **tourist office** are an easy three-minute walk from the train station—just follow the copious signs to the Baroque houses of the Hauptplatz. The **Jugendherberge Neuberg,** Kaplanweg 8 (tel. (03857) 84 95; fax 84 95 4), is a short walk across the bridge and to the left of the train station. With 50 beds and a tennis court, it is frequented by hikers and schoolgroups. The friendly manager is quite hospitable and prizes the sleepy mood of the hamlet he calls home. (150 AS per night. 20 AS for sheets first night only. Curfew 10pm. Call ahead.)

APPROACHING BURGENLAND

South and southeast of Vienna, from the easternmost portion of the Wienerwald to northwest Burgenland, lies a region of rolling hills and dense woodlands. The villages that extend south from Vienna along Autobahn A2 are primarily grape towns, with vineyards to produce world-famous wines and friendly taverns in which to serve them. The area is one of Austria's main industrial centers, with textiles and foodstuff factories, plus major chemical and iron plants, driving the tourist-independent economy. The River Leitha runs along the Burgenland border north of Wiesen to Wiener Neustadt and then onward to nations east. The peaks of the Rosaliengebirge glower over the southern part of this region near the Hungarian border.

Transportation in this region hovers around a Viennese core. **Buses** #1123 and #1115 runs from Vienna to Mödling and Mayerling; #1127 stops in Mödling before proceeding to Heiligenkreuz. Bus #1155 runs from Wiener Neustadt to Forchtenstein approximately every hour; #1140 travels from Baden to Mayerling and St. Pölten. A **train** passes through Semmering and Wiener Neustadt on its way from Graz to Vienna.

■ Forchtenstein and Wiesen

Forchtenstein and Wiesen squat in Austria's **Rosalia Region,** named for the local mountain range. The towns are famed for the delicious **strawberries** cultivated in the valleys; the soil quality and temperate climate supposedly yield strawberries of mythical proportions. Indeed, residents have established a virtual cult of the strawberry, offering libations of strawberry wine to the two strawberry idols in town.

Forchtenstein lives off the renown of the Eszterházy fortress, **Burg Forchtenstein,** built on a huge outcropping in the 13th century and expanded between 1636 and 1652. During the Ottoman Turkish sieges in the 16th and 17th centuries, Forchtenstein prevailed over the foreign invaders; captured Turkish prisoners were put to work digging a 125m well into the rock under the *Burg*. Be sure to hearken to the well's extraordinary echo. The castle is open to the public, with an impressive collection of weapons and armory. (Open April-Oct. 8am-noon and 1-4pm; March and Nov. tours on Sun. 9am-noon and 1-4pm. Admission 50 AS, students 25 AS.) In the summer, the castle hosts regional thematic art exhibitions, under the umbrella exposition Bollwerk Forchtenstein (open May 15-Oct. daily 9am-6pm). Farther up the winding road stands the **Rosalienkapelle,** on a precipice with a view of the western Hungarian plains. The chapel is well-kept but seems curiously isolated by its mountaintop locale. Don't forget to oooooh and aaaaah at the 17th-century gold, black, and green marble altar.

Five kilometers away, **Wiesen** offers a different type of entertainment. This town—literally, "grassy fields"—was known for little beyond strawberries before it first hosted the **International Jazz Festival.** Now, July and August annually attract scores of famous North American, African, Caribbean, and Latin American artists to Wiesen for the all-night open-air concerts. Especially beloved are the **Jazz Fest Wiesen** (2nd weekend in July) and the **Wiesen Reggae Sunsplash** (last weekend in Aug.). Tickets are available through any major Austrian ticket agency, or write to: **Jazz Pub Wiesen,** Hauptstr. 140, A-7203 Wiesen (tel. (02626) 81 64 80; fax 817 69 29). The Jazz Pub is also a hip place to hang out, hear music, and dance year-round.

Tourist information in Forchtenstein is available at the **Gemeindeamt,** Hauptstr. 54 (tel. (02626) 31 25; open Mon.-Fri. 8am-noon and 1-4pm. Branch office at the *Burg.*) In Wiesen, the **Großgemeinde,** Sauerbrunnerstr. 6 (tel. (02626) 33 13), handles tourist information. Both towns have *Privatzimmer,* but Forchtenstein has a greater supply of cheap rooms than its neighbor. **Gasthof Herbert Wutzholfer,** Rosalia 50 (tel. (02626) 812 53), offers comfortable beds with great views, for a reasonable price. (180-220 AS per person with breakfast. Reservations recommended.)

■■■ WIENER NEUSTADT

Once the official residence of Habsburg Emperor Friedrich III, Wiener Neustadt—50km south of Vienna on a plain overlooking the eastern Alps—is now one of Austria's industrial centers and transportation hubs. Wiener Neustadt was called "Neustadt" (new city) long before it had any relation to Vienna; in 1194, Leopold V, Duke of Babenberg, founded "*Nova Civitas.*" When Hungarian King Matthias "Good Sport" Corvinus finally succeeded in conquering 15th-century Wiener Neustadt after a brutal, two-year siege, he chose not to destroy the town; he instead presented the citizens of Wiener Neustadt with a magnificent goblet to honor their extraordinary spirit of resistance—the Corvinusbecher exhibited today in the town hall. In 1459, the Holy Roman Empress visited town, and gave birth to Maximilian I, known to Austrians as the Last Remaining Knight (no relation to the Austrian known to Americans as the "Last Action Hero"). Max managed to return the town to the Habsburgs, and it was his last will to be buried here. The first Austrian airstrip landed a bit north of Wiener Neustadt, prompting the first nationwide Aviation Week, held in town in 1911.

Orientation and Practical Information Trains run regularly from Vienna's Südbahnhof to and through Wiener Neustadt (75 AS). The town is located off Autobahn A2, which runs south from Vienna. The river Fischa meets the Leitha here, before heading north. The **train station** stands right next to the **post office,** the best place to exchange currency. (**Postal code:** A-2700.) The **tourist office** (*Fremdenverkehrsbüro*), Herzog-Leopold-Str. 17, is a short walk from the train station; walk straight one block from the station, take a left at the light onto Porsche-Ring, walk one long block, and take a right onto Herzog-Leopold-Str. The office is in the middle of the *Fußgängerzone* (pedestrian zone). Pick up the pamphlet *Promenade Through the Old Town* from the friendly staff, and follow the green arrows painted on the ground for a self-guided tour. (Open Mon.-Fri. 9am-5pm, Sat. 10am-2pm.)

Accommodations and Food The tourist office has a lodgings pamphlet, which lists *Privatzimmer* around town. Wiener Neustadt's beautiful **Jugendherberge (HI) "Jugendhotel Europahaus,"** Promenade 1, in the park across from the water tower, is almost always full, so call in advance. (Reception open 7-10am and 5-8pm. No curfew; ask for a door key. 115 AS per person. Breakfast 30 AS. Tax 10.50 AS per night.) Another hostel, run by the local priest, lies in the valley near **Pernitz,** 40 minutes from Wiener Neustadt (trains run every hr.). There's really nothing else in Pernitz other than the hostel and the "Oh—it's a Feh®" tissue factory. **Jugendherberge Pernitz,** Hauptstr. 47 (tel. (02632) 723 73), has barracks-like accommodations, with 40 beds whittled from wooden slabs. (Open April-Oct. 80 AS per night.)

Back in Wiener Neustadt, the **Konsum grocery store** at the corner of Herzog-Leopold-Str. and Beethovengasse, at the end of the *Fußgängerzone,* shelves enough groceries to keep you dear mother happy—maybe. ("Eat! You're too skinny! You're wasting away! Look at you, I can see bones..." Open Mon.-Fri. 7:30am-6pm, Sat. 7am-noon.) On Wednesday and Saturday, the **market** comes to town, transforming city squares into a shopper's wonderland.

Sights and Entertainment The most prominent feature in the skyline of the old town—which dates back to 12th-century Babenberg Duke Leopold V—is the **Pfarrkirche.** It had cathedral status from 1469 until 1784, during which time additions such as the life-size wooden figures of the 12 apostles (16th century) and the elaborate high altar (mid-18th century) were constructed. The **water tower,** south of the Burgplatz, also rises above Wiener Neustadt's roofline; it was designed in 1910 to recall the **Becher** (goblet) granted to the town after its capture by Hungarian King Corvinus in 1487. The chalice that served as the tower's model now rests in the **Rathaus.** North of the Burgplatz on Neuklostergasse stands the **Neuklosterkirche,** the 13th-century edifice that hosted the premiere of Mozart's famous **Requiem**.

The **Burgplatz** itself holds the **Theresianische Militärakademie,** the world's oldest existing military academy. Established by Empress Maria Theresa in 1752 in what had been the Habsburg Castle, it was taken over by the Germans, led by General Erwin Rommel (better known as the "Desert Fox"), in 1938. The complex has a number of notable idiosyncracies: inside the courtyard, the **Wappenwand** supports over 100 different coats of arms, only 14 of which have been identified. (These belong to the Habsburg line; the others are either unknown or fictitious.) The statue of Friedrich III inside bears the inscription **A.E.I.O.U.** This impressive display of militant vowels is an acronym for either "*Austriae est imperare orbi universo*," "*Austria erit in orba ultima*," or "*Alles Erdreich ist Osterreich untertan*." All three roughly translate to "Austria will rule the world," an inscription that has inspired more than its share of megalomanic zealots through the years. Above the archway is **Saint George's Church**, built in the 15th century. Maximilian I, the "Last Knight," is buried under the altar's steps; he requested that his remains be placed so that the priest would be "stepping on his heart" during religious services. Honest. (Courtyard open daily; use entrance on the right of the building, and ask the uniformed attendant about tours and information.)

Wiener Neustadt's nightlife is largely a product of would-be Viennese stranded in the suburbs. Observe the Austrian courting rituals at **Leiwaund,** Brodtischgasse 11, two blocks from the Hauptplatz (open Mon.-Wed. 10am-2am, Thurs.-Fri. 10am-3am, Sat. 10am-4am, Sun. 5pm-2am).

■■■ BADEN BEI WIEN

Baden is the favorite weekend getaway spot for Viennese sick of Vienna. Since the age of Roman rule, bathers have cherished the spa for the therapeutic effects of its sulphur springs. All day, every day, a supply of salutary water, with a natural temperature of 36°C, springs from the ground. The Holy Roman Emperors used Baden as a summer retreat; the honor became official when, in 1803, Emperor Franz I decided to move the court here during the summer months.

Under imperial patronage, Biedermeier culture flourished here. City notables generated magnificent specimens of architecture and art and rediscovered the science of horticulture. As a tribute to the Emperor's presence, Baden created a rosarium covering 90,000 square meters of park; the enormous garden contains over 20,000 roses. Here, the 800 different varieties of rose can be admired and studied in their natural environment (or just renamed and smelled for consistency). The park extends from the center of town to the Wienerwald; in one step, you can depart the carefully tended roses and enter the enormous, trail-laced tract of woodland.

Orientation and Practical Information There's only one problem in paradise: Baden is built for an imperial budget. Because it is so well connected to Vienna by public transportation (a mere 16 mi. away), Baden becomes an excellent day trip. A short ride on the "Badener Bahn" from the front of the Viennese Staatsoper brings you to **Josefsplatz,** in the center of the resort (50 AS; every ½-hr.; Eurail valid). Baden's **tourist office** (Kurdirektion) is located at Hauptplatz 2 (tel. (02252) 868 00; fax 807 33. The patient, English-speaking staff will give you all the brochures and information necessary to make a thorough visit. (Open Mon.-Fri. 8am-noon and 2-6pm, Sat. 10am-2pm, Sun 10am-noon.) Baden's **postal code** is A-2500.

Accommodations and Food If you are wholly committed to the full Baden experience despite admonishments from the budget fairy, the tourist office will introduce you to the owner of a *Privatzimmer.* **Gästehaus Baden,** Mühlgasse 65 (tel. (02252) 88 77 85), is a cozy inn with 160 beds and a helpful staff (singles 340 AS, doubles 560 AS. Breakfast included). **Café Damals,** on Rathausgasse in a courtyard on the right facing the Hauptplatz, offers a wonderfully relaxing opportunity to sit and snack in leisurely decadence. Try their cheese baguette (39 AS).

Sights and Entertainment Take Frauengasse north towards the Hauptplatz to find the **Frauenkirche,** the imperial family's church of choice from 1812-1834, on the right. Notice the interior's Neoclassicism and the same "Maria-Theresa yellow" exterior that coats Schönbrunn Palace in Vienna. The **Hauptplatz,** adorned with a Baroque trinity column (1718), holds the **Rathaus** and Franz I's summer residence at #17. Around the corner from the tourist office, at Rathausgasse 10, the **Beethoven Haus** museum marks the famous composer's residence from 1821-23 (open Tues.-Fri. 4-6pm, Sat.-Sun. 9-11am and 4-6pm). He was just one of several Austrian musicians to appreciate Baden's luxury—Mozart, Schubert, Haydn, and Salieri all made their way to the resort.

North of the Hauptplatz via Maria-Theresia-Gasse, lies the glory of Baden, the **Kurpark.** Set into the southeastern edge of the Wienerwald, this park's natural beauty represents much of the town's idyllic simplicity. This meticulously landscaped garden holds monuments to frequent visitors Beethoven and Grillparzer, a casino, an outdoor concert gazebo, and the **Römer Quelle** (Roman Springs), where water gushes forth from the rock. The delightful **Theresiangarten** was laid out in 1792, when the Kurpark was still called "Theresienbad." The **flower clock** in the middle of the Kurpark grass began ticking in 1929. The park became the most important frolic zone in Europe when the Congress of Vienna met in the early 19th century; the most important European political figures were granted permission to escort the Imperial Court here. After Sunday Mass, throngs of townsfolk would gather to watch the mighty personages strut through the park. The **Emperor Franz-Josef Museum,** Hochstr. 51 (tel. (02252) 411 00), perches atop the Badener Berg and holds exhibitions of regional folk art (open April-Oct. Tues.-Sun. 1-7pm; Nov.-March Tues.-Sun. 11am-5pm).

A musical tradition courses through the Baden air. The season opens on May first, with song and music at the **Town Theater** (free on the 1st). Baden's **Beethoven**

Festival takes place from mid-September to early October, with performance by famous Austrian artists; the Town Theater features Beethoven films during the festival. (For ticket reservations, contact: Kulturamt der Stadtgemeinde Baden, Hauptplatz 2, A-2500 Baden, Austria; fax (02252) 86 80 02 10.) From late June to mid-September, the **Summer Arena** offers a magnificent, open-air setting for performances of classic Viennese operettas, including works by Fall and Lehár. On summer days, Baden's **orchestra** performs four or five concerts a week, weather permitting. During Baden's September **Grape Cure Weeks,** the city's historic Hauptplatz is filled with music and folklore. Stands sell fresh grapes and grape juice, and a contest is held in which the winner receives his or her **weight in wine** (see Bludenz in West Austria for a similar, albeit more cocoa-rich, challenge).

■ Mödling

"You must take a good look around Mödling; it's a very nice place."
—Ludwig van Beethoven to the painter August von Kloeber

"Poor I am, and miserable," Beethoven wrote upon his arrival in Mödling. Seeking physical and psychological rehabilitation, he schlepped all this way for the *il ne sait quoi* only mineral-spring could offer. He wrote his "Missa Solemnis" within Mödling's embrace, and his spirits thoroughly improved. Take his happy-camper status as a good omen; whatever the baths' medicinal effects, they certainly offer a soothing respite from travel stress.

About 20 minutes from Vienna by S-Bahn (Eurail valid), Mödling maintains the charm that has drawn nobility and artists since the Babenberg reign. Minstrel Walther von der Vogelweide performed his epics in town. Later, other musical geniuses, including Schubert, Wagner, and Strauss, made their way here to glean inspiration from the stunning scenery. Most of the artists of the *fin-de-siècle,* such as musician Hugo Wolf, poet Peter Altenberg, and painters Egon Schiele and Gustav Klimt, planted at least temporary roots at the spa. In his house on Bernhardgasse, Arnold Schönberg developed his 12-tone chromatic music and posed for the renowned Oskar Kokoschka portrait.

This elegant and serene town of fewer than 20,000 permanent inhabitants is hidden among the trees of the Wienerwald. There are 85km of marked hiking trails in and around Mödling, leading to the ruins of the **Babenbergs' castle,** the Neoclassical **Liechtenstein Palace,** and the Romanesque **Liechtenstein Castle** (both in Maria Enzersdorf, a neighboring town). The well-preserved *Altstadt* proudly presents two Romanesque churches (check out the amazing stained-glass in the **Pfarrkirche St. Othman** and the majestic **Schwarzturm** tower topped by a huge black onion dome) and a charming Renaissance **Rathaus.** Mödling's **City Museum,** Josef Deutsch Platz, displays archaeological finds that trace the town's history back to 6000 BC (open April-Dec. Sat.-Sun. 10am-noon and 2-4pm).

To this day, Mödling remains a favorite recreational destination; the **Stadtbad** (city bath) has huge outdoor and indoor swimming pools, a sauna, sunbathing, massage, and zillions of screaming children climbing on a funky orange **octopus thing.** There are also facilities for golf, tennis, horseback-riding, and fishing. In the evening, summer clientele naturally flock to the *Heurigen,* infinitely more authentic than their counterparts in Vienna.

For information, brochures, and *Privatzimmer* lists, head to the **tourist office** (Gästedienst), Elisabethstr. 2, behind the *Rathaus* (tel. (02236) 267 27). From the train station, walk down Hauptstr. all the way to the *Rathaus* (10 min.). (Office open Mon.-Fri. 9am-noon and 2-6pm, Sat. 10am-2pm, Sun. 10am-noon.) Mödling's proximity to Vienna makes for an excellent day trip. Trains leaving from the Wien Südbahnhof pass through Mödling all day (30 AS), and a bus leaves hourly from Südtiroler Platz in Vienna. The S-Bahn from the Vienna Kennedybrücke also runs into Mödling.

With no hostel in town, overnight stays in Mödling are a bit expensive unless you manage to track down a *Privatzimmer.* Try out **Frühstuckspension Haus Monika,** Badstr. 53 (tel. (02236) 25 73 59; fax 25 73 55). From the train station, stroll down Hauptstr., and make a left on Badstr. (10 min.). Telephones, showers, and toilets adorn every room (singles 400-480 AS; doubles 600-670 AS). For hearty Austrian and grilled cuisine, try **Babenbergerhof,** Babenbergerstr. 6 (tel. (02236) 22 2 46), one block down Elisabethstr. from Schrannenplatz. (Entrees 90-250 AS. Open daily. Major credit cards accepted.) Another option is the **Löwa** market on the corner of Babenbergerstr. and Jasomirgotgasse.

Near Mödling: The Hinterbrühl Seegrotte

Once in Mödling, you might make the jaunt to the neighboring hamlet of Hinterbrühl to visit the Seegrotte. This former mineral mine lies under a mountain flooded with 20 million liters of water in 1912. It was pumped dry by the Nazis during World War II; they used the protected underground complex to assemble the fuselage of the world's first jet fighter. Although the Nazis blew up the factory to cover their tracks, the Seegrotte still exists and is now home to Europe's largest **underground lake.** Officials have to pump out 20,000 liters of water daily to keep the level down. A bus (direction: "Gaaden" or "Heiligenkreuz") runs from Mödling to "Hinterbrühl/Seegrotte." (Open daily; last tour 5pm. Admission 46 AS, including tour in English and German and a boat ride on the lake.)

■ Heiligenkreuz and Mayerling

These two villages, 4km apart in the southeastern Wienerwald, are now sleepy tourist towns with fewer than 1500 permanent inhabitants apiece. Nevertheless, both hold significant places in Austria's imperial history. **Heiligenkreuz** is home to the second-oldest Cistercian abbey in Austria, founded in 1133. The tombs of the Babenberg monarchs rest inside; their family tree is recreated in the stained-glass windows of the Gothic **Brunnenhaus** (Fountain House). The townsfolk tinkered with the abbey until 1739, when the huge Baroque **Dreifältigkeitssäule** (Trinity Column) was erected by Giuliani. This famous Venetian sculptor also decorated the **Totenkapelle** (Chapel of the Dead), where golden skeleton-candelabras guard a coffin and the altar. For a tour of the entire complex, seek out the information office on the right as you enter the **Arkadenhof,** the abbey's central courtyard. (40-min. tours daily 9-11:30am and 1:30-5:30pm. Admission 35 AS, students 20 AS.) The grounds of the abbey are open daily without admission—including the **Waldfriedhof,** where **Mary Vetsera** is buried (see below).

Mayerling boasted no special attraction other than the Habsburgs' hunting lodge, until January 30, 1889. On that day, Crown Prince Rudolf von Habsburg, the only son of Franz Josef and Elisabeth, was found in a pool of blood next to his equally dead 18-year-old mistress, Mary Vetsera. Both were supposedly shot, but no weapon was found (although all the doors and windows were locked when the pair was discovered). This story became the subject of much speculation—double suicide? assassination? Professor Plum, in the conservatory, with a lead pipe? The imperial family tried to avoid a scandal and tore down **Schloß Mayerling** to establish a Carmelite convent. The story leaked out, but all evidence of the affair has since vanished. Prince Rudolf is buried with the rest of the Habsburgs in the Capuchin Vault in Vienna, and Maria Vetsera is buried in Heiligenkreuz. The convent is open for tours, but Mayerling's biggest attraction is its history. (Convent open Mon.-Sat. 9am-5pm, Sun. 11am-5pm. Admission 15 AS.)

Both Heiligenkreuz and Mayerling are accessible by bus from Vienna. From Südtirolerplatz, take the **bus** (#1123, 1127, or 1094) heading to "Alland" (90 min.). Those who want to spend the night should seek out the **tourist office** (Gemeindeamt), across the street from the Heiligenkreuz abbey (tel. (02256) 22 86), for information on *Privatzimmer.* **Hotel Helenenstüberl,** 2354 Helenental-Schwechatback 55 (tel. (02258) 25 35) is located between Heiligenkreuz and Mayerling and offers reasonably priced accommodations (rooms with shower and toilet 330-465 AS). In Mayerling, eat at the **Gasthof "Zum Alten Jagdschloss"** (tel. (02258) 22 72), at the foot of the hill leading to the Carmelite convent (*Champignon Schnitzel* 80 AS; open Mon.-Thurs. and Sat.-Sun. 8am-8pm).

■■■ EISENSTADT

Resting on the southern slope of the Leithagebirge (Leitha Mountains) at the head of the Great Hungarian Plain, Eisenstadt (pop. 11,000) is a gentle hill city with deep roots in Austro-Hungarian history. Once home to the mighty Hungarian Eszterházy family, patrons of the symphonic master Josef Haydn, Eisenstadt today is the capital of the Burgenland province.

Orientation and Practical Information Eisenstadt is a gateway to the Neusiedler See and is situated only 50km from Vienna; Bundesstraße 16 passes through town on its way south from Vienna to Sopron, Hungary. **Trains** run daily to Vienna (60 AS), Neusiedl am See (15 AS), Purbach (15 AS), and other Burgenland destinations. The station (tel. 26 37) rents bikes and stores luggage. (Open Mon. 4:30am-8:30pm, Tues.-Sun. 6:30am-8:30pm.) No buses run from the station to the town center—just walk 10 blocks up Bahnhofstr., Elßler-St.-Martin, and then Hauptstr., or take a taxi. The **bus station** (tel. 2350) is located on the Domplatz next to the *Dom,* down Pfarrgasse from Esterházyplatz. **Buses** run daily to Vienna (80 AS), Rust (30 AS), and other points throughout Burgenland. (Open Mon.-Fri. 6:30am-6:25pm, Sat. 8am-noon.)

The staff at the local **tourist office** (*Fremdenverkehrsamt*), Hauptstr. 35 (tel. 673 90; fax 673 91), in the *Rathaus,* makes room reservations for no fee and distributes materials in English. (Open daily 9am-6pm; Sept.-June Mon.-Fri. 9am-6pm.) A regional tourist office, **Landesfremdenverkehrsverband für das Burgenland,** in Schloß Esterházy (tel. 33 84), offers oodles of information on the entire *Land.* (Open daily 8am-6pm; Sept.-June Mon.-Fri. 8am-5pm.) The **post office,** on Semmelweißgasse between Pfarrgasse and St.-Rochus-Str. (tel. 22 71), has the best **exchange** rates. (Open Mon.-Fri. 7am-7pm, Sat. 7am-4pm, Sun. 8-10am. **Postal Code:** A-7000.) **Telephones** are at the post office, behind the information kiosk on Esterházy Platz, at the bus station, and at the intersection of Hauptstr. and Fanny-Elßler-Gasse. (**City code:** 02682.) Call 133 for the **police,** 141 for an **emergency doctor** and 144 for an **ambulance.**

Accommodations and Food With no youth hostel in the vicinity, the most economical option is to rent a *Privatzimmer* (starting at 150 AS). The tourist office helps make reservations and has an invaluable list of families who speak English. During July and August, strongly consider booking in advance to avoid getting shut out by itinerant throngs. A friendly manager tends bar at **Hotel Mayr Franz,** Kalvarienbergplatz 1 (tel. 627 51), directly across from the Bergkirche. (Singles and doubles 300 AS per person; triples 250 AS per person; quads 200 AS per person. All rooms have shower and toilet. Breakfast included. Reservations recommended.) **Wirsthaus zum Eder,** Hauptstr. 25 (tel. 626 45) is a pleasant, centrally located hotel with a *gemütlich* garden restaurant. (Singles 400 AS, doubles 225 AS per person; both with toilet, shower, and breakfast.)

Gasthaus Kiss, Esterházystr. 16, cooks up huge servings of hearty Austrian food in a snug inn (baked pork *Schnitzel* with salad 70 AS). **Milchstrube,** 26 Pfarrgasse, one block off Hauptstr., provides an endless variety of fresh sandwiches (11 AS), *Strudel,* and its namesake milk-based beverages. The proprietor sings show-tunes while whipping up frappes. (Open Mon.-Fri. 6:30am-6pm, Sat. 6:30am-noon.) **Zum Eulenspiegel,** 10 Neusiedler Str., serves up yummy *Gulasch* (55 AS), *Spätzle* and salad (48 AS), or pizza on a terrace complete with geranium-filled window boxes, rattan screens, and an odd blue mural (open Mon.-Fri. 10am-10pm, Sat. 10am-2pm). Eisenstadt also has two grocery stores: **Spar Markt,** at Esterházystr. 38 (open Mon.-Fri. 7am-12:30pm and 2:30-6pm, Sat. 7am-noon), and **Billa,** at Domplatz 20 (open Mon.-Thurs. 7:30am-6:30, Fri. 7:30am-8pm, Sat. 7am-1pm).

Sights and Entertainment Eisenstadt sprawls out in three directions from **Schloß Esterházy** in Esterházy Platz, a 15-minute walk up Bahnhofstr. from the train station. The *Schloß* is still owned by the Esterházys, an aristocratic family claiming descent from Atilla the Hun (every family has a wacky great-uncle...), but after falling on hard times, they leased the family home to the provincial government as office space. Built on the footings of the Kanizsai family's 14th-century fortress, the castle contains the **Haydnsaal** (Haydn Hall), where the hard-working composer conducted the court orchestra almost every night from 1761 to 1790 (that's *five times* Lou Gehrig's record—and Haydn had to walk uphill through the snow...both ways ...to get to the concerts). The Haydnsaal is considered *the* acoustic Mecca for classical musicians. (Tours of the *Schloß* daily every hr. 9am-4:30pm; 20 AS, students and seniors 10 AS. Tour lasts 40 min. and includes 2 concert halls and 6 exhibition rooms.) The *Kapellmeister's* modest residence has been converted into the **Haydn-Haus,** Haydngasse 21 (tel. 26 52), exhibiting some of his manuscripts and other memorabilia. (Open Easter-Oct. daily 9am-noon and 1-5pm. Admission 20 AS, students 10 AS.)

The **Bergkirche,** an elaborate Baroque church on Kalvarienbergplatz, is another Haydn residence of sorts—his body has de-composed here since 1932, though his head didn't arrive until 1954. Admirers had stolen the composer's noggin 150 years earlier and put it on display in the Vienna Music Museum, where necrophiliac tourists were allowed to touch it. (Church open Easter-Oct. daily 9am-noon and 1-5pm.) The **Kalvarienberg** is an annex to the Bergkirche; inside the vaulted structure is an exact replica of Calvary Hill, where Jesus Christ was crucified. (Open daily April-Oct. 9am-noon and 2-5pm. Admission 15 AS, students 10 AS.)

Two of Eisenstadt's museums will especially interest history buffs. The **Landesmuseum,** Museumgasse 5 (tel. 626 52) comprehensively exhibits Burgenland's cultural history, including an amazing archaeological collection. The **Judisches Museum,** Unterbergstr. 6 (tel. 51 45), celebrates the Austrian Jewish heritage, with an emphasis on religious holidays. A small synagogue and a disturbing black room, with a Nazi banner proclaiming Jewish undesirability, complete the collection (open late May to late Oct. Tues.-Sun. 10am-5pm).

Another renowned composer, Franz Liszt, was born in 1811 in the nearby village of **Raiding** in what is now called the **Franz-Liszt-Geburt-Haus** (tel. (02619) 72 20). This small domicile has been turned into a museum displaying photographs, documents, and the old church organ on which Liszt learned his art as a child. (Open Easter-Oct. daily 9am-noon and 1-5pm. Admission 15 AS, students and seniors 8 AS.) **Buses** to Raiding from Eisenstadt depart from Domplatz (74 AS); another bus (54 AS) runs from Eisenstadt to Forchtenstein.

Every summer Eisenstadt hosts a concert series, the **Haydn Festspiele**—featuring music of Haydn and his contemporaries—culminating in the **Haydn Tage** from September 11 to 20. Some concerts are free; for others, tickets range up to 1200 AS. For information call 618 66.

NEUSIEDLER SEE

Covering 320 square kilometers, the Neusiedler See is a vestige of the body of water that once blanketed the entire Pannenian Plain. With no outlets and no inlets save underground springs, this steppe lake is nowhere more than two meters deep; it periodically recedes to expose thousands of square meters of dry land—indeed, in the mid-19th century, the lake desiccated entirely. Warm and salty, the lake is a haven for birds and humans alike. More than 250 species of waterfowl dwell in the thickets formed by the reeds, and every summer thousands of vacationers flock to various resorts for swimming, sailing, fishing, and cycling.

■ Neusiedl am See

Less than an hour from Vienna by express train, Neusiedl am See is the gateway to the Neusiedler region. Indeed, the streets bustle with almost as much pedestrian and vehicular traffic as the Austrian capital. There's really nothing to do here except enjoy the various pleasures of the lake; to arrive at its celebrated shores, walk down Untere Hauptstr. from the Hauptplatz and turn right on Seestr., a 1km-long causeway that cuts through a thicket of reeds to reach the beach. The beach is a bit rocky, but still pleasant (admission 12 AS, children 4 AS). You can rent **motorboats** (120 AS per hr.), **paddleboats** (80 AS per hr.), and **sailboats** (90 AS per hr.) at **Bootsvermietung Leban,** at the end of Seestr. Next door, **Bootsvermietung Baumgartner** runs cruises of the lake (round-trip 50 AS, children 25 AS). **Buses** to the beach from the *Bahnhof* and the Hauptplatz run hourly until 6pm.

The **tourist office** (*Fremdenverkehrsbüro*), in the *Rathaus* on the Hauptplatz (tel. 22 29), distributes pamphlets about the resort town, provides assistance with accommodations, and offers advice on boat and bike rental. From the train station, walk down Eisenstädterstr. until it becomes Obere Hauptstr., which leads to the Hauptplatz (10 min.). (Open daily 8am-7pm; Sept.-June Mon.-Fri. 8am-noon and 1-5pm.) The **post office,** on the corner of Untere Hauptstr. and Lisztgasse, has a small **telephone center** (**City code:** 02167) and **changes money** at the best rates in town (Open Mon.-Fri. 8am-noon and 2-6pm, Sat. 8-10am. **Postal Code:** A-7100.) **Trains** run frequently to and from Eisenstadt (15 AS) and Vienna (60 AS). The **train station** and adjacent **bus station** are an arduous hike down Obere Hauptstr. and Eisenstädterstr. from the center of town. Fortunately, a train ticket garners a free bus ride to the Hauptplatz. Dial 133 in an **emergencies.**

Because of Neusiedl's proximity to Vienna, finding accommodations can be trying. To reach the newly renovated **Jugendherberge Neusiedl am See (HI),** Herberggasse 1 (tel. 22 52), walk down Bahnhofstr. from the station, take a right on Eisenstädtersstr., a left on Wienerstr., and a left on Herberggasse. The hostel sports 86 beds in 20 quads and three doubles. (Open March-Oct. Reception open 8am-2pm and 5-10pm. 111 AS; under 19 93 AS. Sheets 15 AS. Breakfast included. Key deposit 100 AS. Reservations recommended.) **Gasthof zur Traube,** Hauptplatz 9 (tel. 423), has a cordial staff and huge, wood-paneled rooms. Every room has a shower and toilet (280-320 AS per person; breakfast included). A stroll down **Obere Hauptstraße** and **Untere Hauptstraße** presents an array of bakeries, fruit markets, butcher shops, and restaurants. **Rathausstüberl,** around the corner from the *Rathaus* on Kirchengasse, has a lovely shaded courtyard and great food, including plenty of fish and vegetarian options (entrees 70-150 AS; open May-Oct. daily 10am-10pm). Rathausstüberl doubles as a sunny *Pension,* as well—rooms cost 250-280 AS per person with breakfast buffet (reservations recommended). The **Zielpunkt grocery store,** Untere Hauptstr. near the post office, is the place for cost-efficient comestibles (open Mon.-Fri. 8am-noon and 2-6pm, Sat. 7:30am-noon).

■ Purbach am See

Purbach, on the western shore of the **Neusiedler See,** has fermented grapes since the Roman era. Parts of the city walls, built in the 17th century to protect the town from imperial Turkish ravages, still exist. One militant Turk lent his visage to the **Purbacher Turke,** the bust that has become the town's symbol. In 1532, a Turkish soldier fell into a drunken stupor as his raiding comrades left Purbach for Vienna; when the citizens of Purbach returned from the kills after the raid, they discovered the soldier battling his roaring hangover. The townfolk agreed not to kill him if he converted to Christianity; the soldier complied and was kept as a slave by the farmer in whose house he was found. The Turk became well-loved by the citizens after his conversion, and after his death, this monument to the townfolk's successful colonial venture was erected.

A vacation spot for many outdoor enthusiasts, Purbach is shamelessly tourist-friendly. The **tourist office,** An der Bundesstr., in the lobby of Pauli's Stuben (tel. (02683) 225), organizes daily activities for visitors, including tours through the town and its vineyards (50 AS). They can help book you a *Privatzimmer,* but the hostel at **Camping Purbach** (May-Aug. tel. (02683) 51 70; Sept-Oct. and April tel. 55 38; fax 55 90 85) is much more lively. Return to the days of sixth-grade summer camp, *sans* poison ivy and Parents' Visiting Day. The campsite is near the Hallenbad (public swimming complex) and the Neusiedler See. The Minimarket on the grounds is open daily. (Curfew 10pm. 3-4 beds per room. 150 AS per person. Breakfast included. Sheets 25 AS. Washing machine 40 AS per load. 4 tennis courts, 110 AS per hr.) **Pauli's Stuben,** next to the tourist office, offers excellent Austrian and Hungarian cuisine in a soothing atmosphere (entrees 57-180 AS). At night, sample the renowned Burgenland wine at one of the *Buschenschanken* lining Kellergasse. Tourists here love to bike around the lake, but if prepubescent waifs screaming through hostel hallways at dawn have drained your endurance, catch a **ferry** at various points on the lake to cut down the distance. Don't forget your passport if you plan to hop the Hungarian border.

■■■ RUST

During the summer, tourists inundate tiny Rust (pop. 1700)—one of the self-appointed wine capitals of Austria—to partake of the fruit of the vine. In 1524, the Emperor granted the wine-growers of Rust the exclusive right to display the letter "R" on their wine barrels, a tradition that survives today on all Rust wine-corks. The income from wine production enabled the citizens of Rust to purchase their freedom from the crown in 1681; the town thereafter became a free borough. The town's economic structure is still based largely on the production of its high-quality wines—fully one-quarter of the population is employed by the local vintners. Rust residents give vineyard location most of the credit for the excellent quality of the town beverage; most of the vineyards are situated on gentle slopes that incline toward the lake. In the morning, dawn sunbeams are reflected from the lake's surface to the hills, where the vines bathe in the diffused, gentle rays—and photosynthesize like mad. Most of the soil is sandy loam over a fertile lime base, which stores moisture well.

Orientation and Practical Information Rust is 10km east of Eisenstadt on the Neusiedler See. **Buses** connect the two towns (30 AS) several times per day; they discharge passengers at the **post office,** Franz Josef Platz 14. (Open Mon.-Fri. 8am-noon and 2-6pm. **Postal code:** A-7071.) The historic city center is across Oggauerstr. and toward Conradplatz, by the Renaissance **Rathaus.** The **tourist office** (Gästeinformation), inside the *Rathaus* (tel. (02685) 502), hands out maps, plans bicycle tours, arranges wine tastings, and can usually land you a room with an English-speaking family. (Open Mon.-Fri. 8am-noon and 2-6pm, Sat. 10am-3pm, Sun. 10am-noon.) The nifty electronic board outside displays all of the best accommodations, with green and red lights indicating vacancy. If the board looks like Boston on St. Patrick's Day, you're in good shape; just avoid the green bagels. A telephone connects you to the *Privatzimmer* proprietors for free (open 24 hrs.). Hour-long **tours** featuring discussions of Rust's history, culture, wine, and storks begin May-Sept. Wed. and Sat. at 10am at the tourist office (20 AS, with guest card 15 AS). **Information boards** grace the inside of the *Rathaus* arcade, the corner of Franz Josef Platz and Feldgasse, and Conradplatz.

Accommodations and Food Room prices climb when European tourists pack Rust in July and August. Rust's hostel recently closed, so the most economical option is to rent a *Privatzimmer.* Stroll down Feldgasse and look for vacancies, or check with the tourist office. Surrounded by rolling hills and vineyards, **Pension Magdalenenhof,** Feldgasse 40 (tel. (02685) 373) is a warm and cozy *Pension* just 15 minutes from the bus stop by foot. The friendly proprietor speaks some English. (Reception open noon-7pm. Singles 250 AS. Doubles 230 AS per person; with shower, toilet, and balcony 280 AS. Breakfast included. Reservations recommended.) **Prieler Doris,** St. Ägidigasse 6 (tel. (02685) 461), left off Feldgasse, is an eight-room establishment with a motherly proprietor (210 AS the first night, 10 AS less each night thereafter, down to 160 AS). Camp at **Ruster Freizeitcenter** (tel. (02685) 595), which offers warm showers, washing machines, a game room, a playground, and a grocery store. (Reception open 7:30am-10pm. 25-35 AS per person, children 10-20 AS; 20-30 AS per tent, 25-30 AS per car. Showers included.)

Most taverns in Rust offer superb wine and jolly company; try the G'würztraminer halb-suß wine for an especially savory treat. In addition to hefty daily specials, **Zum Alten Haus,** at the corner of Raiffeisenstr. and Franz Josef Platz, serves a mean *Topfenpalatschinken* (37 AS) or *Wiener Schnitzel* with salad (71 AS; open Tues.-Sun. 9am-10pm). For those with more creativity than cash, the **A & O Markt Dreyseitel,** on Weinberggasse between Mittergasse and Schubertgasse, sells the raw materials for a meal (open Mon.-Fri. 7am-noon and 3-6pm).

Sights and Entertainment During the day, visitors sun themselves on the beaches of the lake's western shore, then migrate to the *Heurigen* to imbibe a few glasses of the renowned Ruster Blaufränkisch wine. Some hop over to Hungary, just a few miles east, and a select few come solely to bird-watch. Rust's most famous residents are the white storks who nest atop the town's chimneys; signs on the corner of Seezeile and Hauptstraße indicate their rooftop hangouts. The stork population has diminished each year, but in 1987, Rust and the World Wildlife Federation initiated a special joint program to protect the storks and eventually increase their number. At the same time, Rust gave birth to a second post office, the "Storks' Post Office, A-7073 Rust," dedicated to the program. You know you're helping the birds if your mail is delivered on special postcards with the storklicious postmark.

Rust's name is derived from the word for "elm tree," as is its Hungarian moniker, "Szil." Early morning strolls down the 16th-century elm-lined streets of the *Altstadt* are accompanied by chiming church bells and crowing roosters. Rust's **Fischerkirche,** around the corner from the tourist office, was built between the 12th and 16th centuries; it's the oldest church in Burgenland (admission 10 AS, students 5 AS; add 5 AS for tour).

Many town vintners (*Weinbauer*) offer wine tasting and tours of their cellars and vineyards. **Rudolf Beilschmidt,** Weinberggasse 1 (tel. (02685) 326) is one such proprietor (tours May-Sept every Friday at 5pm). **Familie Just,** Weinberggasse 16 (tel. (02685) 251) also offers vineyard tours and tastings (April-Sept. every Tues. at 6pm; 60AS).

Near Rust: Mörbisch

The tiny village of Mörbisch lies 5km along the Neusiedler See to the south, easily within cycling distance from Rust. Whitewashed houses, brightly painted doors, and dried corn hanging from the walls mark the village, the last settlement on the western shore of the lake before the Hungarian border. The town has its own beach and "curative" mineral springs. Each summer, it hosts an operetta festival—the **Mörbisch Seefestspiele.** For more information, contact the Mörbisch **tourist office** (Fremdenverkehrsbüro; tel. (02685) 8430).

■ Rohrau

Musical pilgrims constitute the majority of Rohrau's tourism; Josef Haydn was born here in 1732, one of 12 children raised by the cook for the Count in the local castle. Although Haydn left town in 1740, Rohrau still reaps the benefits of those eight precious years. The straw-roofed **Haydn House** (tel. (02164) 22 68), is now a museum, displaying the composer's modest beginnings and spectacular career through original music scores and childhood mementos. (Open Tues.-Sun. 10am-5pm. Admission 20 AS, students 10 AS.) **Harrach Castle,** where Haydn's mother worked, dates back to the 13th century. Owned by the Harrach diplomats since 1524, it is now home to one of Austria's finest private art galleries (tel. (02164) 22 52), with an excellent collection of Spanish, Neapolitan, and Flemish art from the 17th and 18th centuries. (Open April-Oct. Tues.-Sun. 10am-5pm. Admission 40 AS, students 20 AS.) A rolling lawn circumscribes the castle on the site of the original moat; look for the **Schloßtaverne** restaurant on the other side of the moat area. (Entrees 68-178 AS; 90 AS for the Rohrauer Kulturjause: a Haydnlocke pastry, a Melange, and a visit to the gallery. Open Tues.-Sun. 10am-9pm. Major credit cards accepted.)

Forty-five kilometers from Vienna, Rohrau is accessible by bus from **Bruck an der Leitha.** (Take the train from the Wien-Ost Bahnhof to Bruck.) Rohrau's **tourist office** (tel. (02164) 22 04) is in the Gemeindeamt building, on the second floor. (Open Mon.-Thurs. 7:30am-noon and 1-3:30pm; Fri. 7:30am-noon.) **Gasthof/Fremdenzimmer Arnold & Ingeborg Frey,** Gerhaus 23 (tel. (02164) 22 49) offers clean rooms at low prices (180 AS per person). To sample the local culture, visit one of the many *Buschenschenken* on Pachfurth; these wine gardens are analogous to Vienna's famed *Heurigen*.

THE DANUBE (DONAU)

The "Blue Danube" is largely the invention of Johann Strauss's ¾ imagination, but this mighty, muddy-green river still merits a cruise. The **Erste Donau Dampfschiffahrts-Gesellschaft (DDSG)** runs ships daily from May to late October. The firm operates offices in **Vienna,** Handelskai 265, by the Reichsbrücke (tel. (0222) 217 50; fax 218 92 38); in **Linz,** at Untere Donaulände 10 (tel. (0732) 78 36 07 or 77 10 90; fax 783 60 79); and in **Passau,** Germany, Im Ort 14a, at the Dreiflußeck (tel. (0851) 330 35; fax 330 32). Cruises run from Vienna to Grein, passing Krems and Melk *en route,* and between Linz and Passau, on the German border. East of Vienna, hydrofoils run to Bratislava, Slovakia and **Budapest,** Hungary. All of the cruises are expensive (at least double the train fare); fortunately, Eurail passes are valid on river jaunts from Vienna to Grein and from Linz to Passau, and Rabbit Card holders receive a 30% discount. Everyone pays full fare for the eastbound hydrofoils. Families may travel for half-price (minimum 1 parent and one child ages 6-15; children under 6 accompanied by a parent travel free). **Bicycle rental** is possible at the Melk, Spitz, and Krems docks (combined with cruise 35 AS, each additional day 70 AS; without a cruise 150 AS; bring the bike on board for 25 AS). Pets pay half the regular fare; dogs must wear muzzles, available on board, at all times during the cruise.

The **ferries** run from Vienna to Krems (5 hr. upstream, 4 hr. downstream; one way 294 AS, round-trip 442 AS) and from Krems to Melk (3 hr. upstream, 2 hr. downstream; one way 220 AS, round-trip 330 AS). Take the train to Krems (1 hr. from Vienna) or Melk (2 hr. from Vienna) and walk to the dock. You can also sail from Vienna to Melk (8 hr. upstream, 6 hr. downstream; one way 490 AS, round-trip 736 AS). Few make the full Vienna-Grein run (11 hr. upstream, 8 hr. downstream; one way 686 AS, round-trip 1030 AS). For 80 AS, one can ride the boat either way for one stop between Krems and Linz—children and seniors are eligible for a further 50% off. The **Donau Spezial Ticket** (500 AS) allows users unlimited passage on the

Krems-Grein ferry for four days within any 10-day period. See the DDSG and tourist offices for prices on other special ship/bus and ship/train ticket combinations.

Cyclists should take advantage of the **Lower Danube Cycle Track,** a velocipede's Valhalla. This riverside bike trail between Vienna and Naarn links several Danube villages, including Melk and Dürnstein. The ride offers captivating views of crumbling castles, latticed vineyards, and medieval towns, but your attention is inevitably drawn back to the majestic current of the river. Ask at any area tourist office for a route map and bike rental information. Many of the train and ferry stations grant DDSG ticket holders a discount on bicycle rentals.

Between Krems and Melk along the Vienna-Grein route, numerous ruined castles testify to the magnitude of Austria's glorious past. One of the most dramatic fortresses is the 13th-century **Burg Aggstein,** which commands the Danube from a high pinnacle. The castle was formerly inhabited by Scheck von Wald, a robber baron known by fearful sailors as **Schreckenwalder** ("terrible forest man"). The lord was wont to impede the passage of ships with ropes stretched across the Danube, and then demand tribute from his ensnared victims. According to legend, he forced many of his prisoners to jump from the castle ramparts into the river valley more than 300m below.

■ Klosterneuberg

Klosterneuberg is 25 minutes east of Tulln (train 30 AS) and sits on the other side of the Kahlenberg from Vienna. Its claim to fame is the monstrous Augustinian Abbey, **Stift Klosterneuberg,** which sits atop the hill that bisects the town. Built on the 11th-century foundations of the castle of Babenberg Count Leopold III, this abbey was, curiously, coeducational until the mid-16th century. The tours progress through the obscenely ornate Rococo church, the arcaded courtyard, the "Room of Emperors," and the **Marble Hall.** (Obligatory tours Mon.-Sat. 9-11am and 1:30-5pm, Sun. 11am-5pm.) **St. Leopold's Chapel** contains the famous **Verdun Altar,** with 51 enameled panel paintings by Nikolaus of Verdun. The *Stift*'s deed includes acres of vineyards; the volume of wine produced by this religious order hints at a propensity to enjoy at least one worldly pleasure. The abbey's **Stiftskeller** serves the heavenly vintage with regional cuisine.

Klosterneuberg's **tourist office** (tel. (02243) 20 83; fax 867 73) is located conveniently in the train station "Klosterneuberg-Kierling" (*not* "Klosterneuberg-Weidling"). This busy little office provides plenty of pamphlets on the town's history and activities, and the accommodating staff can help you make room reservations. (Open April-Oct. Mon.-Fri. 9am-6pm, Sat.-Sun. 10am-6pm.) Klosterneuberg's **postal code** is A-3400.

Klosterneuberg's **Jugendherberge (HI)** is located on Hüttersteig 8, in Maria Gugging (tel. (02243) 835 01). Take the bus from in front of the train station (direction: "Maria Gugging") to "Hüttersteig" (15 AS); you'll see a *Jugendherberge* sign and a cheesy-looking disco on the right. (Buses every ½ hr. until 6pm, hourly after 6pm, last bus from downtown at about midnight.) Run by the CVJF (the Austrian equivalent of the YWCA), this secluded hostel has a plush garden and a ping-pong table. (Open May-Aug. Reception open from 4pm. Members only. Call ahead.) **Donaupark Camping Tulln und Klosterneuberg** (tel. (02243) 858 77) also has a site in Klosterneuberg, on In der Au, across the tracks from the Klosterneuberg-Kierling train station. (See listing in Tulln, below, for rate information.) **Julius Meinl,** Stadtplatz 26, is ready and willing to sate your nutritive needs (*Semmelbrot* 11 AS; open Mon.-Tues. 7:30am-6pm, Fri. 7:30am-7pm, Sat. 7am-noon).

■ Tulln

On the southern shore of the Danube lies Tulln, a popular daytrip destination for tourists visiting the capital, and a convenient rest stop for tired and hungry cyclists on the Danube trails. The town is just 30km upstream from Vienna (45 AS by train

Let's Go wishes you safe and happy travels

These people are only a third of the 150 students who bring you the *Let's Go* guides. Most of us were still out on the road when this photo was taken, roaming the world in search of the best travel bargains.

Of course, *Let's Go* wouldn't be the same without the help of our readers. We count on you for advice we need to make *Let's Go* better every year. That's why we read each and every piece of mail we get from readers around the globe — and that's why we look forward to your response. Drop us a line, send us a postcard, tell us your stories. We're at 1 Story Street, Cambridge, Massachusetts 02138, USA. Enjoy your trip!

on the Franz-Joseph Bahnlinie), and thereby labors under the shadow of the nearby megalopolis. Tulln has been a *Siedlung* (settled area) since 1000 BC and is known as the birthplace and first capital of Austria, but ever since the ruling families packed up and left for Vienna, the city's significance has waned considerably. The staff of the **tourist office,** Albrechtsgasse 32 (tel. (02272) 58 36), will expound on the magnificence of the city's history until they're red, white, and red in the face. The office is an easy walk from the "Tulln Stadt" train station—walk down Bahnhofstr. and make a left onto the Hauptplatz, then make a right onto Lederergasse, and you'll run right into Albrechtsgasse. Choose from among mounds of information about activities, culture, restaurants, and accommodations in Tulln. (Open May-Oct. Mon.-Fri. 9am-noon and 2-8pm, Sat.-Sun. noon-6pm; Nov.-April, contact the Stadtamt on Nußallee 4, tel. (02272) 42 85 or 42 44).

The office abuts the 18th-century **Minoritenkirche;** this former convent, now beautifully renovated, comprises a huge complex that reaches almost to the Danube. Check out the **Neue Turm** (the tower on the southwest corner, with a clock taken from St. Pölten's city gates) and the overly Rococo **Kirchenraum** (chapel). Walk along the Danube to find the funky granite **Donaubrunnen** fountains; nobody's quite sure *what* they represent. A few steps further, at Donaulände 28, is the recently-opened **Egon Schiele Museum** (tel. (02272) 45 70). Located in the former county jail where the painter Schiele was imprisoned for corrupting minors with erotic nude portraits of pubescent girls, the museum holds an excellent collection documenting the life of this infamous "Son of Tulln." (Open Tues.-Sun. 9am-noon and 2-6pm. Admission 30 AS; under 19 15 AS.) *Fun fact*: Kurt Waldheim is another Son of Tulln, born and bred in town. Coincidence? You be the judge.

The most beloved landmark of Tulln is the 1700-year-old **Römerturm,** a watchtower built by Roman Emperor Diocletian for the town's security. To the south, the Pfarrplatz supports the **Pfarrkirche** and the famous 14th-century **Karner/Dreikönigskappelle,** built in the Norman style of western France. Roam among the bones in the spooky **Krypt** underneath the chapel.

Tulln has no hostel, so if you have an aversion to *Privatzimmer,* look to the *Jugendherberge* in Klosterneuberg or head to **Donaupark Camping Tulln und Klosterneuberg,** on Hafenstr. (tel. (02272) 5200). (Car, tent, hot showers, and toilets 135-145 AS. Add 50 AS per adult, 40 AS per child. Over 15 10.50 AS tax per night. Tent rental with pitch 250 AS per night.)

■■■ KREMS

Combining *Gemütlichkeit* with a well-preserved Renaissance port town, Krems much like a living museum. In recent years, the city has mounted a huge effort to restore the beauty and integrity of its old churches, houses, and pedestrian zones, while private businesses have endeavored to increase the quantity of creature comforts. They certainly won't need help in the realm of wine production—120 different brands are already produced from the Krems vineyards. Franz Liszt's mother lived in Krems, six hundred years after the oldest Austrian coin, the Kremser Pfennig, was minted in town.

Orientation and Practical Information Krems is accessible by **train** and **ferry** (although most visitors arrive on bicycles); from the *Bahnhof,* take a left onto Kingstr. and then a right onto Martin-J.-Schmidt-Str. to reach the center of town. From the ship landing, walk on Donaulände until it becomes Ringstr., and then take a left onto Martin-J.-Schmidt-Str.

Krems's **tourist office** is housed in the Kloster Und on Undstr. 6 (tel. (02732) 82 76; fax 70 011). The friendly staff shares oodles of information on accommodations, sports, and entertainment, as well as the indispensable Heurigen Kalendar (which lists the opening times of regional wine taverns). This region of the Wachau once cradled vineyards owned by religious orders from all over Europe; the tourist office will happily book a **wine tour** for 130 AS. (Office open Mon.-Fri. 8am-6pm, Sat.-Sun. 10am-noon and 1-6pm; mid-Nov. to March Mon.-Fri. 8am-5pm.) **Oberbank,** Obere Landstr. 29, is a good place to **exchange** money; there's a 24-hour ATM for credit card cash advances outside (open Mon.-Fri. 9am-3pm). The **post office** (tel. (02732) 826 06), is right off Ringstr. on Brandströmstr. (Open Mon.-Fri. 8am-noon and 2-6pm, Sat. 8-11am; **Postal code:** A-3500.)

Accommodations and Food No matter where you stay, ask your hosts for a **guest card** that makes you eligible for a cornucopia of discounts. The **Jugendherberge (HI),** Ringstr. 77 (tel. (02732) 834 52), accommodates 52 in comfortable quads and six-bed rooms. (Reception open 5-10pm. Lockout 9am-5pm. Members only. 170 AS. Tax, breakfast and sheets included.) **Donau Camping,** Wiedengasse 7 (tel. (02732) 844 55), rests on the Danube, right by the marina. (Reception open July-Aug. 7:30-10:30am and 4-8pm, April-June and Sept. to mid-Oct. 8-10am and 4:30-5:30pm. 35 AS per person plus 10.50 AS tax, children 25 AS; 20-40 AS per tent, 35 AS per car. Warm showers included.) You can rent **bikes** at the campground (40 AS per ½-day, 60 AS per day), at the ferry landing (80 AS per day, 35 AS per day with a valid ship ticket), or at the train station (same prices as at the ferry landing).

The area around the pedestrian zone hosts many cute restaurants, but the cheapest eats in town are available at the **Zielpunkt grocery store,** Obere Lanstr. 31 (open Mon.-Fri. 8am-6pm, Sat. 7:30am-12:30pm).

Sights and Entertainment A two-hour audio walking tour provides a painfully comprehensive presentation of Krems history; pick up the cassette tape and player (60 AS, passport required) from the tourist office. The center of town—and of **Stein an der Donau,** the neighboring village overtaken by expanding Krems—is the 800m *Fußgängerzone* of **Obere Landstraße.** This pedestrian zone, lined with pastel-colored townhouses, extends east of the Romanesque **Steinertor** on Südtirolerplatz. Take Kirchengasse north to Pfarrplatz to find the onion-domes of the **Pfarrkirche St. Veit.** Just north of Pfarrplatz is Frauenbergplatz, where you can climb the covered stairway to the 15th-century **Piaristenkirche,** a light Gothic structure with ornate Baroque altars.

The **Motorrad-Museum Krems-Egelsee,** idling at Ziegelofengasse 1 (tel. (02732) 41 30 13), will keep you entranced for an afternoon. The museum features an extraordinary collection of exhibits on the history of motorcycles and motor technology. (Open daily 9am-5pm; Sept.-June Sat.-Sun. 9am-5pm. Admission 40 AS, students 20 AS.) The **Dominikanerkloster** at Theaterplatz contains the **Historical Museum,** the **Vintners' Museum,** and the **Modern Gallery.** Every two years, Krems hosts the international folklore festival that is the **Niederösterreich Landesmesse.**

■ Dürnstein

Dürnstein is a jewel of a town. The Danube rumbles slowly by. Medieval houses cling to angular crags. Venerable stone walls wind around equally aged buildings. Terraced vineyards stretch out beneath the ancient castle ramparts. And one lonely *hombre viejo* with gnarled hands hauls in a half-eaten marlin from a tiny wooden rowboat.

This ancient, decadent wine community fosters continuously relaxed revelry. The ruins of the **Kuenringer Castle** now crumble atop the mountain overlooking Dürnstein, but the stronghold was once mighty enough to keep King Richard the Lion-Hearted prisoner. A 20-minute hike up the hill (take the first right after entering the city walls, and walk up the staircase) affords amazing vistas of the most impressive portions of the Wachau region. Perch atop the hill at dusk to partake of the last sun rays streaming through the misty valley. Within the town itself, the most enchanting building is without question the Baroque riverside **Chorherrenstift** (Augustinian Abbey Church), originally founded by the daughter of the penultimate heir of the Kuenringer dynasty (admission 15 AS).

Dürnstein is accessible by **train** on the St. Pölten-St. Valentin line; trains to Krems run every hour (14 AS). The downtown is a five-minute walk from the train station; stroll down the hill and turn right on Hauptstr., which leads directly into town. Use the underground walkway to avoid the cars screaming out of the auto tunnel. Boat passengers arrive at the **Erste Donau Dampfschiffahrts-Gesellschaft (DDSG)** station on the Donaupromenade. To reach midtown from the landing, turn right on Donaupromenade, and then left on Anzuggasse, which skirts one side of the village and intersects Hauptstr., the main street. Dürnstein is almost wholly a pedestrian zone, except for gangs of cycling tourists streaking through the sloped streets, frenetically ringing their shrill bells.

The **tourist office** (*Zimmervermittlung*) is housed in a small shed in the east parking lot (Parkplatz Ost; tel. (02711) 200), down the hill from the station. Ask the staff for the English brochure that lists town restaurants and *Privatzimmer.* The office will book wine-tastings in **Unterloiben,** which, along with the suburb **Oberloiben,** is incorporated under Dürnstein's bureaucratic aegis. Both suburbs are famous for their Riesling wine (8 samples on a wine tour, 50 AS); the tourist office has a complete calendar listing the open *Heurigen* (taverns) in the area. (Office open Easter-Oct. daily 3-5pm.) From Oct.-April, contact the Gemeindeamt Dürnstein (tel. (02711) 219) in the *Rathaus*, on Hauptstr. (Open Mon.-Fri. 9am-noon and 1-4pm.)

The closest hostel lies in Krems (7km downstream), but **Pension "Altes Rathaus,"** Dürnstein 26, on the Hauptstr. behind the *Rathaus* (tel. (02711) 252), boasts a fine garden and clean, quiet rooms. (Singles 250 AS, doubles 420-550 AS. Breakfast included. Call ahead.) **Haus Maria Wagner,** Dürnstein 41 (tel. (02711) 265), is just down the road. The *Privatzimmer* here are comfortable and convenient (180-200 AS, breakfast and showers included). Although most *Heurigen* serve snacks, **Gasthaus Goldener Strauss,** Dürnstein 18, straight ahead on Hauptstr. as you enter the city walls (tel. (02711) 267), serves typical Wachauer cuisine in a cozy, low-ceilinged tavern or a shaded *Gastgarten.* (Entrees 35-150 AS. Open March to mid-Jan. Mon. and Wed.-Sun. 10am-10pm.) **Gasthof Cafe-Gols** is another Hauptstr. option. Try the *Rindgulasch* (60 AS) with a local bread, the *Wachauer Stuberl* (4 AS).

■ Spitz

Framed by vineyards, orchards, and ancient ruins, Spitz an der Donau is perhaps the embodiment of Wachau charm. Built at the foot of a hill carved by the Danube, Spitz's land and climate create the perfect conditions for producing the most lofty of high quality wines—in a good year, this tiny town of 2000 inhabitants produces 56,000 liters of fermented grape juice. Now a market village, Spitz's history dates back to the Celtic age, when consonants ruled the earth and warlords roamed the town. Carolingian monks also made Spitz their home, and a number of churches display the erstwhile religious glory. The late-Gothic **Stadtpfarrkirche,** on Kirchenplatz, is especially noteworthy; tremendous statues of the 12 apostles encircle the organ that faces the magnificent Baroque altar. The **Schiffartsmuseum Spitz/Donau,** in the Erlahof (tel. (02713) 2246), presents the history of rowing and sailing on the Danube (open April-Oct. Mon.-Sat. 10am-noon and 2-4pm, Sun. 1-5pm).

Inquire at the **tourist office,** Hauptstr. 8 (tel. (02713) 32 62 or 32 63), about the various sporting activities and lodging information (open Mon.-Tues. and Thurs.-Fri. 7am-noon and 3-6pm, Wed. and Sat. 7am-noon). At **Frühstückspension "Donaublick,"** Schopperplatz 3 (tel. (02713) 25 52), a stone's throw from the river, guests can rent bicycles from the owner. (Singles and doubles with bathroom and balcony 220-250 AS per person. Extra bed 180 AS. Breakfast included.) Where to go for food fixings? Alimentary, my dear Watson, alimentary. **Nah und Frisch,** Mittergasse 1, has groceries galore (open Mon.-Fri. 7:15am-12:30pm and 3-6pm, Sat. 7:15am-noon).

Spitz is accessible from Vienna by **train** and **ferry;** trains are less expensive and run more frequently, but a dally on the Danube cruise is worth every extra *Schilling.* The **train station** is around the corner from the tourist office. To reach the town center, take a left on Bahnhofstr., and follow it to the intersection with Hauptstr. (3 min.). From the **ferry landing,** walk upstream on the Promenade, and take a right on Hauptstr (5 min.). The **post office,** Hauptstr. 17, is the best place to exchange money. (Open Mon.-Fri. 7:30am-noon and 2-5:30pm, Sat. 8:30-10:30am.)

■■■ MELK

"If I had never come here, I would have regretted it."
—Empress Maria Theresa to the abbot during her visit to Melk

A popular destination for cyclists touring the Wachau, and a mandatory sojourn for religion buffs, Melk sprawls along the southern shore of the Danube, upstream from Krems. Each year, 300,000 guests visit Melk, mostly to see the Baroque **Benedictine Abbey** that dominates the town from its rocky foundation above the Danube. Cowering below the abbey are Renaissance houses in narrow pedestrian zones, romantic cobblestone streets, old towers, and remnants of the old city wall from the Middle Ages.

Orientation and Practical Information Melk's **tourist office,** on the corner of Babenbergerstr. and Abbe-Stadler-Gasse, next to the Rathausplatz (tel. (02752) 23 07 32 or 23 07 33), is equipped with plenty of pamphlets and maps to edify travelers about town history and athletic activities in the Wachau region. The office is located eight minutes by foot from the train station; walk down Bahnhofstr. and then straight on Bahngasse, which spills into Rathausplatz. (Open July-Sept. daily 9am-7pm; April-June Mon.-Fri. 9am-noon and 3-6pm, Sat.-Sun. 10am-2pm.) The **post office** is at Bahnhofstr. 3. (Open Mon.-Fri. 8am-noon and 2-6pm, Sat. 8-10am. **Postal code:** A-3390.) **Trains** link Melk to Amstetten and St. Pölten; there is no rail service to Krems. Bike rental, currency exchange, and luggage storage is available at the station. Take **bus** #1438 to travel from Melk to Spitz, #1451 from Melk to Krems, and #1538 from Melk to St. Pölten.

Accommodations and Food Melk's **Jugendherberge,** Abt-Karl-Str. 42 (tel. (02752) 26 81; fax 42 57), is renovating for 1994, which should improve the bare-bones lodgings. The building, adjacent to the Westbahn tracks, is slated to have 104 beds, all in quads with showers and toilets. (Reception open 5-10pm. 134 AS per night, 117 AS after 2 nights; under 19 114 AS, 97 AS after 2 nights. 10.50 AS tax per night. Breakfast included.) You'd probably do better to head to **Camping Melk** (tel. (02752) 32 91), overlooking the Danube next to the ferry landing. (Reception open 8am-midnight. 35 AS per person, children 20 AS; 35 AS per tent, 25 AS per car, 10.50 AS tax. Showers 15 AS.) **Gasthof Goldener Stern,** Sterngasse 17 (tel. (02752) 2214), has respectable rooms and hearty Austrian fare at the restaurant downstairs. Try the specialty—*Linsen mit Speck, Würstel, und Semmelknödel* (lentils with bacon, sausage, and dumplings; 75 AS). (Singles 270 AS; doubles 230 AS per person; triples 220 AS per person; quads 210 AS; quints 200 AS. All rooms 10% off after first night. Breakfast included. Restaurant open Mon. and Wed.-Sun. 7am-1am; off-season Mon.-Fri. and Sun. 7am-11pm.) Another budget option is to head down the river to the **hostel** in **Oberndorf an der Melk.** (1 hr. by private bus (tel. (07483) 226) leaving Melk at 9am and 5:30pm. 60 beds. 100 AS per person. Sheets and shower included. Breakfast 20 AS. Tax 10.50 AS per night. Call ahead.)

Restaurants abound on the Rathausplatz, but look elsewhere for less tourist-oriented fare. A five-minute walk west through the Hauptplatz brings you to **Restaurant zum "Alten Brauhof,"** Linzer Str. 25 (tel. (02752) 22 96), with a charming outdoor seating area that almost looks out on the Danube. Try the *Grillbendl* (roasted chicken; 70 AS). Admire the synthetic palm trees at **Il Palio,** Wienerstr. 3 (tel. (02752) 47 32). Great beer, great ice cream—not so great together (open Mon.-Thurs. and Sat.-Sun. 10am-1am, Fri. 10am-2am). **SPAR Markt,** Rathausplatz 9, has pears to share, apples to grapple, oranges to...silly, nothing rhymes with "oranges." (Open Mon. and Wed.-Fri. 7am-6pm, Tues. 7am-noon and 2:30-6pm, Sat. 7am-noon.)

Sights and Entertainment Melk is dwarfed by the recently restored **Benediktinerstift,** which perches resplendent atop a hill between the Danube and the **Rathausplatz.** On March 21, 1089, the Austrian Margrave Leopold II bestowed the Babenberg church and castle atop the cliff upon the Benedictine *abbé* Heitler and his monks; this act marked the birth of the monastery at Melk. The imperial chambers, which once served as shelter for such notable personages as Emperor Karl VI, Pope Pius VI, and Napoleon, contain exhibits on the abbey's history. Miniatures of the building's different architectural stages and a tiny display of Empress Maria Theresa's visit after her coronation are special treats.

The first *Hof* you enter is framed by four portals, decorated with strange, post-modern frescoes vaguely resembling chalk drawings of the Terminator. From the balcony, you can clearly see the rolling hills that envelop the Danube Dam north of Melk. The stunning **abbey library** is brimming with sacred texts that were hand-copied by monks. The upper level of books, above the gallery, is fake—the friars sketched book spines onto the wood to make the collection appear more formidable. The church itself, maintained by 38 active monks, is a Baroque masterpiece. Figurines of opulent skeletons reclining in the same position as Goya's "clothed-" and "nude Maja" adorn two of the side altars. They are said to represent most un-monkly "decadent eroticism." (Monastery open daily 9am-5pm; Nov.-April daily 9am-4pm. Guided tours in all major European languages daily (in English at 3pm). Admission 45 AS, students 20 AS. 40-min. tour extra 10 AS.) See if you can swing by Melk in June—the **Pentecost Concert** in the abbey is a cultural fixture of Lower Austrian life.

Near Melk: Schloß Schallaburg

Five kilometers out of town is Schloß Schallaburg (tel. (02754) 63 17), one of the most magnificent Renaissance castles in central Europe. The *Schloß* is a 10-minute bus ride away; by foot, take Kirschengraben, off Lindestr. and Bahnhofstr., out of town and turn right under the Autobahn. The castle's architecture is reason enough to visit; Romanesque, Gothic, Renaissance, and Mannerist influences converge in the terra-cotta arcades of the main courtyard. The floor consists of a 1600-piece **mosaic** (remember, there was no puzzle box top to help the designer). This castle is also known as the International Exhibition Center of Lower Austria; the staff pulls out all the stops in bringing foreign cultures to life. The 1994 display is entitled "Art and Hedonism"; a special exhibit, curiously, will recreate the decidedly austere early days of Christianity and Islam in Syria. (Open May-Sept. Mon.-Fri. 9am-5pm, Sat.-Sun. 9am-6pm. Admission 50 AS, students 15 AS. Buses leave from Melk's *Bahnhof* daily at 10:30am and 3:10pm; each departs from the castle 15 min. later. One way 30 AS, students half-price.)

Near Melk: Danube Strolls

Hikers can enjoy the network of trails surrounding Melk that wind through tiny villages, farmland, and wooded groves. Ask at the tourist office for a *Bezirk Melk* map, which lists area sights and hiking paths, and for the handouts on the 10km Leo Böck trail, 6km Seniorenweg, and 15km Schallaburggrundweg. **Cyclists** might enjoy a tour along the Danube on the former canal-towing path, in the direction of Willendorf. A figure of the **Venus,** one of the world's most famous fertility symbols, was discovered there. After a short stop at the site, you can pedal on to Spitz (see above). Then, perhaps, take a ferry to the other side of the Danube to **Arnsdorf,** where a drink and snack (known as Hauerjause, the vintners' special) will load enough carbos to send you through the vineyards and apricot orchards back towards Melk. On the return trip, you will pass an unusual forest called the **Marriage Woods.** The romantic city awards newlyweds who marry in Melk a young sapling tree, which the happy couple plants and tends for the rest of their lives.

Another cycling route will take you by the mystical basin stones scattered in the Dunkelstein woods and in small streams. According to legend, these stones are pieces of a footstep left behind by the devil. Strange stones also figure in the **cow and calf.** Looking down towards the Danube from the **Schobühel** monastery when the water is relatively low, you can see two rocks in the middle of the river. People in the region have named two rocks the cow and the calf; brave swimmers periodically swim out and "ride" them, though the beasts never seem to budge.

Near Melk: The Mostviertel and Amstetten

The area most foreigners call the Ybbs Valley Alpine Foreland is, in official Austrian parlance, the **Mostviertel.** Its name derives from *Most,* a beverage of apples or pears. These alpine foothills protuberate only 30 miles west of Vienna and comprise the area up to the borders with Upper Austria and Styria. The landscape ranges from gentle hills south of the Danube full of daffodils, through the Ybbs Valley, to the Alpine region itself, with mountains nearly 2000 meters high.

The town of **Amstetten** (pop. 22,000) grew around a central square in the middle of the 13th century. Its market began to thrive in 1858 with the inauguration of the Empress Elisabeth East-West Railway Line. In 1872, the Crown Prince Rudolf Line, which runs from Amstetten to the Ybbs and Enns valleys, was opened. Amstetten remains an important railway junction; the excellent rail network and the town's auspicious location between provincial capitals Linz and St. Pölten are responsible for Amstetten's remarkable prosperity. Nearby, the **Mostviertler Bauernmuseum** (tel. (07479) 334), with over 10,000 exhibits, holds the largest private collection of art, craft, and folklore in Austria. It is housed in the **Oedhof,** a working farm built in the traditional four-sided style. The museum bears fertile witness to the arduous tasks of cultivation and the farmers' inventive responses to their labor.

THE WALDVIERTEL

Off the beaten tourist route, the Waldviertel is a vast tract of mountains and trees stretching between the Danube and the Czech Republic. Though the regional villages and hamlets are treasure troves of history, the chief attractions are the densely forested woodlands, interspersed with lakes and pools, where hiking paths meander hundreds of miles over hill and dale.

Enjoy the forest, but beware: dangerous ticks have been known to fall from the trees onto anything or anyone walking beneath. These ticks carry a virus that results in *Gehirnsentzundung* (literally, inflammation of the brain; it's a disease similar to meningitis). This affliction can lead to paralysis, brain damage, and even death. Most Austrians are **inoculated** yearly against the disease, but foreigners are usually not. To decrease the chances of a tick consummating a relationship with your blood stream, anyone not vaccinated and strolling in the forests should wear at least a hat. Long-sleeved shirts and long pants are also recommended; hiking boots can't hurt. (See Essentials: Health for more preventative advice.)

■ Zwettl

This small village sits in the heart of the Waldviertel, at the junction of the **Kamp** and **Zwettl** rivers. Zwettl has been historically and culturally pivotal in this forested region ever since Babenberg ministers first set up shop in 1137. The major attraction in town is a remnant of the ecclesiastic forefathers—the schizophrenic Romanesque (or is it Baroque?) abbey **Stift Zwettl** (tel. (02822) 550 17), 3km east of the town center. This Cistercian abbey was built in the early 12th century and has since presided piously over the surrounding fields of wheat, corn, and sunflowers. The exterior is exquisite, especially the Baroque **Turmfassade;** the interior, graced by an ornate organ and a serene, arcaded courtyard, is no less spectacular. The abbey explodes in concert every July, as the **International Organ Festival** arrives in town. Buses from the town center to the abbey run twice daily. (Tours May-Oct. 40 AS, students 20 AS.) Zwettl, which prides itself on its Sabbath-esque lack of industry, is home to one important factory—the **Zwettler Brauerei,** keeping the locals' blood alcohol level at an acceptable level. (Hmmm, you seem to be down a quart....) About 10km west of Zwettl is the magnificent and Baroque **Schloß Rosenau** (tel. (02822) 82 21), home to Austria's only freemasonry museum (open April-Oct. daily 9am-5pm; tours 40 AS, students 20 AS).

Zwettl's tiny **tourist office,** Dreifältigkeitsplatz 1 (tel. (02822) 22 33), is in the middle of the *Altstadt.* Ask the staff about bicycle rental to ease transport in and around town. From the train station, walk down Bahnhofstr., and take a left onto Landstr. The tourist office in on the other side of the **Plague Column** that anchors Dreifältigkeitsplatz. Zwettl is a mere 125km from Vienna but can only be accessed by **train** through a regional line from Schwarzenau. **Buses** from Krems to Zwettl leave every few hours, depending on the day of the week. **Gasthof "zum Deutschen Dichter Robert Hammerling,"** Galgenbergstr. 3 (tel. (02822) 523 44), has a breakfast buffet spread as long as its name. From the tourist office, take a left onto Landstr., cross the bridge, take a left onto Syrnauerstr., and follow the road to Galgenbergstr. (5 min.). The peaceful rooms have TVs, telephones, and bathrooms (250-320 AS per person; breakfast buffet included).

Pick an eatery to match your gastronomic whim from among the countless pubs and restaurants of the **Dreifältigkeitsplatz.** If all else fails, the **Julius Meinl supermarket** is around the corner from the tourist office on Landstr. (open Mon.-Fri. 8am-noon and 1-6pm, Sat. 7:30am-noon).

Near Zwettl: Gmünd

Gmünd is a hamlet just northwest of Zwettl, easily accessible by bus or train through **Schwarzenau.** Little Gmünd (usually written Gmünd NÖ or Gmünd Niederösterreich to differentiate the town from Gmünd near Carinthia's Millstätter See) is best known for the beauty of the surrounding forest. Because the town is in the northernmost section of the Waldviertel, just minutes from the border of the Czech Republic, the town culture is richly endowed with the history of Austria's relationships with Bohemia. Especially *sehenswert* (worth seeing) are the ornate **Sgraffito houses** of the Stadtplatz (see Drosendorf, below, for a description of the style), and the **Glasmuseum,** exhibiting the extraordinary Bohemian glasswork. The **Naturpark Blockheide,** flanking the *Altstadt,* displays a more laborious craftsmanship; the enormous natural granite formations were hewn by the winds of millennia. For more information, visit the town **tourist office** in the Stadtgemeinde, Schremserstr. 6 (tel. (02852) 525 06). From the *Bahnhof,* walk up Bahnhofstr. for seven blocks, and make a left turn onto Schremserstr. The nearest hostel, **Jugendherberge Neunagelberg (HI),** Neunagelberg 114 (tel. (02859) 476), is just a short bus ride away. Fifty-nine beds house mostly hikers and youth groups (103 AS, 123 AS for the first night; call ahead).

■ Horn

In the middle of the Waldviertel, at a major junction of local highways, Horn is a natural magnet for tourists. Remnants of the walls and towers that protected the former fortress town from raiding Turks still shield well-preserved Renaissance and Baroque domiciles. The collections of art that celebrate Waldviertel history set Horn apart; the **Höbarth Museum** and the **Mader Museum,** both in the former Burgspital, Wienerstr. 4 (tel. (02982) 23 72), have collections of ancient artifacts unparalleled in Lower Austria. (Open April-Nov. Tues.-Sun. 9am-noon and 2-5pm. Admission 25 AS, students 10 AS, family 50 AS. Ticket good for both museums.)

The friendly museum staff also undertakes duties normally ascribed to a **tourist office** (open daily 9am-noon and 2-5pm). They will furnish you with maps, information, and guides revealing the treasures of Horn and its environment. Few *Privatzimmer* exist, and there's nary a hostel in the town proper; head to **Pernegg,** a sleepy hamlet about 15 minutes from Horn, for the cheapest rooms in the region. The **Jugendherberge Pernegg-Hötzelsdorf** (tel. (02913) 253) is a charming youth hostel within a convent; 120 beds await in bright, clean rooms. Take the bus from Horn's Hauptplatz (direction: "Drosendorf") to Hötzelsdorf, and walk over the hill. (105 AS per person. Breakfast 20 AS. Sheets 25 AS. Call ahead.) In Horn itself, your best bet is **Hotel-Restaurant "zum Weißen Rössel,"** Hauptplatz 16 (tel. (02982) 23 98), which offers tidy and comfortable rooms with showers, toilets, phones, and TVs. (Singles 380 AS, doubles 290 AS per person. Breakfast included.) The restaurant downstairs serves hearty regional cuisine (entrees 60-130 AS; open Mon.-Sat. 7am-10pm, Sun. 7am-2pm). **Pizza Restaurante "Maria,"** Pragerstr. 10 (tel. (02982) 34 95), is a garden restaurant serving pizza specials and Austrian cuisine at the foot of the historic Stephansberg. (Entrees 50-105 AS. Open Wed.-Mon. 10am-midnight; Sept.-April Mon. 10am-2:30pm, Wed.-Sun. 10am-midnight). At **Das Lokal,** Rathausplatz 7 (tel. (02982) 46 25), dark-stained wood brightened by huge windows makes this, literally, "*the* spot" to drink a beer (*Seidel* 22 AS), have a snack, and listen to classic rock (open Sun.-Wed. 10am-midnight, Thurs.-Sat. 10am-2am). **Julius Meinl,** Hauptplatz 9, is a centrally located market extraordinaire (open Mon.-Fri. 8am-noon and 2-6pm, Sat. 7:30am-noon).

Horn is easily accessible from Krems by **train** (45 AS, 35 min.). City buses (15 AS) run regularly from the Horn station to the town center; disembark at "Burgspital/Museen" to reach the tourist office. Buses leave from the Hauptplatz for destinations throughout the northern Waldviertel. **Sparkasse,** Kirchenplatz 12, is the best place to **exchange currency;** it has a 24-hour ATM (open Mon.-Thurs. 8am-4:30pm, Fri. 8am-5pm). The **Sgraffitohaus** is just down the street, at Kirchenplatz 3. Its 16th-century façade was decorated with various coats of arms and scenes that bear a strange likeness to Renaissance cartoon strips. The **Pestsäule** (Plague Column) is a memorial to the thousands who died in the various epidemics that hit 17th-century Horn.

The next station along the train route from Horn to Krems is **Rosenburg,** home to the majestic **Schloß Rosenburg.** This 12th-century castle sits atop a bluff overlooking the Kamp river. (Tours April-Oct. daily 9am-6pm; Nov-March by appointment only. Call (02982) 29 17 for information.)

■ Drosendorf

Less than half an hour from the border of the Czech Republic, Drosendorf is a tiny romantic town atop a hill surrounded on three sides by the **Thaya River.** The city walls that protected the border town from attack in bygone centuries still stand, though they are now considerably less formidable. In some places, there are three layers of fortifications that once kept the enemy at bay. Drosendorf's impermeability was almost vindicated in the late 13th century, when 1000 soldiers held out for over a fortnight against a siege by King Ottokar of Bohemia and his 18,000 troops. The white hats, led by Rudolf von Habsburg, reclaimed the town three weeks later, after Ottokar was killed in battle.

Drosendorf's elongated **Hauptplatz** is lined with flawless examples of Renaissance and Baroque architecture. Especially noteworthy is the Renaissance **Rathaus,** with its *sgraffito* façade; *sgraffiti* is created by carving material away to reveal a design (preferred medium: stained wood), in contrast to *graffiti*, created by adding material to a surface (preferred medium: N.Y.C. subway cars).

The tourist office is in the *Rathaus,* at Hauptplatz 1 (tel. (02915) 213); the staff is especially well-versed in selecting good hiking trails for this part of the Waldviertel.

The most economical option for staying overnight is the **Jugendherberge Drosendorf (HI),** Badstr. 25 (tel. (02915) 22 57). From the *Rathaus,* walk straight down the Hauptplatz, out the archway of the city walls, and continue straight until the street becomes Badstr. (10 min.). This immaculate hostel offers bright, modern rooms—all with shower and toilet—and is located next to a *Sportsplatz* with swimming pools, a soccer field, a mini-golf course, and a bicycle rental shop. The amenities draw plenty of attention; the hostel is almost always full, so make reservations as far in advance as possible. (50 beds in 2-, 4-, 6-, and 8-bed rooms. Open April-Oct. 134 AS per night, 117 AS per night after 2; under 19 114 AS per night, 97 AS per night after 2. Breakfast included. Lunch 55 AS.) **Schloß Drosendorf,** Schloßplatz 1 (tel. (02915) 232 10 or 321; fax 23 21 40) is a bed and breakfast that offers more upscale accommodations—from family apartments to single bedrooms—in a regal yellow castle overlooking the town. The spacious rooms have showers, TVs, and toilets and offer access to a kitchen and sauna (singles 320-340 AS; doubles and apartments 280-300 AS per person).

Drosendorf is accessible from Vienna by **train** (through Hollabrunn; 174 AS; 2½ hrs.; last train back to Vienna leaves at 7:20pm), or by **bus** from Horn (departing daily 10:10am and 5:15pm; 65 AS; 40 min.). The town **train station** lies five minutes from the *Rathaus*—walk to the left out of the station, down the hill, straight past the rotary, and then through the city walls. The *Rathaus* is on the right as you walk into the Hauptplatz, just past the bus terminal.

Most of Drosendorf's **Gasthöfe** linger in the Hauptplatz—any of them can prepare a filling meal for 60-120 AS per entree. **A & O Markt,** Hauptplatz 17, is the place for veggie-friendly groceries. (Open Mon. and Thurs.-Fri. 7am-noon and 3-6pm; Tues.-Wed. and Sat. 7am-noon.)

Vienna (Wien)

A relentlessly self-absorbed metropolis even when it ruled over a vast and heterogeneous empire, Vienna (pop. 1,615,000) dwarfs the rest of the country—culturally, historically, and demographically—to a degree unmatched even by Paris or London. Vienna, the *prima donna* metropolis, governs a nation but inhabits a world all its own. And though most of the old Habsburg empire lay east of what is now Austria, the Viennese made no secret of their contempt for the subject peoples. "The Orient," declared Prime Minister Metternich, "begins at the Landstraße," the street leading east out of town. The empire's standing trailed the rising stars of Viennese society; as history was created and rewritten within the Ringstraße, the Viennese acquired a sense of self-importance at once grossly inflated and wholly justified.

Before the First World War, Vienna balanced a troubled allegiance between the imperial tradition of Kaiser Franz Josef and the optimistic liberalism of a burgeoning bourgeoisie. While 19th-century aesthetes sought to regenerate society through art, the Pan-German League and Christian Socialist Party found social renewal in xenophobic exclusion. Karl Lueger, the Christian Socialist leader, was repeatedly elected mayor on a rabidly anti-Semitic platform and was kept out of office (temporarily) only by the intervention of the Kaiser. The 20th century saw the shredding of the empire and the brief liberal tradition, as intellectuals struggled to define a national identity within the new bureaucratic ethic of modernization. While artistic luminaries sparred over stylistic approaches, the young Adolf Hitler, rejected from the Viennese Academy, walked the streets admiring the gargantuan sprawl of the Ringstraße. When Hitler returned as the master of the very avenues he once paced in shame, he arrived to throngs of cheering Austrians. Today, the Viennese struggle with the same *Vergangenheitsbewältigung* (confronting the past) that haunts many Germans. The old bitterness, fostered by the Allied bombing that devastated the city, still remains, but it is smothered under layers of self-imposed silence; all of the heated protests and denials cannot efface the Third Reich's rose-strewn path into Austria—memories of condoned atrocities still plague the national conscience.

Despite its checkered political history, Vienna can look with unabashed pride on the art and culture pulsing through every cobblestone. Almost all composers in the classic Germanic tradition lived here at some point and subsequently lent their names to every third street in the *Altstadt*. Don't leave Vienna without paying homage to the musical scene, once the stomping ground of Mozart, Schubert, and Mahler. The birthplace of the Viennese waltz is still abuzz with balls from December to March. Monuments to playwrights, musicians, and poets are scattered throughout the city on desultory corners. Woody Allen would be just another *Mensch* without the pioneering work of Viennese native and repressed doctor extraordinaire Sigmund Freud. And the city's museums...so much art, so little time.

ORIENTATION AND PRACTICAL INFORMATION

Vienna's layout reflects both its history and a fundamental respect for tradition. The city is divided into 23 **districts** (*Bezirke*); the oldest area, die Innere Stadt, is district number one. The city expanded from its center, but many of the outer *Bezirke* existed as independent suburbs before they were engulfed by the metropolis. The **Ringstraße,** a massive automobile artery encircling the Innere Stadt, separates the first district from the others, replacing the former city walls. Though the Ringstraße (also known simply as the Ring) is identified as a single entity, it consists of many different segments—Opernring, Kärntner Ring, Dr.-Karl-Lueger-Ring, etc. The districts spiral around the city center in a clockwise fashion, following the Ring's one-way traffic. District one is at the hub, districts two through nine lie just outside the Ring, and the remaining districts expand from the outer boundary of the **Gürtel** (literally, "belt"). This two-way thoroughfare is separated into components—Margaretengürtel, Währinger Gürtel, Neubaugürtel, etc.—just like the Ring; the Gürtel and the Ring are both concentric highways that enclose the *Altstadt*. The Bezirk in which one grows up is often associated with social status and background, a stereotype usually containing some basis in fact; furthermore, most Viennese remain in one Bezirk for life—some stay for generations. Street signs indicate the district number, in either Roman or Arabic numerals; for example, "XIII, Auhofstraße" is in the thirteenth district. Postal codes are also derived from district numbers; for example, 1010 stands for the first district, 1020 for the second, 1110 for the eleventh, etc.

The first district *is* Vienna; its ancient pathways boast innumerable attractions. At the intersection of the **Opernring, Kärntner Ring,** and **Kärntner Straße,** one can find the Opera House (Staatsoper), the main tourist office, and the **Karlsplatz** U-Bahn stop, the hub of the public transportation system. This is a metropolis with crime like any other; use common sense, especially if you venture out after dark. Be extra careful in the beautiful Karlsplatz, home to many pushers and junkies—avoid the area after dark. Beware of pickpockets in the parks and on **Kärntner Straße,** the main shopping boulevard (alas, priced far off the scale for most budget travelers); this avenue leads directly to **Stephansplatz** and the **Stephansdom,** the center of the city and its *Fußgängerzone*.

> The Austrian **telephone** network is becoming digitized, and telephone numbers may change without notice after this book goes to press. If a listed number is incorrect, consult the tourist office for the most up-to-date information.

Tourist Offices

Main bureau: (*map*C4*) I, Kärntner Str. 38 (tel. 513 88 92), behind the Opera House. The friendly, English-speaking staff will give you an excellent free city map. Books rooms (350-400 AS) for a 35 AS fee and the first night's room deposit. Open daily 9am-7pm.

Branch offices, which offer similar services, at the:

- **Westbahnhof** (*map*C2*; tel. 83 51 88). Open daily 6:15am-11pm.
- **Airport** (tel. 711 10 28 75). Open daily 9am-11pm; Oct.-May daily 9am-10pm.
- **Exit** "Richtung Wien Zentrum" off Westautobahn A1 (tel. 97 12 71). Open daily 8am-10pm.
- **Exit** "Richtung Wien Zentrum" off Autobahn A2, XI, Trierstr. 149 (tel. 616 00 70). Open daily 9am-7pm.

Wiener Tourismusverband: (*map*C2*) II, Obere Augartenstr. 40 (tel. 211 14; fax 216 84 92). This *über*office oversees all of the above. Save your **big** questions up before you schedule an appointment here.

Jugend-Info Wien (Vienna Youth Information Service): Bellaria-Passage (*map*B4*; tel. 526 46 37). In the underground passage at the Bellaria intersection; enter at the "Dr. Karl Renner Ring/Bellaria" stop (lines #1, 2, 46, 49, D, and J), or at the "Volkstheater" U-Bahn station. The knowledgeable staff has tons of info on cultural events and sells concert and theater tickets at bargain prices. Get the indispensable *Youth Scene* brochure here. Open Mon.-Fri. noon-7pm, Sat. 10am-7pm.

Wiener Stadtinformation: tel. 403 89 89. This information line can answer almost any questions about the city. Open Mon.-Fri. 8am-4pm.

Information stands in the following U-Bahn stations:

- **Karlsplatz** (*map*C4*). Open daily 10am-7pm; Oct.-April Mon.-Fri. 8am-6pm, Sat.-Sun. 8:30am-4pm. Tickets sold year-round Mon.-Fri. 10am-6pm.
- **Stephansplatz** (*map*C3*). Open daily 10am-7pm; Oct.-April Mon.-Fri. 8am-6pm, Sat.-Sun. 8:30am-4pm. Tickets sold year-round Mon.-Fri. 10am-6pm.
- **Praterstern** (*map*D3*). Open daily 10am-7pm; Oct.-April Mon.-Fri. 8am-6pm.
- **Philadelphiabrücke.** Open daily 10am-7pm; Oct.-April Mon.-Fri. 8am-6pm.
- **Landstraße.**Open daily 10am-7pm; Oct.-April Mon.-Fri. 8am-6pm.
- **Volkstheater.** Open daily 10am-7pm; Oct.-April Mon.-Fri. 8am-6pm.

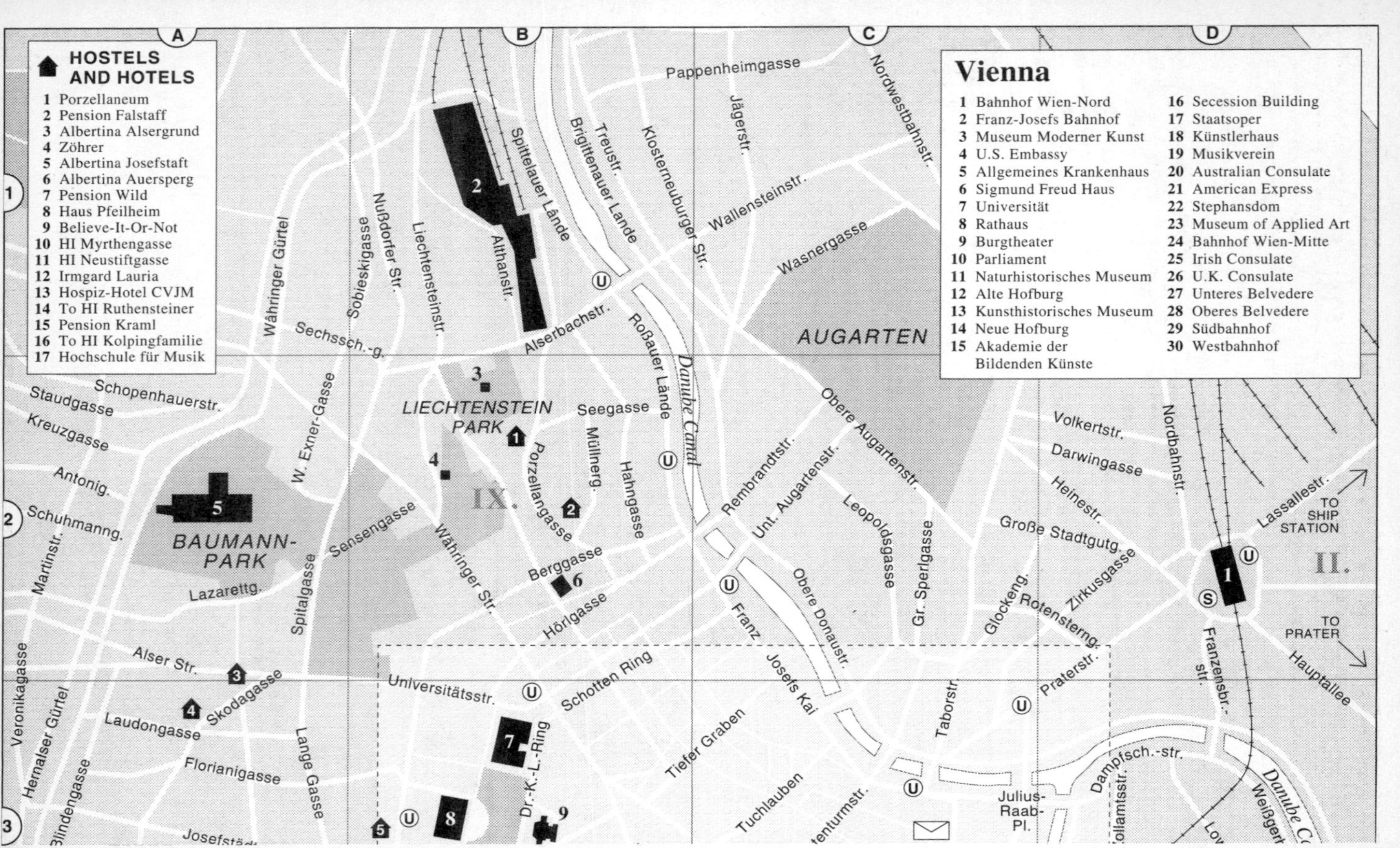
HOSTELS AND HOTELS
1 Porzellaneum
2 Pension Falstaff
3 Albertina Alsergrund
4 Zöhrer
5 Albertina Josefstaft
6 Albertina Auersperg
7 Pension Wild
8 Haus Pfeilheim
9 Believe-It-Or-Not
10 HI Myrthengasse
11 HI Neustiftgasse
12 Irmgard Lauria
13 Hospiz-Hotel CVJM
14 To HI Ruthensteiner
15 Pension Kraml
16 To HI Kolpingfamilie
17 Hochschule für Musik
Vienna
1 Bahnhof Wien-Nord
2 Franz-Josefs Bahnhof
3 Museum Moderner Kunst
4 U.S. Embassy
5 Allgemeines Krankenhaus
6 Sigmund Freud Haus
7 Universität
8 Rathaus
9 Burgtheater
10 Parliament
11 Naturhistorisches Museum
12 Alte Hofburg
13 Kunsthistorisches Museum
14 Neue Hofburg
15 Akademie der Bildenden Künste
16 Secession Building
17 Staatsoper
18 Künstlerhaus
19 Musikverein
20 Australian Consulate
21 American Express
22 Stephansdom
23 Museum of Applied Art
24 Bahnhof Wien-Mitte
25 Irish Consulate
26 U.K. Consulate
27 Unteres Belvedere
28 Oberes Belvedere
29 Südbahnhof
30 Westbahnhof
AUGARTEN
LIECHTENSTEIN PARK
BAUMANN-PARK
Danube Canal
TO SHIP STATION
TO PRATER

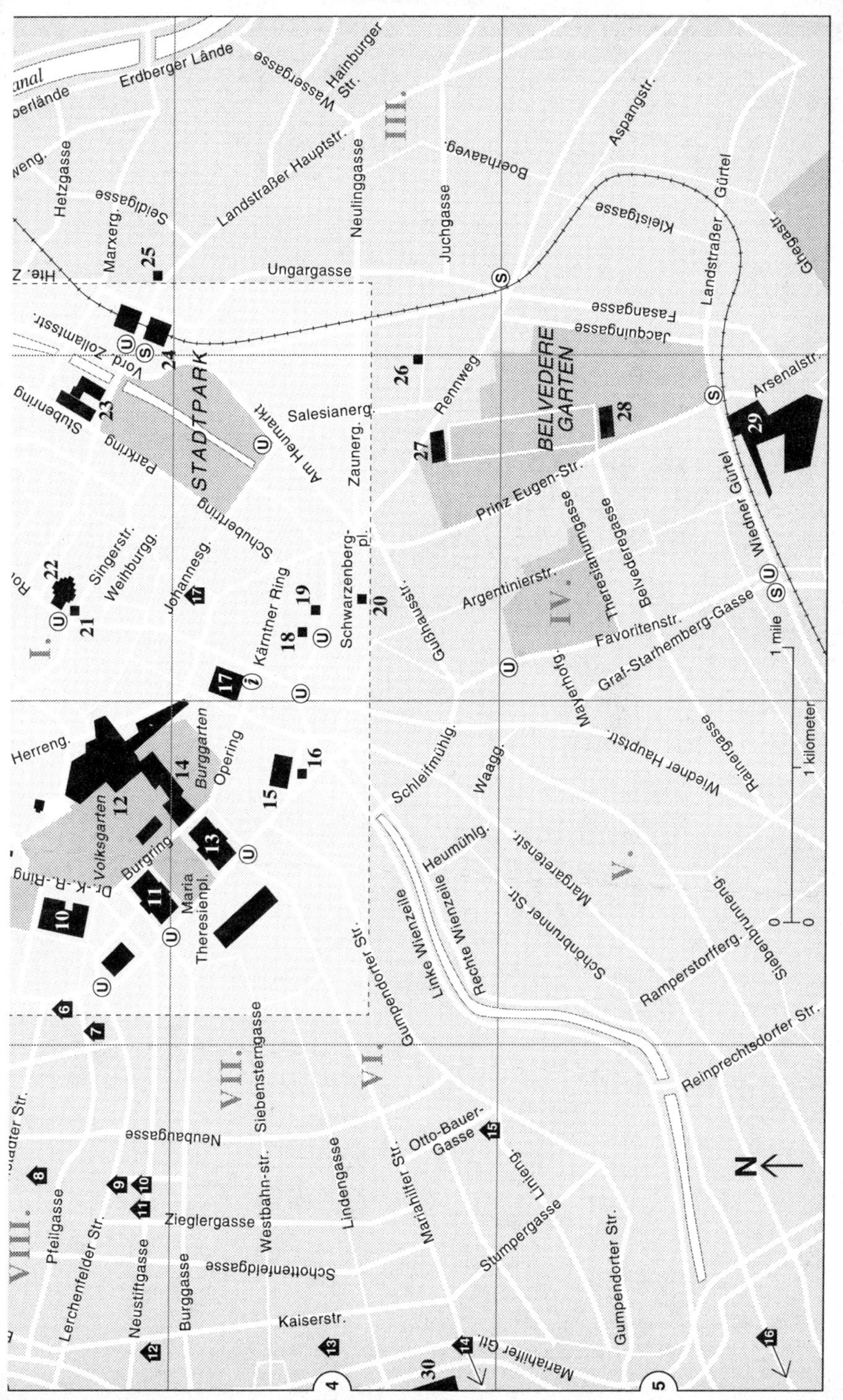
Erdberger Lände
Wassergasse
Hainburger Str.
III.
Hetzgasse
Seidlgasse
Marxerg.
Landstraßer Hauptstr.
Neulinggasse
Boerhaavg.
Juchgasse
Aspangstr.
Kleistgasse
Landstraßer Gürtel
Ghegastr.
Ungargasse
Fasangasse
Jacquingasse
Vord. Zollamtsstr.
Stubenring
Parkring
STADTPARK
Am Heumarkt
Salesianerg.
Renmweg
Zaunerg.
BELVEDERE GARTEN
Arsenalstr.
Prinz Eugen-Str.
Schubertring
Schwarzenberg-pl.
Gußhausstr.
Argentinierstr.
Theresianumgasse
Belvederegasse
IV.
Wiedner Gürtel
Favoritenstr.
Graf-Starhemberg-Gasse
Singerstr.
Weihburgg.
Johannesg.
Kärntner Ring
I.
Herreng.
Burggarten
Opering
Volksgarten
Burgring
Dr.-K.-R.-Ring
Maria Theresienpl.
Schleifmühlg.
Waagg.
Mayerhofg.
Wiedner Hauptstr.
Rainergasse
1 mile
1 kilometer
Heumühlg.
Margaretenstr.
V.
Linke Wienzeile
Rechte Wienzeile
Schönbrunner Str.
Siebenbrunneng.
Ramperstorfferg.
Reinprechtsdorfer Str.
Gumpendorfer Str.
VI.
VII.
Siebensterngasse
Neubaugasse
Westbahn-str.
Lindengasse
Mariahilfer Str.
Otto-Bauer-Gasse
Linieng.
Stumpergasse
Gumpendorfer Str.
VIII.
Pfeilgasse
Lerchenfelder Str.
Neustiftgasse
Zieglergasse
Burggasse
Schottenfeldgasse
Kaiserstr.
Mariahilfer Gü.
N

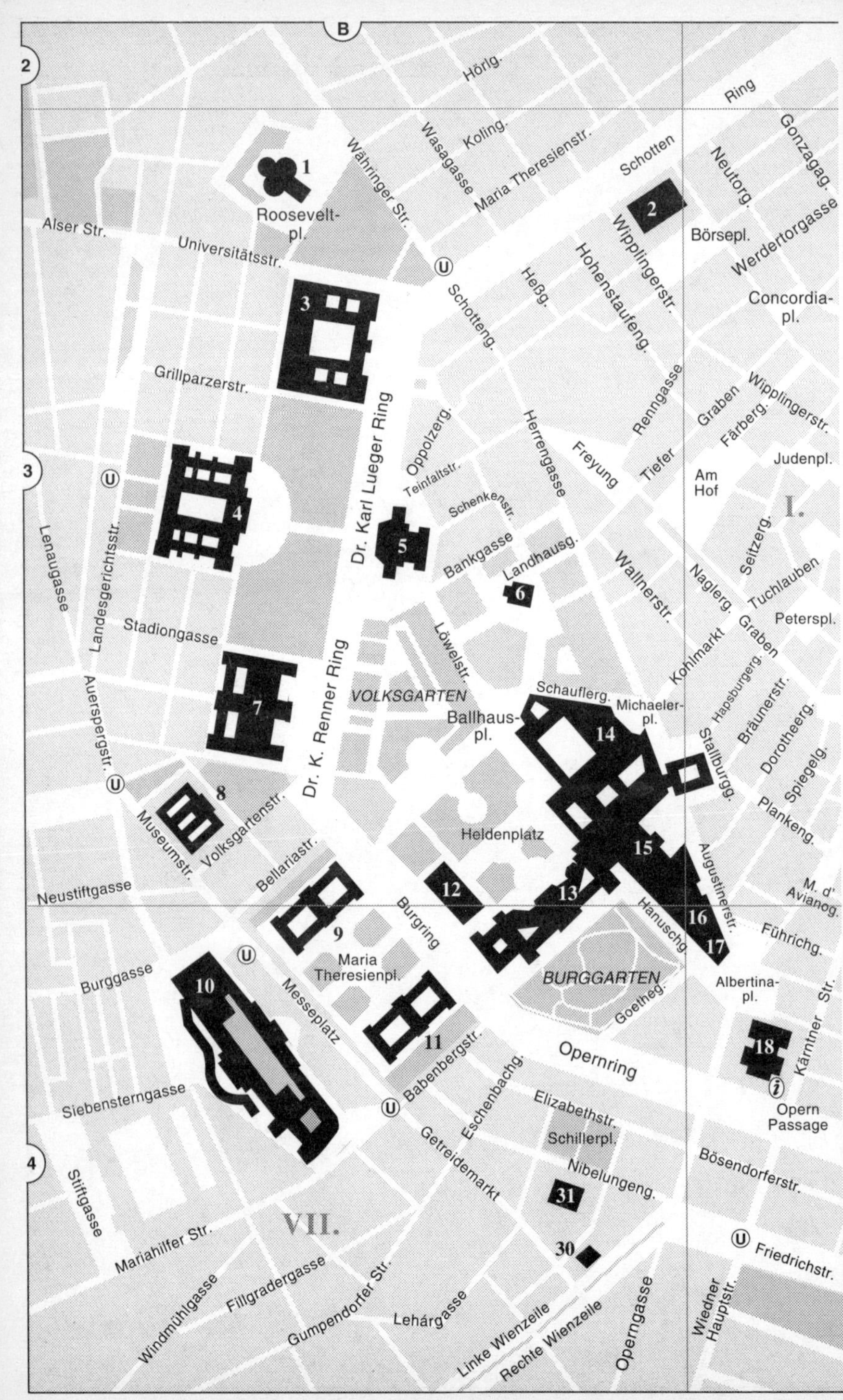
B
2
3
4
Hörlg.
Ring
Wasagasse
Koling.
Maria Theresienstr.
Schotten
Gonzagag.
Neutorg.
Währinger Str.
1
Roosevelt-
pl.
2
Alser Str.
Universitätsstr.
Wipplingerstr.
Börsepl.
Werdertorgasse
Heßg.
Hohenstaufeng.
Schotteng.
Concordia-
pl.
3
Grillparzerstr.
Dr. Karl Lueger Ring
Renngasse
Wipplingerstr.
Graben
Färberg.
Oppolzerg.
Herrengasse
Freyung
Judenpl.
Teinfaltstr.
Tiefer
Am
Hof
4
Schenkenstr.
I.
Lenaugasse
Landesgerichtsstr.
5
Bankgasse
Landhausg.
Wallnerstr.
Seitzerg.
Naglerg.
Tuchlauben
6
Stadiongasse
Löwelstr.
Graben
Peterspl.
Kohlmarkt
Dr. K. Renner Ring
Auerspergstr.
7
VOLKSGARTEN
Schauflerg.
Michaeler-
pl.
Hapsburgerg.
Bräunerstr.
Ballhaus-
pl.
14
Stallburgg.
Dorotheerg.
8
Spiegelg.
Museumstr.
Volksgartenstr.
Heldenplatz
Plankeng.
Augustinerstr.
15
Bellariastr.
12
13
Neustiftgasse
M. d'
Avianog.
Burgring
Hanuschg.
16
Führichg.
9
17
Burggasse
10
Maria
Theresienpl.
BURGGARTEN
Albertina-
pl.
Messeplatz
Goetheg.
Kärntner Str.
11
18
Babenbergstr.
Opernring
Eschenbachg.
Siebensterngasse
Elizabethstr.
Opern
Passage
Schillerpl.
Getreidemarkt
Bösendorferstr.
Nibelungeng.
31
Stiftgasse
VII.
Friedrichstr.
Mariahilfer Str.
30
Fillgradergasse
Windmühlgasse
Gumpendorfer Str.
Lehárgasse
Linke Wienzeile
Rechte Wienzeile
Operngasse
Wiedner
Hauptstr.

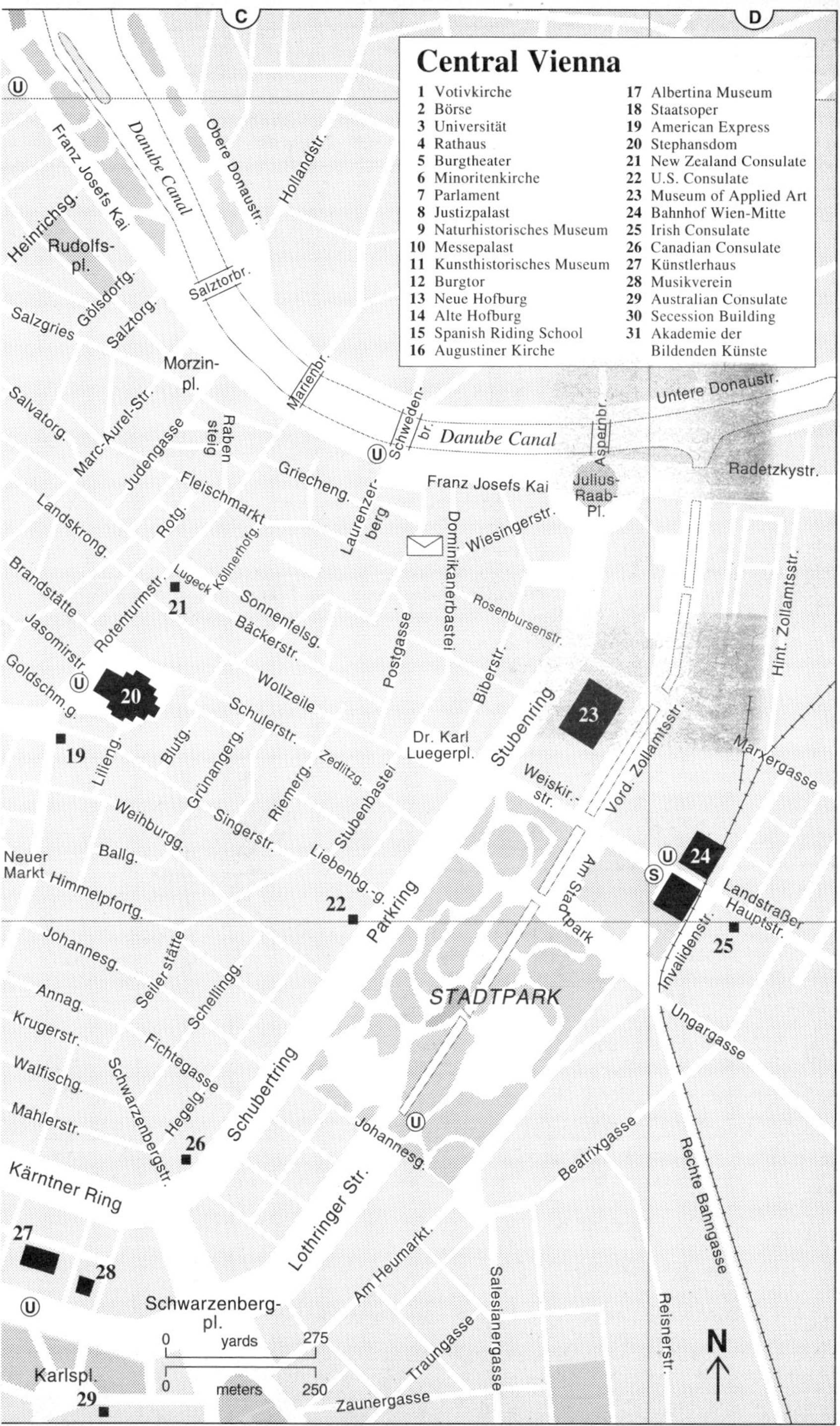
C
D
Central Vienna
1 Votivkirche
2 Börse
3 Universität
4 Rathaus
5 Burgtheater
6 Minoritenkirche
7 Parlament
8 Justizpalast
9 Naturhistorisches Museum
10 Messepalast
11 Kunsthistorisches Museum
12 Burgtor
13 Neue Hofburg
14 Alte Hofburg
15 Spanish Riding School
16 Augustiner Kirche
17 Albertina Museum
18 Staatsoper
19 American Express
20 Stephansdom
21 New Zealand Consulate
22 U.S. Consulate
23 Museum of Applied Art
24 Bahnhof Wien-Mitte
25 Irish Consulate
26 Canadian Consulate
27 Künstlerhaus
28 Musikverein
29 Australian Consulate
30 Secession Building
31 Akademie der Bildenden Künste
Franz Josefs Kai
Danube Canal
Obere Donaustr.
Hollandstr.
Heinrichsg.
Rudolfs-pl.
Gölsdorfg.
Salztorg.
Salzgries
Salztorbr.
Morzin-pl.
Marienbr.
Salvatorg.
Marc-Aurel-Str.
Judengasse
Raben steig
Schweden-br.
Danube Canal
Aspernbr.
Untere Donaustr.
Radetzkystr.
Griecheng.
Laurenzer-berg
Franz Josefs Kai
Julius-Raab-Pl.
Fleischmarkt
Rotg.
Landskrong.
Köllnerhofg.
Lugeck
Wiesingerstr.
Dominikanerbastei
Brandstätte
Rotenturmstr.
21
Sonnenfelsg.
Rosenbursenstr.
Hint. Zollamtsstr.
Jasomirstr.
Bäckerstr.
Postgasse
Goldschm.g.
20
Wollzeile
Biberstr.
Stubenring
23
Schulerstr.
19
Dr. Karl Luegerpl.
Vord. Zollamtsstr.
Marxergasse
Lilieng.
Blutg.
Grünangerg.
Zedlitzg.
Riemerg.
Stubenbastei
Weiskir.-str.
Weihburgg.
Singerstr.
24
Neuer Markt
Ballg.
Liebenbg.-g.
Am Stadtpark
Himmelpfortg.
22
Parkring
Landstraßer Hauptstr.
25
Johannesg.
Seilerstätte
Invalidenstr.
Annag.
Schellingg.
STADTPARK
Krugerstr.
Ungargasse
Fichtegasse
Walfischg.
Schwarzenbergstr.
Schubertring
Hegelg.
Mahlerstr.
26
Johannesg.
Beatrixgasse
Kärntner Ring
Lothringer Str.
Rechte Bahngasse
27
Am Heumarkt.
28
Salesianergasse
Reisnerstr.
Schwarzenberg-pl.
0 yards 275
0 meters 250
Traungasse
N
Karlspl.
29
Zaunergasse

Other Agencies

Budget Travel: Stick with the more established organizations to avoid paying hefty surcharges that quickly multiply the cost of "budget" tour packages.

ÖKISTA (*map*B2*), IX, Türkenstr. 6 (tel. 40 14 80). Discount flight tickets; newsy bulletin boards with personal ads. Open Mon.-Fri. 9:30am-5:30pm. **Branch** at IV, Karlsgasse 3 (tel. 505 01 28) with the same hours and shorter lines.

ÖS Reisen (Austrian Student Travel; *map*B3*), I, Reichsratstr. 13 (tel. 402 15 41), sells cheap train, flight, and bus tickets. Open Mon.-Fri. 9:30am-5:30pm.

Österreichisches Verkehrsbüro (Austrian National Travel Office; *map*B4*), I, Operngasse 3-4 (tel. 588 62 38), opposite the Opera House. Patient English-speaking staff sells BIJ tickets, the *Thomas Cook Timetable* (240 AS), and train timetables for Eastern European countries (100 AS). Open Mon.-Fri. 8:30am-6:30pm, Sat. 9am-noon.

Consulates and Embassies: Unless otherwise indicated, the embassy and consulate for each country are located in the same building. The embassy oversees diplomatic affairs, while the consulates concern themselves with more mundane bureaucratic duties, such as visa and passport services. Consulates provide help in an emergency.

U.S. Embassy (*map*B2*), IX, Boltzmangasse 16, off Währingerstr. **U.S. Consulate** (*map*C3-4*), I, Gartenbaupromenade 2, off Parkring (tel. 31 55 11). Open Mon.-Fri. 8:30am-noon and 1:30-3:30pm.

Canada (*map*C4*), I, Schubertring 12, Sixth floor, near Schwarzenbergplatz (tel. 533 36 91). Open Mon.-Fri. 8:30am-12:30pm and 1:30-3:30pm.

U.K. (*map*C4*), III, Jauresgasse 10, near Schloß Belvedere (tel. 713 15 75). Open Mon.-Fri. 9:15am-noon, for British citizens 9:15am-noon and 2-5pm.

Ireland (*map*D5*), III, Hilton Center, 16th floor, Landstraßer Hauptstr. 2 (tel. 715 42 46 0; tourist line 715 83 17); also serves the **Czech Republic** and **Hungary**.

Australia (*map*C4*), IV, Mattiellistr. 2-4 behind the Karlskirche (tel. 51 28 58 01 64). Open Mon.-Fri. 8:45am-1pm and 2-5pm.

New Zealand (*map*C3*), I, Lugeck 1 (tel. 52 66 36). Open Mon.-Fri. 8:30am-5pm.

South Africa, XIX, Sandgasse 33 (tel. 326 49 30).

Czech Republic, XIV, Penzingerstr. 11-13, in Hütteldorf (tel. 894 37 41 or 894 62 36). Open Mon.-Fri. 9-11am.

Hungary (*map*C3*), I, Bankgasse 4-6 (tel. 533 26 31). Open Mon.-Fri. 8:30am-12:30pm.

Germany (*map*C5*), III, Metternichgasse 3, near Schloß Belvedere (tel. 711 54). Consulate on opposite side of building. Open Mon.-Thurs. 9-10:30am, Fri. 9-9:30am.

Russia (*map*C4*), III, Reisnerstr. 45-47 (tel. 712 12 29). Open Mon., Wed., and Fri. 9am-noon.

Japan (*map*C4-5*), IV, Argentinier Str. 21, behind Karlsplatz (tel. 501 71 0). Open Mon.-Fri. 9am-noon and 2-4pm.

French Embassy (*map*C4*), IV, Technikerstr. 2 (tel. 505 47 47 0); **French Consulate** (*map*B3*), I, Wipplingerstr. 24 (tel. 535 62 09). Open Mon.-Fri. 8:30-11am.

Currency Exchange:

Banks are usually open Mon.-Wed. and Fri. 8am-3pm, Thurs. 8am-5:30pm. Bank and airport exchanges use the same official rates (minimum commission 65 AS for traveler's checks, 10 AS for cash).

Train station exchanges offer longer hours and lighter commission (20 AS or 1%): **Opernpassage** 9am-7pm, **Westbahnhof** 4am-10pm, **Südbahnhof** 6:30am-10pm, **City Air Terminal** 8am-12:30pm and 2-6pm, and at the **airport** 6:30am-11pm.

American Express (see below) charges from 40 AS for traveler's cheques, 15 AS for cash.

Zentralersparkasse (*map*C4*), I, Kärntner Str. 32, and numerous other banks offer cash advance with a Visa card. Zentralersparkasse open Mon.-Wed. 8:30am-12:30pm and 1:30-3pm, Thurs. 8:30am-12:30pm and 1:30-5:30pm.

Thomas Cook (*map*B4*), VI, Mariahilferstr. 20 (tel. 526 58 02), exchanges currency and arranges travel and tourism.

ATMs that accept Mastercard and its affiliate Eurocard are everywhere, including the corner of Führichgasse and Kärntner Str., 1 block from the tourist office. There is also a **bill exchange** machine at the intersection of Graben and Kohlmarkt down the street from Stephansplatz; the rate, however, is less favorable than at the banks.

American Express: (*map*C3*), I, Kärntner Str. 21-23, down the street from Stephansplatz (tel. 515 40; for 24-hr. refund service or lost traveler's cheques call toll-free 066 02 79 or 935 121 152). Will hold mail for 4 weeks (for customers the service is free, otherwise 60 AS charge). Address mail as follows: "Seymour ZELANKO, Client Letter Service, American Express, Kärntner Str. 21-23, A-1010 Vienna, Austria." 40 AS minimum charge to exchange traveler's checks, 15 AS minimum for cash. Theater, concert, and other tickets sold for a 22% commission and a 100 AS deposit. All services open Mon.-Fri. 9am-5:30pm, Sat. 9am-noon.

Post Office:

Hauptpostamt, normally at (*map*E1*) I, Fleischmarkt 19, the big yellow building at the corner of Postgasse—while the building is being renovated, the office has temporarily been relocated to (*map*C3*) I, Barbaragasse 2, on the corner of Barbaragasse and Postgasse. Open 24 hrs.

Branches at the train stations: **Südbahnhof,** open 6am-midnight; **Franz-Josefs Bahnhof,** open 24 hrs.; and **Westbahnhof,** open 24 hrs. All main branches **exchange currency.** Address **Poste Restante** to "Postlagernde Briefe, Hauptpostamt, Fleischmarkt 19, A-1010 Wien." Post office branches are distributed throughout the city; just look for the yellow sign with the trumpet logo.

Postal Codes: Within the 1st district A-1010, in the 2nd A-1020, in the 3rd A-1030, … in the 23rd A-1230.

Telephones: (*map*BC3*) I, Börseplatz 1, near the Schottenring. Open daily 6am-midnight. Also at the **4 main post offices:** the **Hauptpostamt, Südbahnhof, Franz-Josefs Bahnhof,** and **Westbahnhof.** Push the red button on older pay phones to connect when the other party answers. Deposit 1 AS and up for local calls, 9 AS for long-distance calls. Although coin-operated phones are still widely used, *Wertkarten* (phone card) telephones are generally more convenient; **phonecards** are available at post offices and train stations for 48 AS (worth 50 AS of phone calls) and 95 AS (worth 100 AS of phone calls). **City Code:** 0222.

Transportation

Flights: Wien-Schwechat Flughafen (tel. 711 10; for flight info tel. 711 10 22 33), 18km from the city center, is linked by regular buses (60 AS) to the Westbahnhof, Südbahnhof, and City Air Terminal (next to the Hilton Hotel in district III). Take U-Bahn U-3 or U-4 to "Landstr." or trains to "Wien Mitte"; S-Bahn S-7, the metropolitan railway, runs to "Flughafen" each hour from "Wien Mitte" or "Wien Nord" stations (30 AS; Eurail and public transport passes valid). **Austrian Airlines** (tel. 717 99). Open Mon.-Fri. 7:30am-6pm, Sat. and Sun. 8am-5pm.

Trains: tel. 17 17, 24 hrs.; English spoken. There are 5 principal stations in Vienna.

Franz-Josefs Bahnhof (*map*B1*), IX, Althanstr. 10. Handles local trains, and sends 2 per day to **Prague** (5-6hr., 364-370 AS) and Berlin (15hr., 628-654 AS). Streetcar D (direction: "Südbahnhof") runs from the FJB to the Ring.

Westbahnhof (*map*A4*), XV, Mariahilferstr. 132. Sends trains to France, Western Germany, Switzerland, the Netherlands, Belgium, the U.K., Bulgaria, Romania, Hungary, and Western Austria. Showers and baths available at Friseursalon Navratil on the ground floor. (½-hr. shower 40 AS, ½-hr. bath 60 AS. Open Mon.-Sat. 7am-8pm, Sun. 8am-1pm.) To reach the Ring, take U-Bahn U-6 (direction: "Philadelphiabrücke") to "Längenfeldgasse," then U-Bahn U-4 (direction: "Heiligenstadt") to "Karlsplatz"; streetcars #52 and 58 also run to the Ring.

Südbahnhof (*map*C5*), X, Wiedner Gürtel 1a. Trains depart for Italy, Yugoslavia, Greece, the Czech Republic (through Bratislava), and, in summer, Bulgaria and Hungary (Budapest, 4-5 hr., 372 AS plus 80 AS inter-city supplement). To get to the center of town, take streetcar D (direction: "Nußdorf") to the Ring or U-Bahn U-1 (direction: "Kagran") to "Karlsplatz."

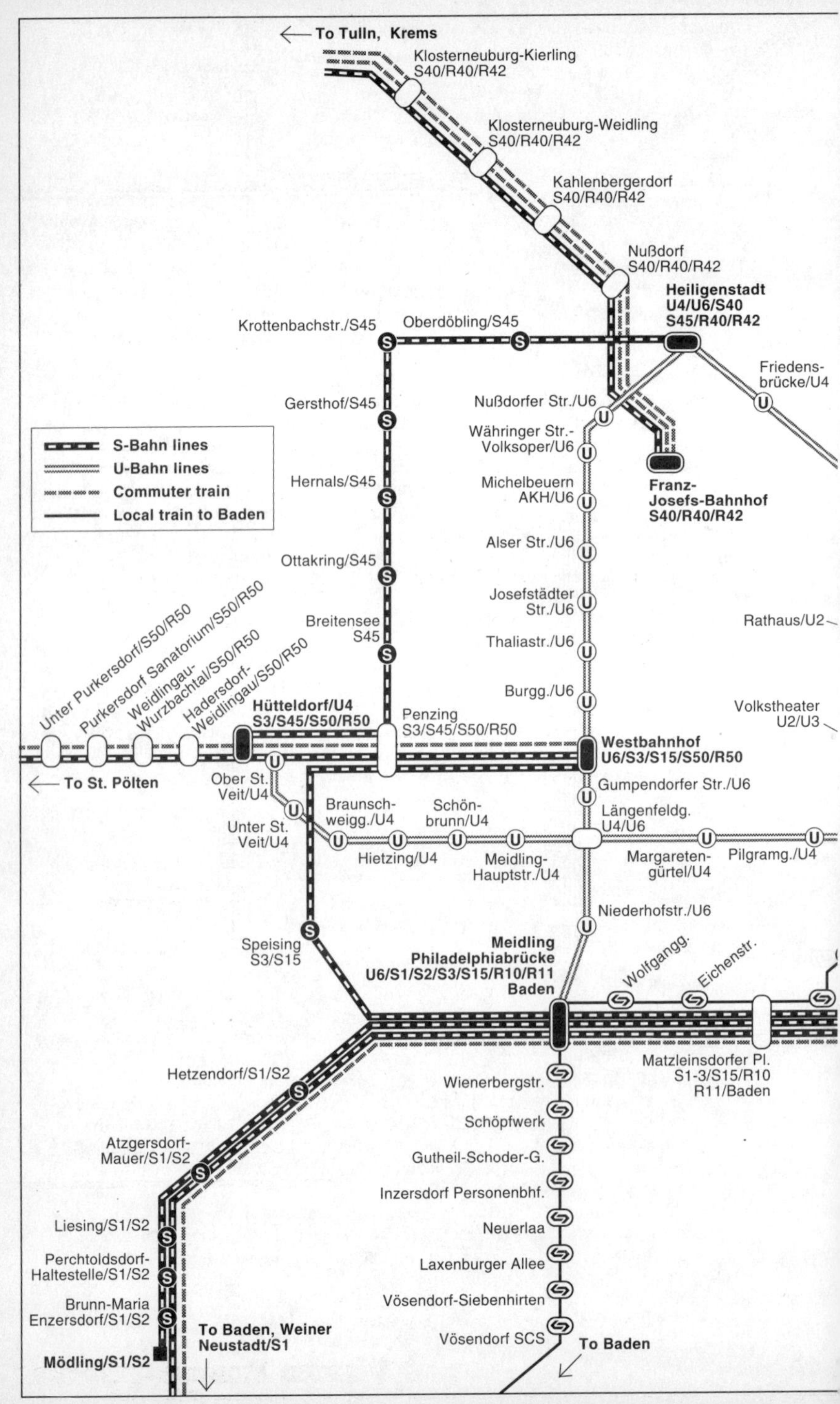

To Tulln, Krems
Klosterneuburg-Kierling S40/R40/R42
Klosterneuburg-Weidling S40/R40/R42
Kahlenbergerdorf S40/R40/R42
Nußdorf S40/R40/R42
Heiligenstadt U4/U6/S40 S45/R40/R42
Krottenbachstr./S45
Oberdöbling/S45
Friedens-brücke/U4
Nußdorfer Str./U6
Gersthof/S45
Währinger Str.-Volksoper/U6
S-Bahn lines
U-Bahn lines
Commuter train
Local train to Baden
Michelbeuern AKH/U6
Hernals/S45
Franz-Josefs-Bahnhof S40/R40/R42
Alser Str./U6
Ottakring/S45
Josefstädter Str./U6
Breitensee S45
Rathaus/U2
Thaliastr./U6
Unter Purkersdorf/S50/R50
Purkersdorf Sanatorium/S50/R50
Weidlingau-Wurzbachtal/S50/R50
Hadersdorf-Weidlingau/S50/R50
Burgg./U6
Hütteldorf/U4 S3/S45/S50/R50
Penzing S3/S45/S50/R50
Volkstheater U2/U3
Westbahnhof U6/S3/S15/S50/R50
To St. Pölten
Ober St. Veit/U4
Gumpendorfer Str./U6
Braunsch-weigg./U4
Schön-brunn/U4
Längenfeldg. U4/U6
Unter St. Veit/U4
Hietzing/U4
Meidling-Hauptstr./U4
Margareten-gürtel/U4
Pilgramg./U4
Niederhofstr./U6
Speising S3/S15
Meidling Philadelphiabrücke U6/S1/S2/S3/S15/R10/R11 Baden
Wolfgangg.
Eichenstr.
Matzleinsdorfer Pl. S1-3/S15/R10 R11/Baden
Hetzendorf/S1/S2
Wienerbergstr.
Schöpfwerk
Atzgersdorf-Mauer/S1/S2
Gutheil-Schoder-G.
Inzersdorf Personenbhf.
Liesing/S1/S2
Neuerlaa
Perchtoldsdorf-Haltestelle/S1/S2
Laxenburger Allee
Brunn-Maria Enzersdorf/S1/S2
Vösendorf-Siebenhirten
To Baden, Weiner Neustadt/S1
Vösendorf SCS
To Baden
Mödling/S1/S2

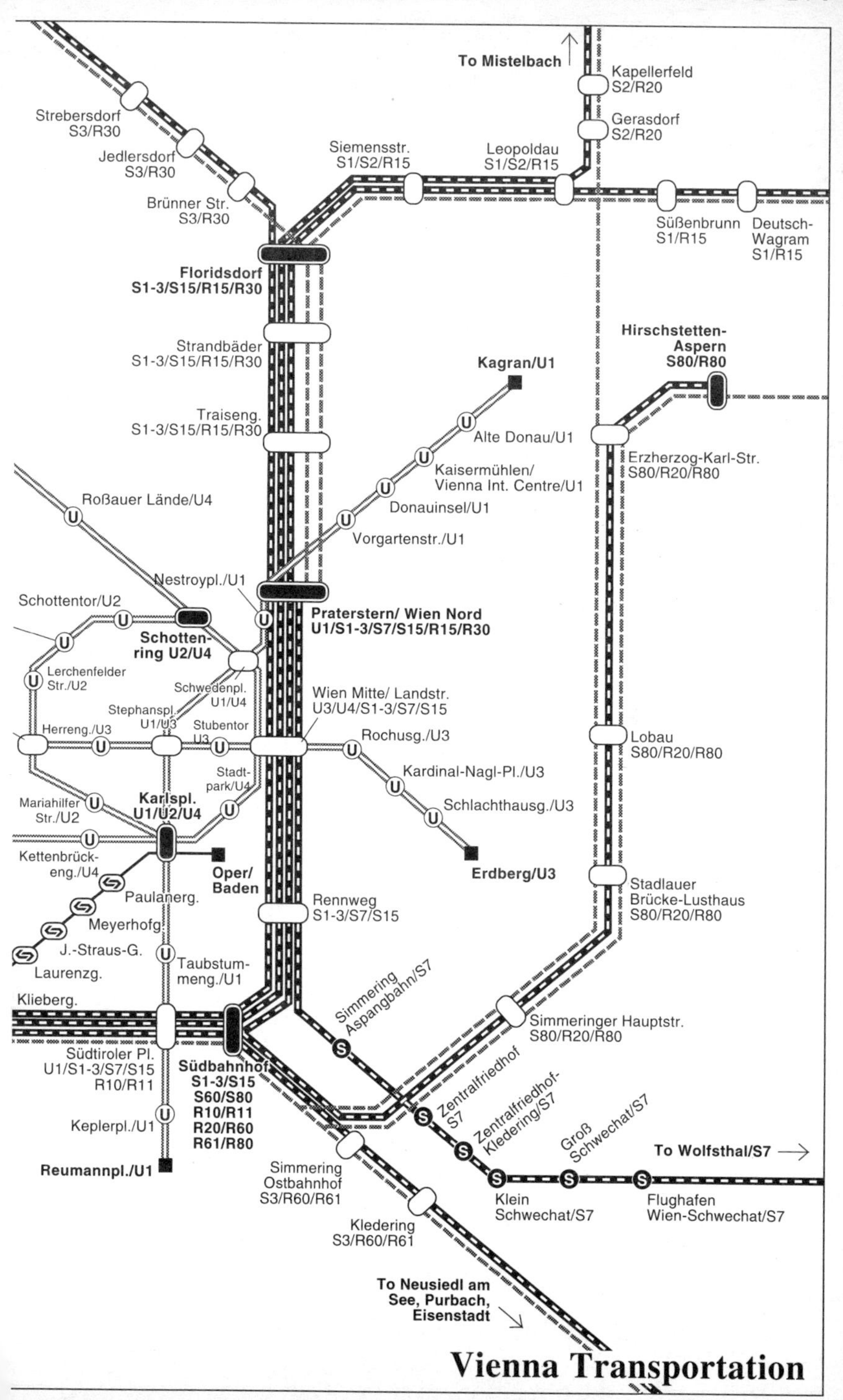

Vienna Transportation

Bahnhof Wien-Mitte (*map*D3*), in the center of town, handles local commuter trains. Also the terminus for the shuttle transportation to the airport.

Bahnhof Wien-Nord (*map*D2*), by the Prater on the north side of the Danube Canal. The main S-Bahn and U-Bahn link for trains heading north, but most of the Bundesbahn trains are funneled through the other rail stations.

Buses: City Bus Terminal (*map*CD3*) at Wien-Mitte rail station. Currency exchange (commission 20 AS or 1%) and lockers available. Domestic BundesBus ticket desk open daily 6:15am-6pm; international private lines maintain travel agencies in the station. For **bus information** daily 6am-9pm, call 711 01 (English-speaking operator available).

Public Transportation: Vienna's U-Bahn, bus, and streetcar system is excellent. Single fares 20 AS; 24-hr. pass 45 AS, 72-hr. pass 115 AS. The 7-day pass (125 AS) requires a passport-sized photo. 8-day ticket 235 AS; it must be stamped for each ride. With this card, 4 people can ride for 2 days, 8 for 1, etc. All passes allow unlimited travel on the system, except on special night buses. To validate a ticket, **punch the ticket immediately** upon entering the bus, tram, etc. in the orange machine; if you possess a ticket but it's not stamped, it is *invalid*, and can incur a fine of up to 490 AS. Tickets can be purchased from *Tabak* kiosks or automats in major U-Bahn stations. Most of the system closes shortly before midnight. Special **night buses** run Fri.-Sat. 12:30-4am between the city center, at Schwedenplatz, and various outlying districts (25 AS, day-transport passes not valid). Night bus stops are designated by "N" signs. Streetcar lines and U-Bahn stops are listed on a free city map, available at the tourist office. There is a **public transportation information** number (tel. 587 31 86, **English-speaking operator** available upon request) that will give you directions to any point in the city by public transportation. Open Mon.-Fri. 7am-6pm, Sat.-Sun. 8:30am-4pm.

Ferries: DDSG Donaureisen, II, Handelskai 265 (tel. 21 75 00; schedule info tel. 15 37). Boats dock at the Reichsbrücke on the New Danube; take U-Bahn U-1 to "Reichsbrücke." Ferries to Budapest April 24-Sept. 18 daily; one way 830 AS, round-trip 1200 AS. Special rates and less frequent service early April and mid-Sept. to Oct. Tickets are available at the tourist offices. Reservations necessary.

Car Rental: Avis (*map*BC4*), I, Opernring 1 (tel. 587 62 41). **Hertz,** Schwechat Airport (tel. (0711) 10 26 61); open Mon.-Fri. 7:30am-11pm, Sat.-Sun. 8am-11pm. Kärntner Ring 17 (tel. 512 86 77); open April-Oct. Mon.-Fri. 7:30am-6:30pm, Sat.-Sun. 8am-4pm; Nov.-March Mon.-Fri. 7:30am-6pm, Sat.-Sun. 9am-3pm. Ungargasse 37 (tel. 713 58 01); open Mon.-Fri. 7:30am-5pm. In the first district, short-term parking is allowed only from Mon.-Fri. 9am-7pm (except holidays) and only for 1½ hr. If your car breaks down, call **ARBÖ** (tel. 123 or 120).

Taxis: tel. 17 12, 313 00, 401 00, 601 60, or 910 11. Accredited taxis have yellow, white, and black signs on the roof. Basic charge 22 AS, plus per mile charge. 10 AS surcharge for taxis called by radiophone; 10 AS surcharge for Sun. rides or Mon.-Sat. 11pm-6am; 10 AS surcharge for luggage weighing more than 20kg, 20 AS for more than 50kg.

Bike Rental: Best bargain at Wien-Nord and the Westbahnhof stations. 90 AS per day; 45 AS with train ticket from the day of arrival, or from 3pm or later on the day before arrival. Elsewhere in the city, such as on the Donauinsel, rentals average 30 AS per hr. Pick up the *Vienna By Bike* brochure at the tourist office for more details.

Mitfahrzentrale Wien: (*map*CD3-4*) III, Invalidenstr. 15, near the Wien-Mitte station (tel. 715 00 66), pairs drivers and riders (Salzburg 190 AS, Innsbruck 240 AS). Open Mon.-Fri. 9am-1pm and 3-6pm, Sat. 10am-2pm; off-season Mon.-Fri. 9am-1pm and 3-6pm, Sat. 10am-1pm.

Hitchhiking: *Let's Go* cannot recommend hitchhiking as a safe mode of transportation. Those headed for Salzburg take U-Bahn U-4 to "Hütteldorf," the highway leading to the Autobahn is about 10km farther out. Hitchers traveling south take streetcar #67 to the last stop and wait at the traffic circle near Laaerberg.

Bisexual, Gay, and Lesbian Organizations

Vienna is not known for its tolerance of gays and lesbians; occasionally, latent tensions erupt in acts of violence directed at people and property. On the other hand, bisexual, gay, and lesbian life in Vienna is more mixed than in other cities; homosexuals are not necessarily segregated to certain "gay clubs." The German word for "gay" is *schwul,* "lesbian" is *lesbisch,* and "bisexual" is *bi* (pronounced BEE). (See Bisexual, Gay, and Lesbian Cafés and Clubs under Nightlife below.)

Rosa Lila Villa (*map**B4*), VI, Linke Wienzeile 102 (tel. 56 81 50). A favored resource for Viennese homosexuals and visiting tourists. Staff provides counseling, information, nightclub listings, and other services. Ask for a copy of the lesbian and gay magazine, *tamtam.* Situated on a main thoroughfare, the large pink and purple building with the inscription "Lesbian and Gay House" makes a rather unique impression on the more conservative passers-by—which, according to the staff, is the whole point. Lending library available. Open Mon.-Fri. 5-10pm.

Homosexuelle Initiative Wien (HOSI) (*map**C2*), II, Novaragasse 40 (tel. 26 66 04). Call the Rosa Lila telephone Tues. and Fri. 6-8pm. Open Tues. from 8pm on. Lesbian group and telephone network Wed. at 7pm. Youth group and telephone network Thurs. at 7pm.

Lesbisch-schwule Studentinnengruppe (*map**B3*), IX, Rooseveltsplatz 5a (tel. 43 93 54). Student and faculty group, able to provide counseling or steer you elsewhere for help. Meets only during the term.

Schwulengruppe der Technische Universität (*map**B4*; tel. 588 01). Another student gay counseling group. Open Fri. 2-4pm. Meets only during the term.

Other Practical Information

Luggage Storage: Lockers at all train stations (20 AS for 24 hrs.). Adequate for sizeable backpacks. Checked luggage 15 AS. Open 4am-midnight.

Lost Property: Fundbüro (*map**BC2*), IX, Wasagasse 22 (tel. 313 44 91 11). Open Mon.-Fri. 8am-noon. For objects lost on the public transit system, call 50 13 00 within 3 days.

Bookstores: Big Ben Bookshop (*map**AB2*), IX, Porzellangasse 24 (tel. 31 64 12). Open Mon.-Fri. 9am-6pm, Sat. 9am-12:30pm. **Shakespeare & Company** (*map**C3*), I, Sterngassse 2. Open Mon.-Fri. 9am-6pm, Sat. 9am-noon. **British Bookshop** (*map**C3*), I, Weihburggasse 8. A bulletin board lists language seminars and other English-language events. Open Mon.-Fri. 9am-6pm, Sat. 9am-noon. **American Discount** (*map**B3*), IV, Rechte Wienzeile 5 (tel. 587 57 72). Open Mon.-Fri. 8:30am-6:30pm, Sat. 8:30am-1pm. Also at (*map**A3-4*) VII, Neubaugasse 39 (tel. 93 37 07). Open Mon.-Fri. 9am-1pm and 2pm-6pm, Sat. 9am-noon.

Laundromat: Münzwäscherei Kalksburger & Co. (*map**D4*), III, Schlachthausgasse 19 (tel. 78 81 91). Wash 90 AS per 6kg, dry 10 AS. Soap 10 AS. Open Mon.-Fri. 7:30am-6:30pm, Sat. 7:30am-1pm. **Münzwäscherei Margaretenstraße** (*map**B4-5*), IV, Margaretenstr. 52 (tel. 587 04 73). Take bus #59A from the U-Bahn U-4 "Margaretengürtel" station to "Kloster-Neugasse." Wash 85 AS per load, dry 10 AS; soap included. Open Mon.-Fri. 7am-6pm; Sat. 8am-noon. **Schnellwäscherei Haydn** (*map**A4*), VI, Stumpergasse 1a (tel. 564 89 14). Open Mon.-Thurs. 7am-5:30pm, Fri. 7am-1pm. Wash per 4kg load, including detergent, 85 AS; dry 16 AS. Many hostels also offer access to a washer, dryer, and soap for about 45 AS.

Crisis Hotlines:

- **House for Threatened and Battered Women,** 24-hr. emergency hotline (tel. 545 48 00 or 408 38 80).
- **Rape Crisis Hotline** (tel. 93 22 22). Open Mon. 10am-1pm, Tues. and Thurs. 6-9pm.
- **Advice Center for Sexually Abused Girls and Young Women,** tel. 523 69 90.
- **Psychological Hotline** (tel. 31 84 19 or 31 84 20). Open Mon.-Sat. 8pm-8am, Sun. 24 hrs.
- **Poison Control,** tel. 43 43 43.
- **English-language Suicide Hotline,** tel. 713 33 74.

Medical Assistance: Allgemeines Krankenhaus (*map**B1*), IX, Währinger Gürtel 18-20 (tel. 404 00). A consulate can provide a list of English-speaking physicians.

Emergencies: Police: tel. 133; Fremdenpolizei (foreign police) headquarters at Bäckerstr. 13 (tel. 63 06 71). **Ambulance:** tel. 144. **Fire:** tel. 122. Alert your consulate of any emergencies or legal problems.

ACCOMMODATIONS AND CAMPING

One of the very few unpleasant aspects of Vienna is the hunt for cheap rooms during peak season (June-Sept.). Most hostels charge up to an extra 40 AS per night to travelers without a Hostelling International (HI) membership card, and some even turn non-members away. Don't leave your shelter to the vagaries of chance; write ahead or call for reservations at least two days in advance. Otherwise, plan on calling from the train station between 6 and 9am during the summer to put your name down for a reservation. If your choice is full, ask to be put on a waiting list, or ask for suggestions—don't waste time tramping around. The list of budget accommodations in Vienna is available at almost every tourist office.

The summer crunch for budget rooms is slightly alleviated in July, when university dorms (*Studentenwohnheim*) are converted into makeshift hostels. Travelers to Vienna should beware proprietors who make offers at train stations. They may try to steer you to their homes by insinuating or outright lying about other accommodations—common refrains include accusations that other lodgings are full, dirty, or brothels (*Bordel*)—and will usually make ambiguous references to their rarefied *Studentenzimmer* (student rooms), often the size of raisins.

The **tourist offices** will set you up in more costly lodgings for a 35 AS fee. They also handle *Privatzimmer* (private homes; 3-day min. stay) in the 180-250 AS range, but many of these are in the suburbs. **ÖKISTA** (see Budget Travel above) finds cheaper rooms and charges no commission. Their accommodations office is at IX, Türkenstr. 4-6 #314 (tel. 34 75 26 23), adjacent to the budget travel office. (Open Mon.-Wed. and Fri. 9:30am-4pm, Thurs. 9:30am-5:30pm.) In summer, the **Mitwohnzentrale** (*map*AB3*), Laudongasse 7 (tel. 402 60 61), will find you an apartment from 500 AS per day (commission included); for a stay of one month or more, rooms can be found for 2500 AS per week, but be sure to book at least four weeks in advance. Bring your passport (open Mon.-Thurs. 10am-5pm, Fri. 10am-1pm).

Hostels and Dormitories

The Myrthengasse Cluster

Myrthengasse (HI) (*map*A3-4*), VII, Myrthengasse 7 (tel. 523 92 49). Same directions as Believe-It-Or-Not, which is across the street. About 15 min. from city center. Sparkling modern rooms with 2-6 beds, washrooms with showers, and big lockers. Coed rooms upon request. Room keys provided. Enthusiastic and attentive staff. Lounge with TV, game room with foosball and ping-pong, outdoor patio, and a party room decorated like a streetcar. 127 beds. Reception open 7:30am-1am. Curfew 1am. Lockout 9am-2pm. 140 AS. Breakfast (7-8:30am) and sheets included. Lunch or dinner 60 AS. Laundry 50 AS per load. Reservations recommended. Wheelchair accessible.

Believe-It-Or-Not (*map*A3*), VII, Myrthengasse 10, apt. #14 (ring bell; tel. 526 46 58). From the Westbahnhof, take U-Bahn U-6 (direction: "Heiligenstadt") to "Burggasse-Stadthalle," then bus #48A (direction: "Ring") to "Neubaugasse." Walk back on Burggasse 1 block, and take the first right on Myrthengasse (15 min.). From the Südbahnhof, take bus #13A (direction: "Skodagasse/Alserstraße") to "Lerchenfelderstraße." Walk back on Neubaugasse 1 block, and make a right on Neustiftgasse; then walk 1 more block, and make a left onto Myrthengasse (25 min.). Camaraderie flourishes in cramped but homey quarters. Easter-Oct. 160 AS, Nov.-Easter 110 AS. Fully equipped kitchen, sheets and down quilts, unlimited hot water, and thoughtful owner. New apartments opened around the corner in 1993. No curfew. Owner will recommend myriad private dormitories when booked. Call ahead.

Neustiftgasse (HI) (*map*A3-4*), VII, Neustiftgasse 85 (tel. 523 74 62). Follow the directions to Myrthengasse—Neustiftgasse is around the corner. Managed by the same friendly people. Access to all Myrthengasse facilities encouraged. Rooms with 2, 4, and 6 beds, all with showers. Coed rooming possible. 118 beds. Members only. Reception open 7:30am-1am. Curfew 1am. Lockout 9am-noon. 140 AS. Breakfast (7-8:30am) and sheets included. Lunch or dinner 60 AS. Hallway lounge with vending machines. Laundry 50 AS per load; soap included. Reservations recommended. Wheelchair accessible.

Other Hostels

Gästehaus Ruthensteiner (HI) (*map*A4-5*), XV, Robert-Hamerlinggasse 24 (tel. 893 42 02 or 893 27 96), 3 min. from the Westbahnhof. Take a right on Mariahilferstr., make your first left on Palmgasse, then your first right onto Robert-Hamerlinggasse, to the middle of the second block. About 15 min. from the city center. Small, sunny rooms, mostly for the younger set. Coed rooming possible. Access to kitchen, dining room, and a tiled and landscaped courtyard with a barbecue pit. 76 beds. Reception open 24 hrs. 4-day max. stay. Members only. No curfew, no lockout. Dorm bed 129 AS (bring your own sheets). Doubles 209 AS per bed, sheets included. Triples, quads, and quints 149 AS per person, sheets included. Breakfast (8-10am) 25 AS. key deposit for big lockers 50 AS. **Bicycle rental** July-Sept. 78 AS per day. Reservations recommended.

Jugendgästehaus Wien Brigittenau (HI) (*map*D1*), XX, Friedrich-Engels Platz 24 (tel. 332 29 40; fax 330 83 79). Efficient and helpful management oversees packs of high-school kids. Take U-Bahn U-1 or U-4 to "Schwedenplatz" and then streetcar N to the end station at "Florisdorfer Brücke/Friedrich Engels Platz." 25 min. from the city center. Big garden and lounge with ping-pong and foosball. 334 beds. Members only. Reception open 24 hrs. Flexible midnight curfew. Lockout 9am-3pm. 140 AS. 3-day max. stay. Sheets and breakfast included. Lunch or dinner 60 AS.

Kolpingfamilie Wien-Meidling (HI) (*map*A5*), XII, Bendlgasse 10-12 (tel. 83 54 87; fax 81 22 130). From the Westbahnhof, take U-Bahn U-6 (direction: "Philadelphiabrücke") to "Längenfeldgasse," and take the "Storchensteg" exit from the station. Walk up Gierstergasse, walk to the right through the square in front of the church, and take a left onto Bendlgasse (5 min.). From the Südbahnhof, take U-Bahn U-1 (direction: "Kagran") to "Karlsplatz," and then U-Bahn U-4 (direction: "Hütteldorf") to "Längenfeldgasse." This well-lit and modern hostel, in an affordable shopping district, has 190 beds. English spoken. Dorm beds 95-140 AS; a la carte breakfast 40 AS, sheets 65 AS, no reservations. Singles with full bath and balcony 520 AS. Doubles with full bath and balcony 390 AS per person. Triples 320 AS per person. Quints 240 AS per person. 6-bed room 220 AS per person. 8-bed room 210 AS per person. Breakfast and sheets included with all private rooms Quiet time after 10pm. Curfew at midnight. Non-members pay 20 AS surcharge. Lunch or dinner 56 AS.

Schloßherberge am Wilhelminenberg (HI), XVI, Savoyenstr. 2 (tel. 458 50 37 00; fax 45 85 03 702; telex 132 008). From the Westbahnhof, take U-Bahn U-6 (direction: "Heiligenstadt") to "Alserstraße," switch to streetcar #44 (direction: "Dornbach") to "Wilhelminenstraße," and then take bus #46B or 146B to "Schloß Wilhelminenberg." About 40 min. from the city center. On a hill and surrounded by forest, this *Jugendgästehaus* abuts a beautiful palace, boasts a mini-golf course, and offers one of the best views of Vienna. 164 beds in comfortable quads, all with showers and toilets. Reception open 7am-11:45pm. 205 AS. Breakfast included. Wheelchair access.

Hostel Zöhrer (*map*A3*), VIII, Skodagasse 26 (tel. 43 07 30; fax 408 04 09). From the Westbahnhof, take U-Bahn U-6 (direction: "Heiligenstadt") to "Alserstraße," then take streetcar #43 (direction: "Dr. Karl Lueger Ring") 2 stops to "Skodagasse." From the Südbahnhof, take bus #13A to "Alserstraße/Skodagasse." About 10 min. from the city center. The helpful owner tends a rose garden adjacent to a courtyard and furnished kitchen. Crowded but comfortable. 36 beds. Reception open 7:30am-10pm. Checkout 9am. No curfew, no lockout. Front door/locker key deposit 50 AS. 160 AS per person. Singles, 4-, 6-, or 7-bed rooms, each with showers. Breakfast (7:30-9:30am), sheets, and kitchen facilities included. Laundry 40 AS.

Jugendgästehaus Hütteldorf-Hacking (HI), XIII, Schloßberggasse 8 (tel. 877 02 63; fax 877 026 32; telex 112 438). From Karlsplatz, take U-bahn U-4 to the end station "Hütteldorf"; walk over the footbridge and follow the signs to the hostel (10 min.). Weary backpackers take bus #53 from the side of the footbridge away from the station to its stop at the hostel. From the Westbahnhof, take S-Bahn S-50 (Eurail valid, last train 10:15pm) to "Hütteldorf." Located about 35 min. from the city center, this hostel resides in one of Vienna's most affluent districts. Secluded, with great views of northwest Vienna. Huge backyard and a recreation room with ping pong, billiards, and foosball tables. Often packed with student groups. Spotless rooms, coed by floor with hall toilets and showers. Large closets without locks—it's *much* wiser to use the safes available at reception (10 AS per day). 281 dorm beds in 2-, 4-, 6-, and 8-bed rooms. Reception open 7am-11:45pm. Curfew 11:45pm, but it can be loud for an hour or two. Lockout 9am-4pm. 137 AS; nonmembers pay a 40 AS surcharge. The house is being rebuilt during the winter of early 1994, and rooms with showers will cost 20 AS more. Laundry 60 AS per load. Sheets and breakfast included.

University Dormitories

From July through September, the following university dorms are converted into hotels. Expect mass-produced university cubicles.

Studentenwohnheim der Hochschule für Musik (*map*C4*), I, Johannesgasse 8 (tel. 514 84 48; fax 514 84 49). Walk 3 blocks down Kärnterstr. away from the Stephansdom, and turn left onto Johannesgasse. Great location. Dinner and lunch is scrumptious and cheap. Reception open 24 hrs. Singles 380 AS, with bath and toilet 450 AS. Doubles 330 AS per person. Triples 240 AS per person. Quads and quints 220 AS per person. Breakfast and showers included.

Porzellaneum der Wiener Universität (*map*B2*), IX, Porzellangasse 30 (tel. 34 72 82). From the Südbahnhof, take streetcar D (direction: "Nußdorf") and get off at "Fürstengasse." From the Westbahnhof, take streetcar #5 to the Franz-Josefs Bahnhof, then streetcar D (direction: "Südbahnhof") to "Fürstengasse" (20 min.). Recently renovated. Reception open 24 hrs. Singles and doubles 160 AS per person. Triples and quads also available. Sheets and showers included. Reservations recommended.

Haus Pfeilheim (*map*A3*), VIII, Pfeilgasse 6, in the Hotel Avis (tel. 426 37 40). From the Südbahnhof, take bus #13A (direction: "Alserstraße/Skodagasse") to "Piaristengasse." From the Westbahnhof, take U-Bahn U-6 (direction: "Heiligenstadt") to "Thaliastraße," then walk a block north to Pfeilgasse and take a right (15-20 min.). Offers spartan but adequate rooms. 400 beds. Reception open 24 hrs. Singles 240 AS. Doubles 200 AS per person. Triples 180 AS per person. Breakfast included.

Katholisches Studentenhaus, XIX, Peter-Jordanstr. 29 (tel. 34 92 64). From the Westbahnhof, take U-Bahn U-6 (direction: "Heiligenstadt") to "Nußdorferstr.," then streetcar #38 to "Hardtgasse," and turn left onto Peter-Jordanstr. From the Südbahnhof, take streetcar D to "Schottentor," then streetcar #38 to "Hardtgasse." Reception on 2nd floor. Singles 220 AS. Doubles 160 AS per person. Showers and sheets included. Call ahead. An **affiliated dormitory** (with doubles only) charges the same prices at 21 Zaunschertgasse 4 (tel. 38 21 97). Take U-Bahn U-6 from the Westbahnhof (direction: "Heiligenstadt") to "Nußdorferstr.," and switch to bus #34A to "Franz-Jonas-Platz."

Albertina Josefstadt (*map*AB3*), VIII, Buchfeldgasse 16 (tel. 43 52 11), behind the *Rathaus.* Take U-Bahn U-2 to "Rathaus" and walk 1 block up Schmidgasse to Buchfeldgasse. Great location. Bountiful hot water, comfortable beds, cushy rooms, and copious breakfast. Reception open 24 hrs. Singles 395 AS. Doubles 310 AS per person. Triples 300 AS per person. Breakfast included.

Albertina Alsergrund (*map*A2-3*), VIII, Alser Str. 33 (tel. 43 32 31 0), and **Albertina Auersperg,** VIII, Auerspergstr. 9 (tel. 43 25 29 0). Two more branches of the same affiliation that commandeers dorms in the summer. Alsergrund: singles 345 AS, doubles 280 AS per person, triples 275 AS per person, quads 265 AS per person. Breakfast and showers included. Auersperg: singles 345 AS, with shower and toilet 490 AS; doubles 280 AS per person, with shower and toilet 400 AS per person; triples with shower and toilet 390 AS per person. Breakfast included.

Hotels and Pensions

Irmgard Lauria (*map*A3-4*), VII, Kaiserstr. 77, apt. 8 (tel. 5 222 555). From the Westbahnhof, take U-Bahn U-6 (direction: "Heiligenstadt") to "Burggasse-Stadthalle," then take a right onto Burggasse, walk 1 block to Kaiserstr., and take a left (10 min.). From the Südbahnhof, take bus #13A (direction: "Alserstraße/Skodagasse") to "Kellermanngasse," then switch onto bus #45A to "Kaiserstraße" (25 min.). About 15 min. from center. Enchanting, custom-designed rooms. Warm and thoughtful owner and staff. Billowy down quilts, color TVs, spotless kitchen, and front door keys provided. Dorm beds 160 AS. Doubles 530 AS, with bath 700 AS. Triples 700 AS, with bath 800 AS. Quads 850 AS, with bath 940 AS. Coed rooming possible. Reservations strongly recommended but require a 2-day-min. stay. If full, the answering machine suggests other places to try. Major credit cards accepted.

Pension Kraml (*map*A4-5*), VI, Brauergasse 5 (tel. 587 85 88; fax 586 75 73), off Gumpendorferstr. From the Westbahnhof, walk across the Gürtel and up Mariahilferstr., and take the third right onto Otto-Bauer-Str.; make the first left on Königseggasse, then the first right (15 min.). From the Südbahnhof, take bus #13A (direction: "Alserstraße/Skodagasse") to "Gumpendorferstraße/Brauergasse" (15 min.). About 10 min. from the city center. Tidy, comfortable, new, and run by a cordial family. Spotless hallways. Lots o' space in the well-lit larger rooms. 33 beds. Singles 260 AS. Doubles 490-570 AS, with shower 660 AS, with shower and toilet 750 AS. Triples 720 AS, with shower and toilet 930 AS. Quads with shower and toilet 1120 AS. Continental breakfast included. Call ahead.

Hospiz-Hotel CVJM (*map*A4*), VII, Kenyongasse 15 (tel. 93 13 04). From the Westbahnhof, walk 1 block down Stallgasse and turn left on Kenyongasse (3 min.). On a side street with classic, old-Vienna architecture, this could be the quietest hotel in town. Sunny rooms range from medium-sized to huge. Inter-denominational mass every weekend. Singles 320 AS, with shower 360 AS. Doubles 560 AS, with shower 640 AS. Triples 810 AS, with shower 900 AS. Quads 1040 AS, with shower 1120 AS. Keys to rooms and front door provided. Generous breakfast included. Major credit cards accepted. 40 AS surcharge for one-night stands. Call ahead.

Pension Falstaff (*map*B2*), IX, Müllnergasse 5 (tel. 34 91 86 or 34 91 27; fax 34 91 864). From the Westbahnhof, take U-Bahn U-6 to "Heiligenstadt," then U-Bahn U-4 to "Roßauer Lände." Make a right onto Grünentorgasse, walk three blocks, and make a left onto Müllnergasse (15 min.). From the Südbahnhof, take streetcar D to "Schlickgasse," walk up Porzellangasse one block and make a right on Müllnergasse (25 min.). Named after Verdi's only comic opera, Falstaff's walls are adorned with humorous drawings. The high-ceilinged entry and airy dining hall overlook a wooded courtyard. Central heating in winter. Ideal location somewhat countered by the large neon sign and sea green and mustard interior decor. Singles 330 AS, with shower 440 AS. Doubles 540 AS, with shower 650 AS, with shower and toilet 760 AS. Triples 850 AS. Extra bed 200 AS. Breakfast included. Reservations recommended. 10 min. from the city center.

Pension Wild (*map*AB3*), VIII, Lange Gasse 10 (tel. 43 51 74). From the Westbahnhof, take U-Bahn U-6 to "Lerchenfelder Straße," then take streetcar #46 (direction: "Dr. Karl Renner Ring") to "Lange Gasse," and take a left onto Lange Gasse. From the Südbahnhof, take bus #13A (direction: "Alserstraße/Skodagasse") to "Piaristengasse." Take a left onto Lerchenfelder Str., and take the second left onto Lange Gasse. 30 beds, with kitchen access. Soullessly modern. Basement level boasts a "Slender You" figure salon (open Mon.-Fri.), featuring a steambath, sauna, tanning salon (30 AS per hour), and a bar. Singles 380 AS. Doubles 560 AS. Triples 790-810 AS. Breakfast included. Reservations recommended. Call ahead.

Camping

Wien-West I and **II** (tel. 94 14 49), at Hüttelbergstr. 40 and 80, respectively, are the most convenient campgrounds; both lie in the 14th *Bezirk* about 8km from the city center. For either, take U-Bahn U-4 to the end station at "Hütteldorf," then switch to bus #52B (direction: "Campingplatz Wien West"). 58 AS per person, children 33 AS; 53 AS per tent; 53 AS per car. Both offer laundry machines, grocery stores, and cooking facilities. I is open in July and August; II year-round. II also rents four-person bungalows (380 AS).

FOOD

Viennese *haute cuisine* arrived with the Emperor; culinary offerings flourished as imperial landholdings extended far and wide. Many of the specialties betray an association with former provinces. *Serbische Bohnensuppe* (Serbian bean soup) and *Ungärische Gulaschsuppe* (Hungarian spicy beef stew) are two examples of Eastern European influence. Even the famed *Wiener Schnitzel* (fried and breaded veal cutlets) originated in Milan. To get a feel for Austrian budget gastronomy, find a *Beißl* (a pub that offers a few entrees and lots and lots of beer) or a *Würstelstand* (a hot-sausage stand that presents a quick, inexpensive, and tasty alternative for eaters on the go). Vienna is perhaps most renowned for its sublime desserts and chocolates; they're unbelievably rich, but priced for patrons who are likewise blessed. *Sacher Torte, Imperial Torte,* and even *Apfelstrudel* cost up to 40 AS, though most residents adamantly maintain that they are worth every *Groschen*.

The restaurants near **Kärtnerstraße** (*map*C3-4*) are generally overpriced. A better bet is the neighborhood just north of the university and near the Votivkirche (*map*B3*; U-2 stop: "Schottentor"), where **Universitätsstraße** and **Währingerstraße** meet; reasonably priced *Gaststätten*, *Kneipen*, and restaurants are easy to find. The **Rathausplatz** (*map*B3*) hosts inexpensive food stands during special seasons: in the weeks before Christmas, the **Christkindlmarkt** offers hot food and (spiked) punch amidst vendors of Christmas charms, ornaments, and candles. From the end of June until the end of July, the **Festwochen** (weeks of celebration) bring foodstuffs of many nations to the stands erected behind seats for the various art and music films (food stands open daily 11am-11pm). Yet another outdoor option is the open-air **Naschmarkt,** where you can nibble on aromatic delicacies (vegetables, bread, and ethnic food) while shopping at Vienna's premier flea market (U-4 stop: "Kettenbrückengasse"; open Mon.-Fri. 7am-6pm, Sat. 7am-1pm). The Naschmarkt is an especially filling option for vegetarians in this carnivorous city. **Niederhofstraße** (*map*A5*) has an open air market similar to the Naschmarkt, *sans* the Saturday flea market.

Pick out the building blocks of a quality meal at one of the ubiquitous supermarket chains in town: **Billa, Julius Meinl, Konsum,** and **Hofer**—slightly less common are **Ledi, Mondo, Renner,** and **Zielpunkt.** (**Bipa** and **DM** supermarkets specialize in inexpensive toiletries and over-the-counter-drugs.) Many of these have branches in the massive **Lugner City** (*map*A4*) mall, near the Westbahnhof at the U-Bahn U-6 stop "Burggasse/Stadthalle." When you've got sufficient foodstuffs, feel free to roam around the **Stadthalle** (*map*A4*; tel. 98 10 00), next door at Vogelweidplatz 14; there's a bowling alley, an Olympic-size pool (45 AS), sauna (140 AS), and ice rink (60 AS) inside. (Open Mon.-Fri. 8am-9pm, Sat.-Sun. 7am-6pm.) Markets and stores are generally open Mon.-Fri. 8am-6pm, Sat. 9am-12:30pm. From Saturday afternoon to Sunday, try shops in and around the major train stations. Restaurants usually stop serving after 11pm. To conquer summer heat, seek out the **Italeis** or **Tichy** ice cream vendors, or visit the delicious **Gelateria Hoher Markt** (*map*C3*), I, Hoher Markt just off Rotenturmstr. Expatriate Italians flock here to sample all 23 mouth-watering flavors of ice cream (open daily March-Oct. 9am-11pm).

Restaurants

The Innere Stadt

Trzesniewski (*map*C3*), I, Dorotheergasse 1, 3 blocks down the Graben from the Stephansdom. A famous stand-up restaurant, this unpronounceable establishment has been serving open-faced sandwiches for more than 80 years. This was the favored locale of Franz Kafka, among others. Eighteen varieties of spreads on bread, 7 AS per *Brötchen.* Ideal for a snack while touring the city center. Lots of vegetarian options. Open Mon.-Fri. 9am-7:30pm, Sat. 9am-1pm. Another **branch** at VII, Mariahilferstr. 26-30 in the Hermansky department store. Open Mon.-Fri. 9am-6pm, Sat. 8:30am-1pm.

Levante (*map*BC3*), I, Wallnerstr. 2 (tel. 533 23 26). Walk down the Graben away from the Stephansdom, bear left on Kohlmarkt, and then right on Wallnerstr. (3 min.). A hot spot among students, this Greek-Turkish restaurant features myriad affordable dishes, including plenty of vegetarian delights. Entrees 78-130 AS. Try the Levante-Platte for a cornucopia of Turkish specialties. Another **branch** at Josefstädterstr. 14, by the "Rathaus" U-2 stop. Both open daily 11:30am-11:30pm.

Ball (*map*C3*), I, Ballgasse 5, near Stephansplatz, off Weihburggasse (tel. 513 17 54). On a narrow cobblestone lane, this dark restaurant has a 1920s atmosphere and quiet jazz music to put you "In the Mood." *Prix fixe* lunch menu 75 AS. Open Mon.-Fri. 10:30am-midnight.

Zu den 3 Hacken (*map*C3*), I, Singerstr. 28 (tel. 512 58 95), a 2-min. walk down Singerstr. away from the Stephansdom. Even if you don't like Austrian food, you can't help marveling at the local fare served at this 200-year-old establishment. It's been around so long for a reason; the food is remarkable, though not intended for vegetarians. The price of fame: famously high prices. Ask for a menu in English unless you speak Viennese dialect. Has a lovely outdoor pavilion and a room devoted to Schubert. Entrees 76-190 AS. Open Mon.-Fri. 9am-midnight, Sat. 9am-3pm.

Outside the Ring

Schnitzelwirt Schmidt (*map*A3-4*), VII, Neubaugasse 52 (tel. 93 37 71). From the Burgring, take bus #49 to the end station at "Neubaugasse" (5 min.). Offers every kind of *Schnitzel* (55 AS) you could imagine. Huge portions and low, low prices will sate your desires and spare your budget. Open Mon.-Fri. 11am-10pm, Sat. 11am-2:30pm and 5-10pm.

Espresso "Teddy"/Rumpelkammerbar (*map*B1-2*), IX, Liechtensteinstr. 10 (tel. 34 03 86). Take U-Bahn U-2 to "Schottentor," walk up Währingerstr. to Hörlgasse (next to the Votivkirche), make a right, and go 1 block to Liechtensteinstr. (3 min.). Please don't let the restaurant's name scare you off. Incredible food, and so much of it for such amazing prices. The only problem: the menu is so thick you'll finish your first drink before you choose your entree. Though the Rumpelkammerbar is billed as a "steak restaurant," it offers fish, poultry, salads, and vegetarian fare. Giant *Schnitzel* 70 AS. *Cordon Bleu* 80 AS. Walk through the café and head to the basement to enjoy great soul music. Call for a reservation on Fri. and Sat. nights. Open Mon.-Fri. 7am-1am, Sat. 9am-1am.

Tunnel (*map*B3*), VIII, Florianigasse 39 (tel. 42 34 65). Take U-Bahn U-2 to "Rathaus," and turn left onto Florianigasse (10 min.). The Viennese version of the Euro-hip pub hangout, popular among young bohemians. Basement level is a club featuring local musicians. Dark and smoky with wildly colorful paintings and the occasional squishy rug sofa instead of chairs. Very casual. Student crowd whiles the night away drinking beer and nibbling at Italian, Austrian, and Middle Eastern food. Great vegetarian options. Entrees 35-120 AS. Open daily 9am-2am.

Jahrhundert Beisl (*map*B3*), VIII, Florianigasse 37 (tel. 43 67 24), next to Tunnel. Candlelight and roses, chic clientele, and Austrian food prepared to perfection. The name reflects its enchanting Jugendstil decor. Great *Gulasch.* Entrees 68-98 AS. *Palatschinken* 52 AS. Open Thurs.-Tues. 8pm-midnight.

Fischerbräu, XIX, Billrothstr. 17 (tel. 31 962 64). Take streetcar #38 from "Schottentor/Universität" to "Hardtgasse," and walk back about 50m. A favorite hangout for youngish locals who revel in home-brewed beer, fantastic Austrian food, and the shaded outdoor patio. Jazz brunch on Sundays with local musicians. Entrees 35-110 AS. Open Mon.-Sat. 4pm-1am, Sun. 11am-1am.

Schweizerhaus (*map*CD3*), II, Volksprater 116 (tel. (218 0152). Take U-Bahn U-1 from Karlsplatz (direction: "Kagran") to "Praterstern." Operated by the Kolarik family since 1920, "Swiss House" is one of Austria's most loved *Biergarten*. Waiters traverse the floor with trays full of beer and refill your mug as soon as it empties. For the complete experience, try the *Schweinstelze* (enough grilled pork for 3 big bad wolves) with mustard and horseradish. Entrees 50-150 AS. Open March-Nov. daily 10am-midnight.

Pizzeria Restaurant Valentino (*map*B2*), XIX, Berggasse 6 (tel. 319 42 62). Take U-Bahn U-2 to "Schottentor," then walk up Währingerstr. to Berggasse, where you'll take a right (3 min.). The decor, staff, and excellent food generate a distinctly Mediterranean flair. Huge pizzas 40-85 AS; pasta 50-80 AS. Open daily 11:30am-11:30pm.

Pizzeria Ristorante Sardegna (*map*B2*), IX, Servitengasse 14 (tel. 319 77 33). From the U-Bahn U-2 "Schottentor" stop, take streetcar D to "Schlickgasse" (5 min.). Cobblestone Servitengasse is just ahead on the right. With a sidewalk café overlooking a beautiful old church, this restaurant is a pleasant spot for authentic Italian food of all sorts. The monstrous menu provides many vegetarian options. Try the stellar *tiramisù*. Entrees 55-180 AS. Open Tues.-Sun. 11:30am-2:30pm and 6-11:30pm.

University Mensa (*map*B3*), IX, Universitätsstr. 7, on the 7th floor of the university building, midway between U-Bahn U-2 stops "Rathaus" and "Schottentor." Open to all. Ride the groovy old-fashioned elevator (no doors and it never stops; you have to jump in and out). Typical university meals in the dining hall 20-50AS. Open Mon.-Fri. 11am-2pm. Adjacent snack bar open Mon.-Fri. 8am-7pm. Other inexpensive student cafeterias serve their constituencies at:

Music Academy (*map*C4*), I, Johannesgasse 8. Open Mon.-Fri. 8am-7pm.

Academy of Applied Art (*map*C3*), I, Oskar Kokoschka-Platz 2. Open Mon.-Thurs. 9am-6pm; Fri. 9am-4pm.

Academy of Fine Arts (*map*B4*), I, Schillerplatz 3. Open Mon.-Fri. 8:30am-5pm.

Vienna Technical University (*map*C4*), IV, Karlsplatz 13. Open Mon.-Fri. 11am-2:30pm.

Catholic University Student's Community (*map*B3*), I, Ebendorfer Str. 8. Open Mon.-Fri. 11:30am-2pm.

Cafés and Konditoreien

The café is the centerpiece of Vienna's unhurried charm. In the 19th century, it became the place to meet, converse, read newspapers, and while away the afternoon. In *fin-de-siècle* culture, the café provided the setting for budding artistic and social movements. Hermann Bahr's literary roundtable Jung Wien became a permanent fixture in the **Café Griensteidl.** Adolf Loos, prophet of 20th-century minimalism and possibly Vienna's most controversial architect, designed the interiors of the **Café Museum** (1899), now altered beyond recognition, and the **Loos Bar** (*map*C34*), located off Kärntner Str. The leather and mahogany interior of the latter offers a rare glimpse at the designer's persecuted aesthetic.

In some cafés, standard procedure is to choose a pastry at the counter, pay for it immediately, find a place to sit, and give your receipt to the server when you order beverages. The server then returns with your pastry. Coffee can be ordered *schwarzer* (black), *brauner* (a little milk), *melange* (light), and *mazagron* (iced with dollop of rum). Both pastry and coffee can be ordered *mit Schlagobers* (with whipped cream, a few *Schillings* extra). If your server refills your water glass twice before you've ordered another coffee, that means it's time to buy another cup.

Cafés provide the cheapest way to read a newspaper. For the price of a cup of coffee, you can read your way through all the papers in the joint. You can advertise free of charge in Vienna's two main papers devoted exclusively to advertisements, **Bazar** and **Fundgrube,** which appear several times a week and can be purchased at newspaper kiosks and from vendors on the street. Foreign daily or weekly newspapers are sold at kiosks along the Ringstraße, at the railway stations, and from *Tabak* stores.

The Viennese frequent cafés for relaxation, but the cafés themselves are quite tense regarding their cultural territory. Perhaps it's the preponderance of caffeinated substances, but café owners will fight to the death to defend their right to claim that Joe Artist/Author/Composer/Politician ate/drank/made merry/preached to the bourgeois masses within the café's walls. To this day, a court case is pending to determine who created the original **Sacher Torte,** a delicious chocolate-raspberry torte: Demel or Sacher. Demel was the Emperor's official *pâtissier,* but Sacher was (and remains) the premier restaurant in Vienna. The case has generated numerous tragedies, including bankruptcy, the sale of Demel to a corporation, and the suicide of the general manager of Sacher. Dashiell Hammett has recently been linked to a mysterious trenchcoat-clad figure seen rummaging through the dumpsters in an alley behind Kohlmarkt.

The Innere Stadt

Demel (*map**BC3*), I, Kohlmarkt 14. Walk 5 min. from the Stephansdom down Graben. The most famous bakery in Austria, for good reason. Heavenly cakes (35-45 AS) arranged like jewels in glass cases. Consume them in *fin-de-siècle* extravagance. Open daily 10am-6pm.

Hotel Sacher (*map**C4*), I, Philharmonikerstr. 4 (tel. 512 14 87), around the corner from the main tourist information office. This historic sight has been serving the world-famous Sacher Torte (45 AS) in red velvet opulence for years. During the reign of Franz Josef, elites invited to the Hofburg would make late reservations at the Sacher. The emperor ate so quickly and Elisabeth was always dieting—nobody dared eat after the imperial family had finished—so all the guests left hungry, and had a real dinner later at Hotel Sacher. Exceedingly elegant. Jeans and shorts are *not* appropriate; most everyone is refined and bejeweled. Open daily 6:30am-midnight.

Café Central (*map**B3*), I, at the corner of Herrengasse and Strauchgasse, inside Palais Ferstel. Steeped in history, this opulent café was once the favorite hangout of satirist Karl Kraus. Obsolete hero Vladimir Ilych Ulianov (better known by his pen-name Lenin) took tea here. Leon Trotsky played chess here, fingering imperialist miniatures with cool anticipation. (Faulty endgame? Duplicitous red pawn?) Alfred Polgar used the name of the café to skewer the intellectual pretensions of the Viennese bourgeoisie in his essay *Theorie des Café Central.* Still a place to drink coffee and discuss Deep Thoughts. Open Mon.-Sat. 9am-8pm.

Café Hawelka (*map**C3*), I, Dorotheergasse 6, 3 blocks west from the Stephansdom. The artists, intellectuals, and radicals who hang out here devour the irresistible *warme Buchteln* (sweet dumplings filled with preserves, 25 AS; available only after 10pm). Coffee 30-40 AS. Open Mon. and Wed.-Sat. 8am-2am, Sun. 4pm-2am.

Peter's Operncafé Hartauer (*map**C3*), I, Riemergasse 9. Walk down Singerstr. away from Stephansplatz and turn left onto Riemergasse (2 min.). Frequented by members of Vienna's music subculture, often with instruments in hand; also a standby for the Viennese gay community. Signed photographs of opera greats grace the walls from floor to ceiling, and *Lieder* play all day long. Endearing interior with wood floors and worn oriental carpets. The biggest *Mohr im Hemd* in town (50 AS). Open Mon.-Fri. 8am-2am, Sat. 5pm-2am.

Café Secession (*map**BC4*), I, Friedrichstr. 12, behind the Secession building. Be hip, hang out, and ponder one of the most interesting architectural masterpieces in Vienna. Open daily 10am-2am.

Pavillon (*map**B3-4*), I, near Heldenplatz and the Volksgarten. A charming garden café and a popular evening hangout for locals before they go clubbing in the neighboring *Volksgarten* disco (see Nightlife below).

Outside the Ring

Café Sperl (*map**A4-5*), VI, Gumpendorferstr. 11; 15 min. from the Westbahnhof. Built in 1880, Sperl is one of Vienna's oldest and most classically beautiful cafés.

Franz Lehár was a *Stammkunde* (regular) here; he composed operettas at a corner table by the entrance. Also the former homebase for Vienna's Hagenbund, an *art nouveau* coterie excluded from the Secession. Coffee 20-33 AS; cake 28 AS. Billiards daily 9:30am-9:30pm. Open Mon.-Sat. 7am-11pm, Sun. 3-11pm; Sept.-June Mon.-Sat. 7am-11pm.

Europa (*map*AB4*), VII, Zollergasse 8 (tel. 526 33 83). Take U-Bahn U-2 to "Babenbergerstraße," then walk up Mariahilferstr. to Zollergasse, the 4th street on the right (7 min.). A clean, well-lit place, this café is a favorite hangout both for expatriate Americans and the late-night bohemian crowd. Classic rock and soul round off the cosmopolitan atmosphere. Open daily 9am-4am.

Café Florianihof (*map*AB3*), VIII, Florianigasse 45 (tel. 40 22 023). Take U-Bahn U-2 to "Rathaus," then turn left onto Florianigasse (15 min.). This immaculate café, with its comfy leather couches and marble tables, appeals to antisocial intellectuals as well as the student crowd. *Melange* 24 AS. Open daily 9am-2am.

SIGHTS

Viennese streets are laden with memories. You can get the best feel for the city if you simply wander the paths that once supported the likes of Klimt, Herzl, and Mozart. *Vienna from A to Z* (30 AS from tourist office, higher prices in bookstores) provides all you need for a self-guided tour. The array of cultural offerings in Vienna can be mind-boggling; the free *Museums* brochure from the tourist office lists all opening hours and admission prices. Individual museum tickets usually cost 15 AS, but 150 AS will buy you a book of 14.

The Innere Stadt

The **First District** (die Innere Stadt) is Vienna's social and geographical epicenter, enclosed on three sides by the massive **Ringstraße** and on the northern end by the **Danube Canal.** Though "*die innere Stadt*" literally translates to "the inner city," it thankfully carries no connotation of American inner-city ills. Vienna's perfectly preserved *Altstadt,* maintained originally as a display of imperial splendor and later as a representation of national pride, was designed by *artistes;* even the rent-controlled tenement housing—especially the rent-controlled tenement housing—exudes the touch of Austria's most famed architectural masters.

Ecclesiastic Vienna: The Houses of Worship

Start your odyssey at the quintessential cathedral, the Gothic **Stephansdom** (St. Stephen's Cathedral; *map*C3*). The pedestrian zone converges on this wondrous structure; either follow the tower's beacon or take U-Bahn U-1 or U-3 to "Stephansplatz." The smoothly tapering, stone lace spire has become Vienna's emblem, gracing every second postcard. The cathedral was mostly destroyed by bombs in World War II, then slowly rebuilt; a series of photos inside depicts the destruction and painstaking reconstruction. The architectural history of the cathedral begins in the 12th century. The oldest sections, the Romanesque **Riesentor** (Giant Gate) and **Heidentürme** (Towers of the Heathens), were built during the reign of King Ottokar II, when Vienna was a Bohemian protectorate. Habsburg Duke Rudolf IV later ordered a complete Gothic retooling, earning him the sobriquet "the Founder." (Tours of the cathedral in English Mon.-Sat. at 10:30am and 3pm, Sun. and holidays 3pm; June-Sept. also Sat. 7pm; July-Aug. also Fri. 7pm.) You can view the Viennese sprawl from the **Nordturm** (North Tower; elevator ride 30 AS; open daily 9am-5:30pm). Walk downstairs to the entrance to the **Catacombs,** where thousands of Plague-victim skeletons line the walls. Look for the lovely **Gruft** (vault), which stores all of the Habsburg innards. Everyone wanted a piece of the rulers: the Stephansdom got the entrails, the Augustinerkirche got the heads, and the Kapuzinergruft, apparently drawing the short straw, got the leftovers. (Catacombs open Mon.-Fri. 9am-noon and 1-4pm. Obligatory tours, in German, on the ½-hr.; 30 AS.)

From the Stephansplatz, walk up Rotenturmstr. and bear left on Rabensteig to reach Ruprechtsplatz, with a slew of relaxing street cafés and the Romanesque

Ruprechtskirche (*map*C3*). The northern side of the square has a stupendous view of the **Danube Canal,** the waterway that defines the northern boundary of the Innere Stadt. Once you've ripped your gaze from the water, walk down Ruprechtsstiege to Seitenstettengasse, a cobblestone street that slopes to the **Synagogue** (*map*C3*), Seitenstettengasse 2-4. This particular building, one of over 94 temples maintained by Vienna's 180,000 Jews until 1938, was saved from Nazi destruction only because it stood in the middle of a residential block. Most of the other synagogues were destroyed by the Nazis in November of 1938, during the Kristallnacht pogrom. Over 50 years later, fewer than 7000 Jews reside in Vienna, and the synagogue is patrolled by an armed guard.

Stroll back to the Danube Canal, turn left on Salzgries, and then make another left onto Tiefer Graben to find the **Freyung** square (*map*B3*) at the end of the street. The space is dominated by the massive **Schottenkirche** (Church of the Scots; *map*BC3*), founded by Babenberg ruler Henry Jasomirgott in the 12th century. The present Baroque building stands opposite the ornate **Kinsky Palace** (*map*BC3*; Freyung 4) and the **Porcia Palace** (*map*BC3*; Herrengasse 23), the only extant palace in Vienna built in the Italian Renaissance style.

If, rather than turning right into Freyung, you instead turn left at the end of Tiefer Graben, you'll find yourself staring into the grand courtyard named **Am Hof** (*map*BC3*). The Babenbergs used this square as the ducal seat when they brought the palace in 1155 from atop **Leopoldsberg** (in the Wienerwald) to the present site of Am Hof 2. In the medieval era, jousters squared off in Am Hof; once the Habsburgs moved the imperial palace to the Hofburg, construction began in earnest. The square now houses the **Church of the Nine Chairs of Angels** (*map*BC3*; built 1386-1662); at the request of Baron von Hirsch, Pope Pius VI gave the papal blessing here on Easter in 1782, and Emperor Franz II proclaimed his abdication as Holy Roman Emperor in 1806 from its terrace. The 19th-century **Ministry of War** (*map*BC3*) also adorns the square, and, at Am Hof 10, a **Firefighting Museum** (*map*BC3*) sits inside the erstwhile headquarters of the Viennese Fire Brigade. There are also **Roman ruins** (*map*BC3*) in Am Hof (open for visits Sat.-Sun. 11am-1pm). In the middle of the square stands the **Mariensäule** (*map*BC3*), erected to fulfill a vow sworn by Emperor Ferdinand III when the Swedes threatened Vienna during the Thirty Years War. On the pillar, Mary is represented as slaying four beasts, among them hunger, war, and pestilence.

Take a quick jaunt down Steindlgasse from Am Hof and continue onto Milchgasse if you want to discover Petersplatz (*map*C3*), home of the **Peterskirche.** This magnificent edifice was modeled after St. Peter's Basilica in Rome. Charlemagne supposedly founded the first version of St. Peter's on this site in the 4th century, but town architects just couldn't resist tinkering throughout the ages; the present Baroque ornamentation was completed in 1733. Head out Jungferngasse to the **Graben** (*map*C3*), one of Vienna's main shopping drags; this pedestrian zone suddenly exudes *Glühwein* (spiked hot punch) during the freezing Christmas season. If you're reading this book, you probably can't afford anything in the windows. *Graben* (graves) received its name from the cemetery that encircled the old town until the 15th century. In the middle of the *Fußgängerzone* stands the **Pestsäule** (Plague Column; *map*C3*), completed in 1693 as a memorial from Emperor Leopold I to more than 100,000 victims of the Black Plague.

At the western end of the Graben, away from the Stephansdom, Kohlmarkt leads off to the left, past **Demel Café** (*map*BC3*)—though few can pass Demel without a purchase—and the **Looshaus** (1910; *map*B3*). The latter architectural wonder was branded "the house without eyebrows" by contemptuous contemporaries. Admirers of both Classical and Jugendstil styles were scandalized by the elegant simplicity of this building; the bottom two floors are decorated with green marble, and the top four floors are of pale green stucco with (gasp!) no façade decoration. The Looshaus technically sits on **Michaelerplatz** (*map*B3*), named for the **Michaelerkirche** on its eastern flank. The church was purportedly founded by Leopold "the Glorious" of

Babenberg, as an expression of gratitude to God for his safe return from the crusades. The church's Romanesque foundation dates back to the early 13th century, but construction continued until 1792 (note the Baroque embellishment over the doorway). St. Michael's interior reflects the many architectural styles in vogue throughout the five centuries of construction; this building, like so many Viennese structures, fell victim to generational rivalry. In the middle of the Michaelerplatz, visitors discard unwanted *Groschen* by throwing them into the **excavated foundations** of Old Vienna. *Let's Go* cannot recommend this practice as a safe means of keeping a budget.

Imperial Vienna: The Hofburg

The enormous complex rising from the southeast of the Michaelerplatz could only be the **Hofburg** (Imperial Palace; *map*BC3-4*), residence of the Habsburg emperors until 1918 and now administrative office space for the Austrian president. The Hofburg's construction began in 1279 and continued for seven centuries; workers only laid down their tools for the last time in 1913. The *Vienna from A to Z* brochure will help you navigate this monstrous complex, or you can just allot a few hours to lose yourself among the splendor.

You should probably stroll around the outside of the Hofburg before you venture into its imperial magnificence. From the Michaelerplatz, look to the right to find the **Stallburg** (Palace Stables; *map*BC3-4*), home to the Royal Lipizzaner stallions of the **Spanische Reitschule** (Spanish Riding School; tel. 533 90 32). This renowned example of equine breeding is a relic of the Habsburg marriage to Spanish royalty. The Reitschule performances (April-June and Sept. Sun. 10:45am, Wed. 7pm; March and Nov. to mid-Dec. Sun. 10:45am) are always sold out; you must reserve tickets six months in advance. (Write to "Spanische Reitschule, Hofburg, A-1010 Wien." If you reserve through a travel agency, you pay a 22% surcharge. Write only for reservations; no money will be accepted. Tickets 200-600 AS, standing room 150 AS.) Watching the horses train is much cheaper. (March-June and Nov. to mid-Dec. Tues.-Sat. 10am-noon; Feb. Mon.-Sat. 10am-noon, except when the horses tour. Tickets sold at the door at Josefsplatz, Gate 2, from about 8:30am. Admission 50 AS, children 15 AS. No reservations.)

Keep walking around the Hofburg away from the Michaelerkirche to encounter the Baroque **Josefsplatz** (*map*BC3*), with a central equestrian monument to Emperor Josef II. The square also contains the entrance to the stunning Gothic **Augustinerkirche.** In the tug-of-war to divide the remains of the Habsburgs, the Augustinerkirche claimed the imperial heads, which now reside in the church's crypts. Augustinerstr. leads right past the **Albertina** (*map*C4*), the palatial wing once inhabited by Maria Christina (Maria Theresa's favorite daughter) and her husband Albert. The Albertina now contains the Viennese **Collection of Graphic Arts** and a **film museum** (see Museums below).

Upon rounding the tip of the Albertina, cut around the monument to Erzherzog Albrecht and stroll through the exquisite **Burggarten** (Gardens of the Imperial Palace; *map*B4*). The opposite end of the garden opens onto the Ring and the main entrance to the *interior* of the Hofburg, just a few meters to the right. Enter through the enormous stone gate into the sweeping **Heldenplatz** (heroes' square; *map*B3*). The two equestrian statues facing each other were sculpted by Anton Fernkorn; one is of the Archduke Karl and the other is Prince Eugene of Savoy, both great military commanders. To the right is the grandest part of the Hofburg, the **Neue Hofburg** (new palace; *map*B3-4*), built between 1881 and 1913. The double-headed golden eagle crowning the roof symbolizes the double empire of Austria-Hungary. It was from the balcony of the Neue Hofburg that Hitler spoke at a 1938 rally following the Anschluß. The palace now houses the branch of the **Kunsthistorisches Museum** (*map*B4*) that holds antique instruments; among the harps and violins are Beethoven's harpsichord and Mozart's piano, which has a double keyboard—the top for the right hand, the bottom for the left (see Museums below). Also within the Neue Hofburg is the **Nationalbibliothek** (National Library; *map*B34*), which boasts an outstanding collection of papyrus scriptures and musical manuscripts.

The arched stone passageway at the rear of the Heldenplatz leads you to the courtyard called **In der Burg,** surrounded by the wings of the **Alter Hofburg** (Old Palace; *map*B3*). In the center is a monument to Emperor Franz II. Turn left under the arch of red and black stones, crowned by a black eagle on a gilded shield, to arrive at the **Schweizerhof** (Swiss Courtyard; *map*B3*), named for the Swiss mercenaries who stoically guarded the palace. On the right side of this courtyard is the **Schatzkammer** (treasury), which holds the imperial crown of the Holy Roman Empire and the crown of the Austrian Empire. Just ahead is the Gothic **Burgkapelle** where the **Wiener Sängerknaben** (Vienna Boys' Choir) perform (see Music below for more details).

Back at In der Burg, turn right to find yourself under the intricately carved ceiling of the **Michaeler Küppel** (*map*B3*). The solid wooden door on the right leads to the **Schauräume,** the former private rooms of Emperor Franz Josef and Empress Elisabeth (open Mon.-Sat. 8:30am-noon and 12:30-4pm, Sun. 8:30am-12:30pm; tours 25 AS, students 10 AS). The door on the left opens to reveal the **Hofsilber und Tafelkammer,** displaying the outrageously ornate cutlery, trays, and pitchers that once adorned the imperial dinner table. You've *never* seen so much flatware. (Open Tues.-Fri. and Sun. 9am-1pm; admission 30 AS, students 5 AS.)

Monumental Vienna: The Ringstraße

The Hofburg's Heldenplatz gate presides over the northeastern side of the Burgring segment of the **Ringstraße.** In 1857, Emperor Franz Josef commissioned this 187-foot-wide and 2½-mile-long boulevard to replace the city walls that separated Vienna's center from the suburban districts. The military, still uneasy in the wake of the revolution attempted nine years earlier, demanded that the first district be surrounded by fortifications; the erupting bureaucratic bourgeoisie, however, protested for the removal of all formal barriers. Imperial designers struck a unique compromise; the walls would be razed to make way for the Ringstraße, a sweeping circle of traffic at once efficient for the large-scale transport of forces and yet visually unobtrusive and thereby non-threatening. The mass traffic of the Ringstraße creates a psychological "edge" or border, isolating life inside from that without; the street is a pathway around the inner city without a specific destination.

As the ethic of lionizing the archetypal craftsman and artisan swept through Vienna in the 1870s, the *artistes* rebelled against the constraining utilitarianism imposed by the Ringstraße. In the space created by the destruction of the old city walls, urban planners pledged to erect monuments to the staples of culture (scholarship, art, theater, politics), recently transferred from the ranks of nobility to the realm of the bourgeoisie; these buildings would serve as landmarks to punctuate the aimless current of the Ring. Traffic would flow linearly, *toward* and *past* grandiose bastions of artistry, rather than *around,* but with both starting point and destination unclear. The magnificent structures commissioned to ground the Ringstraße in newly established values spawned a slew of architectural masterpieces, now known simply as the "Ringstraße style."

The Hofburg, the nexus of Vienna's imperial glory, extends from the right side of the Burgring. On the left is **Maria-Theresien-Platz** (*map*B4*), flanked by two of the monumental foci of culture: the **Kunsthistorisches Museum** (Museum of Art History; *map*B4*) and, on the opposite side of the square, the **Naturhistorisches Museum** (Museum of Natural History; *map*B3-4*). When construction was completed on the museums, the builders stepped back and gasped in horror; they had put Apollo, patron deity of art, atop the Naturhistorisches Museum, and Athena, goddess of science, at the crown of the Kunsthistorisches Museum. An intellectual cover-up was soon manufactured—tour guides still claim that each muse is intentionally situated to *look upon* the appropriate museum (see Museums below). The throned Empress Maria Theresa, surrounded by her key statesmen and advisers, is immortalized in a large statue in the center of the square. The statue purportedly faces the Ring so that the Empress may extend her hand to the people (or flag down a cab).

As you continue clockwise around the Ring, the stunning rose display of the **Volksgarten** (*map*B3-4*) is on your right (see Gardens below), across the Ring from the **Parlament** (parliament) building (*map*B3*). This gilded lily of Neoclassical architecture, built from 1873-83 by Hansen, is the first of the four principal structures designed to fulfill the program of bourgeois cultural symbolism. Now the seat of the Austrian National and Federal Councils, until 1918 it was the meeting place for elected representatives to the Austro-Hungarian Empire; all of the architectural forms in this edifice were created to evoke the great democracies of ancient Greece. Pallas Athena is a fitting stony guardian for this temple of representative government. Before the *fin-de-siècle* artistic revolution, the city planners demanded that architecture be firmly grounded in (a romanticized version of) history; every capital on the Neoclassical Parlament refers to an idealized age of citizen equality.

Just up the Dr. Karl-Renner-Ring is the **Rathaus** (*map*B3*), another masterpiece of rampant historical symbolism. The building is an intriguing remnant of the late 19th-century neo-Gothic style, with Victorian mansard roofs and red geraniums in the windows. The Gothic reference is meant to recall the favored style of the *Freistädter* (free cities) of old; the first grants of trade-based municipal autonomy appeared at the height of the Gothic period in the early 12th century. The Viennese of the Ringstraße, emerging from imperial constraints through the strength of the growing bureaucratic middle class, saw fit to imbue their city hall with the same sense of budding freedom.

The **Burgtheater** (*map*B3*), across the Rathauspark and the Ring, grants drama the same level of symbolic reference as politics. The building's Baroque and Rococo flourishes harken back to the age when theater courted audiences of all social strata. In the early eighteenth century, drama was the ultimate *Gesamtkunstwerk* (total work of art); plays by luminaries such as Goethe and Lessing were emotional events intended for everyone, performed in vast open arenas. The Baroque construction of the Burgtheater attempted to capture this spirit of art of the people, by the people, for the people. Inside, frescoes by Gustav Klimt, his brother, and his partner Matsch depict the interaction between drama and history through the ages. In his representation of Shakespearean theater, Klimt paints himself as a member of the audience, again establishing a link between patron and provider of art.

Immediately to the north, on Karl-Lueger-Ring, is the **Universität** (*map*B3*). This secular cradle of rationalism is rendered unequivocally in Renaissance style. The university was the source of the failed 1848 bourgeois uprising, and thereby received the most careful attention; above all, the architectural symbolism had to be *safe*. It was necessary to dispel all of the ghosts of dissatisfaction and revolt in the building's design. Therefore, the planners took as their model the cradle of state-sponsored liberal learning—Renaissance Italy. In that culture, there existed the quintessential safe blend of discovery *sans* subversion; the Renaissance generated intellectual pursuits in the name of, not in confrontation with, the state. Inside the university (also known as the **Schottentor**) is a tranquil courtyard with busts of famous departed professors filling the archways.

The surrounding side streets gush the typical assortment of university-bred cafés, bookstores, and bars. To the north, across Universitätsstr., the twin spires of the **Votivkirche** (*map*B3*) come into view. This neo-Gothic wonder is surrounded by rose gardens where students study and sunbathe in warm weather. Frequent classical music concerts afford opportunities to see the chapel's interior; look for posters announcing the dates throughout the year. The Votivkirche was commissioned by Franz Josef's brother Maximilian as a gesture of gratitude after the Kaiser survived an assassination attempt in 1853. The Habsburgs habitually strolled around town with a full retinue of bodyguards—supposedly incognito, though everyone knew who they were. The emperor *demanded* that his subjects pretend to not recognize the imperial family. On one of these constitutionals, an assassin leapt from nearby bushes and attempted to stab the emperor; Franz Josef's collar was so heavily starched, however, that the knife never grazed skin, and the crew of bodyguards dispatched the would-be assailant before he could strike again.

Modern Vienna: Near the Donaukanal

From Rooseveltsplatz, Schottenring runs right to the Danube Canal. Halfway to the shore is the neo-Renaissance **Börse** (Austrian Stock Exchange; *map*BC4*), on the corner with Wipplingerstr.; this massive monument to capitalism was built by Theophil Hansen, the architect who designed Parlament and the Musikverein. **Wipplingerstraße** (*map*BC3*), one of the most expensive residential streets in Vienna, runs east from the Börse back into the center of town. On the left side of the street, you'll pass the **Altes Rathaus** (*map*C3*), Wipplingerstr. 8, used from 1316 until 1885, when the government relocated to the Ringstraße. In the building's courtyard is a fountain by Georg Raphael Donner, displaying a scene from the legend of Andromeda and Perseus. Donner's depiction of Medusa's head is rendered in a distinctly Austrian style; if you look directly into her eyes, you'll turn to *Schnitzel*. **Judenplatz** (*map*C3*), directly opposite the Rathaus, responds to the Donner fountain with a statue of Jewish playwright Ephraim Lessing. The statue, originally erected in 1935, was destroyed by Nazis and only returned to Judenplatz in 1982.

The **Hoher Markt** (*map*C3*), once the center of the Roman Vindobona encampment (c. 50 AD), is just a few feet further down Wipplingerstr. The **Josefsbrunnen** fountain anchors the middle of the square. Try to swing by Hoher Markt at noon, to catch the **Ankeruhr** clock (*map*C3*; on the bridge connecting Hoher Markt 10 and 11) in full glory. This mechanical timepiece, built in 1911, has 12 historical figures that rotate past the old Viennese coat of arms. The figures depict city history from the era of Roman encampment up to Joseph Haydn's stint in the Boys' Choir. (One figure per hr., except at noon, when all appear in succession, accompanied by music from their respective eras.)

If you walk straight out Lichtensteg from the Hoher Markt and turn left onto Rotenturmstr., you can take the second right onto tiny **Griechengasse** (*map*C3*). This little cobblestone lane, framed by *faux* gas street lamps, was named for the scores of Greek merchants who settled here in the 18th century and the simple Greek Orthodox church at the street's end. Take a left at the intersection of Griechengasse and Fleischmarkt, and saunter to the main post office straight ahead. Around the office, on the left, squats Otto Wagner's **Postsparkasse** (Post Office Savings Bank; *map*C3*), Georg-Coch-Platz 2. The Postsparkasse is a bulwark of modernist architecture, raising formerly concealed elements of the building, like the thousands of symmetrically placed metallic bolts on the rear wall, to positions of exaggerated significance. This was Wagner's greatest triumph of function over form; don't miss—you can't miss—the heating ducts. The distinctly *art nouveau* interior is open during banking hours free of charge (Mon.-Wed. and Fri. 8am-3pm; Thurs. 8am-5:30pm). The Postsparkasse's façade looks out on Stubenring; its contemporary, the **Imperial War Ministry** (*map*C3*), stares back from across the street. Note the ministry's striking green roof, a symbolic reference to the Hofburg dome.

Three blocks down Stubenring and off to the right waits **Dr.-Karl-Lueger-Platz** (*map*C3*); the tiny little monument marking the square is dedicated to Lueger, the *fin-de-siècle* mayor renowned for both "municipal socialism" and anti-Semitism. From there, you can wander up **Wollzeile** (*map*C3*), the lane to the left of Dr.-Karl-Lueger-Platz, back to Stephansplatz. On the way, be sure to notice the wrought-iron "guild" signs hanging from the building façades; these are trademarks of establishments in the first district.

Cosmopolitan Vienna: Kärntner Straße and the Staatsoper

Just southwest of the Stephansdom, you'll find little **Stock-im-Eisen-Platz** (*map*C3*), named for the square's 16th-century tree trunk impaled by enormous nails. **Kärntner Straße** (*map*C3-4*), Vienna's other primary pedestrian street, leads away from the opposite end of Stock-im-Eisen. This grand boulevard, the epicenter of the city's elegant shopping district, is lined with cafés, boutiques, and street musicians, who play everything from Bolivian mountain music to Dylan to Schubert. A small detour, to the right on Donnergasse will bring you to the spectacular **Neuer Markt** (*map**C3*). In the middle stands the **Donnerbrünnen,** a fountain by Georg Raphael Donner, wherein the graceful Providentia is surrounded by four gods representing the Danube's tributaries. The 17th-century **Kapuzinerkirche** springs from the southwest corner of the square. Inside is the **Imperial Vault** (Gruft), securing the remains (minus head and entrails) of all the Habsburg rulers since 1633 (see the Stephansdom above and the *viscera* inside). Empress Maria Theresa, buried next to her husband Franz Stephan of Lorraine, rests in a domed room encrusted with unmistakably overdone Rococo ornamentation (open daily 9:30am-4pm).

Tegetthoffstraße runs from the Neuer Markt parallel to the pedestrian zone, one block to the west of Kärntner Str. Stroll south, toward the Hofburg, to find Alfred Hrdlicka's poignant 1988 sculpture **Monument Gegen Krieg und Faschismus** (Memorial Against War and Fascism; *map**C3-4*). This work, in the Albertinaplatz, memorializes the suffering of Austria's people—especially its Jews—during World War II. The cast-iron figure scrubbing the sidewalk with a toothbrush is a reminder of related events in Viennese history. In 1938, Liberals and Social Democrats painted anti-Nazi slogans on the streets in preparation for an upcoming referendum on union with Germany. After the Anschluß preempted the plebiscite, Viennese Jews were forced to scrub the streets clean. The same sculptor also created a similarly troubling, ambulatory reminder of Vienna's checkered past: his *Horse Against Amnesia,* sporting a Nazi cap, followed erstwhile Austrian President Kurt Waldheim, a former Nazi, everywhere he went. The horse once appeared in Rome, where Waldheim had an audience with the Pope, accompanied by placards reading, "Don't forget to resign."

The **Staatsoper** (City Opera House; *map**C4*) reigns over the southeast corner of the Albertinaplatz. The glorious building was originally completed in 1869, but was leveled in 1945 by Allied air raids. The renovation, conducted with meticulous reference to the original plans, continued until 1955 (the Staatsoper was reopened before the Stephansdom, which drew harsh criticism of the residents' priorities from the Pope). The list of former directors is formidable, including Gustav Mahler, Richard Strauss, and Lorin Maazel. If you miss the operas, at least tour the glittering gold, crystal, and red-velvet interior—it was featured as the lavish backdrop for the movie *Amadeus* (tours July-Aug. daily 11am-3pm on the hour; Sept.-June upon request). *Fêtes* overwhelm the Opera House from December through March, culminating in the annual **Opernball**—the height of Viennese Romanticism—every February; card-carrying members of European high society waltz the night away, while outside members of the counterculture demonstrate against the class enemies within. (See Music and Entertainment below for more information.)

Outside the Ring

Operngasse, the street perpendicular to the Opernring, conveys traffic through the erstwhile city wall directly to the greatest monument of *fin-de-siècle* Vienna, the **Secession Building** (*map**B4*). This amazing edifice was built by Otto Wagner's pupil Josef Maria Olbrich to accommodate artists who scorned historical style and broke with the rigid, state-sponsored Künstlerhaus. Note the inscription above the door: *"Der Zeit, ihre Kunst; der Kunst, ihre Freiheit"* (to the age, its art; to art, its freedom). With the pared-down simplicity of a Greek temple, the domed building heralds the Secessionist program of a regenerative aesthetic religion. The Secession exhibitions of 1898-1903, seeking truth (*Nuda veritas*) through the new Jugendstil, drew in the work of cutting-edge European artists, led by Gustav Klimt. His painting, *Nuda Vertitas* (naked truth) became the icon of this ideal. Wilde's *Salomé* and paintings by Gauguin, Vuillard, van Gogh, and others created an island of cosmopolitanism amidst a sea of withering Habsburg kitsch. The exhibition hall remains firmly dedicated to the display of cutting-edge art (see Museums below). If you have been ensnared by the tendrils of Jugendstil, there are plenty of other *fin-de-siècle* works in Vienna—ask the tourist office for the *Art Nouveau in Vienna* pamphlet, with color photos and a discussion of the style's top addresses in town.

The **Künstlerhaus** (*map*C4*), Karlsplatz 5, from which the Secession seceded, is just to the east, down Friedrichstr. This is the conservative Viennese museum, as indicated by the statues of Old Masters flanking the entrance. Every year the primary exhibit changes; in 1993 it was Aztec and Mayan art. Next door thrums the acoustically miraculous **Musikverein** (*map*C4*), home of the **Vienna Philharmonic Orchestra.** The blue and gold interior, graced by rose-colored walls, is reminiscent of a sumptuously wrapped chocolate box (see Music below). The **Karlskirche** (*map*C4*) lies on the other side of Friedrichstr., across the gardens of the Karlsplatz. Completed in 1793, this stunning church was built to fulfill a vow Emperor Karl VI made during a plague epidemic in 1713. Many Baroque masters contributed to the interior embellishments. The exterior figures prominently in the city skyline; Byzantine wings flank Roman columns, and a Baroque dome towers atop a classical portico in the amalgam of architectural styles. The reflecting pool and modern, semi-abstract sculpture in front of the church were designed by Henry Moore, after the **Karlsplatz U-Bahn station** (*map*C4*) was completed in 1970.

Wagner and his Disciples

Moore's additions to the subterranean subway station complemented the genius of Otto Wagner, the architect responsible for the massive **Karlsplatz Stadtbahn Pavilion** (*map*C4*) above. This is just one of the many enclosures that he produced for the city's rail system when the structure was redesigned at the turn of the century. All of the U-Bahn U-6 stations between Längenfeldgasse and Heiligenstadt still hold true to Wagner's designs. His attention to the most minute details on station buildings, bridges, and even lampposts gave the city's public transportation a dignified air. Wagner's two arcades in Karlsplatz are both still functional: one as an entrance to the U-Bahn station, the other as a café. Wagner diehards should also visit the acclaimed **Majolicahaus** (*map*B4*) at Wienzeile 40, a collaborative effort by Wagner and Olbrich. Olbrich's Jugendstil ornamentation complements Wagner's penchant for geometric simplicity. The wrought-iron spiral staircase is by Josef Hoffmann, founder of the Wiener Werkstätte.

Otto Wagner's **Kirche am Steinhof,** XIV, Baumgartner Höhe 1, rules from high on a hill in northwestern Vienna. This acclaimed church combines streamlined symmetry and Wagner's signature functionalism with Neoclassical and Renaissance elements. The church has, at 27 seconds, the longest reverb in the world—it's a terror to sing in. Koloman Moser, vanguard member of the Secession, designed the stained-glass windows, while the Jugendstil sculptor Luksch fashioned the statues of Leopold and Severin poised upon each of the building's twin towers. The floor is sloped to facilitate cleaning, and the holy water runs through pipes to keep it pure. Even the pews are functionally designed; they give nurses easy access to the worshipers, a relic of the days when Steinhof served as the mental hospital for the wealthy. (Take bus #48A to the end of the line. Guided tours in German only, Sat. at 3pm.)

The Schwarzenberg and Belvedere Palaces

The elongated **Schwarzenbergplatz** (*map*C4*) is just a quick jaunt from Karlsplatz along Friedrichstr., which becomes Lothringer Str. During the Nazi era, the square was called "Hitlerplatz." At the far end of the square, a patch of landscaped greenery surrounds a fountain and a statue left to the city as a "gift" from Russia. The Viennese have attempted to destroy the monstrosity three times, but this product of sturdy Soviet engineering refuses to be demolished. Behind the fountain is the **Schwarzenberg Palace** (*map*C4*); originally designed by Hildebrandt in 1697, it is now a swank hotel. Rumor has it that daughters of the super-rich annually travel here to meet young Austrian noblemen each year at a national debutante ball—mum's the word.

Directly behind the Schwarzenberg Palace begin the landscaped gardens of **Palais Belvedere** (*map*C4-5*), the summer residence of Prince Eugene of Savoy. Eugene was respected in Vienna for his heroism in a victory over the Ottoman Turks in the late 17th century, but little else of his demeanor pleased the Court; he was a small, ugly, impetuous man. The Belvedere summer palace (originally only the **Untere** (Lower) **Belvedere**) (*map*C4*) was ostensibly a gift from the emperor in recognition of Eugene's military prowess. More likely, the building was intended to get Eugene out of the imperial hair. After a few years, Eugene decided to construct the **Obere** (Upper) **Belvedere** (*map*C5*), a beautiful building topographically higher than the Hofburg. The symbolism of Eugene looking down on the Emperor and the rest of the city incensed the Habsburgs. To top it off, the roof of the Obere Belvedere supports a facsimile of an Ottoman tent, which called undue attention to Eugene's only glory. After Eugene's death, the Habsburgs acquired the building (he never married or had children), and Archduke Franz Ferdinand lived there until he was assassinated in 1914 in Sarajevo. The grounds of the Belvedere, stretching from the Schwarzenberg Palace to the Südbahnhof, now contain three spectacular gardens (see Gardens below) and an equal number of well-endowed museums (see Museums below).

Hundertwasser and Public Housing

Two creations of environmental activist and master of "Fantastic Realism" Friedensreich Hundertwasser await to the northeast, near a bend in the Danube Canal. The **Hundertwasser Haus** (*map*D3*), III, at the corner of Löwengasse and Kegelgasse, was completed in 1985; this was the culmination of the architect's quest for viable municipal housing. Continuing in the tradition of "Rot Wien" (Red Vienna; the socialist republic from 1918 until the Anschluß), when affordable public housing was constructed on a mass scale, Hundertwasser made both an artistic and a political statement with this building. Trees and grass are built into the undulating balconies to bring life back to the "desert" the city had become. Irregular windows, oblique tile columns, and free-form color patterns all contribute to the eccentricity of this blunt rejection of architectural orthodoxy. Take streetcar N from "Schwedenplatz" (direction: "Prater").

KunstHaus Wien (*map*D3*), another Hundertwasser project, is just three blocks away at Untere Weißgerberstr. 13. The house is a museum devoted to the architect's graphic art (see Museums below); it's worth a visit just for a walk on the uneven floors and a drink of *Melange* in the terrace café (open 10am-midnight; use the entrance on Weißgerberlände after museum hours). True Hundertwasser fanatics may want to check out the **Müllbrennerei** (incinerator) visible from the U-4 and U-6 lines to "Heiligenstadt." This is a huge jack-in-the-box of a trash dump, with a high smokestack topped by a golden disco ball.

The **Karl-Marx-Hof,** XIX, Heiligenstädterstr. 82-92, is also properly dedicated to state-sponsored productivity; you must see this mammoth building to appreciate the scale of public housing projects during the Austrian Social Democratic Republic, from 1919 to 1934. This ¾-mi.-long complex encompasses over 1600 apartments, with community space and interior courtyards to garnish the urban-commune atmosphere. The Social Democrats used this Hof as their stronghold during the civil war of 1934, until army artillery broke the resistance down. Take U-Bahn U-4 or U-6 to the end station at "Heiligenstadt."

Museums

Art in Vienna until the 19th century reflected the many styles and nationalities that mingled in the imperial capital. From the Metternich regime onwards, art became a medium for political expression, either belonging to a movement with unified and directed intent, or directly confronting the ruling movement of the day. **Biedermeier** art reflects the repression and censorship of the Metternich years. The **Ringstraße** credo of monumental historical forms was, in some ways, an attempt to bestow a false strength and beauty on Vienna to cover the growing political disorder. The **Secession** seceded from just that tradition, and devoted itself to art of flowing Jugendstil ambiguity. The **Rot Wien** ethic was a full retreat to the security of socialism; artists responded to the excesses of Secession fluidity by reverting to practical, concrete geometric forms. All of these distinctly Viennese schools, and many other styles culled from myriad nations and epochs, await in Vienna's world-class assortment of exceptional museums.

Art Museums

Kunsthistorisches Museum (Museum of Fine Arts; *map*B4*), across the Burgring from the Heldenplatz. Home to one of the world's most amazing art collections, including entire rooms of prime works by Brueghel, Rembrandt, Rubens, Titian, Dürer, and Velázquez, as well as Caravaggio's famed *Madonna of the Rosary* and Vermeer's *Allegory of Painting*. Cellini's famous golden salt cellar is here, along with a superb collection of ancient art and a stolen Egyptian burial chamber. Gustav Klimt decorated the lobby; his mural characteristically employs various female figures to chronicle artistic progress from the Classical era to the 19th century. Painted before his break with the Künstlerhaus, the mural is a fine example of the artist's early historicist style. Open Tues.-Fri. 10am-6pm, Sat.-Sun. 9am-6pm; Nov.-March Tues.-Fri. 10am-4pm, Sat.-Sun. 9am-4pm. Admission 95AS, students and seniors 45AS. Another **branch** of the museum resides in the Neue Hofburg, at the eastern end of the Heldenplatz; the collection includes the antique instruments that Viennese virtuosi used to hone their skills. Their assemblage of arms and armor is the second-largest in the world.

Austrian Gallery (in the Belvedere Palace; *map*C4-5*), III, Prinz-Eugen-Str. 27, behind Schwarzenbergplatz. The collection is split into two parts. The **Upper Belvedere** (built in 1721-22 by Hildebrandt) houses Austrian Art of the 19th and 20th centuries. Especially well represented are Waldmüller, Makart, Schiele, Kokoschka, and Klimt (whose gilded masterpiece, *The Kiss,* has enthralled visitors for just under a century). Also check out the breathtaking views of the city from the upper floors. Use the same ticket to enter the **Lower Belvedere,** where the **Baroque Museum** has an extensive collection of sculptures by Donner, Maulbertsch, and Messerschmidt (his *Schnabelkopf* will make you smile in decadent disgust). The Lower Belvedere also cradles the **Museum of Medieval Austrian Art;** Romanesque and Gothic sculptures and altarpieces abound. Both Belvederes open Tues.-Sun. 10am-5pm. Admission 60 AS, students 30 AS.

Museum Moderner Kunst (Museum of Modern Art; *map*B2*) in the Liechtenstein Palace, IX, Fürstengasse 1. Take streetcar D from the Ring (direction: "Nußdorf") to "Fürstengasse." These are the same Liechtensteins who own that tiny country near France. They still hold the deed to this palace and another inside the First *Bezirk*, as well as others throughout the country. The manicured garden *Schloß,* surrounded by a manicured garden, boasts a superb collection of 20th-century masters, including Klimt's *Portrait of Adele Bloch-Bauer*. Alliterative commentators have quipped "*Mehr Blech als Bloch*" (More tin—colloquially "rubbish"—than Bloch) in response to Klimt's liberal use of metallic pigments in this painting; through his exquisite textures, Klimt transforms his subject into a figment of her auspicious husband's wealth. The museum also features Egon Schiele's *Portrait of Eduard Kosmack*, a Picasso *Harlequin*, and various Magrittes, Légers, and Ernsts. Open Wed.-Mon. 10am-6pm. Admission 28AS.

Secession Building (*map*B4*), I, Friedrichstr. 12 (on the western side of Karlsplatz). Once, it was the stronghold of the Secession program; today, the malleable exhibition space shows works by sundry contemporary artists. Klimt's **Beethoven Frieze** still anchors the collection—this 30m-long work is Klimt's visual interpretation of Beethoven's *Ninth Symphony*. A series of streamlined scenes depict humanity's weaknesses and desires, but conclude triumphantly with a couple embracing amidst a chorus of angels. See sights: Outside the Ringstraße above. Open Tues.-Fri. 10am-6pm, Sat.-Sun. 10am-4pm. Admission 20AS, 10AS for Frieze only.

Österreichisches Museum für Angewandte Kunst (Austrian Museum of Applied Art; *map*C3*), I, Stubenring 5 (tel. 711 36). Take U-Bahn U-3 or U-4 to "Landstraße." The oldest museum of applied arts in Europe. Otto Wagner furniture and Klimt sketches sit amidst crystal, china, furniture, and rugs dating from the Middle Ages to the present. Don't miss Josef Engelhart's exquisite *art nouveau* fireplace depicting Adam, Eve, and their serpentine tormentor, who winds seductively below the mantle. Open Wed.-Mon. 11am-6pm. Last entry 5:30pm. Admission 30AS, students 15AS.

KunstHaus Wien (*map*D3*), III, Untere Weißgerberstr. 13. A Hundertwasser project, just 3 blocks to the left of the Hundertwasser Haus. Opened in 1991, the interior of this building is open to the public, along with a permanent collection of Hundertwasser graphic art and various temporary international exhibits. Open daily 10am-7pm. Admission for the Hundertwasser exhibition 50 AS, students 40 AS.

Albertina (*map*BC3-4*), I, Augustinerstr. 1, behind the Opera House. Named for Duke Albert of Saxony-Techsen, the husband of Princess Maria Christina (Maria Theresa's favorite daughter). Houses the **Collection of Graphic Arts,** one of the most comprehensive in the world. With a collection dating from the 15th century, this museum boasts 200,000 original etchings and prints and 20,000 drawings and watercolors, including works by da Vinci, Raphael, Michelangelo, Rubens, and Rembrandt. Many of the best known works, however, are facsimiles. Open Mon.-Tues. and Thurs. 10am-4pm, Wed. 10am-6pm, Fri. 10am-2pm, Sat.-Sun. 10am-1pm; July-Aug Mon.-Sat. only. Admission 30 AS. Also in the Albertina is the **Austrian Film Museum,** which shows classic and avante-garde films of historical significance. Open Oct.-May Mon.-Sat. 6pm and 8pm.

Akademie Der Bildenen Kunst (Academy of Fine Arts; *map*B4*), I, Schillerplatz 3, near Karlsplatz. Designed in 1876 by Hansen, famed for the Parlament, Musikverein, and Börse. The building has a collection that contains Hieronymus Bosch's *Last Judgment* and works by a score of Dutch painters, including Rubens. Open Tues. and Thurs.-Fri. 10am-2pm, Wed. 10am-1pm and 3-6pm, Sat.-Sun. 9am-1pm. Admission 30 AS, students 15 AS.

Other Collections

Schloß Schönbrunn, the painfully yellow Habsburg summer residence. The building holds the **Wagenburg** (coach collection), displaying the coronation carriage and the imperial hearse. The palace tour brings you to the **Bergl** rooms, where frescoes of peacocks perched on rose bushes create the impression of a refined royal jungle. Tours July-Sept. 8:30am-5:30pm, April-June and Oct. 8:30am-5pm, Nov.-March 9am-4pm. Admission 50 AS, students 20 AS.

Museum für Völkerkunde (Ethnology Museum; *map*B3-4*), across the Ring in the Neue Burg on Heldenplatz. Exhibitions present civilizations outside Europe, especially African and South American, dating to the 1600s. Open Mon. and Wed.-Sun. 10am-4pm.

Naturhistorisches Museum (Natural History Museum; *map*B4*), across from the Kunsthistorisches Museum. Displays the usual animalia and decidedly unusual giant South American beetles and dinosaur skeletons. Open Mon. and Wed.-Sun. 9am-6pm; in winter, first floor only 9am-3pm.

Sigmund Freud Haus Museum (*map*B2*), XIX, Berggasse 19, near the Votivkirche. Take U-Bahn U-3 to "Schottentor." This meager museum, where a cigar is just a cigar, was Freud's home from 1891 until the Anschluß. Almost all of Freud's original belongings moved with him out of the country. Even the patients' couch is now in London—you decide if that *means* anything. Open daily 9am-3pm. Admission 60 AS, students 40 AS.

Historisches Museum der Stadt Vienna (Historical Museum of the City of Vienna; *map*C4*), IV, Karlsplatz 5, to the left of the Karlskirche. This museum has a collection of historical artifacts and paintings that document the city's evolution from the Roman Vindobona encampment through 640 years of Habsburg rule to the present. Memorial rooms to Loos and Grillparzer, plus temporary exhibitions on different Viennese themes that clarify the history of the former imperial capital. Open Tues.-Sun. 9am-4:30pm. Admission 30 AS, students 10 AS.

Gardens and Parks

Gardens, parks, and forests are common Viennese attractions, brightening the urban landscape with scattered patches of greenery. Post-World War II plots of land in sections of the 14th, 16th, and 19th districts were distributed to citizens short on food, to let them grow their own vegetables; although the shortage is long gone, these community *Gärten* still exist, marked by the small huts of the original beneficiaries. The city's primary public gardens were opened and maintained by Habsburgs throughout the last four centuries, but the many palace gardens became public property only recently. Especially noteworthy are the gardens of **Schloß Schönbrunn, Palais Belvedere,** and the **Augarten.** These three precisely groomed Baroque wonders have admirably preserved the intentions of their 18th-century landscapers.

Palatial Gardens

The **Schönbrunner Schloßpark** (XIII, behind the palace) covers almost three-quarters of a square mile. Its symmetrical paths reveal a fantasia of imperial delights. One pathway leads to the **Roman ruins,** home of the **Wiener Kammeroper** summer performances. Another wanders to the **Schöner Brunnen** fountain, built over a natural spring. The **Gloriette** is perhaps the most glorious landmark of the Habsburg reign; this huge Neoclassical archway sits atop the hill, framed by fountains, curving paths, and trees rising from the main garden. From the arch, a monument to the Austrian victory over Prussia at the Battle of Kolin (1757), Maria Theresa surveyed her imperial city on hot summer days. The view is astounding, spanning the palace, Western Vienna, the Kahlenberg, and the Wienerwald. Schönbrunn's **zoo** (*Tiergarten*) is down the slope and to the left of the Gloriette. The complex was designed and built in 1752 for Maria Theresa's husband, Emperor Franz Stephan. Many of the older buildings—such as the octagonal pavilion at the center—still exist, but the animals live largely in more modern, natural accommodations. (Open May-Sept. 9am-6:30pm; April 9am-6pm; March 9am-5:30pm; Feb. and Oct. 9am-5pm; Nov.-Jan. 9am-4:30pm. Admission 60 AS, students 25 AS, ages 5-12 15 AS.)

Belvedere Palace (*map*C4*), III, off Rennweg and behind Schwarzenbergplatz, was built in the early 18th century by Johann Lukas von Hildebrandt for Prince Eugene of Savoy, the renowned conqueror of the Turks. Prince Eugene used Belvedere as his summer palace, and his beautiful Baroque garden stretches between the **Upper Belvedere** (home to the Austrian Gallery) and the **Lower Belvedere** (home to the Baroque Museum). The garden is built on a slight grade and is designed with wide walkways, terraces, and fountains. Also in the area are the **Botanical Gardens,** containing thousands of rare plants, and the **Alpine Garden,** a rock garden liberally sprinkled with plants from Alpine Europe. (Both of these gardens are open only in summer.)

The **Augarten** (*map*C1-2*), II, Obere Augartenstr., is the oldest extant Baroque garden in Austria; it was commissioned by Kaiser Josef II in the 17th century as a gift to the citizens of Vienna. Children play soccer on the lawns between flowers, and various athletic facilities (including a swimming pool and tennis courts) were opened in 1940. Of interest in the Augarten are the **Vienna China Factory,** founded in 1718, and the **Augarten Palace,** residence of the Vienna Boys' Choir. You can't miss the **Flakturm,** a daunting concrete tower constructed as an armory for the Nazis during World War II. This structure, and other similar creations in parks around the city, were so sturdily constructed that demolition would require hazardous explosives; the Austrian state has decided, instead, to let them stand as sad memorials to the country's intimate relationship with the Third Reich. To reach the park, take streetcar N (direction: "Friederich-Engels-Platz") from "Schwedenplatz" to "Obere Augartenstraße" and walk to the left down Taborstr.

By the Danube

The **Danube** provides a number of recreational possibilities northeast of the city. The recurrent floods became problematic once settlers moved outside the city walls, so the Viennese stretch of the Danube was restructured from 1870 to 1875, then again from 1972 to 1987. This generated recreational areas, such as new tributaries (including the **Alte Donau** and the **Donaukanal**) and the **Donauinsel,** a thin slab of island, stretching for kilometers. The Donauinsel is devoted to bicycle paths, swimming, barbecue areas, boat rental, and summer restaurants, and is ideal for a romantic evening stroll. Take U-bahn U-1 (direction: "Kagran") to "Donauinsel" or "Alte Donau."

The **Prater,** extending southeast from the Wien-Nord Bahnhof, is a notoriously touristed amusement park that functioned as a private game reserve for the Imperial Family until 1766. The park is squeezed into a riparian woodland between the Donaukanal and the river proper; it boasts ponds and meadows and is composed of various rides, arcades, restaurants, and casinos (entry to the complex is free, but each attraction charges admission). The most famed Prater feature is the **Riesenrad** (Giant Ferris Wheel), which dominates the northeastern skyline and enjoys a cameo role in Carol Reed's postwar thriller, *The Third Man.* This wheel of fortune *par excellence* is cherished by locals as one of the more obscure city symbols. At night, the Prater becomes a hotbed of prostitution.

The Danube Canal branches into the tiny river **Wien** near the Ring; this sliver of a waterway extends to the southwest, past the Innere Stadt and Schloß Schönbrunn. First, however, the Wien, replete with ducks and lilies at its narrowest point, bisects the **Stadtpark** (City Park). Built in 1862, this was the first municipal park outside the former city walls. The sculpted vegetation provides a soothing counterpoint to the central bus station and Bahnhof Wien-Mitte, just yards away. (Take U-Bahn U-4 to "Stadtpark," or walk down Parkring.)

Along the Ring

Stroll clockwise around the Ring to reach the **Burggarten** (Gardens of the Imperial Palace; *map*B4*), a wonderfully-kept park with monuments to such Austrian notables as Emperor Franz Josef and Emperor Franz I. The **Babenberger Passage** (*map*B4*) leads from the Ring to the **Mozart Memorial** (1896; *map*B4*), which features Amadeus on a pedestal, surrounded by instrument-toting cherubs. In front of the statue is a lawn with a treble clef crafted of red flowers. Reserved for the imperial family and members of the court until 1918, the Burggarten is now a favorite for young lovers and lamentably hyperactive dogs.

The Heldenplatz, farther up the Ring, abuts the **Volksgarten** (*Fahrvergnügen*; *map*B3*), once the site of the Bastion Palace destroyed by Napoleon's order. Be sure to seek out the "Temple of Theseus," the monument to Austrian playwright Franz Grillparzer, and the **Dolphin Fountain.** This latter watery conduit was contributed by Fernkorn, a sculptor also renowned for his equestrian monuments to Prince Eugene and Archduke Karl. The Volksgarten's monument to Empress Elisabeth, assassinated in 1898 by an Italian anarchist, was designed by Hans Bitterlich. The throned empress casts a marmoreal glance on Friedrich Ohmann's goldfish pond. The most striking feature of this space, though, is the **Rose Garden,** populated by thousands of different rose species.

Suburban Plots

South of the city, the **Zentralfriedhof** (Central Cemetery), XI, Simmeringer Hauptstr. 234, is the place to pay respects to a favorite departed Viennese composer. The second gate (**Tor II**) leads to the graves of Beethoven, Wolf, Strauss, Lanner, Schönberg, Moser, and an honorary monument to Mozart. Amadeus's true final resting place is an unmarked mass paupers' grave in the **Cemetery of St. Mark,** III, Leberstr. 6-8 (Zentralfriedhof open May-July daily 7am-7pm; March-April and Sept.-Oct. daily 7am-6pm; Nov.-Feb. daily 8am-5pm). **Tor I** of the Zentralfriedhof leads to the **Jewish Cemetery** and Arthur Schnitzler's burial plot. Various structures erected throughout this portion of the burial grounds memorialize the millions slaughtered in Nazi death camps. The state of this section evinces the fate of Vienna's Jewish population—many of the headstones are cracked, broken, or lying prone and neglected. Since the 1940s, this section of the cemetery has become overgrown with weeds—the families of most of the dead are no longer in Austria to tend the graves. However, a youth group has recently dedicated itself to restoring the area. To reach the Zentralfriedhof, take streetcar #71 from "Schwarzenbergplatz" (35 min.).

West of the 13th *Bezirk* is the **Lainzer Tiergarten** (Lainz Game Preserve). Once an exclusive hunting preserve for the Habsburgs, this park is enclosed by a 15-mi. wall and has been a protected nature park since 1941. Wild animals (boar, deer, elk, buffalo?) roam the grounds freely. Aside from hiking paths, restaurants, and spectacular vistas, this park encloses the **Hermes Villa.** The complex was once a retreat for Empress Elisabeth, but has since been co-opted for exhibitions by the Historical Museum of the City of Vienna. Ride U-Bahn U-4 (direction: "Hütteldorf") to "Hietzing," change to streetcar #60 to "Hermesstraße," and then take bus #60B to "Lainzer Tor." (Open April-Nov. Wed.-Sun. 8am-sunset.)

The **Türkenschanz Park,** in the 18th *Bezirk,* attracts a plethora of leashed dachshunds bristling at the peacocks. The manicured garden is a wonderful pit-stop on the way up to the *Heurigen* of the 19th district. Find your way to the well-tended lawns through the entrance at the corner of Hasenauerstr. and Gregor-Mendel-Str.

Far to the south and west of Vienna sprawls the famous **Wienerwald** (Wally World). In this beautiful forest, an Austrian, Polish, and German force under Polish leadership decisively defeated invading Ottomans in 1683. In addition to the historical significance of the event—it marked the end of the Ottoman conquest—the lifting of the Siege of Vienna left two important culinary legacies. First, the *croissant,* baked to resemble the crescent symbol of the Ottoman Empire, was invented to celebrate the victory. Second, the Ottomans retreated in such a hurry that they left behind sacks of coffee, which fell into the hands of the Viennese. The beverage was a hit, and Vienna has been slightly high-strung ever since. Take streetcar #38S to the "Grinzing" terminus, and continue by bus #38A to "Kahlenberg," where you have a view of the city and the Danube; you can follow in Beethoven's footsteps by wandering into the woods on the well-marked trails.

ENTERTAINMENT

Music

It seems only natural, with such a long list of virtuosi (Haydn, Mozart, Beethoven, Schubert, Mahler, Liszt, and Schönberg, to name just a few), that Vienna is known as the capital city of classical music. Every Austrian child must learn an instrument during his or her schooling, and the **Konservatorium** and **Hochschule** are world-renowned for the high quality of tneir musical instruction.

Opera, still one of Vienna's main attractions, is accessible to the budget traveler throughout the year. Standing room (*Stehplätze*) tickets for the **Staatsoper** (*map*C4*), at the intersection of Kärntner Str. and the Ring, are available on the day of performance. Get in line early at the entrance on Operngasse, on the western side of the Opera House, to get tickets for the center—you'll see nothing standing at the side. The tickets for standing room go on sale three hours before a performance, so be prepared to camp out around 3:30 or 4pm for a 7pm show. The standard protocol, after buying a ticket, is to go immediately and save a place by tying a scarf on the rail. (Standing-room tickets 15 AS for balcony, 20 AS for orchestra.) Costlier advance tickets (100-850 AS) go on sale three weeks before performance and are available at the **Bundestheaterkassen** (*map*C4*), I, Goethegasse (tel. 514 44 22). They also sell tickets for the three other public theaters: the **Volksoper, Burgtheater,** and **Akademietheater** (open Mon.-Fri. 8am-6pm, Sat. 9am-2pm, Sun. 9am-noon). The Volksoper shows Viennese operas and operettas; the other two feature classic dramas in German. Discount tickets go on sale 30 minutes before performance, at the individual theater box offices (50-400 AS, under 27 50 AS). **Horse and carriage rides** are available around the Ring from behind the Staatsoper, to journey home from a performance in style; agree on a price with the driver beforehand—a 40-minute ride can cost as much as 800 AS.

The **Wiener Philharmoniker** (Vienna Philharmonic Orchestra; *map**AB4*) is known worldwide for its excellence; regular performances take place in the **Musikverein** (*map**C4*), I, Dumbastr. 3, on the northeast side of Karlsplatz. The Philharmoniker also play at every Staatsoper production. Tickets to Philharmoniker concerts are mostly available on a subscription basis, so the box office of the Musikverein normally has few tickets for sale. Write to the "Gesellschaft der Musikfreunde, Dumbastr. 20, A-1010 Wien" for more information.

The **Wiener Sängerknaben (Vienna Boys' Choir)** is perhaps the most famous and beloved musical attraction in town. The lads perform Sundays at 9:15am from September to June in the **Burgkapelle** (Royal Chapel; *map**BC3-4*), the oldest section of the Hofburg. Reserve tickets at least two months in advance; write to the "Verwaltung der Hofmusikkapelle, Hofburg, Schweizerhof, A-1010 Wien." Do not enclose money. Tickets may be picked up at the Burgkapelle on the Friday before Mass from 11am to noon, or on the Sunday of the Mass by 9am. Unreserved seats go on sale from 5pm on the preceding Friday, with a maximum of two tickets per person. **Standing room is free.** Sunday High Masses in the major churches (Augustinerkirche, Michaelerkirche, Stephansdom) are accompanied by (free) choral or organ music that approaches the celestial.

The Sängerknaben and the four Bundestheater (see above) vacation during July and August, but music lovers will still find plenty to do during the summer season. The **Wiener Kammeroper** (Chamber Opera) performs Mozart during the summer in the Schönbrunner Schloßpark (near the Roman ruins). Orchestral concerts can be heard in the **Arkadenhof** (*map**BC3-4*), the courtyard inside the **Rathaus** (July-Aug. Tues.-Thurs. at 8pm. Admission 120 AS.) In front of the building, films of great conductors performing classical favorites play daily in the flower-filled **Rathausplatz;** depending on the weather, films begin after sunset late June to July. The Staatsoper and Volkstheater will host the annual **"Jazzfest Wien"** during the first weeks of July in 1994, featuring such artists as Ray Charles, Bill Selig, Herbie Hancock, Manhattan Transfer, and Los Lobos. **Open-air jazz concerts** are also held at the **Museumsquartier** at the Messepalast behind Maria-Theresien-Platz. Discount tickets are available for students after June 1 from the **Tageskasse,** I, Friedrich-Schmidt-Platz 1, Mon.-Fri. 10am-6pm. Also try *Jugend-Info Wien* (see Tourist Information above), or pick up a brochure on *Wiener Musiksommer* from the tourist office for concert and discount ticket information.

Theater

In the past few years, Vienna has made a name for itself as a city of musicals, with productions of West End and Broadway favorites such as *Phantom of the Opera* and *Les Miserables.* The **Theatre an der Wien** (*map**B4*), VI, Linke Wienzeile 6 (tel. 588 30 265) once produced musicals of a different sort; this 18th-century edifice hosted the premieres of works such as Beethoven's *Fidelio* and Mozart's *Magic Flute.* The nobility found that Mozart had crossed the line of good taste by composing an opera in German (such an *ugly* language), so they blocked the scheduled premiere—the masterpiece was finally performed in the Theatre an der Wien. The peasants were thrilled, because they could finally understand the plot. The theater now houses contemporary productions, such as *Elisabeth,* a dramatization of the life of Empress Elisabeth, wife of Franz Josef, the last true Austrian Emperor. (Performances Mon.-Tues. and Thurs.-Sun. 7:30pm; 100-990 AS.)

English-language drama is offered at **Vienna's English Theatre** (*map**A3*), VIII, Josefsgasse 12 (tel. 402 12 60 or 42 82 84; box office open Mon.-Sat. 10am-6pm, evening box office opens at 7pm; tickets 150-420AS, students 100AS on night of performance), and at the **International Theater** (*map**B2*), IX, Porzellangasse 8 (tel. 31 62 72; tickets 220AS, under 26 120AS). Look for the posters around the city. Films subtitled in English usually play at: **Schottenring Kino** (*map**BC2-3*), I, Schottenring 5 (tel. 34 52 36); **Burg Kino** (*map*BC4*), I, Opernring 19 (tel. 587 84 06; last show usually around 8:30pm, Sat. around 11pm; tickets 55-80AS); **Top Kino** (*map*AB4*), VI, Rahlgassel, at the intersection with Gumpendorferstr. (tel. 587 55 57; open Sun.-Thurs. 3pm-10:30pm, Fri.-Sat. 3pm-midnight; tickets 50-80AS); and **De France** (*map*B2*), IX, at the intersection of Hohenstaufengasse and Mariatheresienstr., two minutes from the Schottenring subway stop.

Heurigen (Wine Gardens)

Vienna is almost as famous for its *Heurigen* as for its art and music. These traditional wine gardens typify the suburban Viennese state of mind; walk through the door under the sprig of fresh pine, sit outside at weatherbeaten picnic tables, and hoist a mug of house wine to celebrate whatever first comes to mind. The word *Heuriger* is derived from *Heujahr* (this year), which refers to the wine produced during the current year. By imperial dictate, Heuriger are only allowed to sell their current crop of wine on their own premises. This practice dates back to one of Empress Maria Theresa's seven children, Emperor Josef II; in a fit of noble largesse, he allowed local vintners to serve their wine in their homes at certain times of the year. Occasionally, you'll run across a *Buschenschank;* these wine gardens are similar to *Heurigen*, but (gasp!) may serve older wine as well.

The mood at the *Heurigen* is festive and informal; in most places, you can carry out food served at the indoor buffet or have a picnic (except at specially designated "restaurants," which serve food to your table). People don't drink to get drunk here—they *savor* the fruit of the vine. Most *Heurigen* are inhabited by aged and slightly drunk musicians who move among the tables playing *Schrammelmusik* (Austrian folk music) on the violin, accordion, and other folk instruments while locals sing along.

In the middle of the summer, Stürm (cloudy, unpasteurized wine) is available at the *Heurigen*; the drink is very sweet, but quite potent. At the end of August or the beginning of September in **Neustift am Wald,** now part of Vienna's 19th district, the Neustifter Kirtag mit Winzerumzug rampages through the wine gardens; local vintners march in a mile-long procession through town, carrying a large crown adorned with gilt nuts. After the **Feast of the Martins** on November 11, the wine remaining from last year's crop becomes "old wine," no longer proper to serve in the *Heurigen*; the Viennese do their best to spare it this fate by consuming the beverage in Herculean quantities before time's up. Grab a Martinigansl (goose) and a liter of wine to help the locals in their monumental task.

Heurigen freckle the northern, western, and southern Viennese suburbs, where the famous grapes are grown. **Grinzing** (in the 19th district; take U-Bahn U-4 or U-6 to the end station at "Heiligenstadt," then bus #38A to the end station at "Grinzing") is more renowned, but the atmosphere is more authentic in **Nußdorf** (streetcar D from the Ring), **Sievering, Neustift am Wald,** and **Salmannsdorf.** Ask the tourist office for its extensive list of *Heurigen.* Most are open daily 4pm-midnight. Wine costs about 30 AS per mug; informal dress is fine.

Franz Mayer am Pfarrplatz Beethovenhaus, XIX, Pfarrplatz 3. Take streetcar #37 to the last stop, walk down Wollergasse and through the park, take a right, and then make your first left on Pfarrplatz. Near the home of Beethoven, this *Heuriger* boasts one of the most festive atmospheres in Vienna.

Buschenschank Heinrich Niersche, XIX, Strehlgasse 21. Take bus #41A from the U-Bahn U-6 station "Währingerstraße/Volksoper" to "Pötzleindorfer Höhe"; walk one block and make a left on Strehlgasse. Hidden from tourists and therefore beloved by locals. Its beautiful garden overlooks the fields of Grinzing; low prices complete the relaxed atmosphere. Weiße G'spritzter (white wine with tonic water) 14 AS. Open Thurs.-Mon. 3pm-midnight.

Zum Krottenbach'l, XIX, Krottenbachstr. 148 (tel. 44 12 40). Take bus #35A (direction: "Salmannsdorf") from the U-Bahn U-6 "Nußdorferstraße" station to "Agnesgasse." With a terraced, multi-level garden next to a vineyard, this might be the most beautiful pub in Vienna. The tavern looks like a swiss chalet and offers a delicious hot and cold buffet. Weiße G'spritzter 17 AS. Open daily 3pm-midnight.

Sieveringer Kellerg'wölb, XIX, Sieveringer Str. (tel. 32 11 09). Take bus #39A from the U-Bahn U-4 or U-6 end station "Heiligenstadt" to "Karthauserstraße." The main building is recessed from the street—you have to walk through a gravel parking lot and a comfortable courtyard with wooden picnic tables to reach the house. The bright, L-shaped room is overseen by a friendly staff that dispenses the house wine, Grüne Veltliner; ¼-liter for 24 AS. Open Tues.-Sat. 4pm-midnight.

Weingut Heuriger Reinprecht, XIX, Cobenzlgasse 22 (tel. 32 14 71). Take U-Bahn U-4 or U-6 to "Heiligenstadt," then bus #38A to "Grinzing." This *Heuriger* is a fairy-tale stereotype—picnic tables as far as the eye can see under an ivy-laden trellis, with Schrammel musicians strolling from table to table. Although this is one of the more touristed establishments, don't be surprised to hear whole tables of nostalgic Austrians break into verse with the accordion. Note the incredible bottle-opener collection as you walk in. ¼-liter of red wine runs 30 AS. Open March-Nov. daily 3:30-midnight.

Nightlife

Younger visitors to Vienna commonly complain that the nightlife is deficient. The truth is, if you don't know where to look for it, Vienna's nightlife will seem quite elusive. But make no mistake—Vienna is a city that parties until dawn, even though the public transportation closes at midnight. There is a raging club scene every day of the week, and the changing themes in many discos allow almost everyone to find what he or she seeks. The "in" music of 1993 was 1970s disco and soul, "techno," house, and hip-hop; 1994 Vienna may see a surge in "grunge" rock following a short lag behind U.S. fad styles.

The pub scene is quite varied; some Viennese prefer quiet, intimate bars and cafés where they can schmooze, while others prefer the loud, crowded, and smoky *Lokalen,* where they can consume excellent beer in large quantities. Either way, be prepared to top the night off with a *Strudel* or a *Toast* at an all night *Beißl* or café before turning in.

Students tend to lose themselves in the swirling nightlife of the area known as the **Bermuda Dreieck** (Triangle; *map*C3*), the area northwest of Stephansplatz, bordered by Rotensturmstr. and Wipplingerstr. It is not unknown for visitors to the district to disappear from the outside world, only to resurface at dawn. A host of small bars and hangouts cluster here; you can sit at tables outside in the summer in what the Viennese call *Schanigärten.* The action moves indoors at 10pm, until 2am or even 4am. Other locals congregate in the region surrounding **Bäckerstraße** (*map*C3*), behind the Stephansdom. Here you will also find one nightspot after another, with wall-to-wall beer mugs. Bäckerstraße is where the underground surfaces to join the intellectuals in pondering empirical whatnot and whatnot theory. The **8th District** behind the university, is also a target area for thirsty night-owls.

The Innere Stadt

Benjamin (*map*C3*), I, Salzgries 11-13 (tel. 533 33 49). In the heart of the Bermuda Dreieck, this bar has 2 separate areas: on the left is the relaxed space where people drink with friends to the beat of soul and early-80s music. On the right is the rowdy section, with blaring rock music and beckoning bar stools. The student crowd drinks Kapsreiter beer (in the cool bottle, 34 AS) while chanting song lyrics in broken English. Open daily 7pm-2am.

Zwölf Apostellenkeller (*map*C3*), I, Sonnenfelsgasse 3, behind the *Stephansdom* (tel. 52 62 77). To reach this underground tavern, walk into the archway, take a right, go down the long staircase, and discover grottoes that date back to 1561. Arched brick and mortar support structures "round off" the ancient atmosphere. One of the best *Weinkeller* in Vienna, and a definite must for catacomb fans. The complex has many levels—the lowest is the liveliest. Beer 34 AS. Open Aug.-June daily 4:30pm-midnight.

Esterházykeller (*map**C3*), I, Haarhof 1, off Naglergasse (tel. 533 34 82). Perhaps the least expensive *Weinkeller* in Vienna; try the Grüner Veltliner wine from Burgenland (24 AS). Open Mon.-Fri. 10am-1pm and 4-9pm, Sat.-Sun. 4-9pm.

Santo Spirito (*map**C3*), I, Kampfgasse 7 (tel. 512 99 98). From Stephansplatz, walk down Singerstr. and make a left onto Kumpfgasse (5 min.). This bar will change your idea of classical music forever. Instead of blasting Falco, or even Ostbahn Kurti, the stereo here pumps out Rachmaninoff's second piano concerto while the excited patrons conduct along. Little busts on the wall pay homage to famous composers. Open daily 5pm-2am.

Jazzland (*map**C3*), I, Franz-Josefs-Kai 29 (tel. 533 25 75). Jazz music—Austrian style. Get there early to get a good seat. Cover 50-100 AS. Open Tues.-Sat. 7pm-2am.

Opus One (*map**C4*), I, Mahlerstr. 11 (tel. 513 20 75). More jazz. Cover 50-100 AS. Open daily 9:30pm-4am.

Outside the Ring

Fischerbräu, XIX, Billrothstr. 17 (tel. 31 962 64); see Restaurants above. The stained and lacquered hardwood interior and the leafy garden outside provide a comfortable and festive milieu in which to drink the homemade brew. Open Mon.-Sat. 4pm-1am, Sun. 11am-1am.

Europa (*map**B4*), VII, Zollergasse 8 (tel. 526 33 83); see Cafés above. Adorned with concert posters and funky light fixtures, the hip twenty-something crowd of Vienna hangs out here late at night on the way to further intoxication. Open daily 9am-4am.

Tunnel (*map**B3*), VIII, Florianigasse 39 (tel. 42 34 65); see Restaurants above. Frequented by students for the bohemian, Euro-chic atmosphere and live music (daily from 8:30, cover 30-100 AS, Mon. free). The upper level holds a regular bar/restaurant with a plethora of drinks and food. Open daily 9am-2am.

Donau (*map**AB3*), VII, Karl Schweighofergasse 10 (tel. 93 81 05). From the U-Bahn U-2 "Babenbergerstraße" station, walk up Mariahilferstr. and take the first right (3 min.). Hip-hop and techno music keep the energy high, while the student crowd grooves on the dance floor or poses at the bar. Prepare to be checked out by the eclectic masses. Open daily 8pm-4am.

Roxy (*map**BC4*), IV, Operngasse 24 (tel. 587 26 75), 1 block from Karlsplatz. Opened in 1993, this bar/club is already a huge hit with the retro-crowd. Soul, funk, and 70s disco are the staples of this dark and stylish disco, where a red light has supplanted the disco ball. No cover. Open daily 9pm-4am.

Discos and Dance Clubs

U-4, XII, Schönbrunnerstr. 222 (tel. 85 83 18). Around the corner from the U-Bahn U-4 "Meidling Hauptstraße" stop. In earlier days, this was *the* disco in Vienna, and it's still very crowded after about 1am. The two separate dance areas, slide shows, and dancer's cage provide necessary variety. Rotating theme nights please a varied clientele. Tues.: Rock 'n Roll. Thurs.: Gay men night. Sat: Hip-hop. Sun: Soul and disco. Cover 50 AS. Open daily 11pm-5am.

Volksgarten (*map**B3*), I, Burgring/Heldenplatz (tel. 63 05 18). Nestled on the edge of the Volksgarten Park, this huge club has 2 levels and comfy red couches placed so wallflowers can watch the Viennese shake their *hintern.* The club has a retractable ceiling, so you can dance under the stars. The best nights are Mon. ("Soul Seduction") and Fri. ("Reggae Night"). Cover 80 AS. Open Mon. and Fri.-Sat. 10pm-5am, Thurs. 7pm-5am.

Titanic (*map**AB4*), VI, Theobaldgasse 11 (tel. 587 47 58). From the U-Bahn U-2 "Babenbergerstraße" station, walk up Mariahilferstr. and take the third left. Once you get past the fashion-conscious doorman, you'll find a number of interconnected rooms with bodies undulating to hip-hop and techno. The café upstairs sports a casual atmosphere. No cover. Open Sun.-Thurs. 6pm-2am, Fri.-Sat. 6pm-4am.

P1 (*map**C3*), I, Rotgasse 3, 2 blocks north of the Stephansdom (tel. 535 99 95). A younger crowd dances the night away to techno music, before or after visiting the plentiful bars and pubs in the neighboring Bermuda Dreieck. Open Mon.-Thurs. 9pm-4am, Fri.-Sat. 9pm-5am.

Bisexual, Gay, and Lesbian Cafés and Clubs

For recommendations, support, or just to make contacts, call or stop by the **Rosa Lila Villa** (see Practical Information above). The helpful staff can give you lists of events, clubs, cafés, and discos (available in English). They also sponsor *Frauenfeste* (women's festivals) four times per year; ask for details on the program and dates (open Mon.-Fri. 5-8pm).

Certain Viennese locales have become more recognized meeting places for homosexuals, though very few are exclusively so. These include the Albertinapassage, Opernpassage, Babenbergerpassage, Esterhazypark, Karlsplatzpassage, Staatsoper, Rathauspark, Schweizer Garten, St. Augustin, Venedifer Au, and Waldmüllerpark. In some Viennese clubs, "darkrooms" are set up specifically for casual liaisons.

Café Willendorf (*map*B4*), VI, Linke Wienzeile 102, in the Rosa Lila Villa (tel. 587 17 89). A café, bar, and restaurant with an outdoor terrace. Open daily 7pm-2am.

Frauencafé (*map*A3*), VIII, Langegasse 11 (tel. 43 37 54). For women only. Reading terrace has several lesbian newspapers and magazines. Open Mon.-Sat. 7pm-1am, Sun. 10:30am-3pm; in summer, Mon.-Sat. 8pm-1am.

Why Not (*map*C3*), I, Tiefer Graben 22 (tel. 535 11 88). A relaxed bar/disco for men. "Mann intim" Wed. 11pm-3am. Karaoke Sun. 11pm-3am. Open Fri.-Sat. 11pm-5am. Women only one Thurs. per month, 11pm-3am.

Eagle Bar (*map*AB4*), VI, Blümelgasse 1 (tel. 587 26 61). A bar for men. Diverse clientele from within the leather and/or denim set. Open Mon.-Thurs. and Sun. 8pm-4am, Fri.-Sat. 9pm-4am.

Nightshift (*map*AB4*), VI, Corneliusgasse 8 (tel. 586 23 37). A bar for men. Open Sun.-Thurs. 9pm-4am, Fri.-Sat. 9pm-5am.

Clubhouse Wiener Freizeit (*map*B5*), V, Franzengasse 2. A hangout for both gays and lesbians. Fri. and Sat. night: disco. Open Tues.-Thurs. 8pm-4am, Fri.-Sat. 8pm-5am.

U-4, XII, Schönbrunnerstr. 222 (tel. 85 83 18); see Discos above. Thurs. nights are "Gay Heavens Night," 11pm-4am.

Festivals (Feste)

New Year's Day is celebrated with a huge feast and dancing throughout the streets of the Innere Stadt. Midnight is marked by Johann Strauss's *Blue Danube Waltz,* the unofficial Austrian anthem. Instead of lighting firecrackers, some sublimate their pyrotechnical yen into food for the Third World, through a campaign called "Bread Instead" (Brot statt Böller). A map and a program of events are published in the daily newspapers. **Pummerin,** at 21 tons, the second-largest bell in the world, tolls in the north tower of the Stephansdom to inaugurate the new year. Cast from the iron of Turkish cannon, the original Pummerin rang for the first time in 1712 at the coronation of Emperor Karl VI, father of Empress Maria Theresa. In 1945, as St. Stephen's burned just before the end of World War II, the bell crashed to the ground and was smashed to pieces. The New Year's **concert** by the Vienna Philharmonic Orchestra, a tradition since the 18th century, is broadcast the following morning by the ÖRF (Austrian Broadcasting Corporation). In the countryside, the Viennese music is performed by New Year's fiddlers and brass bands.

During the first two weeks of December, an exhibition of **Christmas crèches** is arranged in the crypt of St. Peter's. Old and new Nativity scenes are included—the new creations result from the efforts of the "Society of the Friends of the Christmas Crèche," which encourages people to make their own displays. On **Christmas** (Christtag), most institutions are closed. The traditional **Christkindlmarkt** invades the Rathausplatz with tinsel and overpriced *Kitsch*—remember those little glass balls you shake to see snow flurries? Wander through the square to window-shop, and warm your heart with some of the hot (spiked) punch.

THE CZECH REPUBLIC

US$1	**= 28.6 koruny (kčs)**	**10 kčs =**	**US$0.35**
CDN$1	**= 21.5 kčs**	**10 kčs =**	**CDN$0.46**
UK£1	**= 43.6 kčs**	**10 kčs =**	**UK£0.22**
IR£1	**= 40.8 kčs**	**10 kčs =**	**IR£0.25**
AUS$1	**= 18.5 kčs**	**10 kčs =**	**AUS$0.54**
NZ$1	**= 15.5 kčs**	**10 kčs =**	**NZ$0.64**
SAR1	**= 8.47 kčs**	**10 kčs =**	**SAR1.18**
DM1	**= 17.6 kčs**	**10 kčs =**	**DM0.57**
SK1	**= 0.88 kčs**	**10 kčs =**	**SK11.4**
AS1	**= 2.51 kčs**	**10 kčs =**	**AS3.99**
FT1	**= 0.31 kčs**	**10 kčs =**	**FT32.4**

Country Code: 42 **International Dialing Prefix: 00**

New Year's Day 1993 saw the dissolution of a haphazard partnership, established in the post-war tumult of 1918; on that day, the independent Czech and Slovak Republics subsumed former Czechoslovakia. The two regions were never close friends, but they parted fond acquaintances. Indeed, the division was a peaceful and orderly resolution of nationalist and ethnic tensions, virtually unimaginable in the New World Disorder. The Czech Republic now comprises Bohemia and Moravia, the cradle of a German-speaking intellectual culture that nurtured artists such as Rilke, Kafka and Dvořák. The mountains in the east form a natural border that divides the Czech Republic from Slovakia, a region manacled for centuries as an Austro-Hungarian fiefdom.

The notion of self-determination in the budding Czech Republic is a new concept; from the Holy Roman Empire to the Nazis and the Soviets, foreign powers have dictated the country's internal affairs. The 1960s witnessed a flourish of Democratic Socialism under Alexander Dubček, which culminated in the so-called "Prague Spring." In 1968 the Soviet Union put an end to the thaw with the iron rumble of tanks. After a 21-year winter under the Soviet puppet government of Gustav Husák, Czechoslovakia blossomed quietly and exuberantly in the Velvet Revolution of 1989. Czechs and Slovaks rallied in enormous demonstrations against the Communist government, which unilaterally stepped down under the force of the popular sentiment.

The natural successor was political activist and playwright Václav Havel, who led the anti-Communist dissident movement, founded the human-rights group Charter 77, and then emerged from prison to stage-manage the revolution before assuming the mantle of president. Though his dramas speak passionately against totalitarianism, Havel-as-president was criticized for his leniency toward former Party members and the secret police and the hesitant caution of his conversion to a market-oriented economy.

The rapid Communist industrialization of previously agricultural Slovakia made the region tragically dependent on outdated and ecologically unsound factories and heavy industry, and the continuing Prague-oriented centrism of Czechoslovakia's intellectual and political life left Slovaks feeling underrepresented and underappreciated—an uneasy federation, at best. After more than three quarters of a century of relatively unabrasive coexistence, the Czech and Slovak republics suddenly faced the brink of dissolution. Slovaks voiced their growing discontent by supporting anti-union/pro-independence candidate Vladimir Meciar in the heated elections of 1992, and on July 20, President Václav Havel left office, anticipating what he termed the "historical necessity" of the country's dissolution.

Today, Havel is back in power in the wholly autonomous Czech Republic; the poet-playwright-politician-humanitarian enjoys the enthusiastic support of most Czech citizens. He leads the country in a steady current of Westernization, and the people—numb by now to reform and transformation—are content to tag along for the ride. To most Czechs, the changes seem natural consequences of freedom, and few harbor deep regrets. No notable sentiments for Moravian separatism have surfaced, and there's little cause for alarm that the Czech Republic will go the way of the mad ethnic carnage in the former Yugoslavia. The Czech nation seems to understand the difference between nationalistic pride and fanatic aggression. Not surprisingly, few Czechs miss the Soviet dominance. Many are chomping at the bit to Westernize, trying economically and socially to recover as soon as possible from the Communist debacle.

Czech culture has also been regenerated of late; most of the region's contributions in the past had been co-opted in the name of the ruling central European regime. The language was all but dead for many years under a hegemonic German influence—German was spoken by everyone except the lowest strata of society. All but the most common words fell out of use and were lost, until a 19th-century resurgence of Czech nationalism. The Austro-Hungarian Empire, and then the Soviets, linguistically stormed the country; now that the republic is occupied only by the Czechs, the Slav alphabet is swiftly replacing any lingering Cyrillic. Czech national heroes include the composers Smetana and Dvořák, the first Czech president Masaryk, and the pioneers who revived the language. The name Kafka is ubiquitous in Prague; at least a dozen buildings graced by his presence proudly display their tenuous connection. This enthusiasm is somewhat misleading and is aimed primarily at tourists; Kafka wrote in German, and his works were banned from translation into Czech until the Velvet Revolution. Before then, most Czechs had never heard of him—he's hardly the Czech Twain you'd expect from all the hype.

Many tourists only delve into the Czech Republic as far as the Prague city line. Prague is a metropolis akin to New York—certainly a nexus of culture and industry, but hardly representative of the entire country. An itinerary devoted entirely to Prague would lead to an incomplete view of the Czech Republic as a whole. Consider visiting some of the cities listed in the Near Prague section. They certainly beat Long Island and the Jersey Turnpike.

Essentials

The importance of **Čedok,** the official state tourist company and a relic of centralized communist bureaucracy, has largely diminished since the 1989 revolution. **CKM,** its junior affiliate, remains helpful for the student and budget traveler by serving as a clearinghouse for youth hostel beds and by issuing ISIC and HI cards. The quality and trustworthiness of private tourist agencies varies; use your instincts. **Information offices** in major cities provide heaps of printed matter on sights and cultural events as well as lists of hostels and hotels. City maps (*plán mésta*) are available for almost all tourist destinations (19-45 kčs).

There is no longer any mandatory foreign **currency exchange** requirement, but keep a couple of exchange receipts in order to change money back upon leaving. Still in operation, the **black market** for hard cash is graying around the temples; because the official exchange rate has almost reached street levels, it is hardly worth the risk. Bring some western currency in small denominations—it's still the preferred payment in larger hotels and private accommodations in larger cities. Banks are generally open from 7am to 3pm. Czech money is no longer valid in Slovakia.

Shopping in the Czech Republic inevitably culminates at the world-class crystal crafted in Bohemia. Less fragile souvenir items are the fine lace and wood-carved crafts that typify the country's folk art. Be sure to bring your own film, batteries and feminine hygiene supplies.

The country's **climate** ranges from relatively mild winters (about 30°F or -1°C) to warm summers that average 70°F or 21°C. **Crime** has climbed dramatically since the 1989 revolution; be especially aware of snatch-and-run purse thieves and pickpockets. Yes, Virginia, there is a moral code: lost wallets and purses sometimes appear at embassies with only the cash missing. In **emergencies,** notify your embassy or consulate; local police may not be well versed in English. The **emergency phone number** throughout the country is **158.**

GETTING THERE AND GETTING AROUND

By Train

EastRail became valid in the Czech Republic in 1991, and Eurail may be accepted by 1994, pending approval from the powers-that-be. Because rail travel remains such a bargain (about 48 kčs per 100km on a second-class *rychlik* train), however, rail passes are less of a necessity here than in Western Europe. The fastest trains are the *expresný.* The *rychlík* trains cost as much as the express, while the few *spešný* (semi-fast) trains cost less; avoid *osobný* (slow) trains. **ČSD,** the national transportation company, publishes the monster *Jízdní řád* (train schedule, 74 kčs), helpful if only for the two-page English explanation in front. *Odjezd* (departures) are printed in train stations on yellow posters, *prijezd* (arrivals) on white. **Čedok** gives ISIC holders up to 50% off international tickets bought at their offices. If you're heading to **Austria** or **Hungary,** it's generally less expensive to buy a Czech ticket to the border, and then buy a separate ticket from the crossing to your destination once inside the foreign country. Seat reservations (*místenka,* 6 kčs) are required on almost all express and international trains, and for all first class seating; snag them at the counter labeled by a boxed "R." A slip of paper with the destination, time, date, and a capital letter "R" expedites the transaction. Be sure to have valid transit visas if you plan to go through Slovakia—or route your trip through red-tape-free Vienna instead.

By Bus and Thumb

Buses can be significantly faster and only slightly more expensive than trains, especially near Prague and for shorter distances; be sure to check the number of stops on your intended route. **ČSAD** runs national and international bus lines. From **Prague,** buses run a few times per week to Munich, Milan, and other international hubs; buses depart from **Brno** to **Linz,** in Austria. Consult the timetables posted at stations or buy your own bus schedule (25 kčs) from bookstores and newsstands.

Because of the inherent risks, *Let's Go* cannot recommend hitchhiking as a safe means of transportation. Hitchhikers find that hitching is popular in the Czech Republic, especially during the morning commuting hours (6-8am).

TEACHING ENGLISH

Native English-speakers, especially those willing to teach outside of Prague, have several conduits to land a position as an English teacher in the Czech Republic. The message board at the **American Hospitality Center** (see Prague: Tourist Offices) posts requests, as does the classified section of Prague's English-language newspaper, *Prognosis.* Also czech out the **Academic Information Agency,** nám. Max. Gorkého 26 (tel. (02) 26 70 10), in Prague. Terms of employment vary from monthly stipends plus housing to lunch money and Czech lessons. Organizations that recruit teachers include **Education for Democracy/USA,** P.O. Box 40514, Mobile, AL 36640-0514 (tel. (205) 434-3889; fax 434-3731), and **The Foundation for Civil Society,** 1270 Avenue of the Americas #609, New York, NY 10020 (tel. (212) 332-2890; fax 332-2898), formerly the Charter 77 Foundation. A bachelor's degree and experience teaching English as a Second Language may be required.

COMMUNICATING IN THE CZECH REPUBLIC

Russian *was* every student's mandatory second language. These days, English will earn you more friends. A few German phrases go even further, especially in Prague. Pronunciation of Czech words can be difficult for tongues accustomed to English; see the Language section of the Appendix for more help. English-Czech dictionaries are indispensable; before you leave home, pick up a *Say it in Czech* phrasebook. A few handy phrases in Czech will make you sound like less of an oaf: "*Dobrý den!*" (doh-BREE den, "hello"); "*Na shledanou*" (nah-SLEH-dah-noh-oo, "goodbye"); "*Dékuji*" (DYEH-koo-yih), "thank you"); "*Prosím*" (PROH-seem, "please" and "you're welcome"); "*Kolik?*" (KOH-lik, "how much?"); and "*Zaplatíme*" (ZAH-plah-tyee-meh, "We're ready to pay"). Just this once, "*no*" (NOH) or "*ano*" (ah-NOH) means "yes," and "*ne*" (NEH) means "no." There's more—so much more—in the Glossary at the back of the book.

The Czech Republic's **postal system** has been converted to capitalist efficiency; that postcard to Cousin Janine will reach home just *fine*. **International phone calls** are possible, though finding a gray and blue pay phone that works can be challenging. Look for a phone with a globe above it; most of the booths in post offices work. Buy the invaluable **phone cards** (100 kčs) at most newsstands, at the main post office, and at shops displaying the yellow and blue sign. Inserting the coin at the precise time in **Czech phones** is an art. In the **gray phones,** place the change in the holding slot and dial; as soon as the other party answers, push in the coin. In the **orange boxes,** the coin will fall automatically when you connect. Local calls cost 1 kčs regardless of length. For inter-city calling, insert additional coins when the warning tone sounds. Use an international long-distance system to avoid the hefty charges of the Czech telephone bureaucracy—calls run 25 kčs per minute to Austria; 31 kčs per minute to Britain, Italy, or France; 63 kčs per minute to the U.S., Canada, Australia, or Japan; and 94 kčs per minute to New Zealand. To reach the **AT&T USA Direct operator,** dial 00 42 00 01 01 for the U.S., 00 42 00 01 51 for Canada, or 00 42 00 44 01 for Britain. For **MCI,** dial 00 42 00 01 12.

ACCOMMODATIONS AND CAMPING

Converted **university dorms** under the auspices of **CKM** are the cheapest option in July and August. Comfy two- to four-bed rooms go for 150 to 250 kčs per person. CKM also runs **Junior Hotels** (year-round hostels loosely affiliated with HI, which give discounts to both HI and ISIC cardholders) that are comfortable but often full. Wildcat hostel operations have usurped CKM's monopoly on youth lodgings but have not necessarily surpassed its reliability. Showers and bedding are almost always included at these hostels, and occasionally breakfast is too, especially outside of the Prague city limits.

Across the country, **private homes** have become a legal and feasible lodging opportunity. In Prague, hawkers offer expensive rooms (US$11-25, but don't agree to more than US$20), sometimes including breakfast. Scan train stations for "hostel," "*Zimmer*," or "accommodations" ads. Quality varies widely; *don't* pay in advance. Make sure anything you accept is easily accessible by public transport; be prepared for a healthy commute to the center of town. Outside of Prague, **Čedok** handles most private room booking, although private agencies are burgeoning around train and bus stations. If you're sticking to **hotels,** consider reserving ahead of time from June to September in Prague and Brno, even if it requires pre-payment. Outside of the major cities, it is easier to find a bed. Hotels come in five flavors: A-star, A, B-star, B, and C. As cities scramble to attract tourists, many of the grungy C hotels have begun to disappear. In 1993, singles in a B hotel averaged 500 kčs, doubles 750 kčs (within Prague 800 kčs and 1200 kčs, respectively).

Inexpensive **camping** is available everywhere, ranging from 40-85 kčs per person (most sites are open only mid-May to September). The book *Ubytování ČSR,* in decodable Czech, comprehensively lists the hotels, inns, hostels, huts, and campgrounds in Bohemia and Moravia. Bookstores also sell a fine hiking map of the country, *Soubor Turistických Map,* with an English key.

FOOD AND DRINK

The health-food craze has yet to hit the Czech Republic: the four basic food groups here are sausages (*párek, klobosa*), cheese (*sýr*), ice cream (*zmrzlina*), and beer (*pivo*). The *Hotová Jidla* (ready dishes) section on menus consistently includes variations on *gulaš*, pork or beef doused in a creamy sauce. Some key words are: *vepřová* (pork), *hovězi* (beef), *kuře* (chicken), *ryby* (fish), *kapr* (carp), *pstruh* (trout), and *zelenia* (vegetables). *Smáženy* means fried. Signs that should command your salivary attention are *bufet, samoobsluha* (self-service), and *občerstveni,* all variations on the stand-up snack bar. A *hostinec* caters to a steady clientele of beer drinkers; *kavárny* and *cukrárny* serve coffee and exquisite pastry, but note that *káva* (coffee) is often a thick layer of grounds topped with boiling water. A *pivnice* is a beer hall and a *vinárna* a wine bar, usually specializing in fine Slovak wines; both are good places to eat. Czech beers are among the world's best. The most famous are plzeňský Prazdroj (Pilsner Urquell) and Budvar (the original Budweiser), but the Velképopovický is a local favorite.

From Saturday noon to Sunday morning, all grocery stores and some restaurants close. It is customary to round the bill up a few kčs—often it will be done for you. At finer eateries, you should add a 10% tip as you pay; do not leave the tip on the table. **Vegetarians** can munch on *smaženy sýr* (fried cheese), a scrumptious Czech specialty sold at food stands, and produce from *ovoce zelenina* stores (green-grocers) or *potraviny* (general grocery stores). Vegetarian restaurants have begun to sprout in larger cities. See Food in the Glossary for more information.

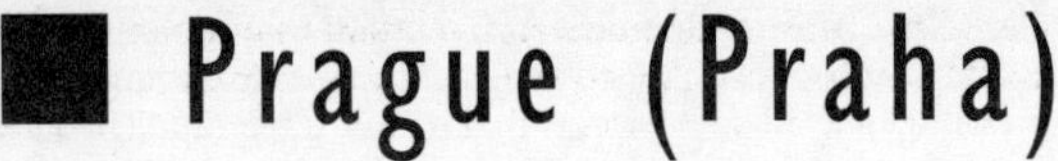

Prague (Praha)

> Prague is planning a much-needed telephone-system overhaul in 1994; many of the numbers listed may change.

The Princess Libuše stood atop one of seven hills overlooking the River Vltava and declared, "I see a city whose glory will touch the stars; it shall be called Praha (threshold)." From its mythological inception to the present, benefactors have placed Prague on the cusp of the divine. Founded at the end of the 8th century, Prague became the capital of the Holy Roman Empire six centuries later. Karel IV, King of Bohemia, Holy Roman Emperor, and Grand Poobah at Large, envisioned a royal seat worthy of his rank. He rebuilt 14th-century Prague into the "city of a hundred spires"—with soaring cathedrals and lavish Baroque palaces—elevating the city to an imperial magnificence eclipsed only by Rome and Constantinople.

Prague's lively squares and avenues give the city a festival atmosphere few can rival, and its museums, concert halls, and ballet and opera performances are world-class. Artists and musicians have always been drawn here. Mozart himself believed that only in Prague was he fully understood (and he didn't even speak Czech). The capital has waltzed through the 20th century as if charmed; not of major strategic importance in either World War, it escaped the ravages suffered by comparable cities. Since the Velvet Revolution of 1989, the city has exploded from relative obscurity and isolation behind the Iron Curtain into a tourist destination surpassing the great capitals of Western Europe. Unlike those bastions of capitalist enterprise, Prague allows a glimpse back into a world that politics rendered inaccessible for decades.

Over 20,000 Americans now make their home in Prague, and more than 750,000 visited last year. While many locals can't keep up with the rising prices, Prague is still a fabulous bargain by Western standards. Just don't flaunt your affluence and thereby offend proprietors and residents. Struggling locals don't need to hear how inexpensive items might seem to you. Instead, immerse yourself as seamlessly as possible into the humbling magnificence of this 1000-year-old metropolis.

ORIENTATION AND PRACTICAL INFORMATION

Prague is a sumptuous blend of nature and architecture in the center of Czech Bohemia. The town is built on seven hills; seventeen bridges span the River **Vltava** ("Moldau" in German) on its course through the city. Direct rail and bus service links Prague easily with Vienna, Berlin, Munich, and Warsaw. All train and bus terminals are on or near the excellent **Metro** system; the **nám. Republiky** Metro B station (*map*E3*) is closest to the principal tourist offices and accommodations agencies. For maps, go to a *tabak* stand or bookstore and buy an indexed *plán města*. Prague's two **English-language newspapers,** *Prognosis* and *The Prague Post,* both provide numerous tips for visitors along with the usual news.

At the top of the west bank of the Vltava lies **Hradčany** (*map*AB1*), Prague's castle and main landmark. Below the fortress are the lovely palaces and gardens of **Malá Strana** (Lesser Town; *map*A3*) originally built and populated by Prague's urban gentry. From Malá Strana, the pedestrian-only **Karlův Most** (Charles Bridge; *map*C3*) crosses the river and leads into **Staré Mésto** (Old Town; *map*E3*) at the center of which is the huge, architecturally resplendent plaza, **Staroměstské náměstí.** Gothic spires representing 600 years of construction rise from every corner in this section of town. North of Staroměstské náměstí is **Josefov,** the old Jewish quarter. The rich 19th-century façades of **Nové Mésto** (New Town; *map*D5*), established in

1348 by Karel IV, lie to the south. Most of Prague's architectural monuments are in the castle district and the Old Town—Nové Mésto is busier and more commercial.

The center of Prague is dominated by three streets that form a leaning *T.* The long stem of the *T,* separating Old and New Towns, is **Václavské náměstí** (Wenceslas Square; actually a grand boulevard; *map*E45*). At the bottom of the *T* towers the glistening **National Museum** (*map*EF5*). The busy pedestrian street **Na přikopé** (*map*E3-4*) forms the right arm and leads to **náměstí Republiky** (*map*E3*). On the left, 28. října becomes **Národní** (*map*C5-D4*) after a block, leading to the **National Theater** (*map*C5*) on the river. A maze of small streets leads to Staromêstské nám. two blocks above the *T.* There are two prominent **St. Nicholas cathedrals,** one in Malá Strana (*map*A3*) near the castle and another in Staromêstské nám. (*map*D3*), and two **Powder Towers,** one in the castle (*map*AB2*) and another in the nám. Republiky (*map*E3*).

Tourist Offices

CKM (*map*DE6*), Žitna 12 (tel. 299 94 15), next to the Junior Hotel Praha. Has information, accommodations, and transportation tickets. Metro C: "I.P. Pavlova." Open daily 9am-1pm, 2-6pm. **Branch office** (*map*E4*) at Jindřisská 28 (tel. 26 85 07). Metro A or B: "Můstek." Sells ISICs and HI cards. Open Mon.-Fri. 9am-1pm, 2-5pm, Sat. 9am-noon.

Čedok (*map*E3-4*), Na přikopé 18 (tel. 212 71 11). No longer essential, but a convenient place to buy train and bus tickets. Processing can take over an hour in high season. Open Mon.-Fri. 8:30am-6pm, Sat. 8:30am-12:30pm.

Pražská Informační Služba (Prague Information Service; *map*E3-4*), next door to Čedok at Na přikopé 20 (tel. 54 44 44). Grab a handful of brochures on upcoming concerts and city sights. Open Mon.-Fri. 9am-7pm, Sat. 9am-6pm.

American Hospitality Center (*map*DE4*), Na Mustkú 7 (tel. 26 15 74 or 26 20 45), just north of the end of Vácklavske nám. Message board posted with requests for English tutors, cycling companions, notes to friends, and lots of whatnot. Nurse a coffee and chat with folks who think they're in 1920s Paris. CNN, MTV, popcorn, and pizza. No apple pie. Open daily 10am-10pm.

Other Organizations

Embassies: Pickpocketing is rampant in Prague, especially among the milling throngs at the clock in the Old Town Square and on the way to the Castle. Many other highly touristed sights are particularly prone, as are trams. Police usually speak little English; if you've been robbed, try your embassy or consulate first for advice on how and where to report the theft. All Western embassies will hold mail. All embassy and consular services are contained in the same building, unless otherwise noted.

U.S. (*map*A3*), Tržiště 15, Praha 12548 (tel. 53 66 41, ext. 2362 for consular services). Metro A: "Malostranská." Cross the Charles Bridge and enter Malostranské nám. (castle side), then turn left on Karmelitská and right on Tržiště.

Canada (*map*B1*), Mickiewiczova 6 (tel. 312 02 51). Open Mon.-Fri. 8:30am-noon, 2-4pm.

U.K. (*map*B2-3*), Thunovská 14 (tel. 53 33 47). Open daily 9am-12pm and 2:45-4pm. Travelers from **Australia** and **New Zealand** should contact the British embassy in an emergency.

Hungary (*map*D5-6*), Badeního 1 (tel. 36 50 41). Same-day visa for citizens of **Australia** and **New Zealand** US$20 plus 2 photos. Open Mon.-Wed. and Fri. 9am-noon.

Poland (*map*B2*), Valdštejnská 8 (tel. 53 69 51); **Polish consulate** (*map*E4-5*), Václavské nám. 49 (tel. 26 44 64). Same-day visa service. Citizens of **Australia** and **New Zealand** pay US$28 plus 2 photos; students US$21 with ISIC. Open Mon.-Fri. 9am-1pm.

Russia (*map*C1*), Pod kaštany 1 (tel. 38 19 41). **Russian consulate** (*map*C1*), around corner at Korunovačni 34 (tel. 37 37 23). Visas US$25 with proper preparation; citizens of **Australia** pay US$50. Open Mon., Wed., and Fri. 9:30am-1pm.

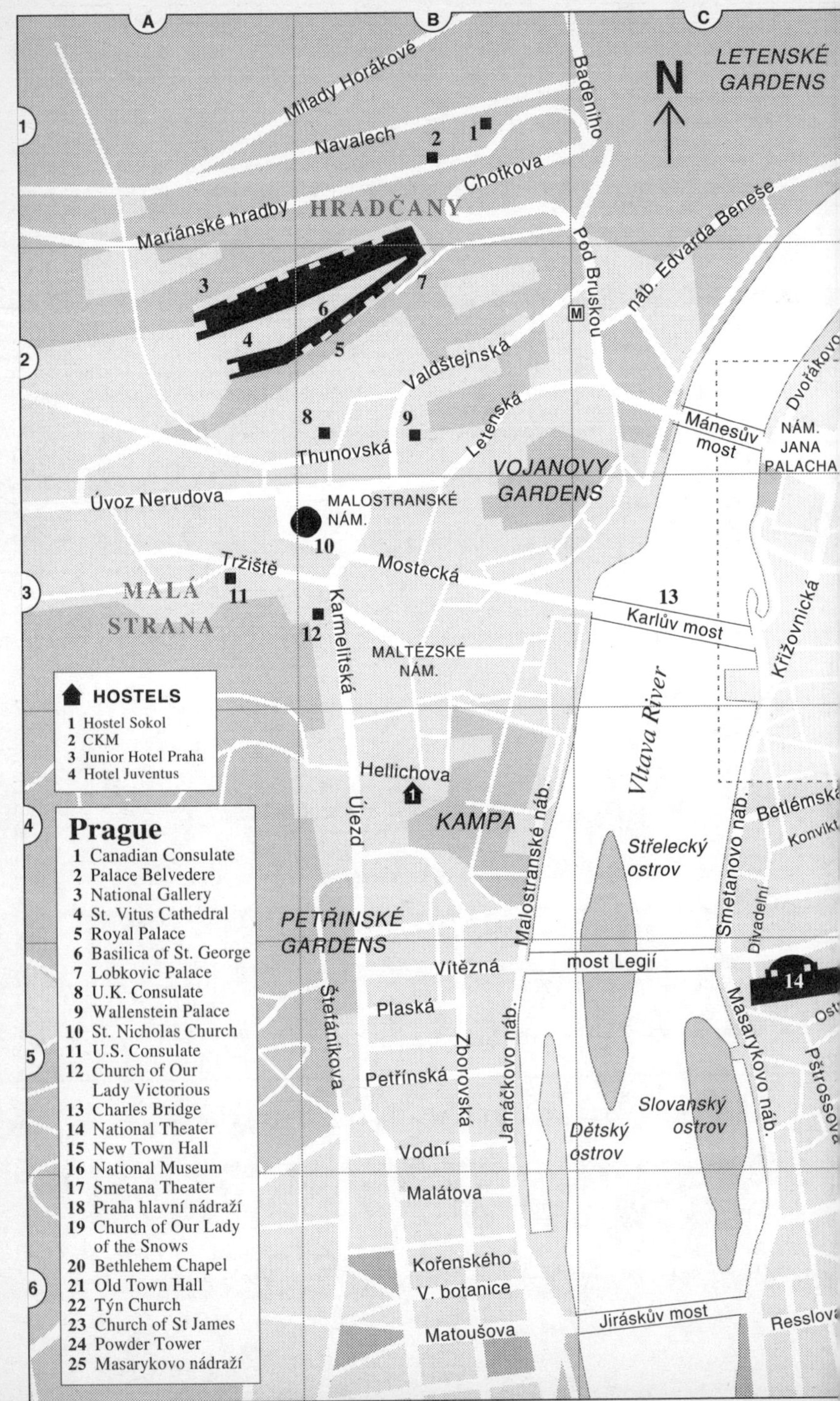
A
B
C
1
2
3
4
5
6
N
LETENSKÉ GARDENS
Mílady Horákové
Navalech
Badeniho
Chotkova
Mariánské hradby
HRADČANY
náb. Edvarda Beneše
Pod Bruskou
Valdštejnská
Letenská
Thunovská
VOJANOVY GARDENS
Mánesův most
NÁM. JANA PALACHA
Dvořákovo
Úvoz Nerudova
MALOSTRANSKÉ NÁM.
Tržiště
Mostecká
MALÁ STRANA
Karmelitská
Karlův most
Křižovnická
MALTÉZSKÉ NÁM.
Vltava River
Hellichova
Újezd
KAMPA
Malostranské náb.
Střelecký ostrov
Smetanovo náb.
Betlémská
Konvikt
Divadelní
PETŘINSKÉ GARDENS
Vítězná
most Legií
Plaská
Štefánikova
Zborovská
Petřínská
Janáčkovo náb.
Masarykovo náb.
Pštrossova
Slovanský ostrov
Dětský ostrov
Vodní
Malátova
Kořenského
V. botanice
Matoušova
Jiráskův most
Resslova
HOSTELS
1 Hostel Sokol
2 CKM
3 Junior Hotel Praha
4 Hotel Juventus
Prague
1 Canadian Consulate
2 Palace Belvedere
3 National Gallery
4 St. Vitus Cathedral
5 Royal Palace
6 Basilica of St. George
7 Lobkovic Palace
8 U.K. Consulate
9 Wallenstein Palace
10 St. Nicholas Church
11 U.S. Consulate
12 Church of Our Lady Victorious
13 Charles Bridge
14 National Theater
15 New Town Hall
16 National Museum
17 Smetana Theater
18 Praha hlavní nádraží
19 Church of Our Lady of the Snows
20 Bethlehem Chapel
21 Old Town Hall
22 Týn Church
23 Church of St James
24 Powder Tower
25 Masarykovo nádraží

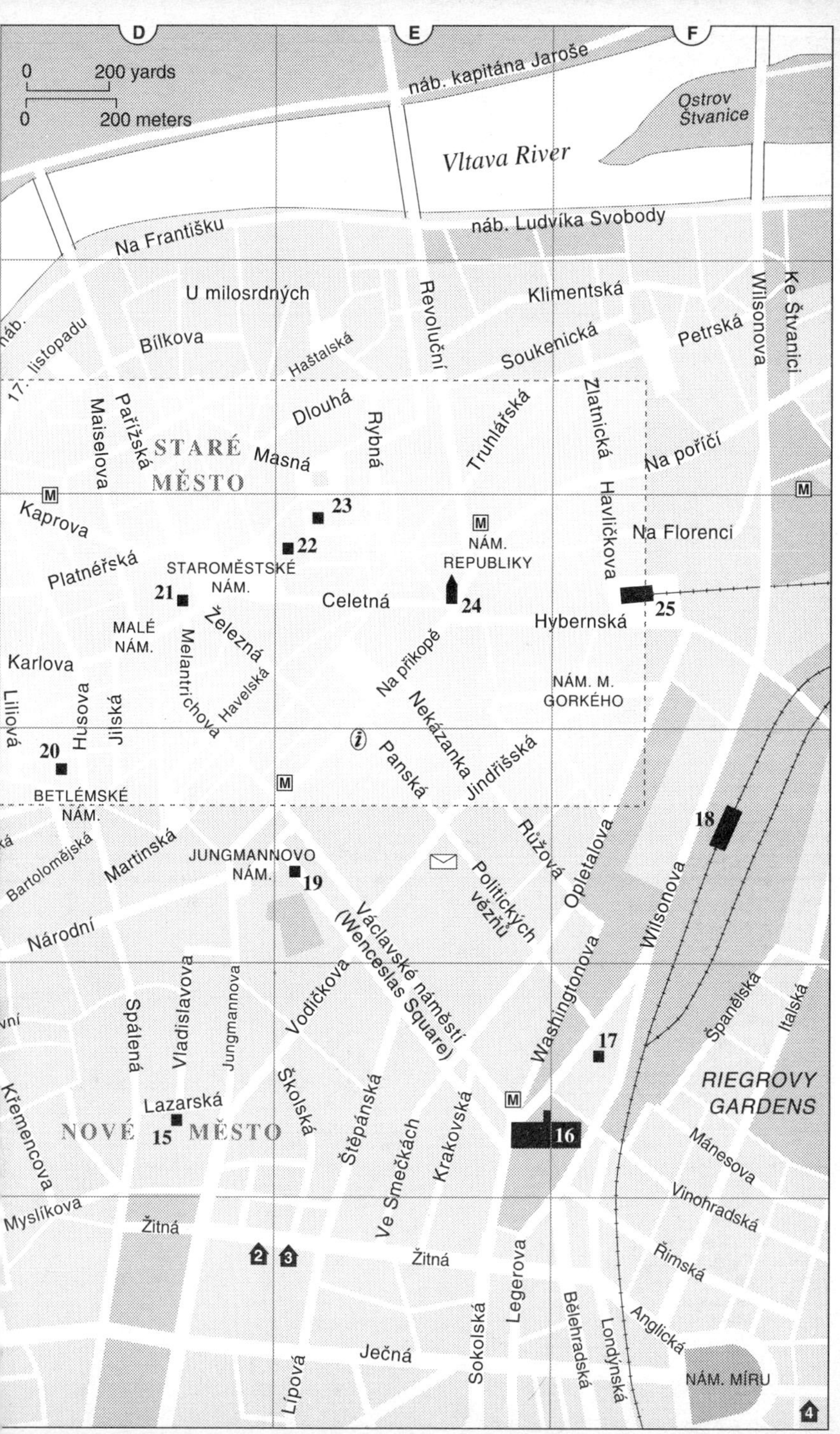
D
E
F
0 200 yards
0 200 meters
náb. kapitána Jaroše
Ostrov Štvanice
Vltava River
náb. Ludvíka Svobody
Na Františku
U milosrdných
Revoluční
Klimentská
Wilsonova
Ke Štvanici
náb.
17. listopadu
Bílkova
Haštalská
Soukenická
Petrská
Dlouhá
Rybná
Truhlářská
Zlatnická
Maiselova
Pařížská
STARÉ MĚSTO
Masná
Na poříčí
Havlíčkova
Kaprova
23
22
NÁM. REPUBLIKY
Na Florenci
Platnéřská
STAROMĚSTSKÉ NÁM.
21
Celetná
24
25
Hybernská
Železná
MALÉ NÁM.
Melantrichova
Karlova
Havelská
Na příkopě
NÁM. M. GORKÉHO
Nekázanka
Liliová
Husova
Jilská
20
Panská
Jindřišská
BETLÉMSKÉ NÁM.
18
Růžová
Bartolomějská
Martinská
JUNGMANNOVO NÁM.
19
Politických vězňů
Opletalova
Wilsonova
Národní
Václavské náměstí (Wenceslas Square)
Washingtonova
Vodičkova
Spálená
Vladislavova
Jungmannova
Španělská
Italská
17
RIEGROVY GARDENS
Školská
Štěpánská
Křemencova
Lazarská
NOVÉ MĚSTO
15
Ve Smečkách
Krakovská
16
Mánesova
Vinohradská
Myslíkova
Žitná
2
3
Žitná
Římská
Legerova
Sokolská
Bělehradská
Londýnská
Anglická
Ječná
Lípová
NÁM. MÍRU
4

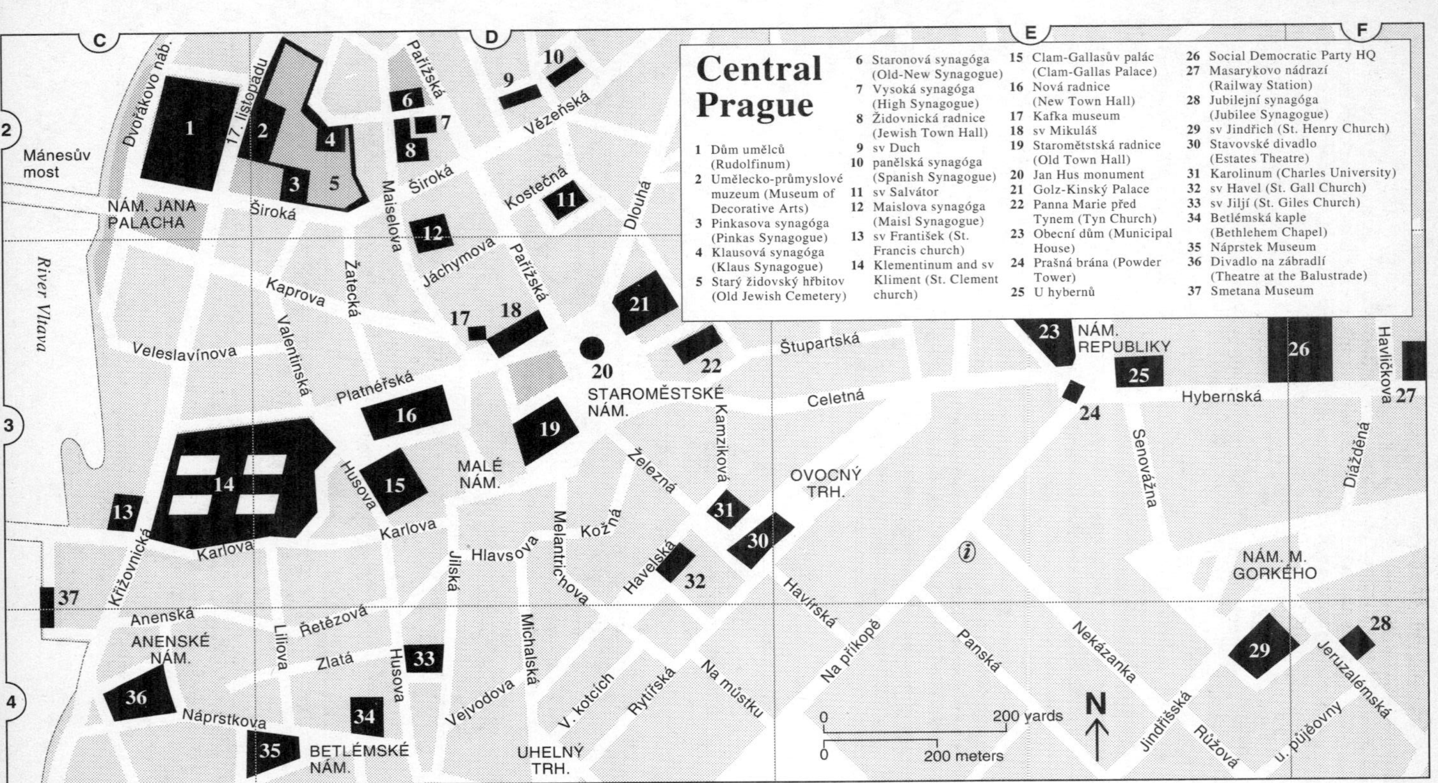
Central Prague
1 Dům umělců (Rudolfinum)
2 Umělecko-průmyslové muzeum (Museum of Decorative Arts)
3 Pinkasova synagóga (Pinkas Synagogue)
4 Klausová synagóga (Klaus Synagogue)
5 Starý židovský hřbitov (Old Jewish Cemetery)
6 Staronová synagóga (Old-New Synagogue)
7 Vysoká synagóga (High Synagogue)
8 Židovnická radnice (Jewish Town Hall)
9 sv Duch
10 panělská synagóga (Spanish Synagogue)
11 sv Salvátor
12 Maislova synagóga (Maisl Synagogue)
13 sv František (St. Francis church)
14 Klementinum and sv Kliment (St. Clement church)
15 Clam-Gallasův palác (Clam-Gallas Palace)
16 Nová radnice (New Town Hall)
17 Kafka museum
18 sv Mikuláš
19 Staroměststská radnice (Old Town Hall)
20 Jan Hus monument
21 Golz-Kinský Palace
22 Panna Marie před Tynem (Tyn Church)
23 Obecní dům (Municipal House)
24 Prašná brána (Powder Tower)
25 U hybernů
26 Social Democratic Party HQ
27 Masarykovo nádrazí (Railway Station)
28 Jubilejní synagóga (Jubilee Synagogue)
29 sv Jindřich (St. Henry Church)
30 Stavovské divadlo (Estates Theatre)
31 Karolinum (Charles University)
32 sv Havel (St. Gall Church)
33 sv Jiljí (St. Giles Church)
34 Betlémská kaple (Bethlehem Chapel)
35 Náprstek Museum
36 Divadlo na zábradlí (Theatre at the Balustrade)
37 Smetana Museum
C
D
E
F
2
3
4
Mánesův most
River Vltava
Dvořákovo náb.
17. listopadu
NÁM. JANA PALACHA
Široká
Pařížská
Maiselova
Vězeňská
Kostečná
Dlouhá
Jáchymova
Žatecká
Kaprova
Valentinská
Veleslavínova
Platnéřská
Husova
Karlova
Křižovnická
MALÉ NÁM.
STAROMĚSTSKÉ NÁM.
Štupartská
Celetná
Kamzíková
Železná
Kožná
Melantrichova
Hlavsova
Jilská
Havelská
OVOCNÝ TRH.
Havířská
Na příkopě
Panská
Nekázanka
Senovážna
Hybernská
NÁM. REPUBLIKY
Havlíčkova
Dlážděná
NÁM. M. GORKÉHO
Jeruzalémská
Jindřišská
Růžová
u. půjčovny
Anenská
ANENSKÉ NÁM.
Řetězová
Liliova
Zlatá
Náprstkova
BETLÉMSKÉ NÁM.
Michalská
Vejvodova
V. kotcích
Rytířská
Na můstku
UHELNÝ TRH.
0 200 yards
0 200 meters
N

Ukraine (tel. 37 43 66).

Lithuania (tel. 312 46 19).

Currency Exchange: Beware the **black market.** The recent influx of Western currency has all but killed it, so unless you are an expert on Czech currency, you may end up with a wad of counterfeit bills no one will accept. **Banks** offer better rates than the private *bureaux de change* that overrun Prague's streets. If you are having difficulty reconverting your crowns into your own currency, contact the **Komerčni bank,** at Na příkopé 42. Most banks are open from 8am-noon and 1-6pm. On weekends and holidays, exchange counters in large hotels will convert money.

Čedok (*map*E3-4*) offers the best rates on cash, in spite of a 2% commission.

State bank (*map*E3-4*), Na příkopé 14 (a stone's throw from Čedok) cashes U.S. dollar or German D-Mark traveler's checks. Open Mon.-Fri. 7:30am-noon and 1-3:30pm.

Živnostenská bank (*map*E3-4*), Na příkopé 20. Also gives cash advances on Visa and MasterCard. Commission 1% on notes, 2% on traveler's checks. Open Mon.-Fri. 8am-9:30pm, Sat. 9:30am-12:30pm and 1:30-5:30pm.

Chequepoint offices are located in all of Prague's highly touristed areas. About 10% commission on top of a service charge–egad! The Chequepoints at the intersections of Václavské nám. and Vodicková and of Václavské nám. and 28 října are open 24 hrs. for travelers in a jam.

American Express: (*map*E5*) Václavské nám. 56 (tel. 26 17 47). Metro A or C: "Muzeum." Free, helpful city maps. If the line extends out the door, just walk 5 min. up Václavské nám. to one of the bank branches listed above. Address mail as follows: "Joshua Egan GROSS, American Express, Client Letter Service, Václavské nám. 56, 113 26 Praha 1, Česka Republika/Czech Republic." Mail held at U.S. visitors counter. Cardholders' personal checks cashed for kčs only. Mastercard advances. Express cash machine. Open Mon.-Fri. 9am-7pm, Sat. 9am-3pm.

Thomas Cook: (*map*E5*), Václavské nám 47 (tel. 26 66 11; fax 26 56 95).

ATMs: CIRRUS network machine in the "Můstek" Metro A or B station, at the intersection of Na mustku and Wenceslas Square; also on Na Přikope, across from the Kino Sevastopol. **PLUS** network machine near the corner of Havelská and Melantrichova; also in the lobby of Hotel Panorama, at the "Pankrác" Metro C stop. For **lost credit cards,** contact: **Visa** and **Diner's Club,** tel. 236 66 88, **MasterCard,** tel. 23 92 21 35, or **American Express** above.

Post Office: (*map*E4*), Jindřišská 14. Metro A or B: "Můstek." Address *Poste Restante* as follows: Alan BLAYNE, Jindřišská 14, 110 00 Praha 1, Czech Republic. *Poste Restante* at window 28, stamps at windows 20-23, letters and parcels under 2kg at windows 10-12. Open 24 hrs. Parcels over 2kg can be mailed only at **Pošta-Celnice,** Plzeňská 139. Take tram #9 west. A bureaucratic pain in the ass. Airmail should arrive within 10 days from the U.S. Open Mon.-Tues. and Thurs.-Fri. 7am-3pm, Wed. 7am-6pm, Sat. 8am-noon.

Telephones: At the post office and most train and Metro stations. Phone cards (100 kčs) available at the post office and at many newsstands; about 2-min. calling time to the U.S. **Prague is planning a much-needed telephone-system overhaul in 1994; many of the numbers listed may change. City code:** 02.

Transportation

Flights: Ruzyné Airport (tel. 334 33 14), 20km northwest of city center. Take bus #119 from the "Dejvická" Metro A station. **ČSA** (tel. 36 78 14), the national airline of the Czech Republic, runs buses to the airport every 20-30 min. from the back of Revoluční 25, 5 blocks north of the "nám. Republiky" Metro B station. Buses run 6am-6:30pm; buy tickets (20 kčs) on the bus.

Trains: *Nádraží* means "station." There are 4 train stations in Prague. Always ask what your point of departure will be—the information may not be volunteered. Czech speakers can call **train information** (tel. 24 44 41 or 26 49 30).

Praha-Holešovice, the main international terminal–you'll probably arrive here or at hlavní nádraží. Metro C "Nádraží Holešovice."

Praha hlavní nádraží (a.k.a. Woodrow Wilsonova station). Metro C: "Hlavní nádraží." Some international and many domestic routes. To: Vienna (5 per day, 5 hr.), Budapest (6 per day, 9 hr.), Berlin (6 per day, 6 hr.), Warsaw (2 per day, 10 hr.).

Masarykovo nádraží, on Hybernská. Metro B: "nám. Republiky." Serves only domestic routes.

Praha-Smíchov, across the river. Metro B: "Smíchovské nádraží."

Buses: ČSAD has 3 terminals (Autobusové nádraží). The central one is **Praha-Florenc** (*map*F2-3*), on Křižíkova (tel. 22 86 42 or 22 26 29), behind the Masarykovo nádraží railway station. Metro B or C: "Florenc." Informace desk staff speaks little English, but posted schedules are legible and extensive. Buy tickets at least a day in advance; they often sell out. Daily to Vienna; to Venice, 4 per week; to Milan and Munich, 2 per week. Extensive service throughout the Czech Republic and Slovakia. Open Mon.-Fri. 6am-6:30pm, Sat. 6am-1pm, Sun. 8:30am-noon and 12:30-3:30pm.

Public Transportation: tel. 22 95 52. The **Metro, tram,** and **bus** systems serve the city well. Bus routes frequently shift for street repairs. **Tickets,** good for all forms of transportation, cost 4 kčs. Stock up at **newspaper stands** and **tabak** shops—the orange automat machines in Metro stations require exact change. **Čedok** also sells handy **tourist passes,** good on all 3 modes of transport (1 day 30 kčs; 2 days 50 kčs; 15 kčs per additional day). Another Čedok pass, the **Prague Card,** is valid for 3 days of unlimited city transport and free admission to 36 museums and sights in Prague (360 kčs, students 260 kčs). **Punch your ticket** when boarding, and punch a new ticket when switching vehicles—except in the Metro, where your ticket is valid for 1 hr. after punching on all lines, as long as you don't go above ground. If you're caught without a punched ticket when exiting, you'll be fined 200 kčs. Ouch. The Metro has three main lines: on city maps, line A is green, line B is yellow, and line C is red. "Můstek" (lines A and B), "Muzeum" (lines A and C), and "Florenc" (lines B and C) are the primary junctions. The system runs daily 5am-midnight. Night trams #51-58 and buses #500-510 run midnight-5am (every 40 min.); look for the dark blue signs at transport stops.

Taxis: tel. 35 03 20 or 35 04 91. Regular taxis cost 8 kčs per km, and larger taxis available in front of the airport and hotels charge 18 kčs per km. As is wise in all cities, ask for a price before entering the cab. Always check to see that the meter starts at "0." On shorter trips, make sure the meter is running, and for longer trips set a price beforehand. Request that the driver put on the meter by saying, "*Zapněte taxametr, prosím.*" If problems arise, ask the driver for a receipt before paying: "*Prosím, dejte, mi paragon.*" Receipts usually state the distance traveled and the price paid. Downtown to airport about 300 kčs, to the hostels average 150-200 kčs.

Car Rental: Esocar (*map*F3*), Husitská 58 (tel. 691 22 44 or 691 23 96; fax 691 22 48). Open Mon.-Fri. 8am-noon and 1-5pm. **Avis** (*map*D2*), E Krasnohorsue 9/134 (tel. 231 78 65). **Hertz,** 3 locations: Prague Airport Ruzyne (tel. 312 07 17). Open daily 8am-8pm. Hotel Palace (*map*E4*), Panska 12 (tel. 236 16 37 or 331 41 74). Open daily 8am-8pm. Central Railroad Station (*map*F4*), Wilsonova 8 (tel. 42 22 36 30 75). Open daily 6am-2:30pm and 3-10:30pm.

Bike Rental: Rent-a-Bike (*map*E5*), Školská 12 (tel. 22 10 63), 150m from the McDonald's on Vodičkova. 280 kčs per day, 700 kčs for 3 days. Open daily 9am-8pm.

Hitchhiking: *Let's Go* cannot recommend hitchhiking as a safe means of transportation. Hitchhiking in and around Prague has become increasingly dangerous; fortunately, cheap and extensive train and bus service render it largely unnecessary. Travelers going east take tram #1, 9, or 16 to the last stop. To points south, they take Metro C to "Pražskeho povstání," then walk left 100m, crossing námésti Hrdinů to 5 Kvétná (also called highway D1). To Munich, hitchers take tram #4 or 9 until the intersection of Plzeňská and Kukulova/Bucharova, then hitch south. Those going north take a tram or bus to "Kobyliské nám.," and then bus #175 up Horňátecká.

Other Practical Information

Luggage Storage: Lockers in every train and bus station (4 kčs). Those in the main train station are usually full, so try 24-hr. baggage storage in the basement (9.50 kčs per day for first 15kg). Beware of nimble thieves who might relieve you of heavy baggage while you set your 4-digit locker code.

Laundromat: In some private flats, tenants ask if their laundry can be included with the family's. Often, underwear will come back darned and ironed. If you're on your own, go to **Laundry Kings** (*map*B1*) at Dejvická 16, 1 block from the "Hradčanská" Metro A stop. Cross the tram *and* railroad tracks, then turn left onto Dejvická. Self-service wash 40 kčs per load, dry 15 kčs per 8 min. Soap 10-20 kčs. Full-service is an additional 30 kčs and takes 24 hr. in peak season. Filled with similarly soiled and thirsty travelers. You can throw back a few cold ones while you wait. Open Mon.-Fri. 6am-10pm, Sat.-Sun. 8am-10pm.

Bookstore: The Globe Bookstore, Janovského 14. Metro C: "Vltavská." From the Metro, walk under the overpass on your right, then turn right onto Janouského. Large selection of used English-language paperbacks (about 80 kčs each). Will trade and buy used books. Open daily 9am-5pm. **International Bookstore Praha** (*map*D2*), at the corner of 17. Listopadu and Pařížská. Specializes in English-language art, literary, and reference books. Open daily 10am-7pm. At the **American Center** (*map*EF3*) on Hybernská 7a, you can peruse books and current periodicals. Metro B: "nám. Republiky." Open Mon.-Thurs. 11am-5pm, Fri. 11am-3pm.

Pharmacy (*Lékárna*): (*map*E3-4*) Na příkopé 7 (tel. 22 00 81). Open 24 hrs.

Police: headquarters at Olšanská 2 (tel. 21 21 11 11). Metro A: "Flora," then walk down Jičinská and turn right onto Olšanská; the station is about 200m ahead on your right. Or take tram #9. Come here for a visa extension. Open Mon., Tues., and Thurs. 8am-3pm, Wed. 8am-5pm, Fri. 8am-2pm.

Emergencies: Medical Emergency Aid in English and German, tel. 29 93 81. **Na Homolce (foreigners' medical assistance),** tel. 52 92 21 46, after hours 52 92 21 91. **Ambulance,** tel. 155. **Fire,** tel. 150. **Police,** tel. 158. Notify your embassy in case of legal emergencies.

ACCOMMODATIONS

The **Prague Information Service Guide Office** (Pražská Informační Služba; *map*E3-4*), Panská 5 off Na Přikopě, displays a list of all hotels, hostels, and campgrounds (open daily 9am-6pm). Prices in Prague are rising rapidly, so expect considerable increases over the prices listed below (perhaps 50-100 kčs). Luckily, beds are plentiful. A growing number of Prague residents are renting spare rooms to travelers, either on their own or through private agencies (see below). Many travelers lodge at the homes of proprietors who accost them at the train station. Other than private flats, budget travelers have three main options: a bed in a youth hostel, a class B (2-star) or class C (1-star) hotel room, or a campground. In late June, universities empty for the summer, freeing up hundreds of sterile and boxy—albeit cheap—rooms. If CKM is mobbed, head directly to the dorms.

Official Agencies

CKM (*map*DE6*), Žitná 12 (tel. 29 99 41 or 29 99 45, fax 235 48 59). Metro C: "I.P. Pavlova," and then backtrack down Žitná, or walk down Štépánská from Václavské nám. The definitive place to find youth-hostel-esque accommodations. Lists local dormitories and youth hostels that currently have available beds (220-450 kčs) and also provides Metro and tram directions. Open daily 9am-1pm, 2-6pm.

Universitas Tour (*map*F3-4*), Opletalova 38 (tel. 22 35 431 or 22 35 50), 2 blocks north of the main train station. Metro C: "Hlavní nádraží." In July and August, the office books rooms in the hostel/dorm on premises. (300 kčs per person in singles, doubles, triples, and quads; hall baths.) During the rest of the year, the staff will scout out a *penzión* (350 kčs per person including breakfast and bath) or private room (450-600 kčs). Open July-Aug. Mon.-Sat. 8:30am-8:30pm, Sept.-June Mon.-Sat. 8:30am-6pm.

Pragotur (*map*E3*), U Obecního domu 2 (tel. 231 70 00, 232 51 28), a side street off nám. Republiky, across from the Hotel Paříž. Metro B: "nám. Republiky." B- and C-class hotels (600-900 kčs per person) and private homes. Spontaneously finding 2 or 3 roommates usually speeds things up. No min. stay. Private rooms in the center of town run singles 665 kčs, doubles 875 kčs. Open Mon.-Fri. 8am-7pm, Sat. 9am-6pm, Sun. 9am-3pm.

Private Agencies

When you first arrive in Prague, you may be besieged by individuals offering private rooms. Many of these hawkers are actually agents for other people. The going rate hovers at about US$10-15 (250-450 kčs), depending primarily on proximity to the town center. Try haggling. These are generally safe arrangements, but if you're wary of bargaining on the street, you can try private agencies that set up shop seemingly overnight in prominent areas of town. Keep your eyes open, and make sure any rooms you accept are within reach of public transportation. Payment in U.S. dollars or German D-Marks is usually preferred and sometimes required, though Czech koruna are generally accepted.

Top Tour (*map*E3*), Rybná 3 (tel. 231 40 69 or 269 65 26), 1 block west of nám. Republiky. Dorm hostels (400 kčs per person, 3 beds per room) and private rooms (singles 630-700 kčs, doubles 1050-1150 kčs). Open Mon.-Fri. 9am-8pm, Sat.-Sun. 10am-7pm.

Vesta (*map*F4*), Wilsonova (tel. 236 81 28), on the top floor of the Hlavní Nádraží train station. Make sure you understand just what sort of room you are paying for, and have the staff write it down. Private rooms (350-500 kčs per person), hostels near the center (250 kčs per person), and hotels (500-800 kčs per person). Open Mon.-Sat. 8:30am-7:30pm, Sun. 8:30am-4:30pm.

AVE Ltd. (*map*F4*), Wilsonova (tel. 24 22 32 26 or 24 22 35 21), next to Vesta. Convenient and speedy. Hostels from 200 kčs, private rooms from 400 kčs, hotels from 800 kčs (singles) and 1100 kčs (doubles). Also in Nádraží Holešovice. Open daily 6am-11:30pm; Sept.-June daily 6am-10pm.

Hello Ltd. (*map*F3*), Gorkého-Senovážné nám 3 (tel. 22 42 83). From nám. Republiky, walk down Hybernská and turn right on Dláždéná. Choose rooms from photos (private rooms 400-600 kčs, private flats 800-900 kčs per person). Open daily 9am-10pm.

Prague Suites (*map*D4*), Melantrichova 8 (tel. 26 77 70 or 26 93 84), 2 blocks north of the intersection of Václavské nám and Na příkopě. The lodging service of the American Hospitality Center. Private rooms US$15-20. Also handles long-term accommodations. Open 24 hrs.

Primo Agency (*map*D5-6*), Žitná 17 (tel. 249 10 340), down the street from CKM. Hostels for 235 kčs, private rooms from 700-1000 kčs (doubles), flats from 900 kčs per night total—a steal for groups. Open daily 9am-10pm; Sept.-June daily 11am-8pm.

Hostels (Studentska Kolej)

An enormous cluster of dorms/hostels west of the river in the Strahov neighborhood, next to the Olympic stadium, frees up for travelers from July to mid-September. Expect limited room the rest of the year. These western hostels may be the best bet for travelers who arrive in the middle of the night *sans* clue. Call ahead and inquire about vacancies before you schlepp all the way out there.

ESTEC Students House, "Kolej Strahov," Vaníčkova (was Spartakiádní), blok (building) 5 (tel. 52 73 44). Take bus #217 or 143 from the "Dejvická" Metro A stop or bus #176 from the "Karlovo nám." Metro B stop to "Stadion Strahov" (every hr.). Then walk around the stadium to the right. Registration open July-Aug. 24 hrs., Sept.-June 5-10pm. Check-out 10am. No curfew. 500 beds from July to mid-Sept.; limited first-floor space available mid-Sept. to June. Doubles 240 kčs per person. Breakfast 50 kčs. 3 lively bars and discos—who needs to go downtown? Laundry machines available. **Post office** (Mon.-Fri. 8am-3pm) and student **grocery store** (Mon.-Fri. 7:30am-7pm, Sat.-Sun. 7:30am-noon) next door.

Oasa, Posepného nám. (tel. 792 63 15). Take Metro C to "Roztyly" or ride bus #505 from "Muzeum Metto." Lockers, kitchen facilities, sauna, and weight room. Reception open 24 hrs; no curfew. 120 kčs for a space to lay your sleeping bag, 165 kčs for a bed. Showers included. 10% discount for stays of more than 2 days.

TJ Slavoj, V náklích (tel. 46 00 70). Take tram #3 or 17 to the end station at "Braník." Lonely 10-min. walk from the tram stop; look for it in the daytime. 48 beds in a boathouse by the river. 3- to 5-bed rooms. 170 kčs. Hearty meals 40 kčs. No curfew, no lockout. The kind proprietors will leave your laundry folded on the bed for 30 kčs.

Hostel Sokol (*map*B4*), Hellichova 1 (tel. 53 45 51, ext. 397). Metro A: "Malostranská." Take tram #12 or 22 to "Hellichova" and follow the signs. Just 5 min. from the Charles Bridge. Offers clean and comfortable 10- to 15-bed rooms, co-ed by floor. Open June-Sept. Reception open 6-10am and 3pm-12:30am. Curfew 12:30am, 18 kčs charge to let you in after that. 180 kčs. Breakfast 20 kčs. Storage room for valuables.

Pensión V podzámčí, V podzámčí 27 (tel. 472 27 59), next to the TJ Sokol Krč gym. Take Metro C to "Budějovická," then bus #192 to the third stop. 6 rooms, each with 2 beds plus double twin-mattress loft. Clean and comfortable; grateful travelers have been known to leave flowers for the gracious hosts. Reception open Mon.-Fri. 7:30am-10pm, Sat.-Sun. 7am-11pm. No lockout. 225 kčs. Breakfast 30 kčs. Kitchen facilities. Make reservations.

TJ Sokol Karlin, Malého 1 (tel. 22 20 09), behind the Praha-Florenc bus station. Metro B or C: "Florenc." 5- to 12-bed dorms plus cots in a gymnasium. Not elegant, but there's usually room. Reception open 6pm-midnight. Check-out 7am. Lockout 8am-6pm. 170 kčs; cots 110 kčs.

Domov Mládeže, Dykova 20 (tel. 25 06 88 or 25 14 29). Take tram #16 from "Ječná" to the fourth stop, or ride Metro A to "nám. Míru," and switch to tram #16 to the second stop. At the streetcar stop, head right on Nitranská, and turn left on Dykova. Hall showers. 60 beds in the peaceful Vinohrady district. No lockout or curfew. 250 kčs. Breakfast 30 kčs. Open 24 hrs.

Hostel Braník, Urbova 1233 (tel. 46 26 41 or 46 26 42; fax 46 26 43). Metro B: "Smíchovské nádraží," then take bus #196 or 198 to "Ve Studeném" and walk 100 yards up the hill. 180 beds in singles, doubles, triples, and quads. Reception open 24 hrs.; no lockout or curfew. 280 kčs per person, including breakfast.

Pension Novodvorská, Novodvorská 151 (tel. 47 18 414). Take Metro B to "Smíchovské nádraží," and then ride bus #196 or 198 to "Sídl. Novodvorská." Many floors of student housing, often full. Reception open 24 hrs. 420 kčs, with breakfast.

Hotels

With so many relatively affluent Western tourists infiltrating Prague, hotels are upgrading both service and appearance. As privatization accelerates, dependable budget hotels are fading faster than you can say *demokracia.* The difference in price between B- and C- hotels and pensiones is often dramatic, though quality levels are comparable. Beware that hotels sometimes try to bill you for a more expensive room than the one you in which you stayed. Come prepared with pen, paper, and receipts.

Hotel Madape, Malešická 74 (tel. 89 31 04). Take bus #234 from the "Želivského" Metro A station 5 stops to "Vackow." Beside the cemetery where Kafka is buried. B-category. Private baths. Doubles off hospital-like corridors an outstanding 290, yes, 290 kčs per person. Some German spoken.

Hotel Juventus (*map*F6*), Blanická 10 (tel. 25 51 51 or 25 51 52), one block from the "nám. Míru" Metro A stop. Ideal location near the city center, between Francouzská and Korunní. Hall showers. Singles 695 kčs, doubles 1110 kčs.

Junior Hotel Praha (*map*D5-6*), Žitná 10 (tel. 29 29 84), right next to CKM. Rooms on the cutting edge of 1970s revival decor. Private showers and baths. Singles 980 kčs, doubles 1260 kčs. Breakfast included. Reserve in advance.

Camping

The **Pražská Informační Služba** (Prague Information Service) has a list of all Prague campgrounds. Call ahead to make sure there's room. German is usually spoken, English less frequently. There is a cluster of campgrounds north of the center in the Troja district of Prague. The largest of these is **Sokol Troja,** Trojská 171 (tel. 84 28 33). Take bus #112 from the Metro C stop "Nádraží Holešovice"; disembark at "Kazanka," the fourth stop, and walk 100m. (90 kčs per person, 70 kčs per small tent, bungalows 170 kčs per bed. Reservations recommended.) Or try **Sokol Dolní Počernice,** Dolní Počernice, Nad rybníkem (tel. 71 80 34). Take tram #9 to the end of the line, then hop on bus #109 and ask for the campground.

FOOD

Restaurants in Prague eat careless travelers alive. After numerous hidden charges are added in, the bill can be nearly twice what you expected. Always ask to see a menu—most restaurants post them outside. Don't be fooled: *anything* they offer you to go with your meal (such as french fries) will cost extra, and you'll be charged for everything they place on your table, including bread and even ketchup. Finally, take more care than usual to check the bill. Tipping involves rounding the bill up a few kčs. At posher places, a 10% gratuity is adequate. Include the tip as you pay; don't leave it on the table. Traditional Czech dishes are generally cheapest; look for "Hotová Jídla." Keep as much distance as possible between package-tour thoroughfares and your low-budget stomach. For a quick bite, the numerous window stands selling tasty *párek v rohlíku* (sausage in a small roll with mustard) for 7-15 kčs are a bargain. Many an outlying Metro stop becomes an impromptu marketplace during the summer; look for the daily **vegetable market** (*map*D3-4*) at the intersection of Havelská and Melantrichova in the Old Town.

Czech Cuisine

Lucerna Barrandor (*map*E5*), Štepanská 61 (tel. 232 22 16). From Vaclávské nám., facing the statue of Václav, turn right onto Štepanská and then right again into an arcade called Lucerna. The restaurant is on the right. Basic eats—Czech fast-food, with a Soviet flair. For the laborer who wants pork and potatoes without any fuss. Eat at stainless steel counters with Prague's proletariat and condemn the System. 25-30 kčs for a full meal. Open Mon.-Fri. 8am-10:30pm, Sat. 10am-8pm.

Restaurace Černý Kůň (Black Horse; *map*E5*), Vodicková 36 (tel. 22 41 53). Metro A or B: "Můstek." Situated downstairs in the Lucerna Bar complex. High ceiling and carved dark wood. Czech dishes 60 kčs, veggie dishes 50 kčs, European cuisine 90-130 kčs. Open daily 11am-11pm.

Slovanska Hospada (*map*E3-4*), Na Příkopě 22 (tel. 25 12 10). Metro B: "nám. Republiky." No-nonsense Czech fare. Owners headed the Czech National AIDS Awareness Week. Dishes about 40 kčs. Open Mon.-Sat. 11am-10pm.

Pivnice Ve Skořepce (*map*D4*), Skořepka 1 (tel. 22 80 81). Take Metro B to "Národní třída," walk up Na Perštýné, and take the 2nd right. A wood-paneled pub serving savory Czech dishes (75-150 kčs) and embarrassingly large liter jugs of beer (60 kčs). Try the *Maloštransky port* (69 kčs) with traditional ***knedelky*** (15 kčs) on the side. Open Mon.-Fri. 11am-10pm, Sat. 11am-8pm.

Plzeňská Restaurace (*map*E3-4*), Na Příkope 17 (tel. 22 08 06). Right down the road from Slovanska Hospada. Southern Bohemian cuisine runs 80-180 kčs. Open daily 10am-10pm.

Café Bar Bílý Orel (White Eagle; *map*AB3*), Malostranské Naměstí, Minská 10 (tel. 53 17 37). Right by the streetcar stop. Stylish and touristy. Outdoor seating in the thick of Malá Strana's hustle and bustle—tourists everywhere, trams whizzing by, cars speeding in reverse, small children shouting imprecations. For people who

like to eat *in* the city. Tasty food (meal 80-140 kčs). Extensive breakfast menu. Beware the price of beer, which is exorbitant here (29 kčs per less-than-½-liter). Kitchen closes at midnight, so as not to tempt the Gremlins. Open daily Mon.-Fri. 9am-4am.

Bistro v Soudním Dvoře (*map*B3*), Karmelitská 19 (tel. 53 00 54). From the "Malostranská" Metro A stop, walk south along Karmelitská until you spot a free-standing chalk-board on the right. Bravely enter the alleyway, take your first left, and then make a right (2 min. from Malostranské Náměstí). One-horse bistro home to many a quiet conversation. Few tourists; nothing resembling English. Meals 60 kčs per person. Beer 9 kčs. Open Mon.-Fri. 10am-11pm.

Černý Pivovar (*map*D6*), Korlovo Náměstí 15 (tel. 29 44 52 3). Metro B: "Karlovo Náměstí." An enormous mural runs the length of the wall, depicting good comrades happily sweating in the brewery that runs the restaurant. Czech and Czech-vegetarian fare, 40-80 kčs. Open daily 11am-11pm.

Malostranská Hospoda (*map*B3*), Karmelitská 25 (tel. 53 20 76). Serves standard Czech pub meals only 2 blocks from Malostranské nám. *Gulaš* 40 kčs. Open daily 10am-11pm.

"Exotic" and "Ethnic" Fare

Jo's Bar (*map*AB3*), Malostranské Náměstí 7. You can bet the ranch that everyone in here will speak English (and carry a camera, and have 2.6 kids and an Oldsmobile...). Burritos, quesadillas, and nachos 75-200 kčs.

Buffalo Bills, Voldičkova 9 (tel. 235 00 21). One of Prague's newest Tex-Mex restaurants, complete with "authentic" country and western music. Excellent fajitas, taco salads, etc., considering that they are 10,500km northeast of the border. Meals 100-200 kčs. Open daily 11am-11pm.

Red, Hot & Blues (*map*D2*), Jakubská 12 (tel. 231 46 39). For those with a superhuman attachment to the jalapeño pepper. Chips, salsa, burgers, and chili all about 80-150 kčs. Open daily 11am-11pm.

Poříčská Pekárna (*map*E3-4*), 28 Na Poříčí. Metro B: "nám. Republiky." Piles of freshly baked breads and pastries (4–8 kčs), as well as carni-, omni-, and herbivorous sandwiches, all for less than a Twix bar back home (19 kčs). Open Mon.-Fri. 7am-7pm, Sat. 8am-1pm.

Café FX, Bělehradská 120, above the Radost Club. Metro C: "I.P. Pavlova." Stylish vegetarian café; a sanctum for angst-ridden expatriates and healthy travelers alike. Proprietors spearheaded the Czech National AIDS Awareness Week. PC with a vengeance, and just a little too aware of the writeup in *Time* and *Smithsonian*. Fresh muffins and chocolate cake, and a divine cappuccino. Greek salad 50 kčs. Juices 20kčs. English poetry readings in the back, Sundays at 6pm. Open daily 11am-5am.

Gafrujola Fruit Shop (*map*F6*), Budečská 35. A wide variety of veggie, pasta, and fruit salads. Fruit drinks, fruit desserts, fruit cocktails, Fruit Roll-ups, Fruit of the Loom®.... Dishes run 40-100 kčs. Open Mon.-Sat. 11am-7pm, Sun. noon-7pm.

Košer Restaurant Shalom (*map*D2-3*), Maiselova 18 (tel. 231 89 96). Right across the street from the Old Jewish Graveyard and Synagogue in Staré Mésto. Excellent kosher food, for a price. Entrees about 300 kčs.

Elite (*map*F6*), Korunní 1 (tel. 25 71 50). The huge dining room is adorned with paintings, molded woodwork, and monstrous chandeliers. Some of the best Italian food in town. Pasta 100-200 kčs. Open daily 11am-11pm.

Pizzeria Kmotra (*map*CD5*), V Jircharich 12 (tel. 24 91 58 09). Pizza. Cheap. Plain pies run 44 kčs, add everything but the kitchen sink for 93 kčs. Beer 18 kčs. Open daily 11am-1am.

Pizzeria Corto (*map*DE4*), Havelská 15, right near the Old Town Square. Large pizzas will set you back 70-120 kčs. Open daily 11am-midnight.

Indický Snack Bar Mayur, Štěpánská 63 (tel. 236 99 22), beside the more expensive restaurant of the same name. This snack bar offers sit-down dining, with a limited menu from next door. Tandoori meats, veggie dishes, and mounds of nan 75-200 kčs. Open daily noon-11pm.

Restaurace Peking (*map*D5-6*), Legerova 64 (tel. 29 35 31), right outside the "I.P. Pavlova" Metro C station. Respectable chicken in honey sauce (130 kčs) and rice (20 kčs). Menu in English. Open daily 11:30am-3pm, 5:30-8pm, and 8:30-11pm.

Queenz Grill Bar (*map*DE4*), Havelská 12 (tel. 26 00 95). Fantastic falafel, great gyros, klassic kebabs 25-75 kčs. Open Mon.-Sat. 10am-10pm, Sun. noon-10pm.

Today's Restaurants Were Brought to You by the Letter...

U Banky, Moskevská 30, in Vršovické Náměstí (tel. 73 51 96). From Metro A "Náměstí Míru," take tram #22 downtown 3 stops in the outbound direction. Well off the beaten path. Watch MTV while you eat. Cheap and extensive international menu, 30-120 kčs.

U Benedikta (*map*E2*), Benediktská 11 (tel. 231 15 27). Take Metro B to "nám. Republiky," then walk down U Obecního domu and right on Rybná. Slightly upscale restaurant serving Czech and other European cuisine. Entrees 60-150 kčs. Open daily 9am-midnight.

U Čízků (*map*D6*), Karlovo Náměstí 34 (tel. 29 88 91). Cannot be beat for top quality Czech food. Pork, beef, duck, dumplings, you name it. Unfortunately, the German touring bus hordes have "discovered the restaurant"; call ahead for reservations. Entrees 150-250 kčs. Open daily noon-3:30pm and 5-10pm.

U Govindy, Na hrázi 5 (tel. 82 14 38). Ride Metro B to "Palmovka," then right off Zenklova. Hearty vegetarian meals in a restaurant founded by Hare Krishnas. Often packed. Full meal costs about 50 kčs. Open Mon.-Fri. noon-6pm.

U Kiliána (*map*B4*), Všehrdova 13. From Malostranské Namĕstí, walk south down Karmelitská; Všehrdova is the fourth street on the left. Only serves 14 typical Czech dishes, but the fried cheese is outstanding. Menu in Czech and English. Meals about 50-85 kčs per person. Open daily 10am-10pm.

U Paleãka, Nitranská 22 (tel. 25 13 00). From the Metro A stop "Jiřího z Poděbrad," cross Vinohradská; Nitranská is the first street to the left. Gourmet Czech cuisine in an intimate setting. Pork steak smothered in cheese, ham, and asparagus (75 kčs). Order the entire menu for just 180 kčs. Dress is casual but neat. Try to make reservations for dinner. Open daily 11am-midnight.

U Zuticů, Strossmayerovo nám., in the shadow of towering St. Antonina. From the Metro C stop "Vltavská," head right under the overpass and follow the white and black towers. Relaxing atmosphere, just outside the city center. Baked chickens 48 kčs. Open daily 11am-11pm.

Markets 'n More

Pomona supermarket (*map*E4-5*), Václavské nám. 52, next to American Express. Open Mon.-Fri. 7am-9pm, Sat. 9am-2pm, Sun. noon-9pm.

Casa Pascual supermarket (*map*D4*), Národní 27. Metro B: "Národní třída." Open Mon.-Fri. 8am-7pm, Sat. 8am-1pm.

Bio Market (*map*B3*), Mostecká 3, across the Charles Bridge on the castle side. Open Mon.-Sat. 6:30am-10pm, Sun. 10am-10pm.

Krone department store (*map*E4*), on Wenceslas Square at the intersection with Jindrišska (tel. 26 94 35 or 24 23 04 77). Look for the snack bar on the first floor. Open Mon.-Wed. and Fri.-Sun. 8am-7pm, Thurs. 8am-9pm.

Kotva department store (*map*E3*), at the corner of Revoluční and Náměstí Republiky (tel. 24 21 54 62 or 235 00 02). Metro B: "nam. Republiky." The state keeps Kotva consistently well-stocked; the basement grocery store has everything you'll need. Open Mon.-Wed. and Fri.-Sun. 8am-7pm, Thurs. 8am-9pm.

Máj department store (*map*D4*), at the corner of Národní and Spálena (tel. 24 22 79 71 or 26 23 41). Metro B: "Národní třída." K-Mart recently bought this formerly state-owned chain.'Nuff said. Open Mon.-Wed. and Fri.-Sun. 8am-7pm, Thurs. 8am-9pm.

SIGHTS

> *"I've taken my grandchildren to the top of Wenceslas Square where St. Wenceslas looks over the entire square. I tell them to imagine all the things St. Wenceslas might have seen sitting there on his horse: the*

trading markets hundreds of years ago, Hitler's troops, the Soviet tanks, and our Velvet Revolution in 1989. I can still imagine these things; it's the boulevard where much of our history, good and bad, has passed."

- Bedřich Šimáček—driver of tram #22 for 9 years—quoted in the Prague Post

Wenceslas Square

Václavské náměstí (Wenceslas Square; *map*E4-5*) has become Prague's focal attraction somewhat by accident; after all, this boulevard was designed as a quiet promenade, not an iconographic repository of the avant-garde or a cultural center of gravity. Yet St. Wenceslas's statue, at the southeast end, has presided over innumerable demonstrations and five full revolutions in the last century alone. The "square" has been gripped by bloody tragedy and elated triumph since its christening after the Czech patron saint; it seems that good king Wenceslas has instilled a powerful sense of Dylan-esque dissatisfaction among his subjects.

Wenceslas Square spreads from the "Můstek" Metro A or B stop, at Na příkopě and 28. října, to the **National Museum** (*map*EF5*), on the Wilsonova highway. The latter six-lane monstrosity was originally named Vitězného února (Victorious February), after the 1948 Communist coup; when the spirit of freedom rampaged through town in 1989, the street was renamed to honor President Woodrow Wilson, who was primarily responsible for breaking the Habsburg hold over the Czech lands. The **Radio Prague Building** (*map*EF5*), behind the National Museum, was the scene of a tense battle between Soviet tanks and Prague's citizens, who attempted to protect the studios by forming human and non-human barricades. The radio had succeeded in transmitting "free" and impartial updates for the first 14 hours of the invasion. The **Wenceslas Monument** (*map*EF5*), an anchor amidst all of the political tumult, sits in front of the National Museum on a small plaza by the "Muzeum" Metro A or C stop. The present version of this equestrian statue of sv Václav was completed in 1912, though a Wenceslas monument of some sort has graced the square since 1680. The statue was the site for student Jan Palach's 1969 self-immolation protesting Soviet intervention in the Prague Spring; his sacrifice sparked a series of similar demonstrations around the country.

Stretching north from the monument, art nouveau houses are scattered among the modernist offices at the sides of the Václavské náměstí. The premier example of Czech Jugendstil is the 1903 **Hotel Evropa** (*map*E4*), just before the intersection with Jindřišská on the right-hand side. Most of the other art nouveau structures along the square were designed by Jan Kotěra, the noted disciple of Viennese architectural giant Otto Wagner. Kotěra's stylistic development closely mirrored Wagner's progression: his early works are completed in flowing Secession grandeur, followed by a rather abrupt turn to strict functionalism, and finally turning at the end of his career to modules of Art Deco.

From the northern end of the Václavské nám., take a quick detour to Jungmannovo nám. and the **Panna Marie Sněžná** (Church of Our Lady of the Snows; *map*E4*). Founded by King Karel IV in 1347, this edifice was intended to be the largest church in Prague; the Gothic walls are, indeed, higher than any other house of worship, but the rest of the structure is still unfinished—there was only enough cash to complete the choir. It still feels tiny, despite the Baroque altar and the magnificently vaulted ceiling. (Open daily 7am-6pm.) Enter the **Františkářská zahrada** (*map*D4*) through the arch at the intersection of Jungmannova and Národní. These gardens, once the rose fields of Franciscan friars, offer quiet detachment amid the shrubbery just minutes from the bustle of Wenceslas Square. (Open daily 7am-9pm.) Under the arcades halfway down Národní stands a **memorial** (*map*D4*) that honors hundreds of Prague's citizens beaten on November 17, 1989. Marching in a government-sanctioned protest, they were greeted by a line of shield-bearing, truncheon-armed police. After a stalemate, the "protectors of the people" bludgeoned the marchers viciously, injuring hundreds. This event marked the inception of the

Velvet Revolution. The **Magic Lantern Theater** (*map*D4*) housed the headquarters of the vanguard of the Velvet Revolution. From within the bowels of this theater, Václav Havel and other dissident leaders delivered their latest releases to the press and developed their peaceful program to topple the Soviet regime.

Staroměstské náměstí

Na můstku and Melantrichova lead up from Wenceslas Square through a labyrinth of Old World alleyways into **Staroměstské náměstí** (*map*D3*), the "other" center of town. This sweeping space is dominated by the **Staroměstská radnice** (Old Town Hall; *map*D3*), which expanded from the original 14th-century tower to annex several neighboring buildings. To gain permission to found a Town Hall, the councillors of Prague traveled to Paris and presented their request to the, er, remote Czech King John of Luxembourg. Beside the Town Hall, **crosses** on the ground mark the spot where 27 Protestant leaders were executed on June 21, 1621, for their (failed) rebellion against the Catholic Habsburgs. The **Old Senate** (*map*D3*), with a magnificent coffered ceiling, boasts a Baroque stove with a figure of Justice and a sculpture of Christ. An inscription reads, "Judge justly—sons of Man." The town hall once encroached upon the St. Nicholas Church, but the extension was demolished by Nazi tanks on the very last day of World War II; today only a patch of grass remains. Townspeople and tourists gather on the hour to see the town hall's fabulous **Astronomical Clock** (*orloj; map*D3*), with 12 peering apostles and a bell-ringing skeleton representing death. The clockmaker's eyes were put out by his patron so he could not craft another. A statue of martyred Czech theologian and leader **Jan Hus** occupies the place of honor in the center of the square; the monument was unveiled in 1915, on the 500th anniversary of his death.

Jan Palach Square (*map*D3*), next to the Staroměstská metro station, was known as Red Army Square before the 1989 revolution. Palach was a philosophy student at Charles University, still located on this square. On the left corner of the philosophy department's façade is a copy of Palach's death mask, erected as a memorial after his self-immolation. Eight hundred thousand citizens followed his coffin from the Old Town Square to the Olšany Cemetery, where he is buried today.

Across from the Town Hall is **Týn Church** (Panna Marie před Týnem; *map*DE3*). The tower on the right represents Adam, who shields Eve, the tower on the left, from the midday sun. Type A astronomer Tycho de Brahe is buried inside; Brahe's tables laid the foundation for Johannes Kepler's planetary discoveries. To the left of the church, the **House at Stone Bell** (Dům U kamenného zvonu; *map*DE3*) shows the Gothic core that may lurk under many of Prague's Baroque façades. To its left, the **Goltz-Kinský Palace** (*map*DE3*), basks in its reputation as the finest of Prague's Rococo buildings. **Sv Mikuláš** (St. Nicholas Church; *map*DE3*), sits just across Staroměstské nám. The church was built in only three years by Kilian Ignaz Dientzenhopfer; Dientzenhopfer and his dad then ran with the idea, and immediately built the **sv Mikuláš** (St. Nicholas Church; *map*AB3*) in Malá Strana, right by the castle. Between Maiselova and Týn Church is **Franz Kafka's** former home (*map*DE3*), marked with a plaque. (Hard-core Kafka devotees can visit the writer's final resting place at the Jewish Graveyard right outside the "Želivského" Metro A stop.)

Malá Štupartská, behind Týn Church, supports **Kostel sv Jakuba** (St. Jacob's Cathedral; *map*DE3*), home to 21 altars. The rotund interior is bloated with garish Baroque ornamentation. Note the decaying limb dangling from the wall next to the entrance; it's a would-be thief's arm. City legend holds that the 15th-century thief attempted to pilfer one of the gems from the **Virgin Mary of Suffering** statue, whereupon the figure came to life and seized the thief's arm at the elbow. The bewildered burglar remained in the Holy Mother's clutches until the cathedral monks arrived for morning services; then came the grisly reproach—Mary wrenched off his arm. The monks took pity on the repentant, profusely bleeding soul, and invited him to join their order. He accepted, and remained faithfully pious;

the arm hung around as a constant reminder of the great potential for movie rights. (Church open daily 6:45am-4:30pm.)

Elsewhere around Staré Město: The Charles Bridge Plus

Take a short detour down Jilská from Staroměstské nám. to arrive at the **Bethlehem Chapel** (Betlémská kaple; *map*D4*). This was the ecclesiastic haunt of Jan Hus, who preached to a fanatically loyal congregation from 1402 until he was burnt at the stake. It's rare to find criticism of Jan, in any medium; the city's canonization of the hero was certainly well done.

Josefov (*map*D2*), the traditional Jewish quarter surrounding Pařížská and Maiselova (Metro A: "Staroměstská"), lost 80,000 of its 90,000 inhabitants to Nazi death camps during World War II. The desolate remains of this formerly vibrant community are reproduced in the scattered buildings of the **Státní Židovské Muzeum** (State Jewish Museum; *map*D2*), Jáchymova 3. (See Museums below.) Tours to the **Terezín ghetto,** a sham "model village" constructed by the Nazis to satisfy the International Red Cross (all Terezín residents were murdered after the Red Cross visit), depart every Sunday and Thursday at 10am from the Jewish Town Hall, Maiselova 18, and return at 3pm. Buses #17 and 20 also leave Florenc bus station; the ride takes about an hour. (Terezín museum open daily 9am-4:30pm.) Near the Florenc metro station stands the former **Communist Party Central Committee Headquarters** (*map*F2*). All the pivotal Czech leaders of the Prague Spring maintained offices here—until Soviet special forces surrounded the building and arrested Dubček and the other liberal members of the Politburo, taking them away in handcuffs to Moscow. Today the building serves as the Ministry of Transportation.

Karlův most (Charles Bridge; *map*C3*) may be Europe's most festive. Artisans and street musicians fill the bridge day and night above a bevy of swans. The musical tradition is ancient; even Austrian minstrel Dan von der Kuper once wandered the planks of the Charles. At the center of the bridge, the eighth statue from the right, is a monument to legendary hero **Jan Nepomucký.** At the statue's base is a depiction of hapless Jan, being tossed over the side of the Charles for faithfully guarding his queen's confidences. Jan was Queen Žofie's confessor, you see, and when King Wenceslas IV grew suspicious about his wife's activities, Jan refused to produce a transcript of the private confession sessions. Torture by hot irons and other devices failed to loosen Jan's lips, so the King ordered the saint to be drowned in the Vltava. Local lore further claims that a halo of five gold stars appeared as Jan plunged into the icy water. The right-hand rail, from whence the saint was supposedly ejected, is now marked with a cross and five stars between the fifth and sixth statues. Place one finger on each star and make a wish; not only is your wish *guaranteed* to come true, but, if you act now, just look what else you get—any wish made on this spot will at some point in the future whisk the wisher back to Prague.

A stone bridge on the site of Jan's murder was ravaged by flood waters in 1342, and King Karel IV decided to build a bridge of unprecedented proportions—520m by 10m. The foundation stone was laid at 5 hours and 31 minutes on the morning of July 9, 1357, the most significant astrological point for Leo, which symbolizes the Kingdom of Bohemia. The cosmological order is formed by the odd numbers, 1, 3, 5, 7, 9, 7, 5, 3, 1. Other supernatural powers inhabit the Karlův most as well—385 spooks, spectres, and things that go bump in the night, according to a resident "ghost expert." The **Waterman** waits in the sludge underneath the bridge for a young lass to spot one of his brightly colored ribbons; when the maiden reaches for the bauble, she is abducted by the fiend and never seen again. More sinister underworld spirits are connected with the construction of the bridge; legend has it that the builder made a pact with the devil in order to complete the massive project. Satan was allotted the first soul to cross the completed bridge, but the builder's wife and newborn babe unwittingly traversed the finished structure first; the devil could not take the baby's pure soul, so he instead cast a spell over the bridge. In the evening, you may now hear the faint cry of an infant, the ghostly wails of a surrogate spirit child—or is it the plaintive whining of prepubescent hostel youth?

Just south of the bridge, **Anenské nám.** (Anne's Square; *map*C3*) claims to be the most haunted district in town. Look toward the back of the square to find a well with its mesh cage torn and the door swinging loose; the **Hairy Man,** one of the most fiendish and allegedly most pungent spirits, prefers to use this well as an exit from his subterranean dwelling among the city sewers.

Climb the Gothic **defense tower** (*map*BC3*) on the Malá Strana side of the bridge for a superb view of the city. (Open daily 10am-5:30pm. Admission 20 kčs, students 10 kčs.) Head down the stairs on the left side of the bridge (as you face the castle district) to **Hroznová** (*map*BC3-4*), where a mural honors John Lennon and the peace movement of the 1960s. **Slovanský ostrov** (*map*C4-5*), **Dětský ostrov** (*map*B5-6*), and **Střelecký ostrov** (*map*C5-6*) islands are accessible from Janáčkovo nábřeží and the **most Legií** bridge. From the Charles, you can see rowboat outlets renting the vessels necessary to explore these islands and the remainder of the **Vltava.** (Boat rental open daily 11am-9pm; 40 kčs per hr.)

Malá Strana

The **Malá Strana** (Lesser Town; *map*A3*) is rich in palaces, ornate gardens, and grand Baroque churches. The fairest of them all is the 18th-century **St. Nicholas' Church** (sv Mikuláš; *map*AB3*), the highest achievement of Czech Baroque art. Mozart tickled the organ's ivories here; concerts of his work are held almost every night at 5pm (100 kčs). (Admission 20 kčs, students 10 kčs. Open daily 9am-5pm.) Nearby on Karmelitská rises the more modest **Panna Marie Vítězné** (Church of Our Lady Victorious; *map*B3*). This holy edifice is the repository of the world-famous porcelain statue of the **Infant Jesus of Prague,** which reputedly bestows miracles on the faithful. The figurine has an elaborate wardrobe of over 380 outfits; every sunrise, the Infant receives swaddling anew from the nuns of a nearby convent. The statue first arrived in town in the arms of a 17th-century Spanish noblewoman who married into the Bohemian royalty; mysteriously, the plague bypassed Prague shortly thereafter. In 1628, the Barefooted Carmelite nunnery gained custody of the Infant and allowed pilgrims to pray to the statue; the public has been infatuated with its magic ever since. Try asking the statue for a special favor—it's probably more reliable than a Magic 8 Ball. (Church open 10am-7:30pm.)

Designed by Kristof and Kilian Ignaz Dientzenhopfer, the charming duo responsible for the Břevnov Monastery's undulating façade (see below), the **St. Thomas Church** (*map*B2-3*) reposes at Letenská, off Malostranské náměstí, toward the Vltava. True to form, the structure's rolling front face introduces the presence of another master of the ornate Baroque—Rubens facsimiles await within, adjacent to the saint reliquaries adorning the fascinating side altars. (Open daily 7am-6pm.) A simple wooden gate just down the street at Letenská 10 opens onto the **Valdštejnská zahrada** (Waldstein Garden; *map*B2*), one of Prague's best-kept secrets. This tranquil 17th-century Baroque garden is enclosed by old buildings that glow golden on sunny afternoons. General Albrecht Waldstein, owner of the palace of the same name, held his Tupperware® parties here among Vredeman de Vries's classical bronze statues—when the works were plundered by Swedish troops in the waning hours of the Thirty Years War, Waldstein replaced the original casts with facsimiles. Frescoes inside the arcaded loggia depict your favorite episodes from the Trojan War. (Open daily 9am-7pm.) Across the street from the Malostranská metro stop, a marker in a small park, called the **Charousková Memorial** (*map*AB3*), is the sole memorial to the slain of 1968. It commemorates Marie Chaousková, a graduate student who was machine-gunned by a Soviet soldier for refusing to remove from her shirt a black ribbon protesting the invasion.

Prague Castle

You can spend days wandering about the structures that comprise the **Pražský hrad** (Prague Castle; *map*AB2*), just to the north. The complex is a full-scale architectural museum; every style since Prague's founding contributes to the castle's splendor. Director Miloš Forman thought that the aged passageways appeared more Viennese than Vienna—most of the movie *Amadeus* was filmed here. The fortress houses the **National Gallery of Bohemian Art** (see Museums below), but there is no doubt that the primary attraction is the soaring **Katedrála sv Vita** (St. Vitus's Cathedral), completed in 1930 after 600 years of construction. You must pass through two castle courtyards and into a third in order to arrive at the Czech Republic's largest church, a curious blend of weathered Gothic and *faux*-weathered neo-Gothic. To the right of the high altar stands the **tomb of St. John of Nepomuk** (Jan Nepomucký), three meters of solid, glistening silver, weighing in at two tons. The enormous silver sepulchre is crowned by an angel holding a silver tongue in her hand; supposedly, this tongue was the only part of Jan Nepomucký still recognizable when his body was discovered by fishermen in the spring after his execution. The queen thereafter placed his tongue in the notorious cathedral confessional to commemorate its faithful silence; eventually, it was silvered and put on display.

Below the cathedral lies the ominous **Royal Crypt,** which houses the tombs of various Bohemian Kings; the four wives of Karel IV all share a tomb beside him. (Entrance to choir and crypt 20 kčs, students 10 kčs. Quads available for spouses of royalty. Open daily 9am-5pm. If you plan to visit the rest of the castle, the **combined ticket** (65 kčs, students 30 kčs) is a worthy investment.) The walls of the **St. Wenceslas Chapel** are lined with precious stones and a painting cycle that depicts the legend of the eponymous saint. The brilliance and purity of the massive stained-glass windows, manufactured in 1930, are astounding. A massive door leads from the chapel to a room where the Czech coronation jewels are stored, but you'll have to ask Mr. Havel for the keys.

Exit the cathedral and stroll across the third interior courtyard to enter the **Starý královský palác** (Old Royal Palace). Inside is the vast **Vladislav Hall,** with ample room for the jousting competitions that once took place here. Climb the 287 steps of the **Cathedral Tower** for a breathtaking view of the castle and the city. (Open daily 10am-4pm; admission 15 kčs, students 8 kčs.) In the nearby **Czech Chancellery,** two Catholic Habsburg officials were lobbed out the window by fed-up Protestant noblemen in 1618. Though a dungheap broke their fall, the die was cast, and war ravaged Europe for the next 30 years. Built in 1485 to enhance the castle's fortifications, the **Powder Tower** (Mihulka) houses a reconstructed alchemist's laboratory (admission 10 kčs, students 5 kčs).

The Romanesque **Basilica of St. George** (Bazilika sv Jiří) was erected in 921 just behind the Starý královský palác. Immediately on the right as you enter, note the wood and glass tomb enclosing St. Ludmila's skeleton. When the basilica was first commissioned, the convent sponsoring the operation unknowingly hired a dishonest architect. That ankle bone's connected to the...shin bone; that shin bone's connected to the...knee bone; that knee bone's connected to the—the thigh bone had mysteriously vanished. One week later, the architect was found dead; the two architects who were hired to complete the job both died within a year. Finally, the original architect's son discovered the thigh bone among his father's personal effects; he snuck into the convent, returned the skeletal link, and thereby ended the curse. (Basilica open daily 9am-4:45pm.)

The **Lobkovic Palace,** at the bottom (northeast) of Jiřská, contains a replica of the Czech coronation jewels and an exhibit recounting the history of the Slavs (admission 30 kčs, students 15 kčs; not included in the combined admission ticket). Halfway up is a tiny street carved into the fortified wall—Kafka held an office on this **Zlatá ulička** (Golden Lane), where the court alchemists supposedly toiled. (All palace-related buildings open Tues.-Sun. 9am-5pm; Oct.-March Tues.-Sun. 9am-4pm.)

Exiting the castle grounds across the **Prašný most** (Powder Bridge), you'll see the entrance to the serene **Royal Garden** (Královská zahrada), sculpted in 1534 to include the glorious Renaissance palace **Belvedér** (renovated in 1993). The Garden was devastated during the Thirty Years War, when the Saxons and Swedes burned the growths and destroyed the various structures; today, it features an **Orangery** and **Fig Garden.** (Open Tues.-Sun. 10am-5:45pm. Admission 5 kčs, students 2 kčs.) If, instead, you exit the castle through the main gate and walk straight for 200 yards, the lovely **Loreto** will be on your right. An aggrandized replica of Jesus' birthplace and a diamond mine of a treasury imperiously anchor the complex, constructed by the ubiquitous Dientzenhopfer family of architects. (Admission 30 kčs, students 20 kčs. Open Tues.-Sun. 9am-4:30pm.) For more information on the entire castle complex, seek out the **Informační středisko** behind the cathedral.

Outer Prague

A model of the **Eiffel Tower** tops the **Petřínské sady** gardens (*map*A4*) on the hills just to the south of the castle. (Open daily in May 9am-10pm; July-Aug. daily 9am-11pm. Admission 20 kčs, students 5 kčs.) The funicular to the top (4 kčs—look for *lanová dráhy* signs) leaves from just above the intersection of Vítězná and Újezd. The neo-Gothic building next to the Tower is a wacky little castle offering juvenile bliss—a **hall of mirrors** awaits inside this **Bludiště.** (Open daily April-Oct. 9am-6pm. Admission 10 kčs, students 5 kčs.) Just east of the park lies **Strahov Stadium,** the world's largest, enclosing the space of 10 soccer fields.

Take tram #22 west of the castle to "Břevnovský klášter," and you'll find yourself staring down the **Břevnov Monastery,** Bohemia's oldest Benedictine order. The monastery was founded in 993 by King Boleslav II and St. Adalbert; both were independently guided by a divine dream to create a monastery atop a bubbling stream. They surprised each other at the indicated site the next morning and instantly agreed to begin construction. **St. Margaret's Cathedral** (Kostel sv Markéty), a Benedictine chapel, waits inside the complex. Beneath the altar rests the tomb of St. Vintíř, who vowed to forego all forms of meat. On one particular diplomatic excursion, St. Vintíř met and dined with a German king, a fanatical hunter; the main course was an enormous pheasant slain that morning by the monarch's own hand. The saint prayed for delivery from the myriad *faux pas* possibilities, whereupon the main course sprang to life and flew out the window.

The green bell tower and red tile roof of the monastery building are all that remain of the original Romanesque construction; the complex was redesigned in High Baroque by the Dientzenhopfer father and son team. During the Soviet occupation, the monastery was allegedly used to store truckloads of secret police files—there may be more to the monks' vow of silence than you think. See if you can graft yourself onto a guided tour of the grounds, the crypt, and the prelature to dig up more dirt on the monastery's history. (Tours daily 10am-6pm; 50 kčs.)

Bus #112 winds from the "Nádraží Holešovice" Metro C station to "Troja," the site of French architect J.B. Mathey's masterful **chateau.** The pleasure palace, overlooking the Vltava from north of the U-shaped bend, includes a terraced garden, a unique oval staircase with monuments attesting to Olympian magnificence, and an admirable collection of 19th-century Czech paintings. Drop by the tourist office to pick up a copy of the schedule of **free concerts** in the Chateau's great hall. (Chateau open daily 9am-5pm.)

A half-hour walk south of Nové Město is the quiet fortress **Vyšehrad,** the Czech Republic's most revered landmark. It's delightfully tourist-free. On the mount above the river, the fortress encompasses a neo-Gothic church, a Romanesque rotunda, and the **Vyšehrad Cemetery** (home to the remains of Smetana and Dvořák). Take Metro C to "Vyšehrad." Even the subway stop has a movie-sweep vista of Prague. (Complex open 24 hrs.)

For a magnificent view of the Old Town and castle from the east, stroll up forested **Pohled z Vítkova** (Vítkov Hill), topped by the world's largest equestrian monument. From this perch, one-eyed Hussite leader Jan Žižka scans the terrain for Crusaders, whom he stomped out on this spot in 1420. Take Metro B to "Křižíkova," walk down Thámova, through the tunnel, and up the hill. (Open 24 hrs. Free.)

Although less a pilgrimage destination than the Old Jewish Cemetery, the **New Jewish Cemetery,** far to the southeast, is one of the largest burial grounds in central Europe. Kafka is interred here; obtain a map of the enormous complex from the attendant before you start hunting for the tombstone. The cemetery's main entrance is at the "Želivského" Metro A stop. (Open daily 8am-6pm.)

Museums

National Museum (*map*EF5*), Václavské nám. 68 (tel. 26 94 51). Metro A or C: "Muzeum." Vast collection including meteorites, enormous minerals, and fossils; don't miss the skeleton horse and rider. Soviet soldiers, thinking this landmark at the top of Wenceslas Square was the main government building, made the mistake of firing on it; traces of the gunning are still visible. Five months later, in January 1969, 20-year-old student Jan Palach set himself on fire here to protest the Soviet quashing of the Prague Spring. Open Mon. and Wed.-Fri. 9am-5pm, Sat.-Sun. 10am-6pm. Admission 20 kčs, students 10 kčs.

State Jewish Museum (Státní Židovské Muzeum; *map*D2*), tel. 231 06 81, Jáchymova 3, tel. 231 06 81. Metro A: "Staroměstská." Includes 5 synagogues, a cemetery, and a collection of artifacts from Bohemia and Moravia. Hitler ordered that these relics of Judaica be preserved for an intended museum of the extinct Jewish race. A unique collection of children's drawings and poems from the Terezín camp also survives. The fascinating underground **Staronová Synagóga** is the oldest synagogue in Europe; parts date from 1270. Next to the synagogue is the pink Rococo **Jewish Town Hall,** with a Hebrew clock that proceeds counterclockwise. The **Pinkas Synagogue** houses a memorial to the Czech Jews who perished in the Holocaust. Communists plastered over the monument; each name is now being reinscribed. A Torah scroll from this synagogue is on permanent loan to Temple Beth Torah in Dix Hills, NY; many Central European synagogues have donated their scrolls to synagoges in the United States and Israel. The **Klausova Synagogue** houses an incongruously merry relic; look for the cycle of paintings of the Prague Burial Society, depicted happily undertaking various duties of the order. The nearby **Jewish cemetery** ripples with 12,000 melancholy tombstones. Town Hall and Staronová Synagóga open Mon.-Fri. and Sun. 9:30am-5pm. Admission 30 kčs, students 15 kčs. Cemetery and other synagogues open Mon.-Fri. and Sun. 9:30am-5:30pm. Admission 80 kčs, students 30 kčs.

National Gallery: collections are housed in 9 different historical buildings. The **National Gallery of European Art** is in the **Šternberk Palace** (*map*AB2*), Hradčanské nám. 15, just outside the front gate of the Prague Castle. Includes works by Rubens, Breughel, Dürer, Picasso, and your favorite Impressionists. The **National Gallery of Bohemian Art** (*map*AB2*), Gothic to Baroque, is housed in **St. George's Monastery** inside the Castle. Showcases works by Czech artists including Master Theodorik, court painter for Karel IV. More Bohemian creations are exhibited at the **Anežský areal.** (*map*D2*), at the corner of Anežka and Řásnovka; the structure was the Cloister of St. Agnes for centuries. All collections open Tues.-Sun. 10am-6pm. Admission to either gallery 40 kčs, students 10 kčs.

Muzeúm Mozart (*map*A6*), Mozartova 169 (tel. 54 38 93). Take Metro B to "Anděl," make a left on Pleňská, and turn left on Mozartova. In the Villa Bertramka, where Mozart lived in 1787 and reputedly wrote *Don Giovanni*. Open daily 9:30am-6pm. Garden concerts in July and Aug. on Fri. at 7:30pm; call ahead for tickets. Admission 50 kčs, students 30 kčs.

The Prague Municipal Museum (Muzeum hlavního města Prahy; *map*EF2-3*), Na poříčí 52 (tel. 236 24 50). Metro B or C: "Florenc." Holds the original calendar board from the Town Hall's Astronomical Clock, but the highlight is a 1:480 scale model of old Prague, meticulously precise to the last window pane on over 2000 houses and all of Prague's great monuments. Come see what your hostel looked like in 1834. Other exhibits from the same collection reside in the **House at Stone Bell,** in Staroměstské nám. just to the left of Týn Church. Both buildings open Tues.-Sun. 10am-6pm. Admission 10 kčs, students 5 kčs.

Museum of National Literature (*map*AB2*), Pohořelec 8, in the Strahov Monastery (tel. 53 88 41). Walk straight from the castle's main gate and bear left. The star attraction here is the Strahov library, with its magnificent **Theological and Philosophical Halls.** The frescoed, vaulted ceilings and lavish, Baroque grandeur of the two reading rooms were intended to spur enlightened monks to the loftiest peaks of erudition; great pagan thinkers of antiquity oversee their progress from the ceiling in the Philosophical Hall. Oohs and aahs guaranteed. Open daily 9am-noon and 1-5pm. Admission 20 kčs, students 5 kčs.

Military Museum (*map*AB2*), Hradčanské nám. 12, in the seemingly envelope-covered **Schwarzenberg Palace,** just outside the castle's main gate. All of the more aggressive implements of Bohemian warfare throughout the ages. Open Tues.-Sun. 10am-6pm. Admission 20 kčs, students 10 kčs.

Museum of Decorative Arts (*map*D2-3*), 17. Listopadu 2, (tel. 232 00 51). Metro A: "Staroměstská"; right behind the Old Jewish Cemetery. Includes exquisite ceramics and richly carved and bejewelled furnishings from Renaissance and Baroque palaces. The second floor houses one of the world's largest glasswork collections (closed to the public in 1993, but should be open, at least on weekends, in 1994). Open Tues.-Sun. 10am-6pm. Admission 20 kčs, students 10 kčs.

ENTERTAINMENT

Václavské náméstí (*map*E4-5*) thumps with numerous dancespots, but the best way to enjoy Prague at night is to find a *pivnice* (beer hall) or a *vinárna* (wine hall).

Pivnice and vinárna (Beer Halls and Wine Halls)

U Fleků (*map*EF5*), Křemencova 11-12. Behind the National Theater; look for the huge clock. Prague's touristy answer to the German brew house, with home-brewed brown ale (30 kčs cover to sit outside for the oom-pah band). Open daily 9am-11pm.

Moravský Šenk (*map*E4*), Jindrišská 11 (tel. 235 88 62). The small tavern, decorated with painted Moravian ceramics, specializes in delectable Moravian wines. 12-14 kčs per glass. Open daily 9am-10pm.

U sv. Tomáše (*map*B2-3*), Letenská 12. Swinging monks founded it in 1358 as a monastery brewery. This *pivnice* serves perhaps Prague's best beer—no small feat. 20 kčs per glass. 15 kčs cover charge for the Czech folk band. Open 11am-midnight.

Krušovická Pivnice (*map*DE3*), Široká 20, 2 blocks from Staroměstské nám. off Pařížská. Traditional Czech *pivnice*, serving light, dark, and half-and-half. Beer 13 kčs. Open Mon.-Sat. 11am-midnight.

Pivnice Ve Skořepce (*map*D4*), Skořepka 1 (tel. 22 80 81). See Food and Drink above. Imbibe monstrous jugs of beer in wood-paneled chambers. Open Mon.-Fri. 11am-10pm, Sat. 11am-8pm.

Cafés

Nebozízek (*map*B4-5*), Petřínské sady 411 (tel. 53 79 05). A somewhat expensive café, but the view of Prague from the terrace is unparalleled. Take the funicular from Újezd street, between Všehrdova and Říční, to the midpoint of the Petřín summit. The lift stops only twice: at Nebozízek and at the mockup of the Eiffel Tower (see above). Café open daily noon-6pm and 7-11pm.

Café Nouveau (*map*E3*), Náměstí Republiky 5 (Obecní dům; tel. 232 58 58). A monstrous coffee house, with live jazz. Open daily 11am-midnight.

Café Savoy (*map*B5*), Vítězná 1 (tel. 53 94 90). Raise your spirits (brandy, 20 kčs) with a toast inside. The lofty ceiling features outrageously ornate restored paintings and intricate woodwork. Open daily noon-midnight.

U Zlatých Nůžek (*map*AB2*), Na Kampě 6, near the castle (tel. 24 51 01 10). Non-smokers frequent this bastion of caffeination. Fresh baked goods complement over 50 teas and coffees. Open daily 10am-8pm.

The Globe Coffeehouse, Janovského 14, inside Prague's newest and largest English-language bookstore. Peruse a *Let's Go* as you sip a hot beverage and contemplate literary self-reference. Open daily 10am-midnight.

Clubs and Bars

Rock Club Bunkr (*map*F2*), Lodecká 2. From the "nám. Republiky" Metro B stop, walk down Na Poříči, and take a left on Zlatnická. Hot Czech and American rock-n-roll bands in an erstwhile Communist-regime nuclear bunker. Cover varies (around 50 kčs). Open daily 7pm-5am. Café upstairs open daily 11am-3am.

Repre Club (*map*E3*), downstairs in the Obecní Dům, nám. Republiky 5. Huge, open nightclub in the basement of the beautiful *art nouveau* Municipal House. Maybe the prettiest building you'll ever get wasted in. Live music nightly until midnight, DJ after that. Cover 50 kčs. Open daily 9pm-5am.

Žíznivý Pes (The Thirsty Dog; *map*E3*), on U Obecního domu, around the corner from the Repre and owned by the same folks. Swathed in wild, energetic murals. Swap stories with other travelers over cheap drafts (15 kčs).

Radost FX, Bělehradská 120, (tel. 25 12 10), below Café FX. An alternative dance club, becoming swiftly mainstream and *hating* every ounce of extra popularity. Replete with a "virtual reality light show" and driving techno beat. Cover 50 kčs. Open 9pm-6am daily.

Jo's Bar (*map*AB3*), Malostranské nám. 7, right in the shadow of St. Nicholas Church in Malostranské nám. You won't practice your Czech here, but you'll get friendly service and surprisingly yummy Mexican food. Nachos 70 kčs, beer 30 kčs. Kitchen open Sun.-Thurs. until 11pm, Fri.-Sat. until midnight. Open Mon.-Sat. 11am-2am, Sun. 11am-1am.

Reduta (*map*CD4-5*), Národní 20 (tel. 20 38 25). A good jazz club with live music nightly and a clientele of artists drowning in tourists. Cover 80 kčs. Open Mon.-Sat. 9pm-2am.

Rock Café (*map*CD4-5*), right next to Reduta (tel. 20 66 56). MTV pumped in on satellite, and the occasional rockumentary. Sadly, *This Is Spinal Tap* doesn't survive the translation into Czech. Open Mon.-Fri. 10am-3am, Sat. noon-3am.

Bar Club (*map*E3*), Hybernská, between Obecního domu and nám. Republiky. Reggae and South American music, with a rare injection of classic rock. The first 10 people in the door at 9pm get in for free. Slowpokes pay 20 kčs cover. Open daily 9pm-5am.

Both the *Prague Post* and *Prognosis* include an invaluable listing of opera, ballet, and theater performances, as well as all concerts in town. The grandest of Prague's theaters are the **Národní Divadlo** (National Theater; *map*C5*), Národní třida 2 (tel. 20 53 64; box office open Mon.-Fri. 10am-8pm, Sat.-Sun. 3-8pm) and the **Státní Opera** (State Opera; *map*F4-5*), Wilsonova třida, between the "Muzeum" Metro A or C stop and Hlavnínádraži (tel. 26 53 53; box office open Mon.-Fri. 10am-6pm, Sat.-Sun. noon-6pm). Mozart conducted the premiere of his own *Don Giovanni* in 1787, at the newly renovated **Stavovské Divadlo** (Estates Theater; *map*DE4*). The theater sits on Ovocnýtrh, at the "Můstek" Metro A or B stop between Celetná and Železná (tel. 22 86 58 or 22 72 82; box office, in the Kolowrat Palace around the corner, open Tues.-Sat. 10am-6pm, Sun.-Mon. noon-6pm). All three theaters showcase world-class opera, drama, and ballet productions almost every night at 7pm; the Stavovské Divadlo provides earphones for simultaneous English translation. (Tickets run about 40-400 kčs; unsold tickets are available ½ hr. before showtime. Scalpers near the National Theater charge around 200 kčs per ticket.)

From mid-May to early June, the **Prague Spring Festival** draws musicians from around the world. Tickets (270-540 kčs) can be bought at **Bohemia Ticket International** (*map*E3-4*), Na příkopé 16 (tel. 22 87 38), next to Čedok. (Open Mon.-Fri. 9am-6pm, Sat. 9am-3pm, Sun. 9am-2pm.) Backed by a Prague tradition over two centuries old, **marionette theater** thrives at **Říše Loutek** (National Marionette Theatre) at žateckal in the Old Town (tel. 232 34 29; box office open Mon. and Tues. 2-8pm). A star tourist attraction is the **Laterna Magica** (*map*CD4-5*), Národní 4 (tel. 20 62 60), a cutesy but clever integration of film, drama, and dance. (Performances Mon.-Fri. at 8pm, Sat. 5pm and 8pm. Box office open Mon.-Sat. 3-6pm. Tickets 300-450 kčs. Often sold out in summer 2 weeks in advance.)

Near Prague: Karlstejn

The Central Bohemian hills surrounding Prague contain 14 castles, some built as early as the 13th century. A 45-minute train ride southwest from Prague (8 kčs) brings you to **Karlstejn,** a walled and turreted fortress built by Karel IV to house his crown jewels and holy relics. The **Chapel of the Holy Cross** is decorated with more than 2000 inlaid precious stones and 128 apocalyptic paintings by medieval artist Master Theodorik. Trains cart gawkers hourly from Praha-Smíchov station. (Metro B: "Smíchovské nádraži." Open Tues.-Sun. 9am-4pm. Admission with foreign-language guide 90 kčs, students 40 kčs; in Czech 10 kčs, students 5 kčs.) A **campground** (tel. (0311) 942 63) is located on the left bank of the River Berounka (open 24 hrs).

Near Prague: Konopište

Animal-rights activists might wish to avoid mighty **Konopiště,** south of Prague in **Benešov** (bus from Praha-Florenc station, 1½ hr.), a Renaissance palace with a luxurious interior preserved from the days when Archduke Franz Ferdinand bagged game here—more than 300,000 animals. Fittingly, the **Weapons Hall** contains one of the finest collections of 16th- to 18th-century European arms.

Near Prague: Kutná Hora

Ninety minutes east of Prague by bus is the former mining town, **Kutná Hora.** Soon after a lucky miner struck a silver vein here in the 13th century, a royal mint—**Vlašský dvůr**—was established to produce the Prague *groschen* (silver coin). The uninteresting coin museum has commentary written entirely in Czech, but up the stairs from the courtyard is a magnificent **Gothic Hall** with frescoes and lovely carved wooden triptychs. The most convincing evidence of the wealth that once flowed through the town is the fantastic, begargoyled **Cathedral of St. Barbara,** built to rival St. Vitus in Prague. Buses leave nearly hourly from Prague's Metro A: Želivského, platform #2 and from Praha-Florenc station.

WESTERN BOHEMIAN DAYTRIPS

Bohemia, the western half of the Czech Republic, is the traditional homeland of the Czech people. Common heritage did little to prevent squabbles, to which hundreds of prickly castles guarding former feudal principalities testify.

■ Karlovy Vary

Essential to a Bohemian itinerary are the springs of **Karlovy Vary** ("Karlsbad" in German), whose guest list is a roster of 19th-century political and cultural icons: Goethe, Schiller, Tolstoy, Gogol, Beethoven, Metternich, and Marx sampled the waters here. *Bon vivants* still throng to the town to cure their ailments and enjoy the air of Victorian luxury and grandeur. Each tappet draws from a different spring with its own documented, supposedly curative minerals. Libation from the "thirteenth spring" is a potent liqueur with a pastoral after-taste called Becherovka, made from herbs and Karlovy Vary water. A fitting accompaniment to all Karlovy Vary rituals are the circular *oplatký* wafers that resemble 20cm beer coasters; they taste divine either plain or chocolate-covered.

The Teplá River winds through the town, which lies in a narrow valley caught in the folds of steep hillsides. On the banks above the modern thermal sanatorium is a **public swimming pool.** (Open Mon.-Sat. 8am-9:30pm, Sun. 9am-9:30pm, 20 kčs per hr.) The many-pillared **Mill Colonnade** on Mlýnské nábřeží contains a few thermal faucets. Bring your own cup, or buy one in a souvenir shop. The heart of Karlovy Vary is the **Vřídelní Colonnade** on Vřídelní, with a gushing 12m fountain. Try the faucet's scalding water. The baroque **Church of Mary Magdalene** overlooks the colonnade. Hiking paths and the **Diana Funicular Railway** on Mariánská lead up to the **Diana Tower** at the top. (Railway departures daily every 15min. 10am-6pm. Round-trip 35 kčs. Tower admission 5 kčs.) The moderately-priced **Diana Restaurant** and **Kavárna** sit atop the mountain. (Open daily 10:30am-6pm.) Hiking trails also appear on the Karlovy Vary city map (19 kčs), available in bookstores. Check out the white **Russian Orthodox Church,** which glitters with gold.

The cheapest place to stay in Karlovy Vary is the attractive **Junior Hotel Alice (HI)** at u. Pétiletky 147 (tel. (017) 243 79), which was undergoing renovations in 1993. Set amid the oaks and squirrels, the hotel is a 3km hike out of town. From the city bus station (near the market), take bus #7 about 12 stops. Reserve in advance. (Members and ISIC holders 215 kčs person, nonmembers in singles 420 kčs. Prices are from 1991, when hostel was last open.) One stop past J. H. Alice is the **Sport Hotel Gejzír,** at bus stop Gejzír. (Singles 305 kčs, doubles 550 kčs.) For less expensive lodgings, Čedok recommends reserving three to four months in advance, although the hotels listed below often have rooms available when you arrive.

A three-minute walk from the main bus station, up the hill, left on T. G. Masaryka, then right on Dr. Davida Bechera, at #18, is **Hotel Turist** (tel. (017) 268 37; doubles 750 kčs, triples 1095 kčs). The **Čedok** closest to the waters, at Karla IV 1 (tel. (017) 261 10), books pensions for 40 DM per person. Take bus #13 from bus station to Lázně III. (Open Mon.-Fri. 9am-5pm, Sat. 9am-noon; Oct. to mid-May Mon.-Fri. 9am-4pm, Sat. 9am-noon.) **"W,"** nám. Republiky 3 (tel. (017) 277 68), near the bus station, also books private rooms (US$10-15; open Mon.-Fri. 9am-7pm, Sat. 10am-7pm). Look for the **občervstení grill** on Stará Louka, two bridges past the colonnade exit, to score cheap eats (pork cutlets 32 kčs; grilled sausages 15-19 kčs). The **Fortuna Restaurant,** at Zámecký vrch 14, cooks up Italian favorites (pizzas 59-90 kčs; open daily 11am-10pm).

The **bus** is your ticket from Prague to Karlovy Vary (2 hr., 56 kčs). Buses leave Praha-Florenc every few hours, but buy tickets early; they sell out two or three days in advance. Leave your bags at **dolní nádraží** train station, 300m down Varšovká (which becomes Západní) from the bus station.

■ Mariánské Lázné

Forty km south of Karlovy Vary (80 min. by bus, 17 kčs), Mariánské Lázné ("Marienbad" in German) is another spa popular among ailing European gentry, though cheaper and less touristy its northern neighbor. The town is a stately park, designed and landscaped by Václav Skalník. At the **Lázeňska Colonnade,** the faucets magically spurt on and off when you wave your hand over them. There is a fountain concert every hour (open daily 6am-noon and 4-6pm).

The **Čedok** office is next to the Hotel Evropa on Třebízského (tel. (0165) 25 00), in the center of town; take bus #5 from the station and get off at stop #6, "Centrum" (open Mon.-Fri. 8am-5pm). The finest pad is easily CKM's beautiful **Junior Hotel Krakonoš (HI)** 3km southeast of town in a gorgeous wooded location (tel. (0165) 26 24). From the train station, take bus #5 to "Centrum," then bus #12 to the top of the mountain. (HI members and ISIC holders 239 kčs, nonmembers 350 kčs; reserve in advance.) Several **hotels** line the main street (singles 450-600 kčs, doubles 600-900 kčs). The cheapest is the **Hotel Evropa** at Třebízského (tel. (0165) 20 63 or 20 64; singles 350 kčs, with bath 550 kčs; doubles 550 kčs, with bath 850 kčs). Hotel restaurants are fairly similar in price and setting (full meals 150-250 kčs). **Kavárna Charlie** (tel. (0165) 29 47) on Anglická 11 is outstanding and cheaper than most (full meal 150 kčs; open daily 11am-midnight). Express **trains** come hither along the Prague-Nuremberg rail line (3 per day, 3 hr., 105 kčs).

■ Plzeň

Eighty kilometers southwest of Prague, Plzeň is immortalized as the birthplace of beer and as the source of Plzeňsky Prazdroj (Pilsner Urquell). Improve the industrial view with several rounds of the town's finest at the **Pivnice Prazdroj,** U Prazdroja 1 (tel. (019) 356 08), right outside the brewery gates and within walking distance from the train station (open Mon.-Fri. 10am-10pm, Sat.-Sun. 11am-9pm). If the art of beer-making enthralls you, visit the **Brewery Museum,** housed in a 15th-century brewery at Veleslavínova 6, in the town center. (Open daily 10am-6pm. Admission 30 kčs, students 10 kčs.) The heart of Plzeň is **náměští Republiky.** The lone bronze tower of the Gothic **Cathedral of St. Bartholemew** is the highest in Bohemia (102m)—its mate was destroyed by lightning in 1525.

To spend the night, contact **Čedok,** at the corner of Sedláckova and Prešovská (tel. (019) 366 48; open Mon.-Fri. 9am-noon and 1-5pm, Sat. 9am-noon). The **Sport Hotel,** U Borského porku 21 (tel. 27 17 70) borders on Borský park, just south of the center. (Private bath, tennis courts, and TV. 380 kčs.) From the train station, take tram #1 or 2 to the right (north), get off at the post office, then cross the major street and take tram #4 to the left (south) to the last stop.The **Bíla Hora autocamping** at 28 října (tel. (019) 356 11) has bungalows (400 kčs per person). Take bus #20 5km north of town (open May-Sept.). Plzeň lies conveniently on the Prague-Munich **train** line; from Mariánské Lázné it will set you back two hours and 38 kčs.

SOUTHERN BOHEMIAN DAYTRIPS

■ České Budéjovice

Founded in 1265 as a royal town at the confluence of the rivers Vltava and Malše, České Budéjovice grew fat in the 16th century and then thinned out during the Thirty Years War; it earned its fame as the original home of **Budvar** (Budweiser) beer. The Budéjovice-Linz horse-drawn railway was the first in Europe. The center is **nám. Přemysla Otakara II,** one of the largest squares in Europe, flanked by pastel Renaissance and Baroque houses and lorded over by the 72m **Black Tower,** which rewards a hefty climb with a nifty view (6 kčs; open Tues.-Sun. 10am-6pm; July-Aug. daily 10am-7pm). Once Gothic, **St. Nicholas's Cathedral** next door was pampered with a Baroque facelift during 1641-1649.

Čedok, in the southwest corner of nám. Přem. Otakara II (tel. (038) 323 81), does little but change money (open Mon.-Fri. 9am-6pm, Sat. 9am-noon). **CKM,** Karla IV 14, books hostels (open July-Aug. Mon.-Fri. 9am-6pm). **CTS International Travel Service,** at the northwest corner of the square at Krajinská 1 (tel. (038) 250 61), books private rooms in town and all over southern Bohemia (singles 170-300 kčs; open daily 9am-7pm). **AT Pension,** Dukelská 15 (tel. (038) 529 34), has fabulous two- and three-bed rooms, some with private bath, in two buildings near the center. (350 kčs per person includes excellent breakfast. Reception 24 hrs.) From the train station walk down Žižkova, then left on U tří lvů, and left on Dukelská. The famous **Masné Krámy beer hall** crams tables into former Renaissance meat shops and is the most interesting spot in town for people-watching. (Entrees 35-100 kčs. Budvar 15 kčs per ½L. Open Sun.-Thurs. 10am-11pm, Fri.-Sat. 10am-midnight.) **U Paní emy,** Široká Ulice 25, is a local favorite (entrees 40-90 kčs; open daily 10am-3am).

From Prague, **buses** run almost hourly to České Budéjovice (3 hrs., 48 kčs), which makes a superb springboard for visits to nearby towns such as becastled **Tábor, Jindřichuv Hradec,** and **Tréboň.** Many Czechs come to České Budéjovice to visit the fairy-tale palace of **Hluboká nad Vltavou,** 12km to the north. Several buses per day make the trip (open Tues.-Sun. 8am-noon and 1-5pm).

Near České Budéjovice: Český Krumlov

Scenic Český Krumlov, 24km southwest of České Budéjovice, seems frozen in time. It was declared by UNESCO second only to Venice in historical value. The 13th-century **castle** walls hide a lavish interior; don't miss the Eggenberg's golden carriage or the festively painted **Masquerade Hall.** (Castle grounds open 24 hrs. Interior rooms only with guided tour: May-Sept. Tues.-Sun. 8am-4pm; April, Oct. Tues.-Sun. 9am-3pm. One per day in English, at around 2pm—ask when you arrive.) The **Vltava**—more moat than river in these parts—cradles the town, with the castle crowning the northern perimeter. To reach thc town center, **nám. Svornosti,** from the bus station, simply head towards the castle watchtower, visible from the parking lot. Once there, you'll find a number of restaurants, including the one at the **Hotel Krumlov** at #14 (entrees 60-150 kčs; open daily 11am-10pm). For cheaper rooms, try the **Tourist Service** office (tel. (0337) 46 05), just inside the castle grounds at Zámek 57 (open daily 9am-6pm), which arranges stays in private rooms (60-400 kčs). In addition, **CTS Travel Service** has an office at Latrán 67 (tel. (0337) 28 21), but a better idea is to arrange a room at the CTS office in České Budéjovice if you're coming from there. The tiny hostel, **U Vodníka,** Povodě 55, along the banks of the Vlatava, has room for six lucky guests (180 kčs per person; write ahead to U Vodníka, Povodě 55, 381 01 Český Krumlov, to reserve).

■ Brno

Midway on the rail line between Prague (3¼hr.; 96 kčs) and Bratislava (90 min.; 60 kčs), Brno is the third-largest city in the Czech Republic and the political and cultural capital of Moravia, the wine-making eastern half of the Czech Republic. To find the principal sights, simply look up. The **Cathedral of Sts. Peter and Paul** rears above the city in a kaleidoscope of stained-glass. Atop the hill behind the cathedral, the **Špilberk Castle** fell to both Napoleon and Hitler; the latter used it as SS headquarters and executed more than 80,000 prisoners in the castle's dungeons. (Castle was under renovations in summer 1993; dungeon open Tues.-Sun. 9am-6pm; box office closes at 5:15pm. Admission 20 kčs, students 10 kčs.) The 41 mummified bodies of the **Capuchin Cloisters** repose in Kapucínské nám., downhill from the cathedral. (Open Tues.-Sat. 9-11:45am and 2-4:30pm, Sun. 11-11:45am and 2-4:30pm. Admission 10 kčs, students 7 kčs. Not for the faint of heart.) Across the street is the **Reduta Theater,** where the 11-year-old Mozart conducted in 1767. (Closed for renovations in 1993.) **Nám. Zelný trh** hosts the daily **produce market** and the **Dietrichstein Palace,** which holds the **Moravian History Museum** at #8. (Open Tues.-Sun. 9am-6pm. Admission to permanent exhibit 20 kčs, to temporary exhibits 30 kčs; students 10 kčs and 16 kčs, respectively.)

The **Čedok** for foreigners is at Divadelní 3 (tel. (42) 21 30 66; open Mon.-Fri. 9am-6pm, Sat. 9am-noon). **CKM,** Česká 11 (tel. (42) 21 31 47), one block northwest of nám. Svobody, books hostel rooms for 200 kčs, 180 kčs for students (open Mon.-Fri. 10am-noon and 1-4pm). The cheapest hotel is the **Hotel Avion,** Česká 20 (tel. (42) 21 50 36; fax (42) 21 40 55). Some rooms even come with their own TVs (singles 425 kčs, with bath 615 kčs; doubles 750 kčs, with bath 990 kčs). **Hotel U Jakuba,** Jakubské nám. 6 (tel. 229 91), in the shadow St. Jacob's Church, has singles for 886 kčs and doubles for 1307 kčs, all with private bath. Sample from the stand-up food factory known as the **Sputnik bufet,** Česká 1/3, right off nám. Svobody, where a full meal won't run more than 30-40 kčs (open Mon.-Fri. 7am-7pm, Sat. 7am-2pm). The **San Marco** Restaurant, near the skinny end of nám. Svobody on Panská 6, has a stunning wine list and a selection of Czech and Italian dishes (entrees 30-70 kčs; open daily 10am-midnight).

Near Brno: Moravian Kras

Just 20km from Brno are the stalagmites and stalactites of theMoravian Kras (caves), home to four main networks of caverns open to visitors year-round. From Brno, take the bus to Blansko (7 per day; 1 hr.; 15 kčs), then hop on a bus to the caves. The 8am and 11am buses make a four-hour tour that hits all of the major caverns (May-Sept.). Other runs go only so far as the **Punkevní jeskyné** (4 kčs one way), a main cavern offering a 75-minute tour of the gaping **Macocha Abyss,** created when the cave roof fell in, as well as a boat ride on the subterranean Punkva River. (Open

Mon.-Fri. 7am-4:30pm, Sat.-Sun. 7:30am-4pm; Oct.-March Mon.-Fri. 7:30am-3pm, Sat.-Sun. 7:30am-4pm. Admission 20 kčs, students 10 kčs.) Bring a sweater or jacket; it gets mighty chilly, even in summer.

Near Brno: Telč

A major stop on the bus line from České Bedéjovice and Brno is the magnificently preserved Renaissance town of Telč (2 hrs. from either city; 42 kčs). Its pastel archways and stone watchtowers create a truly lovely square, **nám. Zachariáše z Hradce,** which is surprisingly free of gawking tourists. The main attraction here is **Telč Castle,** erected in the late 14th and early 15th centuries. (Open Tues.-Sun. 8am-noon and 1-5pm; April and Sept.-Oct. 9am-noon and 1-4pm. Admission 25 kčs, students 10 kčs.) The castle complex, at the far, narrow end of the town square, also houses a **museum** of Moravian and Telč history (same hours as above; admission 8 kčs, students 4 kčs), and a **gallery** of modern art by Jan Zrzavý, who once held the title of National Artist of Czechoslovakia. (Same hours as above, plus Nov.-March Tues.-Fri. and Sun. 9am-noon and 1-4pm, Sat. 9am-4pm. Admission 10 kčs, students 5 kčs.) To reach the town square from the bus center, take a left out of the parking lot; at the end of the street, turn left down Masarykova and look for the green, red, and yellow trail markers at Na parkane. (Go? Stop? Caution?) Follow the cobblestones to the left, then cross the stone bridge on the right. The **Hotel Černý orel** at #7 (tel. (066) 96 22 21) maintains comfortable rooms (singles 430 kčs, with bath 490 kčs; doubles 580 kčs, with bath 750 kčs), and a restaurant with patio seating on the square. (Entrees 25-150 kčs; menu in English. Open Mon.-Sat. 7am-11pm, Sun. 7am-10pm.)

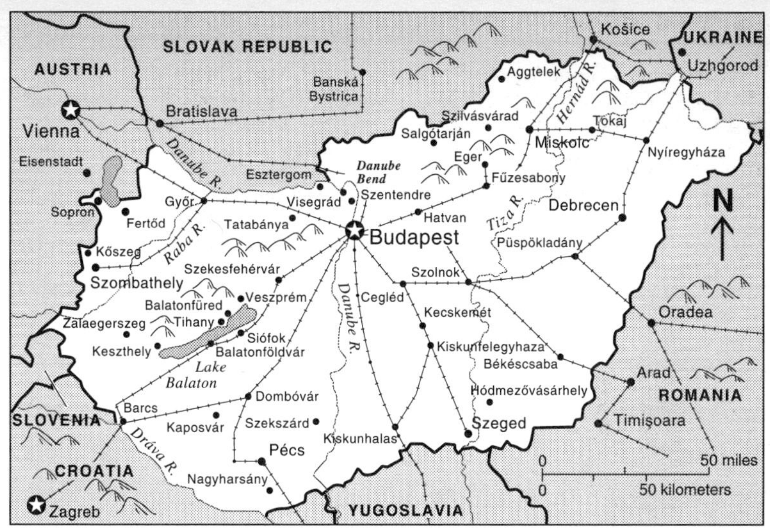

HUNGARY

US$1	**= 92.6 forints (Ft, or HUF)**	**10 Ft =**	**US$0.11**
CAD$1	**= 69.8 Ft**	**10 Ft =**	**CAD$0.14**
UK£1	**= 141 Ft**	**10 Ft =**	**UK£0.07**
IR£1	**= 132 Ft**	**10 Ft =**	**IR£0.08**
AUS$1	**= 59.9 Ft**	**10 Ft =**	**AUS$0.17**
NZ$1	**= 50.3 Ft**	**10 Ft =**	**NZ$0.20**
SAR1	**= 27.5 Ft**	**10 Ft =**	**SAR0.36**
DM1	**= 57.1 Ft**	**10 Ft =**	**DM0.17**
SK1	**= 2.8 Ft**	**10 Ft =**	**SK3.5**
KČS1	**= 3.2 Ft**	**10 Ft =**	**KČS3.1**
AS1	**= 8.1 Ft**	**10 Ft =**	**1.2AS**

Country Code: 36 **International Dialing Prefix: 00**

The people of Hungary (*Magyarország*) seem to combine the best of north and south; their exacting attention to detail balances a warm Mediterranean affability that has miraculously survived the apathy associated with the late Communist system. This easygoing nature has repeatedly subjected the country to the whim of the local bully; academics will marvel at the ancient tension between Magyar ethnicity and foreign domination. In the 13th century, Mongols ravaged the country. From the 16th to the 19th century, Ottomans and Habsburgs plundered it. In the 20th century, World War I redistributed two thirds of its territory. Most recently, after World War II, the Soviet Union transformed Hungary into a buffer state with a puppet government. In 1956, Hungarian patriots led by Imre Nagy rose up against this repression with a passion that was crushed only by Soviet tanks; the bullet holes that dot so many of Budapest's buildings recall this bloody uprising.

In the fall of 1989 the Hungarian people fulfilled the aspirations of the previous generation and broke away from the Soviet orbit in a bloodless revolution. Eager to further privatize Hungary's hybrid economy (called "goulash socialism"), the ruling party relinquished its monopoly on power and took the ironic "People's" out of the

People's Republic of Hungary. Elections have since transferred power to the Hungarian Democratic Forum. Change continues at a dizzying pace, but Hungarians have adapted admirably since the last Soviet troops departed in June 1991.

Although still aglow with their political triumphs, Hungarians are beginning to experience a vicious economic hangover. Inflation is rapidly reducing one quarter of the population to poverty. High prices for daily necessities, widespread unemployment, and yawning inequities in wealth harshly remind Hungarians of the competitive side of liberty. Realizing that there are no quick solutions, most Hungarians are resigning themselves to a painful decade of transition.

In the wake of the Communist abdication, Hungary struggles to dispel its reputation as an underdeveloped, "Eastern bloc" nation. In fact, the 45 years of isolation and relative powerlessness under Soviet rule is a mere blip in Hungary's prolific 1100-year history, and traces of socialism are evaporating with each passing iron-free day. Aside from transitional economic woes, the most visible vestiges of the old regime are benevolent; efficient public transportation, clean parks and streets, and a low incidence of violent crime. In addition, the Communists mercifully preserved the architectural integrity of Hungary's beautiful city centers, although somber, cement apartment blocks now skirt the major cities like so many massive gravestones.

Hungarian culture has flourished throughout the country's tumultuous history. Hungary has fostered such musical masters as 19th-century composer Ferenc (Franz) Liszt and 20th-century geniuses Zoltán Kodály and Béla Bartók. Many current musical groups enjoy worldwide respect, and theater and film also thrive under the direction of such luminaries as István Szabó and Miklós Jancsó. Folk music collectors should look for tapes by Sebestyén Márta.

Roman Catholics constitute 65% of the populace, Protestants 25%, Greek Catholics 3%, and Jews 0.3%. With a fifth of Hungary's population, Budapest dominates the country, though the capital by no means has a monopoly on cultural attractions. No provincial center is more than a three-hour train ride through fertile corn and sunflower fields from Budapest. Try not to forsake the beauty of the countryside for a whirlwind tour of the capital—you'll have skirted the heart of the country but will have missed its soul entirely.

■ Essentials

Perhaps the best word for foreigners in Hungary to know is **IBUSZ,** the Hungarian national travel bureau. Their offices throughout the country can make room arrangements, change money, sell train tickets, and charter tours. Snare the pamphlet *Tourist Information: Hungary* and the monthly entertainment guides *Programme in Hungary* and *Budapest Panorama* (all free and written in English). **Express,** the former national student travel bureau, handles youth hostels and changes money. Regional travel agencies are more helpful than IBUSZ and Express in the outlying areas. **Tourinform** is a fantastically helpful non-profit information service with locations in 15 of Hungary's 19 counties. They have many free and helpful brochures and answer all your questions about Budapest and the rest of Hungary, often serving as interpreters.

GETTING THERE AND GETTING AROUND

Budapest's **Ferihegy airport** handles all international traffic, including **Malév,** the national airline. Hungary's domestic transportation network revolves around a Budapest hub; most rail lines swerve through the capital. Use buses to travel among the outer provincial centers, or plan on returning to Budapest to make connections.

Hungarian **trains** (*vonat*) are reliable and inexpensive; Eurail is valid here. *Személyvonat* are excruciatingly slow; *gyorsvonat* trains (listed on schedules in red) cost the same and move at least twice as fast. All of the larger provincial towns are accessible by the blue express rail lines (*sebesvonat* or *expressz*). The express fare from Budapest to any of the provincial cities should cost between 300-700 Ft each way, including a seat reservation (required on trains marked with an "R" on schedules). Some basic vocabulary will help you navigate the rail system: you should know *érkezés* (arrival), *indúlás* (departure), *vágány* (track) and *állomás* or *pályaudvar* (station, abbreviated *pu.*). All travelers under 26 are eligible for a 33% discount. An ISIC commands discounts on international tickets from IBUSZ, Express and station ticket counters. (Book several days in advance.) If you run up against a non-English-speaking ticket conductor at a train station, just flash your ISIC and repeat "student," or the Hungarian, "*diák*" (pronounced DEE-ahk); you can often get a 50% discount. International tickets are no longer the bargain they once were (from Budapest to: Vienna one way second-class US$26; Prague US$46; Warsaw US$52). Berlin is 16 hr. away by train, Bucharest 19 hr. A trans-Siberian ticket, once US$48, now runs about US$300. When traveling between countries in Eastern Europe, buy a ticket to the border, and then buy another on the train once you've crossed the border; it another, on the train, from the border station to your destination sometimes proves to be less expensive than a ticket.

The extensive **bus** system is cheap but crowded; most routes between provincial cities pass through Budapest. The **Erzsébet tér** bus station in Budapest posts schedules and fares. Inter-city bus tickets are purchased on the bus (get there early if you want a seat), while tickets for local city buses must be bought in advance from a newsstand (18-27 Ft) and punched on board. The Danube **hydrofoil** is the most enjoyable (and most expensive) way to go to Vienna, but no longer runs to Bratislava. The trip between Vienna and Budapest costs about US$70, round-trip US$105 (payment in Austrian *Schillings*). Tickets are cheaper at the IBUSZ travel bureau in Vienna, Kärntner Str. 26, than at the dock; from the Viennese travel agent, you might be able to procure a 50% discount with a Eurailpass. Some travelers **cross the Austrian border** by hitching on Highway E5, the main thoroughfare between Vienna and Budapest. *Let's Go* cannot recommend hitchhiking as a safe method of transportation. Hitching around Budapest, especially, has become significantly more dangerous in the past few years. It is a four-hour drive capital-to-capital. Avoid crossing the border on foot.

Either IBUSZ or Tourinform can provide a brochure about **cycling** in Hungary that includes maps, suggested tours, sights, accommodations, bike rental locations, repair shops and recommended border-crossing points. Write to the tree-huggers at the **Hungarian Nature-Lovers' Federation (MTSZ),** 1065 Budapest, Bajcsy-Zsilinszky út 31, or the **Hungarian Cycling Federation,** 1146 Budapest, Szabó J. u. 3, for more information. Some rail stations rent bicycles to passengers.

PRACTICAL INFORMATION

Change money only as you need it. Make sure to keep some Western cash to purchase visas, international train tickets and (less often) private accommodations. Hard currency may grease the wheels to lower prices and better service. **American Express** offices in Budapest, and IBUSZ offices around the country, convert traveler's checks to cash for a six percent commission. Cash advances on credit cards are available at a few locations in Budapest. All major credit cards are accepted at more expensive hotels and at many shops and restaurants; the smaller ones accept only American Express. The best exchange rates during summer 1993 could be found at branches of the OTP, IBUSZ, and Agricultural banks. New Zealand dollars cannot be exchanged here, so pack another currency. At the few exchange offices with extended hours, the rates are generally poor. The maximum permissible commission for currency exchange (cash to cash) is one percent. Black market exchanges are both illegal and strikingly common, but the rates offered are rarely favorable enough (an extra 10%) to risk the large chance of being swindled—even outside Budapest.

Many addresses are shedding their Russian names in the wake of the 1989 revolution. Tourist brochures, subway-station signs and even street signs may not reflect the latest purges, so it's advisable to get the most recent maps available. Hungarian addresses usually involve one of the following: *utca,* abbreviated *u.* (street); *út* and the related *útja* (avenue); *tér* and the related *tere* (square, but may be a park, plaza, or boulevard); *híd* (bridge); and *körút,* abbreviated *krt.* (ring-boulevard). A single name such as Baross may be associated with several of these in completely separate parts of a city—i.e. Baross út, Baross u., Baross tér, etc. Numbers on either side of the street are not always in sync; some streets are numbered odd and even, some are numbered up one side and down the other, some are numbered in consecutive primes....

COMMUNICATING IN HUNGARY

The official tongue, Hungarian, belongs to the obscure Finno-Ugric family of languages. Elementary German, though linguistically unrelated, can be a great advantage when traveling here due to the years of Austrian occupation. English works in Budapest, but in the countryside, especially in Eastern Hungary, even German may fail. "*Hallo*" is often used as an informal greeting or farewell. Those long-latent Charades skills may yet come in handy; you'd be amazed what acting out your question can accomplish. Beware certain idiosyncracies, though; for example, if you want to visually express numbers, remember to start with the thumb for "one"—holding up your index finger means "wait." (See the Glossary and the Language section of the Appendix for more details about Hungarian speech.)

Western newspapers and magazines are available in many Budapest newsstands and in large hotels. Hungary's English-language paper *Daily News* is supposedly published weekly. Used bookstores *(antikvárium)* often have English books at fire-sale prices. English-language radio and TV programming is found most easily in the English language *Budapest Week,* which has excellent listings, survival tips, helpful hints, and insightful articles about life in Hungary. The paper (62 Ft) comes out every Thursday and is free at American Express offices and larger hotels.

Almost all telephone numbers in the countryside now have a "3" as their first digit. Hungary's pay **phones** require five forints every three minutes for local calls. Wait for the tone and dial slowly. For long distance, dial 06 before the area code (two digits long, except in Budapest). **International calls** require red phones or new, digital-display blue ones, found at large post offices, on the street and in metro stations. At 200 Ft per minute to the U.S., telephones suck money so fast you need a companion to feed them. Direct calls can also be made from the telephone office in Budapest, with a three-minute minimum to the U.S. To call collect, dial 09 for the international operator. For **AT&T's USA Direct,** put in a 20 Ft coin (which you'll get back), dial 00, wait for the second dial tone, then dial 36 01 11. **Australia Direct** is 36 61 11 after the second tone; **Canada Direct** 36 11 11; **U.K. Direct** 36 44 11. Though the blue phones are more handsome than their red brethren, they tend to cut you off after 3-9 minutes. Unfortunately, red phones are more difficult to find. June 1992 saw the installation of new telephones that used a **phonecard,** available at post offices; these card phones are slowly becoming more and more prevalent. Fax service, as well, is getting more reliable.

The Hungarian **mail** system is perfectly reliable (airmail—*légiposta*—to the U.S. takes 5-10 days). Note that if you're mailing to a Hungarian citizen, the family name precedes the given name, as in "Doe John." Because Hungary's per capita telephone rate is the second-lowest in Europe (Albania wins), it is very common to send telegrams, even across town. Ask for a telegram form (*távirati ürlapot*) and fill it out before returning to the counter. Post offices are indicated by the sign **POSTA** and are generally open Mon.-Fri. 8am-7pm, Sat. 8am-1pm.

General **business hours** in Hungary are Monday to Friday from 9am to 6pm (7am-7pm for food stores). Banks now close around 3pm on Friday, but hours continue to expand as Marx gives way to Mammon. Larger shopping centers and food stores may sell food on Sundays; also try the numerous 24-hour private food stores. Tourist bureaus usually open Monday-Saturday 8am-5pm in the summer (some are open until noon on Sun.); in the winter these hours shrink to Monday to Friday 10am to 4pm. Museums are usually open Tuesday to Sunday 10am to 6pm, with occasional free days on Tuesday. Students with ISIC often get in for free or pay only half-price. Nothing is open on national holidays—including Christian festivals, May 1, and August 20. The upheaval in 1989 produced two new holidays, March 15 and Oct. 23, and threw out two Soviet-inspired ones (April 4 and November 7).

Should you get sick, contact your embassy for lists of English-speaking doctors. Some travelers have supported themselves for years, usually in Budapest, by teaching English at an English-language school or through private tutoring. Contracts run for a semester. For more information, contact the English Teachers' Center through the American Embassy, or look for listings in the libraries of the American and British embassies. You can also try calling the myriad private schools that advertise in *Budapest Week* or on posters.

ACCOMMODATIONS AND CAMPING

Most travelers stay in private homes booked through a tourist agency (singles 700-1200 Ft, doubles 800-2000 Ft). If you stay fewer than four nights, you must pay a 30% surcharge. Singles are scarce—it's worth finding a roommate, because solo traveler's often must pay for a double room. Agencies may initially try to foist off their most expensive quarters on you; be persistent. Outside of Budapest, the best and cheapest office is usually the regional one (such as Egertourist in Eger). After staying a few nights, you can often make arrangements to stay on with the owner directly, thus saving the tourist agencies' 20-30% commission. You can also ditch the agencies and find your own room where there is a sign for *szoba kiadó* or *Zimmer frei.* Make sure any private room you rent is near the center or easily accessible by public transport. While quality of rooms varies widely, most are at least passable, and some are quite lovely. Unfortunately, renting a private room sometimes seems less an introduction to Hungarian life than a business transaction. Many owners keep their quarters and lives walled off from the traveler; you receive a front-door key and sometimes kitchen access. Others, however, will offer a gracious welcome, and, just possibly, lifetime friendship you won't find in any hostel.

Some towns have cheap hotels (doubles 1200-1600 Ft); most are rapidly disappearing. As the hotel system develops and room prices rise, hosteling will become more attractive. Many hostel rooms can be booked at **Express** or sometimes the regional tourist office (250-700 Ft). From late June through August, university dorms metamorphose into hostels. Locations change annually; register through an Express office in the off-season, or at the dorm itself during the summer. The staff at Express generally speaks German, sometimes English. Offices in one city cannot book hostels in another. Hostels are usually large enough to accommodate peak-season crowds. In 1993 hostels required neither HI cards nor sleepsacks, though that may change as Hungary's tourist industry integrates with Western Europe's.

Over 100 **campgrounds** are sprinkled throughout Hungary, charging about 500 Ft per day for two people. You can often rent two-person bungalows for 800-1200 Ft and four-person jobs for about 2000 Ft, but you must pay for unfilled spaces. Most sites are open from May through September. Tourist offices offer the comprehensive booklet *Camping Hungary,* which is revised annually. For more information and maps, contact the **Hungarian Camping and Caravanning Club** or **Tourinform** in Budapest.

FOOD AND DRINK

With fantastic concoctions of meat, spices and fresh vegetables, many find Magyar cuisine among the finest in Europe. Paprika, Hungary's chief agricultural export, colors most dishes red. In Hungarian restaurants, called *vendéglő* or *étterem,* you may begin with *gulyásleves,* a delicious and hearty beef soup seasoned with paprika—often a meal in itself for only 100-120 Ft. *Borjúpaprikás* is a veal dish with paprika, often accompanied by small potato-dumpling pastas called *gnocchi.* Vegetarians can find the tasty *rántott sajt* (fried cheese) and *gombapörkölt* (mushroom stew) on most menus. *Túrós táska* is a chewy pastry pocket filled with sweetened cottage cheese. *Somlói galuska,* Hungarian sponge cake, is a fantastically rich and delicious concoction of chocolate, nuts and cream. Hungarians claim that the Austrians stole the recipe for *rétes* and called it *strudel.*

Few Hungarians can afford restaurants; finding a genuine, "local" eatery is a stretch. Piped gypsy music often spells tourist trap; it may be worth your while to plow through a few crowds and find a more remote ethnic eatery. Menus are posted outside most every restaurant; be sure to check your bill, although discrepancies are rare. Bread is generally included in the meal. A 10% gratuity has become standard, even if the bill includes a service charge (which goes to the management); tip as you pay. A roving musician expects about 150 Ft from your table, depending on the number of listeners; the more quickly you pay, the less the expense. A *csárda* is a traditional inn, and a *bisztró* an inexpensive restaurant. To see what you order, try an *ön kiszolgáló étterem*—translation: cheap cafeteria. Since precious few menus outside Budapest are written in English, a dictionary can spare you from a point-and-pray meal. For pastry and coffee, look for a *cukrászdá,* where you can fulfill the relentless desire of your sweet-teeth for dangerously few forints. *Kávé* means espresso. **Salátabárs** vend deli concoctions. Restaurants outside Budapest frequently offer higher quality and lower prices.

Vegetarians may have trouble filling up in Hungarian restaurants, but fresh fruit and vegetables abound on small stands and produce markets. Supermarkets (heralded by "**ABC**" signs) sell dry goods and dairy products; the fresh milk is delectable but curdles within 48 hours. **Julius Meinl** is the largest national supermarket chain. Except "non-stops," most supermarkets and grocers close at 1pm on Saturday and reopen on Sunday morning.

Hungarians are justly proud of their wines. Most famous are the red Egri Bikavér ("Bull's Blood of Eger") and the white Tokaji vintages (150 Ft per bottle at a store, 300 Ft at a restaurant). Fruit schnapps *(pálinka)* are a national specialty; you can sample them in most cafés and bars. Local beers are excellent; the most common is Dreher.

Budapest

At once a cosmopolitan European capital and the stronghold of Magyar nationalism, Budapest (area 525 sq. km, pop. 2,018,000) defies distinctions between East and West. After a four-decade Communist coma, the city has spiritedly awakened and seems destined to recapture its accustomed role as a European powerhouse. Endowed with an architectural majesty befitting the number-two city of the Habsburg empire, Budapest will astound veteran and novice tourists alike. Budapest's intellectual and cultural scene has often been compared to that of Paris. Like Vienna, Budapest bears the architectural stamp of Habsburg rule. But unlike its fastidious Western neighbors, Budapest retains a worn-at-the-elbows charm in its squares and cafés. World War II punished the city; from the rubble, Hungarians rebuilt with the same pride that fomented the ill-fated 1956 uprising, that weathered the Soviet response (invasion), and that overcame the subsequent decades of socialist subservience. Today, the city manages to maintain charm and a vibrant spirit—refusing to buckle under the relentless siege of Western glitzification—while pursuing the total abnegation of all things Russian.

ORIENTATION AND PRACTICAL INFORMATION

Budapest straddles the **Danube River** (Duna) in north-central Hungary, about 250km downstream from Vienna. Regular trains and excursion boats connect the two cities. Budapest also has direct rail links to Belgrade to the southeast, **Prague** to the northwest and other metropolises throughout Eastern Europe. The old Orient Express, recently resurfaced and completely refitted, still chugs through Budapest on the way from Berlin, Germany, to Bucharest, Romania. Budapest is enclosed by a ring of traffic, more concrete to the east of the Danube—where St. Istvan körút, Teréz körút, Erzsébet körút, József körút, and Ferenc körút firmly link arms—than in the nebulous layout of the west. **Óbuda** (Old Buda), in the northwest, was the center of the original Roman settlement. **Buda,** on the west bank, embraces the **Castle District;** it brings to mind trees, hills, and high rents. On the east side buzzes **Pest,** the commercial heart of the modern city. Here you'll find shopping streets, banks, Parliament, and theaters—and even the Budapest Grand Circus. The heart of the city, **Vörösmarty Square** (*map*C4*), was once situated just to the north of the medieval town wall. These four-meter-high constructions are still visible in many places, including the corner of Veres Pálné and Bástya streets or inside the Korona Passage restaurant.

Three central bridges bind the halves together. The **Széchenyi lánchíd** (Chain Bridge; *map*B4*) connects Roosevelt tér to the cable car, which scurries up to the Royal Palace. To the south, the slender, white **Erzsébet híd** (Elizabeth Bridge; (*map*C5*) departs from near Petőfi tér and Március 15 tér; it runs up to the colonnaded monument of St. Gellért near the base of Gellért Hill. Farther along the Danube, the green **Szabadság híd** (*map*C5*) links Fövám tér to the southern tip of Gellért Hill, topped by the Liberation Monument. In the alternately exasperating and endearing European fashion, streets arbitrarily change names from one block to the next—the giant semi-circular avenue that encloses Pest's inner city from Margit híd to Petőfi híd elusively camouflages itself under five different names.

Moszkva tér (Moscow Square; *map*A2*), just five minutes north of the Castle district, is Budapest's transportation hub. Too many people are familiar with its name; were the square any less pivotal, the despised title would surely change. Virtually all trams and buses start or end their routes here. One Metro stop away, **Batthány tér** (*map*B2*) lies opposite the Parliament building on the west bank; this is the starting node of the HÉV commuter railway, which leads north through Óbuda and into Szentendre (see Danube Bend below). Budapest's three Metro lines converge at **Deák tér** (*map*C3-4*), beside the main international bus terminal at **Erzsébet tér** (*map*C4*). Deák tér lies at the core of Pest's loose arrangement of concentric ring boulevards and spoke-like avenues. Walk two blocks west toward the river to Vörösmarty tér. As you face the statue of Mihály Vőrösmarty (the renowned nationalist poet), **Váci utca** (*map*C4*), the main pedestrian shopping zone, extends to the right.

As in Vienna, addresses in Budapest begin with a Roman numeral that represents one of the city's 22 districts. Central Buda is I; downtown Pest is V. In mailing addresses, the middle two digits of the postal code correspond to the district number. Many street names occur more than once in town; always check the district as well. Because many streets are in the process of shedding their Communist names in favor of the original, pre-Soviet ones, an up-to-date **map** is essential. The **American Express** and **Tourinform** offices have excellent, free tourist maps, or pick up the *Belavâros Idegenforgalmi Térképe* at any metro stop (80 Ft). Anyone planning an exhaustive visit should look into purchasing András Török's *Budapest: A Critical Guide.*

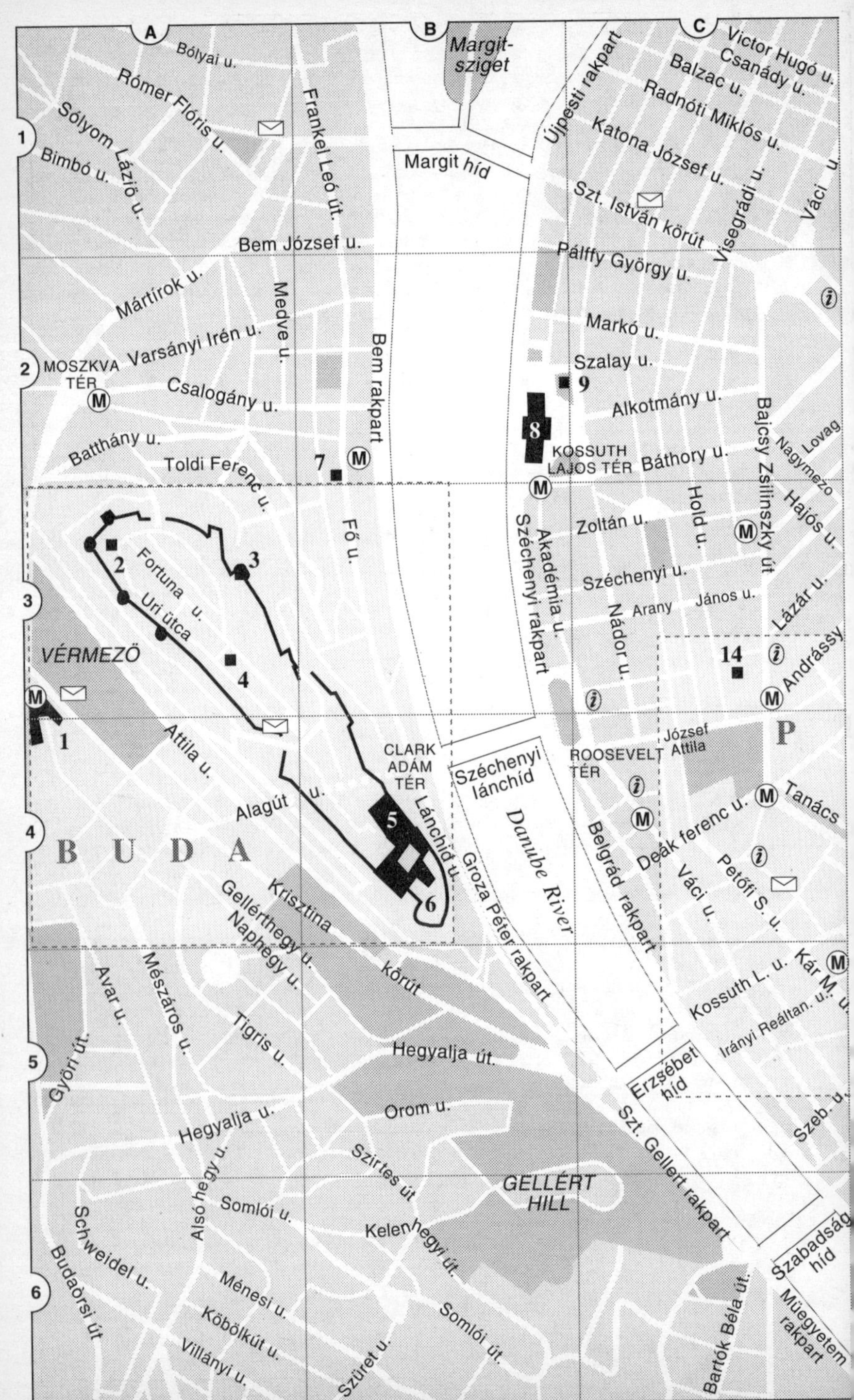
A
B
C
1
2
3
4
5
6
Bólyai u.
Rómer Flóris u.
Sólyom Lázió u.
Bimbó u.
Frankel Leó út
Margit-sziget
Margit híd
Újpesti rakpart
Victor Hugó u.
Csanády u.
Balzac u.
Radnóti Miklós u.
Katona József u.
Szt. István körút
Visegrádi u.
Váci u.
Bem József u.
Pálffy György u.
Mártírok u.
Medve u.
Bem rakpart
Markó u.
Szalay u.
MOSZKVA TÉR
Varsányi Irén u.
Csalogány u.
Batthány u.
Toldi Ferenc u.
Alkotmány u.
Bajcsy Zsilinszky út
Lovag
Nagymező
KOSSUTH LAJOS TÉR
Báthory u.
Fő u.
Zoltán u.
Akadémia u.
Széchenyi rakpart
Hold u.
Hajós u.
Fortuna u.
Uri ütca
Széchenyi u.
Arany János u.
Nádor u.
Lázár u.
VÉRMEZŐ
Andrássy
Attila u.
CLARK ADÁM TÉR
Széchenyi lánchíd
ROOSEVELT TÉR
József Attila
P
Alagút u.
Lánchíd u.
Danube River
Tanács
BUDA
Deák ferenc u.
Belgrád rakpart
Krisztina körút
Gellérthegy u.
Naphegy u.
Groza Péter rakpart
Váci u.
Petőfi S. u.
Avar u.
Mészáros u.
Tigris u.
Kossuth L. u.
Kár M. u.
Irányi Reáltan. u.
Hegyalja út
Győri út
Erzsébet híd
Orom u.
Hegyalja u.
Szeb. u.
Szirtes út
Szt. Gellert rakpart
Alsó hegy u.
Somlói u.
GELLÉRT HILL
Kelenhegyi út
Szabadság híd
Schweidel u.
Budaörsi út
Ménesi u.
Somlói út
Kőbölkút u.
Villányi u.
Szüret u.
Bartók Béla út
Müegyetem rakpart
1
2
3
4
5
6
7
8
9
14

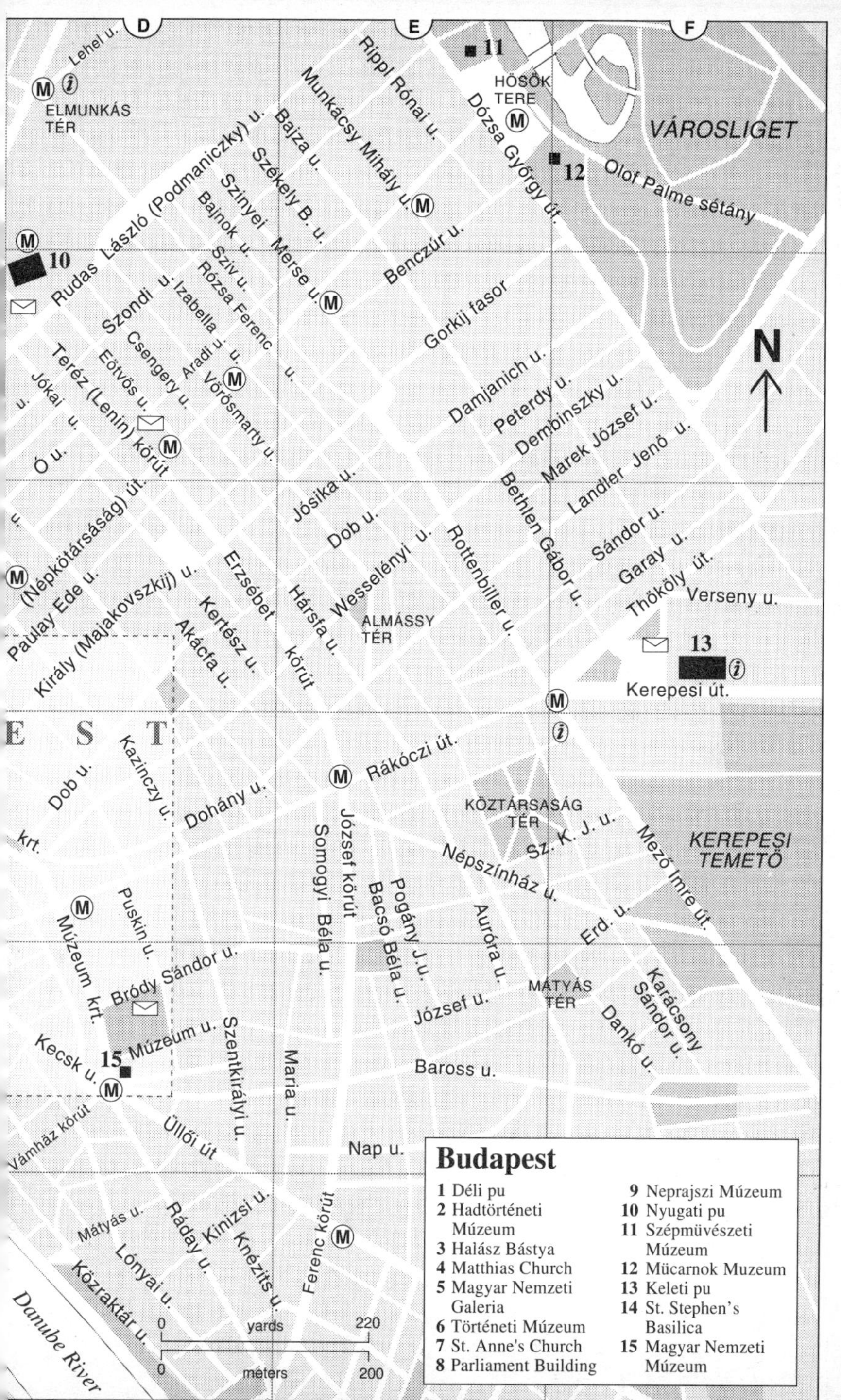

Budapest

1 Déli pu
2 Hadtörténeti Múzeum
3 Halász Bástya
4 Matthias Church
5 Magyar Nemzeti Galeria
6 Történeti Múzeum
7 St. Anne's Church
8 Parliament Building
9 Neprajszi Múzeum
10 Nyugati pu
11 Szépmüvészeti Múzeum
12 Mücarnok Muzeum
13 Keleti pu
14 St. Stephen's Basilica
15 Magyar Nemzeti Múzeum

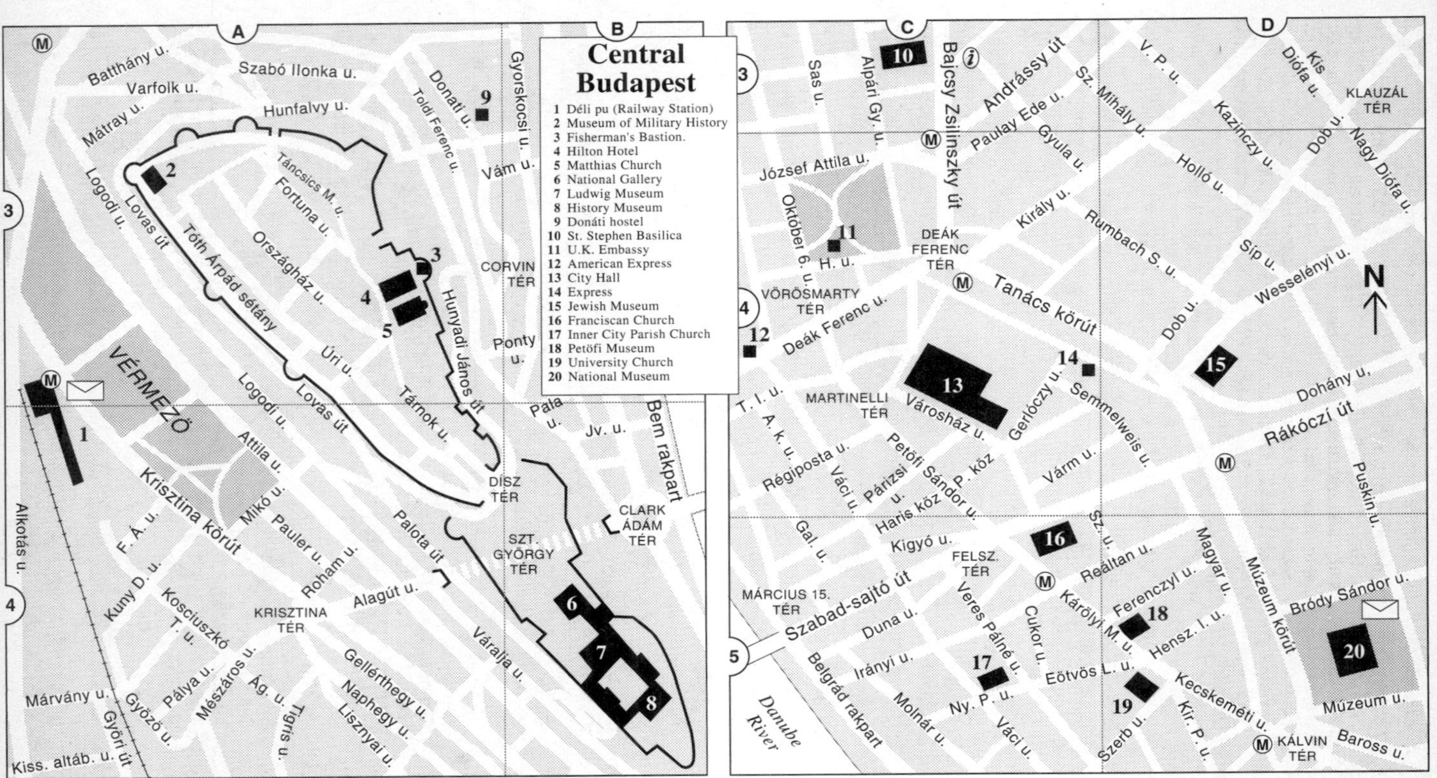
Central Budapest
1 Déli pu (Railway Station)
2 Museum of Military History
3 Fisherman's Bastion.
4 Hilton Hotel
5 Matthias Church
6 National Gallery
7 Ludwig Museum
8 History Museum
9 Donáti hostel
10 St. Stephen Basilica
11 U.K. Embassy
12 American Express
13 City Hall
14 Express
15 Jewish Museum
16 Franciscan Church
17 Inner City Parish Church
18 Petőfi Museum
19 University Church
20 National Museum
VÉRMEZŐ
Krisztina körút
Tóth Árpád sétány
Hunyadi János út
Bem rakpart
Bajcsy Zsilinszky út
Andrássy út
Tanács körút
Rákóczi út
Múzeum körút
Szabad-sajtó út
Belgrád rakpart
Danube River

Agencies

Tourist Offices: Tourinform (*map*C3-4*), V, Sütö u. 2 (tel. 117 98 00). Located off Deák tér around the corner from Porsche Hungaria. Metro: "Deák tér." This remarkably helpful, multilingual tourist office provides information ranging from sight-seeing tours to opera performances to the location of Aikido dojos. Open daily 8am-8pm. Sight-seeing, Coleopterist, accommodation bookings and travel services available at **IBUSZ, Coleopterist** and **Budapest Tourist** (offices in train stations and tourist centers). Ask for their free and very helpful quarterly *For Youth.*

Budget Travel: Express (*map*B3*), V, Zoltán u. 10, 2 blocks south of the Parliament building (tel. 111 64 18). Metro: "Kossuth Lajos." Some reduced international plane fares for the under-26 crowd. Also youth and ISIC reductions on certain international rail fares to Eastern European destinations (same reductions are available at station ticket offices). Open Mon.-Thurs. 8:30am-4:30pm, Fri. 8:30am-3pm. Around the corner at the Express **main office** (*map*C3*), V, Szabadság tér 16 (tel. 131 77 77), pick up ISIC (250 Ft). Open daily 7am-7pm. The Express **accommodations office** in Keleti station (tel. 142 17 72) may be licensed to sell reduced travel tickets by 1994. Open daily 8am-7pm.

Embassies: Unless otherwise noted, embassy and consulate services are contained in the same building. Visit **KEOKH** (*map*C3*), the Foreign Nationals Office, VI, Andrássy út 12 (Metro: "Bajcsy-Zsilinszky"), to get your visa extended or renewed if it has expired. Open Mon.-Wed. 8:30am-noon, Thurs. 2-5pm, Fri. 8:30am-noon.

U.S. (*map*C3*), V, Szabadság tér 12 (tel. 112 64 50, after hours 153 05 66). Metro: "Kossuth Lajos," then walk 2 blocks down Akademia and take a left on Zoltán. Check out the plaque honoring Cardinal Jozef Mindszenty, an important figure in the 1956 revolt who spent his remaining years as a refugee in the embassy. Open Mon.-Fri. 8:30am-noon and 2-4pm.

Canada, XII, Budakeszi út 32 (tel. 176 77 11). Take bus #22; 5 stops from "Moszkva tér." Open Mon.-Fri. 8am-4pm.

U.K. (*map*C4*), V, Harmincad u. 6, near Café Gerbeaud (tel. 266 28 88). Metro: "Vörösmarty tér." Open Mon.-Thurs. 9am-4:30pm, Fri. 9am-1:30pm. **New Zealanders** should contact the British embassy.

Australia (*map*E1-2*), VI, Délibáb u. 30 (tel. 153 42 33), parallel to Andrassy ut., 1 block to the south (i.e. away from the Museum of Fine Arts). Metro: "Hösök tér." Open Mon.-Fri. 8am-4pm.

Austria (*map*E1-2*), VI, Benczúr u. 16 (tel. 269 67 00).

Czech Republic (*map*D2*), VI, Szegfű u. 4 (tel. 142 17 54). Open Mon.-Fri. 8:30am-1pm.

Slovakia, XIV, Stefánia út 22-24 (tel. 251 18 60).

Belgium (*map*A2*), I, Toldy Ferenc u. 13 (tel. 201 17 62).

Denmark, XII, Határőr út 37 (tel. 155 73 20).

France (*map*E1*), VI, Lendvay u. 27 (tel. 132 49 80).

Germany, XIV, Stefánia u. 101-103 (tel. 251 89 99).

Greece (*map*D2*), VI, Szegfű u. 3 (tel. 122 80 65).

Italy, XIV, Stefánia u. 95 (tel. 121 24 50).

Japan (*map*A1*), II, Rómer Flóris u. 58 (tel. 156 45 33).

Poland (*map*D2*), VI, Városligeti fasor 16 (tel. 122 84 37).

Russia (*map*E1-2*), VI, Bajza út. 35 (tel. 252 12 28). Open Mon., Wed., Fri. 9am-3pm.

Spain (*map*D2*), VI, Eötvös u. 13 (tel. 153 10 11)

Sweden, XIV, Ajtósi Dürer sor 27A (tel. 268 08 05).

Switzerland, XIV, Stefánia út 107 (tel. 122 94 91).

Turkey (*map*A4*), I, Úri u. 45 (tel. 155 07 37).

Currency Exchange: The bureaus with longer hours generally have less favorable rates. Larger exchange offices will turn traveler's checks into hard currency for 6% commission (all open Mon.-Fri. 8am-6pm).

OTP Bank or **Penta Tours** (*map*C4*), on Váci u. 19-21. Probably the best rates in town. Open Mon.-Fri. 9am-12:30pm and 1:30-5pm.

IBUSZ (*map*C5*), at V, Petőfi tér 3, just north of Elizabeth (Erzsébet) Bridge, is open 24 hrs. Cash advances on Diners Club and Visa (forints only). Performs most AmEx banking services.

Magyar Külkeres Kedelmi Bank (Foreign Trade Bank; *map*C3*), V, Szent István tér 11. Open Mon.-Thurs. 8am-2pm and Fri. 8am-1pm. Another **branch** (*map*C4*) at V, Türr István u. 9, 1 block south of Vörösmarty tér. Open Mon.-Fri. 8am-8pm and Sat. 9am-2pm. Both offices give Visa and Mastercard cash advances (forints only) and cash traveler's checks in US$ for 2% commission.

Dunabank (*map*C2*), V, Báthory u. 12. Metro: "Kossuth Lajos"; then walk away from the river. Offers Mastercard and Eurocard cash advances (forints only). Open Mon.-Fri. 8am-5pm).

MÁV Tours, in the Keleti Station, may seem slightly offbeat, but offers excellent rates and is extraordinarily convenient for rail travelers.

American Express (*map*C4*), V, Deák Ferenc u. 10 (tel. 266 86 80). Metro: "Vörösmarty tér," next to the new Kempinski Hotel. Sells traveler's cheques for hard cash, Moneygrams or cardholders' personal cheques. ATM, for AmEx cards only; cashes travelers' cheques in US$ for a 6% commission. Cash advances only in forints. Free maps; on Thurs. and Fri. pick up the free *Budapest Week* here as well. Holds mail. Address mail as follows: "ZUCKERMAN Naomi, American Express, Hungary Kft., Deák Ferenc u. 10, H-1052 Budapest, Hungary." Open Mon.-Fri. 9am-6pm, Sat. 9am-2pm; Oct.-June Mon.-Fri. 9am-5pm, Sat. 9am-1pm.

Thomas Cook (*map*C4*), V, in the IBUSZ travel office on Vigadó u. 6 (tel. 118 64 66; fax 118 65 08).

Post Office: *Poste Restante* at (*map*C4*) V, Városház u. 18 (tel. 118 48 11). Open Mon.-Fri. 8am-8pm, Sat. 8am-3pm. 24-hr. **branches** at Nyugati station (*map*D2*), VI, Teréz krt. 105-107 and Keleti station (*map*F3*), VIII, Baross tér 11c. After-hours staff does not speak English. You may be better off sending mail via American Express.

Telephones (*map*C4*), V, Petőfi Sándor u. 17. English-speaking staff. Fax service. Open Mon.-Fri. 8am-8pm, Sat.-Sun. 8am-3pm. At other times, try the post office. Budapest numbers begin with 1 or 2. **Local operator:** 01. Use **red phones** for **international calls** (see Essentials above). **City code:** 1.

Transportation

Flights: Ferihegy Airport, tel. 157 21 22 for reservations, 157 71 55 for general information, 156 65 78 for departures, and 157 84 06 for arrivals. Easily reached by Volánbusz, the bus that runs every ½-hr. daily 5am-9pm to and from Erzsébet tér (Metro: "Deák tér"; ½- hr., 150 Ft). Or take Metro line 3 to "Kőbánya-Kispest," then bus #93. Both the black and red buses go to terminal 1, but only the reds go to departures at terminal 2. **Youth** (under 26) as well as **standby** (under 25) **flight** tickets are available at the **Malév** office (tel. 118 51 22 or 118 43 33), V, Dorottya u. 2, on Vörösmarty tér (open Mon.-Fri. 7:30am-4:30pm) or any other travel agency. Other airlines flying out of Ferihegy (including Aeroflot, Air Canada, Air France, Air India, Air Italia, Austrian Airlines, Balkan, British Airways, Delta Air, KLM, Lot, Lufthansa, Swissair, ElAl, and SAS) offer additional discounts. There's also a **hostel** (Asmara Youth Hostel, Bajcsy Zsilinszky u. 51) at the airport for early birds who fly at dawn.

Trains: (tel. 122 78 60 for domestic trains, 142 91 50 for international trains). The word for train station is *pályaudvar,* often abbreviated *pu.* Those under 26 are eligible for a 33% discount on international train tickets. You generally must show your ISIC; the English word "student" may not be understood. The 3 main stations—**Keleti pu.** (*map*F3*), **Nyugati pu.** (*map*D2*), and **Déli pu.** (*map*A3-4*)—are also Metro stops. Trains to and from a given location do not necessarily stop at the same station; for example, trains from Prague may stop at Nyugati or Keleti. Each station has schedules for the others; go and check. Second class to **Vienna** (10 per day; 3½ hr.; US$27), **Prague** (5 per day; 8 hr.; US$47), Warsaw (2 per day, US$53), Berlin (5 per day, US$62), Belgrade (4 per day, US$26) and Bucharest (6 per day, US$88). Catch the **Orient Express** in Budapest—1 train per day arrives from Berlin and continues on to Bucharest. Purchase **tickets** from: **Metro entrances** in Keleti and Nyugati stations. Domestic tickets only.

IBUSZ (see above). International and domestic tickets available. Should also have generous discounts on other Eastern European rail tickets. Several days advance purchase may be necessary for international destinations.

MÁV Hungarian Railways (*map*CD3*), VI, Andrássy út 35 (tel. 122 90 35). Any discount available at Express should also be available at the station. Be insistent and whip out all your student/youth IDs. International and domestic tickets. Open Mon.-Fri. 9am-6pm.

Wagons-lits (*map*C4*), at V, Dorottya u. 3, near Vörösmarty tér (tel. 266 30 40). Sells discount tickets for seniors and youth. 25-50% off, depending on the route. Open Mon.-Fri. 9am-12:45pm and 1:30-5pm.

Buses: Volánbusz (tel. 117 29 66 for domestic service, 117 25 62 for international service.) **Main station** (*map*C4*), V, Erzsébet tér. Metro: "Deák tér." Luggage storage available. Several buses per week to Istanbul (US$50) and Venice (US$55), and Bucharest. Buses to the Czech Republic, Slovakia, Poland, Romania, Turkey and Ukraine depart from the **Népstadion** terminal on Hungária körút 48-52. Metro: "Népstadion." Domestic buses are usually cheaper than trains, but may take slightly longer. Buses to the Danube Bend leave from the **Árpád Híd** station.

Public Transportation: The **Metro** has been consistently rapid and punctual for just under a century; built in 1896, it was the first in continental Europe. The Communists certainly deserve kudos for their efforts in public transportation; Hungarians may have waited several hours for bread or toilet paper, but they could choose a 3-block line anywhere in the city and be whisked there for next to nothing. The subway comprises 3 numbered lines—line 1 is yellow, line 2 is red, and line 3 is blue. An "M" indicates a stop, but you will not always find the sign on the street; it's better to look for stairs leading down. All *Trafik* shops and some sidewalk vendors sell yellow tickets *(villamos jegy,* 25 Ft) for buses, trams and the Metro. These tickets are valid through Óbuda; beyond that you'll have to buy one on the train. You're supposed to punch your ticket on board trams and buses, but few people do; the enforcement largely appears at the beginning of the month. **Monthly passes** (1100 Ft) are valid from the first of one month through the fifth of the next. Some buses mimic the Metro lines after the subway shuts down (Metro open 4:30am-11:10pm). Watch your limbs in the rapidly closing doors. The **HÉV commuter rail** runs between Batthyány tér in Buda and Szentendre, 40 min. north on the Danube Bend. Trains leave about every 15 min.

Hydrofoils: MAHART International Boat Station (*map*C4-5*), V, Belgrád rakpart (tel. 118 12 23), near the Erzsébet bridge, has information and ticketing. Open Mon.-Fri. 8am-4pm. Or try the **IBUSZ** office (*map*D4*) at Károly Krt. 3 (tel. 122 24 73). Metro: "Astoria." Open Mon.-Fri. 9am-5pm. Arrive at the docks 1 hr. before departure for customs and passport control. Be sure to inquire about prices before setting off on an international voyage; the return ticket may be astronomically expensive. Eurailpasses may garner a discount on tickets bought through the Austrian company **DDSG.** Budapest to Vienna daily 8am and 1:30pm; 5½ hr.; 730 AS, students 590 AS.

Car Rental: Avis, Reservation office, tel. 36 11 18 41 58, 36 11 18 42 40, or 36 11 18 46 85. Ferihegy Airport, tel. 38 11 57 29 22. **Hertz,** Reservation office, 111 61 16. Ferihegy Airport, tel 157 86 29 (open daily). **Fotaxi Rent-A-Car** (*map*C4*), Aranykez u. 4-8, tel. 117 77 88 (open daily 7am-7pm).

Taxis: Fötaxi (tel. 111 61 16; 32 Ft per km) or **Volántaxi** (tel. 166 66 66; 36 Ft per km). 20 Ft base charge plus distance. Stay away from other companies, and especially avoid the Mercedes-Benz taxis, which charge double the jalopy fee.

Hitchhiking: *Let's Go* cannot recommend hitchhiking as a safe method of transportation. Hitching in the Budapest area has become especially dangerous of late. Those who are hitching south to Szeged and Belgrade (along M5 and E75) take tram #2 from "Soroksári út" to the end of the line; they then switch to bus #23, then bus #4. Hitchers heading west to Győr and Vienna or southwest to Lake Balaton and Zagreb take bus #12 from "Moszkva tér" out to "Budaörsi út," then switch to bus #72. The highway splits a few kilometers outside Budapest; M1 heads west and M7 goes south. **Kenguru,** VIII, Kofarago u. 15 (tel. 138 20 19; Metro: "Astoria") is a carpool service charging 4 Ft per km. Open Mon.-Fri. 8am-6pm, Sat. 8am-2pm.

Other Practical Information

Bookstore: Kossuth Könyvesbolt (*map*C4*), V, Vörösmarty tér 4, to the right of Café Gerbeaud. Sells English-language tourist books and paperback novels. Open daily 10am-6pm. Leaving this store, turn left and walk straight down Váci u., where 3 bookstores beckon on the left within 2 blocks. All have English books.

Laundromat: Mosószalon (*map*C4*), V, József Nádor tér 9. Wash: 5kg for 210 Ft. Dry: 90 Ft per 15 min. Look for the gumball-hue tile column in the window. Open Mon., Wed., and Fri. 7am-3pm, Tues. and Thurs. 11am-7pm.

Gay and Lesbian Services: tel. 138 24 19; open daily 8am-4pm. Gay life in Budapest is almost underground; cafés and bars open and close in the course of a few weeks. Public tolerance is lacking, and attacks from skinheads are not uncommon.

Pharmacies: The following are open 24 hrs.: (*map*A2*) I, Széna tér 1 (tel. 202 18 16); (*map*D2*) VI, Teréz krt. 41 (tel. 111 44 39); IX, Boráros tér 3 (tel. 117 07 43); and IX, Üllöi út 121 (tel. 133 89 47). At night, ring the bell to rouse the sleepy owner; you will be charged a slight fee for the service.

Emergencies: Police: tel. 07. **Fire:** tel. 05. **Ambulance:** tel. 04. Emergency medical care is free for foreigners. A list of English-speaking doctors is available at the U.S. embassy. **24-hr. Emergency Medical Service** (English spoken) tel. 118 82 12.

ACCOMMODATIONS AND CAMPING

Travelers arriving in July and August will inevitably be swarmed at the train station by representatives of various hostels, some offering to shuttle you directly to their accommodations. If you'd rather rent a private room or flat, seek out a less voracious onlooker; just make sure the room is near public transportation and that you see your chamber before you pay (generally 600-1000 Ft per person).

Private Accommodations Services

Many other folks will accost you with offers of their private accommodations, though they are not nearly as voracious as their youthful competitors in hostel T-shirts. It's a veritable feeding frenzy, especially during the summer; get your bearings before you even nod assent to *anyone.* Nascent accommodation services and new branches of established organizations are springing up like wildfire. The rates (700-1200 Ft per person) depend on the category (which usually refers to the standard of the bathroom) and location. Always make sure the room is easily accessible by public transportation—preferably tram or Metro, which arrive more frequently than buses. Be careful of accepting rooms deep in Buda or Pest. You can demand that the solicitor show you on a map where his or her lodging is located. Though the runners at the train station are generally both legitimate and reliable, make sure that you actually see the room before you hand over any cash.

Be stubborn about securing the lowest possible price. Arrive early (around 8am) and you may get a single for 600 Ft or a double for 900 Ft. It's hard to find a cheap, centrally located room for only one or two nights. At the end of a day, the only thing left may be doubles for 2000 Ft. Travelers who stay for more than four nights sit in the bargaining driver's seat. Because they represent four nights of income, they can haggle for a delicious rate.

IBUSZ, at all train stations and tourist centers. **24-hr. accommodation office** at (*map*C5*) V, Petőfi tér 3 (tel. 118 39 25 or 118 57 76). An established accommodations service offering the most rooms in Budapest. The streets outside IBUSZ offices swarm with Hungarians pushing "bargain" rooms; quality varies widely, but they're perfectly legal. The little old ladies asking "*Privatzimmer?*" are the ones vending private rooms.

Budapest Tourist (*map*BC3-4*), V, Roosevelt tér 5 (tel. 117 35 55), near the Forum Hotel, 10 min. from Deák tér, on the Pest end of the Chain Bridge. Another well-established enterprise. Requires no min. stay and offers singles for 800-1000 Ft and doubles for 1600-3000 Ft. Open Mon.-Fri. 8am-6pm, Sat. 8am-2pm; Oct.-June Mon.-Fri. 8am-6pm. Branch offices around the city keep the same hours.

Coleopterist (*map*D2*), VI, Bajcsy-Zsilinszky út 17 (tel. 111 70 34 or 111 32 44), supplies doubles (1200-1600 Ft) and triples (1500 Ft). Claims that all of the rooms are located in districts VI and VII. Stays of fewer than 3 nights incur a 30% surcharge. English spoken. Open Mon.-Fri. 9am-5pm.

Duna Tours (*map*D2*), next to Coleopterist (tel. 131 45 33 or 111 56 30), allows travelers to see rooms before accepting them (doubles 1500 Ft, quads 1600-1800 Ft). The English-speaking staff claims their rooms are located only in district V and VI. Open Mon.-Thurs. 9:30am-noon and 12:30-5pm, Fri. 9:30am-noon and 12:30-4pm, Sat. 9am-1pm; Oct.-April Mon.-Fri. 8am-4:15pm.

To-Ma Tour (*map*C3*), V, Oktober 6. utca 22 (tel. 153 08 19), promises to find you a central room, even if only for 1 night (doubles 1200-2000 Ft depending on location, with private bathroom 2400 Ft; triples 2200 Ft). Reservations during the summer are recommended. Open Mon.-Fri. 9am-noon and 1-8pm, Sat.-Sun. 9am-5pm.

Orient Tours (*map*F3*), in Keleti station. Private rooms and hostels, but they may be way out in Never-never-land. Singles from 380-650 Ft, doubles from 900-1500 Ft. Open daily noon-10pm.

Hostels

Most hostel-type accommodations, including university dorm rooms, are under the aegis of **Express.** Try their office at (*map*C4*) V, Semmelweis u. 4 (tel. 117 66 34 or 117 86 00); leave Deák tér on Tanács krt., head right on Gerlóczy u., and the first left is Semmelweis u. Or try the branch at (*map*C3*) V, Szabadság tér 16, between the Arany János and Kossuth Lajos metro stops. Individual hostels advertise in the Budapest train stations on billboards and small photocopied notices. Most publicly advertised hostels are legal **Kollegiums** (university dorms). You may also see the standard HI symbol outside buildings. Private hostels began to appear *en masse* in 1990, wedging many people into diminutive two-room apartments. Before accepting lodging at the rail station, make sure you're not being brought to one of these sardine cans.

Open Year-round

Diaksportszálló, XIII, Dózsa György u. 152 (tel. 140 85 85 or 129 86 44). Entrance on Angyaföldi, 50m from the "Dózsa György" Metro stop. Dirt cheap, and exceptionally social. Fun international crowd. Bar open, and occupied, 24 hrs., as is reception. Quiet upstairs—don't worry. 8-bed rooms 360 Ft per person, quads 460 Ft per person, doubles 480 Ft per person. This is hostel #4 of the "More Than Ways Company"—ask for it by name.

Back Pack Guesthouse, XI, Takács Menyhért u. 33 (formerly Antal János u.; tel. 185 50 89). From Keleti pu. or the city center take bus #1, 7 or 7A (black numbers) heading toward Buda and disembark at "Tétenyi u.," immediately after the rail bridge. From the bus stop, head back under the bridge, turn left, and follow the street parallel to the train tracks for 3 blocks. Look for the small green signs. One of the homiest hostels in the area. 26 beds; it's best to call ahead. The staff is young, friendly, and very helpful. 5- and 8-bed rooms. No curfew. 450-520 Ft per person. Hot showers, breakfast, private locker, use of kitchen and TV included. Sheets 50 Ft. The bulletin board lists special trips, programs and information. Bike rental available; tennis courts are a 10-min. walk.

ASMARA youth hostel, XVIII, Bajcsy Zsilinszky u. 51, near the airport. Metro: "Köbánya-Kispest." From the Metro stop, take bus #93 and get off at "Majus 1. tér"; Bajcsy Zsilinszky u. is 2 blocks to the right. 560 Ft per person. Common bathroom and kitchen. There's a supermarket, restaurant, and swimming pool in the area.

Donáti (*map*D2*), I, Donáti u. 46 (tel. 201 19 71). Metro: "Batthyány tér." Walk up Batthyány u. for 3 blocks, and cross the little park. Good location. Uncrowded rooms. 72 beds in 6 12-bed dorms. Reception open 24 hrs. 460 Ft per person.

Summer Hostels

These are all university dorms and are mostly of comparable quality. All are open only in July and August. Almost all dorms of the **Technical University** (Műegyetem) become youth hostels in summer; these are conveniently located in district XI, around Móricz Zsigmond Körtér. Take the Metro to "Kálvin Ter," then ride tram #47 or 49 across the river to "M. Zsigmond." For more information, call the **International Student Center** at 166 77 58 or 166 50 11, ext. 1469. During the summer the center also has an office in Schönherz.

Schönherz, XI, Irinyi u. 42 (tel. 166 54 60), one Metro stop after "Universitas." With 1300 beds, the largest dorm around. This high-rise has well-kept quads with bathrooms and refrigerators. Tries to be the most helpful, state-of-the-art hostel. Sauna in building (100 Ft; open 7-9pm). 500 Ft per person. These quads can also be booked as doubles (700 Ft per person) or triples (600 Ft per person). 50 Ft surcharge without HI membership. Breakfast 100-250 Ft. Information office open 8am-midnight.

Strawberry Youth Hostels (*map*D5*), IX, Ráday u. 43-45 (tel. 138 47 66) and Kinizsi u. 2-6 (tel. 117 30 33). Metro: "Kálvin tér." 2 converted university dorms within a block of one another in Pest, on a smaller street running south out of Kálvin tér. Reception open 24 hrs. Checkout 10 am. Doubles 750 Ft per person. triples and quads 590 Ft per person. Refrigerators in rooms. **Free T-shirt** if you stay more than 3 nights.

Baross (*map*C5*), XI, Bartók Béla út 17 (tel. 185 14 44), a block from Géllert tér. From simple singles to quads with sink and refrigerator in the room. Hall bathroom. Lived-in college dorms, Madonna pin-ups and all. Reception 24-hr. Checkout 9am. 520 Ft. per person. Spanking new Maytag washer (120 Ft) and dryer (60 Ft).

Vasarhely (*map*C5*), XI, Krusper utca 2-4 (tel. 185 37 94), on the southwestern corner of the Technical University. One of the fairest dorms of them all—all rooms have a refrigerator and private shower. Doubles 700 Ft per person, quads 600 Ft per person.

Martos (*map*C5*), XI, Stoczek utca 5-7 (tel. 181 11 18), opposite Vasarhely. Checkout 9am. Doubles 920 Ft; dorm beds 403 Ft each, though these require student ID. Hall bathroom.

Bakfark hostel (*map*A2*), I, Bakfark u. 1-3 (tel. 201 54 19). Metro: "Moszkva tér." Centrally located. From the Metro stop, stroll along Margit krt. (formerly Mártírok utja); take the first side street after Széna tér. 88 beds. Reception open 24 hrs. No curfew. Checkout 9am. Dorm beds 460 Ft per person. Sheets, locker, storage space and use of washing machine included. The hostel van will pick backpackers up at the Keleti rail station; call ahead.

Universitas, XI, Irinyi utca 9-11 (tel. 186 81 44). At the first stop after "Petőfi híd" on tram #4 or 6. Large, square dorm with comfortably clean doubles. 500 beds. Checkout 9am. 620 Ft. Hall bathroom. Refrigerator in all rooms. Laundry machines 180 Ft.

Bercsényi, XI, Bercsényi u. 28-30 (tel. 166 66 77), one more stop on tram #4 or 6 past Schönherz, on the side street next to the large **Skala supermarket**. 65 doubles (650 Ft per person) with sink and fridge. Newly refurbished. Hall bathrooms. Reception open 24 hrs. Free parking. Washing machine (120 Ft) available.

Kek (*map*AB5*), XI, Szüret u. 2-18 (tel. 185 23 69). Take bus #27 two stops from "Móricz Zsigmond Körtér." In a very peaceful and green neighborhood on the side of the Gellért Hill. Doubles 780 Ft per person, 1120 Ft per person with shower. Kitchen facilities available.

Hotels

Budapest still has a few inexpensive hotels, frequently clogged with groups. Call ahead. Proprietors generally speak English. All hotels should be registered with Tourinform.

Hotel Citadella (*map*B5*), atop Gellért Hill (tel. 166 57 94). Take tram #47 or 49 three stops into Buda to "Móricz Zsigmond Körtér," and then catch bus #27 to "Citadella." Perfect location. Dorm beds 420 Ft; quads with bathroom 2740 Ft. Usually packed, so call ahead.

Lido Hotel, III, Nánási u. 67 (tel. 188 68 65). Metro: "Arpád híd," then bus #106 to "Nánási." Near the river bank and the Aquincum ruins. Singles 1550 Ft, doubles 2350 Ft. Hall bathroom. Breakfast included.

Aquincum Panzió, III, Szentendrei u. 105 (tel. 168 64 36). Take the HÉV from "Batthyány tér" to "Köles út." Presentable rooms with hall bathrooms. Singles 2300 Ft, doubles 2600 Ft. Breakfast included.

Hotel Kandó, III, Bécsi út 104-108 (tel. 168 20 36). Take bus #60 seven stops from "Batthyány tér." Apartments with private showers and refrigerators. Open July-Aug. Doubles 1800 Ft, triples and quads 2000 Ft.

Unikum Panzió, XI, Bod Péter u. 13 (tel. 186 12 80). Metro: "Deli pu.," then bus #139 south to "Zólyom Köz"; walk 2 blocks on Zólyom Köz and turn left. 15 min. south of the castle. Singles with shower 2250 Ft, doubles with shower 3000 Ft. Breakfast included.

Camping

Camping Hungary, available at tourist offices, describes Budapest's campgrounds.

Zugligeti Niche Camping, Zugligeti út 101. Take bus #158 from "Moszkva tér" to the last stop. A chairlift at campground entrance ascends the Buda hills. Lovely wooded location. Open March 15-Oct. 15. 330 Ft per person. English spoken.

Római Camping, III, Szentendrei út 189 (tel. 168 62 60). Metro: "Batthyány tér," then take the HÉV tram to "Római fürdö." A whopping 2000-person capacity. Disco, swimming pool, and huge green park on the site; Roman ruins nearby. Reception open year-round 24 hrs. Bungalows mid-April to mid-Oct. 960 Ft for a bunk bed, 1490 for 2 beds side by side. Tents 425 Ft per person, students 390 Ft.

Hárs-hegy, II, Hárs-hegy út 5 (tel. 115 14 82). Take bus #22 from "Moszkva tér" 7 stops to "Dénes utca." 2-person tent 780 Ft; 2-person bungalows 1040 Ft; cars 260 Ft. Good, cheap restaurant on the grounds.

Diák Camping, III, Királyok útja 191. Take HÉV from "Batthyány tér" to "Római fürdö," and then ride bus #34 for 10 min. until you see the campground. 160 Ft per person, 80 Ft per tent. Doubles, triples, quads, and 10-bed dorm rooms 240 Ft per person. Owner also rents bikes (30 Ft per hr., 180 Ft per day) and canoes (40 Ft per hr., 240 Ft per day).

FOOD

Even the most expensive restaurants in Budapest may be within your budget, though less costly family eateries may offer superior cuisine. Many restaurants have menus in German, some in English. Keep your eye out for restaurants with Hungarian-only menus; the Glossary at the back of this book should guide you through the more common basics. An average meal runs 400-600 Ft. Cafeterias lurk under **Önikiszolgáló Étterem** signs (vegetarian entrees 50 Ft, meat entrees 120-160 Ft). The listings below are just a nibble of what Budapest has to offer. Seek out the *kifözde* or *kisvendégl* in your neighborhood for a taste of Hungarian life.

Pizzerias overrun the city, though the version they serve is closer to the Italian pie than the popular American conception. The world's largest branch of the culinary behemoth—Burger King—is located on the Oktogon, while co-conspirators Pizza Hut and McDonald's lurk nearby. Though hardly Hungarian, these juggernauts can prove life-savers with their late hours and quick service. McWhatever is generally cheap (100-150 Ft) and filling; just don't subsist on thy daily burger—*please*. Be as adventurous as you can; your intrigued palate will bless you for the extra effort. Ask your hotel or hostel management to recommend a local favorite in order to avoid the many tourist traps—few locals can afford to eat in restaurants, so most are tourist-oriented. A 10% tip has come to be expected in many establishments.

Travelers may also rely on markets and raisin-sized 24-hour stores, labeled "Non-Stop," for staples. Take a gander at the **produce market** (*map*CD5*), IX, Vámház krt. 1-3 at Fövám tér (open Mon. 6am-3pm), the **ABC Food Hall** (*map*B2*), I, Batthyány tér 5-7 (open Sun. 7am-1pm) or the **Non-Stops** at (*map*C3*) V, Oktober 6. u. 5 and at (*map*C4-5*) V, Régi Posta u., off Váci u. past McDonald's.

Restaurants

Central Pest

Vegetárium (*map*C5*), V, Cukor u. 3 (tel. 138 37 10). Metro: "Ferenciek tér." A block and a half from the Metro stop; walk up Ferenciek tér (formerly Károlyi M. u.) to Irány u. on the right; a quick left puts you on Cukor u. Vegetarian and macrobiotic dishes (tempura dinner 300 Ft). A great place to detox after a week of meat. Classical guitar in the evening. Vigorously smoke-free environment. Menu in English. Open daily noon-10pm.

Alföldi Kisvendéglő (*map*D5*), V, Kecskeméti u. 4 (tel. 117 44 04). Metro: "Kálvin tér," 50m past the Best Western. Traditional Hungarian folk cuisine—even the booths are paprika-red. The sumptuous homemade rolls (24 Ft each) should be reason enough to dine here. Entrees 180-300 Ft. Open daily 11am-midnight.

Claudia (*map*D5*), V, Bástya u., off of Kecskeméti u. (tel. 117 19 83). Metro: "Kálvin tér." Subterranean family restaurant with hearty, inexpensive food (entrees 220-510 Ft). Generous helpings of exotic specials are a highlight. Open daily 11am-11pm.

Golden Gastronomie (*map*C4*), V, Bécsi u. 8 (tel. 117 21 97), 2 doors down from American Express. The enticing deli fixings are provocatively displayed. You can sample the salads (60-85 Ft per 100g) before making a choice and devour your selection under a cool artificial tree. English spoken. Open 24 hrs.

Paprika (*map*C4*), V, Harmincad u. 4, just north of Vörösmarty tér, at the big red pepper. Hungarian fast food and a picture menu to help speed eye-hand-mouth coordination. Entrees 80-130 Ft. Open Mon.-Fri. 11am-6pm, Sat.-Sun. 11am-4pm.

Apostolok (*map*C5*), V, Kígyó u. 4-6 (tel. 118 37 04). Visible from the "Ferenciek tér" Metro stop, on a pedestrian side-street toward the bridge. An eclectic, expensive evening of Gothic ambience and superb food in an old beer hall. Entrees 400-700 Ft. Open daily 11am-11pm.

Szindbád (*map*C4*), V, Markó út 33 (tel. 132 29 66), at the corner of Bajcsy-Zsilinszky. 2 blocks from the "Nyugati tér" Metro stop. Impeccable elegance and stupendous desserts, but you pay for the quality. Book 2 days ahead and look sharp. Open Mon.-Fri. 11:30am-3:30pm and 6:30pm-midnight, Sat.-Sun. 6pm-midnight.

Flanking the Pest körút

Restaurant Hanna (*map*CD4*), VII, Dob u. 35, a 10-min. walk from Deák tér. Wholesome kosher food in an Orthodox Jewish time-warp. Dress Conservatively. Open Mon.-Fri. and Sun. 11am-3pm.

Shalom Restaurant (*map*CD4*), VII, Klauzál tér 2, same directions as for Hanna above (tel. 122 14 64). Reform your palate at this elegant but inexpensive Kosher restaurant in the traditionally Jewish section of town. Entrees 300-400 Ft. Open daily noon-11pm.

New York Bagels (*map*DE5*), IX, Ferenc körút 20 (tel. 215 78 80). A 200m walk toward the river from the "Ferenc körút" Metro stop, near the Petőfi Bridge. Eastern Europe's first and only bagel shop, with 9 more branches in the works. Serves wide-eyed Hungarians and elated tourists alike. Assorted bagels baked hourly (36 Ft), with freshly made spreads (140 Ft). Yes, they even have lox (276 Ft). Owned by a former *Let's Go* Researcher-Writer. Open 24 hrs.

Sirály (*map*C4*), VI, Bajcsy-Zsilinszky út. 9 (tel. 122 88 64 or 122 88 80). Metro: "Deák tér." Well-prepared Hungarian food (entrees 250-400 Ft) and imported beer. Just the place to partake of some potent paprika. Fast and friendly service. Menus and service in English. Open daily noon-midnight.

Megálló ("Bus stop"; *map*C5*), VII, Károly krt. 23, two doors to the left of the IBUSZ office. Metro: "Deák tér." Look beyond the ratty bearskin on the wall to the

130-item menu (available in English) which includes such temptations as "rump-steak with gizzard in red wine." Dinner about 400 Ft. Open daily 11am-11pm.

Bagolyvá (*map*F1*), XIV, Allatkerti Körut 2 (tel. 121 35 50). Metro: "Hősök." Directly behind the Museum of Fine Arts—a perfect place to deconstruct the chromatic schema presented on your supper plate. Exceptional Hungarian cuisine, yet remarkably affordable. Enrees 300-400 Ft. Open daily noon-10pm. The Gundel Restaurant next door is Budapest's most famous—and most expensive.

Across the Danube

Söröző a Szent Jupáthoz (*map*A2*), II, Dékán u. 3 (tel. 115 18 98). 50m from the "Moszkva tér" Metro stop, with an entrance on Retek. Venture down the modest stairway, then right back up into a lively garden. Portions are huge—be ready to roll yourself home. "Soup for Just Married Man" 139 Ft. Entrees 200-500 Ft. Open 24 hrs.

Marxim (*map*A2*), II, Kis Rókus u. 23 (tel. 115 50 36). Metro: "Moszkva tér." With your back to the Lego-esque castle, walk 200m along Margit körút and turn left. KGB pizza and Lenin salad are just a few of the revolutionary dishes served in structurally constrained, barbed-wire-laden booths. Food prepared by the staff according to their abilities, consumed by the patrons according to their needs. Join the locals in thumbing their nose at the erstwhile oppressive vanguard. Open Mon.-Fri. noon-1am, Sat. noon-2am, Sun. 6pm-1am.

Marcello's (*map*C5*), XI, Bartók Béla út 40 (tel. 166 62 31). May be the only pizzeria in Budapest to use tomato sauce rather than ketchup. Pizzas 160-340 Ft; salad bar as well. Reservations suggested. Open Mon.-Sat. noon-10pm.

Cafés

The café in Budapest is like grandmother's house—more a living museum of a bygone era than just a place to be spoiled by scrumptious desserts and coffee. These amazing institutions were the pretentious haunts of Budapest's literary, intellectual, and cultural elite. If you lounge in the hallowed eateries long enough, you'll be smothered by the atmosphere. A leisurely repose at any one of Budapest's cafés is a must for every visitor; best of all, the absurdly ornate pastries are inexpensive, even in the most genteel establishments.

Café New York (*map*C4*), VII, Erzsébet krt. 9-11 (tel. 122 38 49). Metro: "Blaha Lujza tér." This remarkably embellished café was the favored locale of turn of the century "starving" *artistes*. Exquisite gilded ceilings. Best of all, no sign of Koch or Sharpton. Cappuccino 100 Ft. Ice cream and coffee delights 100-350 Ft. Open daily 9am-midnight.

Lukács cukrászda (*map*D2*), VI, Andrássy út 70. Metro: "Vorosmarty utca," near Hösök tere. One of the most stunning cafés in Budapest. Dieters will wish the heavenly cakes and tortes (30-50 Ft) were more expensive. Seated service costs more. Open Mon.-Fri. 9am-8pm.

Ruszwurm (*map*AB3*), I, Szentháromság u. 7. Confecting since 1826 and strewn with period furniture. An excellent café. Stop by to relax after the majesty of Mátyás Cathedral down the street in the castle district. You won't be hurried on your way. Best ice cream in Budapest 20 Ft per scoop. Cakes 50-70 Ft. Open daily 10am-8pm.

Gerbeaud Cukrászda (*map*C4*), V, Vörösmarty tér 7. Metro: "Vörösmarty tér." Formerly the meeting place of Budapest's literary elite, this café retains a stunning 19th-century elegance. Service is a bit relaxed, but what's your rush? About 90 Ft. Open daily 7am-9pm.

Wiener Kaffeehaus (Bécsi Kávéház; (*map*C4*), Apáczai Csere János u. 12-14, inside the Forum Hotel on the Danube. Budapest's *crèmes de la cake* tantalize from glass cases. You'd be amazed by what you can savor for 90 Ft. Everything served by pink-clad Magyar maidens. Open daily 9am-9pm.

SIGHTS

Hungary celebrated its 1000-year anniversary in 1896. The various constructions for this Millenary Exhibition, still so prominent in the city, attest to the vast wealth and power of the Austro-Hungarian Empire at the turn of the century. Among the architectural marvels commissioned by the Habsburgs are the Parliament and the adjacent Supreme Court Buildings (now the Ethnographic Museum), Heroes' Square, Szabadság (Liberty) Bridge, Vajdahunyad Castle, and the first Metro station in continental Europe. The domes of both Parliament and St. Stephen's Basilica (completed several years later) are 96m high—vertical referents to the historic date.

Castle Hill

Strategically perched 100m above the Danube, Budapest's **Castle District** (*map*AB3-4*) rests atop the 2km mound called **Várhegy** (Castle Hill; *map*A3*). Cross the **Széchenyi lánchíd** (chain bridge; *map*B4*) and ride the *sikló* (cable car) to the top of the hill (daily 7:30am-10pm, 80 Ft). The upper lift station sits just inside the castle walls. Built in the 13th century, the castle was leveled in consecutive sieges by Mongols and Ottoman Turks. Christian Habsburg forces razed the rebuilt castle in overthrowing the Turks after a 145-year occupation. Reconstruction was completed just in time for the Germans, whose last stand here in 1945 left the fortress again in ruins. Determined Hungarians pasted the castle together once more, only to face the new Soviet menace; bullet holes in the palace façade recall the 1956 uprising. In the post-post-war period, sorely needed resources were channeled into its immediate reconstruction—evidence of its symbolic significance to the city and nation. During this rebuilding, extensive excavations revealed artifacts from the earliest castle on this site; they are now housed in the **Budapest History Museum** in the **Budavári palota** (Royal Palace; *map*B4*), The palace, just to the left of the cable car peak station, holds numerous other collections as well (see Museums below for more information).

From the palace, stroll down Színház u. and Tárnok u. to breach **Trinity Square** (*map*A3*), site of the Disney-esque **Fisherman's Bastion** (*map*A3*). This arcaded stone wall supports a squat, fairy-tale tower with a magnificent view across the Duna. Behind the tower stands the neo-Gothic **Mátyás templom** (Matthias Church; *map*A3*), converted into a mosque literally overnight on September 2, 1541, when the Turks commenced their occupation of Buda; it remained a mosque for 145 years. These days, High Mass is celebrated Sundays at 10am with orchestra and choir (come early for a seat), and organ concerts lob melodies into the valley below on summer Fridays at 8pm. The church's richly painted interior defies description. (Open daily 7am-7pm.)

The holy edifice also boasts a **crypt** and a **treasury;** descend the stairway to the right of the altar. The treasury contains primarily ecclesiastic relics, but don't miss the stunning marble bust of Queen Elizabeth, next to the entrance to the **St. Stephen chapel.** The marble was hewn from the Italian Carrara mine, reputed to hold the world's finest carving stone—Michelangelo's master sculptures were all crafted from the material. (Treasury open daily 9am-5:30pm. Admission 30 Ft.) A second side chapel contains the tomb of King Béla III and his wife, Anna Chatillon; this was the only sepulchre of the Árpád line of kings spared from Ottoman imperial looting. Outside the church is the grand **equestrian monument** of King Stephen, with his trademark double cross.

Next door sits the presumptuous **Budapest Hilton Hotel** (*map*A3*), which incorporates the remains of Castle Hill's oldest church, an abbey built in the 13th century. Intricate door-knockers and balconies adorn the Castle District's other historic buildings; ramble through **Úri utca** (Gentlemen's Street; *map*A3*) with its Baroque townhouses, or **Táncsics Mihály utca** (*map*A3*) in the old Jewish sector. You can command a tremendous view of Buda from the Castle District's western walls. By **Vienna Gate** (*map*A3*) at the northern tip of the District, frequent minibuses run to Moszkva tér, though the walk down Várfok u. only takes about five minutes.

Elsewhere in Buda

The **Liberation Monument** crowns neighboring **Gellért Hill** (*map*B5*), just south of the Castle. This 100-foot bronze statue is dedicated to the Soviet soldiers who died while "saving" Hungary from the Nazis. Hike up to the **Citadella** (*map*B5*) from beside Gellért Hotel at the base of the hill, or take bus #27 from "Móricz Zsigmond Körtér" to two bus stops beyond the hotel. The Habsburgs built the Citadella after the Revolution of 1848 to remind the populace just who held the reigns of power. The view from the top is especially spectacular at night, when the Duna and its bridges shimmer in black and gold.

Overlooking the Elizabeth bridge near the base of Gellért Hill is the statue of **St. Gellért,** complete with colonnaded backdrop and glistening waterfall. Bishop Gellért was sent by the pope to the coronation of King Stephen, the first Christian Hungarian monarch, to assist in the conversion of the pagan Magyars. Many were not intrigued by his message; some disgruntled nonbelievers hurled the good bishop to his death from atop the hill that now bears his name.

Further forestry awaits in the suburban Buda Hills, far into the second and twelfth districts. Catch bus #56 from "Moszkva tér," north of the Castle, and ride up Szilagyi Erzsébet fasor and Hűvösvölgyi út to the end station. There you'll find the **Vadaskert** (Game Park), where boar roam while deer and antelope play—here, people speak optimistically and the skies are supposedly cloudless.

The fabulous **Pál-völgyi caves** hide east of the Vadaskert. Even if you've never before spelunked, you can enjoy the 15m-high caverns, remarkable stalactite formations, and such attractions as the Cave of the Stone Bat and the 25m-deep Radium Chamber. Be sure to wear your long johns, even in the summer—it's quite cool inside. Take the HÉV rail line from "Batthyány tér" two stops to "Szépvölgyi," and walk away from the river to Kolosy tér; then take bus #65 or 65a, across from the yellow church, five stops to "Pál-völgyi barlang." (Guided 45-min. tours leave May.-Sept. Tues.-Sun. on the hour 9am-4pm; Oct.-Dec. and Feb.-April Sat.-Sun. on the hour 9am-4pm. Admission 50 Ft, students 30 Ft.)

Between the caves and the Castle, the **Margit híd** (*map*B1*) spans the Duna to the lovely **Margitsziget** (*map*B1*). This vast island, off-limits to private cars, offers capacious thermal baths, luxurious garden pathways, and numerous shaded terraces. According to legend, the island is named after the daughter of King Béla IV; he vowed to rear young Margaret as a nun if the nation survived the Mongol invasion of 1241. The Mongols left Hungary decimated but not destroyed, and Margaret was confined to the island convent. Take bus #26 from "Szt. István krt." to reach the island.

Pest

Cross the Danube to reach Pest, the throbbing commercial and administrative center of the capital. Its heart is the **Inner City** (*map*C4*), an old section rooted in the pedestrian zone of Váci u. and Vörösmarty tér. Pest's river bank sports a string of modern luxury hotels leading up to the magnificent neo-Gothic **Parliament** (*map*B2*) in Kossuth tér. One cannot grasp its magnitude from across the river; step out from the Metro stop "Kossuth tér" and marvel at one of Europe's most impressive structures (arrange tours at IBUSZ and Budapest Tourist; 1200-1500 Ft).

St. Stephen's Basilica (*map*C3*), just two blocks north of Deák tér, is by far the city's largest church, with room for 8500 worshipers under its massive dome. A very Christ-like depiction of St. Stephen (István) adorns the high altar. St. Stephen's holy **right hand,** one of the nation's most revered religious relics, is displayed here. (Basilica open daily 8am-7pm. Free. Hand visible Mon.-Sat. 9am-5pm, Sun. 1-4pm; Oct.-March Mon.-Sat. 10am-4pm, Sun. 1-4pm.) On the other hand, you may want to visit the Budapest **Synagogue** (*map*D4*), on the corner of Dohány and Wesselényi streets, a five-minute walk from the IBUSZ office on Tanács körút. It is the largest active synagogue in Europe. The gravestones at the rear of the building form an alarming collection amassed in the 1940s. The ethereal harmonies of organ and mixed choir float through the enormous chamber during Friday evening services from 6-7pm. Next door, the **Jewish Museum** (*map*D4*) devotes one haunting room to photos and documents from the Holocaust. (Open April-Oct. Mon. and Thurs. 1-4pm, Tues.-Wed. and Fri. 10am-1pm.)

Andrassy utja (*map*CD2-3*), probably the nation's grandest boulevard, extends from the edge of the Bélvaros in downtown Pest and arrives in **Hősök tere** (Heroes' Square; *map*E1*), some 2km away. A stroll down Andrassy út from Hősök tere toward the inner city best evokes Budapest's golden age, somewhat tarnished by Soviet occupation in recent decades. The grandest stretch is between Hősök tere and the Oktogon, where the world's largest Burger King marks the frontier of commercialism. Metro line 1 runs directly underneath Andrassy. Hősök tere is dominated by the **Millennium monument** (*map*E1*), which showcases the nation's most prominent leaders and national heroes from 896 to 1896, when the structure was erected for the great 1000th Anniversary celebration. The seven fearsome horsemen, with Prince Árpád at the helm, represent the seven Magyar tribes who settled the Carpathian Basin. Soaring above is the Archangel Gabriel, who, according to legend, offered Stephen the crown of Hungary in a dream. It was King (later Saint) Stephen who made Hungary an officially Christian state with his coronation on Christmas Day, 1000. Stephen (István) is the first of the figures on the colonnade.

Behind the monument, the **Városliget** (City Park; *map*F1*) contains a permanent circus, an amusement park, a zoo, a castle, and the impressive **Széchenyi Baths**. The **Vajdahunyad Castle** was also created for the Millenary Exhibition of 1896. Originally constructed of canvas and wood, the castle was redone with more durable materials in response to popular outcry. The façade, intended to chronicle 1000 years of architecture, is a stone collage of Romanesque, Gothic, Renaissance, and Baroque. The castle now houses the **Museum of Agriculture** (see Museums below). Rent a **rowboat** (June to mid-Sept. daily 9am-8pm; 150 Ft per hr.) or **ice skates** (Nov.-March daily 9am-1pm 60 Ft; daily 4-8pm 100 Ft) on the lake next to the castle. Outside the Museum (oink) broods the hooded statue of **Anonymous,** the secretive scribe to whom we owe much of our knowledge of medieval Hungary, and, after Ibid., the most-quoted figure in history.

The ruins of the northern Budapest garrison town, **Aquincum,** continue to crumble in the outer regions of the third district. These are the most impressive vestiges of the Roman occupation, which spanned the first four centuries AD. The settlement's significance increased steadily over that time, eventually attaining the status of **colonia** and becoming the capital of Pannonia Inferior; Marcus Aurelius and Constantine were but two of the Emperors to bless the town with a visit. The **museum** on the grounds contains a model of the ancient city as well as musical instruments and other household items. (Open April-Sept. 9am-6pm, Oct. 9am-5pm. Admission 20 Ft.) The remains of the **Roman military baths** are displayed to the south of the Roman encampment, beside the overpass at Florian tér near the "Árpád híd" HÉV station. From the stop, just follow the main road away from the river.

Museums

Buda Castle (*map*B4*; tel. 175 75 33). Leveled by Soviet and Nazi combat at the end of World War II, the reconstructed palace now houses an assortment of fine museums. Wing A contains the **Museum of Contemporary History** and the **Ludwig Museum,** a collection of international modern art. Open Tues.-Sun. 10am-6pm. Admission 100 Ft, students 50 Ft. Wings B-D hold the **Hungarian National Gallery,** a vast hoard containing the best in Hungarian painting and sculpture over a millennium. Open Tues.-Sun. 10am-6pm. Admission 60 Ft, students 30 Ft. One ticket is valid for all 3 wings. Wing E comprises the **Budapest History Museum,** which chronicles the development of Óbuda, Buda, and Pest over the years. Open Wed.-Sun. 10am-6pm. Admission 60 Ft, students 30 Ft.

Museum of Fine Arts (Szépművészti Múzeum; *map*EF1*), XIV, Hősök tere (tel. 142 97 59). Simply spectacular. One of Europe's finest collections of artworks, from Duccio to Picasso. An immense Italian exhibit. Highlights include an entire room devoted to El Greco and an exhaustive display of Renaissance works. Cameos from all your favorite Impressionists, too. Open Tues.-Sun. 10am-6pm.

Museum of Ethnography (Néprajzi Múzeum; *map*BC2*), V, Kossuth Tér 12, across from the Parliament building (tel. 132 63 40). Outstanding exhibit of Hungarian folk culture, from the late 18th century to the First World War. It covers the whole cycle of peasant life and customs, from childhood to marriage (to taxes) to death. Though slightly skewed in presentation, the 2nd floor houses an exceptional collection of cultural artifacts from Asian, African, and Aboriginal peoples. One of Budapest's best museums; located in the erstwhile home of the Hungarian Supreme Court. Open Tues.-Sun. 10am-6pm. Admission 50 Ft, students free; everyone admitted free on Tues.

Hungarian National Museum (*map*D5*), VIII, Múzeum Krt. 14-16 (tel. 138 21 22). Includes a chronicle of Hungarian settlements, as well as the **Hungarian Crown Jewels,** supposedly the very crown and scepter used in the coronation of King Stephen on Christmas Day in 1000 AD. Don't miss Mihály Munkácsy's enormous "Golgotha" canvas in the room at the top of the stairs. Open Tues.-Sun. 10am-6pm. English guide book 75 Ft. Admission 50 Ft, students 20 Ft.

Museum of Military History (*map*A3*), I, Tóth Árpád sétány 40, in the northwest corner of the Castle District. An intimidating collection of ancient and modern weapons, from the most functional to the most ornate. Some swords seem too splendid to sully with petty disembowelments. The upper floor presents the military history of World War II and a compelling day-by-day account of the 1956 Uprising, from the student protests to the Soviet invasion. Don't miss the severed fist from the massive Stalin statue toppled in the uprising or the memorial to the revolutionaries caught Red-handed thereafter. Open Tues.-Sat. 9am-5pm, Sun. 10am-6pm. Admission 20 Ft.

Vásárhely Museum, III, Szentlélek tér 1. Take the HÉV train from the "Batthyány tér" Metro to "Árpád híd." Room after room filled with the arresting work of Viktor Vásárhely, a pioneer of Op-Art (optical art). Open Tues.-Sun. 10am-6pm Admission 30 Ft.

Museum of Agriculture, XIV, in the Vajdahunyad Castle. Offers exhibits like the "History of Pig Breeding." Also displays stuffed domestic animals and artificial fruit. Open Tues.-Sun. 10am-6pm. Admission 50 Ft, free with ISIC and on Tues.

ENTERTAINMENT

Budapest offers a vast cultural program year-round. Pick up a copy of the English-language monthly *Program in Hungary* or *Budapest Panorama,* both available free at tourist offices; they contain daily listings of all concerts, operas, and theater performances in the city. The "Style" section of the weekly English-language *Budapest Sun* is another excellent source for schedules of entertainment happenings.

The **Central Theater Booking Office** (*map*D3*), at VI, Andrassy u. 18, next to the Opera House (tel. 112 00 00), and the branch at Moszkva tér (tel. 135 91 36) both sell tickets without commission to almost every performance in the city. (Open Mon.-Thurs. 10am-1pm and 2-6pm, Fri. 10am-3pm.) An extravaganza in the gilded, neo-Renaissance **State Opera House** (*map*D3*), VI, Andrássy út 22 (tel. 153 01 70; Metro: "Opera") can cost as little as 50 Ft; the box-office sells any unclaimed tickets for amazing discounts (up to half-price) a half hour before showtime. (Ticket office open Tues.-Sun. 10am-7pm.) The city's **Philharmonic Orchestra** is also world renowned; their concerts thunder through town almost every evening from September to June. The **National Philharmonic Ticket Office** (*map*C4*), Vörösmarty tér 1 (tel. 117 62 22) is next to the Opera House (open Mon.-Fri. 10am-6pm, Sat. 10am-2pm; tickets 600 Ft).

When the weather turns warm, the Philharmonic takes a summer sabbatical, but the tide of culture never ebbs; **summer theaters** are located throughout the city. Classical music and opera are performed in the **Hilton Hotel Courtyard** (*map*A3*), I, Hess András tér 1-3 (tel. 175 10 00), next to the Matthias Church in the Castle District. The **Margitsziget Theater** (*map*B1*), XIII, on Margaret Island (tel. 111 24 96), features opera and Hungarian music concerts. Take tram #4 or 6 to "Margitsziget."

Try **Zichy Mansion Courtyard,** III, Fö tér 1, for orchestral concerts. **Mátyás Church** (*map*A3*) holds regular organ and choral recitals (tickets 100-320 Ft). The **Pest Concert Hall** (Vigadó; *map*C4*), V, Vigadó tér 2, on the Danube bank near Vörösmarty tér, hosts operettas almost every other night (tickets 150-500 Ft).

Folk-dancers stomp across the stage at the **Buda Park Theater,** XI, Kosztolányi Dezsö tér (tel. 117 62 22). Brochures and concert tickets flood from the ticket office at Vörösmarty tér 1. (Open Mon.-Fri. 11am-6pm; tickets run 70-250 Ft.) For a psychedelic evening, try the laser shows at the **Planetarium,** Metro: "Nepliget" (tel. 134 11 61). Performances—yup, they even play Floyd on occasion—are Tues. to Sat. 6:30 and 9pm (admission 350Ft). The **Budapest Spring Festival,** in late March, provides an excellent chance to see the best in Hungarian art and music. The autumn **Budapest Arts Weeks** is another major festival.

Hungary has an outstanding cinematic tradition; most notable among its directors are Miklós Jancsó and István Szabó. Movie theaters abound in Budapest, screening the latest Hungarian and foreign films. The English-language *Budapest Sun* lists a surprising number of reasonably current movies in English; check the kiosks around town. If *szinkronizált* or *magyarul beszélö* appears next to the title, the movie has been dubbed. Tickets are largely a bargain, compared to the monstrous admission at American theaters (100-150 Ft).

To soak away weeks of city grime, crowded trains, and yammering camera-clickers, sink into a **thermal bath,** a constitutive part of the Budapest experience. The post-bath massages vary widely from a quick three-minute slap to a royal half-hour indulgence. Many baths are meeting places for, but by no means exclusively for, Budapest's limited gay population. The **Király** baths, II, Fö u. 84 (tel. 115 30 00), date from Turkish times. (Thermal bath and sauna 120 Ft. 10-min. massage 130 Ft. Open Mon.-Sat. 6:30am-6pm; Mon., Wed., Fri. for men; Thurs. and Sat. for women.) The **Gellért** (*map*B5*) baths are located inside Hotel Gellért at the base of Gellért Hill. Women and men frolic nude in separate baths. (Thermal bath and sauna 140 Ft. 15-min. massage 160 Ft. Open Mon.-Sat. 6am-7pm, Sun. 6am-4pm.) The gorgeous **Széchenyi** spread, XIV, Állatkerti u. 11 (tel. 121 03 10), beckons in the main city park (Városliget), near Heroes' Square. Metro: "Széchenyi Fűrdó." Their thermal baths (130 Ft) command a devoted following among the city's venerable gentry, while the large **outdoor swimming pool** (200 Ft) delights their grandchildren.

Nightlife

Budapest's citizens are rapidly catching up on 35 years of foregone revelry. The clubs around the university generally attract the liveliest patrons.

Morrison's Music Pub (*map*D3*), VI, Révay u. 25 (tel. 269 40 60), just to the left of the State Opera House. Metro: "Opera." Half pub, half hip dance club with cheap beer (80 Ft). A young, international crowd. This may be the one place in Europe that Jim's *not* buried. Cover 100-200 Ft. Functional English red telephone booth inside. Open noon-4am.

Fregatt Pub (*map*C4*), V, Moluár u. 26 (tel. 118 99 97), off Váci u. near the "Ferenciek tér" Metro station. Popular pub, usually filled with English-speaking twentysomethings. Beer 110 Ft. Shuts down at midnight.

Véndiák (Former Student), V, (*map*D5*) Egyetem tér (tel. 117 46 03). Metro: "Kálvin tér," then walk up Kecskeméti u. This late-night bar also has a lively dance floor. Popular with local students. Really picks up around 2am. Cover 100 Ft. Open 9pm-4am.

Tilos az Á ("A" is forbidden), VIII, (*map*D5*) Mikszáth Kálmán tér 2 (tel. 118 06 84). Walk down Baross u. from the "Kálvin tér" Metro station for 2 blocks, then turn left. This cryptic Magyar name should strike a chord with hard-core Winnie the Pooh fans. Live music and dancing until the wee hours. Open daily 8pm-4am.

Jazz Café (*map*BC2*), V, Balassi Bálint u. 25 (tel. 132 43 77). Metro: "Kossuth tér," then walk across the square past the Parliament building. Live jazz under blue lights nightly at 8pm. Club closes at midnight.

Táncház, an itinerant folk-dancing club, where you can stomp with Transylvanians. They invariably have a beginners' circle and an instructor. Locate them in *Pesti Mùsor* (Budapest's weekly entertainment guide, in Hungarian) or ask at Tourinform.

KEK (*map*C5*), the "official" club of Eötvös Loránt University, V, Károlyi Mihály u. 9 (tel. 117 49 67). Metro: "Ferenciek tér." In July-Aug. open Tues. 6-10pm and Thurs. 7pm-midnight.

Local (*map*D3*), VII, at the intersection of Dob u. and Kertész u. just off Erzsébet körút. A gay club.

DAYTRIPS INTO THE DANUBE BEND

North of Budapest, the Danube sweeps south in a dramatic arc, called the Danube Bend (Dunakanyar), as it flows east from Vienna along the Slovakian border. Roman ruins from first-century settlements dapple the countryside, and medieval palaces gaze upon the river **Esztergom** and **Visegrád.** An artist colony thrives today amidst the museums and churches of **Szentendre.** Lying within 45km of Budapest, the region offers winsome daytrips and overnights from the capital.

Hourly **buses** from Budapest's Árpád Híd metro station link these three towns with the capital. If you are traveling directly to Esztergom, take the bus through Dorog; this 70-minute shortcut subtracts an hour from the route that winds along the river through Visegrád (139 Ft, stretches between the 3 cities cost 74 Ft each). The suburban **railway** (HÉV) to Szentendre (every 15 min.; 40 min., 64 Ft) starts from Batthyány tér in Budapest (M: Batthyány tér). The river boats from Budapest are a pleasurable, if painstaking, way to visit the region. **Boats** cast off from Budapest's Vigadó tér dock four times per day and steam upriver to Visegrád (3 hr., 105 Ft) and Esztergom (5 hr., 120 Ft), making short stops along the way. Not all boats stop at Szentendre (1 hr., 75 Ft). **Dunatours,** V, Bajcsy-Zsilinszky út. 17 (tel. 131 45 33), in Budapest, books private rooms in Szentendre. (Open Mon.-Thurs. 9:30am-noon and 12:30-5pm, Fri. 9:30am-noon and 12:30-4pm.)

■ Szentendre

Twenty kilometers north of Budapest, Szentendre's diminutive pastel townhouses and superior galleries attract rampaging legions of tourists to its artsy streets. From the HÉV and bus station, use the underpass and continue ten minutes up Kossuth Lajos u. to the triangular center of the old town, **Fö tér.** Branching off the top of the square to the right is Bogdányi u. The **IBUSZ** office, Bogdányi u. 11 (tel. (26) 31 35 96-7) finds rooms (doubles 1300 Ft) and rents bicycles (800 Ft per day). (Open Mon.-Sat. 9am-4pm; Sept.-June Mon.-Fri. 9am-4pm). At **Dunatours,** Bogdányi u. 1 (tel. (26) 31 13 11), you might encounter rough-hewn English, but you can usually secure a comparably priced room, should IBUSZ fail. (Open Tues.-Sun. 10am-12:30pm and 1:30-6pm.) Camping is available at **Pap-szigeti Camping** (tel. (26) 31 06 97), 800m north of Fö tér (2 people with tent 520 Ft; open May-Sept.).

On **Templomdomb** (Church Hill) above Fö tér is Szentendre's first stone church, built in the 13th century. Redone in the Baroque style in the 18th century, the church has retained its original Romanesque character. Across Alkotmány u. is the rival **Serbian Orthodox Church;** the church is open only for Sunday services, but the grounds house a museum of 18th-century Serbian religious art, collected from abandoned churches when the area's Serbs returned home after the Ottoman Turkish threat had passed (open Wed.-Sun. 10am-6pm; 30 Ft). The most impressive of Szentendre's museums is the **Kovács Margit Múzeum,** at Vastagh György u. 1, which exhibits brilliant ceramic sculptures and tiles by the 20th-century Hungarian artist Margit Kovács (including the renowned Pound Cake Madonna; 60 Ft, students free). Also worthwhile is the **Czóbel Museum,** atop Church Hill, displaying the works of Hungary's foremost Impressionist, Béla Czóbel. (Museums open Tues.-Sun. 10am-5:30pm. Admission 30-40 Ft, sometimes free to students.)

■ Visegrád

Thirteen km upriver between the Pilis and Börsöny mountains, Visegrád was once the high-water mark of the Roman Empire. After suffering one too many Mongol invasions, King Béla IV built a **citadel** in 1259 on the hilltop—hike up to "Fellegvár" from the statue of King Matthias near the wharf (40 min.; open daily 9am-5:30pm). Hourly buses run from the town's first stop to the citadel in July and August (44 Ft). For nearly two centuries, Visegrád and Buda alternated as the capital of Hungary. Below the citadel, **Solomon's Tower** once formed part of a lower castle for regulating river traffic. The museum inside holds relics from the royal palace (open May-Oct. Tues.-Sun. 9am-4:30pm; 30 Ft). From the tower, cavort on Fö u. to the terraced ruins of the 14th-century **palace** of King Charles Robert. As you wander through the rubble, don't miss the remarkable red-marble wall **fountain,** in the Lion Court on the top level. (Open Tues.-Sun. 9am-5pm; Nov.-March 8am-4pm. Admission 30 Ft.)

Few tourists sleep in Visegrád, a town with only two major streets. The first of the bus's three stops is nearest the Tower and Palace; the second is closer to the hostel and **campground** (along the river road; 450 Ft per 2 people and tent; tel. (26) 32 81 02; open May-Sept.). Otherwise, walk into town away from the river and take the first right after the green-tipped church for the Széchenyi u. **campground** and **hostel** (330 Ft per 2 people and tent; hostel bed 300 Ft). At both sites, an ISIC nets a 10% discount. Fö u. runs parallel to the Danube and the main road to the cathedral at the other end of town. Near the church around Fö u. 100, several houses rent private rooms for about 1000 Ft per person. The snack bar at the foot of the citadel is open during visiting hours and is better and cheaper than many of its breed.

■ Esztergom

Esztergom witnessed the birth and coronation of Hungary's first king, Saint István (Stephen) in 1000. Strategically located 20km beyond Visegrád at the western edge of the Danube Bend, Esztergom has endured invasions by Mongols, Turks, and the Austrian Habsburgs. Today it is best known as a stronghold of the Catholic church.

Esztergom Cathedral, the largest church in Hungary, majestically crowns **Várhegy** (Castle Hill) to the north. Franz Liszt composed and conducted the consecration mass for this colossal structure, begun in 1010 and completed in 1856. Enter ye, and be engulfed in a sea of gray marble. The **treasure room** contains the cross upon which all the kings of Hungary until 1916 pledged their oath (admission 50 Ft, students 10 Ft; open daily 9am-4:30pm). From the cupola you can look across the river into Slovakia (admission 20 Ft, students 10 Ft). The **Keresztény Múzeum (Christian Museum),** on Berényi Zsigmond u. at the foot of Castle Hill, houses an exceptional collection of Hungarian and Italian religious artwork. (Open Tues.-Sun. 10am-6:30pm. Admission 50 Ft, students 30 Ft.) Experience the country-town atmosphere of this one-time capital at the daily **vegetable market** on Simor János u. near the bus station (6am-5pm).

IBUSZ, Lőrinc u. 1 (tel. (33) 31 25 52) has city maps (31 Ft) and books doubles for 1300 Ft (open Mon.-Fri. 8am-11:50am and 12:30-4pm, Sat. 8-11am). From the bus station, walk up Simor János u. to the center, where it confronts Rákóczi in Széchenyi tér. Up the street at Lőrinc u. 6, **Komtourist** (tel. (33) 31 20 82), has rooms in pensions (doubles 1200-2000 Ft; open Mon.-Fri. 8am-4pm, Sat. 8-11am). **Express** is nearby at Széchenyi tér 7. (Open Mon.-Wed. 8am-noon and 12:30-3pm, Thurs. 8am-noon and 12:30-3:30pm, Fri. 8am-noon and 12:30-2:30pm.)

In general, rooms for a few nights are easy to find. Walk along Lőrinc u. from Rákóczi tér until you reach a bridge. Turn left before crossing it. **Márta Panzió,** Bocskoroskúti út 1 (tel. (33) 31 19 83), offers double rooms with bathroom and breakfast for 1800 Ft. Closer to the town center is **Pansion Platán,** Kis Duna sétany 11 (tel. (33) 31 13 55), where a double with bathroom goes for 1378 Ft. **Vadvirág Camping** (tel. (33) 31 22 34), one of three sites in town, is a 10-min. bus ride outside the city (take the Visegrád bus). From IBUSZ, walk down Lőrinc u. to the Danube and turn right (250 Ft per person; 4-person bungalows with bathroom 2200 Ft). A closer, if more crowded, campground is Gran Camping. From Rákóczi tér, walk down Lőrinc u. across the bridge and continue to the other side of the island; then go left. (Open May to mid-Oct. 280 Ft per person, plus 250 Ft per tent. 4-person bungalow with bath 3200 Ft. ISIC discount 10%. Students-only dorm beds 320 Ft.)

For fish specialties, continue on Mártirok u. across the bridge and look left—under a straw roof, **Halászcsárda** serves the catch of the day for 140-250 Ft (open daily noon-10pm). **Alabárdos** on Bajcsy-Zsilinszky út 49 (tel. (33) 31 26 40) serves reasonably priced Hungarian specialties with old photos of the city on its walls. (Entrees 350-500 Ft. Open daily noon-11pm. Menu in English.)

■■■ EGER

A thousand years of invasions and bacchanalian revelry have left their mark on Eger, one of the most beguiling towns in Hungary. Eger has a wealth of historical sights, cheap lodgings, and the potential for exceptional dining experiences. Two hours northeast of Budapest by train, Eger is a launch pad for exploring the Baradla caves in Aggtelek and the Bükk and Mátra Mountains, the loftiest in the country.

Orientation and Practical Information Trains from Budapest-Keleti station go directly to Eger or make a tight connection in Füzesabony (about every 3 hr., 2 hr., 402 Ft). Trains split in Hatran, so beware. From the train station, try to catch the (infrequent) #3 bus two stops, or walk to the right on Deák Ferenc út to the tremendous yellow cathedral on Eszterházy tér. Turn right on Kossuth Lajos u., then take a quick left along Eszterházy tér to reach Széchenyi István u. **OTP Bank,** on Széchenyi u., posts information for all **exchange bureaus** in town.

Accommodations and Food **Express,** Széchenyi István u. 28 (tel. (36) 31 07 57) relays information about summer youth hostels in university dorms (office open Mon.-Fri. 8am-4pm). **Egertourist,** Bajcsy-Zsilinszky u. 9 (tel. (36) 31 17 24) finds private rooms (singles from 750 Ft; doubles from 960 Ft; open Mon.-Fri. 8am-7pm, Sat. 8am-2pm). Bajcsy-Zsilinsky u. starts right at the beginning of Széchenyi u. Egertourist also runs **Egercamping** at Rákóczi u. 59-79 (tel. (36) 31 05 58), 1.2km out of town. Go directly there on city buses #5, 10, 11, or 12. Through the archway next to Egertourist is **IBUSZ,** Bajcsy-tömb belsö (tel. (36) 31 14 51) where doubles fetch 950 Ft. (Open Mon.-Thurs. 8am-noon and 1-4pm, Fri. 8am-noon and 1-3pm.) Both Egertourist and IBUSZ sell city map (20 Ft).

You can go directly to the dormitories for rooms, priced from 250 Ft. Consider the **Berzeviczy Gizella Kollégium,** Leányka u. 2 (tel. (36) 31 23 99), and nearby **Kun Béla Kollegium,** Leányka u. 6; both lie near the castle. Ascend the steps to the right of the castle entrance; you can see the white Berzeviczy form there; Kun Béla is the gray block around the corner. Or try the **Eszterházy Károly** dorm on Egészségház u. 4 (tel. (36) 31 23 77), off Kossuth Lajos u. (250 Ft per person). The **Hotel Unicornis** (tel. (36) 31 28 86) earns only one star for its one horn and has rooms at Dr. Hibak Károly u. 2 (doubles 1220 Ft, with shower 1450 Ft; breakfast included).

In the shadow of the cathedral, **Kazamata** restaurant hibernates in a concrete cave. (Stuffed meat pancakes 90 Ft. Entrees 130-400 Ft. Open daily 10am-11pm. Disco/bar 10pm-4am.) Country women hawk produce and flowers in the cavernous **indoor market,** near Centrum áruház department store in the center (open Mon.-Fri. 6am-6pm, Sat. 6am-1pm, Sun. 6-10am). Upstairs, fabulous barbecued ribs sell for a paltry 100 Ft (open Mon.-Fri. 8am-7:30pm, Sat.-Sun. 8:30am-7:30pm). For quick and inexpensive gourmet food, go to the **HBH** (Bayerische Hofbräuhaus), Bajcsy Zs. u. 19, next to Dóbo Jér. Meals are well-prepared and the portions enormous. Wash them down with local beer in the back of the restaurant. (Open daily 10am-10pm; Nov.-March Mon.-Sat. 10am-10pm. Entrees 170-350 Ft. Menus in English.)

Sights and Entertainment The potent **Egri Bikavér** (Bull's Blood) wine flows from Eger, the red-wine capital of Hungary. The **Szépasszonyvölgy** (Valley of Beautiful Women), in the southwestern part of the town, shelters hundreds of wine cellars, of which **Ködmön** is the most famous, but not necessarily the best. Locals say that in the valley the wine is watered down; you'll have to judge for yourself. From Deák Ferenc U. and Eszterházy tér, go west away from the center on Telekessy István, which becomes Bacsó Béla u. and eventually Szépasszonyvölgy u. Keep walking straight for 20 minutes until you reach the bottom of the hill; it's the first restaurant on your left. Rowdy Hungarians drink and sing along with gypsy violinists in the candlelight, and the inexpensive food is as fine as the atmosphere. (Entrees 150-300 Ft. Egri Bikavér costs only 100 Ft per ½L. Order white wine at your own risk. Open daily noon-10pm, but kitchen closes around 8pm.)

Eger's most venerable buildings date from the Baroque and Ottoman periods. At medieval **Eger Castle,** István Dobó and his fighters repelled the unified Ottoman army in 1552, halting their advance for another 44 years. Hungarians still revere it as a symbol of national pride. The **István Dobó Museum** displays excavated doorways, weapons and pottery. (Open Tues.-Sun. 9am-5pm. Admission 60 Ft, students free.) The castle's innards include subterranean barracks, catacombs, and a crypt. Reach the castle from Kossuth u. In Dobó tér, the comely Baroque **Minorite church** overlooks a statue of Captain Dobó and two co-defenders—one a woman poised to hurl a rock upon an unfortunate Turk. The other end of Kossuth u. leads to the yellow **cathedral,** the second-largest church in Hungary, on Eszterházy (open daily 9am-6pm; free). It's well-nigh impossible to distinguish the real marble from the painted illusions. Opposite the cathedral, the Rococo 18th-century **Lyceum** stages operettas and other performances (100 Ft). Inside the Lyceum (now a teacher's college) is the magnificent **library** in room #48, whose frescoed ceiling depicts the Council of Trent, which spawned the edicts of the Counter-Reformation. A **Museum of Astronomy** on the sixth floor, a great view from a balcony on the eighth, and a **periscope** on the ninth, which projects live images onto a table in front of you, all await your touristic pleasure. (Lyceum open Tues.-Fri. 9:30am-1pm, Sat.-Sun. 9:30am-noon. Admission 60 Ft, students 15 Ft. Capture another Egerian Kodak Moment™ from the **Turkish minaret,** the northernmost Turkish monument in Europe. (Ascend the huge stone pencil daily 10am-6pm for 20 Ft.) The 18th-century **Serbian church** on Vitkovics u. (at the northern end of the center, parallel to Szechenyi u.) displays a magnificent altar and beautiful murals (open daily 10am-4pm; free).

■■■ GYŐR

Though usually associated with heavy industries such as the Rába truck factory, Győr (pronounced "dyur") is not without charm: it is still possible to see a horse-drawn firewood cart clogging rush-hour traffic. Győr's status as a major tourist town, boosted by a rich cultural atmosphere, no doubt stems from its fortuitous position on the Vienna-Budapest rail line. All of Győr's major sights are within easy walking distance and can be seen in an afternoon. Three rivers that eventually flow into with the Danube meet here, adding to the pleasant atmosphere.

Orientation and Practical Information Győr is two hours from Budapest-Keleti train station (6 per day; 402 Ft) and an easy daytrip from Sopron (6 per day; 1hr.; 254 Ft). From the bus station, take the underpass to the train station (signs say Belváros), and emerge 40m to the right of the train station's main entrance. Straight ahead is Aradi Vértanúk u. and one of the public bus stops. One block up from the train station, along Aradi Vértanúk u., at the intersection with Szent István út, is **Ciklámen Tourist,** Aradi u. 22 (tel. (96) 31 15 57 or (96) 31 67 01), where an

English-speaking staff rents singles for 750 Ft, doubles for 1300 Ft, and gives away a map (open Mon.-Thurs. 8am-4:30pm, Fri. 8am-3:30pm, Sat. 8am-1pm).

Accommodations and Food A right from Aradi onto Szent István for two blocks will bring you to Szent István út 29-31, where **IBUSZ** (tel. (96) 31 17 00 or 31 42 24) rents singles from 770 Ft and doubles from 880 Ft. (Open Mon.-Tues. and Thurs. 8-11:50am and 12:30-4pm; Wed. and Fri. 8-11:50am and 12:30-3:30pm.) Two blocks into the tourist area, take a right to Bajcsy-Zsilinszky út 41 (past the theater) where **Express** (tel. (96) 32 88 33) offers friendly service. (Open Mon.-Fri. 8am-noon and 12:30-3:45pm; has doubles.)

Try **Hotel Aranypart** at Áldozat u. 12, five stops on bus #16 from Szabadság tér (doubles without bathroom 1800 Ft). In July and August you can find beds in the unmarked but brightly colored **Kollegium** (tel. (96) 31 36 55) on Liszt Ferenc u. 42, which runs out of Széchenyi tér (300 Ft per person). **Szárnyaskerék Hotel** (tel. (96) 31 46 29), on Révai Miklós u. 5 at the railway station, has clean rooms but a non-English-speaking staff (doubles 1500 Ft, with bathroom 1700 Ft). There is a **post office** down the street at Bajcsy-Zsilinszky út 46 (open Mon.-Fri. 8am-8pm). Bus #8 stops at **Kiskút-ligeti Camping** (formerly called Ciklámen Camping), Kiskút-liget (tel. (96) 31 89 86). Camping and bungalows are open April 15-October 15, and the motel is open year-round (2-person bungalows 1500 Ft, 300 Ft per person in tent).

Vaskakas (Iron Rooster) **Tavern,** in the dungeon of the castle on Köztársaság tér, has music and a great location (platters 150-520 Ft; open 11am-4am). **Várkapu,** at Bécsikapu tér 7, serves excellent paprika garnished lightly with food (entrees 200-450 Ft; open daily 10am-11pm; English menu). **Komédiás** at Czuczor G. u. 30 (tel. (96) 31 90 50), on the west side of the theater, is a cozy, family-run restaurant with a limited selection but excellent service and reasonable prices (entrees 150-380 Ft). A **Biergarten** huddles around the back (beer 90 Ft).

Sights and Entertainment About 10 minutes up Aradi vértanúk from the station lies **Köztársaság tér** (Republic Square), site of the very yellow **Carmelite Church** and the remains of a medieval castle. Follow Alkotmány u. away from the river to Széchenyi tér, the old town center, to drink *kávé* and people-watch. The marketplace on the river transmogrifies into a **bazaar** on Wednesday, Friday, and Saturday mornings. Győr frolics away its **summer festival** in late June and early July with theater, ballet and concerts.

The town's **Cathedral** dates from the 11th century. Consider it an open-air museum of architectural styles; elements of the Romanesque, Gothic, and Baroque are all present. Inside, dozens of golden cherubim and the magnificent frescoes make it one of the nation's loveliest churches. Don't miss the wide-eyed bust of Saint László in the Hédervári Chapel, a masterwork of Gothic goldsmithery.

The **Margit Kovács Museum** on Rözsa Ferenc u. 1, one block north of Széchenyi tér, is one of Győr's hidden treasures, displaying the artist's distinctive ceramic sculptures and tiles. (Open Tues.-Sun. 10am-6pm, Nov.-March Tues.-Sun. 10am-5pm. Admission 20 Ft, students 10 Ft.)

■■■ SOPRON

Sopron is the Hungarian metropolis closest to Austria both geographically and culturally, lending the denizens of the city an air of snobbery over their compatriots. One of the most expensive towns in all Hungary, Sopron is still cheap enough for the Austrians who flock here for a nearby jaunt. The pillaging Ottoman Turks bypassed Sopron, leaving its medieval buildings and Roman foundations intact.

Orientation and Practical Information Sopron rises from fertile farmland only a few rail hours from Budapest's Déli station (5 per day, 3 hr., 656 Ft) and Vienna's Südbahnhof (7-9 per day, 90 min., US$17). From **Gysev pu.** (the terminus for all trains from Vienna), walk north on Mátyás Király út for 10 minutes to reach Várkerület, or take bus #1, 2 or 12 for three stops (22 Ft at newsstands, 30 Ft on the bus). The bus station is a short hop north of Ciklámen Tourist on Lackner Kristóf. A **post office** is on Széchenyi tér, at the southern end of the old town (open Mon.-Fri. 8am-8pm, Sat. 8am-noon).

Accommodations and Food On the left side of the street is **Lokomotiv,** Várkerület 90 (tel. (99) 31 11 11) where you can get doubles for 1000-1200 Ft (open Mon.-Fri. 8am-4pm, Sat. 8am-noon). The **IBUSZ** office at Várkerület 41 (tel. (99) 31 24 55), offers excellent exchange rates as well as singles and doubles for 1000 Ft (open Mon.-Fri. 8am-4pm, Sat. 8am-noon). At **Ciklámen Tourist,** Ógabona tér 8 (tel. (99) 31 20 40) doubles go for 1300 Ft the first night, 1200 Ft each night thereafter. (Open Mon.-Thurs. 7:30am-4pm, Fri.-Sat. 7:30am-8pm, Sun. 8:30am-noon; mid-Sept. to May Mon.-Fri. 7:30am-4pm, Sat. 7:30am-3:30pm.)

Talizmán Panzió is 1.5km west of the center at Ady Eudre u. 85, but the comfortable rooms with TV and private shower are a steal at 800Ft per person. From the train station, walk up Mätyas Kiraály one block to Csengery, then catch bus #10 going left (west) on Csengery; the stop is right in front of the *panzió* on your left.

In the comfortable *panzió* above the **Taverna** (see below), show 'em your *Let's Go* and earn a 200 Ft discount on rooms (doubles 1200 Ft without bath, 1500 Ft with bath). Showers and TVs in every room, coupled with no curfew, make this a great spot to set up camp for a night or two. **Lövér Campground** (tel. (99) 31 17 15) on Köszegi u. at the south end of town, is often crammed (bungalow doubles 1100 Ft, bungalow triples 1400 Ft). Take bus #12 from Várkerület, and ask the driver to let you off at the campground (buses every 30 min. until 10:15pm).

Go to **Deák Étterem** at Erzsébet u. 20 on Deák tér (tel. (99) 31 16 86) to meet the English club, which comes here for a chat and beer every Tuesday evening from September to June. In the huge green garden, you can try to decipher your meal from the very rich, non-English menu. (Entrees 150-480 Ft. Open Mon.-Sat. 10am-midnight, Sun. 10am-10pm.) To get there, walk toward the train station along Erzsébet u. from Széchenyi tér, where the main post office is located. **Taverna** is a mighty restaurant at Táncsics M. utca 15. Take bus #19 three stops from the train station. A huge wine cellar serves excellent food at very reasonable prices (entrees 140-450 Ft). Eat before the orchestra starts or you just might choke with laughter (restaurant open Mon.-Sat. 8am-10pm).

There is a **Non-Stop** grocery store on the corner of Móricz Zsigmond u. and Magyar u. and a larger **Julius Meinl** grocery store on Várkerület.

Sights and Entertainment Most of Sopron's historic sights lie within the oval Old Town, bounded by Széchenyi tér in the south, Vár kerület to the east and north, and Öguabona tér to the west. Within the ring cluster four churches, two synagogues, and 10 museums. Fö tér is an oval in the old town, circled by Várkerület and oozing aged houses and museums. Enter under the tall green fire tower (*tüztorony*), which presides over the shingled roofs of the old town. (Sights open Tues.-Sun. 10am-6pm. Museum admission 40 Ft, 20 Ft with ISIC.) On the right, **Storno-Ház,** a Renaissance palace, houses a marvelous collection of Baroque items. Across the street on the right is the **Bencés Templom** (Goat Church), built by a happy herder whose goats found gold. Inside, stone goats jut out from the walls like domesticated gargoyles. The small Franciscan **monastery** next door dates from the late 13th century. Its textbook Gothic architecture is enriched by 10 symbolic sculptures of human sins and taped Gregorian muzak chants (open Sat.-Thurs. 10am-noon and 2-5pm; free). Walk down Új u. to two rare 14th-century **synagogues** at #11 (under renovation in 1994) and #22, which evoke daily life in the local Jewish community, expelled in 1526 (open Wed.-Mon. 9am-5pm). Ten minutes outside the old town at the intersection of Május 1 and Csatkai Endre is the **Liszt Ferenc Muzeum** (Franz Liszt Museum). Don't be fooled; it's an ethnographic museum and has nothing to do with the composer. During the **Sopron Festival Weeks** (June-July), the town hosts a profusion of opera, ballet, and concerts, some set in the **Fertörákos Quarry** caverns, 10km away. (1 bus per hr. from main bus terminal. Admission to quarry 10 Ft for students. Concerts 300-400 Ft. Buy tickets for all events from the Festival Bureau on Széchenyi tér. across form the post office. Open Mon.-Fri. 10am-1pm and 2-5pm, Sat. 10am-1pm.)

Near Sopron: Fertöd

Twenty-seven km east of Sopron, in tiny **Fertöd,** stands the magnificent Rococo **Eszterházy Palace,** nicknamed the "Hungarian Versailles" and easily the finest in Hungary. Miklós Eszterházy, known as Miklós the Sumptuous before he squandered his family's vast fortune, ordered the palace built in 1766 to hold his multi-day orgiastic feasts. Josef Haydn wrote and conducted here, and stellar concerts still resound within (open Tues.-Sun. 8am-4pm). Buses leave hourly for Fertöd from stage five in the station on Lackner Kristóf in Sopron (45min., 105 Ft). Fertöd has dorm beds and a few doubles, but groups often fill them. Book with Ciklámen Tourist in Sopron.

Near Sopron: Kőszeg

Roadside shrines and thriving farms lie along the bus route from Sopron to **Kőszeg** (take the Szombathely line; 3 per day, 90 min., 172 Ft). Kőszeg is also served by trains from Szombathely (about 15 per day, 30 min., 72 Ft).The town's central Jurisics tér retains its medieval cityscape; **St. James Church** is one of the country's most significant Gothic treasures. The bus from Sopron stops first at the train station and then closer to the center. Step off and turn right on Kossuth Lajos u.; one block up is **Várkör** (Castle Ring), the ovoid main street. From the train station, cross the little bridge and bear right up Rákóczi u. about 1km into the center. **Savaria Tourist** on Várkör 69 (tel. (94) 36 02 38), offers doubles in private homes for 1100 Ft (only German spoken). Next door, at the corner of Városház u. is an **Express** office (tel. (94) 36 02 47; open May-Oct.) with hotel rooms (doubles 1300 Ft, with bathroom 1800 Ft; 10% off with HI card). Twenty meters farther, **IBUSZ,** Városhaz 3 (tel. (94) 36 03 76), has doubles from 900 Ft. (All tourist offices open Mon.-Fri. roughly 8am-4pm, Sat. 8am-noon.) There is also a **campground** in town near the beach on route #87. The **castle** (tel. (94) 36 02 27) at Rajnis u. 9 in Jurisics tér has tourist dorm rooms for 280 Ft per person. **Irottkö Restaurant,** Fö tér 4, is good (entrees 180-430 Ft; open daily 7am-10pm), and the more authentic **Kulacs Restaurant,** Várkör 12, one blocks from Irottkö, is better yet (entrees 140-440 F; open daily 9am-10pm).

LAKE BALATON

Shallow Balaton (600 sq. km) is the largest lake and one of the most coveted vacation spots in Central Europe. The first villas appeared during the Roman Empire, and when a railroad linked Lake Balaton to its surroundings in the 1860s, it mushroomed into a favored summer playground. Today, mobs of Germans, Austrians, and Hungarians invade the region for its rich scenery and comparatively low prices.

Long and narrow, Lake Balaton is easily accessible from Budapest through Balatonfüred on the northern shore or Siófok on the southern shore (5 trains per day, 350-400 Ft). These two centers sate vacationers with discos and bars but leave little for rainy days. Buses run from Balatonfüred to the quieter Tihany (1 per hr. from 6am-10pm, 44Ft), while ferries link the three towns. **MAHART ferries** are the most convenient and enjoyable way to travel to nearby towns on the lake; student status saves you half off all fares (1 per hr. from mid-April to mid-Oct.; Siófok to Balatonfüred 1 hr., to Tihany 80 min., 156 Ft, students 78 Ft). Bundles of tourist agencies book private rooms at the bus and train stations, and there are numerous *Zimmer Frei* signs for rooms for rent on the street.

■ Tihany

Perched on a peninsular hilltop, Tihany (pronounced TEE-haw-nee) is the most luscious spot on Lake Balaton. The discos of the lowlands give way to the town's venerable Baroque church and the inland lakes and hiking trails that lace the rolling hills. The price of paradise is predictably high; further, Tihany's isolation means fewer hedonistic diversions.

The two ferry landings, Tihany and, to the southwest, Tihanyi-rév, are easy to confuse; don't. The village is at the top of the hill, marked by the twin-towered church. The view from atop the village is the best anywhere on the lake.

Take the bus (departing frequently from both ferry wharves, or stay on the bus from Balatonfüred) up to town, or hike up the winding paths toward the church. Lording over the peninsula, the magnificent 1754 **Abbey Church** has Baroque altars, pulpit, and organ. (Open daily 10am-5pm. Admission 20 Ft, students 10 Ft.) Buried in the crypt is Andrew I, one of Hungary's first kings and the only King of the Árpáp line who lies in his original resting place. His grant establishing the first church on the site in 1055 is one of the oldest extant Hungarian texts. Inquire about occasional organ concerts during the summer. Next door, an 18th-century monastery has been reincarnated as the **Tihany Museum,** with psychedelic dreamscapes, colorized etchings, and Roman inscriptions displayed in a cool, subterranean **lapidarium** (room with stone carvings). (Open March-Oct. Tues.-Sun. 10am-6pm; admission 30 Ft.) Far from the madding crowd is the bizarre **garage-gallery** of "painter artist, writer, professor" Gergely Koós-Hutás, at Füdötelep 43, a five-minute climb from the Tihany wharf. Works include massive canvases of a didactic Lenin and several of the artist himself in front of famous edifices around the world, such as Grauman's Chinese Restaurant in Hollywood. Signed photos are a steal at 20 Ft.

Balatontourist, the **post office** and the church all huddle next to the bus stop. Balatontourist, Kossuth u. 20 (tel. (86) 34 85 19) arranges private rooms in the village. (Doubles 1570 Ft; private apartments with kitchen, bath, and two double rooms 3500-4000 Ft. Open in summer Mon.-Sat. 8am-6:30pm, Sun. 8am-1pm.) Set up your own room at the numerous houses posting *Zimmer* signs. A room close to the lake (4000-5000 Ft) is not worth it, since the village is but a hop, skip, and jump away. The promenade behind the church also leads to the beach (follow the "strand" signs). For an indoor panorama, choose **Echo Rest,** the round building at the end of the promenade (250-550 Ft; open daily 10am-11pm). Next to the abbey, **Rege Presso** (Panorama Teraze) has a more restricted view, but the most succulent pastries on the peninsula (50-60Ft; open daily 9am-7pm). The beach is open daily 7am to 7pm (admission 50 Ft), though the side gate remains unlocked after hours.

■ Keszthely

The lake's largest port, Keszthely (pronounced KESS-tay), can be a refreshing stopover. Five trains per day head to the Budapest-Déli station (546 Ft), skirting the south shore of the lake. Be careful when arriving from Budapest; only the first three or four carriages of the train actually go to Keszthely. Once at the train station, ignore the signs for MÁV tours and *Privatzimmer dienst;* these bureaus are largely unhelpful. The bus station is at the front of the train station. Walk straight ahead along Martirok útja until you reach the main street, Kossuth Lajos. Turn right and head for its pedestrian section. Arriving by bus from a different Balaton city, you may be let out on Szalasztó u. near Kossath Lajos u. If so, turn right down Kossuth Lajos to the pedestrian zone and tourist office. Try **IBUSZ** at Széchenyi u. 1-3 for doubles from 1100 Ft. Beware of rooms far from the shore, which cost the same. (Open Mon.-Fri. 8am-6pm, Sat. 8am-1pm and 4-8pm, Sun. 9am-1pm; mid-Sept. to May Mon.-Fri. 8am-4pm.) A **Tourinform** is at Kossuth Lajos u. 28 (open Mon.-Sat. 9am-7pm, Sun. 9am-1pm). There's also a **private-room bureau** at Római u. 2 near the train station (open May-Sept. Mon.-Fri. 5-8pm, Sat. 8am-8pm, Sun 9am-1pm). Other bureaus include **Zala Volán,** Kossuth u. 43 (open Mon.-Sat. 9am-5pm) and

Zalatour, Fő tér 1 (open Mon.-Sat. 8am-9pm, Sun. 8am-noon). All tourist offices are located within a block of Fő tér. Mr. Attila Lukics's cosy **panzió** is at Jókai Mór u. 16 (tel. 31 12 32), a block down from Fő tér. Look for the signs. The three triples and three doubles each have bathrooms; *Let's Go* readers receive a 20% discount. In July and August, head to the **Pethe Ferenc Kollégium** at Festetics György út 5 (tel. 31 12 90), the continuation of Kossuth Lajos in the southern part of Keszthely (triples with hall bathroom 300 Ft per person), or try the **Helikon Tourist Hotel** (tel. 31 14 24), Honvéd u. 22, for dorm beds with breakfast (500 Ft each). **Sport Camping** (tel. 31 37 77) is a five-minute walk south from the train station and across the tracks; it has doubles for 700 Ft (with bathroom 1500 Ft); a tent for two runs 550 Ft per day. *Zimmer Frei* signs are most common in the neighborhood of the tourist hotel.

Restaurants here aim to make their yearly profits in the tourist season; don't hemorrhage upon seeing the higher prices. **Béke Vendéglő,** Kossuth u. 50 (tel. 31 24 47), has a large shady garden and reasonable prices (entrees 140-460 Ft). Gypsy music plays in the evenings (open daily 8am-10pm). **Park Vendéglő**Ąis at Vörösmarty u. 1/a (tel. 31 16 54). From Fö tér, follow Vöröscsillag u. until it comes across Vörösmarty. *Let's Go* readers get yet another discount here: 10% off or a free glass of wine (entrees 280-550 Ft; open daily 11am-11pm; English menu). **Reform,** at Rákóczi tér 3, is one of a handful of Hungary's vegetarian restaurants. Pay 55 Ft per 100g of whatever you choose (open daily 11am-9pm).

The **Balaton Museum** at the corner of Kossuth Lajos and Mártinok u. displays Balaton's indigenous wildlife and an ethnographic regional history. (Open Tues.-Sun. 9am-6pm. Admission 50 Ft, students 30 Ft.) Keszthely's pride is the **Festetics Palace;** of the 360 rooms, tourists can only see the central wing. Built by one of the most powerful Austro-Hungarian families, it exemplifies the beauty and grandeur of the Baroque. Concerts are often held in the mirrored ballroom hall during summer. (Open Tues.-Sun. 9am-6pm. Admission 250 Ft, 50 Ft with ISIC.) The surrounding park is a vast and well-kept strolling ground. The **Georgikon Major Múzeum** at Bercsényi u. 67 is an extremely amusing apotheosis of Gyorgy Festetics, who founded Europe's oldest agricultural university here in 1797. (Open April-Oct. Tues.-Sat. 10am-5pm, Sun. 10am-6pm. Admission 30 Ft, free with ISIC.)

Near Keszthely: Hevíz

Hevíz, just 8km northwest of Keszthely, is home to the world's second largest hot-water lake. With a surface area of 47,000 square meters and a temperature of around 34°C (93°F), this gigantic hot tub is renowned for its medicinal mud at the bottom and its red water lilies floating up top. **Buses** leave from the Keszthely station twice per hour from 5:30 to 10:30pm (32 Ft).

■■■ PÉCS

Spiced with minarets from the Ottoman occupation and home to over a dozen museums and galleries, Pécs (pronounced PAYTCH) could well be the cultural capital of Hungary. In the Middle Ages, the city's walls encircled an area larger than modern-day Vienna. Pécs's architecture retains a pleasing mix of Central European and Mediterranean styles.

Orientation and Practical Information Several trains per day chug from Budapest-Déli station (3 hr., 632 Ft). The bus and train stations are about 800m apart at the bottom of the town's historic district. Bus #34 connects both with Széchenyi tér, the town's tourist center.

Accommodations and Food Rent a private room at the **MÁV travel office** (tel. (72) 32 45 23) in the railway station, 10 minutes from the city center by bus. (Open Mon.-Thurs. 9am-4:30pm, Fri. 9am-4pm; Sept.-May Mon.-Thurs. 8am-4:30pm, Fri. 8am-3:30pm. Doubles 1100 Ft. English spoken.) Alternatively, take any bus that goes to Széchenyi tér (including #30 and 34) and head into one of the tourist offices on or just below the square. **IBUSZ,** Széchenyi tér 8 (tel. (72) 31 21 76), has doubles for 1100 Ft. (Open Mon.-Thurs. 8am-noon and 12:30-4pm, Fri. 8am-noon and 12:30-3pm, Sat. 8am-noon.) **Tourinform,** Széchenyi tér 1 (tel. (72) 41 33 15; fax 41 26 32) is open Mon.-Fri. 8am-6pm; Oct.-May Mon.-Fri. 8am-4pm. The staff at **Mecsek Tourist,** just across from IBUSZ at Széchenyi tér 1 (tel. (72) 31 33 00), speaks more English, has doubles for 1050 Ft, and runs a campground (listed below). Disdain the 180 Ft map from Meczek Tourist in favor of the 20 Ft model from IBUSZ. Be sure to spell out exactly how long you plan to stay. The **Express** office, Bajcsy-Zsilinszky u. 6, on the other side of the indoor market from the bus station, can provide general information and employs English-speakers, but is otherwise rather useless.

For **student accommodations** call the AIESEC Center at the Economics University (tel. (72) 31 14 33, ext. 273 Mon.-Fri. 9am-4pm). Go directly to **hostels** (July-Aug. only) and you'll pay less (office open Mon.-Thurs. 8am-4pm, Fri. 8:15am-2pm). The **student dorm** on Rákóczi út 52 across from the Konzum department store (tel. (72) 31 59 57) is bare but still liveable (doubles, triples and quads 400 Ft per person). The best **hostel** is the farthest away, at Szántó Kovács u. 1 (tel. (72) 32 42 34); take bus #27 from Konzum Aruház. **Szent Mór Kollégium,** on 48-es tér 4 (tel. (72) 31 11 99), has doubles (800 Ft) and triples (1150 Ft) in a gorgeous old building. In the **Kollégium** on Rókus u. 2 (tel. (72) 32 42 77, ext. 174), sunny quads with bunkbeds go for 400 Ft per person and doubles for 450 Ft apiece (550 Ft with bath). Take bus #30 to the fourth stop after Széchenyi tér. Early in the day or outside of peak season, take bus #34 directly to the **campground** (tel. (72) 31 59 81), in the hills above the city, where tent sites (500 Ft for 2 people), three-bed bungalows (1600 Ft) and doubles (2000 Ft) in a one-star hotel are located at the entrance to hiking trails into the Mecsek Hills. (Camp open mid-April to mid-Oct.) Call the campsite for same-day reservations. For advance reservations, call Mescek Tourist (see above).

For cheap **food** near the center, try **Liceum Sörözö** (tel. (72) 32 72 84), in a cellar off Kossuth Lajos u. 35, opposite the Liceum church. (Entrees 220-360 Ft. Open Mon.-Fri. 11am-10pm. English menu.) **Iparos Kisvendéglő** (tel. (72) 33 34 00) hides behind a house at Rákóczi út 24. Go through the inner yard. Food is well prepared and reasonably priced (entrees 190-520 Ft), though you may have trouble selecting the excellent steaks from a menu written only in Hungarian, German, or Croatian (open Sun.-Thurs. 11:30am-10pm, Fri.-Sat. 11:30am-midnight). **DÓM Restaurant** inhabits a two-level wooden model of a church. (Entrees 130-400 Ft. Open daily 11am-11pm. Menu in German.) **Caflisch Cukrászda,** at Kossuth Lajos u. 32, spoils visitors with delightful Hungarian sweets (30-55 Ft; open Sun.-Thurs. 8am-10pm, Fri.-Sat. 8am-11pm).

Sights and Entertainment Remnants of the Ottoman occupation are more visible in Pécs than in many other Hungarian cities. The main square, **Széchenyi tér,** is dominated by the nation's largest **mosque,** dating from the 16th century. Today it serves as the Inner City Parish Church—the stone window grilles alone betray its former faith. An impressive **synagogue** (Kossuth tér) recalls a once-thriving Jewish community. (Open May-Oct. Sun.-Fri. 9:30am-1pm and 1:30-5pm. Admission 35 Ft, students 25 Ft, including highly educational booklet.) West of Széchenyi lies the distinctive four-towered **Cathedral,** whose earliest parts date back to the 4th century; it was restored in Romanesque style from 1881-92. (Open Mon.-Sat. 9am-1pm and 2-5pm, Sun. 1-5pm. Admission 40 Ft, students 20 Ft.) Cycles of neglect and regeneration, traced in the building's different styles, mirror the city's schizophrenic history. The **Archeological Museum,** behind the Inner City Parish Church, at Széchenyi tér 12, traces the history of the city. Eight more museums and galleries, some quite exceptional, are all clustered along Káptalan u. and can be seen on a leisurely but nonetheless rewarding afternoon stroll. The museums are distinctive enough that you could literally see every one without encountering any redundancy. All are open Tuesday to Sunday 10am to 6pm, and admission is free with ISIC. The **Zsolnay**

Porcelain Museum houses some exquisite creations, while the **Viktor Vásárhely Museum** showcases arresting works by the famous Hungarian op-artist. Not to be missed is the **Csontváry Museum,** which houses the works of Tivadar Csontváry Koszka (1853-1919), Hungary's two-eared answer to Van Gogh. Snag a view of Pécs from the TV tower that looms above it (take bus #35; admission 50 Ft). Pécs holds a regional **international folk festival** each autumn.

Near Pécs: Nagyharsány

From Pécs, consider a daytrip to the incredible sculpture park in **Nagyharsány,** hard by the Croatian border 37km to the south. Located by a former quarry, the park contains pieces by artists from around the world. Facing the quarry, follow the path on the right for a climb to even better views of the town and the fruited plains below. First take a train to Villány (several per day; 1 hr.; round-trip 220 Ft); from the station, turn left and follow the main road (towards Siklós) about 4km. There is a map across from the ABC supermarket 1km along, or just ask for the szoborpark.

■■■ SZEGED

Szeged's easy-going charm belies its status as Hungary's only planned city and a somewhat dynamic center of the great southeastern plain. Glorious *art nouveau* buildings are sprinkled amongst row after row of colorful neo-Renaissance façades. The savory scent of sweet paprika and spicy fish soup (*halászlé*), for which Szeged is famous, perfumes the city.

Orientation and Practical Information A brutal day-trip from Budapest, Szeged is an excellent stop for those spending a longer stretch in Hungary. When going to Budapest-Nyugati from Szeged, make sure to board the right car—the train splits midway (6 express trains per day, 2 hr., 576 Ft). Romania-bound trains pass through Békéscsaba, which has regular connections with Szeged.

With your back to the train station, follow the tracks outside the front entrance (going right) for 15 min., or take tram #1 to Széchenyi tér (5 stops). One block back, on the other side of Híd u., is Klauzál tér, the pedestrian center where **tourist agencies** live.

Accommodations and Food Head for the less-expensive **Szeged Tourist** at Klauzál tér 7. (Tel. (62) 32 18 00. Singles 500-600 Ft. Doubles 900-1200 Ft. Open Mon.-Fri. 8:30am-5pm, Sat. 9am-1pm; Sept.-June Mon.-Fri. 9am-5:30pm, Sat. 8am-noon.) Across the street, the staff at **IBUSZ,** Klauzál tér 2 (tel. (62) 47 11 77) sells train tickets and finds rooms. IBUSZ also sells an accurate city map. (150 Ft. Singles and doubles 1000 Ft per person. Open Mon.-Fri. 8am-4pm, Sat. 8am-1pm, 45-min. lunch break around noon.) **Tourinform** is located on Victor Hugo u. 1, on the corner of Oskola u. (open Mon.-Fri. 8am-6pm, Sat. 10am-2pm). There are several decent **kollégiums** in Szeged (open July-Aug.). The most luxurious is **Apáthy István Kollégium,** Ápáthy Ístvan u. 1 (tel. (62) 32 31 55), with its perfect location right next to Dóm tér and its triples with private bathroom (singles and doubles 1400 Ft, triples 1800 Ft). Also in a prime location is the **Eötvös Loránd Kollegium** on Tisza Lajos Krt. 103, just down the road from Hösök Kapuju (tel. (62) 31 06 41), with singles for 477 Ft and doubles for 901 Ft. **Károly Mihaly Kollégium,** Kossuth Lajos sugarút 72b (tel. (62) 32 53 22), lies a little farther away from the city center but is easily reachable by tram #1. (10 stops from the train station. Triples 380 Ft or 160 Ft per person. Sheets 50 Ft. Reserve in advance.) Other options include **Béke Kollégium,** Béke u. 11-13 (doubles 700 Ft, triples 850 Ft, quads 1000 Ft). The **Talent Center,** Fürj u. 92b, in Újszeged (tel. (62) 31 27 11), has a very green campground and motel open all year. The motel has four- and six-bed rooms with bunk beds (320 Ft per person). Eight-bed tents house people for 150 Ft from May 1 to September 30; a tent for two people costs only 275 Ft per night (breakfast 100 Ft, lunch 120 Ft, dinner

110 Ft). To get there take bus #71 (every 20 min.) for six stops from Széchenyi tér. Tram #1 takes you to another year-round motel: **Napfény,** at Dorozsmai út 4 (tel. (62) 32 58 00; doubles 750 Ft; quads 1900 Ft). Debark at the last stop, then ascend the steps of the overpass behind you, and walk to the right.

Two cafeteria-style establishments have low-priced food (entrees 100-150 Ft): **Fesztival** (open daily 10am-9pm), on Oskola u. across the street from the Votive Church, is a little snazzier than **Boszorkány Konyhu** (The Witch's Kitchen), just off Széchenyi tér at Híd u. 8 (open 9am-9pm). For an upscale dining evening, try **Alabárdós,** Oskola u. 11, two blocks from Klauzal tér at the other end of Oroszlán. (280-700 Ft. Open Mon.-Sat. 11:30am-2pm and 6pm-midnight.) Solid Hungarian food, vegetarian options, and pasta are served at **Restaurant Botond,** on the same side of the square at #12. (Menu in English. Entrees 140-420 Ft. Open daily noon-midnight.) By far the busiest place in town is the **Kisvirág Cukrászda** in Klauzúl tér, which serves excellent pastries (50 Ft) and an endless dollop of ice cream (15 Ft per scoop; open daily 8am-10pm). The city's youth hang at the **Mojo Club,** Batthyány u. 12, and on the banks of the Tisza (open daily 6pm-2am).

Sights and Entertainment In 1879, the River Tisza burst its banks, destroying almost everything in town. Survivors of the flood constructed the neo-Romanesque **Votive Church** in Dóm tér, whose brick dome and 91m twin towers dominate the city's skyline. One of the largest churches in Hungary, its organ sports over 10,000 pipes. (Open daily 9am-6pm, except during services Sun. 10-11am. Free.) Kissing the church is the 12th-century **Demetrius Tower,** Szeged's oldest monument. Note the sculptures of great Hungarian heroes in front of the cathedral. Behind the Votive Church is the less imposing **Serbian Church,** with its precious Orthodox icons. In the center of town is **Széchenyi tér,** where the yellow **Town Hall** was restored after the deluge to its present eclectic form. Walk along the Vörösmarty u. side of the square to see the lavish, *art nouveau* **gyógyszertár** (pharmacy) building. Just southwest of Széchenyi tér, in Aradi Vértanúk tér, stands **Hösök Kapuja** (Heroes' Gate), guarded by stone likenesses of the fascist soldiers it was originally meant to honor. In Roosevelt tér along the river is the **Móra Ferenc Museum,** a huge Neoclassical building that houses cultural and artistic accomplishments from the region, as well as a fascinating display on the long-vanished Avar tribe that occupied the Carpathian Basin from the 6th to 9th centuries. From July 20 to August 20 every year, the country's largest open-air festival, the **Szeged Weeks** in Dóm tér, tickles tens of thousands of visitors with opera, ballet, and folklore performances (tickets purchased through the tourist offices 100-500 Ft).

■ Siófok

Siófok is the largest city on the southern shore of Lake Balaton and the tourist capital of the whole lake region. Several high-rise, high-priced hotels line the crowded beachfront, making Siófok the most modern, if least scenic, of Balaton's resorts. The bus and train stations are next to each other off the town's main drag, **Fő u.** From the stations, go right down Fő u. toward the large octagonal water tower. **Tourinform** is inside the tower's base (open Mon.-Fri. 8am-9pm, Sat. 8am-1pm and 4-8pm, Sun. 10am-noon). **IBUSZ,** nearby at Fő u 174 (tel. (84) 31 10 66), has doubles near the center for 1500 Ft per night (open Mon.-Fri. 8am-6pm, Sat. 8am-8pm, Sun. 8:30am-1pm). Across the street at Szabadság tér 6, **Siotour** (tel. (84) 31 09 00) has doubles for 1000 Ft per night (open Mon.-Sat. 8am-8pm, Sun. 9am-noon and 4-7pm). Camping is available 5km east of the center at **Aranypart Camping** (tel. (84) 31 18 01), where two people can occupy a site near the water for 630 Ft. You can also pitch a tent in the backyard of the **Tuja Panzió,** Szent László u. 74 (tel. (84) 31 49 96), for 400 Ft per person. The *panzió,* meanwhile, has doubles for 1200 Ft per person. **Szent László u.** is just one block from the beach and is lined with *panziós* and *Zimmer Frei* signs; doubles here fetch 1500-2700 Ft—search around until you find one that suits you. The **Csárdás Restaurant,** Fő u. 105, offers traditional Hungarian dishes in a friendly atmosphere (entrees 275-500 Ft; open mid-May to mid-Oct. 11:30am-midnight.) The outdoor cafeteria-style counter near the ferry station serves a respectable spaghetti bolognese for 120Ft.

Public and private **beaches** (60 Ft) alternate along Siofók's expensive coastline; both are packed in the summers. Nightclubs line the lakefront, while amphibious lounge lizards revel on the **Disco Boat** from July 10 to August 22, which leaves the docks at 9:30pm (250 Ft). **MAHART ferry** boats leave almost hourly to nearby ports from the docks next to the verdant **Jókai Park,** just 10 minutes from the train station. **Trains** leave from Budapest-Deli station roughly every hour (2 hr.; 304 Ft).

APPENDIX

PHONE COMMUNICATION

This appendix is meant for quick reference; for a detailed and informative description of international calling, and of the Austrian, Czech, and Hungarian national phone networks and calling options, see Essentials: Telephones at the beginning of this book.

In **Austria,** for **local information,** dial 16 11. Dial 09 for assistance with **local calls.** For the **police** anywhere in Austria, dial 133; for an **ambulance,** dial 144; for the **fire department,** dial 122.

In the **Czech Republic,** the national **emergency phone number** is 158.

For Austrian telephones, a constant tone is the dial tone, long beeps indicate ringing, and three ascending tones signal a malfunction. Many foreigners are fooled by the ringing sound—which, let it be stressed, is *not* a busy signal; the busy signal is a rapid series of short, staccato beeps. Austrian phonebooks are user-friendly and are available in phone booths. The beginning section lists phone codes for international dialing. If a call won't go through, check to see if you are using the correct area code. A complete list of city codes appears below.

■ Making International Calls

In Austria, for **assistance with international calls,** dial 08. If you are calling North America from abroad, you can dial one of these service numbers, which connect you instantly to an operator back home:

AT&T USA Direct:

From Austria: tel. 022 903 011. In Austria, the connection to the AT&T operator is a local call—you must keep dropping in 1 AS per minute for the length of the call.

From the Czech Republic: tel. 00 42 00 01 01. You must wait for a dial tone after you dial the first two zeros.

From Hungary: tel. 00 800 01 111. You must wait for a dial tone after you dial the first two zeros.

MCI Call USA:

From Austria: tel. 022 903 012. Also a local call—1 AS per minute.

From the Czech Republic: tel. 00 42 000 112. You must wait for a dial tone after you dial the first two zeros.

From Hungary: 00 800 01 411. You must wait for a dial tone after you dial the first two zeros.

Making international calls directly is relatively painless. Follow these steps:

1. Dial the **international access code** for the country from which you are calling:

Austria: 900 from Vienna, 00 from elsewhere
Czech Republic: 00
Hungary: 00
United States and **Canada:** 011
United Kingdom: 010

Republic of Ireland: 00
Australia: 001
New Zealand: 00
South Africa: 09

Wait briefly; in some countries, such as the Czech Republic and Hungary, there will be a second dialtone after you have dialed the international access code. Then:

2. Dial the **country code** for the country you are calling:

Austria: 43
Czech Republic: 42
Hungary: 36
United States and **Canada:** 1
United Kingdom: 44
Republic of Ireland: 353
Australia: 61
New Zealand: 64
South Africa: 27

3. Dial the **area code** or **city code** for the establishment you are calling. When calling Austria, the Czech Republic, and most other countries (but excluding the U.S., Canada, and Hungary) *from outside the country,* omit the first number of this code, usually 0, 1, or 9. Consult the list below for city codes in Austria; for example, when calling Austria from outisde the country, omit the 0.

4. Dial the establishment's number.

> Note: Austria's telephone system is currently being converted to a digital network. Some phone numbers may change in the near future, particularly in Innsbruck and Vienna.

■ Reservations by Phone

Mastery of the following phrases should help you reserve a room by telephone. Remember that many proprietors, particularly in larger cities, are used to dealing with the minimal German of callers; even in the most trying of situations, with a little patience and politeness you should be able to make yourself understood. See Language below for more tips on securing accommodations.

German

Servus!	(phone greeting)
Sprechen Sie Englisch?	Hopefully, the answer is "Ja," or better yet, "Yes." If not, struggle bravely on...
Haben Sie ein Zimmer (Einzelzimmer, Doppelzimmer) frei...	Do you have a room (single, double) free...
für heute abend?	for tonight?
für morgen?	for tomorrow?
für einen Tag / zwei Tage?	for a day / for two days?
vom vierten Juli...	from the fourth of July...
bis zum sechsten Juli?	until the sixth of July?
mit W.C./ Dusche?	with bathroom/ shower?
Wieviel kostet es?	How much does it cost?
Ich heiße... (ikh HIGH-suh)	My name is...
Ich komme gleich	I'm coming immediately.
Ich komme um acht Uhr am Morgen/Abend.	I'm coming at eight in the morning/evening.

Return phrases to watch out for:

Nein, es ist alles besetzt / voll.	No, we're booked / full.
Es tut mir leid.	Sorry.
Wir machen keine Vorbestellungen / Reservierungen am Telephon.	We don't make reservations by phone.
Sie müssen vor zwei Uhr ankommen.	You have to arrive before two o'clock.

Hungarian

Halo.	Hello.
Beszél angolol?	Do you speak English?
Van maguknak egy hálószobájuk?	Do you have a room?
Van maguknal egy kítszobás lakásuk?	Do you have an apartment with two rooms?
Ma estére?	For tonight?
Holnapra?	For tomorrow?
Egy, vagy két napra?	For a day or two days?
Julius negyedikétől...	from the fourth of July...
Julius hatódikáig?	until the sixth of July?
Van frdőszoba ees zúhanyzó?	With bathroom and shower?
Az een nevem...	My name is...
Yövök mindjárt.	I'm coming immediately.
Rezzel, Este nyólcra itt beszek.	I'm coming at eight in the morning/evening.

Those nasty responses:

Ninch több űres szobáuk.	No, we are booked full.
Sajnealom.	Sorry.

■ Austrian Telephone and Postal Codes

Village/Town/City	Telephone Code	Postal Code
Admont	03613	A-8911
Aigen	07281	A-4160
Altenmarkt	06452	A-5541
Attersee	07666	A-4864
Bad Aussee	03622	A-8990
Bad Ischl	06132	A-4820
Bad Kleinkirchheim	04240	A-9546
Bad Leonfelden	07213	A-4190
Baden bei Wien	02252	A-2500
Badgastein	06434	A-5640
Braunau am Inn	07722	A-5280
Bludenz	05552	A-6700
Bregenz	05574	A-6900
Bruck an der Mur	03862	A-8600
Drosendorf	02915	A-2095
Dürnstein	02711	A-3601
Ebensee	06133	A-4802
Egg	05512	A-6863
Ehrwald	05673	A-6632
Eisenstadt	02685	A-7000
Feldkirch	05522	A-6800
Forchtenstein	02626	A-7212
Friesach	07942	A-9360
Freistadt	07942	A-4240
Fulpmes	05225	A-6166
Gerlos	05248	A-6281

Gmunden	07612	A-4810
Graz	0316	A-8010 through 8036
Hallein	06245	A-5400
Hallstatt	06134	A-4830
Haslach an der Mühl	07289	A-4170
Heiligenblut	04824	A-9844
Heiligenkreuz	02258	A-2532
Horn	02982	A-3580
Hinterstoder	07564	A-4573
Igls	0512	A-6080
Innsbruck	0512	A-6020
Jenbach	05244	A-6200
Kitzbühel	05356	A-6370
Klagenfurt	0463	A-9020
Klosterneuberg	02243	A-3400
Krems	02732	A-3500
Kremsmünster		A-4550
Krimml	06564	A-5743
Kufstein	03328	A-6330
Lambach	07245	A-4650
Landeck	05442	A-6500
Landskron	04242	A-7341
Lech	05583	A-6764
Leoben	03842	A-8700
Lienz	04852	A-9900
Linz	0732	A-4020 through 4040
Maria Saal	04223	A-9063
Maria Wörth	04273	A-9082
Mariazell	03882	A-8630
Mauthausen		A-4310
Mayerling	02258	A-2534
Mayrhofen	05285	A-6290
Melk	02752	A-3390
Mellau	05518	A-6881
Millstatt	04766	A-9872
Mödling bei Wien	02236	A-2340
Mörbisch	02685	A-7072
Murau	03532	A-8850
Nassereith	05265	A-6465
Neusiedl am See	02167	A-7100
Neustift	05226	A-6167
Obertauern	06456	A-5562
Obertraun	06131	A-4831
Peggau	03127	A-8120
Pfunds	05474	A-6542
Pörtschach	04272	A-9210
Purbach	02683	A-7083
Radstadt	06452	A-5550
Reutte	05672	A-6600
Riegersburg	03153	A-8333
Rohrau	02164	A-2471
Rust	02685	A-7071
St. Anton am Arlberg	05446	A-6580
St. Florian Abbey		A-4490
St. Gilgen	06227	A-5340
St. Jakob	05354	A-6391
St. Johann im Pongau	06412	A-5600
St. Johann in Tirol	05352	A-6380
St. Michael	06477	A-5582
St. Pölten	02742	A-3100

St. Veit an der Glan	04212	A-9300
St. Wolfgang	06227	A-5360
Salzburg	0662	A-5020
Schärding	07712	A-4780
Schladming	03687	A-8970
Schlägl	07281	A-4160
Schwaz	05242	A-6130
Seefeld in Tirol	05212	A-6100
Semmering	02664	A-2680
Spital am Pyhrn	07563	A-4582
Spittal an der Drau	04762	A-9800
Spitz	02713	A-3620
Stams	05263	A-6422
Steyr	07252	A-4400
Tamsweg	06474	A-5580
Tulln	02272	A-3430
Ulrichsberg	07288	A-4161
Vienna	0222	A-1010 through 1230
Villach	04242	A-9500
Wels	07242	A-4600
Wiener Neustadt	02622	A-2700
Wiesen	02626	A-7203
Zell am See	06542	A-5700
Zell am Ziller	05282	A-6280
Zürs	05583	A-6763
Zwettl	02822	A-3910

SIGNIFICANT DIGITS

■ Climate

Austria's climate throughout the year resembles chilly New York weather. Just ask yourself, "What would Al Sharpton be wearing today?" and you'll ably ascertain the appropriate duds. Temperatures depend largely on altitude; as a rule, they decrease an average of 3°F (1.7°C) for each additional thousand feet of elevation. Unless you're on a mountain, Austria doesn't usually get brutally cold, even in the dead of winter. Warm sweaters are the rule September to May, with a parka, hat, and gloves added on in the winter months. Winter snow-cover lasts from late December to March in the valleys, from November to May at about 6000 ft., and becomes permanent above about 8500 ft. Summer temperatures can reach 100°F (38°C) for brief periods, although summer evenings are usually cool. In much of Austria, the prevailing winds are westerly and northwesterly. Summertime brings very frequent rains—almost one day out of two in Salzburg—so suitable raingear is a must. Budapest, on the other hand, glistens under approximately 2015 annual hours of sunshine.

The following are average low and high temperatures, in degrees Fahrenheit, provided by the **International Association for Medical Assistance to Travelers** (see Essentials: Health for more information). IAMAT provides world climate charts that also include recommended seasonal clothing and information on the sanitary condition of local water, milk, and food.

	July	October	January	April
Bad Aussee (2,290 ft.)	58-67°	38-52°	27-34°	41-49°
Bad Ischl (1,539 ft.)	52-79°	35-54°	19-39°	39-64°
Bregenz (1,450 ft.)	57-79°	43-57°	25-34°	43-63°
Bruck a. d. Mur (1,591 ft.)	52-79°	34-63°	19-34°	37-61°
Eisenstadt (640 ft.)	68-76°	47-54°	27-31°	49-56°
Graz (1,237 ft.)	57-77°	43-57°	23-34°	41-59°
Kitzbühel (2,568 ft.)	57-73°	50-57°	16-34°	39-59°
Klagenfurt (1,470 ft.)	55-77°	41-57°	16-30°	37-59°
Krems a. d. Donau (745 ft.)	59-77°	43-58°	25-36°	41-59°
Kufstein (1,667 ft.)	54-77°	37-61°	21-36°	39-63°
Innsbruck (1,909 ft.)	55-77°	41-59°	19-34°	39-61°
Lienz (2,217 ft.)	51-76°	37-57°	17-33°	36-58°
Linz (853 ft.)	57-75°	42-57°	25-34°	41-58°
Neusiedl am See (423 ft.)	68-76°	45-54°	27-31°	49-56°
Salzburg (1,427 ft.)	55-75°	40-57°	22-35°	39-58°
St. Anton (4,278 ft.)	52-68°	34-57°	18-30°	34-52°
Seefeld (3,950 ft.)	57-70°	39-57°	23-36°	41-54°
Vienna (666 ft.)	59-77°	45-57°	25-34°	43-59°
Villach (1,614 ft.)	63-74°	41-56°	23-29°	47-56°
Zell am See (2,474 ft.)	54-73°	39-55°	14-28°	36-55°
Zell am Ziller (1,919 ft.)	50-75°	32-61°	16-37°	36-64°
Bratislava (502 ft.)	61-79°	45-59°	27-36°	43-61°
Brno (732 ft.)	57-77°	39-57°	23-34°	39-59°
Budapest (456 ft.)	61-82°	45-61°	25-34°	45-63°
České Budějovice (1,270 ft.)	54-75°	37-57°	23-36°	37-57°
Prague (860 ft.)	55-75°	41-55°	25-36°	39-58°

And, for *déjà vu* fans, now in metric:

	July	October	January	April
Bad Aussee (698m)	14-19°	3-11°	(-3)-1°	5-9°
Bad Ischl (469m)	11-26°	2-12°	(-7)-4°	4-18°
Bregenz (442m)	14-26°	6-14°	(-4)-1°	6-17°
Bruck a. d. Mur (485m)	11-26°	1-17°	(-7)-1°	3-16°
Eisenstadt (195m)	20-24°	8-12°	(-3)-(-1)°	9-13°
Graz (377m)	14-25°	6-14°	(-5)-1°	5-15°
Kitzbühel (783m)	14-23°	10-14°	(-9)-1°	4-15°
Klagenfurt (448m)	13-25°	5-14°	(-9)-(-1)°	3-15°
Krems a. d. Donau (227m)	15-25°	6-14°	(-4)-2°	5-15°
Kufstein (508m)	12-25°	3-16°	(-6)-2°	4-17°
Innsbruck (582m)	13-25°	5-15°	(-7)-1°	4-16°
Lienz (676m)	11-24°	3-14°	(-8)-1°	2-14°
Linz (260m)	14-24°	6-14°	(-4)-1°	5-14°
Neusiedl am See (129m)	20-24°	7-12°	(-3)-(-1)°	9-13°
Salzburg (435m)	13-24°	4-14°	(-6)-2°	4-14°
St. Anton (1304m)	11-20°	1-14°	(-8)-(-1)°	1-11°
Seefeld (1204m)	14-21°	4-14°	(-5)-2°	5-12°
Vienna (203m)	15-25°	7-14°	(-4)-1°	6-15°
Villach (492m)	17-23°	5-13°	(-5)-(-2)°	8-13°
Zell am See (754m)	12-23°	4-13°	(-10)-(-2)°	2-13°
Zell am Ziller (585m)	10-24°	0-16°	(-9)-3°	2-18°
Bratislava (153m)	16-26°	7-15°	-3-2°	6-16°
Brno (223m)	14-25°	4-14°	-5-1°	4-15°
Budapest (139m)	16-28°	7-16°	-4-1°	7-17°
České Budějovice (387m)	12-24°	3-14°	-5-2°	3-14°
Prague (262m)	13-24°	5-13°	-4-2°	4-14°

■ Weights and Measures

Like the rest of the civilized world, Austria, Prague, and Budapest use the metric system. So does *Let's Go.* Austrians also commonly use some traditional measurements, but they have been modified to match the metric system more closely. Thus, a *Pfund* is half a kilogram and a *Meil* is two kilometers. All you really need to know to get around is that a meter is a little more than a yard, a kilometer is two-thirds of a mile, a liter is a little more than a quart, a kilogram is a little more than two pounds, and 100 grams of cheese or sausage is plenty for lunch. The following are more precise metric equivalents of common English measurements. To convert from Fahrenheit degrees into Celsius, subtract 32 and multiply by 5/9; from Celsius to Fahrenheit, multiply by 9/5 and add 32.

1 millimeter (mm) = 0.04 inch	1 inch = 25mm
1 meter (m) = 1.09 yards	1 yard = 0.92m
1 kilometer (km) = 0.62 mile	1 mile = 1.61km
1 gram (g) = 0.04 ounce	1 ounce = 25g
1 kilogram (kg) = 2.2 pounds	1 pound = 0.45kg
1 liter (L) = 1.06 quarts	1 quart = 0.94L

FESTIVALS AND HOLIDAYS

The *International Herald Tribune* lists national holidays in each daily edition. If you plan your itinerary around them, you encounter the holidays that entice you and circumvent the crowds visiting the ones you'd rather bypass. Also, you should be sure to arrive in any country on a non-holiday, when most services are operating. Check the individual town listings for information on the festivals below.

1996 is Austria's Millenium; it marks 1,000 years since the name Ostarrichi, meaning Empire of the East, first appeared in a document. The nation is currently planning festivities and oodles of whatnot to celebrate the occasion.

Austria

Summer

June: *Tyrol.* Summer Bonfires.
June: *Upper and Lower Austria.* Fires of St. Peter.
June 2: Public Holiday. Corpus Christi Day.
June 28: *Tauern and Pinzgau regions.* Pilgrimage over the mountains.
Last Sunday in July, every third year: *Oberndorf.* Historic Pirates' Battle.
Sundays in July, some years: *River Salzach near Oberndorf.* Boatmen's Fights.
End of July: *Salzburg.* Salzburg Festival.
late July to mid-August: *Bregenz.* Festival.
late July to late August: *Salzburg.* Salzburg Music Festival.
around August First: *Villach.* Folklore fair.
First Monday and Tuesday in August: *Graz.* Fröhlichgasse
Eve of the First Feast of the Assumption: *Wörther See.*
August 15: *Upper Austria.* Meeting of the Piper.
August 15: Public Holiday. Feast of the Assumption.
Monday and Tuesday following September 1: *Graz.* Rag Fair.
Third Sunday of September: *Carinthia.* Croats' Sunday.

Autumn

Last Sunday in September: Foreigner's Sunday.
October 26: Public Holiday. Flag Day.
November 1: Public Holiday. All Saints' Day.
November 11: St. Martin's Day.

Sunday following November 25: Kathreinsonntag. .
late-Novermber to Christmas Eve: Advent.
December 8: Public Holiday. Feast of the Immaculate Conception.

Winter

December 25: Public Holiday. Christmas Day.
December 26: Public Holiday. St. Stephen's Day.
January 1: Public Holiday. New Year's Day.
January 5: *Upper Austria.* Running of the Figures with Special Caps.
January 5 and 6: *Upper Austria.* The Ride of the Three Kings.
January 6: Twelfth Night or Epiphany.
January 6 and 7: *Salzburg.* Dancers on Stilts.
January: *Kitzbühel.* World Cup Ski Races.

Spring

April 3: Public Holiday. Easter Sunday.
April 4: Public Holiday. Easter Monday.
April 4-11: *Salzburg.* Easter Festival.
May 1: Public Holiday. Labor Day.
mid-May to mid-June: *Vienna.* Vienna Festival.
May 12: Public Holiday. Ascension Day.
Saturday and Sunday after Corpus Christi: *Tamsweg.* Procession of Samson.
May 22-23: Public Holiday. Whit Sunday and Monday.

Prague

The National Theater closes in July and August across the Czech Republic.

Summer

July 5: Public Holiday. Cyril Methodius Day.
July 6: Public Holiday. Jan Hus Day.
June 10: Public Holiday. Corpus Christi Day.
August 15: Public Holiday. Feast of the Assumption.

Autumn

October 28: Public Holiday. Independence Day.
November 1: Public Holiday. All Saints' Day.

Winter

December 24: Public Holiday. Boxing Day.
December 25: Public Holiday. Christmas Day.
December 26: Public Holiday. St. Stephen's Day.
January 1: Public Holiday. New Year's Day.

Spring

April 3: Public Holiday. Easter Sunday.
April 4: Public Holiday. Easter Monday.
May 1: Public Holiday. May Day.
May 9: Public Holiday. Anniversary of Soviet Liberation Day.
May 20: Public Holiday. Ascension Day.

Budapest

Summer

June to August: Open-air Theater programs.
June to September: Organ concerts in Matthias Church.
August 20: Public Holiday. Constitution Day.

Autumn

October 23: Republic Day.
November 7: Public Holiday.

Winter

December 25: Public Holiday. Christmas Day.
December 26: Public Holiday.
January 1: Public Holiday. New Year's Day.

Spring

March: Budapest Spring Festival.
March 15: Public Holiday. National Uprising of 1848.
April to October: Folk dance performances by the Budapest Dance Ensemble.
April 3: Public Holiday. Easter Sunday.
April 4: Public Holiday. Easter Monday.
May: Budapest International Fair.
May to October: Operetta concerts.
May 1: Public Holiday. Labor Day.
May to June: Whitsun Monday.

LANGUAGE

Life is too short to learn German.
—Thomas Love Peacock, "Gryll Grange"

As the Germanic peoples extend their commercial tentacles into more and more ventures, German stakes a firmer claim to the status of international language. Nevertheless, it is a difficult tongue for many English speakers to learn, with three genders, four cases, and five ways of saying "the." Fortunately, most Viennese speak at least a smattering of English, and quite a few speak it better than the typical American college student. (The situation is considerably different in isolated villages of the Alps, where proprietors are considered proficient if they can regurgitate "hello," "good-bye," and "dollars.") All schoolchildren are required to take English, and most are quite anxious to practice. Don't, however, assume that all Austrians speak English, especially outside the major cities; always preface your questions with a polite "*Sprechen Sie Englisch?*"

If the answer is negative, don't be afraid to wade in with a bit of Austrian; a few phrases will go a long way. Locals will generally appreciate your effort to acknowledge their culture, and will usually be significantly more helpful once they've heard a bit of their native language. There are a few caveats, though; German is an extremely polite and formal tongue, and it's fairly easy to unintentionally offend. Keep these few simple rules in mind to maintain the good graces of your listener. Always address an aquaintance with *Herr* (Mr.) or *Frau* (Ms.) and his or her surname, and always use the formal prounoun *Sie* with the plural form of the verb. *Fräulein* is used to address a younger waitress or stewardess only. The transition from formal to informal (*dutzen*) is occasion for a major ceremony in Austria; never assume that you are on informal terms—you will be *told*. Those who have achieved post-collegiate degrees or civic positions should be addressed with "Mr." or "Ms." *and* their secondary title, e.g. Frau Doktor Puka or Herr Bürgermeister Zabusky.

The good news is that Austrians are also forgiving towards foreigners who butcher their mother tongue; this is probably because the natives butcher the mother tongue as well. The Austrian dialect, incorporating a bit of Italian from the neighbors, a bit of French from the Imperial court, and a bit of Hungarian from the immigrants, is a far cry from *Hochdeutsch* (High German). Indeed, if both speak in the local vernacular, a Wiener and an Innsbruckener can hardly understand each other. More educated Austrians will be able to spot you floundering in dialect and will switch to High German automatically. Barring that, you can always return to the old standby—don't underestimate the power of pencil, paper, and body language.

By and large, residents don't mind if you experiment with the langauge, but keep one important exception in mind—place names. If you learn no other facet of the language, learn to pronounce the names of the locales properly. Austria (Österreich) is roughly pronounced "OOES-tuh-raich." Burgenland is "BOOR-gun-lahnt," Carinthia (Kärnten) is "KAIRN-tun," East Tyrol (Osttirol) is "aust-tee-ROHL," Lower Austria (Niederösterreich) is "NEE-dur OOES-tuh-raich," Styria (Steiermark) is "STAI-er-mahrk," Tyrol (Tirol) is "Tee-ROHL," Upper Austria (Oberöesterreich) is "OH-bur OOES-tuh-raich," and Vorarlberg is "for-AHRL-bayrg." Graz is "GRAHTS," Innsbruck is "INNS-brook", Lienz is "LEENTS," Linz is "LINTS," Salzburg is "ZAHLTS-boorg," Vienna (Wien) is "VEEN," Prague (Praha) is "PRAH-hah," and Budapest is "BOO-dah-pesht."

■ Pronunciation

German

Although you cannot hope to speak grammatically correct German without studying the language for years, you can make yourself understood by learning only selected key phrases. The first step is to master the pronunciation system. Unlike English, German pronunciation is perfectly consistent with spelling; once you learn the rules, everything is easy. Other than the occasional H, there are no silent letters.

Consonants

Consonants are pronounced the same as in English with the following exceptions:

B	"Weib"	Pronounced as P at the end of a word.
C	"Camping"	Exists in German only in borrowed foreign words.
CH	"Milch"	See below.
	"Rauch"	See below.
CHS	"Lachs"	Pronounced as KS.
D	"Bad"	Pronounced as T at the end of a word.
G	"König"	See below.
	"Tag"	See below.
	"General"	See below.
H	"gehen"	Silent in the middle of a word.
J	"ja"	Pronounced as the consonant Y.
K	"Kneipe"	Always pronounced, even before an N.
P	"Pfund"	Always pronounced, even before an F or an S.
QU	"Quittung"	Pronounced as KV.
S	"Salz"	Pronounced as Z at the beginning of a word.
SCH	"Schule"	Pronounced as SH.
SP	"Spiel"	Pronounced as SHP at the beginning of a word.
ST	"Stein"	Pronounced as SHT at the beginning of a word.
TH	"Theater"	Pronounced as T.
TSCH	"Tschüß"	Pronounced as CH.
V	"Volks"	Pronounced as F.
W	"Wagen"	Pronounced as V.
X	"Xerokopie"	Pronounced as KS.
Z	"zahlen"	Pronounced as TS.

The R sound is quite tricky for untrained English-speaking vocal cords. In German, the R is gutteral, spoken from the back of the throat, almost as if you were gargling. There's nothing quite like it in English—your best bet is, as always, to listen closely to the natives and attempt to mimic their pronunciation. The CH sound is also a linguistic challenge. After A, O, U, or AU, it is pronounced as in the Scottish "loch." After other vowels and consonants, CH sounds like the English H in "huge" or "hubris" if you draw out this sound before saying the U. If you can't hack it, use an

SH sound to approximate the Austrian dialect. *Let's Go* uses KH to indicate the pronunciation of the German CH, but that isn't strictly accurate. In German words ending "-ig," the G also takes on the extended-H sound of CH. When G ends a word and is preceded by any other vowel, it is pronounced as a K. At all other times, G is hard, as in "good," never soft, as in "germ." German has one consonant which does not exist in English, "ß," which is pronounced as an S, and may be written as a double-S (*Strasse* or *Straße*).

Vowels

German vowels and dipthongs are also pronounced differently:

A	"Vater"	Pronounced as in "father."
short Ä	"Länder"	See below.
long Ä	"Fähre"	See below.
short E	"Bett"	Pronounced as in "bed."
long E	"dem"	Pronounced as the AY in "hay."
schwa	e in "Bitte"	Pronounced as both A's in "America."
short I	"Sitz"	Pronounced as in "sit."
long I	"Bibel"	Pronounced as the IE in "thief."
short O	"Gott"	Pronounced as the OU in "thought."
long O	"Dom"	Pronounced as in "dome."
short Ö	"öffnen"	See below.
long Ö	"schön"	See below.
short U	"Mutter"	Pronounced as the OO in "foot."
long U	"zu"	Pronounced as the OO in "boot."
short Ü	"Glück"	See below.
long Ü	"Tür"	See below.
Y	"Typ"	See below.
AA	"Haar"	Pronounced as the A in "father."
AI	"Mai"	Pronounced as the I in "wine."
AU	"Haus"	Pronounced as the OU in "mouse."
ÄU	"Läufer"	Pronounced as the OI in "boil."
EE	"Allee"	Pronounced as the AY in "hay."
EI	"Wein"	Pronounced as the I in "wine."
EU	"Heurigen"	Pronounced as the OI in "boil."
IE	"hier"	Pronounced as in "thief."
OO	"Boot"	Pronounced as the O in "dome."

An H following a vowel usually makes that vowel long (as in "weh" or "gehen"). An *umlaut* over a letter (e.g. Ü) changes the pronunciation entirely. An *umlaut* is often replaced by an E following the vowel, e.g. "schön" becomes "schoen." In the speech of most Austrians, long Ä is the equivalent of an American long A (as in "hay"). The short Ä is more akin to American short E (as in "bed"), but hold the vowel for slightly longer than in English. To make the long Ö sound, round your lips to say "oh," freeze them in that position, and try to say "a" as in "hay." Short Ö adds a bit of the American short I sound (as in "bit"). To make the short Ü sound, round your lips to say "ooh," freeze them in that position, and try to say "ee" instead. The long Ü adds a slight inflection of long OO as in "boot". To make the Y sound, round your lips to say "you," freeze them in that position, and try to say "ee" instead. Put it all together ... and at least you'll be close.

Czech

The rest of the republic may be unaccustomed to mass quantities of foreigners mangling the language, but Prague residents are quite jaded by now. As always, even an attempt at Czech will earn you points; locals are becoming increasingly adept at deciphering the best efforts of foreign tourists. If you don't know the word, try **sound**ing it out **phon**etically, and stress the first **syl**lable. If you don't wish to try on some Czech, German should be acceptable, especially with the older generations. Russian was once the second tongue of almost every citizen, but the language has since been identified with the occupation; English now will get you farther.

Consonants

Consonants are pronounced the same as in English with the following exceptions:

C	Pronounced as TS.
Č	Pronounced as CH.
CH	See below.
Ď, ď	Pronounced as DY, with Y as a *consonant*.
G	See below.
J	Pronounced as the consonant Y.
KD	Pronounced as GD.
MĚ	Pronounced as MNYE.
Ň	Pronounced as NY, with Y as a *consonant*.
R	See below.
Ř	See below.
Š	Pronounced as SH.
Ť, ť	Pronounced as TY, with Y as a *consonant*.
W	Pronounced as V.
Ž	Pronounced as the S in "pleasure."

The R sound is quite tricky for untrained English-speaking vocal cords. In Czech, the R is gutteral, spoken from the back of the throat, almost as if you were gargling. Ř is even worse for foreigners. The sound is a curious blend of a rolled, guttural English "r" and the hard English ZH, as the S in "pleasure." There's nothing quite like it in English—your best bet is, as always, to listen closely to the natives and attempt to mimic their pronunciation. The CH sound is also a linguistic challenge; it's pronounced much like the German CH, as in the Scottish "loch." G always represents a hard consonant, as in "good," never soft, as in "germ."

Vowels

Czech vowels and dipthongs are also pronounced differently:

A	Pronounced as the U in "cup."
Á	Pronounced as in "father."
E	Pronounced as in "bed."
É	Pronounced as the AY in "hay."
Ě	Pronounced as the YE in "yes."
I	Pronounced as in "sit."
Í	Pronounced as the IE in "thief."
O	Pronounced as the OU in "thought."
Ó	Pronounced as the OO in "door."
U	Pronounced as the OO in "foot."
Ú	Pronounced as the OO in "boot."
Ů	Pronounced as the OO in "boot."
Y	Pronounced as in "sit."
Ý	Pronounced as the IE in "thief."
AU	Pronounced as the OU in "mouse."
OU	Pronounced as the O in "dome."

Hungarian

Compared to Hungarian, German and Czech are mind-bogglingly easy. Hungarian belongs to the Finno-Ugric family of languages; you haven't heard of it because it is completely unrelated to any other European form of speech. Wade in slowly.

A little elementary German can be a great advantage when traveling in Hungary. English works in Budapest, but in the countryside, especially in Eastern Hungary, even German may not work. Learning a bit of the Hungarians' language will not only make you a better person, but may also endear you to the natives. Keep in mind: in personal names, the surname precedes the given one, as in Doe John or Doe Jane.

Consonants

Consonants are pronounced the same as in English with the following exceptions:

C	"cukor"	Pronounced as TS.
CS	"vacsora"	Pronounced as TCH.
GY	"gyufa"	Pronounced as DY, with Y as a *consonant.*
J	"jég"	Pronounced as the consonant Y.
LY	"lyuk"	Pronounced as the consonant Y.
NY	"nyár"	Pronounced as NY, with Y as a *consonant.*
S	"sál"	Pronounced as SH.
SZ	"szó"	Pronounced as S.
TY	'kutya"	Pronounced as TY, with Y as a *consonant.*
ZS	"rizs"	Pronounced as the S in "pleasure."

Vowels

Hungarian vowel and dipthong sounds are also pronounced differently:

A	"alma"	See below.
Á	"banán"	Pronounced as the A in "car."
E	"emelet"	Pronounced as in "ten."
É	"édes"	Pronounced as the AY in "hay."
I	"hitel"	Pronounced as in "sit."
Í	"híd"	Pronounced as the IE in "thief."
O	"bor"	Pronounced as the OU in "thought."
Ó	"tó"	Pronounced as the O in "dome."
Ö	"zöld"	Pronounced as the short Ö in German.
Ő	"erős"	Pronounced as the long Ö in German.
U	"puha"	Pronounced as the OO in "foot."
Ú	"húsz"	Pronounced as the OO in "boot."
Ü	"szürke"	Pronounced as the short Ü in German.
Ű	"fű"	Pronounced as the long Ü in German.

The Hungarian short A is perhaps most troublesome for English speakers. You can approximate the sound by mimicking the O in the British "hot" or "gone"; it is a blend of OO as in "book" and O as in "corn."

■ Spelling

Character	German	Czech	Hungarian
a	ah	ah	o
b	bay	beh	be
c	say	tseh	tsay
č		cheh	
cs			tche
d	day	deh	de
ď		dyeh	
e	ay	eh	ay
f	eff	eff	ayf
g	gay	geh	ghe
gy			dye
h	hah	hah	hay
ch		*ch*ah	
i	ee	ee	ee
j	yut	yeh	ye
k	kah	kah	kay
l	ell	ell	ayl
ly			eep-se-lon
m	em	em	aym
n	en	en	ayn
ň		en-yeh	
ny			eny
o	oh	aw	aw
p	pay	peh	pe
q	koo	kveh	kew
r	air	er	ayr
ř		erzh	
s	ess	ess	aysh
š		esh	
sz			ays
ß	ess-tset		
t	tay	teh	te
ť		tyeh	
ty			tye
u	oo	oo	oo
v	fau	veh	ve
w	vay	dvo-yiteh veh	doop-l-o-vay
x	iks	iks	
y	oopsilon	ipsilon	
z	tset	zet	ze
ž		zhet	
zs			zhe

■ Numbers

Arabic	German	Czech	Hungarian
0	null	nula	nulla
1	eins	jedna, jeden	egy
2	zwei (zwoh)	dvě, dva	két, kettő
3	drei	tři	három
4	vier	čtyři	négy
5	fünf	pět	öt
6	sechs	šest	hat
7	sieben	sedm	hét
8	acht	osm	nyolc
9	neun	devět	kilenc
10	zehn	deset	tíz
11	elf	jedenáct	tizenegy
12	zwölf	dvanáct	tizenkettő
13	dreizehn	třináct	tizenhárom
14	vierzehn	čtrnáct	tizennégy
15	fünfzehn	patnáct	tizenöt
16	sechzehn	šestnáct	tizenhat
17	siebzehn	sedmnáct	tizenhét
18	achtzehn	osmnáct	tizennyolc
19	neunzehn	devatenáct	tizenkilenc
20	zwanzig	dvacet	húsz
21	einundzwanzig	jedenadvacet	huszonegy
30	dreißig	třicet	harminc
40	vierzig	čtyřicet	negyven
50	fünfzig	padesát	ötven
60	sechzig	šedesát	hatvan
70	siebzig	sedmdesát	hetven
80	achtzig	osmdesát	nyolcvan
90	neunzig	devadesát	kilencven
100	(ein) hundert	sto	száz
101	hunderteins	sto jedna	százegy
200	zweihundert	dvě stě	kettőszáz
300	dreihundert	tří sta	háromszáz
400	vierhundert	čtyří sta	négyszáz
500	fünfhundert	pět set	ötszáz
600	sechshundert	šest set	hatszáz
700	siebenhundert	sedm set	hétszáz
800	achthundert	osum set	nyolcszáz
900	neunhundert	devět set	kilencszáz
1000	(ein) tausend	tisíc	ezer
2000	zwei tausend	dva tisíce	kétezer
1,000,000	ein million	milión	millió
1st	erste	první	első
2nd	zweite	druhý	második
3rd	dritte	třetí	harmadik
4th	vierte	čtvrtý	negyedik
5th	fünfte	pátý	ötödik
6th	sechste	šestý	hatodik
7th	siebte	sedmý	hetedik
8th	achte	osmý	nyolcadik
9th	neunte	devátý	kilencedik
10th	zehnte	desátý	tizedik

There are a couple of peculiarities in the way Europeans render numbers that can trip up the unwary American. A space or period rather than a comma is used to indicate thousands, e.g. "10,000" is written "10 000" or "10.000". Instead of a decimal point, most Europeans use a comma, e.g. "3.1415" is written "3,1415". Months and days are written in the reverse of the American manner, e.g. "10.11.92" is November 10, not October 11. The numeral 7 is written with a slash through the vertical line, and the numeral 1 is written with an upswing, resembling an inverted "V." Ordinal numbers are written with a period after the digit, e.g. "1st" is written "1.".

Note that, in German, the number in the ones place is pronounced *before* the number in the tens place; thus "zweihundertfünfundsiebzig" is 275, not 257. This can be excrutiatingly difficult to remember if you're not used to the system.

■ Time

Austria, Prague, and Budapest all use Central European time (abbreviated MEZ in German). Add six hours to Eastern Standard Time and one hour to Greenwich Mean Time. Subtract nine hours from Eastern Australia Time and 11 hours from New Zealand Time. Austria uses the 24-hour clock for all official purposes: 8pm equals 20.00.

	German	Czech	Hungarian
Phrases			
six o'clock	sechs Uhr	šest hodiny	hat óra
At what time...?	Um wieviel Uhr...?	Kdy...?	Mikor?
What time is it?	Wie spät ist es?	kolik je hodin?	Hány óra?
What's the date?	Der wievielte ist heute?	kolikátého je dnes?	Ma milyen nap van?
June 1st	ersten Juni	prvního června	június első
quarter past seven	viertel acht	čtvrt na osm	hét óra múlt tizenöt perccel
twenty past seven	zwanzig nach sieben	sedm dvacet	hét óra múlt húsz perccel
half past seven	halb acht	půl osm	fél hét
twenty to eight	zwanzig vor acht	za dvacet budou osm	nyolc óra lesz húsz perc múlva
quarter to eight	dreiviertel acht	třičtvrtě na osm	háromnegyed nyolc
am	vormittags	ráno	délelőtt
pm	nachmittags	odpoledne	
morning	Morgen	ráno	reggel
noon	Mittag	poledne	dél
afternoon	Nachmittag	odpoledne	délután
evening	Abend	večer	este
night	Nacht	noc	éjszaka
midnight	Mitternacht	půlnoc	éjfél
day	Tag	den	nap
week	Woche	týden	hét
month	Monat	měsíc	hó, hónap
year	Jahr	rok	év, esztendő
peak season	Hauptsaison	vrchalná sezóna	főszezon
post-season	Nachsaison	po sezóně	utoszezon
pre-season	Vorsaison	před sezonou	előszezon
yesterday	gestern	včera	tegnap
today	heute	dnes	ma
tomorrow	morgen	zítra	holnap
now	jetzt	nyní	most
soon	bald	brzy	rövidesen
late	spät	pozdě	késő

GLOSSARY

The Countries

Austria	Österreich	Rakousko	Ausztria
Czech Republic	die Tschechei	Česká Republika	Cseh Köztársaság
Hungary	Ungarn	Uhry	Magyarország
Slovakia	die Slowakei	Slovensko	Szlovákia

Emergency

hospital	das Krankenhaus	nemocnice	kórház
	das Spital		
pharmacy	die Apotheke	lékárna	patika
sick	krank	doplňku	beteg
doctor	der Arzt	lékař	orvos
police	die Polizei	státní správa	rendőrséget
Help!	Hilfe!	Pomoc!	Segítség!
Caution!	Achtung!	Pozor!	Óvatosan!
	Vorsicht!	Obezýelost!	
Danger!	Gefahr!	Nebezpečí!	Vigyázat!
Fire!	Feuer!	Oheň!	Tűz
Stop!	Halt!	Stůj!	Megállni
consulate	das Konsulat	konsulát	konzulátus

Basic Expressions

English (language)	Englisch	Anglický	angolul
German (language)	Deutsch	Německý	németül
Hungarian (language)	Ungarisch	Madarský	magyarul
American (person)	der Amerikaner/in	Američan/ka	Amerikai
Australian (person)	der Australier/in	Australan/ka	Ausztráliai
Briton (person)	der Engländer/in	Anglicán/ka	Brit
Canadian (person)	der Kanadier/in	Kanadán/ka	Kanadai
Irish (person)	der Irländer/in	Ir/ka	Ír
New Zealander (person)	der Neuseeländer/in	Novozélanďan/ka	Új-Zálendi
South African (person)	der Südafrikaner/in	Jihoafričan/ka	Dél-Afrikai
Good morning	Guten Morgen	Dobré jitro/ráno	Jó reggelt
Good day	Servus		Szervusz
	Grüß Gott		Jó napot
	Guten Tag		Jó napot kívanok
	Tag	Dobrý den	Jó napot
Good evening	Guten Abend	Dobrý večer	Jó estét
Good night	Gute Nacht	Dobrov noc	Jó éjszakát
Goodbye	Tschüß	Nashledanou	Szía
	Auf Wiedersehen		Viszlát
	Auf Wiederschauen		A viszontlátásra
Hello	Hallo	Haló	Jó napot
Please	Bitte	prosím	Kérem
Thank you	Danke	Děkuji	Köszönöm
You're welcome	Bitte	prosím	Szívesen
Excuse me	Entschuldigung	Promiňte	Bocsánat
Yes	Ja	ano	igen
No	Nein	ne	nem
Sir	Herr	pane	úr
Madam	Frau	paní	asszony
Gentlemen	Herren	pánové	férfiak
Ladies	Damen	dámy	nők
I'm sorry.	Es tut mir leid.	Je mi líto.	Sajnálom.
I don't speak…	Ich spreche kein…	Nemluvím…	Nem beszélek…
Do you speak English?	Sprechen Sie Englisch?	Mluvíte anglicky?	Beszél angolul?

Can you help me?	Können Sie mir helfen?	Můžetemi řiči?	Segitsél?
I don't understand.	Ich verstehe nicht.	Nerozumlín.	Nem értem.
Do you understand?	Verstehen Sie?	Rozumíte mi?	Értesz engemet?
Please speak slowly.	Sprechen Sie langsam.	Mluvte pomaleji.	Elmondaná lassabban
How do you say…in…	Wie sagt man…auf…?	Jak se řekne česky?	Hogy mondják ezt...?
What did you say?	Wie, bitte?	Co íste řikae?	Mit mondott? Megismételné?
My name is…	Ich heiße …	Jmenuji se…	A nevem...
I would like…	Ich möchte…	Chci…	Kérek…
How much does…cost?	Wieviel kostet…?	Koliktostojí.	Mibe kerül
I'd like to pay.	Zahlen, bitte.	Platit prosím.	Fizetni szeretnék.
Where is…?	Wo ist…?	Kde je?	Hol van?
When is…?	Wann ist…?	Kdy?	Mikor van?
Non-smoking	Nichtraucher	Kovření zakázáno.	Nem dohányzó
Smoking	Raucher	Kouření.	Dohánzyó

Days of the week

Monday	Montag	(Mo.)	pondělí	hétfő
Tuesday	Dienstag	(Di.)	úterý	kedd
Wednesday	Mittwoch	(Mi.)	středa	szerda
Thursday	Donnerstag	(Do.)	čtvrtek	csütörtök
Friday	Freitag	(Fr.)	pátek	péntek
Saturday	Samstag	(Sa.)	sobota	szombat
Sunday	Sonntag	(So.)	neděle	vasárnap

Months

January	Januar (Jänner)	leden	január
February	Februar (Feber)	únor	február
March	März	březen	március
April	April	duben	április
May	Mai	květen	május
June	Juni	červen	június
July	Juli	červenec	július
August	August	srpen	augusztus
September	September	zaří	szeptember
October	Oktober	říjen	október
November	November	listopad	november
December	Dezember	prosinec	december

Directions

direction	die Richtung	směr	irány
left	links	nalevo	bal
right	rechts	naprovo	jobb
straight ahead	geradeaus	přímo	egyenesen
here	hier	indy	itt
there	da	tam	ott
far	fern	vzdálený	távol
near	nah	blízký	kőzel

Travel

travel ticket	die Fahrkarte	jízdenka	menetjegy
reservation	die Reservierung	rezervace	foglalás
one-way	einfacher Fahrt	jednosměrný	egy irányban
round-trip	Hin- und Rückfahrt	zpáteřní	oda és vissza
window seat	der Fensterplatz	okno	ülőhely az ablaknál
arrival	die Ankunft	příjézd	érkezés
departure	die Abfahrt	odjézd	indulás
schedule	der Fahrplan		táblázat
baggage	das Gepäck	zavazadla	poggyász

airplane	das Flugzeug	letadlo	repülőgép
airport	der Flughafen	letiště	repülőtér
airport gate	der Flugsteig	nástupište	repülő határ
customs	der Zoll	celní úřad	vám
train	der Zug	vlak	vonat
train station	der Bahnhof	nádraži	vonat állomás pályaudvar
main train station	der Hauptbahnhof	hlavní nádraží	főpályaudvar
(train) track	das Gleis	koleje	vágány
train platform	der Bahnsteig	(perón) nástupíště	pályaudvar
express train	der Eilzug	rychlík	sebesvonat
railway	die Bahn	železnice	vasút
subway	die U-Bahn	metro	metróva
tram, trolley	die Straßenbahn	tramvaj	trolli
urban railway	die S-Bahn	trolejbus	villamos
mountain cable car	die Seilbahn	lanovka	drótkötélpálya
ferry	die Fähre	převoz trajekt	hajó
bus	der Bus	autobus	busz
bus station	der Busbahnhof	autobusová zastávka	autóbusz állomás
(bus, subway) stop	die Haltestelle	zastávka	buszmegálló
car	das Auto	auto	autó
expressway	die Autobahn	dálnice	seves autó ut
federal highway	die Bundesstraße	obresní silnice	sebes országi autó ut
one-way street	die Einbahnstraße	jednosmeřný	egyirányú utca
dead-end street	die Sackgasse	slepá ulice	zsákutca
bicycle	das Fahrrad	kolo	bicikli
moped	das Moped	moped	moped
motorcycle	das Motorrad	motocykl	motorkerékpár

The Tourist Office

tourist office	das Verkehrsamt der Verkehrsverein das Tourismusbüro die Kurverwaltung das Gemeindeamt	cestovní koncelář	turista iroda idegenforgalmi- hivatal utazási iroda
hiking map	die Wanderkarte	mapa	térkép
to find a room for	vermitteln	najít misto pro	egy szobát keresek
theater ticket	die Karte	lístek do dívadla	színházjegy
visitors' newspaper	die Gästezeitung	příručha	látogatok újságja
register of lodgings	das Gastverzeichnis	registrace noclehů	vendégkönyv

The Post Office

post office	dic Post	pošta	posta
main post office	das Hauptpostamt	hlavní pošta	főposta
address	die Adresse	adresa	címzés
express	der Eilboten	spéšná zásilku expres	expressz
air mail	die Luftpost	leteckov poštou	légiposta
letter	der Brief	dopis	levél
parcel	das Paket	balík	postacsomag
postcard	die Postkarte	pobled	képeslap
Poste restante	Postlagernde Briefe	posté restante	postán maradó
stamp	die Briefmarke	známka	bélyeg
telegram	das Telegramm	telegram	távirat
telephone	das Telefon	telefon	telefon
telephone number	die Telefonnummer	telefonní číslo	telefonszám
to exchange	wechseln	vyměnit	váltani
money	das Geld	penize	pénz

Accommodations

toilet	die Toilette	záchad	tojlet
	das WC	WC	WC
shower	die Dusche	sprcha	zuhany
key	der Schlüssel	klič	kulcs
house	das Haus	dům	ház
youth hostel	die Jugendherberge	kolej	diákszállás
campground	der Campingplatz	tábořište	táborhely
guest-house	die Pension	penzion	panzió
hotel	das Hotel	hotel	hotel
inn	das Gasthaus	hostinec	szálloda
private apartment	das Privatzimmer	byt	panzió
bed-and-breakfast	die Frühstückspension	penzion	szoba reggelivel
bed	das Bett	postel	ágy
single	das Einzelzimmer	jednol ůž ková	egyágyas szoba
double	das Doppelzimmer	dvohlůžkový	kétárgyas szoba

Dining

diabetic	der Diabetiker	diabetik	diabetikus
vegetarian	der Vegetarier	vegetariañ	vegetáriánus
hungry	hungrig	míthlad	éhes
meal	das Essen	jídlo	étel
lounge, café	die Kneipe	kavárna	vendéglő
snack or fast-food stand	der Imbiß	občerstvení	önkiszolgáló
pastry shop	die Konditorei	cukrárna	cukrászda
restaurant	die Gaststätte	restaurace	étterem
waiter	der Kellner	číšník	pincér
waitress	die Kellnerin	číšnice	pincérnő
bill, check	die Rechnung	účet	számla
breakfast	das Frühstück	snídaně	reggeli
lunch/dinner	das Mittagessen	obéd	ebéd
supper	das Abendessen	večeře	vacsora
fork	die Gabel	vidlička	villa
knife	das Messer	nůž	kés
spoon	der Löffel	lžičko	kanál

The Town

metropolis	die Großstadt	metropole	főváros
town, city	die Stadt	město	város
village	der Ort	vesnice	falu
health spa	der Kurort	lázné	városi fürdő ház
hamlet	das Dorf	vesnička	falucska
town map	der Stadtplan	mapa mésta	város térkép
old city	die Altstadt	staré město	régi város
quarter	das Viertel	čturť	negyed
square	der Platz	náměstí	tér
main square	der Hauptplatz	hlavní ndméstí	főtér
market	der Markt	trh	piac
center	das Zentrum	střed	központ
pedestrian zone	die Fußgängerzone	péší zóna	sétálóutca
bridge	die Brücke	most	híd
avenue	die Allee	ulice	körút
street	die Straße	ulice	utca
lane	die Gasse	ulice	út
passage	die Durchgang	pasáž	keskenyút
path	der Weg	stezka	átkelés
quay or waterfront	der Kai	nábřezí	rakodópart

Sights

diocese	das Stift	diecéze	egyházmegye
abbey	das Abtei	opatstuí	apátság
cloister	das Kloster	klášter	kolosto
cathedral	der Dom	katedrála	székesegyház
parish church	die Pfarrkirche	farní kostel	plébániatemplom
church	die Kirche	kostel	templom
treasury	die Schatzkammer	pokladnice	kincstár
castle	die Burg	zámek	vár
palace	das Schloß	palác	palota
fortress	die Festung	pevnost	erőd
gate	das Tor	vchod, brána	kapu
door	die Tür	dveře	ajtó
tower	der Turm	věž	torony
wall (free-standing)	die Mauer		fal
fountain	der Brunnen	fontána	forrás
town hall	das Rathaus	radnice	városháza
arsenal	das Zeughaus	zbrojnice	fegyverraktár
provincial gov't hall	das Landhaus	oblastní úřad	ország háza
opera house	die Oper	opera	operaház
theater	das Schauspielhaus	divadlo	szinház
brewery	die Brauerei	pivovar	sörfőzde
monument	das Denkmal	pomník	emlék
museum	das Museum	muzeum	múzeum
open-air museum	das Freilichtsmuseum	skanzen	szabadtéri
museum of local history	das Heimatmuseum	mistaí historiché	történeti múzeum

A Freilichtmuseum is usually an assortment of 16th- and 17th-century peasant houses, kept in authentically working order by a staff that mimics the life of the era. The houses are usually arranged as a small village, on a huge meadow or other open tract of land. A Heimatmuseum is usually a collection of town artifacts, displaying the daily life of town peasants and nobles. The exhibits are usually arranged, within the museum, in rooms—each room is decorated with the appropriate trappings of a particular social station in a certain era.

Architecture

courtyard	der Hof	dvor, náclvoří	udvar
nave	das Schiff	kostelní loď	templombajó
column	die Säule	sloulz	oszlop
chapel	die Kapelle	kaple	kápolna
pulpit	die Kanzel	kazatelna	szószék
apse	die Apsis	apsida	apszis
altar	der Altar	oltář	oltár
vestibule	die Vorhalle	vestibul	előszoba
room	der Saal	sál	szoba
choir	der Chor	kůr	énekkar
arch	der Bogen	ark, oblouk	bolthajtás
window	das Fenster	okno	ablak
stained-glass	das Buntglas	barevné sklo	szines üveg
wall (of a building)	die Wand	zeď	fal
flying buttress	der Strebebogen	pilír	külső támiv

Geography

mountain	der Berg	hora	hegy
brook	der Bach	potak	patak
river	der Fluß	řeka	folyó
lake	der See	jezero	tó
sea	die See	moře	tenger
forest	der Wald	les	erdő
shore	das Ufer	břéh	tengerpart
beach	der Strand	pláž	tópart
pond	der Teich	rybnik	kistó patak

valley	das Tal	údolí	völgy
gorge	die Schlucht	rokle	torok
glacier	der Gletscher	svah	gleccser
mountain range	die Gebirge	horsképásmo	hegység
crag	der Fels	lítes	köszirt
spring	die Quelle	zřídlo	tavasz
island	die Insel	ostrou	sziget
cave	die Höhle	jeskyné	barlang

Holidays

New Year's Day	Neujahr	Nouý Rok	Újév
Easter	Ostern	Velikonoce	Húsvét
Ascension	Christi Himmelfahrt	Nanebevstoupérí	Felszált a Menyekbe
Whitsun	Pfingsten	Letnice	
Assumption	Mariä Himmelfahrt		Mária Gelszált a
All Saints	Allerheiligen	Vsech svatých	Az Összes Szentek
Christmas	Weihnachten	Vánoce	Karácsony
New Year's Eve	Silvester	Silvestr	Újéc Este

Colors

white	weiß	bílý	fehér
yellow	gelb	žlutý	sárga
pink	rose	propíchnouti	rózsaszinű
green	grün	zelený	zöld
blue	blau	modrý	kék
orange	orange	pomorani	narancs
red	rot	červený	vörös
brown	brown	hnědý	barna
grey	grau	šedý	szürke
black	schwarz	černý	fekete

Miscellany

entrance	der Eingang	vchod	belépés
exit	der Ausgang	východ	kijárat
open	geöffnet	otevřeno	nyílt
closed	geschlossen	zavřeno	zárva
emperor	der Kaiser	císař	császár
knight	der Ritter	rytíř	lovag
saint	der Heilige/r	svatý	szent
the Trinity	the Dreifaltigkeit	Trojice	szentháromság
more	mehr	vice	több
less	weniger	méné	kisebb
good	gut	dobrý	jó
bad	schlecht	šnatný	rossz
big	groß	velký	nagy
small	klein	malý	kis
hot	heiß	horký	forró
cold	kalt	chladný	hideg
and	und	a	és
but	aber	ale	de
or	oder	nebo	vagy
what	was	co	mi
very	sehr	velmi	nagyon
without	ohne	ben	nélkül

One important note concerning Austrian vernacular: phrases like "I am hot" or "I am hungry" often carry unintended sexual connotations. (We kid you not.) It's better to be safe—say "Es ist mir heiß/kalt" (It is hot/cold to me) rather than "Ich bin heiß/kalt"; say "Ich habe Hunger/Durst" (I have hunger/thirst) rather than "Ich bin hungrig/durstig."

■■■ FOOD AND DRINK

Mixed hors-d'oeuvres	Gemischte Vorspeise		

Vegetables	**Gemüse**	**Zelenina**	**Zöldség**
Artichokes	Artischoken	artyčoky	articsóka
Eggplant	Aubergine		padlizsán
Sweet potatoes	Bataten	sladké brambory	edes burgonya
Beans	Bohnen	fazole	bab
Mushrooms	Champignons	houby	gomba
Breaded mushroom caps		obalované houby	rántott gombafejek
Peas	Erbsen	hrásek	borsó
Stuffed green peppers	Gefüllte Paprika	plnéhá paprika	töltött paprika
Cucumber	Gurke	okurky	uborka
Cauliflower	Karfiol	květák	karfiol
Carrots	Karotten	mrkev	sárgarépa
Potato	Kartoffeln Erdäpfel	brambory	burgonya
Garlic	Knoblauch	česnek	fokkagyma
Brussels sprouts	Kohlsprossen		kelbimbó
Lettuce	Kopfsalat	hlávkový salát	saláta
Cabbage	Kraut Kohl	zelí	káposzta
Corn on the cob	Kukuruz	kukuřice	csöves kukorica
Pumpkin	Kürbis	dýné	tök
Lentils	Linsen	čočka	lemcse
Corn	Mais	obilé	kukorica
French fries	Pommes frites	hranolky	sült krumpli
Leek	Poree	pórek	póré
Radish	Rettich	ředkvička	retek
Red beets	Rote Ruben	červená řepa	cékla répa
Red cabbage	Rotkohl	červená zelí	vorös káposzta
Salad	Salat	salát	salata
Celery	Sellerie	celer	zeller
Asparagus	Spargel	chřest	spárga
Broccoli	Spargelkohl	brokolice	brokkoli
Spinach	Spinat	špenát	spenót
Tomatoes	Tomaten	jablíčka	paradicsom
Truffles	Trüffeln	lanýž	szarvasgomba
Turnips	Weiße Rüben	tuřín	feher répa
Zucchini	Zucchini	cuketa	zucchini
Onions	Zwiebeln	cibule	hagyma

Fruits	**Obst**	**Ovece**	**gyümölcs**
Pineapples	Ananas	ananas	ananász
Apple	Apfel	jablko	alma
Orange	Apfelsine	pomeranč	narancs
Apricot	Aprikose	meruňky	sárgabarack
Prune	Backpflaune	šbestka	szilva
Pear	Birne	hruška	körte
Blackberry	Brombeere	ostružina	földiszeder
Strawberry	Erdbeere	jahody	eper
Grapefruit	Grapefruit Pampelmuse	grapefruit	grépfrut
Blueberry	Heidelbeere	barůvky	áfonya
Raspberry	Himbeere	maliny	málna
Cherry	Kirsche	třešně	cseresznye
Stewed fruit	Kompott		kompót
Peach	Pfirsich	broskev	őszibarack
Plum	Pflaume	švestka	szilva
Cranberry	Preiselbeere	brusinka	
Red currants	Ribisel	rybíz	ribizli
Raisins	Rosinen	rozinka	mazsola

Grapes	Trauben	hrozsové vino	szőlő
Lemon	Zitrone	citrón	citrom
Nuts	**Nüsse**		**Dió**
Peanuts	Erdnuss	burské oříšky	mogyoró
Assorted nuts	Gemische Nüsse		begyes dió
Chestnut	Kasanie	kaštak	gesztenye
Almond	Mandel	mandle	mandula
Walnuts	Walnüsse	vlašskéořechy	dió
Eggs	**Eier**		**tojás**
Scrambled eggs	Eierspeise	míchaná vejce	tojásrántotta
Fried eggs	Spiegeleier	smažená vejce	sült tojás
Stuffed eggs	Gefüllte Eier	plnéna vejce	töltött tojás
Hard-boiled eggs	Hartgekochte Eier	vejcenaturdo	kemény tojás
Cheese omelette	Käse-Omelett	sýrová omeleta	omlett sajttal
Poached eggs	Pochierte Eier	sázená vejce	buggyantott tojás
Soft-boiled eggs	Weiche Eier	vejce na měkko	lágy tojás
Cheese	**Käse**	**Sýr**	**sajt**
Goat cheese	Ziegenkäse	kozí sýr	kecske sajt
Hungarian cream cheese			körözött
Bread	**Brot**	**Chleba**	**kenyér**
Roll	Brötchen	houska rohlík	péksütemény zsemle
Sweet rolls	Plundergebäck	sladký rohlík	édes péksütemény
Toast	Toast	opečený chléb	piritos kenyér
Whole wheat bread	Vollweizenbrot	celck chléb	barna kenyer piritós
White bread	Weißbrot	pšeničný chléb	feher kenyér
Rusk biscuits	Zwieback	suchary	
Pancakes	Palatschinken	palačinka	hortobágyi palacsinta
Soups	**Suppen**	**Polévky**	**Leves**
Cream of mushroom	Champignoncremesuppe	žampiónová polévka	tejfeles gombaleves
Stew	Eintopf	hovězí vývar	párol
Sliced pancakes broth	Fritattensuppe		zöldségesleves
Vegetable soup	Gemüsesuppe	zeleninová polévka	zöldsegesleves
Semolina dumpling sp.	Grießnockerlsuppe		grizes nokedli
Goulash soup	Gulaschsuppe	gulášová polévka	gulyásleves
Chicken broth	Hühnerbrühe	slepičí polévka	újházi tyúkhúsleves
Potato soup	Kartoffelsuppe	bramborová polévka	burgonyakrémleves
Liver dumpling broth	Leberknödelsuppe	polévka jattroufmi knedlíéký	májgombócleves
Dumpling soup	Markknödelsuppe		guyás leves
Noodle soup	Nudelsuppe	nudlová polévka	tészta leves
Ragout of oxtail, celery	Ochsenschwanz-Ragout mit Sellerie	ragú	
Garlic soup	Knoblauchsuppe	césneková polévka	fokhagymás leves
Tomato soup	Tomatensuppe	rajská polévka	paradicsomleves
Fish soup		ryví polévka	halászlé
Onion soup	Zwiebelsuppe	cibulová polévka	hagymas leves
Beef	**Rindfleisch**	**Hovézí**	**Marhahús**
Boiled ribs of beef	Beinfleisch	vařená hovézí žebra	főttborda
Beef filet and vegetables	Rinderfilet nach Gärtnerin-Art	hovězí na zeleniné	marhaszelet zöldséggel
Braised beef	Rindsbraten	dušené hovézí	dinsztelve
Goulash of beef	Rindsgulasch	hovézí guláš	marha gulyás
Rolled beef steaks	Rindsroulade	hovézí roláda	marha hús rostélyon sült
Boiled rump	Tafelspitz	varéná kýta	főve

Beef cutlet with onions	Zwiebelrostbraten	hovézí kotletas cíbulí	hagymással sült marha hüs
Veal	**Kalbfleisch**	**Telecí Maso**	**Borjú**
Leg of lamb	Gebratene Lammkeule	jehnéčí noha	bárány comb
Stuffed breast of veal	Gefüllet Kalbsbrust	plnéná telecí prsa	söttöt borjú máj
Sweetbreads	Kalbsbries		mandola
Goulash of veal	Kalbsgulasch		borjú gulyas
Brains fried in butter	Kalbshim		agy velő vajjal
Breaded calf's liver	Kalbsleber gebacken		kirántott borjú máj
Escalloped veal in wine	Kalbsschnitzel in Weisswein		borjú szeletek boros szósszal
Knuckle, in sour cream	Kalbsvögerl mit Rahm		disznócsülök tejfelesen
Veal scallop sauteed	Naturschnitzel		
Roast loin of veal	Nierenbraten		sült borjú bélszin
Breaded veal cutlet	Wiener Schnitzel		borjú szelet kirántva
Pork	**Schweinefleisch**		**Diszno**
Roast suckling pig	Gebratenes Spanferkel		sült malac
Smoked ham	Geräucherter Schinken		füstölt sonka
Breast, with horseradish	Krenfleisch		bordás sertés
Ham	Schinken	šunkou	sonka
Pork scallop	Schweinsschnitzel		csonka
Bacon	Speck	slaninou	szalonna
Sausage	Wurst	párek	kolbász
Poultry	**Geflügel**	**Drůbež**	**Szárnyas**
Fried chicken	Backhuhn	pečené kuré	sült csirke
Roast chicken	Brathuhn	grilované kuré	rántott csirke
Duck	Ente	kachua	kacsa
Pheasant	Fasan	bažant	fácán
Goose	Gans	pusa	liba
Roast goose	Gänsebraten	pečená husa	rántott liba
Roast duckling	Gebratene Ente	pečená kachňátko	rántott kacsa
Chicken	Huhn Hendl	kuré	csirke
Broiled hen with bacon	Huhn vom Rost mit Speck	pečené slepice na slanině	rántott csirke szalonnaval
Chicken liver	Hühnerleber	kurěcí játra	csirkemáj
Paprika chicken		kurěcí na paprice	csirkepaprikás
Goose liver		husí játra	libamáj
Capon	Kapaun Masthahn	kapsum	tyúk
Turkey	Pute Truthahn	krocan	pulyka
Roast turkey	Puterbraten	pešený krocan	sült pulyka
Partridge	Rebhuhn	koroptev	fogoly
Pigeon	Taube	holub	galamb
Quail	Wachtel	křepelka	fürj
Game	**Wild**		**Vadas Állatok**
Hare	Hase	zajíc	nyúl
Stew of marinated hare	Hasenpfeffer		nyúl pörkölt
Saddle of hare	Hasenrücken	zaječí hřbet	nyúl oldal
Deer	Hirsch	sračí	szarvas
Saddle of deer	Hirschrücken		szarvas oldal
Deer stew	Hirschragout	dicíeuí srnzcí	szarvas pörkölt
Shoulder of deer	Hirschschulter	srnzcí rameno	
Rabbit	Kaninchen	králík	házinyúl
Venison	Reh	kvěřína	szarvashús
Saddle of venison roast	Rehrücken gebraten		sütött szarvas oldal
Boar	Wildschwein		vaddisznö

Fish	**Fisch**	**Ryby**	**Hal**
Eel	Aal	úhoř	angolna
Oysters	Austern	ústřice	osztriga
Flounder	Flunder	okoun	tengeri hal
Pike/perch	Fogosch		hideg fogas
Trout	Forelle	pstruh	pisztráng
Pike	Hecht		hideg fogas
Halibut	Heilbutt	halibut	
Lobster	Hummer	humr	tengeri rák
Scallops	Jakobsmuscheln		kagylóhéj
Cod	Kabeljau	treska	tőkehal
Carp	Karpfen	kapr	
Crab	Krebs	krab	tengeri rák
Salmon	Lachs	losos	lazac
Mackerel	Makerele	makrela	makrahal
Herring	Matjes	sleď	hering
Mussels	Muscheln	mořské mušle	kagyló
Smoked salmon	Räucherlachs	uzený losos	füstölt lazac
Anchovies	Sardellen	aněsvičky	ajóka
Haddock	Schellfisch		tőkehal
Snails	Schnecken		csiga
Perch	Seebarsch		hideg fogas
Sole	Seezunge		talp
Turbot	Steinbutt		naphal
Squid	Tintenfisch		
Tuna in oil	Thunfisch in Olivenöl	tuňák olejí	olayyal tonalt
Whiting	Weißfisch		tőkehal
Pasta	**Teigwaren**		Tészták
Noodles	Bandnudeln	nudle	metélt
Gnocchi	Nockerl		nokedli
Pasta in cream sauce	Schlipfkrapfen		tészta krémszós
Spaghetti	Spaghetti		spagetti
Dumplings		knedlíky	nokedli
Pizza Toppings			
green peppers	Pepperoni	paprika	zöldpaprika
pepperoni	Salami	saláui	szalámi
Desserts	**Mehlspeisen**		**Dizört**
Apple strudel	Apfelstrudel	jablkový zóvin	rétes
Soufflé	Auflauf	nákyp	szuflé
Baked apple	Bratapfel	pečený jablko	sült alma
Breadcrumb noodles	Bröselnudeln		
Jam-filled dumplings	Buchteln	ovocné knedlíky	lekváros gombóc
Caramel-top gâteau	Dobos-Torte		Dob os torta
Ice cream	Eis	zmzlina	fagylalt
Strawberries, ice cream	Erdbeeren mit Eis	jahodavá	eper
Neapolitan ice cream	Gemischtes Eis		
Sourdough dumplings	Germknödel		nokedli németesen
Semolina noodles	Grießnudeln		grizes tészta
Omelette imperial	Kaiserschmarren		Császáros omlet
Dumplings	Knödel	knedlíky	gombóc
Stewed fruit	Kompott	kompot	kompot
Cake	Küchen	koláč	torta
Nut, trellis-top gâteau	Linzer Torte	linecké koláčky	linzer
Malakoff	Malakofftorte		malokov
Pancakes with jam	Marmeladepalatschinken Pfannkuchen Konfitüre	Palačinky sdžěmem	palacsinta lekvárosan
Poppy-seed noodles	Mohnnudeln	čokoládzý dort	mákos nudli
Sponge cake,choc. sauce	Mohr im Hemd		
Nut gâteau	Nußtorte	oříškovy dort	diós torta
Stuffed roll fritters	Pofesen		

Plum jam turnovers	Powidltascherl		szilvás strudel
Profiteroles in chocolate	Profiterolen		
Sponge cake, rum filling	Punschtorte	punčovy dort	rumos torta
Choc./raspberry cake	Sacher Torte	čokoládová malinaký dort	csokoládé szamóca torta
Salzburg soufflé	Salzburger Nockerl		
Whipped cream	Schlagsahne Schlagobers		
Chocolate mousse	Schokolade-Mousse	čokoládová péna	csokoládé puding
Chocolate cream	Schokoladencreme	čokoládova krém	csoki krém
Cottage cheese dumpling	Topfenknödel	tvarohové knedlíky	turos nokedli
Cottage cheese strudel	Topfenstrudel	tvarohový závin	turos strudel
Gâteau	Torte		torta
Plum dumplings	Zwetschkenknödel	šrestkové knedlíký	szilvás gombóc

Seasonings		**Koření**	**Fűszer**
Basil	Basilikum	bazalka	bazsalikom
Butter	Butter	máslo	vaj
Vinegar	Essig	ocet	ecet
Honey	Honig	med	méz
Garlic	Knoblauch	česnek	fokhagyma
Jam	Konfitüre	džem	lekvár
Pepper	Pfeffer	pepř	bors
Salt	Salz	sůl	só
Mustard	Senf	hořčice	mustár
Syrup	Sirup	siry/z	szirup
Sugar	Zucker	cukrcukor	cukor

Beverages	**Getränk**	**Nápoje**	**Ital**
Bottle	Flasche	láhev	üveg
Cup	Tasse	šálek	csésze
Glass	Glas	skleničku	pohár
I am tipsy.	Ich bin geschwippst.	Hotam se.	Jol érzem magam.
I am drunk.	Ich bin blau.	Jsem opilý.	Részeg vagyok..
I am very drunk.	Ich bin sehr besoffen.	Jsem mám dost.	Nagyon részeg vagyok.
I am more drunk than I have ever been before.	Ich bin zelman.	Jsem zělmán.	Zélmán vagyok.
I am sick.	Ich bin krank.	Je mi špatně.	Beteg vagyok.
He was drunk.	Er war gut darauf.	Bye opilý.	Ő részeg volt.
to pick (someone) up at a social gathering	aufreißen		

Beer	**Bier**	**Pivo**	**Sör**
Beer hall	Bierstube	pivnice	söröző
Cheers! (beer)	Prosit!	nazclravž	egészségedre!
1/3 liter (beer)	Seidel	trétikna	
1/2 liter (beer)	Krügerl	půl litru	fél liter
1 liter (beer)	Maß	litr	egy liter
Draft beer	Bier vom Faß	světlé černé	csapolt sör
Dark beer	Ein Dunkles	černé pivo	barna sör

Wine	**Wein**	**Víno**	**Bor**
Wine hall	Weinstube	vinárna	borozó
Cheers! (wine)	zum Wohl!	Na zdraví!	Egészségedre
1/8 liter (wine)	Achterl	osmihka	egy decit
1/4 liter (wine)	Viertel	čturt litru	negyed liter
Sweet	süß	sladký	édes
Mild	mild	jemný	gyenge
Dry	trocken	suchý	száraz

Chilled	eiskalt	ehlazené	jéghideg
Room temperature	Zimmertemperatur	pokojová teplota	szoba hőmérsékletű
Mulled claret	Glühwein		must
Red wine	Rotwein	červené víno	vörös bor
White wine	Weißwein	bílé víno	fehér bor
Sparkling wine	Sekt	šampaňské	pezsgő
Wine and soda water	ein G'spritzter	vinný střik	bor szodavizzel
Coffee and Tea	**Kaffee und Tee**		**Kávé és Tea**
Coffee, very little milk	ein Brauner	káva strochow mléka	kávé kevés tejjel
Black, whipped cream	Einspänner	káva se šlehačkow	fekete kávé tejszinhabbal
Coffee with ice cream	Eiskaffee	káva se zmrzlina	kávé fagylatal
Light espresso	ein Gestreckter ein Verlängerter	espresso	eszpresszo
Coffee	Kaffee	káva	kávé
Coffee with cream	Kaffee mit Sahne	káva se smetanou	tejszines kávé
Coffee, whipped cream	Kaffee mit Schlag		tejszinhabos kávé
Camomile tea	Kamillentee	heřmánkový čaj	kamilla tea
Decaffeinated coffee	Koffeinfreier Kaffee	káva bez kofeinu	koffein mentes kávé
Strong espresso	ein Kurzer	silný espresso	erős kávé
Espresso with milk	Macchiato	espreso a mléko	tejes exzpresszo
Cold coffee, ice, rum	Mazagron		
½ Coffee, ½ milk	Melange		fél kávé fél tej
Mocha	Mokka	móka	mokka
Black coffee and rum	Mokka gespritzt	černy káva s rum	rumos kávé
Mint tea	Pfefferminztee	mentalovy čaj	mentalos tea
Black coffee	ein Schwarzer	černá káva	fekete kávé
Tea	Tee	horký čaj	tea
Milk with little coffee	Teeschale gold	mléko a trochou kávy	keves kávé tejjel
Milk, very little coffee	Teeschale licht		
Other beverages	**Andere Getränke**		**Különleges italok**
Cider	Apfelwein	jábleéný mošt	alma lé
Bottled sodas	Brauselimonaden	sodou	szoda
Cola	Cola	cola	cola
Egg liquor	Eierlikör	vájeéný koňak	tojás likör
2% milk	Fettarmemilch		tej két százalék
Fruit juice	Fruchtsaft	št áva	gyümölcske
Brandy	Brandy	brandy	brandy
Tap water	Leitungswasser	voda	csap viz
Liqueur	Likör	likér	likör
		koňak	
Soft drink	Limonade	limonáda	lemonádé
Mineral water	Mineralwasser	minerálka	ásványvíz
Hard cider	Most	mošt	
Fruit brandy	Obstler	ovocná čtáva	gyümölcs brandy
Schnapps	Schnapps		pálinka
Scotch	Scotch	Skotský	skács
Soda	Soda	soda	szóda
Whole milk	Vollmilch	mléko	tej
Water	Wasser	minerálky	víz
Vermouth	Wermut	versusúte	ürmös
Skim milk	Forget it.	uizkotúcné mléko	lefölözött
Preparation			***Elökészülés***
to fry	backen	smažeňý	süt
chilled	eiskalt	chlareny	hűtött
rare	Englisch	dokrvava	félig sült
medium	etwas durch	nemoc vypečený	közepes
liquid	flüssig	tékulý	folyékony

baked	gebacken	pečený	sült
to roast	gebraten	pečený	süt
steamed	gedünstet	dušěný	gőzöl
grilled	gegrillt	pečený narožni	rácsos
boiled	gekocht	vařený	főtt
smoked	geräuchert	uzený	füstöl
salted	geselcht	slaný	besózott
well done	gut durchgebraten sehr durch	hodně vypečený	jól átsütött
hard	hart	tvrdé	kemény
to add	hinzufugen	přidat	hozzáad
deep-fried	in Backteig	smažené	olajban sült
sautéed	in Butter geschwenkt	dušený	hirtelen fözve
cold	kalt	chladný	hideg
boil	kochen	vařený	forral
breaded	paniert	obalovaný v housce	kenyérbél
straight	pur	přímo	egyenes
raw	roh	nedovařené	nyers
very rare	sehr Englisch	do krvava	nagyon nyers
sweet	süß	sladký	édes
soft	weich	měkčíé	lágy
to season	wurzen	připravovakorěnit	megfüsserezve
temperature	temperatur	teplota	hőmérséklet

■■■ FINAL FOOD FOR THOUGHT

A taste of Austria before you arrive. Or a remembrance of meals past after you return. Or something to assuage your bitterness after nine hours of airline cuisine. Or, perhaps, a vacation for travelers who prefer to experience another culture from their own kitchen. For all these reasons and more, we have provided recipes to transport you, culinarily, to Vienna.

■ An Austrian Meal

Eisbein mit Sauerkraut (Pig's Knuckles)

This dish makes a hearty main course and serves a crowd with ease. A traditional favorite worth trying at least once in Austria, even if you don't have the guts (or the knuckles) to cook it at home.

2½ pounds fresh pig's knuckles
½ tablespoon salt
½ teaspoon ground pepper
1 bay leaf
3 carrots
1 stalk celery
½ parsnip
2 large onions
1½ pound sauerkraut
2 peeled and diced apples
¾ cup dry white wine
2½ tablespoons minced parsley

Wash the pig's knuckles thoroughly to eliminate all strains of salmonella, and remove bristles by scraping with a sharp knife. Cover with water in a large saucepan. Add salt, pepper, bay leaf, carrots, celery, parsnip, and one whole onion. Boil, cover, and cook over low heat for three hours.

Meanwhile, chop remaining onion, and cook with undrained sauerkraut and apples. Cook over low heat 1½ hours, stirring occasionally.

Drain knuckles and arrange on a heated serving dish reserving the stock; keep warm. Strain and measure two cups of stock into a saucepan. Combine the flour and the wine; stir until smooth, then add to the stock. Cook over low heat, then add to the sauerkraut mixture. Combine and pour over the knuckles. Serve immediately. Drink with a good beer to stave off queasiness.

Wiener Schnitzel (Viennese Veal Cutlet)

This delicious recipe has been appropriated by many other cuisines. You just can't go wrong. Variations include frying an egg over the cutlet (for a cholesterol-laden treat) or substituting fine breadcrumbs for flour. Serve with a red wine such as the renowned Blauburgunder.

3 pounds veal shoulder, thinly sliced
1 egg
½ cup flour
1 teaspoon salt
½ teaspoon pepper
¼ pound (1 stick) margarine
4 tablespoons fresh lemon juice, plus fresh lemon for garnish
4 tablespoons chopped parsley

Pound veal slices between two sheets of wax paper with a meat mallet until very thin. Mix flour, salt, and pepper on another sheet of wax paper. Lightly beat the egg. Dip each slice of veal in egg and then lightly coat with flour mixture.

Melt margarine in a large frying pan. Cook veal over low heat until tender and well-browned, about five minutes on the first side and ten minutes on the other. Add lemon juice and pan juices. Transfer to a platter and garnish with lemon and parsley. Serves four.

Linzer Torte

A crowd-pleasing party dessert. The Linzer Tortes are simple yet elegant, and delicious as well as beautiful. Try making Linzer cookies with leftover dough and jam.

2 nine-inch tortes

Pastry crust

3 cups sifted all-purpose flour
1 ½ teaspoons cinnamon
8 ounces butter, sliced
1¾ cups sugar
4 cups walnuts, finely ground
2 eggs
grated lemon rind

Adjust rack one-third up from the bottom of the oven. Preheat oven to 400°F. Butter two nine-inch round layer cake pans with removable bottoms. Cut two sheets of wax paper to fit the pans by tracing the outline onto the paper. Line the pans with the wax paper and butter again.

Mix flour and cinnamon in a mixing bowl. Cut the butter into the flour with a pastry blender or two knives until small crumbs form, and add the sugar, walnuts, lightly beaten egg and lemon rind. Knead the dough slightly, pour it onto a lightly floured surface, and squeeze it until it sticks together. Form a ball of dough, and push off small pieces with the heel of your palm until all dough is separated. Repeat. Divide the dough into quarters, and place a quarter in each pan, gently spreading it with your fingers. Evenly distribute over the bottom of the pan and 1½ inches up the sides. Bake for 15 minutes or until light brown.

While the crust is baking, roll the rest of the dough between two sheets of wax paper to ¼-inch thickness. Leave the dough between the paper and slide it onto a cookie sheet. Chill in the freezer for 15 minutes.

Remove crust from the oven. Reduce temperature to 350° and elevate rack up a third of the oven.

Fruit filling

¼ cup fine bread crumbs
2 cups raspberry jam

Sprinkle two tablespoons of the crumbs over the bottom of each crust. Stir jam and divide evenly between the two pans. Set filled pans aside.

Remove remaining dough from the freezer. Remove the top sheet of wax paper and place on cutting board. Cut into ½-inch strips. Lift strips by wax paper underneath. Lay the first strip over the center of the torte, paper side up, and peel off the paper when the dough is in place. Place strips ½ inch apart, forming a lattice. Use excess dough to cover gaps around the edges. Press edges into place; score edges.

Nutty topping

1 egg yolk
1 teaspoon water
1 cup slivered almonds

Mix egg and water; carefully brush the glaze over the dough. Sprinkle half the almonds over the tortes. Bake for one hour until lightly browned. Cool on racks in pans. Delicately remove tortes by sliding a sharp serrated knife between the torte and the pans. Let stand for several hours; tortes will keep for a couple of days. Sprinkle with confectioner's sugar just before serving.

■ Beer

Dusty are our books,
the stein makes us more clever;
beer gives us joy,
books frustration ever.

- Johann Wolfgang von Goethe

And what Austrian meal would be complete without a cold, frothy brew? Beer was first documented over 6000 years ago, as a staple food of the Sumerians, and has both fascinated and intoxicated *Homo sapiens* ever since. In the Babylonian epic Gilgamesh, soldiers of the realm were paid in beer; no records were kept of the soldiers' subsequent battleground performance. More than 20 recipes for the fermentation of beer appear in ancient Egyptian scrolls, but the ancient Teutonic tribes were responsible for creating the celebrated mix of hops, barley, malt, yeast, and water that satiates Austria's present citizenry.

Bockbier

A strong, full-bodied dark amber beer consumed mostly at Christmas and Easter, originally brewed as "liquid bread" because drinking did not *officially* break a religious fast. Ancient imperial beer purity laws mandate that it contain over 16% wort before fermentation and over 6¼% alcohol by volume afterward. Served in a ½-liter mug (*Krügel*).

Spezialbier

Still tangy, but slightly more mellow than *Bockbier*; the beer purity laws mandate over 13% wort before fermentation and over 5% alcohol afterward. Served in a standard bar *Stein* (*Schankglas*).

Lagerbier, Märzenbier

A very mild malt beer with a faint hops aftertaste; it's legal if it had 12-12.8% wort and contains 5% alcohol. Served in a standard bar mug (*Schankglas*).

Schankbier

If you saunter up to a stool and simply request *ein Bier*, this is likely to fill your *Stein*. The fairly mild frothy beverage has a sharp hops aftertaste; regulations mandate 10-12% wort before fermentation and 4.3% alcohol content afterward. Served in a standard bar mug (*Schankglas*).

Pils

If, instead, an Austrian saunters up to the bar stool, the standard order is *ein Pils*; this native staple is slightly stronger than the *Schankbier*, with more malt and hops and thereby more flavor. Imperial bureaucrats decided that a *Pils* should consist of 11-13% wort before the brewing process and 5% alcohol by volume at its end. Served in a tulip glass, with a bowl atop a long glass stem (*Tulpe*).

Dunkel

This ultra-dark beer is powerful with a capital "P"; the bitter taste is generated by the 12-14% wort, which becomes 5% alcohol. Served in a tall tumbler (*Becher*).

Weizenbier

Weizenbier is especially carbonated, either clear (*Kristall* or *Blank*) or clouded by unstrained yeast (*Hefetrüb*). The beer has a lighter taste than the other "full" beers; it's flavorful but has less afterbite. The beer purity laws declared that th beer, also known as *Hefe-weizen*, should have 11-13% wort and over 5.5% alcohol by volume. Served in special fluted conical glasses (*Spezialgläser*).

Leichtbier

This beer is akin to a standard English lite; there's under 9% wort involved, and less than 3.7% alcohol. Served in a tulip glass (*Tulpe*).

Stein ohne Schleim

An Austrian custom, imported from Bavaria years ago, dictates that a rather special ritual be performed on the earliest brew of the season in order to ensure its quality. When the first keg is filled, old wives from the town must dance around the barrel and spit into its frothy contents to bless the remainder of the brewing year. If you sample some of a brewery's first yield, be sure to ask for your *Stein ohne Schleim*.

Try at least some of the following brands during your sojourn in Austria:

Ottakringer	Hirter Morchel
Hofstetten	Steigl
Mühlviertler	Zipfer
Uttendorf	Ratsherrn Trunk
Grieskirchner	St. Peter Bräu
Kapsreiter	Bürger Bräu
Kaiser	Freistädter
Landbier	Clams
Jörger	Gösser
Ritterbräu	Mayr
Fohrenburg	

INDEX

Y

Z

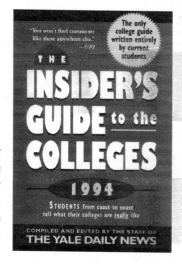

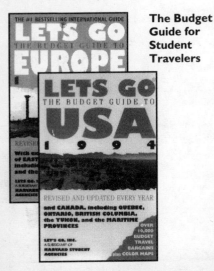